S0-AAA-169

McGRAW-HILL/CONTEMPORARY'S
COMPLETE
PRE-GED

Contributing Writers:

Language Arts, Writing: Judith Gallagher

Language Arts, Reading: Patricia Mulcrone

Social Studies: Kenneth Tamarkin

Science: Karen Harrington

Mathematics: Robert Mitchell

 **Wright Group**

Book Editor: Mitch Rosin
Executive Editor: Linda Kwil
Production Manager: Genevieve Kelley
Marketing Manager: Sean Klunder

Copyright © 2003 by McGraw-Hill/Contemporary, a business unit of The McGraw-Hill Companies, Inc. No part of this book may be reproduced, stored in a retrieval system, or transmitted by any means, electronic, mechanical, photocopying, recording, or otherwise, without prior permission of the publisher.

Send all inquiries to:
McGraw-Hill/Contemporary
130 East Randolph Street, Suite 400
Chicago, Illinois 60601

ISBN 0-07-286356-0

Printed in the United States of America.

12 13 14 15 CUS 15 14 13 12

The **McGraw·Hill** Companies

Table of Contents

LANGUAGE ARTS, READING

SOCIAL STUDIES

SCIENCE

MATHEMATICS

POSTTESTS

Acknowledgments

The editor has made every effort to trace the ownership of all copyrighted material and to secure the necessary permissions. Should there prove to be any question regarding the use of any material, regret is here expressed for such error. Upon notification of any such oversight, proper acknowledgment will be made in future editions.

Excerpt on page 11 is from *Newsweek*, April 19, 2002 © 2002 Newsweek, Inc. All rights reserved. Reprinted by permission.

Excerpt on page 12 is from "A Day's Wait." Excerpted with permission of Scribner, an imprint of Simon & Schuster Adult Publishing Group, from *The Complete Short Stories of Ernest Hemingway*. Copyright © 1933 by Charles Scribner's Sons. Copyright renewed © 1961 by Mary Hemingway. Also from *The Complete Short Stories of Ernest Hemingway*, published by Jonathan Cape. Reprinted by permission of The Random House Group Ltd.

Poem on page 15 is "A Time To Talk," from *The Poetry Of Robert Frost* edited by Edward Connery Lathem. Copyright 1916, © 1969 by Henry Holt and Company, copyright 1944 by Robert Frost. Reprinted by permission of Henry Holt and Company, LLC.

Cartoon on page 20 is from Peter Oakley, "Modern Wonder Cartoons." Reprinted by permission.

Excerpt on page 229 is from "Preface," from *Lake Wobegon Days* by Garrison Keillor, copyright © 1985 by Garrison Keillor. Used by permission of Viking Penguin, a division of Penguin Putnam, Inc.

Excerpt on page 232 is from "7 Money Rules To Break," by William J. Lynott in *Reader's Digest*, August 2002. Adapted from *Money, How To Make The Most Of What You've Got*, by William J. Lynott. Reprinted by permission of the author.

Excerpt on page 236 is from "The Other Wife" from *The Collected Stories Colette* edited by Robert Phelps, and translated by Matthew Ward. Translation copyright © 1983 by Farrar, Straus & Giroux, Inc. Reprinted by permission of Farrar, Straus and Giroux, LLC.

Cartoon on page 241 is from Thomas Brothers. Reprinted by permission.

Excerpt on page 242 is from "What I Have Been Doing Lately" from *At the Bottom of the River* by Jamaica Kincaid. Copyright © 1983 by Jamaica Kincaid. Reprinted by permission of Farrar, Straus and Giroux, LLC and The Wylie Agency, Inc.

Excerpt on page 248 is from *Dave Barry's Complete Guide To Guys* by Dave Barry, copyright © 1995 by Dave Barry. Used by permission of Random House, Inc.

Excerpt on pages 258–259 is from *Soldier's Heart* by Gary Paulsen, copyright © 1998 by Gary Paulsen. Used by permission of Random House Children's Books, a division of Random House, Inc., and Flannery Literary.

Excerpt on page 283 is from "Charles," from *The Lottery and Other Stories* by Shirley Jackson. Copyright © 1948, 1949 by Shirley Jackson. Copyright renewed 1976, 1977 by Laurence Hyman, Barry Hyman, Mrs. Sarah Webster and Mrs. Joanne Schnurer. Reprinted by permission of Farrar, Straus & Giroux, LLC and the Estate of Shirley Jackson.

Excerpt on page 286 is from *Sarah, Plain and Tall* by Patricia MacLachlan. Copyright © 1985 by Patricia MacLachlan. First appeared in *Sarah, Plain and Tall*, published by HarperCollins. Used by permission of HarperCollins Publishers and Curtis Brown, Ltd.

Excerpt on page 287 is from *Obscure Destinies* by Willa Cather. Used by permission of Alfred A. Knopf, a division of Random House, Inc.

Excerpt on page 289 is from *Dragonwings* by Laurence Yep. Copyright © 1975 by Laurence Yep. Used by permission of HarperCollins Publishers.

Excerpt on page 294 is from "Thank You M'am" from *Short Stories* by Langston Hughes. Copyright © 1996 by Ramona Bass and Arnold Rampersad. Reprinted by permission of Hill and Wang, a division of Farrar, Straus and Giroux, LLC and Harold Ober Associates Incorporated.

Excerpt on page 298 is from *Sarah, Plain and Tall* by Patricia MacLachlan. Copyright © 1985 by Patricia MacLachlan. First appeared in *Sarah, Plain and Tall*, published by HarperCollins. Used by permission of HarperCollins Publishers and Curtis Brown, Ltd.

Excerpt on page 298 is from "Thank You M'am" from *Short Stories* by Langston Hughes. Copyright © 1996 by Ramona Bass and Arnold Rampersad. Reprinted by permission of Hill and Wang, a division of Farrar, Straus and Giroux, LLC and Harold Ober Associates Incorporated.

Excerpt on page 298 is from "The No-Guitar Blues" by Gary Soto from *Baseball in April and Other Stories*, copyright © 1990 by Gary Soto, reprinted by permission of Harcourt, Inc.

Excerpt on page 299 is from *Catherine, Called Birdy* by Karen Cushman. Text copyright © 1994 by Karen Cushman. Reprinted by permission of Clarion Books/Houghton Mifflin Company. All rights reserved.

Excerpt on page 300 is from "Two Dreamers" in *Baseball In April and Other Stories*, copyright © 1990 by Gary Soto, reprinted by permission of Harcourt, Inc.

Excerpt on pages 301–302 is from "The Scarlet Ibis," by James Hurst. First published by *The Atlantic Monthly*, July 1960. Copyright © 1988 James Hurst. Reprinted by permission.

Poem on page 305 is from *Chicago Poems* by Carl Sandburg, copyright 1916 by Holt, Rinehart and Winston and renewed 1944 by Carl Sandburg, reprinted by permission of Harcourt, Inc.

Poem on page 306 is ".05," by Ishmael Reed from *Chattanooga*. Copyright © 1973 by Ishmael Reed. Reprinted by permission of Barbara Lowenstein Associates.

Poem on page 308 is "Three Ponies" by Arthur Guiterman from *The Best-Loved Poems of Jacqueline Kennedy Onassis* selected by Caroline Kennedy, 2001. Reprinted with the permission of Richard Sclove.

Poem on page 309 is from "Mending Wall" from *The Poetry of Robert Frost* edited by Edward Connery Lathem, published by Jonathan Cape. Copyright 1930, 1939, © 1969 by Henry Holt and Company, © 1958 by Robert Frost, © 1967 by Lesley Frost Ballantine. Reprinted by permission of Henry Holt and Company, LLC and The Random House Group Ltd.

Poem on page 311 is from *The Prophet* by Kahlil Gibran, copyright 1923 by Kahlil Gibran and renewed 1951 by Administrators C.T.A. of Kahlil Gibran Estate and Mary G. Gibran. Used by permission of Alfred A. Knopf, a division of Random House, Inc. Reprinted by permission of the Gibran National Committee, address: P.O. Box 116-5375, Beruit, Lebanon; Phone & Fax: (+961-1) 396916; E-Mail: k.gibran@cyberia.net.lb.

Poem on page 312 is from *The Collected Poems Of Langston Hughes* by Langston Hughes, copyright © 1994 by The Estate of Langston Hughes. Used by permission of Alfred A. Knopf, a division of Random House, Inc., and by permission of Harold Ober Associates Incorporated.

Excerpt on page 314 is from *Of Mice And Men* by John Steinbeck, copyright 1937, renewed © 1965 by John Steinbeck. Used by permission of Viking Penguin, a division of Penguin Putnam, Inc.

Excerpt on page 316 is from *The Hot L Baltimore* by Lanford Wilson. Copyright © by Lanford Wilson. Reprinted by permission of Hill and Wang, a division of Farrar, Straus and Giroux, L.L.C., and by permission of International Creative Management, Inc.

Excerpt on page 318 is from "Verdict" by Agatha Christie, copyright © Agatha Christie Limited 1958. Reprinted by permission.

Excerpt on page 319–320 is from *The Glass Menagerie* by Tennessee Williams, copyright 1945 by Tennessee Williams and Edwina D. Williams; copyright renewed 1973 by Tennessee Williams. Used by permission of Random House, Inc. *The Glass Menagerie* copyright © 1945 renewed 1973 by The University of the South. Published by New Directions. Reprinted by permission of The University of the South, Sewanee, Tennessee. All rights whatsoever in this play are strictly reserved and application for performance etc., must be made before rehearsal to Casarotto Ramsay & Associates Ltd., National House, 60-66 Wardour Street, London W1V 4ND England. No performance may be given unless a license has been obtained.

Excerpt on page 324 is from *Raiders of the Lost Ark* summary in *Variety Movie Guide 2001*. Used with permission of and copyrighted by © Variety Magazine, owned and published by Cahners Business Information, a division of Reed Elsevier, Inc. All Rights Reserved, and may not be modified, resold, sublicensed or disseminated further without express written permission. Any commercial exploitation of this content is strictly prohibited and infringers will be prosecuted to the full extent of the law.

Excerpt on page 342 is from *A People's History of The United States* by Howard Zinn. Copyright © 1980 by Howard Zinn. Reprinted by permission of HarperCollins Publishers Inc.

Excerpt on page 350 is from *The Black Americans: A History in Their Own Words*, edited by Milton Meltzer. Copyright © 1964, 1965, 1967, 1968 by Milton Melter. Used by permission of HarperCollins Publishers and Harold Ober Associates Incorporated.

Excerpt on page 351 is used with permission from Microsoft Corporation as made available through Microsoft ® Encarta ® Encyclopedia 2000. Located at http://encarta.msn.com.

Cartoon on page 367 is by Mike Keefe, The Denver Post. Reprinted by permission.

Cartoon on page 368 is "Link Between Poverty and Terrorism." Theo Moudakis, Toronto Star. Reprinted by permission.

Excerpt on pages 372–373 is from "Burma's New Dawn," by Zarni. Reprinted by permission of the author.

Excerpt on page 374 is used with permission from Microsoft Corporation as made available through Microsoft ® Encarta ® Encyclopedia 2000. Located at http://encarta.msn.com.

Excerpt on page 375 is from *A People's History of The United States* by Howard Zinn. Copyright © 1980 by Howard Zinn. Reprinted by permission of HarperCollins Publishers Inc.

Circle graph on page 385 is used with permission from NYT Graphics, © 1986. Reprinted by permission of The New York Times.

Excerpt on page 412 is reprinted with permission from *Discouraging Terrorism: Some Implications of 9/11*. Copyright 2002 by the National Academy of Sciences. Courtesy of the National Academies Press, Washington, D.C.

Graph on page 426 is from ACCRA. Graph reprinted by permission of Kansas City Area Development Council.

Graph on page 436 is from *The Secret History of the Industrial Revolution* by Gregory Clark. Reprinted by permission.

Excerpt on page 444 is used with permission from Microsoft Corporation as made available through Microsoft ® Encarta ® Encyclopedia 2000. Located at http://encarta.msn.com.

Graph on page 460 is reprinted with permission from *2002 Britannica Book of the Year*, © 2002 by Encyclopædia Britannica, Inc.

Cartoon on page 461 is "Office of Information Awareness," by Jeff Parker. Reprinted by permission of Jeff Parker, Florida Today.

Cartoon on page 471 is "The Doctrine of Preemption," by Andy Singer. www.andysinger.com. Reprinted by permission.

Cartoon on page 475 is © Tribune Media Services, Inc. All Rights Reserved. Reprinted with permission.

Cartoon on page 476 is by Bruce Beattie. © 1983 Daytona Beach Morning Journal. Reprinted by permission of Copley News Service.

Excerpt on page 850 is from *Woman Hollering Creek*. Copyright © 1991 by Sandra Cisneros. Published by Vintage Books, a division of Random House, Inc., New York and originally in hardcover by Random House, Inc. Reprinted by permission of Susan Bergholz Literary Services, New York and Bloomsbury Publishing Plc. All Rights Reserved.

Excerpts on pages 852–853 are from *My Fair Lady* © 1956 Alan Jay Lerner and Frederick Loewe. Reprinted by permission of the Estate of Alan Jay Lerner.

Cartoon on page 860 is by Mike Keefe, The Denver Post. Reprinted by permission.

Excerpt on page 864 is used with permission from Microsoft Corporation as made available through Microsoft ® Encarta ® Encyclopedia 2000. Located at http://encarta.msn.com.

To the Teacher and the Student

Incorporating the 2002 changes to the GED Test, McGraw-Hill/Contemporary's **Complete Pre-GED** program is designed to develop a firm basis in all the GED subject areas: language arts, writing; language arts, reading; social studies; science; and mathematics. Some special features to note are the Pretests, Posttests, Chapter Reviews, and the Answer Keys.

<u>Pretests and Posttests</u> These tests ask questions in multiple-choice and short-answer format, similar to those found on many tests. Questions are drawn from the entire range of skills and content in each section. Evaluation charts correlated to the chapters help identify areas of strength and weakness for further study.

<u>Chapter Reviews</u> These exercises, also in multiple-choice and short-answer format, review the skills taught in the chapter.

<u>Answer Keys</u> An answer key is located at the end of each section. Answers should be checked as soon as an exercise is completed to ensure mastery of the material.

Language Arts, Writing

This section develops both the process of writing and the conventions of English. In particular, there are four features to note:

<u>Grammar and Usage</u> The first part of each chapter covers specific grammar and usage skills needed for standard English.

<u>Punctuating Perfectly</u> These sections concentrate exclusively on punctuation related to grammar covered in the chapter.

<u>Putting Your Skills to Work</u> These highly structured writing activities follow language skills exercises. The writing focuses on the grammar point that was just taught. This feature provides an opportunity to understand grammar in the context of personal writing.

<u>Your Turn to Write</u> These sections provide a choice of topics and suggestions about how to approach a topic. They are followed by a checklist of the major grammar and usage points in the chapter. The checklist can be used as a guide for writers to edit their own work.

Research has shown that teaching the process of writing in conjunction with grammar and usage is a highly effective way of helping students to become better writers. Students should be encouraged to apply the skills they learn in this section to their daily lives.

Language Arts, Reading

This section develops the critical reading and thinking skills needed to handle a wide range of reading materials including poetry, drama, literature, nonfiction, and business documents. This section provides the reader with a thorough grounding in the organization and comprehension of short reading passages as well as in basic vocabulary skills. Critical reading skills such as making inferences, predicting outcomes, and identifying persuasive techniques are introduced.

The section emphasizes the step-by-step acquisition of skills. Attention is given to comprehension, vocabulary, and study skills, which complement each other and build skills gradually. Thinking-skill questions provide extra practice with the more challenging inferential and predicting skills. Visual aids such as charts, outlines, cartoons, and advertisements reinforce comprehension skills as they relate to daily life.

The short passages in this section provide a thorough introduction to reading, but they are no substitute for other reading opportunities. Short stories, poetry, newspapers, magazines, and any other reading material can supplement the passages in this section. Being comfortable with reading is necessary for lifelong learning.

Social Studies

This section develops the critical reading and thinking skills needed to successfully work with social studies material. Materials introduce how to study reading passages and illustrations such as charts, graphs, maps, and cartoons. Topics such as U.S. history, world history, basic economic principles, and primary source documents are presented through the use of reading passages and graphic illustrations. Higher-order thinking skills— understanding, application, analysis, synthesis, and evaluation—are introduced and practiced.

This section emphasizes the step-by-step acquisition of skills rather than discrete knowledge. Materials from the GED social studies areas—history, civics, government, economics, and geography—are represented throughout the text. Newspapers, magazines, road maps, and anything else you find useful or interesting should be read in addition to the material provided in this text.

Science

This section develops the critical reading and thinking skills needed to read and apply scientific information. While some skills may have already been mastered, each section is important as the science topics assure a solid grounding in key science concepts. Each chapter addresses a different science topic including: the scientific method, living things, human biology, physics, chemistry, and earth and space science.

Various sections introduce how to read and study passages and illustrations such as diagrams, charts, and graphs. Reading and discussing science topics from newspapers, magazines, radio programs, and television shows will help not only in school but also in everyday life.

Mathematics

This section instructs in a range of skills including whole numbers, calculator usage, word problems, decimals, fractions, ratio, proportions, percents, probability, basic algebra, measurement, and geometry. Addition, subtraction, multiplication, and division are applied to each of these skills.

Because word problems are an important component of a math tests, this section pays special attention to the development of problem-solving skills. As computation skills improve with practice, so will the problem-solving skills that are needed to work successfully through the math encountered in daily life.

17. What is the setting of the story?

    (1) a boy's bedroom
    (2) a school
    (3) a hospital
    (4) a doctor's office
    (5) a car

18. What does the title of the story refer to?

    (1) Schatz's application to go to school in France
    (2) the nine-year-old boy's wait for his father
    (3) the boy's wait for a doctor to make a home visit
    (4) the boy's wait for his fever to go down
    (5) the boy's waiting to die from a fever

19. What is the main conflict, or confusion, in the story?

    (1) the father's feeling over possibly losing his son
    (2) the doctor's handling of the boy's illness
    (3) the boy's thinking a fever over 44 degrees is fatal
    (4) the difference between driving miles and kilometers
    (5) the boy's lack of interest in the Pirate book

20. What is the connotation (suggested meaning) of the word poor when the father says, "You poor Schatz"?

    (1) disbelieving
    (2) disgusting
    (3) young
    (4) pitiful
    (5) cowardly

21. What happens at the climax of the story?

    (1) The father makes fun of Schatz's mistake.
    (2) The boy realizes he's not going to die.
    (3) The doctor shakes his head in disbelief.
    (4) The pharmacist calls to check on medication.
    (5) The boy's school friends call him from France.

22. What happens at the conclusion, or end, of the story?
    The boy

    (1) drove at seventy miles an hour
    (2) broke all thermometers in the house
    (3) realized how much he loved his dad
    (4) relaxed and cried easily at little things
    (5) promised to learn the Celcius temperature system

23. Why did Schatz cry easily the next day?
    He was

    (1) still very upset
    (2) relaxed and relieved
    (3) disappointed in his father
    (4) still very ill
    (5) reacting to medication

24. What is the tone up until the end of the story?

    (1) sad
    (2) happy
    (3) scary
    (4) peaceful
    (5) light

25. The theme of the story could involve all except

    (1) experience

Language Arts, Writing

This pretest is a chance for you to test your present writing skills. The pretest will show you the kinds of things you will be studying in this section and will help you identify the areas you should work on most.

Follow the directions before each section of the pretest and answer as many of the questions as possible. Answer each question to the best of your ability. When you have completed the pretest, check your answers on page 6.

Part I: Language Skills

Directions: Each pair of sentences below contains one complete sentence and one fragment or run-on. Circle the letter of the complete sentence in each pair. Then underline the subject of the complete sentence. The first one has been done as an example.

1. **a.** At Dinah's house after the movie.
   (b.) The <u>party</u> starts after the movie.

2. **a.** The role of computers in the plant.
   b. The computers do much of the work.

3. **a.** Roger is going to the office now.
   b. Go to the office this morning, come home in the afternoon.

4. **a.** Will Carla go out with her parents tonight?
   b. Respect your parents they love you.

Directions: Underline the correct noun form in each sentence below.

5. In the spring, the (school, School) will have driver education classes.

6. The (women, womens) are on their way home.

7. The (bus's, bus'es) tires were flat.

8. The (boys, boy's) caught five fish last summer.

9. Tomorrow (aunt, Aunt) Judy will pick you up at 3:00 P.M.

10. All the (doctors', doctors's) offices have gray carpeting.

Directions: Part of each sentence below is underlined. In the blank at the end of the sentence, write the pronoun you could use to replace the underlined part. The first one has been done as an example.

11. Bruno will buy <u>pizza</u>. _____ *it* _____

12. <u>Patty</u> will bring the tapes.
   _____

13. <u>The stereo's</u> speakers are fantastic.
   _____

14. <u>Steve and I</u> will entertain. _____

15. <u>Ethel's</u> best jokes will be told during dinner.
   _____

16. Those jokes will keep <u>the guests</u> laughing.
   _____

3

PRETEST

Directions: In the questions below, draw lines to connect the thoughts that can be combined to make complete, logical sentences. The first one is done as an example.

17. Alex ran for the train,   she missed my party.

18. Rosa lost her wallet;   nevertheless, she forgave us.

19. Tim worked very hard,   but he missed it.

20. Alice was angry;   although he hates music.

21. Because Cathy went to Boston,   so he got the promotion.

22. Mark went to the concert   therefore, she had to borrow money.

Directions: Underline the correct form of the verb to complete each sentence below.

23. The winner (will receive, will receives) $50,000.

24. Yesterday the man (laughs, laughed) at the television show.

25. The letters about the fundraiser (was, were) mailed last week.

26. Mike or Diane (is, are) in charge of the meeting.

27. Everyone (swims, swim) at the local pool.

28. Next time I (will walk, walked) another way.

Directions: Underline the correct word to complete each sentence below.

29. The (intelligent, intelligently) professor wrote a book.

30. After the game, Howard drove home (quick, quickly).

31. Raoul swam (graceful, gracefully).

Directions: Add one punctuation mark to make each sentence below correct.

32. I ordered pizza salad, and coffee.

33. What happened to the hot water

34. After the soccer team won the championship the players celebrated for two days.

35. Mr. Spagnola your help is needed.

36. I said "I am ready for anything."

37. Tim cant go dancing because he broke his leg.

38. Edwin has three daughters and I have two sons.

39. Celeste Wesson a policewoman, will talk about self-defense.

Part II: Writing Skills

Directions: Answer the following questions about yourself in complete sentences.

40. Tell three things you do when you have free time.

_____

_____

41. Write a sentence about what you like to eat for breakfast.

_____

_____

42. Tell why someone you love is very important to you.

_____

_____

43. Describe yourself. You might tell how tall you are, how old you are, what color hair and eyes you have, and how you like to dress.

_____

_____

_____

44. If you could have one wish granted, what would that wish be?

_____

_____

Answers are on pages 6–7.

Language Arts, Writing Answer Key

PART I: LANGUAGE SKILLS

1. **b.** party

2. **b.** computers

3. **a.** Roger

4. **a.** Carla

5. school No specific school is named, so it is not a proper noun and should not be capitalized.

6. women *Women* is a plural noun, so you should not add an *s*.

7. bus's Add *'s* to a singular noun to show possession.

8. boys Add *s* to make most nouns plural.

9. Aunt *Aunt* is used as part of Aunt Judy's name in this sentence, so it should be capitalized.

10. doctors' Several doctors have offices with gray carpeting. Add an apostrophe to a plural noun ending in *s* to show possession.

11. it The pronoun is the object of the sentence.

12. She The pronoun is the subject of the sentence.

13. Its The pronoun must show possession. Note that possessive pronouns are never spelled with an apostrophe. *It's* would be a contraction of *it is*.

14. We The pronoun is the subject of the sentence.

15. Her The pronoun must show possession.

16. them The pronoun is the object of the sentence.

17. Alex ran for the train, but he missed it.

18. Rosa lost her wallet; therefore, she had to borrow money.

19. Tim worked very hard, so he got the promotion.

20. Alice was angry; nevertheless, she forgave us.

21. Because Cathy went to Boston, she missed my party.

22. Mark went to the concert although he hates music.

23. will receive Form the future tense by using *will* with the base verb, *receive*.

24. laughed The time clue *Yesterday* tells you to put the verb in the past tense.

25. were To agree with the noun *letters* (not the noun in the interrupting phrase, *fundraiser*), the verb should be plural.

26. is Because the two parts of the subject are joined by *or*, the verb agrees with the closer part—the singular noun *Diane*.

27. swims Because *everyone* is a singular indefinite pronoun, the verb must end with *s*.

28. will walk The time clue *Next time* tells you to use the future tense.

29. intelligent An adjective must be used to describe the noun *professor*.

30. quickly An adverb must be used to describe the verb *drove*.

31. gracefully An adverb must be used to describe the verb *swam*.

32. I ordered pizza, salad, and coffee.

33. What happened to the hot water?

34. After the soccer team won the championship, the players celebrated for two days.

35. Mr. Spagnola, your help is needed.

36. I said, "I am ready for anything."

37. Tim can't go dancing because he broke his leg.

38. Edwin has three daughters, and I have two sons.

39. Celeste Wesson, a policewoman, will talk about self-defense.

6

PART II: WRITING SKILLS

Answers will vary. Ask your teacher to read your sentences and evaluate your work.

40. I like to jog. I watch TV often. I read the daily newspaper.

41. I like to eat bacon and eggs for breakfast.

42. I love my mother because she has done so many things for me.

43. I am nineteen years old. I am over six feet tall. I have dark hair and green eyes. My favorite clothes are jeans and a T-shirt.

44. If I could have one wish granted, I would wish for more wishes!

Evaluation Chart

After you have checked your answers, find the number of each question you missed and circle it in the second column. As you work through the Language Arts, Writing section, pay special attention to those areas where you missed one or more questions.

Skill		Question Numbers	Number Correct
Chapter 2 **Sentences**	Complete sentences Types of sentences	1, 2, 3, 4 33	_____ / 5
Chapter 3 **Nouns and Pronouns**	Common and proper nouns Singular and plural nouns Possessive nouns Subject and object pronouns Possessive pronouns Contractions	5, 9 6, 8 7, 10 11, 12, 14, 16 13, 15 37	_____ / 13
Chapter 4 **Verbs: Form and Tense**	Verb tenses	23, 24, 28	_____ / 3
Chapter 5 **Subject-Verb Agreement**	Subject-verb agreement	25, 26, 27	_____ / 3
Chapter 6 **Adjectives and Adverbs**	Adjectives and adverbs Quotation marks	29, 30, 31 36	_____ / 4
Chapter 7 **Combining Sentences and Organizing Paragraphs**	Coordinating conjunctions Connectors Subordinating conjunctions	17, 19, 38 18, 20 21, 22, 34	_____ / 8
Chapter 8 **Sentences and Paragraphs**	Commas in a series Direct address Phrases that give additional information	32 35 39	_____ / 3
	Total Correct		_____ / 39

Language Arts, Reading

The purpose of the Language Arts, Reading Pretest is to find your strengths as well as the areas you need to work on. As you take the pretest, don't worry if you have trouble answering a question. When you finish, check your answers with the Answer Key on page 16 and use the evaluation chart to help you and your instructor determine which skills you need to work on most.

Directions: Choose the best answer to each question.

1. Look at the following words: include, chowder, reporter, raven. What is the correct way to divide these words into syllables?

   (1) in-clude, chow-der, re-port-er, ra-ven
   (2) inc-lude, chow-der, re-port-er, ra-ven
   (3) in-clude, chowd-er, re-port-er, ra-ven
   (4) in-clude, chow-der, rep-ort-er, ra-ven
   (5) in-clude, chow-der, re-port-er, rav-en

2. Use your knowledge of roots, prefixes, and suffixes to match each word with its definition at the right.

   (1) antiaircraft
   (2) enfold
   (3) duplicate
   (4) interchangeable
   (5) dissect

   a. cover or surround
   b. make a copy
   c. cut in order to examine
   d. against aircraft
   e. able to be changed

3. Look at each word in **boldface type** on the left. Find its <u>synonym</u> from the four choices to the right.

   (1) slumber   **a.** sleep   **c.** awake
   　　　　　　　　b. work   **d.** read

   (2) gaze   **a.** gazebo   **c.** glaze
   　　　　　　　b. stare   **d.** haze

   (3) plain   **a.** unclear   **c.** vague
   　　　　　　　b. hazy   **d.** clear

   (4) winner   **a.** lost   **c.** victor
   　　　　　　　　b. failure   **d.** struggle

   (5) form   **a.** shape   **c.** from
   　　　　　　　b. produce   **d.** destroy

4. Read the following sentence. Then identify the key words that answer the questions *Who or what?* and *Did what?*

   The busy manager became irritable as the piles of work on his desk grew higher.

   The key words are ＿＿＿＿＿＿＿＿＿

   and ＿＿＿＿＿＿＿＿＿＿＿＿＿＿＿.

5. The earthquake was a calamity. People were trapped under buildings, and bridges had collapsed. *Calamity* means

   (1) disaster
   (2) party
   (3) celebration
   (4) bridge
   (5) surprise

6. Pick the word that best completes the analogy.

   red : stop :: green : ＿＿＿＿＿＿＿＿＿

   (1) yellow
   (2) go
   (3) slow
   (4) yield
   (5) turn

Questions 7–12 are based on the following passage.

People prefer to use self-service pumps at gas stations. As a result, routine car checks that gas station attendants used to do are often neglected. However, you can do these simple checks for yourself to ensure that your car stays in good running order.

Check the oil level with the dipstick, since running a car without sufficient oil can ruin the engine. You should also check other fluid levels such as the brake fluid, the transmission fluid (if your car is automatic), and the power steering fluid (if your car has power steering).

To avoid being burned or scalded, make sure the engine is cold before you check to see whether the radiator needs coolant. Tires, too, should be checked for proper air pressure when cool. Too much or too little pressure can cause tires to wear faster than normal.

These regular checks can save excessive wear on your car and may even prevent a frightening experience on the road.

7. The main idea of this selection is that you should

    (1) check your oil regularly
    (2) make routine car checks
    (3) always check your tire pressure
    (4) always buy gas at self-service pumps
    (5) never use self-service pumps

8. According to the author, why have routine car checks often been neglected?

    (1) Gas station attendants don't like to do routine car checks.
    (2) People are too lazy to bother with routine car checks.
    (3) People use self-service pumps and don't have attendants check their cars.
    (4) Cars are made to function without routine checks.
    (5) People aren't as concerned with safety as they once were.

9. The tone of the article is

    (1) funny
    (2) sad
    (3) informational
    (4) cheerful
    (5) sentimental

10. The passage includes the statement, "Running a car without sufficient oil can ruin the engine." You could also say, "Running a long race without drinking water can harm the body." If you consider both statements, you are

    (1) passing on a rumor
    (2) expressing an opinion
    (3) making a guess
    (4) using a contrast
    (5) making a comparison

11. What is the best title for this selection?

    (1) Getting Gas at a Self-Service Pump
    (2) The Importance of Routine Car Checks
    (3) Checking Car Brakes
    (4) Checking Fluids in Your Car
    (5) Buying a Used Car

12. Fill in the following blanks with details from the selection.

    a. Check the _____ level with the dipstick.

    b. Other fluids that need checking are the _____ fluid, the _____ fluid for automatics, and the _____ fluid.

    c. Your engine should be _____ when you check the radiator.

    d. Tires should be checked for pressure when _____.

Questions 13–16 are based on the following passage.

Everyone will face problems with their eyes at some point in life. For as wonderful as the eyes are, they are also very complicated organs of the human body. You should always be aware of how your eyes look, feel, and see.

How do your eyes FEEL?

There are many factors that can cause your eyes to feel different than they do normally. You should see your doctor if you have pain in or around your eyes, burning or itching, excessive tearing, or if they are unusually sensitive to light.

How do your eyes LOOK?

You should routinely inspect your eyelids and eye lashes. Check if they are crusty or swollen. Are the whites of your eyes bloodshot? Has there been any change to the iris (the colored part of your eye) or to the pupil (the black center of your eye)? Do both eyes look the same, or is one shaped differently.

How do your eyes SEE?

Visual acuity is the term doctors give to how well you see. You should routinely cover one eye, then the other, to determine if you can see objects clearly out of both eyes. Look at things that are both near and far. Can you read letters on signs? Can you clearly see the edges of objects, or do the edges blur?

> —Excerpted from "Extremely Important to Get Your Eyes Checked" by Tedd Mitchell, M.D.

13. To notice possible eye problems, what should you do?

(1) Ask a doctor about lasik surgery.
(2) Pay attention to how your eyes feel, look, and see.
(3) Adjust for your nighttime driving.
(4) Look for new glasses at the drugstore.
(5) Wear your glasses indoors.

14. Match each description below with the correct fact. Write the letter of the fact next to its description.

Description

_____ **(1)** how the eye feels

_____ **(2)** how the eye looks

_____ **(3)** how the eye sees

Fact

a. visual acuity, near and far
b. pain, blurring, itching, sensitive
c. whites, iris, pupil

15. How can you tell if you can see well?

(1) Notice any change in the color of the iris.
(2) Hold this book until the letters blur on the page.
(3) Read a book in very low light.
(4) Look at objects that are both distant and close.
(5) Notice if one pupil is larger than the other.

16. Fill in the following blanks with the correct details from the passage.

a. Who will face eye problems during their life? _____

b. What kind of organs are eyes?

_____

c. What is a problem with the way your eyes look? _____

d. When should you see the eye doctor?

_____

e. Why should you cover one eye, then the other and compare how you see?

_____

f. _____ is how well you see.

Questions 17–25 are based on the following passage.

A Day's Wait

At the house they said the boy had refused to let any one come into the room.

"You can't come in," he said. "You mustn't get what I have."

I went up to him and found him in exactly the position I had left him, white-faced, but with the tops of his cheeks flushed by the fever, staring still, as he had stared, at the foot of the bed.

I took his temperature.

"What is it?"

"Something like a hundred," I said. It was one hundred and two and four tenths.

"It was a hundred and two," he said.

"Who said so?"

"The doctor."

"Your temperature is all right," I said. "It's nothing to worry about."

"I don't worry," he said, "but I can't keep from thinking."

"Don't think," I said. "Just take it easy."

"I'm taking it easy," he said and looked straight ahead. He was evidently holding tight onto himself about something.

"Take this with water."

"Do you think it will do any good?"

"Of course it will."

I sat down and opened the *Pirate* book and commenced to read, but I could see he was not following, so I stopped.

"About what time do you think I'm going to die?" he asked.

"What?"

"About how long will it be before I die?"

"You aren't going to die. What's the matter with you?"

"Oh, yes I am. I heard him say a hundred and two."

"People don't die with a fever of one hundred and two. That's a silly way to talk."

"I know they do. At school in France the boys told me you can't live with forty-four degrees. I have a hundred and two."

He had been waiting to die all day, ever since nine o'clock in the morning.

"You poor Schatz," I said. "Poor old Schatz. It's like miles and kilometers. You aren't going to die. That's a different thermometer. On that thermometer thirty-seven is normal. On this kind it's ninety-eight."

"Are you sure?"

"Absolutely," I said. "It's like miles and kilometers. You know, like how many kilometers we make when we do seventy miles in the car?"

"Oh," he said.

But his gaze at the foot of the bed relaxed slowly. The hold over himself relaxed too, finally, and the next day it was very slack and he cried very easily at little things that were of no importance.

—Excerpted from "A Day's Wait" by Ernest Hemingway

17. What is the setting of the story?

   (1) a boy's bedroom
   (2) a school
   (3) a hospital
   (4) a doctor's office
   (5) a car

18. What does the title of the story refer to?

   (1) Schatz's application to go to school in France
   (2) the nine-year-old boy's wait for his father
   (3) the boy's wait for a doctor to make a home visit
   (4) the boy's wait for his fever to go down
   (5) the boy's waiting to die from a fever

19. What is the main conflict, or confusion, in the story?

   (1) the father's feeling over possibly losing his son
   (2) the doctor's handling of the boy's illness
   (3) the boy's thinking a fever over 44 degrees is fatal
   (4) the difference between driving miles and kilometers
   (5) the boy's lack of interest in the *Pirate* book

20. What is the connotation (suggested meaning) of the word *poor* when the father says, "You poor Schatz"?

   (1) disbelieving
   (2) disgusting
   (3) young
   (4) pitiful
   (5) cowardly

21. What happens at the climax of the story?

   (1) The father makes fun of Schatz's mistake.
   (2) The boy realizes he's not going to die.
   (3) The doctor shakes his head in disbelief.
   (4) The pharmacist calls to check on medication.
   (5) The boy's school friends call him from France.

22. What happens at the conclusion, or end, of the story?
The boy

   (1) drove at seventy miles an hour
   (2) broke all thermometers in the house
   (3) realized how much he loved his dad
   (4) relaxed and cried easily at little things
   (5) promised to learn the Celcius temperature system

23. Why did Schatz cry easily the next day?
He was

   (1) still very upset
   (2) relaxed and relieved
   (3) disappointed in his father
   (4) still very ill
   (5) reacting to medication

24. What is the tone up until the end of the story?

   (1) sad
   (2) happy
   (3) scary
   (4) peaceful
   (5) light

25. The theme of the story could involve all except

   (1) experience
   (2) knowledge
   (3) compassion
   (4) innocence
   (5) greed

Questions 26–29 are based on the following business document.

If you own a home, you know it is important to have homeowner's insurance. Every day, insurance companies decide whether to issue or renew policies. Natural disasters, such as fires, floods, and earthquakes, result in a lot of claims being filed each year. Serious acts of terror may also result in more claims. Insurance companies may not renew the policies of homeowners who have made two or more recent claims. If this happens to you, contact the Department of Insurance in your state. Here is sample information from an Illinois fact sheet.

Illinois Insurance Facts:
If Your Homeowners Insurance Policy Is Nonrenewed
Revised February 2002

Reason for Nonrenewal

A company may nonrenew your homeowner's policy for any reason except age or location of the property, or the age, gender, race, color, ancestry, marital status, or occupation of the occupants.

If the company nonrenews your policy because the property condition has declined, the company must allow you time (not more than 90 days) to make repairs.

A company is prohibited from nonrenewing your homeowner's policy based **solely** on credit report information.

Notice

The company must send you a written notice explaining why it is nonrenewing your policy. The notice must also explain two important items:

1. You have the right to appeal the nonrenewal.
2. You may be eligible to buy insurance from the Illinois FAIR Plan Association if you cannot find coverage elsewhere.

Source: http://www.state.il.us/ins/HomeInsurance/honon.htm

26. Name one thing for which insurance companies may receive numerous claims.

_____

27. If an insurance company decides to nonrenew your homeowner's policy because they think you filed more than two claims last year, what could you argue to reinstate your policy?

(1) your age
(2) your gender (male or female)
(3) your race or color
(4) your occupation
(5) your claim history

28. An insurance company must follow a certain process if it is nonrenewing your policy. What must the company send you?

_____

29. The information about insurance nonrenewal may be called

(1) facts
(2) opinions
(3) beliefs
(4) views
(5) rumors

Questions 30–34 are based on the following poem.

A Time to Talk

(1) When a friend calls to me from the road
And slows his horse to a meaning walk,
I don't stand still and look around
On all the hills I haven't hoed,
(5) And shout from where I am, "What is it?"
No, not as there is a time to talk.
I thrust my hoe in the mellow ground,
Blade-end up and five feet tall,
And plod: I go up to the stone wall
(10) For a friendly visit.

—by Robert Frost

30. What does the poet **not** do when a friend calls to him?

(1) decide it's time for a break
(2) join his friend for a chat
(3) put down his hoe
(4) plod over to the stone wall
(5) stand and look at the work he hasn't done

31. When a friend calls to him, the poet

(1) stops working so that he can talk to his friend
(2) keeps hoeing so he can finish his work
(3) waves at his friend and tells him he is too busy to talk
(4) goes to the barn to milk his cows
(5) pretends not to hear his friend

32. From this poem, you can infer that the poet believes

(1) talking to friends is less important than working
(2) talking to friends is more important than working
(3) plowing fields is hard work
(4) his friend shouldn't bother him while he is working
(5) his friend is a lazy worker

33. The hoe is left

(1) lying on the ground
(2) leaning against the stone wall
(3) stuck upright in the dirt
(4) in the barn
(5) resting against a hill

34. You can predict that, after the visit, the poet will probably

(1) return to hoeing
(2) go home
(3) fall asleep
(4) find another friend to talk to
(5) eat dinner

Answers are on pages 16–17.

Language Arts, Reading Answer Key

1. (1)

2. (1) d **(2)** a **(3)** b **(4)** e **(5)** c

3. (1) a **(2)** b **(3)** d **(4)** c **(5)** a

4. *Who or what?*   *Did what?*
the busy manager   became irritable

5. (1) Clues are "people were trapped under buildings" and "bridges had collapsed." This could only be a disaster.

6. (2) *Red* means to stop and *green* means to go.

7. (2) Choice (2) is the main idea. All other choices are supporting ideas.

8. (3) This idea is stated in the first two sentences of the passage.

9. (3) The facts given in this passage give the passage an informational rather than an emotional tone.

10. (5) The two statements are similar. Both involve having enough liquid (in a car engine and a runner).

11. (2) Choice (5) is not mentioned in the passage. All the other choices refer only to specific details in the passage, not the entire passage.

12. a. oil
b. brake; transmission; power steering
c. cold
d. cool

13. (2) The last sentence of the first paragraph states this information.

14. (1) b
    (2) c
    (3) a

15. (4) The fourth paragraph tells about how to tell if you can see well. It tells you to look at distant objects and closer objects.

16. a. everyone
b. wonderful, extremely complex
c. crusty, swollen, bloodshot, changes to the iris or pupil
d. when you experience changes
e. to see how well you can see near and far
f. Visual acuity

17. (1) The boy is in his bedroom in bed.

18. (5) The story states, "He had been waiting to die all day, ever since nine o'clock in the morning." This explains the title.

19. (3) The boy says, "At school in France the boys told me you can't live with forty-four degrees. I've got a hundred and two." He thought his temperature was fatal.

20. (4) The father understands that his son mixed up two types of thermometers (Fahrenheit and Celsius). *Poor* may mean *pitiful* in this context.

21. (2) Schatz's father tells him, "You aren't going to die. That's a different thermometer."

22. (4) The narrator relates, "The hold over himself relaxed too, finally, and the next day it was very slack and he cried very easily."

23. (2) The boy "cried very easily at little things that were of no importance." This shows that he's relaxed enough to cry and to return to the simple things of a child.

24. (1) The boy is obviously upset and sad because he's ill and thinks he is going to die.

25. (5) There is no connection of greed to the story.

26. natural disasters (fires, earthquakes, floods) or a serious act of terror

27. (5) Choices (1), (2), (3), and (4) may not be used as a condition for nonrenewal.

28. "The company must send you a written notice explaining why it is nonrenewing your policy."

29. (1) The sheet is called "Illinois Insurance Facts." The other choices are not accurate.

30. (5) Lines 3–4 support this choice.

31. (1) Lines 9–10 state that the poet goes "up to the stone wall / For a friendly visit."

32. (2) The poet states that there is always time for "a friendly visit," even when he's busy hoeing. Choices (1) and (4) are directly contradicted by the poem. Choices (3) and (5) are not addressed by the poem.

33. (3) In lines 7–8, the poet sticks his hoe "in the mellow ground, / Blade-end up."

34. (1) The poet does not imply that he thinks hoeing is not important. He says only that he thinks it worth interrupting to talk with a friend who drops by. Therefore, he will probably return to hoeing.

Evaluation Chart

After you have checked your answers, circle the number of each question you missed. This will help you and your instructor decide which chapters you should concentrate on.

	Skill	Item Numbers	Number Correct
Chapter 1 **Gaining Meaning** **from Words**	Syllables Word parts Synonyms and antonyms	1 2 3	_____/3
Chapter 2 **Understanding What** **You Read**	Key words in sentences Words in context Main idea Supporting details	4 5 7, 11, 18 12, 13, 14, 15, 16, 27	_____/11
Chapter 3 **Finding Hidden** **Meaning**	Inference Word connotation Predicting outcomes	23, 32 20 34	_____/4
Chapter 4 **Organizing Ideas**	Fact, opinion, and generalization Sequence Comparison and contrast Cause and effect Analogy	29 28 10 8, 26 6	_____/6
Chapter 5 **Understanding** **Fiction**	Setting Tone Plot: beginning, conflict, climax, and conclusion Theme	17 9, 24 19, 21, 22 25	_____/7
Chapter 6 **Understanding** **Poetry and Drama**	Paraphrasing poetry	30, 31, 33	_____/3

Total Correct _____/34

Social Studies

The Social Studies Pretest is a guide to using the social studies section. The questions will test the social studies reading and reasoning skills covered in this section. When you have completed the pretest, check your answers with the Answer Key on page 27.

Directions: Read each passage or illustration, and then answer the questions that follow.

Questions 1 and 2 are based on the following passage.

Just as George Washington is often considered the founding father of the United States, Simon Bolivar is often considered the "Liberator of Spanish America." However, the lives and legacies of these two men turned out to be very different. Washington died a hero, and the colonies he led to independence became the world's most powerful nation, the United States of America. Bolivar died in disgrace. The colonies he led to independence from Spain eventually split into six independent, but weak, nations: Venezuela, Peru, Columbia, Ecuador, Bolivia, and Panama.

Both Washington and Bolivar were the military leaders of colonial revolts against European powers. Both favored strong central governments and were the first presidents of newly independent countries. After Washington left the presidency of the United States, the nation continued to prosper and grow. By the time Bolivar resigned the presidency of the Republic of Columbia in 1830, his dream of a confederation of Spanish American countries lay in ruins.

1. In what way were Washington and Bolivar similar?

   (1) Both ended their lives in retirement as honored national heroes.
   (2) Both successfully led wars of independence from a colonial nation.
   (3) Both were forced to resign from the presidency of their new nations.
   (4) Both were the first president of nations that became very strong.
   (5) Both were frustrated in their attempts to guide their new nations.

2. What was the most important difference between Washington and Bolivar?

   (1) Washington revolted against the British Empire, while Bolivar revolted against Spanish Empire.
   (2) Washington led a revolt in the late 1700s, while Bolivar led a revolt in the early 1800s.
   (3) Washington believed in a strong central government, while Bolivar favored separate nations.
   (4) Washington was successful as a military leader, while Bolivar was defeated on the battlefield.
   (5) Washington succeeded in creating a united nation from separate colonies, while Bolivar failed.

Question 3 is based on the following passage.

As a word-processing teacher, I often receive telephone calls from companies interested in hiring my students. When they ask for a recommendation, they do not first ask about skills, intelligence, age, or appearance. The first question is almost always about attendance and punctuality. When I tell my students about this question, they are often surprised.

3. What do companies value most in their word-processing employees?

   (1) potential
   (2) attractiveness
   (3) youth
   (4) dependability
   (5) knowledge

Questions 4 and 5 are based on the following cartoon.

"You can take the five years and $60,000 in fines, or you can go for Door Number Two where officer Meryl is standing."

Peter Oakley, "Modern Wonder Cartoons"

Background clues: Prison overcrowding in the United States has forced judges to seek alternative ways of punishing people convicted of crimes. Community service, payments to victims, and boot camps are just some of the alternative sentences judges in the United States have used.

4. When the cartoonist writes, "You can go for Door Number Two where Officer Meryl is standing," he is comparing modern trials to

   (1) birthday parties
   (2) war
   (3) classrooms
   (4) game shows
   (5) horrible ordeals

5. The point of this cartoon is that alternative sentencing

   (1) makes punishment a matter of luck
   (2) helps trials move more smoothly
   (3) is a more humane way of punishing criminals
   (4) discourages potential criminals from committing crimes
   (5) saves the government a lot of money

Questions 6 and 7 are based on the following passage.

   Even though Islamic countries generally have had poor records on women's rights, the three most populous Islamic countries have all had women lead their governments. In 1988, Benazir Bhutto, daughter of former President Zulfikar Ali Bhutto, became the first woman to be elected prime minister of an Islamic country when she won the election in Pakistan. In Bangladesh, Begum Khaleda Zia, the widow of former President Ziaur Rahman, became Prime Minister in 1991. More recently, in 2001, the world's largest Islamic country, Indonesia, elected Megawati Sukarnoputri as president, daughter of founding President Sukarno.

6. What is the main idea of this passage?

   (1) It is very rare for women to gain political influence in Islamic countries.
   (2) Islamic countries are increasingly turning to women for political leadership.
   (3) Political success is improving conditions for women in Islamic countries.
   (4) The three largest Islamic states have all had women lead their countries.
   (5) Benazir Bhutto was the first woman to be elected leader of an Islamic country.

7. The information given in the passage is adequate to make which prediction?

   (1) The next woman to lead an Islamic country will probably be the wife or daughter of a former leader.
   (2) The political success of Islamic women will lead to a fundamentalist backlash in Islamic countries.
   (3) Megawati Sukarnoputri will probably remain in power in Indonesia for many years.
   (4) The next generation of political Islamic women will get their start in local politics.
   (5) As they turn to women leaders, Islamic nations will be less violent.

Question 8 is based on the following passage.

   The United States can be thought of as a land of invention. For example, in the area of transportation, America has been responsible for more progress than any other nation in the world. American firsts include the steamboat, the airplane, and the nuclear submarine. The nineteenth century's most extensive railroad system was built in our country. In addition, the mass production of automobiles began in the United States which led to our highway system being the best in the world.

8. In the area of transportation, the United States has

   (1) been a world leader
   (2) concentrated on the automobile
   (3) neglected the railroads
   (4) followed progress in Europe
   (5) resisted change

Questions 9 and 10 are based on the following graph.

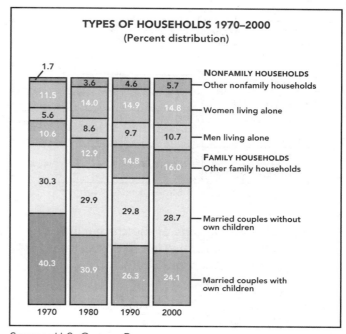

Source: U.S. Census Bureau

9. What type of household had the most dramatic decline from 1970 to 2000?

   (1) other nonfamily households
   (2) people living alone
   (3) other family households
   (4) married couples without own children
   (5) married couples with own children

10. Which of the following is a reasonable conclusion based on this graph?

   (1) Nontraditional households will most likely continue to increase in numbers.
   (2) Traditional families with two parents and children are likely to become more common.
   (3) Planners need to expect an increased demand for large single-family homes.
   (4) Most Americans have decided not to have any children at all.
   (5) The increase in single-parent households totally explains the decrease in two-parent households

Questions 11 and 12 are based on the following chart.

STRATEGIC IMPORTS (Averages in percent)	Platinum group metals	Chromium	Vanadium	Manganese	Gold
Share of U.S. imports originating in South Africa (1990–1993)	47%	43%	13%	24%	NA
South Africa's share of world reserves	89%	60%	50%	92%	26%
South Africa's share of world production (1994)	60%	31%	30%	36%	48%

Sources: U.S. Bureau of Mines; United Nations

11. What percentage of the chromium imported into the United States from 1990 to 1993 came from South Africa?

(1) 13%
(2) 31%
(3) 43%
(4) 47%
(5) 60%

12. Platinum group metals, chromium, vanadium, and manganese are all important to American industry. What does the chart tell you about the relationship of South Africa to the United States in the early 1990s?

(1) The United States had virtually no economic relationship with South Africa.
(2) South Africa relies on the United States for raw materials such as valuable metals.
(3) The United States could get along easily without imports from South Africa.
(4) South Africa provides the United States with important raw materials.
(5) South Africa lacks natural mineral resources needed by its heavy industries.

Questions 13 and 14 are based on the following passage.

In May 1607, the first permanent English colony in what is now the United States was founded at Jamestown, Virginia. The colonists built their village on a terrible swamp, and then the men spent their time looking for gold. The entire colony would have starved if not for the help of the native chief Powhatan, who gave the settlers food.

The colony struggled along until John Rolfe discovered the American tobacco plant. Virginia eventually began to export tobacco to Europe, where it became very popular. The success of the Virginia colony was assured.

13. After building their village, the first settlers

(1) planted tobacco
(2) attacked the Native Americans
(3) searched for gold
(4) planted food crops
(5) befriended and helped the Native Americans

14. The colonists needed help from the Native Americans

(1) because they did not know how to grow tobacco in Virginia
(2) because they did not produce enough food for their needs
(3) to prevent the introduction of slavery into Virginia
(4) to build the houses and storage buildings in the village of Jamestown
(5) to figure out how they could export tobacco to Europe

Questions 15 and 16 are based on the following map.

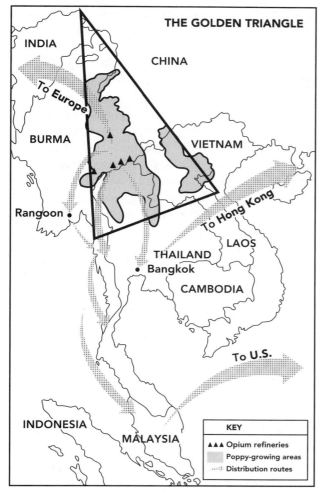

THE GOLDEN TRIANGLE

INDIA
CHINA
To Europe
BURMA
VIETNAM
Rangoon
To Hong Kong
LAOS
THAILAND
Bangkok
CAMBODIA
To U.S.
INDONESIA
MALAYSIA

KEY
▲▲▲ Opium refineries
Poppy-growing areas
······ Distribution routes

15. According to the map, opium refineries in the Golden Triangle were all in

  (1) Bangkok
  (2) Europe
  (3) Rangoon
  (4) India
  (5) poppy-growing areas

16. From Malaysia, heroin was sent to

  (1) Thailand
  (2) Burma
  (3) Hong Kong
  (4) the United States
  (5) Europe

Questions 17 and 18 are based on the following passage.

During the nineteenth century, the plow played a vital role for men searching for the American promise of opportunity and independence. The wilderness was the frontier for American men. As long as they could clear new land, plow it, and grow something on it, the land was theirs. The plow set them free.

However, by the late 1800s, the city was the frontier for American women. The typewriter gave them a way to earn money and the opportunity to set a course of their own. The business office, not the wilderness, would give women the chance to control their own lives.

17. According to the passage, the machine that most helped women gain economic independence was the

  (1) sewing machine
  (2) typewriter
  (3) plow
  (4) electric mixer
  (5) automobile

18. The passage describes different opportunities for American women and American men. The key difference the writer describes is that

  (1) women were usually more dependent on others for help than were men
  (2) women preferred to live in cities while men preferred to live in log cabins
  (3) women preferred the safety of staying at home while men preferred change and adventure
  (4) cities offered women the independence and opportunity that men found in the wilderness
  (5) women were more likely to plan for the future, while men usually lived for the present

Question 19 is based on the following map.

MODERN EUROPE

19. The Age of Exploration was just beginning during the 1500s. Many European countries sent explorers across the Atlantic Ocean to claim lands. Spain, Portugal, France, and England were all major participants in the exploration and colonization of the Americas. Switzerland, however, did not participate in this exploration and colonization. What was the most likely cause for this lack of participation?

    (1) Switzerland was fragmented into many small, weak states.
    (2) Switzerland did not have an interest in other countries until much later.
    (3) Switzerland wanted to conquer Europe, not the Americas.
    (4) Switzerland lacked access to the Atlantic Ocean.
    (5) Cities in Switzerland were not yet interested in trading.

Questions 20 and 21 are based on the following passage.

As in quite a few southern towns, many people in Eastman, Georgia, used to work in a textile mill. After eighty years of operation, the Reeves Brothers mill closed in the mid-1980s, laying off 340 people. The economy of this little town was hurt badly by the loss of jobs and wages from the mill.

Bit by bit, however, the town rebounded from the mill closing. At the time the Reeves Brothers mill closed, the Standard Candy Company was run by fewer than 100 part-time employees. Now Standard Candy has several hundred full-time workers. Another company, Reynolds Aluminum, also added employees to its payroll. A local welding company expanded, and so did another small candy company. In addition, a large discount store opened its doors in Eastman, providing even more jobs.

Perhaps the biggest boost to Eastman's economy was a new Georgia highway that was built right through it. The highway connects Georgia's largest city, Atlanta, with the Georgia seacoast. Because of the highway, products made in Eastman are easier to ship to other places. The highway also allows Eastman to attract tourists driving from Atlanta to the various beaches.

20. Over the next few years, it is likely that

    (1) more new jobs will be created in Eastman
    (2) the population of Eastman will decline rapidly
    (3) many residents of Eastman will turn to farming for a living
    (4) most laid-off mill workers will still be out of work
    (5) a major state highway running through Eastman will close

21. Which of the following strategies could best help another small, Southern town rebound from a mill closing?

  (1) Residents should relocate to areas where mills are still open.
  (2) The town should work to attract new businesses to the area.
  (3) Mill workers who are laid off by the closing should collect unemployment insurance.
  (4) The town should improve schools and recreational programs for children.
  (5) The town should build a new highway.

Questions 22 and 23 are based on the following passage.

At the end of World War I, in 1919, world leaders decided to form a League of Nations to help prevent future wars. Many of the leaders who were writing the Covenant of the League of Nations laughed at including a clause that supported racial equality. One British official, Lord Balfour, said that he could not accept the fact that "a man in Central Africa was created equal to a European." President Woodrow Wilson even voted against including a section about racial equality in the document. The leaders finally extended rights to Europeans but not people living in colonies around the world.

Given such obvious racism in 1919, it seems amazing that the United Nations in 1948 adopted the Universal Declaration of Human Rights. The UDHR is clear that "all human beings are born free and equal in dignity and rights" and plainly states that "distinction of any kind" based on race or color is wrong.

22. What most likely caused the reasoning of Lord Balfour and Woodrow Wilson?

  (1) They concluded that since their countries won World War I, they were superior to others.
  (2) They felt that the technological advancement of European peoples was proof of superiority.
  (3) They thought that full equality for all human beings would not be accepted by others.
  (4) They felt that only whites could be trusted to manage conflicts without using violence.
  (5) They believed that since the population of Europe was so large they were superior to others.

23. Based on the information in the passage, which of the following statements is a fact?

  (1) Woodrow Wilson has an undeserved reputation as a defender of democracy and freedom.
  (2) Wilson resisted equal rights for nonwhite areas in order to gain support in the U.S.
  (3) It is amazing that the world made so much progress in human rights from 1919 to 1948.
  (4) The League of Nations would have succeeded if it had endorsed universal human rights.
  (5) The Universal Declaration of Human Rights was adopted by the United Nations in 1948.

Question 24 is based on the following passage.

During the 1840s, many Americans believed in manifest destiny—the idea that the United States had the right to control all the land from the Atlantic Ocean to the Pacific Ocean. President Polk used the theory of manifest destiny to justify declaring war on Mexico in 1846. As a result of the Mexican War, Mexico lost half of its territory and the United States gained most of its southwestern lands, including California.

24. The main idea of this paragraph is that

(1) the United States used manifest destiny to justify taking over half of Mexico

(2) Mexico lost half of its territory as a result of losing the Mexican War

(3) the American form of government needs an entire continent to function well

(4) the United States was right to conquer half of Mexico in order to spread democracy

(5) Mexico provoked the United States into war by opposing manifest destiny

Answers are on page 27.

Social Studies Answer Key

1. (2) They both successfully led wars of independence from colonial powers.

2. (5) While choices (1) and (2) are also true, Washington's success in creating a unified government while Bolivar failed is the most important difference.

3. (4) The writer tells you that the companies are most concerned with attendance and punctuality. These are signs of dependability.

4. (4) Some game shows offer contestants mystery boxes like the one in this cartoon.

5. (1) The gift-wrapped door represents the alternative sentence. If the defendant is lucky, the sentence will be light; if he's unlucky, the sentence will be heavy.

6. (4) The main idea is that the three largest Islamic countries have all had women leaders.

7. (1) Given the evidence in the passage, the only way currently for a women to become the political leader of an Islamic country is to be the wife or daughter of a former political leader.

8. (1) The passage describes different ways that the U.S. has been a world leader in transportation.

9. (5) "Married couples with own children" had the most dramatic decline from 40.3% in 1970 to 24.1% in 2000.

10. (1) Both "other nonfamily" and "other family" households have had an increasing percentage of total households from 1970 to 2000. It seems likely the trend will continue.

11. (3) The "Share of U.S. imports originating in South Africa" is 43%.

12. (4) These materials are important to U.S. industry. The chart shows that South Africa sells a lot of these materials to the United States.

13. (3) The passage states that the colonists built homes and then spent their time looking for gold.

14. (2) The passage states that the colonists would have starved if Powhatan had not given them food. The settlers were not producing enough food on their own.

15. (5) Opium refineries (triangles) are in the poppy-growing areas (shaded gray).

16. (4) Distribution routes are marked on the map by arrows. The arrow from Malaysia is "to U.S."

17. (2) The passage says that the typewriter gave women a way to earn money.

18. (4) The first paragraph says that men found independence in the wilderness. The second paragraph describes the city as the place where women found the opportunity for independence.

19. (4) The most likely cause for the lack of Swiss participation in the Age of Exploration was the lack of access to the ocean.

20. (1) The passage describes ways in which new jobs are coming into Eastman because of new and expanding businesses.

21. (2) New businesses helped to bring new jobs to Eastman. Other small towns that have lost jobs through mill closings would also benefit if new businesses moved in.

22. (1) At the end of World War I, the winning countries made decisions that impacted the lives of many people around the world.

23. (5) Only choice (5) is a fact. The other choices are either opinions or hypotheses.

24. (1) This choice brings together all the ideas in the paragraph.

SOCIAL STUDIES PRETEST

Evaluation Chart

After you have checked your answers, circle the number of each question you missed on the chart below. Then decide which chapters you should concentrate on.

	Skill	Question Numbers	Number Correct
Chapter 1 Understanding What You Read	Finding details Restating information Summarizing information Main idea Inference Political cartoons	17 14 8 6, 24 12 4, 5	______/8
Chapter 2 Interpreting Graphic Materials	Using charts Using graphs Using maps	11 9 15, 16	______/4
Chapter 3 Applying Information in Social Studies	Application	21	______/1
Chapter 4 Analyzing Social Studies Materials	Sequence Cause and effect Compare and contrast Fact, opinion, and hypothesis Predicting outcomes	13 19 1, 2, 18 23 10, 20	______/8
Chapter 5 Evaluating Social Studies Materials	Adequacy of information Errors in reasoning and propaganda Values	7 22 3	______/3
		Total Correct	______/24

Science

This pretest will check your science knowledge and your ability to think scientifically. When you have completed the pretest, check your answers on page 35.

Directions: Read each passage carefully. Look closely at any illustrations. Then choose the one best answer for each question that follows.

Questions 1 and 2 are based on the following passage.

Everyone knows what a cold is. Most of us will get two to four colds this year. But did you know that the common cold is caused by any one of more than 200 different viruses? The number of cold viruses is one reason a cure for the common cold has yet to be developed. Scientists have not been able to find a remedy that fights every single cold virus.

What can you do when you catch a cold? The best advice is to drink lots of fluids and get plenty of rest. Gargling with warm salt water might soothe your scratchy throat. Inhaling steam might open up your stuffy nose. Taking over-the-counter cold remedies might also help. If those remedies don't help, give yourself time. Most people feel better after a week or two. Meanwhile, get yourself a box of tissues and a nice warm blanket!

1. Which of the following is the best title for this passage?

    (1) Avoiding the Common Cold
    (2) Remedies for the Common Cold
    (3) How to Cure the Common Cold
    (4) Dealing with a Common Cold Virus
    (5) Recognizing the Common Cold Virus

2. Which of the following best explains why a cold is called "the common cold"?

    (1) Many ordinary doctors can cure it.
    (2) It is caused by one common virus.
    (3) Most people catch a cold fairly often.
    (4) Common people catch more colds than famous people do.
    (5) It is commonly treated with over-the-counter remedies.

Question 3 is based on the following passage and chart.

More than 1,000 animals around the world are endangered, or threatened with extinction. About 500 of these are found in the U.S.

Species	Causes of Endangerment
American crocodile	Overhunted for its hide
Black-footed ferret	Poisoning of prairie dogs—its chief prey
Blue whale	Overhunted for blubber, food, and whale oil
Cheetah	Overhunted for sport; habitat destruction
Indian elephant	Habitat destruction; illegal killing for ivory
Snow leopard	Overhunted for its fur; killed in predator-control programs

3. Which of the following is **not** a reason that the animals on the chart are endangered?

    (1) The place where some animals lived was destroyed.
    (2) Too many of some animals were hunted for sport or body parts.
    (3) Some animals died because their main source of food was poisoned.
    (4) Some animals were killed because they are predators.
    (5) Some animals died from a natural cause, such as a change in climate.

Questions 4 and 5 are based on the following passage and diagram.

Keeping the proper amount of air pressure in your automobile tires is important. Incorrect tire pressure can cause extra tire wear. It can also cause accidents. Underinflation can cause a tire to heat up, possibly leading to a blowout on the highway. Overinflation prevents tire tread from fully gripping the road, making the car more likely to skid. Car owners should routinely check the pressure in their car's tires.

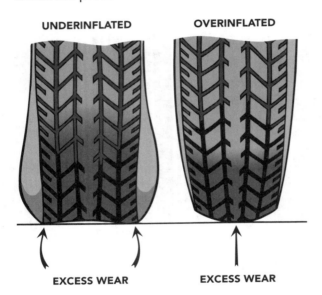

UNDERINFLATED   OVERINFLATED

EXCESS WEAR   EXCESS WEAR

4. Which of the following describes an overinflated tire?

   (1) a tire that costs too much
   (2) a tire that has too little pressure in it
   (3) a tire that is badly worn
   (4) a tire that has too much air in it
   (5) a tire that requires fifty pounds of pressure

5. This passage is most likely to be from which of the following books?

   (1) Cooking Great Meals on the Road
   (2) 1,001 Ways to Save Money
   (3) Choosing the Right Automobile
   (4) Safe Travel in the Air
   (5) Tips for New Car Owners

Questions 6 and 7 are based on the following passage.

People have been making glass for thousands of years using some of the same methods we use today. Ordinary window glass is made from a mixture of sand (SiO_2), soda (Na_2CO_3), and lime (CaO). This mixture is heated until the different chemicals fuse together into a thick semiliquid. The semiliquid can be blown, pressed, or stretched into different shapes before it cools and hardens.

Depending on how it has been mixed and shaped, glass can be used for windows, cups and dishes, lenses in eyeglasses and telescopes, airtight containers for foods and medicines, glass bricks for building, and many other purposes. Glass can even be drawn into a fine thread called fiberglass. Fiberglass can be used for insulation and filters or woven into fabric for curtains and drapes.

6. Which of the following statements is true, according to the passage?

   (1) Sand, soda, and lime are heated separately and mixed to make glass.
   (2) Glass must be cool before it can be shaped.
   (3) The basic materials in glass fuse together after they are heated.
   (4) After the glass is shaped, it is heated to make it strong.
   (5) After it hardens, glass is carved into the desired shape.

7. Oxygen is an element present in sand, soda, and lime. Which of the following is the chemical symbol for oxygen? (**Hint:** Look at the chemical formulas.)

   (1) Si
   (2) O
   (3) Na
   (4) C
   (5) Ca

Questions 8 and 9 are based on the following passage.

When a human enjoys something, cells in the brain release the chemical dopamine. When dopamine travels to other brain cells, called receptors, the person feels pleasure. After a short time, the dopamine is absorbed back into the cells that produced it.

Research indicates that cocaine stops this process. Cocaine keeps dopamine from being reabsorbed. Instead, the dopamine stays near the receptor cells, causing intense pleasure. But after fifteen to twenty minutes, the dopamine has broken up. The user must take cocaine again in order to feel that rush of pleasure.

Every dose of cocaine uses up more of the brain's supply of dopamine. The user must have larger doses to feel the same rush. Also, the brain no longer releases dopamine in response to ordinary enjoyment. The cocaine user can get pleasure only from cocaine.

Obviously, cocaine is not a harmless drug. In fact, cocaine addiction is one of the hardest drug habits to break. Fortunately, research points the way toward new medical treatments that may help users break the cocaine habit.

8. What is this passage mostly about?

   (1) the effects of cocaine on the body
   (2) the reasons people take cocaine
   (3) the treatments available to addicts
   (4) the effects of cocaine on the brain
   (5) the different ways people feel pleasure

9. Which of the following would the author of this passage most likely vote for?

   (1) more government money to pay for drug-related research
   (2) harsher prison sentences for drug users
   (3) cuts in funding for drug education programs
   (4) government programs to supply addicts with dopamine
   (5) shorter prison time for drug dealers

Questions 10 and 11 are based on the following passage and graph.

Weather forecasters use an anemometer to measure the speed of wind. Below is a graph showing one day's anemometer readings at a certain weather station.

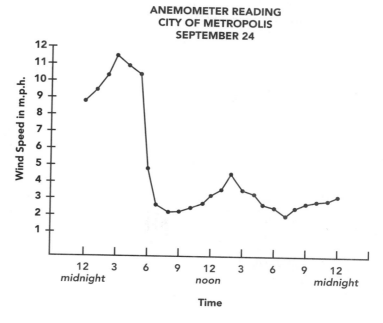

10. Considering that both light and wind are needed to fly a kite successfully, what was the best time to fly a kite in Metropolis on September 24?

    (1) 2 A.M.
    (2) 3 A.M.
    (3) 10 A.M.
    (4) 2 P.M.
    (5) 6 P.M.

11. A thermometer measures temperature, and an anemometer is used to measure wind speed. Which of the following best describes what an altimeter measures?

    (1) the loudness of sounds
    (2) the alternate routes through cities
    (3) the altitude in airplanes
    (4) the amount of liquid in a cylinder
    (5) the speed of light

Questions 12 and 13 are based on the following passage and diagram.

The diagram shows the two main scales used to measure temperature today. The Fahrenheit (F) scale is used by most people in the United States. The Celsius (C) scale is used by most other people in the world as well as by scientists.

TEMPERATURE

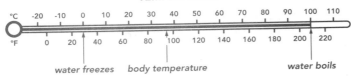

12. What is the boiling point of water on the Celsius scale?

   (1) 0°C
   (2) 60°C
   (3) 98.6°C
   (4) 100°C
   (5) 212°C

13. Which statement correctly reflects the information in the diagram?

   (1) When the temperature outside is 35°C, most people would want to turn on the air conditioner.
   (2) The weather is warmer in the United States than in other countries.
   (3) The Celsius scale is harder for most people to understand.
   (4) Water freezes at a lower temperature on the Celsius scale than it does on the Fahrenheit scale.
   (5) 70°F is warmer than 25°C.

Questions 14 and 15 are based on the following passage.

Yellowstone National Park, in the western United States, was the first national park established in the world. Little was known about this beautiful area, famous for its hot springs, geysers, and spectacular scenery, until after the Civil War, when two different groups of men set out to explore the region.

Cornelius Hedges was a member of one of the expeditions. Around the campfire one night he suggested to his friends that, instead of claiming the land for private profit, they should find a way to preserve the amazing landscape for all people in America to enjoy.

Because of their efforts, Congress passed the Yellowstone Act in 1872: a law that required everything in the park to be preserved in its natural condition. No one would be allowed to cut down trees or to spoil the park in any way. This law was the foundation for the entire system of national parks in the United States, preserving millions of acres of land.

14. Which of the following can you infer from the passage?

   (1) No one had ever seen the Yellowstone area before 1865.
   (2) The president did not want to sign the Yellowstone Act.
   (3) Cornelius Hedges and his friends acted unselfishly.
   (4) Other countries had national parks before the United States had them.
   (5) All the beautiful places in the United States are preserved in national parks.

15. Which of the following is a fact, **not** an opinion?

    (1) Campfires should never be built in forests.

    (2) Natural beauty is more important than private profit.

    (3) The Yellowstone area is famous for its scenery.

    (4) Yellowstone National Park is the most beautiful park in the world.

    (5) Everyone should spend some time in a national park.

Questions 16, 17, and 18 are based on the following passage and diagram.

When you cut down a tree, you can read its life history by counting the number of rings in its trunk. Each ring is one year's growth. The inside rings are the earliest, while the outside rings show the tree's most recent growth. Tree rings are easiest to read in deciduous trees, because these trees have a period of almost no growth each winter after their leaves fall. Coniferous trees do not lose their leaves and their rings are more difficult to read.

In a good year, with plenty of water and sunshine, a tree grows a lot, leaving a wide ring as a record of that year. In a bad year, the tree grows only a little, leaving a thin ring. If the tree is attacked by fire or disease, this evidence too will show in the tree's rings.

16. Look at the tree ring indicated by an arrow in the diagram. This tree ring is a record of

    (1) a good year followed by another good year

    (2) a bad year followed by a good year

    (3) two bad years in a row

    (4) the first year the tree was alive

    (5) a good year followed by a bad year

17. From the passage, which of the following can you infer about deciduous trees?

    (1) They live only in warm climates.

    (2) They lose their leaves in the fall.

    (3) They grow very tall.

    (4) They are very young.

    (5) They stay green all year.

18. Which of the following would most likely cause a conflict of values for a tree lover who had a job studying tree rings?

    (1) cutting down trees to study their rings

    (2) using trees to study human history

    (3) getting paid to study trees

    (4) not really being interested in the work

    (5) not wanting other people to study tree rings

Questions 19 and 20 are based on the following passage.

Asteroids are chunks of rock and metal orbiting the Sun. When asteroids enter Earth's atmosphere, they are called meteors. Caught by the pull of gravity, the meteors plunge toward Earth. Most of them burn up in the atmosphere before they hit the ground. Because the glow of their burning makes them visible, people often call them shooting stars.

Sometimes meteors actually hit Earth. If a meteor hits Earth, it is called a meteorite. One crashed in the Shandong province of China over 1,300 years ago. It weighed four tons and was shaped like an ox. The ancient Chinese regarded the stone as holy, so they built a temple around it. Only recently have researchers determined that the ox-shaped rock is a meteorite.

19. Which of the following explains why people call meteors shooting stars?

(1) They float in space like stars.
(2) The glow they give off while burning makes them visible.
(3) They are the same size as stars.
(4) They light up when they hit the Moon.
(5) They are ox-shaped.

20. What causes meteors to plunge toward Earth?

(1) They bounce off the Moon and onto Earth.
(2) They are part of a comet's tail.
(3) They are attracted by the North Pole.
(4) They are caught by the pull of Earth's gravity.
(5) They collide with stars and fall from the sky.

Answers are on page 35.

Science Answer Key

1. (4) Choice (4) is the best summary of the ideas in the passage. Choices (1) and (5) are not discussed in the passage. Choices (2) and (3) disagree with the information in the passage.

2. (3) Having a cold is a familiar experience for almost everyone. Choice (2) is untrue according to the passage. Choices (1) and (4) are not mentioned in the passage. Choice (5) is not an explanation of the common cold.

3. (5) Dying as a result of natural causes is the only cause not listed in the chart. The other four choices are the result of human activities.

4. (4) This meaning of overinflation can be figured out from the drawing of an overinflated tire and from the meaning of the prefix *over-*, meaning "too much."

5. (5) The paragraph gives helpful information for car owners. Choices (1) and (4) are not mentioned in the passage. Choice (2) is wrong because the passage talks about safety, not about saving money on tire wear. Choice (3) is wrong because the passage does not discuss how to choose an automobile, only how to take care of one.

6. (3) The first paragraph provides the answer. All the other choices are untrue, according to the passage.

7. (2) Oxygen (O) is the only symbol contained in all three chemical formulas.

8. (4) The passage describes how cocaine affects the dopamine supply in the brain. None of the other topics are mentioned.

9. (1) The author would vote for choice (1) because the more we know about drugs, the better prepared we'll be to deal with them.

10. (4) You need daylight and wind to fly a kite successfully. Choices (1) and (2) are wrong because it is dark outdoors at those times. Choices (3) and (5) are incorrect because the graph shows less wind at those times.

11. (3) The two examples, *thermometer* and *anemometer*, show you that the suffix *meter* indicates something used for measurement. The prefix *alti-* comes from the Latin *altus*, meaning *high*.

12. (4) The arrow pointing to "water boils" is at 100°C.

13. (1) According to the diagram, 35°C is equal to about 90°F, a temperature at which most people would want to turn on their air conditioner. Choices (2) and (3) are not shown by the diagram. Choice (4) is impossible. Choice (5) is untrue, according to the diagram.

14. (3) The passage says the team of explorers wanted the land for all the people, instead of just for themselves. Choices (1) and (4) are untrue, according to the passage. Choice (2) is not mentioned at all. Choice (5) is incorrect because you cannot assume that all the beautiful spots are in parks.

15. (3) This fact is mentioned in the first paragraph of the passage. All the other statements are opinions.

16. (5) The indicated ring is wide, showing that it records a good year. The next ring outward is narrow, showing a bad year that followed.

17. (2) This is shown by the phrase "each winter after their leaves fall."

18. (1) The conflict would be a tree lover's desire to preserve trees and a desire to study their history as required by his or her job.

19. (2) The last sentence of the first paragraph states this information.

20. (4) The third sentence in paragraph 1 states that gravity pulls meteors toward Earth.

Evaluation Chart

Use the answer key to check your answers. Then, on the chart below, circle the number of each question that you missed. If you missed many of the questions that correspond to a certain skill, you will want to pay special attention to that skill as you work through this section.

	Skill	Question Numbers	Numbers Correct
Chapter 1 **Science Knowledge** **and Skills**	Scientific method Building vocabulary	15 11	_____/2
Chapter 2 **Living Things**	Understanding illustrations Analyzing ideas Building vocabulary Evaluating ideas	16 3 17 18	_____/4
Chapter 3 **Human Biology**	Understanding what you read Building vocabulary Evaluating ideas	1, 8 2 9	_____/4
Chapter 4 **Physics**	Understanding illustrations Analyzing ideas Building vocabulary Evaluating ideas	12 13 4 5	_____/4
Chapter 5 **Chemistry**	Analyzing ideas Building vocabulary	6 7	_____/2
Chapter 6 **Earth and Space** **Science**	Understanding what you read Understanding illustrations Building vocabulary	14, 20 10 19	_____/4

Total Score _____/20

Mathematics

This Mathematics Pretest will help you find your strengths as well as the areas you need to work on. Answer each question and solve each problem to the best of your ability. When you finish the pretest, check your answers with the Answer Key on page 41.

Whole Numbers

1. Fill in each blank with the correct digit.

   3,062 has _____ thousands

   _____ hundreds

   _____ tens and

   _____ ones.

2. Write the value of the underlined digit.

   2,465 _____

3. Add: 375
               + 147

4. Subtract: 1,259
               − 484

5. Multiply: 38
               × 24

6. Divide: 6)384

7. Estimate the following difference:
                 914
               − 205

8. Estimate the following product:
                 294
               × 41

Solving Word Problems

9. Circle the words that tell what the following problem asks you to find.

   Last week, Stacey earned $24 for baby-sitting 4 hours. In her part-time job at Burger City she worked 12 hours and earned $78. How many total hours did Stacey work last week?

   (1) total amount earned
   (2) average pay rate
   (3) total time worked

10. On the line below the following problem, write the numbers needed to answer the question.

    During league play last week, Kevin played in three basketball games. He scored 12 points in the first game, 17 points in the second game, and 9 points in the third game. In only one game did he score above his game average of 15 points. How many total points did Kevin score last week?

    _____

11. Antonio drove 531 miles in 11 hours. **Estimate** Antonio's average speed, in miles per hour, for this trip. Show the numbers used in your estimate.

12. Four friends shared the cost of a pizza dinner. They ordered 1 large pizza for $17.50, 4 sodas for $1.25 each, and 4 salads. Salads normally cost $1.75 but were on sale: "Buy one, get one free." If the friends split the total cost of dinner equally, what was each person's share?

Decimals

13. Write the following number in words:

0.025 _____

14. Write the following number using digits:

one hundred twenty-six thousandths

_____

15. Write > or < to compare the following decimals:

0.359 _____ 0.42

16. Round the following number to the nearest tenth:

0.273 ≈ _____

17. Add: 6.025
2.6
+ 3.74

18. Subtract: 8.50
− 4.75

19. Multiply: 0.625
×   5

20. Divide: $0.04\overline{)26.4}$

Fractions

21. Write a fraction to show how much of the following group of figures is shaded.

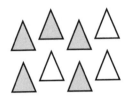

22. Reduce the fraction $\frac{10}{12}$ to lowest terms.

23. Write the mixed number represented by the shaded part of the drawing below.

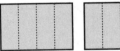

24. Add: $1\frac{1}{2}$

$+ \frac{3}{4}$

25. Subtract: $4\frac{1}{4}$

$- 1\frac{7}{8}$

26. Multiply: $\frac{3}{4} \times \frac{1}{2} =$

27. Divide: $\frac{2}{3} \div 4 =$

Ratios and Proportions

28. Heather's softball team won 12 of 14 games last summer. What is the ratio of games they won to the total number of games they played?

29. Max earns $380 each week for 40 hours of work. What is Max's pay rate in dollars per hour?

30. What is the value of n in the following proportion?

$$\frac{n}{12} = \frac{18}{24}$$

31. A light blue paint is made by mixing 9 fluid ounces of blue color with each 3 quarts of white paint. About how many ounces of blue color should be mixed with 10 quarts of white paint to make the same light blue color?

Percent

32. What percent of $1.00 is represented by the group of coins shown below?

33. Write 83% as a decimal.

34. Write 45% as a fraction. Reduce the fraction to lowest terms.

35. What is 60% of 230?

36. What percent of 25 is 3?

37. 20% of what amount is $6.50?

Data and Probability

Questions 38 and 39 refer to the table below.

Video City Televisions	
Size	**Price**
27 inch	$525
25 inch	425
23 inch	375
21 inch	275

38. Find the mean (average) of the television set prices shown on the table.

39. What is the median of the television set prices shown on the table?

PRETEST

Questions 40 and 41 refer to the circle graph.

Emerald Valley High School
Grades 9–12 (1200 students)

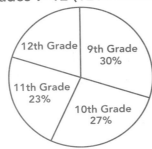

40. What percent of students at Emerald Valley High School are in the 12th grade?

41. How many more students are in the 9th grade than are in the 11th grade?

42. A bag contains 3 blue marbles, 4 red marbles, and 7 white marbles. Suppose you reach into the bag and take a marble without looking. What is the probability that you will select a red marble? Write your answer as a fraction.

Basic Algebra

43. What is the value of 4^3?

44. What is the value of $x + 12$ when $x = 23$?

45. For what value of x is the following equation true?

$x + 9 = 14$

$x = $ _____

46. For what value of n is the following equation true?

$3n = \$36.90$

$n = $ _____

Measurement and Geometry

47. Write 24 fluid ounces as a number of cups.

24 fl oz = _____ c

48. What is the perimeter of the rectangle below?

14 ft

32 ft

49. What is the area of the square below?

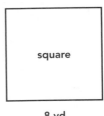

square

8 yd

50. What is the measure of $\angle DBC$?

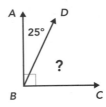

Answers are on page 41.

Mathematics Answer Key

1. $\underline{3}$ thousands, $\underline{0}$ hundreds, $\underline{6}$ tens, $\underline{2}$ ones

2. 4 hundred (400)

3. 522

4. 775

5. 912

6. 64

7. 700 (900 − 200) Any reasonable answer is acceptable.

8. 12,000 (300 × 40) Any reasonable answer is acceptable.

9. **(3)** total time worked

10. 12, 17, 9

11. 50 mph (500 ÷ 10) Any reasonable answer is acceptable.

12. $6.50 $\left[\dfrac{17.50 + (4 \times 1.25) + (2 + 1.75)}{4} = 6.50\right]$

13. twenty-five thousandths

14. 0.126

15. 0.359 < 0.42

16. 0.3

17. 12.365

18. 3.75

19. 3.125

20. 660

21. $\frac{5}{8}$ (5 out of 8)

22. $\frac{5}{6}$ $\left(\dfrac{10}{12} \div \dfrac{2}{2} = \dfrac{5}{6}\right)$

23. $1\frac{3}{4}$

24. $2\frac{1}{4}$

25. $2\frac{3}{8}$

26. $\frac{3}{8}$

27. $\frac{1}{6}$

28. $\frac{6}{7}$ $\left(\dfrac{12}{14}\right)$

29. $9.50 per hour $\left(\dfrac{380}{40} = \dfrac{n}{1}\right)$

30. $n = 9$

31. 30 fluid ounces of blue $\left(\dfrac{9}{3} = \dfrac{n}{10}\right)$

32. 71% (.50 + .50 + .10 + .10 + .01 = .71 = 71%)

33. 0.83

34. $\frac{9}{20}$ $\left(\dfrac{45}{100}\right)$

35. 138 (230 × .60 = 138)

36. 12% $\left(\dfrac{3}{25} = \dfrac{n}{100}\right)$

37. $32.50 $\left(\dfrac{6.50}{20\%} = \dfrac{n}{100\%}\right)$

38. $400 ($1,600 ÷ 4 = 400)

39. $400 [($425 + $375) ÷ 2]

40. 20% (100% − 23% − 27% − 30% = 20%)

41. 84 students (7% of 1200 = 84)

42. $\frac{2}{7}$ $\left(\dfrac{4}{14}\right)$

43. 64 (4 × 4 × 4)

44. 35 (23 + 12 = 35)

45. $x = 5$ (14 − 9 = 5)

46. $n = $12.30 (36.90 ÷ 3 = 12.30)

47. 3 cups (1 c = 8 fl oz; 24 ÷ 8 = 3)

48. 92 feet (32 + 14 + 32 + 14 = 92)

49. 64 sq yd (8 × 8 = 64)

50. 65° (90° − 25° = 65°)

Evaluation Chart

After you have checked your answers, circle the number of each question that you missed. If you missed any questions that correspond to a certain skill, you will want to pay special attention to that skill as you work through the math section of this book.

	Skill	Question Numbers	Number Correct
Chapter 1 **Whole Numbers**	Place value Basic operations Estimation	1, 2 3, 4, 5, 6 7, 8	_____/8
Chapter 3 **Solving Word Problems**	Understanding the question Necessary information Estimation Multistep Problems	9 10 11 12	_____/4
Chapter 4 **Decimals**	Understanding decimals Comparing decimals Rounding decimals Basic operations	13, 14 15 16 17, 18, 19, 20	_____/8
Chapter 5 **Fractions**	Understanding fractions Basic operations	21, 22, 23 24, 25, 26, 27	_____/7
Chapter 6 **Ratios and Proportions**	Understanding ratio Proportion word problems	30 28, 29, 31	_____/4
Chapter 7 **Percent**	Understanding percent Relating decimals, fractions, and percent Solving percent problems	32 33, 34 35, 36, 37	_____/6
Chapter 8 **Data and Probability**	Mean and median Reading a graph Probability	38, 39 40, 41 42	_____/5
Chapter 9 **Basic Algebra**	Powers and roots Evaluating expressions Solving equations	43 44 45, 46	_____/4
Chapter 10 **Measurement and Geometry**	Units of measurement Perimeter and area Measuring angles	47 48, 49 50	_____/4

Total Correct _____/50

LANGUAGE ARTS
WRITING

LANGUAGE ARTS
WRITING

Parts of Speech

In this section, you will examine the five parts of speech: **nouns, pronouns, verbs, adjectives,** and **adverbs.** They are presented here because you often need to be familiar with the parts of speech when studying writing skills.

Nouns

A **noun** names a person, place, thing, or idea.

Here are a few examples of nouns.

People	Places	Things	Ideas
uncle	lake	motorcycle	honesty
Mr. Sanchez	stadium	baseball	excitement
Thuy	ocean	shells	health
lawyer	courthouse	hat	crime
president	White House	dog	love

There are three nouns in the sentence below. Find and circle them.

Aunt Rose wanted to ride her motorcycle to the ocean.

You were right if you circled *Aunt Rose* (a person), *motorcycle* (a thing), and *ocean* (a place). Now try another sentence containing two nouns. One of the nouns is an idea.

My cousin learned that crime doesn't pay.

The nouns in that sentence are *cousin* and *crime.*

EXERCISE 1

Nouns

Directions: Add a noun to each sentence below. Check to see that the nouns you add make sense.

1. Mr. Archer goes to the stadium because he loves the game of _____.

2. On a trip to the _____, Shelley found a new dress.

3. Ms. Willard finds _____ by the ocean.

4. At the town hall, the _____ paid to get her parking permit.

5. _____ was my best friend in school.

6. My _____ thought I was really great.

7. I would like to go on a vacation to _____.

8. _____ is a quality I admire in people.

Answers are on page 177.

Pronouns

Pronouns are words that take the place of nouns.

Pronouns are used like nouns. A pronoun stands for the name of a person, place, thing, or idea.

> **Rosanna** got ice cream. Then **she** went to the park.

Both sentences talk about Rosanna. But in the second sentence, the pronoun *she* takes the place of the noun *Rosanna*.

> Many **cities** get government assistance. **They** use the money for various projects.

Both sentences talk about cities. But in the second sentence, the pronoun *they* takes the place of the noun *cities*.

> That **dog** looks hungry. **It** probably hasn't eaten for days.

Both sentences talk about a dog. But in the second sentence, the pronoun *it* takes the place of the noun *dog*.

Many useful pronouns are listed in the box below. You will study these pronouns in Chapter 3.

Singular Pronouns	Plural Pronouns
I, me, my, mine	we, us, our, ours
you, your, yours	you, your, yours
he, him, his, she, her, hers, it, its	they, them, their, theirs

Find and circle the pronouns in the following sentence.

The landlord wants the rent, and he wants it now.

There are two pronouns in that sentence: *he* and *it*. The pronoun *he* takes the place of *landlord*, and *it* refers to *rent*. Check the box of pronouns above if you aren't sure which words are pronouns.

Find and circle the pronouns in the following sentence.

They are leaving town, but their friends are staying.

You should have circled the pronouns *they* and *their*.

EXERCISE 2

Pronouns

Directions: Replace each noun in parentheses with a pronoun. The first one is done as an example.

1. (The motorcycle) _____*It*_____ has a top speed of 120 mph.

2. (Roberto) _____ goes to the stadium because he loves baseball.

3. She found (the dress) _____ in Paris.

4. He finds (seashells) _____ for us by the ocean.

5. (My friend) _____ paid for my movie ticket.

6. (Health) _____ is important whether you are young or old.

7. (The teacher) _____ warned me about getting into trouble again.

8. The president wanted (his speech) _____ to go over well.

Answers are on page **177.**

Verbs

A **verb** is a word that shows action or being. Some verbs are action words.

> Gloria **rides** her bike every day.
> Jim **mows** the lawn on Saturdays.

Rides is an action that Gloria does. *Mows* is an action that Jim does.

Other verbs are linking verbs—or being verbs. These verbs link a noun or pronoun to words that rename or describe it.

> Our street **is** very noisy.
> Their neighbors **are** Sonia and Larry Petrie.

Is links *noisy* to *street*. *Are* links *Sonia and Larry Petrie* to *neighbors*.

Following are some examples of both kinds of verbs.

Action	Linking
run, go, ride	am, is, are
love, dance, keep	was, were
find, fight, pay	seem, become
drive, laugh	appear

Any time you talk about what something *does* or *is*, you use one or more verbs. Read the sentence below and underline each verb you find.

> Tilly socializes and dances at parties.

Did you underline the action verbs *socializes* and *dances*? Try underlining verbs in another sentence.

> This party is wonderful.

You were right if you underlined the linking verb *is*. The verb links the noun *party* with a describing word, *wonderful*.

EXERCISE 3

Verbs

Directions: Add a verb to each sentence below. Check to see that the verbs you add make sense.

1. Dan _____ a motorcycle to the lake.

2. Mr. Gonzalez _____ to the stadium because he is a fan.

3. Paula bought a beautiful painting when she _____ in Paris.

4. Justin _____ the most honest person I know.

5. Barry _____ his own costume for the play.

6. The stars _____ beautiful tonight.

7. This summer _____ much hotter than last summer.

8. Last night in my sleep, I _____ I was a giant marshmallow.

Answers are on page 177.

Adjectives

Adjectives describe nouns. They tell *which one, what kind,* or *how many.*

You might say to a friend, "Meet me by my car." If your friend doesn't know what your car looks like, he would not be able to meet you. But if you said, "Meet me by the old, blue, convertible Corvette parked next to the brown house," he would know exactly which car you meant.

Using adjectives makes a difference. The adjectives *old, blue,* and *convertible* describe *Corvette.* The adjective *brown* describes *house.* Your friend would be able to find your car because of the specific information that these adjectives provide.

Here are three lists of common adjectives.

What kind	Which one	How many
big, little	this, that	many, few
young, old	these, those	one, two
neat, sloppy		some
happy, sad		
nice, kind		
red, blue, white		

Find and circle the ten adjectives in the following paragraph.

Many people are happy when they see the red, white, and blue flag of the United States. But some people are sad because they think about friends or family who died in a war. Those people fought and died in big and little wars.

Did you find all ten adjectives? Keep in mind that an adjective can come before or after the word it describes. For example, in the sentence "One girl in math class was nice to me," both *one* and *nice* are adjectives that describe *girl*.

You should have circled *many, happy, red, white,* and *blue* in the first sentence; *some* and *sad* in the second sentence; and *those, big,* and *little* in the third sentence.

EXERCISE 4

Adjectives

Directions: Circle all the adjectives in the sentences. Each sentence contains at least two adjectives that describe nouns or pronouns.

1. Amy discovered a new fashion in fuzzy sweaters.
2. Amanda finds big and little shells by the beautiful ocean.
3. The kind teacher paid for lunch at the new cafeteria.
4. The president kept a noisy dog in the busy White House.
5. Mr. Chen takes a slow walk around the small lake each summer evening.
6. The upstairs bedroom is blue and white.
7. The alert cat with a twitching tail watched the brick path.
8. Uncle Carlos thinks skydiving is a good hobby for some people.

Answers are on page 177.

Adverbs

Adverbs describe verbs. Adverbs can tell *how, when,* or *where.*

He writes.

You know that the person writes, but you don't know anything else.

He writes **neatly.**

You learn **how** he writes. The adverb *neatly* describes the verb *writes.*

He writes **daily.**

You know **when** he writes. The adverb *daily* describes the verb *writes.* An adverb often comes right after the verb it describes.

He writes **here.**

You know **where** he writes. The adverb *here* describes the verb *writes.* Notice that not all adverbs end in *-ly.*

In the following sentences, the verbs have been underlined and the adverbs circled. Answer the questions that follow each sentence.

The driver <u>arrived</u> (late).

What did he do? _____

When did he do it? _____

The child <u>sobbed</u> (quietly).

What did she do? _____

How did she do it? _____

You should have answered *arrived* and *late* for the first sentence and *sobbed* and *quietly* for the second sentence.

EXERCISE 5

Adverbs

Directions: Complete the following sentences by writing in adverbs that tell *how, when,* or *where.* You can choose adverbs from the following list, or you can think of your own.

dangerously	early	fast	immediately
loudly	sweetly	daily	upstairs
now	there	softly	outdoors

1. Uncle Don rides _____. (How does he ride?)

2. Mr. Hirsch arrives _____. (When does he arrive?)

3. The kitten plays _____. (Where does it play?)

4. The doctor paid _____. (When did she pay?)

5. Adrian's dog barked _____. (How did it bark?)

6. Mr. Maxwell lives _____. (Where does he live?)

7. Megan sings _____. (How does she sing?)

8. Heather sings _____. (When does she sing?)

Answers are on page 177.

EXERCISE 6

Parts of Speech

Directions: Read the following business memo. Identify the part of speech of each underlined word or group of words. Then write the parts of speech on the lines below the memo.

MEMO

To: All employees
Re: Founders' Day

We <u>would like</u> to announce that the <u>company</u> will be celebrating Founders' Day on April 7 <u>this</u> year. As most of you <u>already</u> know, Elizabeth Blackburn and Miguel Gomez founded Tech World in April 1988. They deeply appreciate how hard you <u>have worked</u> to make this firm the <u>huge</u> success it is <u>today</u>. In recognition of <u>your</u> efforts, <u>we</u> hope you will enjoy the catered <u>lunch</u> on Founders' Day. <u>Then</u> the offices <u>will close</u> early. Each and every employee will get a half-day off with pay.

---

1. would like _____
2. company _____
3. this _____
4. already _____
5. have worked _____
6. huge _____

7. today _____
8. your _____
9. we _____
10. lunch _____
11. then _____
12. will close _____

Answers are on page 177.

Chapter Review

You have had a quick overview of the five parts of speech. As you work through this section, you will continue to study nouns, pronouns, verbs, adjectives, and adverbs. The next exercise is a review of this chapter. Look up any information you need to complete the exercises.

EXERCISE 7

Part 1 **Directions:** Twenty words are listed below. Decide what part of speech each word is. Write each word in the correct column. The first row has been completed for you.

early	neat	Mrs. Kay	listens	he
there	dog	happy	keep	they
baseball	went	slowly	you	old
now	loves	nice	boat	it

Nouns	Pronouns	Verbs	Adjectives	Adverbs
Mrs. Kay	*he*	*listens*	*neat*	*early*

Part 2 **Directions:** Add a word to fill in each blank. After the sentence, tell whether you used a *noun, pronoun, verb, adjective,* or *adverb.*

1. Neil rode his _____ to the lake. _____

2. Ms. White _____ to the stadium. _____

3. Marcia told me about her _____ sweater._____

4. Aunt Dorothy looked _____ for shells. _____

5. Uncle Ted ate _____ dinner. _____

Answers are on page 177.

Your Turn to Write: Writing a Paragraph

Writing Skill: Mapping

Now you are going to write a paragraph of your own. As you write, keep in mind that others will want to understand your writing. Make it as clear and correct as you can. Putting your thoughts down on paper can be difficult at times. You might feel like writing but find that you don't know where to start. One way to begin writing is to map your ideas.

Idea mapping—also called **clustering** or **webbing**—means writing one word in the middle of the page and jotting down around that first word all the thoughts that come to your mind. Don't try to write sentences. Begin by writing words.

An example of idea mapping follows. The subject is **My Favorite Vacation.** Here are the instructions to make an idea map.

1. Write the words **My Favorite Vacation** in the middle of the paper and circle the words.

2. In the space around **My Favorite Vacation,** write any words that pop into your mind on the subject of your favorite vacation and circle those words.

3. Draw arrows connecting the words that seem to go together.

4. Continue doing this until you have all your ideas written down.

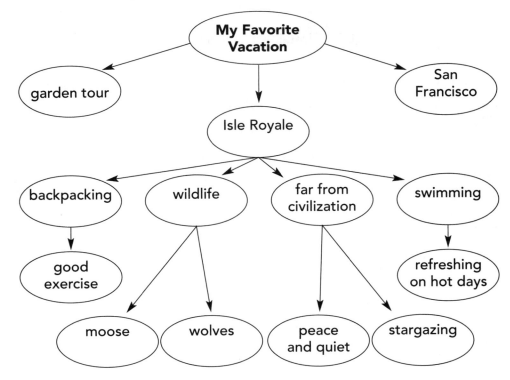

Notice all the circles around the words. Look at the arrows used to join the words. Could some of those words be put together to form ideas and sentences?

You never have to use all the words in an idea map. Just use the ones that give you something to say. Here is an example paragraph using the idea map.

My favorite vacation was one my husband and I took three years ago. We went to Isle Royale National Park. It's an island in Lake Superior that is an eight-hour boat ride from the mainland. We enjoyed the peace and quiet. We backpacked five or six miles every day. Sometimes we saw moose. Then we'd set up camp, fix supper, and go for a refreshing swim. At night the stargazing was great because there were no electric lights. We could hear the wolves howling at night as we fell asleep.

You will have many writing exercises in this section. Put the date at the top of every writing exercise. Then you will have a record of when you did the writing. Keep all your writing exercises in a notebook or folder. This way you will be able to reread what you have written and see how your writing is improving.

Writing Assignment

Directions: Write a story about an event in your life. Write about anything that happened to you, whether it was a very important event or just something that happened the other day. Create an idea map to help you find things to say about the event. Start with the first thing that happened and write down all the information in time order. Here are some suggestions for topics.

My favorite day

A vacation to _____

My best childhood memory

When you finish your paragraph, use the following writing checklist to proofread and correct your writing.

Writing Checklist	Yes	No
Have you said all you wanted to say?	_____	_____
Are there any changes you want to make?	_____	_____
Did you use pronouns to avoid repeating some nouns?	_____	_____
Did you include adjectives and adverbs to make your writing more interesting?	_____	_____

Sentences

Sentences, Fragments, and Run-ons

A **sentence** is a group of words that expresses a complete thought. The words in a sentence make sense. You can understand what the writer is saying. Is the following group of words a sentence?

The man was driving very fast.

That group of words tells a complete thought, so it is a sentence.

A **fragment** does not express a complete thought. The words below do not tell a complete thought. Something is missing. This group of words is called a fragment.

Pulled out behind him.

A fragment leaves a question in your mind. In the example you just read, *who* pulled out behind him? You can add information to a fragment to make it a complete thought.

The motorcycle pulled out behind him.

Now you have a complete thought and a complete sentence.

Complete Sentences:

The motorcycle passed the car.

The driver was speeding.

Each one of those sentences made sense and told a complete thought. You could understand what was being said.

Fragments:

After the game.

Too many people.

Left early.

You might realize that someone is talking about a game, but each group of words leaves out a lot of information. *What happened* after the game? *Where were there* too many people? *Who* left early?

Information can be added to the fragments so that they express complete thoughts. Read the sentences below and compare them with the fragments.

After the game, I wanted to have a good time.

There were too many people at Ori's party.

The house was so crowded that I left early.

A **run-on sentence** is two complete sentences run together without the correct punctuation between them. Sometimes two sentences are run together with only a comma between them.

My uncle was driving his car, my cousin was riding his motorcycle.

Correct this run-on by making two complete sentences beginning with capital letters and ending with periods.

My uncle was driving his car. My cousin was riding his motorcycle.

Sometimes two short, related sentences are made into a run-on sentence.

The movie was sad it made me cry.

To correct this run-on, use a semicolon or a period and a capital letter.

The movie was sad; it made me cry.

The movie was sad. It made me cry.

EXERCISE 1

Sentences, Fragments, and Run-ons

Directions: Some of the following groups of words are fragments, some are run-ons, and some are sentences. If a group of words is a sentence, write *S* on the line after it. If a group of words is a fragment, write *F* on the line after it. If it is a fragment, add some new information to make it a complete sentence. If a group of words is a run-on, write *R* on the line after it. If it is a run-on, divide it into two complete sentences. The first one is done as an example.

1. Took the man to jail. _*F*_
   The police took the man to jail.

2. Locked him up. _____

3. He called his lawyer, she promised to help him. _____

4. He didn't want to spend the night in jail. _____

5. Felt terrible. _____

6. The lawyer. _____

7. She bailed him out, then she drove him home. _____

_____

8. Convicted of driving drunk. _____

_____

9. He joined Alcoholics Anonymous. _____

_____

10. Saved his life. _____

_____

Answers are on page 177.

Punctuating Perfectly: Sentences

A sentence is a group of words that tells a complete thought. It is also a group of words that has a special look. Here is an opportunity for you to do a little detective work with sentences. Read the sentences in this paragraph carefully and then answer the following questions.

A. What kind of letter does the first word of each sentence begin with?

_____

B. What marks do you find at the ends of the sentences?

_____

Did you discover that the first word of each sentence begins with a capital letter? Did you discover that each sentence ends with a punctuation mark? You need to remember these two rules when writing a sentence:

1. The first word of each sentence begins with a **capital letter.**

2. Every sentence ends with one of these three **punctuation marks:**

a period (.)

a question mark (?)

an exclamation point (!)

Every Sentence Has a Purpose

There are four different types of sentences. The first type makes a **statement.** Statements give information. The second type gives a **command.** Commands tell someone to do something. The third type asks a **question.** Questions find out about something. The fourth type is an **exclamation.** Exclamations show strong feeling. Notice how each example sentence begins with a capital letter and ends with an end mark.

STATEMENT: I want to go bowling.

COMMAND: Take me to the bowling lanes.

QUESTION: Did you get my bowling shoes?

EXCLAMATION: You missed every pin!

Statements

Most of the sentences that you write or read are statements. They give you information about a subject. They end with a period.

STATEMENT: Janet bought four bags of groceries.

Write two examples of statements on the lines below.

_____

_____

Commands

Commands tell someone to do something. As you grew up, you heard a lot of commands from parents, teachers, brothers, or sisters.

COMMANDS: Clean your room.   Do your homework.

                Be home by midnight.   Walk the dog.

Think of two more commands. Write them on the next two lines.

_____

_____

In writing, a command often looks like a statement because it ends with a period. However, a statement just gives information. In a command, the writer is telling the reader to do something. You can mentally fill in the missing subject *you* in a command. Below are some examples.

(*You*) Clean your room.   (*You*) Do your homework.

(*You*) Be home by midnight.   (*You*) Walk the dog.

Questions

A question asks something, and it ends with a question mark. Below are some examples of common questions.

QUESTIONS: What time is it?   How are you?

What's for dinner?   Did the mail come yet?

On the lines below, write two questions you asked today.

_____

_____

Exclamations

An exclamation shows strong feeling. It ends with an exclamation point. Exclamations are often made at exciting or frightening times. Sometimes an exclamation is a shouted command. Notice that all exclamations end with exclamation points.

EXCLAMATIONS: It's a touchdown!   Look out for that car!

That dress is gorgeous!   Let's celebrate!

On the lines below, write two sentences that are exclamations. You might want to think of one you used at a game, at a party, or when you accidentally touched a hot stove.

_____

_____

EXERCISE 2

Types of Sentences

Directions: Read the following sentences. Place the correct punctuation mark at the end of each sentence. Use a period, question mark, or exclamation point. Then write whether the sentence is a *statement,* a *command,* a *question,* or an *exclamation.* The first one is done as an example.

1. This is the Rainbow Coffee Shop ___.___   _statement_

2. Would you like to see a menu _____   _____

3. Get me a glass of water _____   _____

4. Do you like the homemade pie _____   _____

5. The special today is meatloaf _____   _____

6. This place is on fire _____   _____

Answers are on page 178.

EXERCISE 3

Mistakes in Sentences

Directions: Some of the following sentences contain mistakes in punctuation or capitalization. Some are fragments. Rewrite each sentence correctly. The first one is done as an example.

1. High rents.

This neighborhood has very high rents.

2. why did they have to tear down our building.

_____

3. most landlords don't allow pets.

_____

4. Can't give up my dog!

_____

5. I've circled some ads for apartments?

_____

6. My old neighborhood

_____

Answers are on page 178.

Putting Your Skills to Work

Directions: In your notebook, write eight sentences. Write two of each kind of sentence that you just studied. After each sentence, indicate whether it is a statement, a command, a question, or an exclamation. When you are finished writing, reread your sentences. Use the following writing checklist to proofread and correct what you have written.

Writing Checklist	Yes	No
Does each sentence begin with a capital letter and end with an end mark?	_____	_____
Do you have two examples of all four kinds of sentences?	_____	_____
Did you use end marks correctly for each kind of sentence?	_____	_____

Every Sentence Has a Subject

The **subject** of a sentence is the person, place, thing, or idea talked about in the sentence. The sentence tells what the subject does or is.

To find the subject of a sentence, look for the **verb** in the sentence. If the verb shows action, figure out *who* or *what* is performing the action. In the following sentence, what is the action verb? Who performs the action?

The skilled dentist pulled my wisdom teeth.

In the sentence above, the action verb is *pulled.* The person performing the pulling is the dentist, so the simple subject is *dentist.*

When the verb in a sentence doesn't show action, it is a linking verb. In that case, ask yourself, "Who or what is this sentence about?"

My mouth was numb for three hours.

The verb *was* is a linking verb. *Numb* describes the writer's mouth, so *mouth* is the simple subject.

EXERCISE 4

Finding the Subject

Directions: In each of the following sentences, find the verb and underline it. Then circle the simple subject. The first one is done as an example.

1. (Chicago) is a big city.

2. Its people live in interesting neighborhoods.

3. They have all kinds of jobs.

4. Commuter trains take many workers downtown.

5. Commuters hurry to the train stations.

6. Many residents were originally from other places.

Answers are on page 178.

Tricky Subjects: Commands and Questions

The subject of a sentence usually comes at the beginning of the sentence—but not always. Sometimes the way a sentence is written makes finding the subject hard. Remember that you can always add the missing word *you* to a command.

Write a letter to your aunt.   (You) Write a letter to your aunt.

The missing *you* is the subject of the sentence.

In a question, part of the verb often comes before the subject. The sentence is inverted. To find the subject, mentally put the sentence back in order as if it were a statement. Below is an example.

Has the president signed the bill?

Here is the question, rearranged as a statement:

The president has signed the bill.

The subject performing the action is *president.*

Tricky Subjects: Confusing Words and Phrases

Sometimes extra words and phrases in a sentence can be confusing when you are looking for the subject. Remember to always look for the verb. If it is an action verb, figure out *who* or *what* is performing the action. If it is a linking verb, figure out *who* or *what* the sentence is about.

In the following sentence, words come between the subject and the verb. What is the verb? What is the subject?

The women at the park play tennis.

The verb is *play.* The performer of the action is *women.* The prepositional phrase *at the park* comes between the subject and the verb. Obviously, a *park* cannot *play*, so the subject cannot be *park.*

Now try another example. The following sentence starts out with some words that are not the subject. Find the verb; then find the subject.

In this park, the trees are tall and old.

The verb *are* is a linking verb. To find the subject, ask "Who or what *are*?" The subject is *trees*.

EXERCISE 5

Finding Tricky Subjects

Directions: Write the subject of each sentence in the blank. Remember that the subject may be the missing word *(you)*. The first one is done as an example.

1. Does Denise come in today? _____ *Denise* _____

2. Give Sarah a coffee break at 10:00. _____

3. Larry, the typist on the left, drinks tea. _____

4. Is the coffee ready to drink? _____

5. At lunchtime, I usually leave the building. _____

6. Change the channel, please. _____

7. The girl in the purple shoes is our best player. _____

8. Would you like to join us? _____

Answers are on page 178.

Every Sentence Has a Predicate

The subject is one important part of a sentence. The **predicate** is the other important part. Everything that isn't part of the complete subject is part of the predicate and tells what the subject *does* or *is*. The predicate gives information about the subject. There is always a verb in the predicate. This sentence contains an action verb:

> The mechanic replaced the car's muffler.

There are two parts to that sentence. *The mechanic* is the complete subject. The predicate is *replaced the car's muffler.* The subject is the person who completed the action. The predicate tells what the subject did. The next sentence contains a linking verb.

> The muffler is expensive.

There are also two parts to that sentence. *The muffler* is the complete subject. The predicate is *is expensive*.

EXERCISE 6

Writing Predicates

Directions: Ten subjects are listed below. Add two-word predicates to them to make complete sentences. You can use either action verbs to tell what the subjects do or linking verbs to tell what the subjects are. The first one has been done for you.

1. Babies _____*cry*_____ _____*sometimes*_____ .

2. Our money _____ _____ .

3. Flowers _____ _____ .

4. Mary _____ _____ .

5. The pool _____ _____ .

6. Birds _____ _____ .

7. Fish _____ _____ .

8. Scissors _____ _____ .

9. My apartment _____ _____ .

10. The tomatoes _____ _____ .

Answers are on page 178.

Putting Your Skills to Work

Directions: Now practice writing sentences. Write a paragraph about someone you know. First, name the person and tell how you know him or her. Second, tell where you spend time together. Third, tell what you do when you spend time together. Finally, tell why you enjoy being with this person. You may want to use an idea map to help organize your thoughts.

When you have completed your paragraph, use the writing checklist below to proofread and correct your writing.

Writing Checklist	Yes	No
Do you have a subject for each sentence?	_____	_____
Do you have a predicate for each sentence?	_____	_____
Have you started each sentence with a capital letter?	_____	_____
Have you used correct punctuation at the end of each sentence?	_____	_____

Chapter Review

EXERCISE 7

<u>Part 1</u> **Directions:** Write the simple subject of each of the following sentences in the blank. The first one is done as an example.

1. Juan wants to find a job. _____*Juan*_____

2. A counselor in the unemployment office helps him. _____

3. Each week, Juan goes on at least one job interview. _____

4. The interviewer talked to the manager. _____

5. Is this person qualified for this job? _____

6. Give Juan a chance. _____

<u>Part 2</u> **Directions:** Read the following groups of sentences. Only one sentence in each group is written correctly. Circle the letter of the correct sentence in each group.

7. **a.** going back to school is not easy.
   b. Students need time to study?
   c. Once the brain is out of gear.
   d. It is difficult to start working again.
   e. takes determination.

8. **a.** In high school my grades.
   b. I knew I was smart, I wasn't dumb.
   c. I hated to study.
   d. teachers didn't like me?
   e. If I try, I can do it

9. **a.** When I was playing volleyball.
   b. my knee hit the ground hard!
   c. Took me to the emergency room.
   d. X rays.
   e. Now I have a plaster cast.

10. **a.** My daughter Naomi was born.
    b. I was 24 at the time?
    c. She was so beautiful?
    d. She was a sweet baby, I love her.
    e. Every time I think of her.

Part 3 **Directions:** Look at the two pictures on this page. Under each picture, write sentences to answer the following two questions:

What is happening in the picture?

What could the characters in the pictures be saying?

Make sure each sentence has both a subject and a predicate. Try to write at least one statement, one command, one question, and one exclamation. Remember to use the correct end punctuation.

11. _____

_____

12. _____

_____

13. _____

_____

14. _____

_____

Answers are on page 178.

Your Turn to Write: Telling a Story

Writing Skill: Brainstorming

Brainstorming is part of a writing process in which you write down your thoughts and then organize them. Write your thoughts down as quickly as possible and in whatever order they pop into your mind. One thought will lead to another. Some of the thoughts may not seem to be a part of the topic. That's all right. You don't need to write complete sentences or worry about correct spelling. Just write words and ideas until you don't have anything else to write.

When you finish, decide if you want to use all the ideas you brainstormed. Cross out any ideas you don't want to use. Then number the remaining ideas in the order in which you want to write about them.

Sample Brainstorming

My Pet

1 cat named Misty

~~doesn't like anyone but me~~

3 went outside and came back pregnant

~~sleeps with me at night~~

2 moved into my first apartment with me

4 became very calm and content

5 made her a box with soft towels

6 had her kittens in my underwear drawer

Notice that each idea has been numbered. Two ideas that will not be included in the paragraph have been crossed out.

> My cat's name is Misty. When I moved into my first apartment, Misty was there to celebrate with me. She was always waiting to welcome me home. Then one day she got outside and came back pregnant. After that, Misty became very content to sleep and lie around all day. When it was time for her kittens to be born, I made her a soft bed with towels in a box. However, she chose to have her babies in my underwear drawer! She has certainly been a problem for me, but I wouldn't want to lose her.

Writing Assignment

Directions: Think about a special day in your life. Use one of the following subjects and brainstorm to create a list of ideas. Cross out any ideas you don't like. Number the remaining ideas in the order you want to use them. Then write your paragraph.

My first day on the job

The day I almost _____

My favorite New Year's Eve (or birthday or _____)

When you have written your paragraph, use the following writing checklist to proofread and correct your story.

Writing Checklist	**Yes**	**No**
Are there are any sentence fragments or run-ons?	_____	_____
Does each sentence have a subject and a predicate?	_____	_____
Did you use capitals and end punctuation correctly?	_____	_____

CHAPTER 3

Nouns and Pronouns

Nouns and pronouns are both naming words. You use them to tell whom or what you are talking or writing about. They both identify people, places, things, or ideas. In the following paragraph, the nouns and pronouns are shown in **boldface type.**

> **Holly** and **Hailey** walked to the **store** near **their house. They** saw **their neighbor Riley** as **he** walked with **his dog.**

Nouns

Nouns identify *who* or *what* is being talked about. In this part of the chapter, you will work with several types of nouns.

Common Nouns and Proper Nouns

Both common and proper nouns name people, places, things, or ideas. But there is an important difference between them.

> A **common noun** is the *general* name of a person, place, thing, or idea.
>
> A **proper noun** is the *specific* name of a person, place, thing, or idea.

Words like *woman, building, airplane,* and *month* are common nouns. Words like *Lin, Empire State Building, Concorde,* and *December* are proper nouns.

A common noun never begins with a capital letter unless it begins a sentence. On the other hand, a proper noun always begins with a capital letter.

Common noun: city   **Proper noun:** Detroit

The word *city* is a common noun because it names a general type of place. You could be talking about any city in the world. But *Detroit* is a specific place, so it is a proper noun. The name *Detroit* begins with a capital letter, while *city* does not.

Study the lists below. Notice that for each common noun on the left, there is a corresponding proper noun on the right.

Common Nouns	Proper Nouns
school	Roosevelt High School
car	Chevrolet
store	Target
restaurant	Mama Leone's
day	Friday

Remember that a common noun is a general name, but a proper noun is a specific name. When you are writing proper nouns of more than one word, you usually capitalize all the words. For example, if you were writing the name of a restaurant, you would write *Country Kitchen,* not *Country kitchen.*

EXERCISE 1

Common and Proper Nouns

Directions: Write the name of a proper noun for each common noun in the list below. The first one is done as an example.

1. car: _____*Honda*_____
2. senator: _____
3. company: _____
4. town: _____
5. minister: _____
6. holiday: _____
7. state: _____
8. country: _____
9. organization: _____
10. doctor: _____

Answers are on pages 178–179.

Specific Names

Many nouns can be either common or proper depending on how they are used. Words that are used as the specific names of people are proper nouns. However, titles like *senator, doctor, judge, sergeant, vice president, lieutenant, pastor,* and *mayor* are common nouns when they refer to the position. For example, you would write:

Kate Jordan is a **senator.**

In that sentence, the word *senator* is used as a job title. It names a position, so it is not capitalized. But you would write:

Many people admire **Senator Kate Jordan.**

In that sentence, *Senator* is used as part of a specific name, so it is capitalized. Titles are capitalized when they are used as part of a person's name.

Words that refer to places or things can also be either common nouns or proper nouns. Words like *building, school, department,* and *road* are capitalized when they are used as part of a name.

Look at the following sentences. Circle all of the proper nouns that should be capitalized.

I went to the doctor.

The nurse said, "doctor rahji will be ten minutes late."

"The doctor had to stop at mercy hospital," the nurse added.

"How far away is the hospital?" I asked.

"It's about two miles down the road," the nurse said.

Just then, a sergeant walked into the office.

"Oh, sergeant jones, you're early," said the nurse.

"There wasn't much traffic on willow road," the sergeant explained.

You should have circled *Doctor Rahji, Mercy Hospital, Sergeant Jones,* and *Willow Road.* These are proper nouns because they are used as the names of specific people and places.

EXERCISE 2

Capitalizing Proper Nouns

Directions: Read the following sentences. If all of the proper nouns in a sentence are capitalized, write *C* for *Correct* on the line. If you find a proper noun or part of a proper noun that should be capitalized, underline it. Some sentences contain more than one proper noun. The first one is done as an example.

_____ **1.** Mrs. Linkowski first saw the <u>washington monument</u> when she was five.

_____ **2.** New year's eve is aunt Betty's favorite holiday.

_____ **3.** The teachers at brookside elementary school wrote a letter to mayor carlson.

_____ **4.** My dentist hasn't missed a green bay packers' game in seven years.

_____ **5.** Who ran for mayor in the last election?

_____ **6.** Ms. Davis is a member of an organization called mothers against drunk driving.

_____ **7.** The oak valley fire department was too late to save the warehouse.

Answers are on page 179.

Singular Nouns and Plural Nouns

Nouns that name one person, place, or thing are **singular nouns.**

Nouns that name more than one person, place, or things are **plural nouns.**

Singular Nouns	Plural Nouns
bird	birds
class	classes
man	men

The following sentences show some ways that singular and plural nouns are used.

It is legal to have one husband but illegal to have two husbands.

Erma wants to have one child, but Steve wants to have four children.

Forming Plurals

There are several rules for making singular nouns plural. Study the following rules. Then practice these rules by filling in the blanks with the correct words.

1. The usual way to make singular nouns plural is to add an *s*.

planet—planets   flower—flowers   balloon—balloons

monkey—_____   cake—_____   clown—_____

2. For nouns that end in *s*, *sh*, *ch*, *z*, and *x*, add *es* to make them plural.

bus—buses   box—boxes   church—churches

dish—_____   waltz—_____   branch—_____

3. For nouns that end with a consonant and *y*, change the *y* to *i* and add *es*.

county—counties   salary—salaries   city—cities

country—_____   enemy—_____   bully—_____

4. Some nouns do not change form at all when they are plural. If you are ever unsure, check the dictionary.

sheep   deer   fish   clothing

5. The plurals of some nouns are not formed according to any set of rules. The only way to learn them is to memorize them.

child—children   goose—geese   man—men

woman—_____   mouse—_____   ox—_____

EXERCISE 3

Changing Singular Nouns to Plural Nouns

Directions: Read the following sentences. In each sentence, cross out the singular noun that should be plural and write the plural form on the line. The first one is done as an example.

1. Many ~~woman~~ work outside the home. *women*

2. Some employer pay women less than men. _____

3. Salary should be the same for all people who do the same job.

   _____

4. Some companies have child-care program. _____

5. Often, several church in a town have day-care centers.

   _____

6. City, counties, and towns should do more to help single mothers.

   _____

EXERCISE 4

Correcting Errors with Nouns

Directions: Two sentences in each group below have mistakes. The mistakes may be with singular and plural nouns or with common and proper nouns. Read each group of sentences and circle the letter of the sentence is correct.

1. **a.** Hungers is widespread.
   b. Many people eat only one meals a day.
   c. Some people do not even get one meal.

2. **a.** What can an american do about the problem?
   b. She can support her local food bank.
   c. Food Bank are often run by religious groups.

3. **a.** They feed any person who is hungry.
   b. Your Religiones is not important.
   c. When parentes have a hungry child, they are not ignored.

Answers are on page 179.

Possessive Nouns

> A noun that shows ownership is a **possessive noun.**

Singular possessive nouns always end in *'s.* Read the following examples of sentences with singular possessive nouns.

To show that Harold owns a van, you could write:

> That is **Harold's** van.

To show that Jess had a brown hamster, you could write:

> **Jess's** hamster is brown.

In both of those sentences, *'s* is added to the noun to show possession.

There are times when more than one person owns something. Then you need a **plural possessive noun.** When a plural noun ends in *s,* just add an apostrophe (') to make it possessive.

To show that two ladies owned a boat, you could write:

> The **ladies'** boat will be launched Tuesday.

As you know, not all plural nouns end in *s.* If a plural noun does not end in *s,* add *'s* to show possession.

To show that several geese laid eggs, you could write this sentence:

> The **geese's** eggs will hatch soon.

Summary of Rules for Possessive Nouns

1. Add *'s* to a singular noun to make it possessive.
   boss's office—one boss has an office
   James's toy—James has a toy

2. Add *'* to a plural noun ending in *s* to make it possessive.
   bosses' offices—several bosses have offices

3. Add *'s* to a plural noun that does not end in *s* to make it possessive.
   children's toys—several children have toys

EXERCISE 5

Writing Possessive Nouns

Directions: Write the possessive form of the first noun in each pair of words. The first one is done as an example.

1. coach signals: _____*coach's*_____

2. army equipment: _____

3. armies conflict: _____

4. women magazines: _____

5. teachers meetings: _____

6. mechanic wrench: _____

7. mice food: _____

8. Tess blouse: _____

Answers are on page 179.

Putting Your Skills to Work

Directions: Practice writing possessive, plural, and proper nouns. Write five sentences based on the following instructions:

In the first sentence, use the possessive form of *Dracula.*
In the second sentence, use the possessive form of *sheep.*
In the third sentence, use the plural form of *city.*
In the fourth sentence, use the plural form of *woman.*
In the fifth sentence, use a proper noun with *Detective.*

When you have finished the five sentences, use the following writing checklist to proofread and correct your sentences.

Writing Checklist	Yes	No
Did you use the correct form of each of the five nouns?	_____	_____
Are all proper nouns and first words of sentences capitalized?	_____	_____
Did you use the apostrophes correctly?	_____	_____

Pronouns

As you learned before, pronouns take the place of nouns. Like nouns, they name people, places, things, and ideas.

Gina is an experienced welder.   **She** is an experienced welder.

She took the place of *Gina* in the second sentence.

The evening sky was covered with **clouds.**   The evening sky was covered with **them.**

Them took the place of *clouds* in the second sentence.

Frank's party lasted only ten minutes.   **His** party lasted only ten minutes.

His took the place of *Frank's* in the second sentence.

Subject pronouns take the place of the subject of a sentence—like *She* in the first example above. **Object pronouns** take the place of nouns that are not the subject of a sentence—like *them* in the second example above. **Possessive pronouns** take the place of possessive nouns—like *his* in the third example above.

The chart below shows the pronouns you will be studying in this section.

Subject Pronouns	Object Pronouns	Possessive Pronouns Used with a noun	Used alone
I	me	my	mine
you	you	your	yours
he	him	his	his
she	her	her	hers
it	it	its	its
we	us	our	ours
they	them	their	theirs

Subject Pronouns

Subject pronouns are used as the subjects of sentences. As you remember from Chapter 2, the subject is the person, place, thing, or idea talked about in a sentence. Every sentence tells what the subject is or does. The subject pronoun is in **boldface type** in each of the following sentences.

Aaron said not to listen to the radio.

He said not to listen to the radio.

Aaron is the subject of the sentence, so the pronoun *He* replaces *Aaron*.

The statements are not true.

They are not true.

Statements is the subject. The plural subject pronoun *They* replaces *statements*.

The children are singing.

They are singing.

Children is the subject. *They* is the plural subject pronoun that replaces *children*.

Object Pronouns

Object pronouns are not subjects and do not show possession. The object pronouns are *me, you, him, her, it, us,* and *them.* See the chart on page 79. The object pronoun is in **boldface type** in each of the following sentences.

Luis gave Ellen a birthday present.

Luis gave **her** a birthday present.

Luis is the subject. Since *Ellen* is not the subject, the object pronoun *her* replaces *Ellen.*

After school, the bus took Artemis and Titus home.

After school, the bus took **them** home.

In this sentence, *bus* is the subject. Since *Artemis and Titus* is not the subject, the object pronoun *them* is used.

EXERCISE 6

Using Subject and Object Pronouns

Directions: On the blank after each sentence, write the subject or object pronoun you could use to replace the underlined noun. The first one is done as an example.

1. <u>Linda</u> encouraged her husband, Paul, to apply for a credit card. _____*She*_____

2. <u>Paul</u> seemed qualified for a card. _____

3. <u>Paul and Linda</u> were surprised by the company's response. _____

4. <u>The letter</u> said that Paul's salary was too low. _____

5. For the third time, Bob glared at <u>the washing machine</u>. _____

6. He wrote down the exact dates of each breakdown and handed the list to <u>his landlady</u>. _____

7. She thanked <u>Bob</u> and promised to speak with the repairman. _____

8. When the machine stayed broken for another week, Bob sent letters to <u>his landlady and the repair company</u>. _____

Answers are on page 179.

Possessive Pronouns

Possessive pronouns have the same purpose as possessive nouns: they show ownership. Unlike possessive nouns, the possessive pronouns do NOT contain apostrophes (').

Some possessive pronouns appear with a noun to show who owns the noun. Those possessive pronouns are *my, your, his, her, its, our,* and *their.* The possessive pronouns are in **boldface type** in each of the following sentences.

That is Harold's van.   That is **his** van.

In that sentence, *his* replaces *Harold's* and appears with *van* to show who owns the van.

The boys' hamster is brown.   **Their** hamster is brown.

In that sentence, *Their* replaces *boys'* and appears with *hamster* to show who owns the *hamster.*

A second group of possessive pronouns can stand alone. These pronouns are *mine, yours, his, hers, its, ours,* and *theirs.* Here are some examples.

The van is Harold's.   The van is **his.**

The brown hamster is the boys'.   The brown hamster is **theirs.**

In those sentences, the possessive pronouns *his* and *theirs* replace the possessive nouns *Harold's* and *boys'.*

EXERCISE 7

Using Possessive Pronouns

Directions: In the blank after each sentence, write the possessive pronoun that can replace the underlined noun.

1. Have you seen <u>the Garcias'</u> new day-care center? _____*their*_____

2. One reason for <u>the center's</u> popularity is that it's just two blocks from the subway. _____

3. The parents like to help out, so many ideas for games are <u>the parents'</u>. _____

4. Every time Lizzy leaves the center, she tries to take a doll or car that isn't <u>Lizzy's</u>. _____

5. The Garcias sort <u>the children's</u> belongings. _____

6. Despite the confusion, Lupe Garcia often thinks, "This place is really <u>mine and my husband's</u>." _____

Answers are on page 179.

Pronoun Agreement

When you replace a noun with a pronoun, the pronoun must agree with the noun in **case** (subject or object). It must also agree with the noun in **gender** (male, female, or neither) and **number** (singular or plural). If the noun is possessive, the pronoun must also be possessive.

If a female's name is replaced, the pronoun must be *she, her,* or *hers.*

> **Eleanor Roosevelt** never went to grade school. But **she** became a world leader. The world respects **her** contributions to society.

A male name must be replaced with *he, his,* or *him.*

> **Albert Einstein** failed math as a child. However, **his** theory of relativity changed the world of science.

The name of a place, thing, or idea must be replaced with *it* or *its.*

> **The United Nations** is in New York City. **It** is a worldwide organization. One of **its** main interests is the children of the world.

Always use a singular pronoun to replace a singular noun and a plural pronoun to replace a plural noun.

> That **book** is interesting. You should read **it.**

> Those **books** are interesting. You should read **them.**

EXERCISE 8

Pronoun Agreement

Directions: Fill in each blank with a pronoun that agrees with the word in **boldface type.** The first one is done as an example.

1. **Will Rogers** hated school and caused extensive damage to school property. In later years, _____*he*_____ became a famous humorist.

2. The composer **Beethoven** was deaf. Although he could not hear _____ music, the world still appreciates it.

3. These **rocks** will make a pretty garden border. I will put _____ around the edges.

4. The **dogs** may dig up the garden. _____ run through the yard all the time.

5. These **flowers** were planted last month. I can see _____ leaves coming up now.

6. **Horace and I** have worked hard in the garden. _____ efforts will make this house more beautiful.

Answers are on page 179.

Punctuating Perfectly: Apostrophes in Contractions

Read the two sentences below. How are they different?

She is a good person.   She's a good person.

The second sentence contains the contraction *She's*. A contraction is formed when two words are combined into one word. An apostrophe (') shows where one or more letters are left out when two words are joined. In the example above, the two words *She is* become one word, *She's*. The letter *i* is dropped from the word *is*, and an apostrophe replaces it.

To make a contraction, replace the missing letter or letters with an apostrophe. Study the examples below and then complete the list.

I am _____*I'm*_____	it is _____
you are _____*you're*_____	she is _____
we will _____	they are _____
he is _____	

The correct contractions are *we'll, he's, it's, she's,* and *they're.*

Negatives are formed the same way.

did not _____*didn't*_____	is not _____
was not _____*wasn't*_____	would not _____
are not _____	had not _____

The correct contractions are *aren't, isn't, wouldn't,* and *hadn't.*

EXERCISE 9

Forming Contractions

Directions: Finish the following list of contractions.

1. was not _____*wasn't*_____

2. does not _____

3. he will _____

4. I am _____

5. we are _____

6. is not _____

7. should not _____

8. they will _____

Answers are on page 179.

Homonyms

A **homonym** is a word that sounds the same as another word but is spelled differently. The chart below shows several homonyms and their meanings. Learn the difference between these words so you can use them correctly in your writing.

Homonym	Meaning	Example Sentence
affect	act upon (verb)	The weather will **affect** his mood.
effect	result (noun)	The new law will have a big **effect.**
knew	was aware of	Caitlin **knew** her subject.
new	not old	She kept up on **new** developments.
passed	went by; succeeded	Time **passed** slowly on Monday.
past	before the present	Don't punish Fido for **past** mistakes.
to	word before a verb or in a direction	Steve wants **to** complain. He went **to** the store.
two	number after one	There can't be **two** winners.
too	also; more than enough	Chan thinks so **too.** He ate **too** much.
weak	not strong	Your logic is **weak.**
week	seven days	I'll finish this job in one **week.**

Contractions, Possessive Pronouns, and Plurals

Several contractions and possessive pronouns are homonyms. For example, read the two sentences below.

> The monarch butterflies are migrating to **their** winter homes in Mexico.

> **They're** strong for such fragile looking creatures.

The first sentence contains the possessive pronoun *their.* The second sentence contains the contraction *they're.* Because the two words sound the same but are spelled differently, they are homonyms. How can you tell which word to use when? Substitute the two words the contraction stands for to see if the sentence makes sense.

> The monarch butterflies are migrating to **they are** winter homes in Mexico.

They are does not make sense here, so use the possessive pronoun *their.*

> **They are** strong for such fragile looking creatures.

They are makes sense here, so use the contraction *they're.*

In the following example, which word correctly completes the sentence?

> (*Its, It's*) cold outside.

As you know, *It's* is a contraction of *It is*. Try substituting *It is*. Does the following sentence make sense?

It is cold outside.

Yes. If you can use *It is,* you can also use the contraction *It's.*

Now read another sentence. Which word is correct?

That dog is hurt. Something is wrong with (*its, it's*) paw.

Try substituting the words *it is* in the sentence.

Something is wrong with **it is** paw.

That sentence doesn't make sense. So the correct word to complete the sentence must be the possessive pronoun *its.*

Something is wrong with **its** paw.

Another common homonym error is using an apostrophe to form a plural noun. In the examples below, which word correctly completes each sentence?

The (*dogs, dog's*) are in the park.

That (*dogs, dog's*) name is Shep.

All of the (*dog's, dogs'*) owners are here.

The first sentence is plural but not possessive, so the word should be *dogs* with an *s* ending but no apostrophe. The second sentence is singular but possessive (*dog's name*), so the word should be *dog's*—a singular noun with an *'s* ending. The third sentence is both plural and possessive (*dogs' owners*), so the word should be *dogs'.*

EXERCISE 10

Homonyms

Directions: There are twelve errors in the paragraph below. All of the mistakes have to do with homonyms, including contractions and possessives. Find each mistake, cross it out, and write the correct word above it. The first error is corrected for you.

~~Its~~ *It's* always a good idea two decorate you're home. Even people who

don't have much spare time can hang pictures on they're wall's and put

up curtains. A knew coat of paint can effect your mood. Of course, its

harder if your working full-time. Gary, a friend of mine, did a nice job on

he's apartment. I hope that he and he's friend Pete will help me out.

Their really talented at decorating.

Answers are on page 179.

Chapter Review

Part 1   **Directions:** Read the three ways of writing each group of sentences. Circle the letter of the sentence that is written correctly.

1. **a.** Many United states citizens do not want nuclear power.
   b. Many united states citizens do not want nuclear power.
   c. Many United States citizens do not want nuclear power.

2. **a.** The residents of Harrisburg live close to the power plant.
   b. The Residents of Harrisburg live close to the power plant.
   c. The residents of harrisburg live close to the power plant.

3. **a.** The residents homes were in danger during the accident.
   b. The resident's home's were in danger during the accident.
   c. The residents' homes were in danger during the accident.

4. **a.** Some of these citizen's are leading the fight to close all nuclear power plants.
   b. Some of these citizens are leading the fight to close all nuclear power plants.
   c. Some of these Citizens are leading the fight to close all nuclear power plants.

Part 2   **Directions:** In each of the following sentences, one or more nouns are incorrect. Write each sentence correctly.

5. Years ago, I went to hear senator Gore speak.

   _____

   _____

6. The year Bush ran for president, dad bought a new ford.

   _____

   _____

Part 3   **Directions:** Fill each blank in the following sentences with one of the pronouns from the list. You should use each pronoun once.

I	ours	his	hers
they	us	she	my

7. After the game, _____ drove my car home.

8. Suzette claimed that the purse was _____.

9. "Throw the Frisbee to _____!" screamed Pablo and Paco.

10. We went to visit the Archers, but _____ weren't home.

11. "Please give me _____ change," requested the diner.

12. "The car that was stolen was _____," cried Ben and Jerry.

Part 4 **Directions:** Underline the correct pronouns in the following paragraphs. The first one is done as an example.

Karen enjoys **(13)** (<u>her</u>, her's) job at the Adult Learning Center. **(14)** (She, Her) is the staff support specialist. She helps Larry with **(15)** (he, his) teaching. Carol teaches there too and is well liked by **(16)** (she's, her) students. The students look forward to coming to **(17)** (their, them) classes.

The directors of the center are Vicki and George. **(18)** (They, Them) count on government grants to fund the center's programs. **(19)** (Their, They're) assistant, Jorge, helps **(20)** (they, them) get funding for the programs. **(21)** (He, Him) is a very important member of the staff. All the Adult Learning Center staff members are quick to say, **(22)** "(Are, Our) goal is education for everybody!"

Answers are on page 179.

Your Turn to Write: Writing a One-Sided Argument

Writing Skill: Topic Sentence

Your opinion is what you think about something. It can be based on facts, ideas, and or information you have received from a number of sources. You also form opinions through personal experiences.

You are going to write a paragraph to share your opinion about something. Your paragraph should begin with a **topic sentence.** That's a sentence that tells what the rest of the paragraph is about. It gives the **main idea** that is going to be explained in the paragraph. All of the other sentences in the paragraph are **supporting sentences.** They add details to support that main idea.

For example, if you want to write your opinion about nuclear power plants, you begin your paragraph with one of the following topic sentences:

Nuclear power plants are a good source of energy that will not destroy our natural resources.

Nuclear power plants are not safe and should be replaced.

Writing Assignment

Directions: Choose a topic from the three below. You can agree or disagree with the topic you choose. There are good points and bad points to everything, but to win this argument you should present only those points that support your side of the issue.

Companies should provide free child care.

Parents should not be responsible for their children's illegal actions.

Drunk drivers should have to serve time in jail.

Write the topic sentence you are going to use for your paragraph at the top of a blank page. Next, brainstorm or map your ideas. Write down all the ways you can think of to support your opinion. Try to think of lots of arguments and specific details and examples. Then read over your work and mark the ideas you want to include in your writing.

On a new page, write your topic sentence again. Then write a sentence for each of your supporting ideas. When you are finished writing, use the writing checklist below to proofread and correct your paragraph.

Writing Checklist	Yes	No
Does your paragraph begin with a topic sentence?	_____	_____
Does every sentence you wrote support your opinion?	_____	_____
Are your nouns used correctly?	_____	_____
Are proper nouns capitalized and common nouns not capitalized?	_____	_____
Do all of your pronouns agree in case, gender, and number with the nouns they replace?	_____	_____
Are possessive nouns and pronouns spelled correctly?	_____	_____
Are all homonyms and contractions spelled correctly?	_____	_____

CHAPTER 4

Verbs: Form and Tense

What Is a Verb?

A **verb** is a word that shows action or being. A verb can be an action word like *run, jump, skip, drink,* or *dance.* It can also be a linking word like *is, am, was,* or *were.*

Underline the verbs in the following sentences.

> The traffic roared through the tunnel.
>
> Drivers honked horns at each other.
>
> Many drivers were impatient.
>
> At the tunnel's exit, a motorcycle cop waited for speeders.

Did you underline *roared, honked, were,* and *waited*? If so, you have a good understanding of verbs.

Below is a list of nouns. In the space next to each noun, write a verb that tells something that the noun does.

husbands _____

friends _____

wives _____

dogs _____

cars _____

Did you write, for example, *dogs bark* and *friends share*? Any word is a correct answer as long as it is a verb.

Verbs Tell Time

When you talk about what you do today, what you did yesterday, and what you will do tomorrow, you use **verb tenses.** You change verb tenses to show when events in your life take place.

Think about this very moment as the present. A verb that tells what you do in the present is a **present tense** verb.

> Right now, I **walk** slowly.

Present tense verbs also tell what you do on a regular basis.

I always **walk** slowly.

Anything that happened before the present—it doesn't matter how long ago—is part of your past. A verb that tells what you did in the past is a **past tense** verb.

Last week, I **walked** slowly.

You also plan to do things tomorrow and weeks, months, and years in the future. A verb that tells what you will do at some later time is a **future tense** verb.

Next week, I **will walk** slowly.

Fill in the blank below with verbs showing things you do every day. Write in the present tense.

Every day I _____*sleep*_____. I also _____.

There are things you did yesterday that you do not do every day. In the blank below, write a verb that shows what you did yesterday or the day before. Write in the past tense.

Yesterday I _____*danced*_____. Then I _____.

Now write a verb that shows what you will do tomorrow or the next day. Write in the future tense.

Tomorrow I _____*will shop*_____. Later in the day, I

_____.

Recognizing the Base Verb

The main verb is called the **base verb**. You form different verb tenses by adding endings or helping verbs to the base verb. In the examples above, you read the verbs *walk, walked,* and *will walk.* In these examples, the present tense verb *walk* is the base verb. You form the past tense by adding an ending, *-ed*, to the base verb. You form the future tense by adding a helping verb, *will*, to the base verb.

Some verbs, like *walk*, change to the present and past tenses according to a regular pattern. These are **regular verbs**. You will learn how to form regular verbs first. Later in the chapter, you will study some **irregular verbs**. Irregular verbs don't follow the regular patterns for changing tenses.

Present Tense of Regular Verbs

The **present tense** shows that something is happening in the present or right now. It is also used to show that something takes place regularly. To form the present tense, use the base verb by itself or the base verb plus -*s*.

The following box shows how the present tense of the base verb *walk* is formed for different subjects. Notice that -*s* is added to the base verb for singular subjects (except for *I* and *you*) to make the verb agree with those subjects.

Subject	Present Tense
I, you, we, they, and all plural nouns	walk (base verb alone)
he, she, it, and all singular nouns	walks (base verb + s)

In the following sentences, the verbs end in -*s* because their subjects are the singular pronouns *he, she, it,* or singular nouns.

> She **looks** great in her new coat.
> Jordan **seems** happy enough.
> The wind **feels** cool.

Complete the following sentences by writing *dance* or *dances* in each blank. In one of the sentences, the verb should end in -*s*.

> My grandparents _____ in a contest every year.
>
> My grandmother _____ very gracefully.

For the first sentence, the correct answer is *dance*, since *grandparents* is a plural noun. For the second sentence, the correct answer is *dances*, since *grandmother* is a singular noun. You will learn more about subject-verb agreement in Chapter 5.

EXERCISE 1

Choosing Present Tense Verbs

Directions: Circle the subject in each sentence. Then underline the correct verb form. The first one is done as an example.

1. (Americans) (like, likes) to see their country grow.
2. I (love, loves) being a citizen.
3. I (find, finds) that many people are willing to help me.
4. They (welcome, welcomes) me with open arms.
5. My parents still (live, lives) in Guatemala.
6. We (write, writes) to each other every week.
7. My sister (live, lives) in California now.
8. (Do, Does) you have relatives in another country?

Answers are on page 180.

Past Tense of Regular Verbs

The **past tense** shows that something took place in the past. Most regular verbs take an *-ed* ending to form the past tense. When regular verbs end in *e*, just add the letter *-d* to form the past tense.

Here are some examples of how to form the past tense of regular verbs.

base verb	+	ending	=	past tense
walk	+	ed	=	walked
spell	+	ed	=	spelled
change	+	d	=	changed
love	+	d	=	loved

Now write some past tense verbs. The following paragraph has three blanks. There is a base verb in front of each blank. Fill in the past tense of each base verb to complete the paragraph.

Two years ago, Al (hate) _____ exercise. Last year, he (walk) _____ one mile a day. Now Al walks three miles a day. He looks physically fit. Two years ago, he (looks) _____ terrible. Now he hates to miss his daily exercise.

You should have written *hated, walked,* and *looked*. What letters did you add to the verbs to make them past tense? _____

The endings that make those verbs past tense are *-d* for *hate* and *-ed* for *walk* and *look*.

Future Tense

The **future tense** shows that something has not happened yet. Below are two sentences using the future tense of the base verbs *fly* and *smile*.

Maria **will fly** to Puerto Rico.

She **will smile** when she sees her family.

What helping verb comes before the base verbs *fly* and *smile* to show the future tense? _____

The helping verb is *will*. You can form the future tense of any verb by using the helping verb *will* in front of it.

EXERCISE 2

Writing the Past and Future Tenses

Directions: Write the past and future tenses of the following base verbs. The first one is done as an example.

Base Verb	Past	Future
1. look	*looked*	*will look*
2. move		
3. live		
4. save		
5. shout		
6. paint		

Answers are on page 180.

Common Irregular Verbs

In Exercise 2, you added *-d* or *-ed* to put each verb in the past tense. But not all verbs change to the past tense according to the regular pattern. There are many **irregular verbs,** mostly in the past tense. The only way to get to know irregular verbs is to study them until you can remember them.

A list of the simple present, simple past, and past participle forms of common irregular verbs appears on the following pages. Verbs that follow similar patterns are grouped together. You may already use most of these verbs correctly. Study this list by following these steps:

1. Cover the second and third columns of the list.

2. Read the simple present form in a short sentence using *I* as the subject. *I go.*

3. Test to see if you know the simple past form by putting the sentence in the past tense. *I went.*

4. Test to see if you know the past participle by putting the sentence in the present perfect. *I have gone.*

5. Check your answers against the forms listed in the second and third columns.

6. Study the forms you missed by repeating the sentences over and over in each tense until you have memorized them.

Simple Present	Simple Past	Past Participle (with *have, has,* or *had*)
cost	cost	cost
put	put	put
read	read	read
set	set	set
bring	brought	brought
buy	bought	bought
think	thought	thought
catch	caught	caught
teach	taught	taught
lay (put or place)	laid	laid
pay	paid	paid
say	said	said

Simple Present	Simple Past	Past Participle (with *have, has,* or *had*)
send	sent	sent
feel	felt	felt
keep	kept	kept
leave	left	left
mean	meant	meant
meet	met	met
sleep	slept	slept
build	built	built
get	got	got, gotten
lose	lost	lost
find	found	found
feed	fed	fed
hold	held	held
hear	heard	heard
sell	sold	sold
tell	told	told
understand	understood	understood
make	made	made
fall	fell	fallen
speak	spoke	spoken
take	took	taken
drive	drove	driven
eat	ate	eaten
give	gave	given
ride	rode	ridden
write	wrote	written
begin	began	begun
drink	drank	drunk
ring	rang	rung
sing	sang	sung
draw	drew	drawn
grow	grew	grown

Simple Present	Simple Past	Past Participle (with *have, has,* or *had*)
know	knew	known
become	became	become
come	came	come
has or have	had	had
run	ran	run
see	saw	seen
go	went	gone
do or does	did	done
lie	lay	lain

EXERCISE 3

Past Tense of Irregular Verbs

Directions: Fill in the past tense of the verbs below. When you have filled in as many as you know, find the others on the chart in this lesson. The first one is done as an example.

Base Verb	Past Tense
1. give	I _____ *gave* _____ last month.
2. tell	I _____ him yesterday.
3. see	I _____ him the day before he left.
4. come	I _____ home late.
5. read	I _____ the paper last Sunday.
6. bring	I _____ a cake to the party.
7. say	I _____ so yesterday.
8. make	I _____ the cake last night.
9. go	I _____ home yesterday.
10. do	I _____ it a minute ago.
11. have	I _____ the book last night.
12. sell	I _____ the car four months ago.

Answers are on page 180.

Avoiding Errors with Irregular Verbs

In Exercise 3, you filled in the blanks with the past tense forms of many irregular verbs. None of these forms needed helping verbs. There are some other past tenses that do require helping verbs, but you will not be studying all of those tenses in this chapter. However, there are some very common mistakes people make when they confuse the different past tenses.

Study the following pair of sentences. The correct sentence uses the form of the past you learned in Exercise 3. It does not require a helping verb. The other sentence contains a mistake because it uses a form that cannot stand alone.

CORRECT: I did my homework already.
INCORRECT: I done my homework already.

The correct past tense of *do* is *did*. The word *done* is used to form a tense that requires a helping verb (like *have*), so *done* is never correct when it is used alone.

Here are some other pairs of similar sentences. Study each pair to be sure you know which past tense form can be used without a helping verb.

CORRECT: She went home yesterday.
INCORRECT: She gone home yesterday.

CORRECT: We came home last night.
INCORRECT: We come home last night.

CORRECT: Jesse was helping me.
INCORRECT: Jesse been helping me.

EXERCISE 4

Choosing the Correct Past Tense Form

Directions: Underline the correct verb to complete each of the following sentences. The first one is done as an example.

1. Angie (seen, <u>saw</u>) a prowler in the parking lot.

2. Last weekend the Karlovskys (ran, run) in a marathon.

3. Horace (was, been) in that bowling league for years.

4. We (went, gone) camping for our vacation.

5. Cathi (sang, sung) in the musical.

6. Mikey (did, done) his best to catch the ball.

Answers are on page 180.

Important Irregular Verbs

There are three very important irregular verbs: *be, have,* and *do.* These verbs are used often in your speech and in writing.

The Base Verb Be

As you already know, the most common linking verbs are forms of *be.* In fact, forms of *be* are also some of the most frequently used helping verbs.

The verb *be* is irregular because its forms change for different subjects in both the present tense and the past tense. The following chart shows the forms of the three tenses for *be.*

Subject	Present	Past	Future
I	am		
he, she, it, and all singular nouns	is	was	will be
you, we, they, and all plural nouns	are	were	

Choose the correct form of *be* to complete the following sentences.

I (be, am) furious with those boys.

Tom (was, were) about to put his brother in the washing machine.

You (is, are) kidding!

In the first sentence, *am* agrees with *I.* In the second sentence, *was* agrees with the singular noun *Tom.* In the third sentence, *are* agrees with *You.*

The Verbs Have and Do

Two other confusing irregular verbs that we use every day are *have* and *do.* You may already know how to use these verbs correctly most of the time. Try to correct the paragraph below to see how much you already know about these two verbs. Draw a line through each verb you think is incorrect and write the correct form above it. There is one mistake in each sentence.

My brother have to quit his job. His wife don't like it when he leaves home at 5 A.M. to go to work. She have to understand that he will get fired if he comes to work late. My brother's children does not understand him either. They has no time to see him.

Here is the corrected paragraph:

My brother **has** to quit his job. His wife **doesn't** like it when he leaves home at 5 A.M. to go to work. She **has** to understand that he will get fired if he comes to work late. My brother's children **do** not understand him either. They **have** no time to see him.

Forms of Have

The following chart shows the forms of all three tenses of the irregular verb *have*.

Subject	Present	Past	Future
I, you, we, they, and all plural nouns	have	had	will have
he, she, it and all singular nouns	has		

Remember that the present tense is either *have* or *has*. The past tense is always *had*, and the future is always *will have*.

Forms of Do

The following chart shows the forms of all three tenses of the irregular verb *do*.

Subject	Present	Past	Future
I, you, we, they, and all plural nouns	do	did	will do
he, she, it, and all singular nouns	does		

Remember that the present tense is either *do* or *does*. The past tense is always *did*, and the future tense is always *will do*.

EXERCISE 5

Forms of Irregular Verbs

Directions: Complete the following sentences using the correct forms of the verbs *be*, *have*, and *do*. The first one is done as an example.

1. (past) They _____*were*_____ married in April.

2. (present) Erika _____ angry about the robbery.

3. (future) The station wagon _____ ready for the junkyard soon.

4. (present) My parents _____ not sure that they want a divorce.

5. (present) Tom _____ a good job.

6. (future) Sue _____ fun at the movies next weekend.

7. (past) After work on Friday, Nate remembered that he _____ to cash a check.

8. (future) The Morrises _____ a picnic every summer.

9. (present) Most people _____ not bother to make a budget.

10. (past) If they _____, they might be surprised by where their money goes.

11. (present) My sister _____ a budget every month.

12. (future) In the future, I _____ a budget each month too.

Answers are on page 180.

Time Clues to Verb Tenses

Often clue words in a sentence will tell you to use the past, present, or future verb tense. Words like *now, this minute*, and *today* tell you that the sentence takes place in the present.

> Right this minute, I attend school.

The clue words are _____ _____ _____.

Words like *yesterday, last year, some time ago*, and *before* tell you that the sentence takes place in the past.

> Last year, I attended school.

The clue words are _____ _____.

Words like *tomorrow, in three hours*, and *next year* tell you that the sentence takes place in the future.

> Next year, I will attend school.

The clue words are _____ _____.

EXERCISE 6

Using Time Clues

Directions: Write the correct form of the base verb to complete each sentence. Underline the time clue in each sentence that tells you what tense to choose. The first one is done as an example.

1. (want) <u>Today</u> many people _____ *want* _____ to lose weight.

2. (work) Last year Rob _____ out to tone up his muscles.

3. (get) We _____ up early every day.

4. (go) Tomorrow Anne _____ to her aerobics class.

5. (run) Yesterday I _____ three miles.

6. (be) The game _____ interesting next week.

Answers are on page 180.

Putting Your Skills to Work

Directions: Complete the following exercise. Pay special attention to the verbs.

Look at the picture. Imagine you are one of the people in the picture. Write a paragraph that tells what happened before the scene in the picture (past), what is happening now (present), and what will happen later (future). Try to use at least two sentences in the past tense, two sentences in the present tense, and two sentences in the future tense. You can use the following sentence as your first sentence. Notice that it is in the past tense.

Matthew and Shaneesha lived in Florida for three years.

When you complete the sentences, use the following writing checklist to proofread and correct your sentences.

Writing Checklist	Yes	No
Do you have two sentences written in the past tense?	———	———
Do you have two sentences written in the present tense?	———	———
Do you have two sentences written in the future tense?	———	———
Are your verb forms correct?	———	———
Did you use correct end punctuation?	———	———

The Continuous Tenses

Another Way to Form the Present

You have already learned to form the present tense by using the base verb or the base verb plus -*s* or -*es*. Another present tense, the **present continuous tense**, shows that an action is continuing in the present. To form the present continuous tense, use *am, is,* or *are* as a helping verb with the base verb plus -*ing*. For example,

The clown **is laughing.**

There are two words in the verb of that sentence: *is laughing.* The helping verb is the word *is.* The base verb is *laugh.* The ending -*ing* is added to *laugh.* Find and underline the verbs in the next two sentences that are in the present continuous tense.

The workers are striking.   I am walking the picket line.

Did you underline *are striking* and *am walking*? They are the verbs in those sentences.

You can add -*ing* to any base verb. On the lines below, combine the verbs *swear, think*, and *choose* with the -*ing* ending. If a base verb ends in *e*, drop the *e* before adding -*ing*.

_____   _____   _____

You should have written *swearing, thinking,* and *choosing*.

Now write the three helping verbs that can be used before the base verb plus -*ing* to form the present continuous tense: _____,

_____, and _____.

The following chart shows all the present continuous forms of the verb *walk*.

Subject	Helping Verb	Base Verb + *ing*
I	am	
he, she, it, and all singular nouns	is	walking
you, we, they, and all plural nouns	are	

Another Way to Form the Past

Compare the two sentences below. How are they alike? How are they different?

Rafael is running.   Rafael was running.

The verb in the first sentence is *is running*. That verb is in the present continuous tense. The action is taking place now.

Look at the second sentence. It also uses the word *running*, but the helping verb *was* has been added. As you know, *was* is a past tense verb. This verb is in the **past continuous tense**, which shows that an action was continuing in the past: *was running*.

The following chart shows how to form the past continuous tense of the verb *walk* for different subjects.

Subject	Helping Verb	Base Verb + *ing*
I, he, she, it, and all singular nouns	was	walking
you, we, they, and all plural nouns	were	

Complete the following sentences by filling in the correct form of the past continuous tense of each base verb.

It ___*was raining*___ hard that day.
     (rain)

Carin _____ when she said that.
     (joke)

The children _____ when we got home.
     (sleep)

You should have written *was joking* in the second sentence because *Carin* is a singular noun. In the third sentence, *were sleeping* agrees with the plural noun *children*.

EXERCISE 7

Using the Continuous Tenses

Directions: Complete each sentence below by filling in the correct form of the present or past continuous tense of the base verb before each blank. The first one is done as an example. Remember, you need to use a helping verb, and the base verb must have an *-ing* ending.

1. In my class, everyone (study) ___*is studying*___ for an important test this week.

2. We (work) _____ at different speeds and are good at different things.

3. Anna (learn) _____ fractions faster than Dave or I right now.

4. Already some students (solve) _____ equations with no trouble.

5. I (enjoy) _____ my math class this year because I understand it.

6. One morning I (drive) _____ to work too fast, and I hit two other cars.

7. Both other drivers said, "We (go) _____ in for repairs anyway, so don't worry."

8. When I got to work, my boss said that she (give)

    _____ me the day off and a big raise.

9. Then suddenly my alarm clock (ring) _____.

10. It turned out that I (dream) _____!

Answers are on page 180.

Punctuating Perfectly: Business Documents

Sometimes in your daily life, you'll need to use your knowledge of punctuation and language to write business documents like letters, memos, meeting notes, and reports. You may also need your knowledge to fill out such forms as job applications, driver's license applications, and voter registration forms.

Writing a Business Letter

A **business letter** is written to take care of a business matter. You might write one to apply for a job, order a gift, or complain about a product or service.

A business letter always uses commas and colons in specific places. Study the following sample business letter.

---

15 Tulip Place	RETURN
Chicago, IL 60604	ADDRESS
July 14, 2003	DATE
Ms. Jane West	
Western Fields Inc.	INSIDE
313 East Street	ADDRESS
Chicago, IL 60607	
Dear Ms. West:	GREETING

Thank you for interviewing me for the server position in your company's dining room. After speaking with you, I am sure I would enjoy working at Western Fields Inc. I believe my past food service experience would make me a valuable asset to the company. I look forward to hearing from you in the near future.   **BODY**

Sincerely,	CLOSING
Ramona Jones	SIGNATURE
Ramona Jones	TYPED NAME

Did you notice how punctuation is used in a business letter?

- The return address and inside address have a comma between the name of the city and the state (Chicago, IL). However, there is no comma between the state and the zipcode.

- The date has a comma between the day and the year (July 14, 2003).

- The greeting has a colon (not a comma) after the name (Dear Ms. West:). Notice that this is a formal greeting (Ms. West), not a friendly greeting (Jane).

- A comma follows the closing (Sincerely,). Formal words are used as closings in business letters. *Sincerely, Cordially,* and *Yours truly* are often used.

- The closing is followed by a handwritten signature and the same name typed for clarity.

EXERCISE 8

Punctuating a Business Letter

Directions: Read the short business letter that follows. Using the letter to Jane West as a sample, add the missing punctuation.

227 March Avenue
Rockport MA 08642
December 13 2003

Ms. S. J. Reed
Lightner's Logging Co.
234 Pine Road
Rockport MA 08642

Dear Ms. Reed

    This is to inform you that the sweater I ordered is too small. I am returning the sweater to exchange it for a size 44. Please send the larger sweater right away.

Sincerely

Hank Greene

Hank Greene

Answers are on page 180.

Filling Out a Job Application

A **job application** is just one of many forms you may need to fill out in your daily life. The most important thing to remember with any form is to fill in every blank with the information asked for. If you list items, such as your previous employers or references, separate them with semicolons (;). Some parts of the form may not require complete sentences, but other parts may. In those sections, make sure you use commas and end punctuation correctly. Read the sample application and notice how it has been filled in.

———— Aguilar Auto Repair ————

Name: *Tony Barrone*

Address: *919 Mulford St., Greensburg, PA 15601*

Phone: *(724) 555-1234*

Job applying for: *Auto mechanic*

Past experience (include phone numbers and dates of employment):
Greensburg Motors (555-4321), 10/1999- present;
Al's Auto Body (555-9876), 8/97 to 10/99;
Vic's Repair Shop (555-6789), 6/96 to 8/97

Education: *Greensburg United High School, Vocational-*
Technical Program, 1994-97

References (include titles and phone numbers): *Marge Miller,*
manager of Greensburg Motors (555-4321); Vic
Dobrowski, owner of Vic's Repair Shop (555-6789)

Why should you get this job? *I've been working on cars since*
I was 12 years old, when I used to help my dad keep
his '83 Honda running. I have experience repairing
all makes and models of cars. I know how to do
computer diagnostics and emissions tests. I'm
knowledgeable and a hard worker.

Read the following blank job application. Complete it using your own information, including the job of your choice. Remember to check your use of punctuation.

Name: _____

Address: _____

Phone: _____

Job applying for: _____

Past experience (include phone numbers and dates of employment):

_____

_____

_____

_____

Education: _____

References (include titles and phone numbers): _____

_____

_____

_____

Why should you get this job? _____

_____

_____

_____

Chapter Review

EXERCISE 9

Part 1 **Directions:** Decide whether each verb in the following list is in the past, present, or future tense. Then put each word in the appropriate column of the chart below. The first row is done as an example.

1.

will find	drive	will write	sang
claim	hopes	jump	is
danced	will paint	will want	looked
had	was	are	saw

Present	Past	Future
drive	*sang*	*will find*

Part 2 **Directions:** Read each sentence carefully. Three different ways of writing the underlined part of each sentence are given. Circle the letter of the choice that makes the sentence correct. Choice **a** is always the same as the original underlined part.

2. The community center <u>beginned</u> a gymnastics program for toddlers.

   a. beginned
   b. began
   c. begin

3. Our neighbors <u>are having</u> a huge argument.

   a. are having
   b. is having
   c. having

4. The circus <u>stop</u> here each year.

   a. stop
   b. will stops
   c. stops

5. Two years ago, my father <u>decide</u> to go back to school.

   a. decide
   b. decided
   c. will decide

6. Daquan <u>walk</u> six miles after his car broke down.

   a. walk
   b. walking
   c. walked

7. We <u>be</u> ready to leave for school now.

   a. be
   b. is
   c. are

8. Velma <u>done</u> the copying three times last week.

   a. done
   b. did
   c. will do

9. Theo <u>turned</u> the radio on when he gets home from work.

   a. turned
   b. are turning
   c. will turn

10. I <u>is</u> sure you can find something better to do than play video games.

   a. is
   b. are
   c. am

Answers are on page 180.

Your Turn to Write: Writing a Business Letter

Writing Skill: Letter Writing

Directions: Write a short business letter requesting a copy of the *Consumer Information Catalog*. Write to Consumer Information Center, P.O. Box 100, Pueblo, CO 81002. If you mail the letter, the Consumer Information Center will send you a free catalog, which lists government publications that may be helpful to you.

Be sure to follow the business letter style that you learned earlier in this chapter. When you have completed the letter, use the following writing checklist to proofread and correct your letter.

Writing Checklist	Yes	No
Does your business letter have		
a return address?	_____	_____
a date?	_____	_____
an inside address?	_____	_____
a greeting?	_____	_____
a body?	_____	_____
a closing?	_____	_____
a signature?	_____	_____
a name?	_____	_____
Is the punctuation correct?	_____	_____
Did you use subjects and pronouns correctly?	_____	_____
Did you use verbs correctly?	_____	_____
Did you write complete sentences?	_____	_____

CHAPTER 5

Subject-Verb Agreement

Subject-verb agreement means that the verb in a sentence must agree with the subject of that sentence. A singular subject needs a singular verb, and a plural subject needs a plural verb. A singular noun or pronoun refers to only one person, place, thing, or idea. A plural noun or pronoun refers to more than one person, place, thing, or idea. In this chapter, you will learn how to make verbs agree with singular subjects and plural subjects.

Except for the irregular verb *be*, which you learned in Chapter 4, verbs change form for different subjects only in the present tense.

Pronouns as Subjects

If the subject of a sentence is a pronoun, the verb must agree with it in number. Here are the subject pronouns with the correct present tense of the verb *swim*.

Pronoun	Verb	Pronoun	Verb
I you, we, they	swim	he, she, it	swims

Which pronouns need a verb that ends in -*s*?

Which pronouns need a verb that does not end in -*s*?

> **Rules for Subject-Verb Agreement with Pronouns**
>
> In the present tense, the verb must end in -*s* if the subject is *he*, *she*, or *it*.
>
> If the subject is *I*, *you*, *we*, or *they*, the verb does not end in -*s*.

Underline the correct verb to complete each of the following sentences.

They (swim, swims) at the beach every Saturday.

He (laugh, laughs) at all my jokes.

In the first sentence, *swim* agrees with *They* because both are plural.

In the second sentence, *laughs* agrees with *He* because both are singular.

Usually you add -*s* to the end of a base verb for the subjects *he, she,* and *it*. However, when the base verb ends in *s, x, z, sh,* or *ch,* you should add -*es*. In the following sentences, the base verbs have -*es* added for subject-verb agreement.

> She **washes** the car on Sunday mornings.　　He **fixes** waffles for breakfast.

Sometimes it is hard to decide if a pronoun is singular or plural. An **indefinite pronoun** does not name a specific person or thing. The following indefinite pronouns are always singular.

Singular Indefinite Pronouns

each (one)	no one	everyone
either (one)	nothing	everything
neither (one)	nobody	everybody
one		
someone	anyone	
something	anything	
somebody	anybody	

Note that singular verbs agree with the following indefinite pronouns.

> Nobody **knows** the trouble I've seen.　　Each of the winners **is** here.

EXERCISE 1

Subject-Verb Agreement with Pronouns

Directions: Underline the correct form of the verb to complete each sentence. Follow the rule for subject-verb agreement with pronouns. The first one is done as an example.

1. He (own, <u>owns</u>) a garage on 42nd Street.
2. We (take, takes) all our cars and trucks to his shop.
3. They (come, comes) back as good as new.
4. If anything (are, is) wrong, the mechanic can fix it.
5. She (thank, thanks) him for taking good care of her car.
6. It's eight years old, but it (perform, performs) like a new vehicle.
7. Everybody (want, wants) a reliable car.
8. Neither of my sisters (have, has) a new car.

Answers are on page 181.

Irregular Verbs

Now you will learn the present tense of one new irregular verb: *go*. Start by looking at the irregular verb you studied in Chapter 4: *have*. Here are the subject pronouns with the correct present tense forms of *have*.

Pronoun	Verb	Pronoun	Verb
I _____ you, we, they	have	he, she, it	has

Which pronouns need the form of the verb that ends in -*s*?

Which pronouns need the form of the verb that does not end in -*s*?

Did you notice that the rule on page 113 still applies, even though *have* is an irregular verb? Even though the spellings are irregular, the form for *he*, *she*, and *it* (the singular form) still ends in -*s*.

Now look at the present tense forms of *go*.

Pronoun	Verb	Pronoun	Verb
I _____ you, we, they	go	he, she, it	goes

As you can see, the forms for *he*, *she*, and *it* still end in -*s*, but an *e* is added before the -*s*. With the irregular verb *go*, as well as with the verb *do*, the -*es* ending is used.

Now try applying the subject-verb agreement rule with irregular verbs. Underline the correct form of the verb to complete each of the following.

He (do, does) the dishes this week.

She (have, has) the shopping list.

They (are, is) in the clothes hamper.

In the first sentence, *does* agrees with *He*. In the second sentence, *has* agrees with *She*. In the third sentence, *are* agrees with *They*.

Only one verb changes form for different subjects in the past tense. That verb is *be*. Look at the past tense forms of *be* for different subjects.

Pronoun	Verb	Pronoun	Verb
I	was		
you, we, they	were	he, she, it	was

Notice that in the past tense, *I was* breaks the subject-verb agreement rule because the verb ends in *-s*. This is the only exception to the rule. Underline the correct past tense form of *be* to complete the following sentences.

It (were, was) done when I left.

They (were, was) on the kitchen table.

You should have underlined *was* in the first sentence (singular) and *were* in the second sentence (plural).

EXERCISE 2

Subject-Verb Agreement with Irregular Verbs

Directions: Underline the correct form of the irregular verb to complete each sentence. Follow the subject-verb agreement rule and refer to the charts of irregular verb forms on the previous pages when needed.

1. We (go, goes) for a walk every day.

2. They (have, has) dinner at 7:00 on most nights.

3. I (am, are, is) ready to sing now, Fred.

4. She (do, does) whatever her friends tell her.

5. He (were, was) on the phone when I arrived.

6. They (do, does) the laundry every weekend.

7. You (were, was) not invited to this party.

8. He (go, goes) to the basketball court every night.

Answers are on page 181.

Nouns as Subjects

The subject of a sentence can be either a subject pronoun, a singular noun, or a plural noun. A singular subject can always be replaced by *he, she,* or *it.* Therefore, a present tense verb must end in *-s* to agree with a singular noun. Cross out the subject of the following sentence and replace it with *he, she,* or *it.* Then underline the correct verb.

The alligator (swim, swims) slowly through the swamp.

Alligator is the singular subject. *The alligator* can be replaced by *It.* Therefore, the verb must end in *-s.* Here is the correct answer:

~~The alligator~~ (swim, <u>swims</u>) slowly through the swamp.
It

A plural subject can always be replaced by *they,* so a present tense verb must not end in *-s* to agree with a plural subject. Cross out the plural subject of the following sentence and replace it with *they.* Then underline the correct verb.

The women (laugh, laughs) loudly.

In this sentence, *women* is the plural subject. *The women* can be replaced by *They.* The verb must not end in *-s* to agree with *They,* so the correct verb is *laugh.*

Here is the subject-verb agreement rule again.

Subject-Verb Agreement Rule

In the present tense, the verb must end in *-s* if the subject is *he, she, it,* or a singular noun. If the subject is *I, you, we, they,* or a plural noun, the verb should not end in *-s.*

It's usually easy to tell whether nouns are singular or plural because most nouns are **countable**. You can have one dog, three cousins, and two radios. However, you cannot count some things and ideas, like *knowledge, pain, love, advice,* and *beauty.* **Uncountable** nouns are singular. If you put a pronoun in the place of an uncountable noun, you use the pronoun *it.*

The subject of the following sentence is an uncountable noun. Since *knowledge* can be replaced with *it,* the verb must end in *-s.*

~~Knowledge~~ (increase, <u>increases</u>) your job skills.
It

EXERCISE 3

Nouns as Subjects

Directions: Underline the correct verb to complete each sentence. The first one is done as an example.

1. Summer (are, <u>is</u>) the best time of the year.
2. Families (move, moves) from city to city.
3. The gardens (look, looks) gorgeous.
4. Carl (guide, guides) tourists through the Everglades.
5. Strength (give, gives) a woman confidence.
6. Carolyn's advice (is, are) always good.

Answers are on page 181.

Tricky Subject-Verb Agreement

Sometimes it's hard to make a subject and a verb agree. This is especially true when the subject of a sentence has two parts, when a phrase comes between the subject and the verb, or when the word order of the sentence is inverted.

When a sentence has a **compound subject**, the subject is in two parts that are always connected by *and, or,* or *nor*. The parts are always nouns or pronouns. The following sentence has a compound subject:

Ed and Joe like to eat breakfast at the local diner.

Ed and *Joe* are the two parts of the compound subject. The two parts are joined by *and*.

In the next example, the two parts of the compound subject are joined by *or*. Identify and underline the two parts of the compound subject.

Either Alice or I have to plan the surprise party for our boss.

The two parts of the compound subject in that sentence are *Alice* and *I. Either* is not part of the subject.

Underline the parts of the compound subjects in the sentences below.

Mrs. Jones and her daughter love Italian food.

The adults or the teenagers bring the snacks.

Neither she nor her brother is likely to win the contest.

You should have underlined *Mrs. Jones* and *daughter, adults* and *teenagers,* and *she* and *brother*. The words *either* and *neither* often appear with compound subjects, but they are never part of the subject.

Compound Subjects Joined by And

Very often, the parts of a compound subject are joined by the word *and*.

> Compound subjects joined by *and* are always plural. They need a verb that agrees with a plural subject.

Underline the parts of the compound subject and circle the verb in each sentence. The first one is done for you.

> <u>Music</u> and <u>art</u> (excite) many people.
>
> Football and baseball thrill millions of sports fans.
>
> Susan and I love movies.

You should have underlined *Football* and *baseball* in the second sentence and *Susan* and *I* in the third sentence. You should have circled *thrill* in the second sentence and *love* in the third sentence. Notice that none of the verbs in the three sentences ends in -*s*.

Compound Subjects Joined by Or and Nor

Deciding which verb to use when the parts of a compound subject are joined by *or* or *nor* takes a little more thought.

> When a compound subject is joined by *or* or *nor*, the verb has to agree with the subject that is closer to the verb.

Underline the two parts of the compound subject in the following sentence. Which part is closer to the verb?

> Either Betsy or you **come** home at 3:00 every day.

The two parts of the subject are *Betsy* and *you*. The part of the subject closer to the verb is *you*. According to the subject-verb agreement rule, the pronoun *you* needs a verb that does not end in -*s*.

Now look at the sentence again, this time with the parts of the subject switched.

> Either you or Betsy **comes** home at 3:00 every day.

Since the part of the subject closer to the verb now is *Betsy*, the form of the verb must agree with a singular subject. According to the subject-verb agreement rule, the singular noun *Betsy* needs a verb ending in -*s*.

When the parts of the subject are joined by *nor*, the verb is chosen the same way. The verb agrees with the part of the subject closer to it. Underline the two parts of the compound subject in the following sentence. Then circle the verb that agrees with the closer part of the subject.

Neither Max nor his brothers (plan, plans) to visit Mother.

The two parts of the compound subject are *Max* and *brothers*. The correct verb is *plan*, which agrees with the closer part of the subject, *brothers*. Remember, a plural subject needs a verb that does not end in -*s*.

Now look at the sentence again with the parts of the subject reversed. Circle the verb that agrees with the closer part of the subject in the new sentence.

Neither his brothers nor Max (plan, plans) to visit Mother.

The correct verb for that sentence is *plans*, which agrees with the singular subject *Max*.

EXERCISE 4

Subject-Verb Agreement with Compound Subjects

Directions: Underline the parts of the compound subject in each sentence. Then circle the correct form of the verb. The first one is done as an example.

1. The local <u>police</u> and the state <u>police</u> (increase), increases) their patrols on holiday weekends.

2. You and your parents (need, needs) to spend more time together.

3. Neither Nan nor I (go, goes) to Canada for Christmas.

4. A local club or business (give, gives) awards for community service.

5. Newspapers and radio (help, helps) people stay informed.

6. Either Greg or Stephanie always (answer, answers) the phone.

Answers are on page 181.

Putting Your Skills to Work

Directions: Write ten sentences using compound subjects. Write about anything or anyone you wish. Pay close attention to subject-verb agreement.

In at least two of your sentences, join the parts of the compound subject with the word *and*. In at least two other sentences, use *or* to connect the parts of the subject. In at least two other sentences, use *nor*.

When you have completed the sentences, use the following writing checklist to proofread and correct your sentences.

Writing Checklist	Yes	No
Do you have at least two sentences using *and*, two sentences using *or*, and two sentences using *nor*?	_____	_____
Do the verbs agree with the subjects?	_____	_____
Did you write complete sentences?	_____	_____

Interrupters

In many sentences, **interrupting phrases** come between the subject and the verb. To make sure the subject and verb agree, you must be able to find the subject and ignore the interrupter. Here's an example.

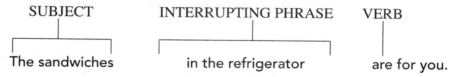

SUBJECT	INTERRUPTING PHRASE	VERB
The sandwiches	in the refrigerator	are for you.

The subject, *sandwiches*, is plural. The verb *are* is correct for a plural subject. Notice that the interrupting phrase, *in the refrigerator*, does not affect subject-verb agreement. The verb should not agree with *refrigerator*, because that noun is not the subject.

Now try making the subject and verb agree in a sentence with an interrupting phrase. Circle the subject of the following sentence and cross out the interrupter. Then underline the verb that agrees with the subject.

The hinges on the door (are, is) rusty.

It makes sense that the hinges would be rusty, so *hinges* has to be the subject of the sentence. The interrupting phrase is *on the door*. The verb must agree with the plural subject *hinges*, not the interrupter *on the door*, so the correct form is *are*.

Now try one more example. Circle the subject of the following sentence and cross out the interrupting phrase. Then underline the verb that agrees with the subject.

A car with bucket seats (hold, holds) fewer passengers.

The correct verb is *holds*. The subject is *car*, a singular noun. The interrupter is *with bucket seats*.

Inverted Word Order

Subject-verb agreement can also be tricky in sentences with **inverted word order**. This often occurs in sentences that contain questions. As you learned in Chapter 2, changing the order of the words in the sentence will help you figure out whether the subject is singular or plural. Which verb is correct in the sentence below?

(Does, Do) many people come to the club?

If you put the subject first, you will quickly see which verb is correct.

Many people **do** come to the club.

The subject is plural (*people*), so the present tense verb does not end in -*s*.

Sometimes inverted sentences begin with question words such as *what* or *why*.

Why (is, are) your parents coming for dinner?
Why (is are) my uncle here?

Your parents **are** coming for dinner.
My uncle **is** here.

When you put the subject first, it's clear that the first sentence needs a plural verb while the second sentence is singular.

Sentences can also be inverted if they begin with an introductory phrase instead of with the subject. What verb is correct in the next sentence?

In the salad (is, are) tomato slices.

Again, change the word order so the subject comes first.

Tomato slices **are** in the salad.

EXERCISE 5

Subject-Verb Agreement with Interrupters or Inverted Order

Directions: Cross out the interrupter. Underline the subject of each sentence. Then choose the correct verb to agree with the subject. Remember to follow the subject-verb agreement rule.

1. The <u>tree</u> ~~with the red and gold leaves~~ (change, <u>changes</u>) color in early October.

2. The children under the tree (pick, picks) up the colorful leaves.

3. The father of one of the girls (arrive, arrives) early today.

4. (Do, Does) the truckers take safety precautions?

5. A truck with bad brakes (have, has) to be repaired immediately.

6. On a long trip (is, are) many distractions.

7. Why (is, are) that diner busy all night long?

8. Under those magazines (lurk, lurks) the dentist's bill.

Answers are on page 181.

Chapter Review

EXERCISE 6

Part 1 **Directions:** Find the mistake in each of the following sentences. Correct it by crossing out the wrong word and writing the correct word above it. The first one is done as an example.

want
1. Lucas and Dena ~~wants~~ to buy a house.

2. A porch or patio give a house an outdoor feeling.

3. The house with the hardwood floors were too expensive.

4. Neither Lucas nor Dena like the less expensive houses.

5. Why does houses cost so much in this city?

6. In this neighborhood is some affordable condos.

7. Each week the newspaper publish a list of mortgage rates at different banks.

8. Financial security are hard to find.

Part 2 **Directions:** Underline the correct verb to complete each sentence.

9. Nutritious meals and rest (help, helps) sick people recover.

10. A grandmother and grandfather (give, gives) tender loving care to their grandchildren.

11. (Is, Are) those blankets for Maggie's bed?

12. You (have, has) no chance of getting away with that.

13. Neither the vegetables nor the meat (look, looks) good to me.

14. Students in our class (learn, learns) how to write clear paragraphs.

15. The beauty of the classes (lie, lies) in the fact that they address real-world situations.

16. Either a colorful poster or flowers (cheer, cheers) up a bare office.

17. At that website (is, are) many good ideas.

18. Where (do, does) these toys of Fido's belong?

Answers are on page 181.

Your Turn to Write: Using the Writing Process

Writing Skill: Revision

Good writers go through the following three main steps of the **writing process** before, during, and after they write. It doesn't matter whether they are writing a few sentences, a paragraph, or a longer essay, they use the same steps of this process.

STEP 1: **Prewriting** is the step that you use before you begin to write. Prewriting includes both gathering ideas and organizing those ideas. Examine the assignment and decide what you want to say about it. What do you know about the topic? What is your opinion?

In Chapter 1 you learned how to map your ideas. In Chapter 2, you learned how to brainstorm ideas. These are both prewriting techniques. Another technique is simply to make notes or write a list of ideas. For example, suppose you decide to write a paragraph persuading people to vote for your candidate for mayor. Your notes might say,

- Olga Koryev got grant money for community center
- wants to have city offer day care at reasonable prices
- has a degree in finance
- has put in many hours volunteering: helping to build playgrounds, organizing Fourth of July celebration, etc.
- promises to fill potholes and plow snow promptly

When you have your ideas listed or mapped or brainstormed, read them over carefully. Cross out any ideas that don't stick to the subject or that are not important. Then number your ideas in a logical order. You might number them in the order that they happened, or you could number them in their order of importance.

Finally, write a topic sentence that states the main idea you are going to write about.

STEP 2: **Writing** is the next step now that you have your ideas organized. Write a rough draft; that means put your ideas down in sentence form. At this stage, don't worry about mistakes in grammar, punctuation, or spelling. Concentrate on content. Begin with your topic sentence and write each supporting idea in a separate sentence. Follow the order that you decided on in the prewriting step. For example, your topic sentence might be, "Henleyville needs Olga Koryev for our mayor." Then each of your supporting sentences would give reasons why Henleyville needs Olga Koryev for mayor.

STEP 3: **Revising** is the final step of the writing process. Now that you have written the paragraph, you need to check your content, grammar, punctuation, and spelling. This is the step where you make sure that you have written complete sentences—not fragments or run-ons. This is also the step to make sure you have the right amount of information in your paragraph. If anything is missing, add it now. If any sentences don't relate to the main idea, remove them. Check your spelling and your punctuation. Make sure your meaning can be understood. You might ask a friend or relative to read what you have written to be sure it's clear. If your teacher has included a writing checklist with the assignment, use that checklist to help with your revision.

Finally, copy or type your paragraph so that it looks neat and readable.

Writing Assignment

Directions: Now try the writing process with an assignment. Choose one of the topics below and write a paragraph telling how you feel about that topic. You may want to convince someone to feel the same way as you do. Follow the steps of the writing process. When you have finished your paragraph, use the writing checklist below to proofread and revise your paragraph.

Vote for _____!

It's best to buy clothes out of season.

A wise car buyer shops around.

Homeless people need our help.

Drugs are everyone's problem.

Writing Checklist	Yes	No
Have you written a good topic sentence that states your opinion or main idea?	_____	_____
Does each sentence belong in the paragraph?	_____	_____
Have you used end punctuation correctly?	_____	_____
Have you used words that convey exactly what you mean to say?	_____	_____
Do you have any fragments or run-on sentences?	_____	_____
Are there any supporting ideas that you have forgotten to include?	_____	_____

CHAPTER 6

Adjectives and Adverbs

Adjectives and adverbs **modify**, or tell more about, other words. In this chapter, you will learn to identify adjectives and adverbs and learn how to tell them apart.

What Is an Adjective?

> **Adjectives** are words that describe nouns. Adjectives tell *what kind*, *which one*, or *how many*. Adjectives make nouns more specific.

For example, if you say, "James bought a motorcycle," you are not being very specific about the type of motorcycle he bought. Here are two different sentences that use adjectives to explain exactly what kind of motorcycle James bought.

> James bought a **shiny, black, powerful** motorcycle.

> James bought a **small, red, inexpensive** motorcycle.

In both sentences, you learn that James bought a motorcycle, but there is a big difference between the two motorcycles. The adjectives make each sentence more specific.

Here are three lists of adjectives that are used often.

What Kind	Which One	How Many
silly	this	none
sleepy	that	some
loud	these	six
fast	those	nine
large		fourteen

Using adjectives from the lists above, fill in the blanks in the following sentence.

After driving a _____ truck for _____
(what kind)   (how many)

hours, Tim was _____.
(what kind)

Your sentence should be similar to this:

> After driving a **large** truck for **fourteen** hours, Tim was **sleepy**.

127

Adjectives make sentences more specific and more interesting. For example, you can say, "I have a dog," or you can say, "I have a friendly, curly-haired dog with a ferocious bark." The second sentence is more specific and gives the listener a much better picture of your dog.

The more specific an adjective is, the better it describes what you are talking about. Below are four adjectives. Next to each one, list at least three other adjectives that could describe someone or something more specifically. You can look up the words in a thesaurus or dictionary to get ideas.

small: *tiny, undersized, trivial* _____

nice: _____

good: _____

big: _____

Putting Your Skills to Work

Directions: At the top of a sheet of paper, write the name of a close friend or relative. Then brainstorm and write the first ten adjectives you can think of that describe the person you named. Finally, use at least five of those adjectives and write a paragraph about the person.

Here is a sample paragraph from a student's list that contained the adjectives *thoughtful, loving, funny, disorganized*, and *oldest*.

Martha is a very **thoughtful** person who never forgets to send birthday cards. She is a **loving** mother and a **funny** person. However, she is also very **disorganized.** She is the **oldest** employee in her company, yet the boss refuses to let her retire.

After you have written your paragraph, use the following writing checklist to proofread and correct your sentences.

Writing Checklist	Yes	No
Have you included five adjectives from your list?	_____	_____
Can you make any of the adjectives more specific?	_____	_____
Does each sentence start with a capital letter and use correct end punctuation?	_____	_____
Do subjects and verbs agree?	_____	_____

Where Do Adjectives Belong?

An adjective often comes right before the noun it describes.

The **happy** child ran through the house.

However, an adjective often can be found in another part of a sentence. You can tell it is an adjective because it describes the noun. It still tells you *what kind, which one,* or *how many.* Here is an example:

Tina is happy.

Which word describes *Tina*?

Even though the word *happy* comes after *Tina*, it is an adjective because it describes what kind of person she is.

EXERCISE 1

Adjectives

Directions: Use adjectives to fill in each blank in the following sentences. The adjective should describe the underlined noun. Part of the first one is done as an example.

1. The ___*middle-aged*___ <u>men</u> play _____
   (what kind)   (how many)

   <u>games</u> of poker each month.

2. They use _____ <u>cards</u> and play on a
   (what kind)

   _____ <u>table</u>.
   (what kind)

3. They play on the _____ <u>Friday</u> of each month.
   (which one)

4. During the _____ <u>game</u>, _____
   (what kind)   (how many)

   <u>pounds</u> of potato chips are eaten.

5. <u>Television</u> can be _____.
   (what kind)

6. _____ <u>people</u> in our family watch the **news**.
   (how many)

7. Sometimes _____ <u>viewers</u> go to sleep.
   (what kind)

8. _____ <u>show</u> about doctors and surgeons is
   (which one)

   _____.
   (what kind)

Answers are on page 182.

What Is an Adverb?

> **Adverbs** are words that describe verbs, adjectives, or other adverbs. Adverbs tell *how*, *when*, or *where*.

Here are three lists of adverbs.

How	When	Where
rapidly	today	outside
angrily	later	inside
happily	daily	there
fast	once	here
very	again	everywhere

   Just as adjectives give more information about nouns, adverbs tell you more about verbs. Look at this sentence without adverbs:

Lin will talk.

That sentence doesn't tell *how*, *when*, or *where* Lin will talk. By adding an adverb after the verb *talk*, you can give more specific information about the verb. The sentence has been rewritten below with an adverb. Continue rewriting the sentence until you have sentences with adverbs that tell *how*, *when*, and *where*. You may use adverbs from the lists above.

Lin will talk _____slowly_____. (how)

Lin will talk _____. (when)

Lin will talk _____. (where)

   Sometimes an adverb will describe an adjective. For example,

Mary is very sick.

Sick is an adjective describing *Mary*. *Very* tells *how* sick, so *very* is an adverb describing an adjective.

   An adverb can also describe another adverb. For example,

The car stopped rather suddenly.

Suddenly is an adverb describing *stopped*. *Rather* tells *how* suddenly, so *rather* is an adverb describing another adverb.

Where Do Adverbs Appear?

An adverb can come right after the verb it describes, or it can be in another part of the sentence. You can tell it is an adverb because it still describes the verb. It tells you *how*, *where*, or *when*. Below are three examples.

Angrily, she turned her back to the group. (how)

Eric bought a car **today**. (when)

Yesterday, the softball team won first place **here**. (when, where)

An adverb that describes an adjective or another adverb will come just before the word it describes. Below are two examples.

Uncle Joe is **seldom** ill. (describes adjective *ill*)

Holly speaks **rather** quickly. (describes adverb *quickly*)

EXERCISE 2

Adverbs

Directions: In this exercise you will write three groups of sentences. In each group of sentences, use adverbs that tell *how*, *when*, and *where*. One from each group is done as an example.

1. In this group, use adverbs with the verb *write*.

   a. (how) _____

   b. (when) _We write daily_.

   c. (where) _____

2. In this group, use adverbs with the verb *dance*.

   a. (how) _Rebecca and Issa dance beautifully_.

   b. (when) _____

   c. (where) _____

3. In this group, use adverbs with the verb *laugh*.

   a. (how) _Andrew laughed nervously_.

   b. (when) _____

   c. (where) _____

4. In this group, use adverbs with the verb *read*.

   a. (how) _____

   b. (where) _Sam will read later_.

   c. (when) _____

Answers are on page 182.

Adjective or Adverb?

Adjectives and adverbs are both words that describe. In many cases, they look alike. Often you can change a word that is an adjective into an adverb by adding two letters. These letters are *-ly*. Here are two examples:

Adjective	**Adverb**
sad	sadly
beautiful	beautifully

However, if an adjective ends in *y*, you must change the *y* to *i* and then add the *-ly*. Here are two examples:

Adjective	**Adverb**
angry	angrily
happy	happily

The way a word is used in a sentence tells you whether to use the adjective or the adverb form. To describe a noun, use an adjective. To describe a verb, use an adverb. To describe an adjective or another adverb, use an adverb.

The **sad** man walked down the street. (adjective modifying *man*)

The man walked **sadly** down the street. (adverb modifying *walked*)

The man walked **rather** sadly down the street. (adverb modifying the adverb *sadly*)

Shelley followed her **usual** route. (adjective modifying *route*)

Shelley **usually** followed that route. (adverb modifying *followed*)

Shelley is **somewhat** worried tonight. (adverb modifying the adjective *worried*)

EXERCISE 3

Choosing Adjectives or Adverbs

Directions: Underline the correct form of the word for each sentence. The first one is done as an example.

1. Football season is (<u>fantastic</u>, fantastically) for avid sports fans.
2. Fans prepare (careful, carefully) for each game.
3. They wait (calm, calmly) for the whistle that starts the game.
4. Around them, the (excited, excitedly) crowd cheers for their team.
5. They applaud (loud, loudly) when their team makes a touchdown.
6. The quarterback throws a (magnificent, magnificently) pass.
7. The pass receiver (smooth, smoothly) dodges tackles.
8. The Super Bowl is the (high, highly) point of football season.

Answers are on page 182.

Punctuating Perfectly: Using Quotation Marks

Quotation marks (" ") are used for a number of things. The main use for quotation marks is to show direct quotes—when someone is speaking.

> **Quotation marks** are used to tell the reader exactly what someone said.

"Don't do anything I wouldn't do," said Lee.

The words between the quotation marks are a direct quote. You know that Lee said the words *Don't do anything I wouldn't do.* A direct quote repeats the exact words that someone used.

"Our team won the championship," said Mike.

Mike said, "Our team won the championship."

Both of those sentences give you the same information. However, in the first example, the direct quote comes first in the sentence. There is a comma (,) after the word *championship* and before the end quotation mark. The period comes after the last word in the sentence, *Mike.*

In the second example, the quote is at the end of the sentence. The comma is after the word *said* and in front of the first quotation mark. The period is still at the end of the sentence, but it is inside the end quotation mark. Also, the first word of the quote (*Our*) always begins with a capital letter.

The sentences below all contain direct quotes. Add quotation marks to show the quotes.

It would take me forever to wax the car, said Pedro.

I really need help with the job, he stated.

Estralita asked, Would you pay me if I helped you?

Then she added, If you drive me to work every day, I'll help you.

Check the first sentence. Do you have quotation marks before the word *It* and after the comma? In the second sentence, you should have quotation marks before *I* and after the comma. In the third sentence, you should have quotation marks before *Would* and after the question mark. In the final sentence, you should have quotation marks before *If* and after the period.

EXERCISE 4

Using Quotation Marks

Directions: The following sentences form a conversation. Add quotation marks wherever they are needed.

1. I think the best years of a person's life are his teens, said Raymond.

2. His mother laughed and said, That's because you're a teenager.

3. Actually, you will have more fun once you're an adult, said his twenty-two-year-old brother, John.

4. What will happen to me once I reach thirty? John wondered.

5. You will be on your way to forty, and believe me, those are really the best years, said Mom.

6. Dad piped in, Oh, I don't know, I think I'm even better looking at fifty.

7. John asked, How were your sixties, Grandma?

Answers are on page 182.

Putting Your Skills to Work

Directions: Write a conversation between two people. You might want to have them talking about the first time they met or about their family. The conversation you write should have at least four sentences.

- Sentence 1 should begin with *She said.*

- Sentence 2 should begin with *He replied.*

- Sentence 3 should end with *she added.*

- Sentence 4 should end with *he said.*

When you complete the sentences, use the following writing checklist to proofread and correct your sentences.

Writing Checklist	Yes	No
Do you have quotation marks at the beginning and end of direct quotes?	_____	_____
Does the first word inside the quotation marks begin with a capital letter?	_____	_____
Is there a comma before the beginning of the quotation in sentences 1 and 2?	_____	_____
Is there a comma before the end quotation marks in sentences 3 and 4?	_____	_____

Chapter Review

EXERCISE 5

Part 1 **Directions:** Find the mistake in each sentence. Circle the mistake and rewrite each sentence correctly in the space provided. The first one is done as an example.

1. Ruth is a (happily) person.

   Ruth is a happy person.

2. The race car moved quick around the track.

   _____

   _____

3. Nuts, bolts, wrenches, and tools were thrown around the shop in a haphazardly fashion.

   _____

   _____

4. The men and the women agreed that life moves too rapid.

   _____

   _____

5. The supervisor angry shipped the last fifty space heaters to Anchorage, Alaska.

   _____

   _____

6. The trustworthily young baby-sitter raised her fee.

   _____

   _____

7. The soldier looked brave into the eyes of his captors.

   _____

   _____

8. It's very clear that both Faizon and Jill are excitedly about the wedding.

   _____

   _____

Part 2 **Directions:** In this exercise, a part of each sentence is underlined. Below the sentence, you will find three possible ways to write the underlined section. The first choice is always the same as the underlined part of the sentence. Circle the letter of the best correction. The first one is done as an example.

9. The little boy played <u>busyly</u> with his building blocks.

   a. busyly
   b. busy
   c. busily

10. Edna put down her glass and bit <u>hungry</u> into the crisp, red apple.

    a. hungry
    b. hungrily
    c. hungryly

11. The <u>tired</u> shopper kept on walking through the store.

    a. tired
    b. tiredly
    c. tiredli

12. The shopper kept on walking <u>tired</u> through the store.

    a. tired
    b. tiredly
    c. tiredli

13. English is a <u>difficultly</u> language to learn.

    a. difficultly
    b. difficult
    c. difficulty

14. The ending of that movie is very <u>mysterious</u>.

    a. mysterious
    b. mysteriously
    c. mysteriousally

Answers are on pages 182–183.

Your Turn to Write: Using Descriptive Language

Writing Skill: Description

When you want to describe something to another person, you need to use details. For example, if you wrote in a letter to a friend, "The park near our new house is beautiful," your friend would know your opinion, but he would not be able to imagine what the park looked like. To paint a word picture, you might write something like this:

> The park near our new house is beautiful. It's a block long, and there are crabapple and cherry trees all around the edges. They're in bloom right now, and the white and pink blossoms smell wonderful. In the center of the park is a garden filled with white crocuses, red tulips, and yellow daffodils. In the center of the garden is a stone fountain. The sound of its water is soothing, and the wind sometimes blows its spray in my face. The park is very quiet and peaceful.

When you include details, think about what you can see, hear, smell, touch, and even taste. The details you add will be adjectives and adverbs. For example, look at this sentence from above: "They're in bloom right now, and the white and pink blossoms smell wonderful." *Right* and *now* are adverbs. *White, pink,* and *wonderful* are adjectives.

Begin *Prewriting* with brainstorming or an idea map to list nouns and their descriptive adjectives as well as verbs and their descriptive adverbs. Think of as many details as possible. Then write a good topic sentence to introduce your description.

In the *Writing* step, write good sentences with three or four adjectives and adverbs per sentence. Do not make sentences with long lists of adjectives. Try to include as much description as possible.

In the *Revising* step, read your description carefully to make sure it makes sense. Have a friend or your teacher read the paragraph. Ask if he or she can picture what you've described. Use his or her comments to help improve your writing.

Writing Assignment

Directions: Using plenty of description, write a paragraph about one of the three topics below. Brainstorm or make an idea map to organize your ideas. Then write a good topic sentence. Be sure each supporting idea has descriptive adjectives or adverbs.

Your classroom

A place you visit often

The place where you work

When you have completed your paragraph, use the following writing checklist to proofread and correct your writing.

Writing Checklist	Yes	No
Have you written a good topic sentence?	_____	_____
Have you included two or three adjectives or adverbs in each sentence?	_____	_____
Have you written complete sentences with subjects and predicates?	_____	_____
Is the first letter of every sentence capitalized?	_____	_____
Is there a suitable punctuation mark at the end of every sentence?	_____	_____
Do you have any misspelled words?	_____	_____

CHAPTER 7

Combining Sentences and Organizing Paragraphs

There are many ways to make your writing more interesting. In this chapter, you will learn how to combine sentences and organize paragraphs.

Combining Simple Sentences

Knowing how to use compound subjects and compound predicates will expand your writing ability. Often two or three short sentences can be combined when they say almost the same thing.

Compound Subjects

A sentence has a **compound subject** when the subject is in two or more parts. The following sentences have compound subjects. The subject in each of the following sentences is in **boldface type.**

> **Ray** and **Ted** have been going to junior college for one year.

> **Their counselors, their teachers,** and **their families** want them to continue to attend school.

In each sentence, the subjects share the same predicate. When you have two sentences with the same or very similar information, often you can combine the subjects. For example,

> **Ray** complained about the cafeteria's food. **Ted** complained about the cafeteria's food.

> **Ray and Ted** complained about the cafeteria's food.

Read the following pair of sentences. Then, on the blank lines, combine them into one sentence with a compound subject.

The dietitian thought they had valid complaints. The cook thought they had valid complaints.

_____

_____

You should have written this sentence: *The dietitian and the cook thought they had valid complaints.*

Compound Predicates

Just as you can combine subjects of sentences with similar or related information, you can combine predicates that have the same subject. When you do this, you have a **compound predicate**. Read the following example sentences.

> Ted **works in the mornings.** Ted **studies in the evenings.**
> Ted **works in the mornings and studies in the evenings.**

> Ray belongs to the Spanish Club. He is its treasurer.
> Ray belongs to the Spanish Club and is its treasurer.

You could shorten that sentence even more. If Ray is the treasurer of the Spanish Club, he must belong to the club, so:

> Ray is the treasurer of the Spanish Club.

Now try combining the following pair of sentences into one sentence with a compound predicate. Write the combined sentence on the blank lines.

> The school library opens early in the morning.

> It quickly fills with students.

_____

_____

You should have written this sentence: *The school library opens early in the morning and quickly fills with students.*

EXERCISE 1

Compound Subjects and Predicates

Directions: Using a compound subject or compound predicate, combine the following pairs of sentences. The first one is done as an example.

1. Sharon wrote a letter to her parents during lunch. She mailed it on her way home.

    Sharon wrote a letter to her parents during lunch and mailed it on her way home.

2. Sharon planned to visit her parents for Thanksgiving. Sharon's brother planned to visit them for Thanksgiving, too.

    _____

    _____

3. They were looking forward to seeing their parents. They could hardly wait to taste their mother's cooking.

    _____

    _____

4. The immigrants met at the airport. Their host families met at the airport, too.

   _____

   _____

5. They were happy to see each other. They were eager to get acquainted.

   _____

   _____

6. American food seems strange to the people from other countries. American clothing seems strange to the people from other countries. American housing seems strange to the people from other countries.

   _____

   _____

Answers are on page 183.

Coordinating Conjunctions for Combining Sentences

Sentences that contain related ideas can be combined to make longer, more interesting sentences. The sentences do not need the same subject or the same predicate to be combined. For example,

> Rosa lost her sewing job. She has no other skills.

> Rosa lost her sewing job, **and** she has no other skills.

In that example, both subjects and both predicates are in the new sentence. You can combine two related sentences by keeping both sentences and putting a joining word between them. These joining words are called **coordinating conjunctions**.

Here are seven common conjunctions and some examples showing how they are used. Notice that a comma comes before the conjunction in each sentence. The comma is needed to show that two complete sentences (each with a subject and a verb) have been combined.

Coordinating Conjunctions

To add information, use *and*.

> The night was stormy, **and** the lights went out.

To show a contrast, use *but* or *yet*.

> The laundromat was closed, **but** the manager let me in.
> This coat is ten years old, **yet** people still admire it.

To show a cause and then the effect, use *so*.

> The drain was clogged, **so** Margaret called a plumber.

To show an effect and then the cause, use *for.*

> They got a new kitten, **for** their cat had disappeared.

To show two alternatives, use *or.*

> Either I'll go to the party, **or** I'll stay home and study.

To show two negatives, use *nor.*

> The sun isn't going to come out, **nor** will it rain.

Choosing the Right Conjunction

When you choose a conjunction, be careful to choose one that shows how the two thoughts are related. For example,

> I ran for the bus, **but** I missed it.

The conjunction *but* shows the contrast between the two thoughts. The person did all he could but was not able to reach the bus in time. If he had written, "I ran for the bus, *so* I missed it," the sentence wouldn't make sense. Now look at another example. Notice the conjunction *and.*

> Allisandra joined an aerobics class, and she loves exercising.

You would not say, "Allisandra joined an aerobics class, *but* she loves exercising." That would make it sound as though aerobics were not exercising.

> Read the following sentences. Choose the best conjunction: *and, but, yet, so, for, or,* or *nor.* Write the correct word in the blank between the two complete thoughts.

> Ed wants to exercise more, _____ he is joining a health club.

Did you choose *so?* If you did, you realized that the first thought is the cause and the second thought is the effect.

> Start helping with chores around the house, _____ you will have to move out.

Did you choose *or?* The two thoughts are alternatives; either one or the other will happen.

Avoid Overusing Commas

As you have seen, when you join two complete thoughts with a conjunction, a comma comes before the conjunction. You do not use a comma before the conjunction when one of the thoughts is incomplete. Remember that a complete thought has *both* a subject and a verb. Here are two sentences that do not contain two complete thoughts. Instead, they have compound predicates.

> I ran for the bus **but** missed it.

The second part of the compound predicate, *missed it,* is not a complete thought, so no comma is used before *but.*

Allisandra joined an aerobics class **and** loves exercising.

The second part of the compound predicate, *loves exercising*, is not a complete thought, so no comma is used before *and*.

Read the three sentences that follow. Only one of them has a conjunction combining two complete thoughts. Find that sentence and put the comma in the correct place.

The car broke down on the highway and Sam had it towed.

The car broke down on the highway but started up again right away.

The car broke down on the highway and was towed.

Did you place your comma in the first sentence after *highway? Car* and *broke* are the subject and verb of the first thought. *Sam* and *had* are the subject and verb of the second thought. The second and third sentences do not have two complete thoughts, so you do not need to add a comma.

EXERCISE 2

Practice Using Coordinating Conjunctions and Commas

Directions: Circle the conjunction in each of these sentences and add commas in the correct places. Each of these sentences contains two complete thoughts. The first one is done as an example.

1. Thrift stores are great places to shop, (and) they have many bargains.

2. Some of the customers who visit them are on tight budgets for they have been laid off.

3. Other customers can afford higher prices yet they enjoy finding good buys.

4. Nice clothes sell quickly so smart customers shop on the day new items are stocked.

5. Men and women go to these stores for clothes but children like to look for toys.

6. Some shops are open at odd hours yet shoppers fill the aisles.

7. Kevin has never been to a thrift shop before nor has Marilyn.

8. I'll go shopping tomorrow or I'll go to the park if the weather's nice.

Answers are on page 183.

EXERCISE 3

Combining Sentences with Conjunctions

Directions: Rewrite the following sentences. Add a conjunction and a comma to each set of sentences to form one combined sentence. The first one is done as an example.

and	but	yet
for	so	
or	nor	

1. Children are fun. Many people enjoy teaching them.

   Children are fun, and many people enjoy teaching them.

2. Horses are farm animals. Some people keep them in cities.

   _____

   _____

3. Drugs are a serious problem. Many teenagers think they are harmless.

   _____

   _____

4. I'll get an A on the history test. I'll get a B.

   _____

   _____

5. Ron can't have a dog. He's allergic to fur.

   _____

   _____

6. The traffic light was red. Norma stopped her car.

   _____

   _____

Answers are on page 183.

Connectors for Combining Sentences

Connectors are another group of joining words you can use to combine sentences. Some common connectors are listed below. Each one has a specific meaning. Notice the punctuation in each sentence.

Word Connectors

To show contrast, use *however, nevertheless,* or *instead.*

> Brad wants to be a team player; **however**, he loves glory.
> Anita was grounded; **nevertheless**, she went out.
> Yim wanted to go to school; **instead**, she got a job.

To add more information, use *furthermore* or *moreover.*

> You are a good friend; **furthermore**, you are my best friend.
> Martin wants to help; **moreover**, he insists on washing the dishes.

To show a cause and then its effect, use *therefore* or *consequently.*

> We love children; **therefore**, we adopted six of them.
> Alan enters every contest he can; **consequently**, he often wins.

Punctuating Connectors

Notice that there is a semicolon (;) in front of each connector and a comma after the connector in each of the sample sentences. Study the following sentences. Circle the connector in each sentence and add semicolons and commas where needed. The first one is done for you.

> Todd's chair broke yesterday; (therefore), he has to fix it.

> Rhonda hurried otherwise she would be late for work.

> Amy is 87 today furthermore she intends to live to be 107.

Did you circle *otherwise* in sentence 2 and *furthermore* in sentence 3? They are the connectors, and each one should have a semicolon in front of it and a comma following it.

Choosing the Right Connector

Always be careful to choose a connector that shows the relationship between the thoughts in the combined sentence. Look at this example. How does *therefore* show the relationship between the two thoughts?

> The women like exercising; **therefore**, they go to the gym often.

In that sentence, *therefore* is used to show that going to the gym is the effect of the women liking exercising.

> Now you try. What connector would work well in the following sentence?

> Steve needs a new car; _____, he has no money.

Did you write *however?* It shows the contrast between needing a new car and not having the money to buy one.

EXERCISE 4

Writing Sentences with Connectors

Directions: Join the following sentences using connectors. Remember that the connector you use has to make sense. Be certain to put the correct punctuation in each sentence.

therefore	nevertheless	furthermore
consequently	moreover	however
instead		

1. The police searched the neighborhood for drugs. They vowed to jail all dealers.

   _____

   _____

2. After the race, the drivers were exhausted. They went to the party.

   _____

   _____

3. The Joneses were evicted from their apartment. Mr. Jones lost his job.

   _____

   _____

4. Dorothy thought she would get a small raise. She was surprised with a ten percent salary increase.

   _____

   _____

5. Electric heat is very expensive. We keep the thermostat turned down to 65 degrees.

   _____

   _____

6. I frequently lose my house keys. I lock my car keys in my car at least once a week.

   _____

   _____

7. Kenny has played the banjo since he was three. He is the best banjo picker in town.

   _____

   _____

Answers are on pages 183–184.

Subordinating Conjunctions for Combining Sentences

Subordinating conjunctions can also be used to combine sentences. When these words are used, one part of the sentence becomes dependent on the other part to make sense. Notice how commas are used with the following list of subordinating conjunctions.

Subordinating Conjunctions

To show cause and effect, use *because* or *since*.

> **Because** she couldn't dance, Sandra stayed home.
> Peter took the job **since** the pay was good.

To show contrast, use *though* or *although*.

> **Though** Harry was elected, he doesn't feel victorious.
> The Bennets rented the apartment **although** it was too small.

To show condition, use *if*.

> **If** Blair gets home on time, we will go to the game.

To show time, use *when*, *after*, or *before*.

> **When** the cows come home, Greta will milk them.
> **After** she milks the cows, Jerry will feed them.
> Kenton will sample the milk **before** Kimmy scrubs the milkhouse.

If the subordinating conjunction is the first word in the sentence, place a comma between the two ideas. If the subordinating conjunction is in the middle of the sentence, do **not** use a comma.

Now practice using the subordinating conjunctions. The following examples show how to combine two sentences using these conjunctions.

To join a cause to an effect:

> **Since** Sam had no money, he couldn't buy a soda.

To show a contradiction between two ideas:

> Herman took the job **though** it meant a huge salary cut.

To show condition and result (If one thing happens, another will happen.):

> **If** the weather is good, we will go swimming tomorrow.

To show time (*When* shows that two actions are taking place at the same time. *After* and *before* show the order of two actions.):

> **When** you do the dishes, I'll vacuum the floor.
> **Before** you vacuum the floor, I'll do the dishes.
> I'll vacuum the floor **after** you do the dishes.

EXERCISE 5

Writing Sentences with Subordinating Conjunctions

Directions: Combine each pair of sentences using one of the subordinating conjunctions listed. If the conjunction starts with a capital letter, put it at the beginning of the sentence. Be sure to punctuate your sentences correctly. The first one is done as an example.

if	Though	Since	When	after	because
Before	although	because	After	since	Although

1. David gets home. We will show him the pictures.

    When David gets home, we'll show him the pictures.

2. Chan went to the doctor yesterday. He doesn't feel any better today.

    _____

3. The Jellybeans recorded their first big hit in 1964. They were completely unknown.

    _____

    _____

4. The police will be able to arrest the purse snatcher. Maura can identify him in a lineup.

    _____

    _____

5. Margaret mowed the lawn. Greg agreed to do the raking.

    _____

6. Jenka gave me the money. She needed it herself.

    _____

7. Bruno will go to work today. He is feeling better.

    _____

8. The examination was over. The doctor wrote the report.

    _____

9. Fast-food restaurants like to hire adults. They are more dependable workers.

    _____

    _____

10. Bob had retired. His employer asked him to return to work.

    _____

Answers are on page 184.

Punctuating Perfectly: Commas and Semicolons in Combined Sentences

You have been combining related sentences by using three types of joining words. When you use conjunctions like *and, but, or*, and *yet* to combine complete ideas, place a comma in front of the conjunction.

Loretta pushed down the brake pedal, **but** the truck didn't stop.

When you use connectors like *however, nevertheless, consequently,* and *moreover*, place a semicolon in front of the connector and a comma after it.

Loretta pushed down the brake pedal; **however,** the truck didn't stop.

You can also use subordinating conjunctions like *because, though, if*, and *after*. If the subordinating conjunction comes at the beginning of the sentence, separate the two thoughts with a comma. If the subordinating conjunction comes in the middle of the sentence, don't use a comma.

The truck roared down the hill **because** its brakes failed.
Because its brakes failed, the truck roared down the hill.

EXERCISE 6

Practicing Punctuation

Directions: Add the correct punctuation to each of the following sentences. The first one is done as an example.

1. Being new in town is not easy; however, there are many support groups.

2. Churches form newcomers' groups and community agencies do the same thing.

3. People go to the meetings because they want to make new friends.

4. Some women feel that they will appear to be looking for men consequently they won't attend these meetings.

5. Many men fear that same thing so they stay home, too.

6. Others are more optimistic therefore they go to meet people of both sexes.

7. When people have interests in common they may develop good relationships.

8. Most people make new friends if they give it enough time.

Answers are on page 184.

Paragraph Organization

Now that you have studied how to structure sentences to make your writing clearer and more interesting, it is time to look at how to write **paragraphs** that achieve the same goal. A paragraph is a group of sentences that work together to communicate one idea. An effective paragraph states a clear **main idea** in a **topic sentence**. Then it gives more details about that main idea in several **supporting sentences**.

For example, you might decide that you would like to write a paragraph on insurance. However, that is a very broad topic. There is life insurance, health insurance, car insurance, home insurance, and many other kinds of insurance. So you can narrow your topic by deciding to write about life insurance. That is still a broad topic and can be narrowed even more. You might decide to write about good reasons to purchase life insurance.

That can be turned into a good topic sentence. It makes the purpose of your paragraph specific. If you wrote the paragraph, you would include only good reasons for buying life insurance. That paragraph might look like this.

> **There are three good reasons for buying life insurance. First, it gives security to your family in case you die. Second, it can give you retirement income. Finally, you can borrow against the policy if you need a loan.**

Is that paragraph effective? What is its topic sentence?

If you said the topic sentence is "There are three good reasons for buying life insurance," you're right. The topic sentence of a paragraph is often, though not always, its first sentence. The paragraph is effective because it communicates one main idea, and its other sentences all provide supporting details that add information to that main idea.

It's important to make sure that each paragraph you write has just the right amount of information in it—not too much and not too little. To do that, you need to learn how to move sentences to different paragraphs, remove sentences altogether, and divide one paragraph into two or more if it has more than one main idea.

Moving Sentences

Sometimes a sentence in a paragraph really belongs in another paragraph. When in doubt, ask yourself two questions. What is the topic sentence of this paragraph? Does this sentence contribute to the main idea? If it does not, ask yourself if it belongs in the following paragraph, or perhaps in the preceding one.

To: All Employees
From: Personnel

Fire Safety Is Everyone's Job

(A)

(1) The fire marshal wishes to remind all employees that fire safety is everyone's job. (2) Each floor of the building has a fire warden who is responsible for conducting periodic drills and for getting people out of the building in an emergency. (3) But every employee should be keeping an eye out. (4) Is there a short in the coffeemaker? (5) Are too many appliances plugged into one outlet? (6) If you see any potential problems, tell your floor's fire warden. (7) There will be a fire drill one morning next week.

(B)

(8) If you don't recall where to go and what to do during a fire drill, review the map and instructions posted in your break room. (9) Your fire warden will be happy to go over the plan with you and answer any questions. (10) Meanwhile, please stay alert. (11) Your safety is important to us.

What is the topic sentence of paragraph A?

It is sentence 1: "The fire marshal wishes to remind all employees that fire safety is everyone's job."

What is the topic sentence of paragraph B?

There is no topic sentence, but it appears to be the last sentence of paragraph A. Sentence 7 reads: "There will be a fire drill one morning next week." This sentence begins a new topic, and therefore should be moved to a different paragraph. The final sentence of paragraph A should be moved to paragraph B because paragraph B is about fire drills.

EXERCISE 7

Moving Sentences

Directions: Read the four paragraphs of this passage. Then answer the questions that follow.

Fixing Up Your Apartment

(A)

(1) Everyone wants an attractive living space. (2) But when you live in an apartment, there are limits to how much you can express yourself in your decor. (3) Here are some guidelines for fixing up your apartment without losing your security deposit. (4) First, read over your lease carefully.

(B)

(5) It probably spells out what you can and cannot do. (6) Notice the clause about what your landlord is required to fix. (7) That leaky shower is probably not your responsibility. (8) Nor is the old, loose window that lets in a breeze even when it's closed. (9) Make a list of everything in your apartment that needs to be repaired. (10) Then show it to your landlord and ask him or her (politely) to take care of the problems. (11) You might point out that fixing them now could save trouble and greater expense down the road. (12) For example, your leaky shower may eventually cause your downstairs neighbor's ceiling to collapse.

(C)

(13) If your landlord pays the heating bills, your loose window could be costing a lot more than insulating or even replacing it would cost. (14) It doesn't hurt to ask about improvements that aren't legally your landlord's responsibility. (15) Suppose you want to repaint your shabby-looking living room. (16) If the room hasn't been painted in years or the last tenant left holes and chips in the wall, the landlord may hire someone to paint it for you.

(D)

(17) At least you may be able to get him or her to pay for the paint if you supply the labor. (18) If you wind up doing the work yourself, be considerate. (19) Don't paint a room such a dark color that it will be hard to paint over when you move out. (20) Don't wallpaper; it's a huge task to remove it. (21) Fill in existing holes in the wall, and don't put too many new ones in when you redecorate. (22) Don't do noisy repair work late at night when your neighbors are trying to sleep.

1. Which revision would improve this piece of writing?

   (1) Move sentence 1 to the end of paragraph D.
   (2) Move sentence 4 to the beginning of paragraph B.
   (3) Move sentence 12 to the beginning of paragraph C.
   (4) Move sentence 18 to the end of paragraph C.

2. Which revision would improve this piece of writing?

   (1) Move sentence 5 to the end of paragraph A.
   (2) Move sentence 12 to the beginning of paragraph C.
   (3) Move sentence 13 to the end of paragraph B.
   (4) Move sentence 16 to the beginning of paragraph D.
   (5) Move sentence 22 to the end of paragraph C.

3. Which revision would improve this piece of writing?

   (1) Move sentence 16 to the beginning of paragraph D.
   (2) Move sentence 17 to the end of paragraph C.
   (3) Move sentence 18 to the end of paragraph D.
   (4) Move sentence 21 to the beginning of paragraph D.
   (5) Move sentence 22 to the end of paragraph C.

Answers are on page 184.

Removing Sentences

Be certain that all the information you include in a paragraph supports the topic sentence. When a sentence does not contribute a supporting detail to the paragraph, remove it completely.

Directions to Carnegie Works Plant Tour

(1) All production people will tour the Carnegie Works in Uniontown on October 14 beginning at 9 A.M. sharp. (2) The plant is located at 1234 Allegheny Avenue, near the Steel Museum. (3) The museum has some wonderful historical exhibits. (4) Here are directions to get there from the Parkway East. (5) Take Exit 9 to the first traffic light—Cedar St. (6) Turn left onto Cedar and go 2.5 miles to Oak St. (7) Make the hairpin turn right onto Oak. (8) Go just under 2 miles on Oak, then turn right again onto Pittsburgh St. which parallels the river. (9) At the third traffic light, turn left onto Carnegie Rd. (10) Follow the signs to Parking Lot B.

What sentence does not belong in that paragraph?

To answer that, you need to figure out the main idea of the paragraph. The main idea is contained in both the title and sentence (4): directions to the plant tour. Sentence (3) should be deleted: "The museum has some wonderful historical exhibits." This sentence does not contribute to the main idea.

EXERCISE 8

Removing Sentences

Directions: Read each of the four paragraphs and underline the topic sentence—the sentence that tells the main idea of the paragraph. Then cross out the one sentence in each paragraph that does not support the topic sentence. The first one is done as an example.

Paragraph 1

<u>Credit cards are convenient, but they can cost large sums of money.</u> Department stores, gasoline stations, banks, and even telephone companies offer credit as a way to encourage spending. Cardholders pay interest on the amount they don't pay off each month. Most cards charge interest rates of 17 to 20 percent or more. ~~Some cards, such as department store cards and gasoline cards, are used to buy items at a specific place.~~

Paragraph 2

Caring for an infant is very demanding. A baby must be fed many times each day. His or her diaper must be changed several times a day. They are so cute and so much fun to watch. Often the baby needs care in the middle of the night. Once a baby arrives, parents find their time is not their own.

Paragraph 3

Avid TV sports fans are called armchair athletes. These armchair athletes get their exercise walking from the armchair to the refrigerator and back. They build biceps by crushing soda or beer cans and by changing channels. Soda is better for them because it doesn't contain alcohol. These people spend great amounts of energy cheering or booing the teams on the screen.

Paragraph 4

Riding the subway takes a great deal of knowledge. The passengers must know how to read train schedules. They must know where the station platforms are located. Eating candy helps brighten up a long ride. They must know whether to get off at the front or back of the train.

Answers are on page 184.

Beginning New Paragraphs

Sometimes the problem involves more than one sentence. Writers can wander off the topic, and several sentences may belong in a separate paragraph of their own. When that happens, you have to figure out where to divide the paragraph.

(1) We're looking for people to help take inventory. (2) On June 23 and 24, we need a group of at least six employees to count every product on the shelves. (3) They'll keep track of every item we carry and compare the quantities on the shelves to those ordered and those sold. (4) Those two days will be long, but workers will be paid time and a half. (5) The next company event, the annual TechStar Family Picnic, is coming up on August 5. (6) We encourage all employees to bring their families. (7) There will be food and fun for everyone. (8) In the afternoon, we'll play softball and frisbee. (9) For the kids, there will be three-legged races, a frog-jumping contest, and face painting. (10) In the evening, the band Pay It Forward, fronted by our own accounting supervisor, Dave Patel, will play.

You probably noticed that the paragraph above is very long—long enough to be hard to read. It also contains two main ideas. The best way to improve that paragraph is to divide it into two paragraphs. The first paragraph is about taking inventory. The second paragraph, beginning with sentence 5, is about the company picnic.

EXERCISE 9

Beginning New Paragraphs

Directions: Read the paragraph below. Underline the topic sentence(s). Then mark where you think a new paragraph should begin.

Performance Reviews

(1) All employees on the production lines will receive their annual performance reviews during the month of April. (2) The supervisor of each line will schedule meetings with each employee in his or her office. (3) Your supervisor will sit down with you and go over your performance for the past year. (4) This is the time for you to share your concerns about the job and your goals for your future. (5) We suggest you bring to the meeting notes about anything you want to discuss. (6) Your supervisor will also discuss the amount of your raise. (7) This year, for the first time, the company is trying a 360-degree review. (8) That means that all employees will be asked to evaluate not just the people who report to them but the people they report to as well. (9) You'll be given a form to fill out rating your supervisor on ten criteria, including organization, communication, and people skills. (10) There will be room on the form for you to write any criticisms or compliments about your supervisor.

Chapter Review

EXERCISE 10

<u>Part 1</u> **Directions:** Read the following sentences. Then combine them, as directed, in three different ways.

Getting up for work is not easy. I am usually late.

1. Use *so* with a comma to combine the two sentences.

_____

_____

2. Use a semicolon with *therefore* to combine the two sentences.

_____

_____

3. Use *Because* and a comma to combine the two sentences.

_____

_____

Directions: The underlined parts of the following sentences may contain errors. Circle the letter of the choice that makes each sentence correct. The first choice will always be the same as the underlined part.

4. Farsighted adults plan for <u>retirement; and they</u> hope to spend many years enjoying themselves.

    a. retirement; and they
    b. retirement, and they
    c. retirement; and, they

5. Businesses offer profit-sharing <u>plans; consequently the</u> employees feel they are a part of the company.

    a. plans; consequently the
    b. plans; consequently, the
    c. plans, consequently, the

6. It is helpful to have <u>savings; instead, you</u> reach retirement age.

    a. savings; instead, you
    b. savings; furthermore, you
    c. savings when you

7. Unfortunately, it is not always possible to save <u>earnings because</u> they are needed to pay bills.

    a. earnings because
    b. earnings; because
    c. earnings. Because

<u>**Part 2**</u> **Directions:** Read the three paragraphs below. Then answer the questions.

Applying for a Job

(A)

(1) There are several steps to follow when applying for a job. (2) More jobs are found through personal contacts than through ads. (3) First, read the help wanted ads and clip all the ones that sound good to you. (4) Tell everyone you know that you're job hunting. (5) When you have a list of four or five jobs, contact each company's human resources office to submit an application and arrange for an interview.

(B)

(6) Arrive for the interview at least five minutes early. (7) Meeting a friend for lunch makes the day more enjoyable. (8) Bring with you phone numbers of all your previous employers and any other references you plan to use. (9) If you have a written resume, bring that too. (10) It's your chance to put your employment history in the most flattering light. (11) Accurately complete the employment application. (12) Be polite and answer all the interviewer's questions completely and honestly.

(C)

(13) Give some thought ahead of time to how you'll answer tricky questions like, "What's your biggest flaw?" (14) When the interview is over, thank the person who conducted the interview. (15) Before the day is over, write a thank you note to the interviewer and restate your desire to work for that company.

8. Which revision should be made to sentence (2) to make paragraph A more effective?

    (1) move sentence (2) to follow sentence (4)
    (2) move sentence (2) to the beginning of paragraph B
    (3) begin a new paragraph with sentence (2)
    (4) remove sentence (2)
    (5) no revision is necessary

9. Which revision should be made to sentence (7) to make paragraph B more effective?

    (1) move sentence (7) to follow sentence (10)
    (2) move sentence (7) to follow sentence (12)
    (3) move sentence (7) to the beginning of paragraph B
    (4) remove sentence (7)
    (5) no revision is necessary

10. Which revision should be made to sentence (13) to make paragraph C more effective?

    (1) move sentence (13) to the end of paragraph B
    (2) move sentence (13) to follow sentence (14)
    (3) move sentence (13) to follow sentence (8)
    (4) remove sentence (13)
    (5) no revision is necessary

Answers are on pages 184–185.

Your Turn to Write: Writing a Paragraph in Time Order

Writing Skill: Paragraph Organization

Many times you will write a paragraph that needs to be told in time order—the order in which events happened. You may be describing something that took place in your life, or you may be giving directions to make something or to find a specific place. You can help your reader follow your thinking by introducing some sentences with time organization words like *first*, *next*, *then*, *later*, and *finally*. Most importantly, you need to keep your ideas or events in the order that they happened.

Writing Assignment

Directions: Pick an event from the list below. You are going to write about an event in your life, telling what happened in time order.

A holiday celebration

A job interview

The first day of school

Moving to a new home

First, brainstorm or map your ideas. Then number your ideas in the order that they happened. Write a topic sentence that introduces your paragraph and tells what you will be describing. Write a paragraph of six or eight sentences, using words like *first, then, next, later,* and *finally* to put the events in order.

When you have completed your paragraph, use the following writing checklist to proofread and correct what you have written.

Writing Checklist	Yes	No
Have you written a good topic sentence?	————	————
Are the ideas told in the order that they happened?	————	————
Do all the sentences stick to the subject of the paragraph?	————	————
Do your subjects and verbs agree?	————	————
Have you used commas and end punctuation correctly?	————	————

CHAPTER 8

Sentences and Paragraphs

Sentence Structure

In this chapter, you will practice writing sentences with describing phrases and with parallel structure. These techniques will help to make your sentences more interesting.

Using Describing Phrases Correctly

A **describing phrase** can tell you something about a noun or a pronoun. Describing phrases must always be placed as close as possible to the word they describe. Read the following sentences.

> Mona entered the office at midnight. She was carrying the stolen papers.

> **Carrying the stolen papers**, Mona entered the office at midnight.

In the combined sentence, the describing phrase *Carrying the stolen papers* tells you something about *Mona*. Therefore, that phrase is placed next to *Mona*.

A describing phrase is **misplaced** if it is not placed next to the noun or pronoun it describes. Here is an example of a sentence with a misplaced describing phrase:

> The cowboy entered the saloon wearing matching pistols.

The describing phrase, *wearing matching pistols*, is placed next to *saloon*. The wording of the sentence tells you that the saloon was wearing matching pistols! But your common sense tells you that the cowboy was wearing them.

> **Wearing matching pistols**, the cowboy entered the saloon.

> The cowboy **wearing matching pistols** entered the saloon.

In both of those examples, the describing phrase *wearing matching pistols* is next to *cowboy,* the word it describes.

Now look at an example of what happens when describing phrases are misplaced. Look at the picture and read the sentence below it.

INCORRECT: Jamal chopped onions while Sue stirred the soup with a dull knife.

Your common sense tells you that Sue is not stirring the soup with a dull knife. The describing phrase should be placed next to the underlined word it describes.

CORRECT: Jamal chopped <u>onions</u> **with a dull knife** while Sue stirred the soup.

Read the three sentences that follow. A describing phrase to insert in each sentence is also given. First, underline the word that each phrase describes. Then rewrite the sentences, placing each describing phrase as close as possible to the word it describes. The first one is done for you.

Please put the <u>presents</u> under the tree. (that you wrapped)

Please put the presents that you wrapped under the tree.

Albert saw a dog chasing a cat. (walking to work)

_____

_____

Danny put the ring on Carmen's finger. (worn by his grandmother)

_____

_____

Did you rewrite the sentences like this?

Walking to work, <u>Albert</u> saw a dog chasing a cat.

Danny put the <u>ring</u> **worn by his grandmother** on Carmen's finger.

EXERCISE 1

Identifying Misplaced Describing Phrases

Directions: Read the following sentences. Circle the letter of the sentence in each pair that is written correctly. In each correct sentence, underline the describing phrase and circle the word it describes.

1. a. The (woman) <u>in purple shoes</u> caught the Frisbee.

    b. The woman caught the Frisbee in purple shoes.

2. a. The desk that is 500 years old was bought in an antique shop near Chicago.

    b. The desk was bought in an antique shop near Chicago that is 500 years old.

3. a. The people yawned through the movie sitting in the front row.

    b. The people sitting in the front row yawned through the movie.

4. a. Quivering with excitement, the kitten pounced on the leaf.

    b. The kitten pounced on the leaf quivering with excitement.

Answers are on page 185.

EXERCISE 2

Writing Sentences with Describing Phrases

Directions: Insert the describing phrase into each of the following sentences. Be sure to place the phrase next to the word it describes.

1. He let the puppy out. (wearing only his pajamas and slippers)

    Wearing only his pajamas and slippers,
    he let the puppy out.

2. The actors were getting ready to face the audience. (in their dressing rooms)

    _____

    _____

3. The salesperson handed the blouse to Geraldine. (with red stripes)

    _____

    _____

4. The team fumbled the ball in the second half. (in blue uniforms)

    _____

    _____

Answers are on page 185.

Parallel Structure

When writing sentences, use **parallel structure** to list two or more things or ideas. Parallel structure means that the items (connected by *and*, *or*, or *but*) are in the same form.

INCORRECT: John likes **to fish** and **boating**.
The forms of the two items are different: *to fish* and *boating*.

CORRECT: John likes **fishing** and **boating**.
The words *fishing* and *boating* both end in *-ing*.

CORRECT: John likes **to fish** and **to boat**.
Both words *fish* and *boat* are introduced by *to*.

Here's another example.

INCORRECT: The cartoon was **funny, short,** and **was unusual**.
The third part of the list contains a verb *(was)* instead of just an adjective.

CORRECT: The cartoon was **funny, short,** and **unusual**.
The words *funny, short,* and *unusual* are all adjectives that describe *cartoon*.

The following sentence contains longer parallel parts.

The employer promised to **increase salaries** and **give more coffee breaks.**

The two phrases are *increase salaries* and *give more coffee breaks*. Both phrases begin with a verb in the same form.

The following sentences do not have correct parallel structure. On the lines below, rewrite each sentence so that it has parallel structure.

1. When he was twenty-one, Richard loved dancing, skiing, and to swim.

   _____

   _____

2. Singing in a rock group and to star in a movie are Claude's goals.

   _____

   _____

Sentence 1 corrected:

When he was twenty-one, Richard loved **dancing, skiing,** and **swimming**.

When he was twenty-one, Richard loved to **dance, ski,** and **swim**.

Sentence 2 corrected:

Singing in a rock group and **starring** in a movie are Claude's goals.

To sing in a rock group and **to star** in a movie are Claude's goals.

EXERCISE 3

Identifying Correct Parallel Structure

Directions: Circle the letter of the sentence that has correct parallel structure in each pair below. Underline the parallel parts in the correct sentence. The first one is done as an example.

1. a. Harold loves working, playing, and to watch good movies.

    (b.) Harold loves <u>working</u>, <u>playing</u>, and <u>watching</u> good movies.

2. a. Burt can't decide if he wants to be a police officer, a paramedic, or a firefighter.

    b. Burt can't decide if he wants to be a police officer, a paramedic, or work for the fire department.

3. a. Mary Jo draws exquisitely and does painting superbly.

    b. Mary Jo draws exquisitely and paints superbly.

4. a. Alice's car always stalls out and is leaving her stranded.

    b. Alice's car always stalls out and leaves her stranded.

Answers are on page 185.

EXERCISE 4

Correcting Parallel Structure

Directions: The following sentences contain errors in parallel structure. Rewrite each sentence with the correct parallel structure.

1. Homer went to Texas, got a job, built a house, and he got married.

    _____

    _____

2. Getting rich and to buy a car are Maxine's only interests.

    _____

    _____

3. Mystery stories have intrigue, excitement, and full of suspense.

    _____

    _____

4. Wendy works very hard but is having fun too.

    _____

    _____

Answers are on page 185.

Paragraph Structure

Just as there are rules for writing sentences, there are rules for writing paragraphs. You have learned that the structure of items in a sentence should be parallel. Now you will learn how to make the verb tenses in a paragraph consistent.

Matching Verbs in a Paragraph

Verb tenses show how things happen in time. In Chapter 4 you studied past, present, and future tenses. When you are writing, the verbs in a paragraph must show the time element of that paragraph.

EXAMPLE—past tense:

Mardi **won** first prize in the cooking contest. She **baked** a shoofly pie. It **looked** scrumptious. The Iowa State Fair judges **thought** it **was** delectable.

Notice that every verb in that paragraph is written in the past tense. That tells you that everything happened in the past.

EXAMPLE—present tense:

The bus **is** very dependable. It **arrives** on time every morning. In bad weather, the driver **drives** cautiously and **gets** all the passengers to work on time.

All the verbs in that paragraph are in the present tense. They show that this information is true in the present time.

EXAMPLE—future tense:

There **will be** a severe blizzard tonight. Cars **will have** trouble staying on the highways. Pipes **will freeze**. Power lines **will break**. Snow emergency plans **will go** into effect. The storm **will cause** many problems.

Since that paragraph was written with future tense verbs, each verb had the helping verb *will* in front of it.

When you are writing, be careful not to shift tenses unnecessarily. For example, you would not want to write these sentences:

There **will be** a blizzard tonight. The storm **caused** many problems.

The first sentence is written in the future tense, while the second sentence is written in the past tense. This shift makes readers wonder whether the storm has already happened or not. As a result, neither sentence makes any sense.

The following paragraph should be written in the past tense. Cross out and change any verbs that are not written in the past tense.

Albert bought a car phone after he saw mine. He had it put into his car, but he didn't like it. The next day, he removes it. The shop owner refuses to refund Albert's money but gave him a store credit.

You should have changed *removes* to *removed* and *refuses* to *refused*.

Sometimes the verbs in a paragraph should be in different tenses because their actions occur at different times. Read the following example:

> Melissa **started** her political career as a city councilor, and now she **is** a state senator. I **believe** she **will run** for president someday.

Notice that the first verb in the first sentence is in the past tense, and the second verb in the first sentence is in the present tense. The first verb in the second sentence is present tense, and the second verb in that sentence is future tense. Yet each verb is in the correct tense for the time of the action it describes.

EXERCISE 5

Checking Verb Tense in a Paragraph

Directions: Read the following paragraphs. Cross out any verb that is written in an incorrect tense and write the correct verb above it. The first one is done as an example.

Paragraph 1

Glenn loves being outdoors in the Wyoming mountains. He feels close to nature. He ~~was~~ *is* a careful camper. Glenn sets up perfect campsites. He will build a log cabin one day.

Paragraph 2

The cabin will have only one big room, and it had a bathroom. It will be furnished very sparsely. Glenn will live in the cabin all year round.

Paragraph 3

A herd of deer lived close to the building spot. They left once the land was cleared. They move to an area close to a nearby stream.

Paragraph 4

Glenn watches the deer when he camps at his homesite. He also observes hawks soaring overhead and trout swimming in the stream. Last year he sees a bear eating blackberries.

Answers are on page 185.

Punctuating Perfectly: Commas

Commas have many uses. They can be used to interrupt a sentence with additional information, to connect or make transitions between ideas, to address a person directly, or to separate items in a series.

Using Commas for Additional Information

When additional information is given about the subject of a sentence, commas are used to set off that information. Notice how a comma comes before and after the additional information in the following example.

Mrs. Kannan, **my sixth-grade teacher**, really loved teaching.

In the following sentence, the phrase that gives additional information comes at the end of the sentence, so only one comma is needed.

One of my best friends is Harry, **the barber on Ninth Street**.

Now try an example. Add one comma to the following sentence to set off the phrase that gives the additional information.

The best person for that job is Ben an experienced carpenter.

Did you put a comma after *Ben*? The phrase that gives the additional information is *an experienced carpenter*. A phrase that gives additional information always comes directly after the noun it describes.

When you punctuate a phrase that gives additional information, always be careful to put a comma both before *and* after the phrase, unless it comes at the end of the sentence. Here is a common error to avoid:

INCORRECT: Ben, an experienced carpenter can do the job.

CORRECT: Ben, an experienced carpenter, can do the job.

Using Commas for Connecting Ideas or Making Transitions

Commas are also used to set off short **interrupting phrases** that connect or make transitions between ideas in a sentence. The following sentences contain examples of these short phrases. Notice that if you take out the words between the commas, the sentence still tells a complete thought.

I could, **for example**, move to San Francisco.

I might, **on the other hand**, move to Phoenix.

In those sentences, the interrupting phrases come in the middle of the sentence. Two commas are needed—one before and one after the interrupting phrase. However, these phrases could also come at the beginning or the end of the sentence. When they do, only one comma is needed.

I could move to San Francisco, **for example**.

On the other hand, I might move to Phoenix.

Here is a list of common interrupting phrases that connect or make transitions between ideas.

Common Interrupting Phases	
of course	for example
in my opinion	in fact
by the way	on one hand
on the other hand	

Using Commas for Direct Address

Names used in **direct address** are set off by commas. When you use a person's name to speak directly to him or her, set off the name with commas.

Charles, would you please help with this project?

A comma sets off the name *Charles* in that sentence. Only one comma is needed because the name comes first in the sentence. The name can also come at the end of the sentence.

You had better think twice about that, **Fred**.

In the following example, the name used in direct address comes in the middle of the sentence. Two commas are needed to set off *Mr. Littlefield*. Put the commas where they belong.

I hope Mr. Littlefield that you will accept this offer.

You should have put commas both before and after *Mr. Littlefield*.

EXERCISE 6

Using Commas

Directions: The following sentences may contain additional information, connecting ideas, or direct address. Insert commas where they are needed. The first one is done as an example.

1. Dan, in fact, shot the winning basket.

2. Melanie you should do well on the test.

3. The soloist is Heather my oldest granddaughter.

4. Riley by the way is the best third-base player we have.

5. We should give Holly an excellent athlete a place on the relay team.

6. Lisa would you like to pitch today?

7. For example Hailey enjoys science more than math.

8. Pam my next-door neighbor has just won the lottery!

Answers are on page 185.

Using Commas in a Series

Sometimes in your writing, you may want to use several adjectives or adverbs to describe one noun or verb. In this case, use commas to separate three or more items in a series.

> The **green, spotted, worm-eaten** apple fell from the tree.

The adjectives describing the apple are separated by commas.

> The chorus began **carefully, quietly,** and **harmoniously.**

The adverbs describing the chorus are separated by commas.

Where would you place commas in the following sentence, which contains three adverbs?

> Nina Totenberg speaks calmly clearly and firmly.

You were right if you put commas after *calmly* and *clearly*.

Now, punctuate another sentence with adjectives.

> The long modern sleek building won an award for its design.

You should have put commas after *long* and *modern*.

Other kinds of words besides adjectives and adverbs can be used in a series. In the following example, three nouns make up a series. Underline the items in the series. Notice how commas separate them.

> Please bring coffee, tea, and cream to the meeting.

The items *coffee*, *tea*, and *cream* are separated by commas. Notice that no comma is placed before the first item *(coffee)* or after the last item *(cream)*.

Rule for using commas in a series

Commas are used *after* every item except the last one in a series of three or more items.

It is also very important to remember not to use a comma between only two items.

> Jan and Mark are working today.

> Cincinnati or Austin will host the next convention.

> Read the two sentences that follow. Add commas where necessary. Be sure not to add any extra commas.

> George swims runs and lifts weights to stay in shape.

> The Tigers and the Redskins will play a game on Monday.

The first sentence contains a series of three verbs: *swims*, *runs*, and *lifts*. Commas are needed after *swims* and *runs*. The second sentence needs no commas since only two teams are named.

EXERCISE 7

More Commas

Directions: The following sentences may contain additional information, direct address, or series. Or they may connect ideas or make transitions. Insert commas where they are needed. The first one is done as an example.

1. The Wizard of Oz, a favorite childhood character, granted wishes.

2. Checkers a game for two is challenging for children and adults.

3. The undercover officer on the case is Detective Blackwell a member of the vice squad.

4. I just learned in fact that I'm eating all the wrong foods.

5. Marlene gave up smoking by the way.

6. Andy in my opinion is not mature enough to live on his own.

7. Terry will you please come for a visit this summer?

8. If I could afford the trip Mary I would surely come.

9. Do you realize how talented you are Paula?

10. The women's club is planning a dinner and a play to celebrate its anniversary.

11. On the menu will be stuffed chicken breasts baked potatoes peas salad rolls ice cream and coffee.

12. Sue Almeda Fran Warner Lillian Rutledge and Vanessa Grogan are in charge of inviting guests.

Answers are on page 186.

Putting Your Skills to Work

Directions: Write the following kinds of sentences:

- Write two sentences with phrases that give additional information. Make certain you use commas correctly. Here is an example:

  Danielle, an eighth-grader, is taking piano lessons.

- Write two sentences with phrases that connect or make transitions between ideas. Use commas carefully. You can choose from the list of phrases on page 167. Here is an example:

  Television, in my opinion, is not worth watching.

- Write two sentences showing direct address. Be careful about comma placement. Here is an example:

  Woody, you are acting like a fool!

- Write two sentences that list items in a series. Make sure the items are parallel and use commas correctly. Here is an example:

  We are looking for talented, hard-working, enthusiastic volunteers.

  When you have completed writing the eight sentences, use the following writing checklist to proofread and correct your sentences.

Writing Checklist	Yes	No
Do you have two sentences showing the use of commas with phrases that give additional information?	————	————
Do you have two sentences showing phrases that connect ideas? Are the phrases set off by commas?	————	————
Do you have two sentences showing the use of commas with direct address?	————	————
Do you have two sentences showing the use of commas in a series?	————	————
Do the subjects of your sentences agree with the verbs?	————	————
Have you used correct end punctuation for your sentences?	————	————

Chapter Review

EXERCISE 8

Part 1   **Directions:** Each of the following sentences contain either a misplaced describing phrase or incorrect parallel structure. Rewrite each sentence so it is written correctly and clearly.

1. The cat meowed, whined, and was scratching the door.

   _____

   _____

2. Getting a new job and to move to another apartment will improve Flo's life.

   _____

   _____

3. The children listened to the story of *The Pokey Little Puppy* eating their cookies.

   _____

   _____

4. Grabbing the ball and fighting to the goal line, we watched the quarterback.

   _____

   _____

5. The family worked, played, and was living in Missouri for six years.

   _____

   _____

6. Everyone should stop, look, and listening before crossing a street.

   _____

   _____

7. Joe paid $500 for the used car of his hard-earned money.

   _____

   _____

Part 2 **Directions:** Read each of the following paragraphs. Cross out any incorrect verb tense you find and write the correct verb form above it. If the paragraph is written with correct verb forms, write *Correct*.

8. Joel was listening to a new CD when the doorbell rang. He got up from his chair and walks over to the door. He looked through the peephole and saw his best friend, so he opened the door.

_____

9. I've made some New Year's resolutions. From now on, I will exercise every day. I will eat lots of fruits and vegetables. I will read at least one book a month, and I will learn how to speak Spanish. I want to be a healthier, more productive person.

_____

10. Barbara is the busiest person I know. She takes care of three kids and worked full-time. She plays basketball in a local league. Somehow she still finds time to volunteer at a soup kitchen.

_____

11. Ellen planted blue morning glories last May. She put them at the base of a trellis by her door. The vines grew quickly. They will climb up the trellis. But the flowers didn't bloom until August.

_____

Part 3 **Directions:** In this exercise, a part of each sentence is underlined. After the sentence, you will find three possible ways to write the underlined section. The first choice is always the same as the underlined part of the sentence. Circle the letter of the best correction. The first one is done as an example.

12. "What time is <u>it."</u> Clayton asked.

    a. it."
    b. it".
    c. it?"

13. Did your doctor say when <u>youre</u> getting the test results?

    a. youre
    b. you're
    c. your

14. Michelle <u>said, "are</u> you going to the concert?"

    a. said, "are
    b. said "Are
    c. said, "Are

15. Mary Distel, my <u>neighbor has</u> two dogs.

    a. neighbor has
    b. neighbor, has
    c. neighbor; has

16. Spring <u>is of course,</u> my favorite season.

    a. is of course,
    b. is, of course
    c. is, of course,

17. Do you want to go to a <u>movie, Ron?</u>

    a. movie, Ron?
    b. movie Ron?
    c. movie, Ron.

18. The <u>frisky, bright-eyed,</u> squirrel ran up the tree.

    a. frisky, bright-eyed,
    b. frisky, bright-eyed
    c. frisky bright-eyed

19. <u>Fish, or chicken</u> would be good for dinner.

    a. Fish, or chicken
    b. Fish or chicken
    c. Fish, or chicken,

20. Jason is <u>tired; moreover,</u> he's hungry.

    a. tired; moreover,
    b. tired; moreover
    c. tired, moreover,

Answers are on page 186.

Your Turn to Write: A Three-Paragraph Essay

Writing Skill: Introduction and Conclusion

You are now going to put all your writing skills to work by writing a three-paragraph essay. A good essay has three parts: an **introduction**, at least one **body paragraph**, and a **conclusion**.

The **introductory paragraph** tells what the essay topic is and gives the main idea you will be presenting. For example, if the essay topic is violence in schools and you think media coverage makes schools seem more violent than they are, you might write the following introduction. The main idea is stated in the last sentence.

> *People are much more worried about violence in schools today than when I was in school, but, in fact, schools are less violent now than they were then. We just hear more about the terrible incidents that happen. We do need to know about these incidents, but excessive media coverage makes the problem seem too big to handle.*

The **body** of the essay gives the details and facts that explain and support your main idea. This is where you'll draw on your own experiences, observations, and knowledge.

> There were actually fewer murders in schools nationwide last year than in 1970. Of course, one murder is too many, but it's important not to lose sight of the facts. Because the media gives so much attention to a few tragedies, we are led to believe that violence happens often and in many schools. Treating entire student bodies like convicted criminals will unjustly punish the many law-abiding students. It may also push troubled kids over the edge. Additionally, too much media coverage gives glory hounds the publicity they crave. We need to teach students conflict resolution skills. We need to make sure no one feels persecuted. We need to help our children find activities and interests that give them a sense of purpose. We need to be good role models for them.

The **concluding paragraph** wraps up what you've already said. It may summarize your body paragraph, or it may draw some broader truths from the facts you've presented. It does not add any new information.

> If schools and families work together to provide safe havens for all our children, especially those in crisis, we can nearly eliminate violence. If we can persuade the media just to report, not over-emphasize what happens, we can face those few tragedies. Who knows which at-risk child, reached in time, will grow up to be the next Martin Luther King, Jr.?

Writing Assignment

Directions: Write a three-paragraph essay that has an introduction, one body paragraph, and a conclusion. You can begin by using one of these topic sentences or chose a topic of your own:

The speed limit of 55 mph should be enforced.

More people should vote in elections.

Parents should spend more time with their children.

First, organize your ideas by mapping or brainstorming. Write your main idea in a topic sentence for the first paragraph. Write your supporting ideas in the body of the essay. You want to be as convincing as possible. Finally, sum up your thoughts in the conclusion. When you have completed your essay, use the following writing checklist to proofread and revise what you have written.

Writing Checklist	Yes	No
Are all forms of punctuation used correctly?	_____	_____
Are all the sentences complete, not fragments or run-ons?	_____	_____
Are describing phrases placed correctly, and are items in sentences parallel?	_____	_____
Are verb tenses consistent throughout the essay?	_____	_____
Are there any sentences that can be combined to sound better?	_____	_____
Does your first paragraph introduce your subject clearly?	_____	_____
Does your second paragraph explain and support your main idea?	_____	_____
Does your final paragraph summarize your essay convincingly?	_____	_____

Answer Key

CHAPTER 1
PARTS OF SPEECH

Exercise 1: Nouns (page 46)
Answers will vary. Compare your answers to these sample answers to see if you used similar nouns.

1. baseball
2. mall
3. seashells
4. woman
5. Jerry
6. dad
7. Bermuda
8. Honesty

Exercise 2: Pronouns (page 47)
1. It
2. He
3. it
4. them
5. She, He
6. It
7. She, He
8. it

Exercise 3: Verbs (page 49)
Answers will vary. Compare your answers to these sample answers to see if you used similar verbs.

1. rode
2. went
3. visited
4. is
5. sewed
6. look
7. is
8. dreamed

Exercise 4: Adjectives (page 50)
1. new, fuzzy
2. big, little, beautiful
3. kind, new
4. noisy, busy
5. slow, small, each, summer
6. upstairs, blue, white
7. alert, twitching, brick
8. good, some

Exercise 5: Adverbs (page 51)
Answers will vary. Make sure the adverbs you chose tell how, when, and where depending on the instructions.

1. dangerously
2. early
3. outdoors
4. immediately
5. loudly
6. upstairs
7. sweetly
8. daily

Exercise 6: Parts of Speech (page 52)
1. verb
2. noun
3. adjective
4. adverb
5. verb
6. adjective
7. adverb
8. pronoun
9. pronoun
10. noun
11. adverb
12. verb

Exercise 7: Chapter Review (page 53)
Part 1

Nouns	Pronouns	Verbs	Adjectives	Adverbs
Mrs. Kay	he	listens	neat	early
dog	they	keep	happy	there
baseball	you	went	old	slowly
boat	it	loves	nice	now

Part 2
Check to see if you added the correct part of speech to the sentences. You might have a different word, but the part of speech will be the same.

1. motorcycle — noun
2. goes — verb
3. fuzzy — adjective
4. carefully — adverb
5. his — pronoun **or**
   some — adjective

CHAPTER 2
SENTENCES

Exercise 1: Sentences, Fragments, and Run-ons (page 58)
Answers will vary. Just make sure that each of your sentences tells a complete thought.

1. F: The police took the man to jail.
2. F: An officer locked him up.
3. R: He called his lawyer. She promised to help him.
4. S
5. F: He felt terrible.
6. F: The lawyer came to the jail.
7. R: She bailed him out. Then she drove him home.
8. F: He was convicted of driving drunk.
9. S
10. F: He said AA saved his life.

Exercise 2: Types of Sentences (page 61)

1.	This is the Rainbow Coffee Shop.	statement
2.	Would you like to see a menu?	question
3.	Get me a glass of water.	command
4.	Do you like the homemade pie?	question
5.	The special today is meatloaf.	statement
6.	This place is on fire!	exclamation

Exercise 3: Mistakes in Sentences (page 62)

1. This neighborhood has very high rents.
   The original group of words was a fragment. The answer must be a complete sentence.
2. Why did they have to tear down our building?
   The end punctuation for this question should be a question mark, not a period. The first word should be capitalized.
3. Most landlords don't allow pets.
   The first letter of the sentence must be capitalized.
4. I can't give up my dog!
   The original group of words was a fragment. Your answer must be a complete sentence.
5. I've circled some ads for apartments.
   The end punctuation for this statement should be a period, not a question mark.
6. I miss my old neighborhood.
   The original group of words was a fragment. Your answer must be a complete sentence. The sentence should end with a period.

Exercise 4: Finding the Subject (page 63)

	Subject	Verb
1.	Chicago	is
2.	people	live
3.	They	have
4.	trains	take
5.	Commuters	hurry
6.	residents	were

Exercise 5: Finding Tricky Subjects (page 65)

1.	Denise	5.	I
2.	(You)	6.	(You)
3.	Larry	7.	girl
4.	coffee	8.	you

Exercise 6: Writing Predicates (page 66)

Answers will vary. Compare your answers to these sample answers to see if you used similar predicates.

1. Babies cry sometimes.
2. Our money is gone.
3. Flowers grow quickly.
4. Mary went home.
5. The pool heated up.
6. Birds sing loudly.
7. Fish swim swiftly.
8. Scissors cut fabric.
9. My apartment is small.
10. The tomatoes are ripe.

Exercise 7: Chapter Review (pages 67–68)
Part 1

1.	Juan	4.	interviewer
2.	counselor	5.	person
3.	Juan	6.	(You)

Part 2

7.	d	9.	e
8.	c	10.	a

Part 3
Answers will vary. Here are some sample answers.

11–12. The clerk is talking to a customer. Those are on sale today. *(statement)* or Do you want only one of those? *(question)*

13–14. A man is talking to his dog. Sit up. *(command)* or Good dog! *(exclamation)*

CHAPTER 3
NOUNS AND PRONOUNS

Exercise 1: Common and Proper Nouns (page 72)
Below are some sample answers. Did you capitalize your proper nouns?

1. Honda
2. Senator Barbara Boxer
3. Sears

4. Orlando
5. Reverend Zeiders
6. Labor Day
7. Vermont
8. China
9. Boy Scouts
10. Dr. Owens

Exercise 2: Capitalizing Proper Nouns (page 74)

1. Mrs. Linkowski first saw the <u>Washington Monument</u> when she was five.
2. New <u>Year's Eve</u> is <u>Aunt</u> Betty's favorite holiday.
3. The teachers at <u>Brookside Elementary School</u> wrote a letter to <u>Mayor Carlson</u>.
4. My dentist hasn't missed a <u>Green Bay Packers'</u> game in seven years.
5. Correct
6. Ms. Davis is a member of an organization called <u>Mothers Against Drunk Driving</u>.
7. The <u>Oak Valley Fire Department</u> was too late to save the warehouse.

Exercise 3: Changing Singular Nouns to Plural Nouns (page 75)

1. women
2. employers
3. Salaries
4. programs
5. churches
6. Cities

Exercise 4: Correcting Errors with Nouns (page 76)

1. c   **2.** b   **3.** a

Exercise 5: Writing Possessive Nouns (page 77)

1. coach's
2. army's
3. armies'
4. women's
5. teachers'
6. mechanic's
7. mice's
8. Tess's

Exercise 6: Using Subject and Object Pronouns (page 80)

1. She
2. He
3. They
4. It
5. it
6. her
7. him
8. them

Exercise 7: Using Possessive Pronouns (page 81)

1. their
2. its
3. theirs
4. hers
5. their
6. ours

Exercise 8: Pronoun Agreement (page 82)

1. he
2. his
3. them
4. They
5. their
6. Our

Exercise 9: Forming Contractions (page 83)

1. wasn't
2. doesn't
3. he'll
4. I'm
5. we're
6. isn't
7. shouldn't
8. they'll

Exercise 10: Homonyms (page 85)

It's always a good idea **to** decorate **your** home. Even people who don't have much spare time can hang pictures on **their walls** and put up curtains. A **new** coat of paint can **affect** your mood. Of course, **it's** harder if **you're** working full-time. Gary, a friend of mine, did a nice job on **his** apartment. I hope that he and **his** friend Pete will help me out. **They're** really talented at decorating.

Exercise 11: Chapter Review (pages 86–87)

Part 1

1. c
2. a
3. c
4. b

Part 2

5. Years ago, I went to hear **Senator** Gore speak.
6. The year Bush ran for president, **Dad** bought a new **Ford**.

Part 3

7. I, she, or they
8. hers
9. us
10. they
11. my
12. ours

Part 4

13. her
14. She
15. his
16. her
17. their
18. They
19. Their
20. them
21. He
22. Our

CHAPTER 4
VERBS

Exercise 1: Choosing Present Tense Verbs (page 92)

1. Americans like
2. I love
3. I find
4. They welcome
5. parents live
6. We write
7. sister lives
8. Do you

Exercise 2: Writing the Past and Future Tenses (page 93)

Past	Future
1. looked	will look
2. moved	will move
3. lived	will live
4. saved	will save
5. shouted	will shout
6. painted	will paint

Exercise 3: Past Tense of Irregular Verbs (page 96)

1. gave
2. told
3. saw
4. came
5. read
6. brought
7. said
8. made
9. went
10. did
11. had
12. sold

Exercise 4: Choosing the Correct Past Tense Form (page 97)

1. saw
2. ran
3. was
4. went
5. sang
6. did

Exercise 5: Forms of Irregular Verbs (page 100)

1. were
2. is
3. will be
4. are
5. has *or* does
6. will have
7. had
8. will have
9. do
10. did
11. does *or* has
12. will do *or* will have

Exercise 6: Using Time Clues (page 101)

Verb	Time Clues
1. want	Today
2. worked	Last year
3. get	every day
4. will go	Tomorrow
5. ran	Yesterday
6. will be	next week

Exercise 7: Using the Continuous Tenses (page 105)

1. is studying
2. are working
3. is learning
4. are solving
5. am enjoying
6. was driving
7. are going
8. was giving
9. was ringing
10. was dreaming

Exercise 8: Punctuating a Business Letter (page 107)

Rockport,
December 13,
Rockport,
Dear Ms. Reed:
Sincerely,

Exercise 9: Chapter Review (pages 110–111)
Part 1

Present	Past	Future
1. drive	sang	will find
claim	danced	will write
hopes	looked	will paint
jump	had	will want
is	was	
are	saw	

Part 2

2. b
3. a
4. c
5. b
6. c
7. c
8. b
9. c
10. c

CHAPTER 5
SUBJECT-VERB AGREEMENT

Exercise 1: Subject-Verb Agreement with Pronouns (page 114)

1. owns
2. take
3. come
4. is
5. thanks
6. performs
7. wants
8. has

Exercise 2: Subject-Verb Agreement with Irregular Verbs (page 116)

1. go
2. have
3. am
4. does
5. was
6. do
7. were
8. goes

Exercise 3: Nouns as Subjects (page 118)

1. is
2. move
3. look
4. guides
5. gives
6. is

Exercise 4: Subject-Verb Agreement with Compound Subjects (page 120)

	Subjects	Verb
1.	police, police	increase
2.	You, parents	need
3.	Nan, I	go
4.	club, business	gives
5.	newspapers, radio	help
6.	Greg, Stephanie	answers

Exercise 5: Subject-Verb Agreement with Interrupters or Inverted Order (page 123)

	Subject	Verb	Interrupter or Changed Word Order
1.	tree	changes	with the red and gold leaves
2.	children	pick	under the tree
3.	father	arrives	of one of the girls
4.	truckers	Do	The truckers do take safety precautions.
5.	truck	has	with bad brakes
6.	distractions	are	Many distractions are on a long trip.
7.	diner	is	That diner is busy all night long.
8.	bill	lurks	The dentist's bill lurks under those magazines.

Exercise 6: Chapter Review (page 124)
Part 1

1. Lucas and Dena **want** to buy a house.
2. A porch or patio **gives** a house an outdoor feeling.
3. The house with the hardwood floors **was** too expensive.
4. Neither Lucas nor Dena **likes** the less expensive houses.
5. Why **do** houses cost so much in this city?
6. In this neighborhood **are** some affordable condos.
7. Each week the newspaper **publishes** a list of mortgage rates at different banks.
8. Financial security **is** hard to find.

Part 2

9. help   The compound subject is *meals* and *rest*.
10. give   The subject is *grandmother* and *grandfather*.
11. Are   The subject is *blankets*.
12. have   The subject is *You.*
13. looks   The closer part of the compound subject is *meat*.
14. learn   The plural subject is *students*.
15. lies   The plural subject is *beauty*.
16. cheer   The closer part of the compound subject is *flowers*.
17. are   The plural subject is *ideas*.
18. do   The subject is *toys*.

CHAPTER 6
ADJECTIVES AND ADVERBS

Exercise 1: Adjectives (page 129)
Your answers should be similar to these.

1. The **middle-aged** men play **forty** games of poker each month.
2. They use **playing** cards and play on a **card** table.
3. They play on the **first** Friday of each month.
4. During the **monthly** game, **two** pounds of potato chips are eaten.
5. Television can be **boring**.
6. **Seven** people in our family watch the news.
7. Sometimes **tired** viewers go to sleep.
8. **That** show about doctors and surgeons is **entertaining**.

Exercise 2: Adverbs (page 131)
Answers will vary. Check to be sure you have used an adverb to modify the verb in each of your sentences.

1. a. We write *quickly*.
   b. We write *daily*.
   c. We write *upstairs*.
2. a. Rebecca and Issa dance *beautifully*.
   b. They dance *all night*.
   c. They dance *outdoors*.
3. a. Andrew laughed *nervously*.
   b. He laughed *this morning*.
   c. He laughed *next door*.
4. a. Sam will read *quickly*.
   b. Sam will read *later*.
   c. He will read *tomorrow*.

Exercise 3: Choosing Adjectives or Adverbs (page 132)

1. *Fantastic* is an adjective describing *what kind* of football season.
2. *Carefully* is an adverb describing *how* fans prepare.
3. *Calmly* is an adverb describing *how* they wait.
4. *Excited* is an adjective describing *what kind* of crowd.
5. *Loudly* is an adverb describing *how* the fans applaud.
6. *Magnificent* is an adjective describing *what kind* of pass.
7. *Smoothly* is an adverb describing *how* the receiver dodges.
8. *High* is an adjective describing *what kind* of point.

Exercise 4: Using Quotation Marks (page 134)

1. "I think the best years of a person's life are his teen years," said Raymond.
2. His mother laughed and said, "That's because you're a teenager."
3. "Actually, you will have more fun once you're an adult," said his twenty-two-year-old brother, John.
4. "What will happen to me once I reach thirty?" John wondered.
5. "You'll be on your way to forty, and believe me, those are really the best years," said Mom.
6. Dad piped in, "Oh, I don't know, I think I'm even better looking at fifty."
7. John asked, "How were your sixties, Grandma?"

Exercise 5: Chapter Review (pages 135–136)
Part 1
You should have corrected the sentences as follows.

1. Ruth is a **happy** person. (Use an adjective to tell *what kind* of person Ruth is.)
2. The race car moved **quickly** around the track. (Use an adverb to tell *how* the car moved.)
3. Nuts, bolts, wrenches, and tools were thrown around the shop in a **haphazard** fashion. (Use an adjective to tell *what kind* of fashion.)
4. The men and the women agreed that life moves too **rapidly**. (Use an adverb to tell *how* life moves.)
5. The supervisor **angrily** shipped the last fifty space heaters to Anchorage, Alaska. (Use an adverb to tell *how* she shipped the heaters, and change the *y* to *i* before adding *ly*.)
6. The **trustworthy** young baby-sitter raised her fee. (Use an adjective to tell *what kind* of baby-sitter she was.)
7. The soldier looked **bravely** into the eyes of his captors. (Use an adverb to tell *how* the soldier looked.)
8. It's very clear that both Scott and Jill are **excited** about the wedding. (Use an adjective to tell *what kind* of people Scott and Jill are.)

Part 2

9. c *Busily* is an adverb telling *how* the boy played, and the *y* is changed to *i*.

10. b *Hungrily* is an adverb telling *how* Edna bit, and the *y* is changed to *i*.

11. a *Tired* is an adjective telling *what kind* of shopper.

12. b *Tiredly* is an adverb telling *how* the shopper walked.

13. b *Difficult* is an adjective telling *what kind* of language it is.

14. a *Mysterious* is an adjective telling *what kind* of ending.

CHAPTER 7
COMBINING SENTENCES AND ORGANIZING PARAGRAPHS

Exercise 1: Compound Subjects and Predicates (page 140)

Your sentences should be very similar to the following sentences.

2. Sharon and her brother planned to visit their parents for Thanksgiving.

3. They were looking forward to seeing their parents and could hardly wait to taste their mother's cooking.

4. The immigrants and their host families met at the airport.

5. They were happy to see each other and eager to get acquainted.

6. American food, clothing, and housing seem strange to the people from other countries.

Exercise 2: Practice Using Coordinating Conjunctions and Commas (page 143)

2. Some of the customers who visit them are on tight budgets, <u>for</u> they have been laid off.

3. Other customers can afford higher prices, <u>yet</u> they enjoy finding good buys.

4. Nice clothes sell quickly, <u>so</u> smart customers shop on the day new items are stocked.

5. Men and women go to these stores for clothes, <u>but</u> children like to look for toys.

6. Some shops are open at odd hours, <u>yet</u> shoppers fill the aisles.

7. Kevin has never been to a thrift shop before, <u>nor</u> has Marilyn.

8. I'll go shopping tomorrow, <u>or</u> I'll go to the park if the weather's nice.

Exercise 3: Combining Sentences with Conjunctions (page 144)

2. Horses are farm animals, <u>yet</u> some people keep them in cities. **or:**
Horses are farm animals, <u>but</u> some people keep them in cities.

3. Drugs are a serious problem, <u>but</u> many teenagers think they are harmless. **or:**
Drugs are a serious problem, <u>yet</u> many teenagers think they are harmless.

4. I'll get an A on the history test, <u>or</u> I'll get a B.

5. Ron can't have a dog, <u>for</u> he's allergic to fur.

6. The traffic light was red, <u>so</u> Norma stopped her car. **or:**
The traffic light was red, <u>and</u> Norma stopped her car.

Exercise 4: Writing Sentences with Connectors (page 146)

Pay close attention to the punctuation in the answers. Make sure your sentence makes sense.

1. The police searched the neighborhood for drugs; <u>moreover</u>, they vowed to jail all dealers. **or:**
The police searched the neighborhood for drugs; <u>furthermore</u>, they vowed to jail all dealers.

2. After the race, the drivers were exhausted; <u>nevertheless</u>, they went to the party. **or:**
After the race, the drivers were exhausted; <u>however</u>, they went to the party.

3. The Joneses were evicted from their apartment; <u>furthermore</u>, Mr. Jones lost his job. **or:**
The Joneses were evicted from their apartment; <u>moreover</u>, Mr. Jones lost his job. **or:**
The Joneses were evicted from their apartment; <u>consequently</u>, Mr. Jones lost his job.

4. Dorothy thought she would get a small raise; <u>instead</u>, she was surprised with a ten percent salary increase. **or:**
Dorothy thought she would get a small raise; <u>however</u>, she was surprised with a ten percent salary increase.

5. Electric heat is very expensive; <u>therefore</u>, we keep the thermostat turned down to 65 degrees.
   or:
   Electric heat is very expensive; <u>consequently</u>, we keep the thermostat turned down to 65 degrees.

6. I frequently lose my house keys; <u>furthermore</u>, I lock my car keys in my car at least once a week.
   or:
   I frequently lose my house keys; <u>moreover</u>, I lock my car keys in my car at least once a week.

7. Kenny has played the banjo since he was three; <u>consequently</u>, he is the best banjo picker in town. **or:**
   Kenny has played the banjo since he was three; <u>therefore</u>, he is the best banjo picker in town.

Exercise 5: Writing Sentences with Subordinating Conjunctions (page 148)

Answers will vary. Check to make sure your punctuation is correct and your sentences make sense.

2. <u>Though</u> Chan went to the doctor yesterday, he doesn't feel any better today.
3. <u>Before</u> the Jellybeans recorded their first big hit in 1964, they were completely unknown.
4. The police will be able to arrest the purse snatcher <u>if</u> Maura can identify him in a lineup.
5. <u>Since</u> Margaret mowed the lawn, Greg agreed to do the raking.
6. Jenka gave me the money <u>although</u> she needed it herself.
7. Bruno will go to work today <u>if</u> he is feeling better.
8. <u>Since</u> the examination was over, the doctor wrote the report.
9. Fast-food restaurants like to hire adults <u>because</u> they are more dependable workers.
10. <u>Although</u> Bob had retired, his employer asked him to return to work.

Exercise 6: Practicing Punctuation (page 149)

2. Churches form newcomers' groups, and community agencies do the same thing.
3. no comma needed
4. Some women feel that they will appear to be looking for men; consequently, they won't attend these meetings.

5. Many men fear that same thing, so they stay home, too.
6. Others are more optimistic; therefore, they go to meet people of both sexes.
7. When people have interests in common, they may develop good relationships.
8. no comma needed

Exercise 7: Moving Sentences (page 152)

1. **(2)** Move sentence 4 to the beginning of paragraph B. This is the topic sentence of paragraph B.
2. **(3)** Move sentence 13 to the end of paragraph B. This sentence gives another example of a problem the landlord should take care of.
3. **(2)** Move sentence 17 to the end of paragraph C. This is another example of a problem the landlord might be willing to take care of.

Exercise 8: Removing Sentences (page 154)

Paragraph 2—Topic sentence: Caring for an infant is very demanding.
   Remove: They are so cute and so much fun to watch.
Paragraph 3—Topic sentence: Avid TV sports fans are called armchair athletes.
   Remove: Soda is better for them because it doesn't contain alcohol.
Paragraph 4—Topic sentence: Riding the subway takes a great deal of knowledge.
   Remove: Eating candy helps brighten up a long ride.

Exercise 9: Beginning New Paragraphs (page 155)

Start a new paragraph with sentence 7. The topic sentence of the first paragraph is sentence (1). The topic sentence of the second paragraph is sentence (7).

Exercise 10: Chapter Review (pages 156–157)
Part 1

1. Getting up for work is not easy, so I am usually late.
2. Getting up for work is not easy; therefore, I am usually late.

3. Because getting up for work is not easy, I am usually late.
4. **b**
5. **b**
6. **c**
7. **a**

Part 2
8. **(1)** move sentence (2) to follow sentence (4)
9. **(4)** remove sentence (7)
10. **(1)** move sentence (13) to the end of paragraph B

CHAPTER 8
SENTENCES AND PARAGRAPHS

Exercise 1: Identifying Misplaced Describing Phrases (page 161)

	Described Word	Describing Phrase
2. a.	desk	that is 500 years old
3. b.	people	sitting in the front row
4. a.	kitten	quivering with excitement

Exercise 2: Writing Sentences with Describing Phrases (page 161)

2. The actors in their dressing rooms were getting ready to face the audience. **or:**
   In their dressing rooms, the actors were getting ready to face the audience.
3. The salesperson handed the blouse with red stripes to Geraldine.
4. The team in blue uniforms fumbled the ball in the second half.

Exercise 3: Identifying Correct Parallel Structure (page 163)

2. **a.** a police officer, a paramedic, a firefighter
3. **b.** draws exquisitely, paints superbly
4. **b.** stalls out, leaves her stranded

Exercise 4: Correcting Parallel Structure (page 163)

There are several ways to correct some of these sentences. If you did not write the same sentences as those listed below, make sure you have written sentences with correct parallel structure.

1. Homer went to Texas, got a job, built a house, and got married.
2. Getting rich and buying a car are Maxine's only interests. **or:**
   To get rich and to buy a car are Maxine's only interests.
3. Mystery stories have intrigue, excitement, and suspense. **or:**
   Mystery stories are full of intrigue, excitement, and suspense.
4. Wendy works very hard but has fun too. **or:**
   Wendy is working very hard but is having fun too.

Exercise 5: Checking Verb Tense in a Paragraph (page 165)

The corrected sentences for each paragraph follow:

Paragraph 2—The cabin will have only one big room, and it **will have** a bathroom.
Paragraph 3—They **moved** to an area close to a nearby stream.
Paragraph 4—Last year he **saw** a bear eating blackberries.

Exercise 6: Using Commas (page 167)

2. Melanie, you should do well on the test.
3. The soloist is Heather, my oldest grandaughter.
4. Riley, by the way, is the best third-base player we have.
5. We should give Holly, an excellent athlete, a place on the relay team.
6. Lisa, would you like to pitch today?
7. For example, Hailey enjoys science more than math.
8. Pam, my next-door neighbor, has just won the lottery!

Exercise 7: More Commas (page 169)

2. Checkers, a game for two, is challenging for children and adults.
3. The undercover policeman on the case is Detective Blackwell, a member of the vice squad.
4. I just learned, in fact, that I'm eating all the wrong foods.
5. Marlene gave up smoking, by the way.
6. Andy, in my opinion, is not mature enough to live on his own.
7. Terry, will you please come for a visit this summer?
8. If I could afford the trip, Mary, I would surely come.
9. Do you realize how talented you are, Paula?
10. no commas needed
11. On the menu will be stuffed chicken breasts, baked potatoes, peas, salad, rolls, ice cream, and coffee.
12. Sue Almeda, Fran Warner, Lillian Rutledge, and Vanessa Grogan are in charge of inviting guests.

Exercise 8: Chapter Review (pages 171–173)
Part 1
There can be more than one way to correct some of these sentences. If you did not write the same sentences as those listed below, make sure you have avoided using misplaced describing phrases or incorrect parallel structure.

1. The cat meowed, whined, and scratched the door.
2. Getting a new job and moving to another apartment will improve Flo's life.
3. The children, eating their cookies, listened to the story of *The Pokey Little Puppy*.
4. We watched the quarterback grab the ball and fight to the goal line.
5. The family worked, played, and lived in Missouri for six years.
6. Everyone should stop, look, and listen before crossing a street.
7. Joe paid $500 of his hard-earned money for the used car.

Part 2

8. He got up from his chair and **walked** over to the door.
9. Correct
10. She takes care of three kids and **works** full-time.
11. They **climbed** up the trellis.

Part 3

13. b	17. a
14. c	18. b
15. b	19. b
16. c	20. a

LANGUAGE ARTS
READING

CHAPTER 1

Gaining Meaning from Words

As you read, you want to understand whole sentences, paragraphs, and passages. However, do individual words ever slow you down? A good vocabulary helps you to understand more of what you read.

There are a number of ways to build your vocabulary. In this chapter you'll look at those ways. First, you'll work on dictionary skills. Then you'll study syllables, word parts, synonyms, and antonyms.

Using the Dictionary

Skillful use of a dictionary is important for adults. It allows you to figure out the meanings of words on your own and to continue to learn in and out of school.

Words represent ideas. If you don't know what a word means, you can't think about that idea, much less read with understanding or have a discussion about it. A good vocabulary is important in making progress in school, on the job, and at home. Being able to use a dictionary well is also useful for parents who help their children with homework.

Basic Alphabetical Order

As you know, the dictionary lists words in alphabetical order by the first letter in each word. Look at the three words that follow. In what order would the dictionary list them?

fan   corn   hit

Look at the first letter of each word. Which letter comes first in the alphabet: *f, c,* or *h*? Since *c* comes before *f* or *h, corn* would be first in alphabetical order. Which letter comes next: *f* or *h*? Since *f* comes after *c* but before *h, fan* would be next. Since *h* comes after *f, hit* would be the last word.

corn   fan   hit

Alphabetizing

Directions: The following groups of words are not in alphabetical order. Rearrange them as they would appear in the dictionary. You need only to look at the first letter of each.

1. broccoli, lettuce, peas, cauliflower, radish, spinach

2. Ford, Chevrolet, Honda, Toyota, Dodge, Kia

3. love, hate, free, control, reject, accept

Answers are on page 327.

You've seen how the dictionary lists words in alphabetical order by the first letter in each word. But many words start with the same letter: *can, cent, chat.*

How does the dictionary sort these words out? Read the following rule.

> **Rule:** If the first letters in the words are alike, alphabetize by the second letters. If the first and second letters are the same, alphabetize by the third, and so on.

For example, look at these five words:

can cent chat chart cereal

Since they all begin with *c*, you must look at the second letter of each word in order to alphabetize them. Before putting them into a final list, look at the third and fourth letters.

The correct order is as follows:

can cent cereal chart chat

Alphabetizing Beyond the First Letter

Directions: Look at each set of words and alphabetize them. If they begin with the same first letter, alphabetize by the second. If the first two letters are the same, alphabetize by the third, and so on.

1. needle, nervous, nerd, need, nest

2. worry, wrench, wreck, worm, worn

3. able, abuse, ache, achieve, about

Answers are on page 327.

Guide Words

Now that you know how to alphabetize words, the **guide words** on a dictionary page will help you locate a word quickly. The guide words are the two words at the top of a dictionary page. The guide word on the left is the first word defined on that page. The guide word on the right is the last word defined on that page. Look at the dictionary page that follows. Note the words *lid* and *lizard* in **boldface type** at the top of the page. By using alphabetical order and guide words, you can quickly decide whether the word you want is on that page, before it, or after it.

---

lid—lizard

lid *n* a cover for the opening
 or top of a container
lift *v* to raise from a lower to a
 higher place
light *adj* easy to carry, having
 little weight
limerick *n* a humorous verse
 having a special rhyme scheme
limp *v* to walk unsteadily or with
 difficulty
linen *n* cloth known for its
 strength and shine
linger *v* to be slow in leaving
link *n* something that connects
 one thing to another
lint *n* fuzz from small pieces
 of yarn and fabric
lion *n* a large, meat-eating cat
lipstick *n* a cosmetic, usually colored,
 for the lips

liquid *n* a substance that
 flows like water
list *n* a record or catalog
 of names or items
listen *v* to pay attention to
 something you hear
listless *adj* having no
 energy
liter *n* a metric unit for
 measuring liquids
literature *n* a body of
 written work, including
 prose, poetry, and drama
litter *v* to scatter trash or
 garbage
lively *adj* energetic, full of
 spirit
lizard *n* any of a group of
 long-bodied reptiles

For example, would *lane* be on this page? No, *la* (in *lane*) comes before *li* (in the guide word *lid*), so you would know to turn back a few pages.

Would *loose* be on this page? No, *lo* (in *loose*) comes after *li* (in the guide word *lizard*), so you would know to turn forward a page or so.

Would *list* be on the page? Yes, *lis* (in *list*) comes after *lid* (the guide word) and before *liz* (the guide word *lizard*). Therefore, you know *list* would be on the page.

EXERCISE 3

Using Guide Words

Directions: Decide whether the words listed in the left column would be on the page, on a page before the guide words, or on a page after the guide words. Write <u>before</u> if the word on the left comes before the guide words. Write <u>after</u> if the word on the left comes after the guide words. Write <u>same page</u> if the word would be on the same page as the guide words. The first one is done as an example.

Part 1   GUIDE WORDS: **combat—command**

Word	Where Word Appears
1. come	*same page*
2. commit	
3. color	
4. college	
5. compass	
6. common	
7. comet	

Part 2   GUIDE WORDS: **hockey—Holmes**

Word	Where Word Appears
8. home	
9. hike	
10. house	
11. hospital	
12. holiday	
13. holdup	
14. hoarse	

Answers are on page 327.

Finding Related Words

Often, dictionaries put the definition of a longer word at the bottom part of the entry for the shorter word from which it's formed. This uses less space than making a separate entry.

What would you look under to find the word *basically*? You were right if you said *basic*. *Basically* is formed from the shorter word *basic*.

EXERCISE 4

Finding Related Forms of a Word

Directions: Look at each word in the left column; then write the shorter, related word under which you could find it. The first one is done for you.

To Find	Look Under
1. hollowness	*hollow*
2. marriageable	_____
3. quickness	_____
4. liquidity	_____
5. guardianship	_____
6. discontentment	_____
7. chargeable	_____

Answers are on page 327.

Pronunciation

Now you'll see how the dictionary can help you pronounce a word that you don't know how to say. For example, look at the word *chic*. It looks like the word *chick* or *chicken*. But just after the word, the dictionary gives you another spelling between parentheses ( ) or slashes / /, depending on your dictionary: *chic (shēk)*.

You already know how to say the *sh* sound at the beginning and the *k* sound at the end of (*shēk*). But you also need to know how to say the *e*, the vowel sound in the middle.

To know how to say the *e*, you look at the dictionary's pronunciation key. The pronunciation key shows you how to pronounce the vowels in a word by giving you sample words whose vowels sound the same. The pronunciation key may be found on a page at the beginning or at the end of your dictionary. A shortened version of it may also appear at the bottom of every other page.

Here is part of the pronunciation key from *Webster's Tenth Collegiate Dictionary.*

Symbol	Word	Symbol	Word
a	ash	ī	ice
ā	ace	ȯ	law
ä	mop, mar	ō	go
e	bet	ü	loot
ē	easy	u̇	foot
i	hit	ə	abut

From this list, find the word with the *e* marked the same as the *e* in (*shēk*): *easy.* Now we know that the *e* in (*shēk*) is said the same way as the *ea* in *easy.* Therefore, *chic* is pronounced *sheek.*

EXERCISE 5

Looking Up Pronunciations

Directions: In your dictionary, look up each of the words. In the middle column, copy the pronunciation given. Then compare the pronunciation to the pronunciation key in your dictionary. Find the word that has the same vowel sound as the word you looked up, and write it in the third column.

Word	Pronunciation from Dictionary	Word from Pronunciation Key that Matches Vowel
1. chute	*shüt*	*loot*
2. reign		
3. aisle		
4. psalm		
5. bias		
6. plague		
7. plaque		

Answers are on page 327.

Using The Dictionary

Dictionaries use the following abbreviations for the different kinds of words and their uses. These labels help you know how to use the word.

n = noun	word used to name people, places, things, or ideas
pron = pronoun	word that can be used in place of nouns
v* = verb	word of action or state of being
adj = adjective	word that describes nouns
adv = adverb	word that describes verbs, adjectives, or other adverbs
prep = preposition	word that gives a position in time and space
conj = conjunction	word that connects other words
*Note: You may see *vb, vt,* or *vi* in the dictionary. These are all verb forms.	

These abbreviations usually appear just after the pronunciation. Sometimes words can be used in more than one way. For example, the word *bat* can be used as a noun and a verb. The second label will appear further down in the entry.

EXERCISE 6

Understanding Dictionary Labels

Directions: In a dictionary, look up each of the following words. Then write the part or parts of speech given. Some words can be used as more than one part of speech. The first one is done as an example.

Word	Part(s) of Speech
1. bat	*noun, verb*
2. cross	_____
3. exhibit	_____
4. liquid	_____
5. around	_____
6. rule	_____
7. about	_____
8. but	_____
9. they	_____

Answers are on page 327.

Multiple Meanings

Many words have more than one meaning. These different meanings are listed in the dictionary by number, with the most common meaning as number 1, the next most common as number 2, and so forth.

For example, one common meaning of *leave* is "to allow to remain," as in "Leave a sip for me." Another meaning of *leave* is "to abandon," as in "How could Bob leave his wife and children by themselves?"

EXERCISE 7

Understanding Multiple Meanings

Directions: In each item, two sentences contain the same word in **boldface type.** However, in each sentence the word has a different meaning. Find the word in the dictionary. Then write the correct meaning on the blank beneath each sentence.

1. **a.** I want to **pose** a question.

   Meaning: *to propose (a question)*

   b. The model held the **pose** for two hours.

   Meaning: *a bodily attitude held for an artist*

2. **a.** Newspapers **report** important events.

   Meaning: _____

   b. I have to **report** for work at 8:00 A.M. daily.

   Meaning: _____

3. **a.** We sat in the third **row** of the movie theater.

   Meaning: _____

   b. We had to **row** ashore when it began to rain.

   Meaning: _____

4. **a.** Get a new **bar** of soap from under the sink.

   Meaning: _____

   b. You can order a milkshake at the snack **bar.**

   Meaning: _____

5. **a.** Tom works at a furniture **plant.**

   Meaning: _____

   b. The flowering **plant** gets enough sunlight in their apartment.

   Meaning: _____

Answers are on page 327.

Syllables

Syllables are word parts that form "beats." Syllables can be combined to make words. Breaking words into syllables sometimes provides clues to the meanings of words. Syllables also help you to spell words correctly. Look at these examples:

walk = 1 beat, or 1 syllable

ideal = i + deal = 2 beats, or 2 syllables

quietly = qui + et + ly = 3 beats, or 3 syllables

information = in + for + ma + tion = 4 beats, or 4 syllables

There are several rules that can help you decide how to break a word into syllables:

- the Prefix/Suffix Rule
- the VC/CV Rule
- the VCV Rule

You will want to use these rules in the order in which they're given here. First, see if the Prefix/Suffix Rule applies to the word you are dividing. In other words, does the word have a prefix or a suffix? If it does, use the rule to divide the word. If it doesn't apply, then go on to the next rule listed.

The Prefix/Suffix Rule

The first rule you need to apply when deciding how to break a word into syllables is the Prefix/Suffix Rule. A **prefix** is a syllable added to the beginning of a word. A **suffix** is a syllable added to the end of a word. Look at the following chart that lists common prefixes and suffixes.

Common Prefixes		Common Suffixes	
pre-	re-	-ing	-ish
ex-	dis-	-er	-est
in-	un-	-ness	-ment
pro-	de-	-ist	-ful
sub-	trans-	-less	-ship
non-	mis-	-tion (say "shun")	-or
pre-	post-		-ly
bi-	tri-		-al
co-	per-		
con-	col-		

The Prefix/Suffix Rule tells you to break a word into syllables in the following way:

Prefix	+	Word or Word Part	+	Suffix
1 SYLLABLE		1 OR MORE SYLLABLES		1 SYLLABLE

To use the Prefix/Suffix Rule, you must first decide whether your word contains a prefix or a suffix.

For example, look at the following word:

redoing

Does this word have a prefix, a suffix, or both? If you look at the chart, you can see that it has both; the prefix is *re–* and the suffix is *-ing*. Now apply the Prefix/Suffix Rule to the word *redoing*.

re-	+	**do**	+	**-ing**
PREFIX		WORD OR WORD PART		SUFFIX

Redoing has both a prefix and a suffix. However, some words may have only a prefix or only a suffix. You can use the Prefix/Suffix Rule for these words as well. For example, the word *export* has only a prefix, so only the prefix part of the Prefix/Suffix Rule is applied, like this:

ex-	+	**port**
PREFIX		WORD OR WORD PART

EXERCISE 8

Applying the Prefix/Suffix Rule

Directions: Break the following words into syllables by breaking the prefix and/or suffix away from the rest of the word. Underline each prefix and/or suffix. Then say each word to yourself. The first one is done as an example.

1. sickness _____*sick - ness*_____

2. subtraction _____

3. prevention _____

4. misspelling _____

5. extended _____

6. retirement _____

7. swiftly _____

8. proposal _____

Answers are on page 328.

The VC/CV Rule

The next rule for breaking words into syllables is the VC/CV Rule. The *V* stands for *vowel;* the *C* stands for *consonant.* The VC/CV Rule tells you that if two consonants come together with vowels on either side, you split the word between the two consonants like this:

VC – CV

Look at how this rule works with the words *rabbit* and *silver.*

In both words, two consonants come together, with vowels on either side. Therefore, the VC/CV Rule tells you to split the words between the two consonants, like this:

rab – bit   sil – ver
VC – CV   VC – CV

Note: The silent *e* at the ends of words and syllables **does not count** as a vowel. Only sounding vowels count. For example, look at the silent *e* in the syllables in the following words:

re – mote̸ – ly   en – gage̸ – ment

In the words *rabbit* and *silver,* you've seen how the VC/CV Rule works with words that have neither a prefix nor a suffix. Now look at how to use the VC/CV Rule with words to which you've already applied the Prefix/Suffix Rule.

re – en – ter – ing   un – hap – pi – ness
PREFIX – VC – CV – SUFFIX   PREFIX – VC – CV – SUFFIX

EXERCISE 9

Applying the VC/CV Rule

Part 1 **Directions:** Use the Prefix/Suffix Rule and the VC/CV Rule to break the following words into syllables. Mark the VC/CV. The first one is done as an example.

1. fragment *frag – ment*
　　　　　　 VC　　 CV

2. remnant _____

3. curtain _____

4. appendix _____

5. budget _____

6. embassy _____

7. consistent _____

8. filter _____

Part 2 **Directions:** Using the Prefix/Suffix Rule and the VC/CV Rule, break the following words into syllables. Underline prefixes and suffixes.

9. abnormal _ab – nor – mal_

10. interviewer _____

11. compartment _____

12. correspond _____

13. organist _____

Answers are on page 328.

The VCV Rule

The third rule to apply when dividing words into syllables concerns one consonant falling between two vowels, as in the following examples:

solo = so – lo   **or**   rapid = rap – id
   V – CV   VC – V

As you can see, the single consonant can go with either the first vowel or the second vowel. To judge which way to place the consonant, figure out the vowel sound. A long vowel will end a syllable. With a long vowel, use V + CV, as in the word *solo.*

sō – lō
V – CV

A short vowel will be followed by one or more consonants. With a short vowel, use VC + V, as in the word *rapid.*

rap – id
VC – V

EXERCISE 10

Applying the VCV Rule

Directions: Divide the following words into syllables using the VCV rule. Mark long vowels with a (ˉ) and silent vowels with a (/).

1. agent _ā - gent_

2. recent _____

3. cabinet _____

4. tomato _____

5. license _____

6. humane _____

7. female _____

8. limit _____

Answers are on page 328.

Prefixes

Prefixes are sometimes added to whole words we already know in order to change the meaning. For example, the prefix *il-* means "not." When we add *il-* to *legal,* we get *illegal,* which means "not legal."

The prefix *inter-* means "in the middle." The Latin word *sect* means "to cross." From the prefix *inter-* and the Latin root *sect* we get the English word *intersection.* This word means "in the middle of the crossing." Following is a table listing some common prefixes and their meanings. Study them carefully.

Prefix	Meaning	Example	Definition
co-, col-, com-	with, together	copilot	person who pilots with another
con-, cor-	with another	correspond	to exchange letters with another person
per-	through	permit	to allow to go through
auto-	self	automobile	vehicle that moves itself
inter-	between, among	international	between or among nations
intra-	inside	intravenous	inside the vein
re-	back, again	return, redo	turn back; do again

EXERCISE 11

Adding Prefixes

Part 1 **Directions:** Make a word by adding one of the prefixes from the table above to each of the words in the following list. With some words, you may be able to use more than one prefix to make a word.

	Prefix	Word or Root	New Word
1.	*re –*	use	*reuse*
2.	_____	section	_____
3.	_____	worker	_____
4.	_____	graph	_____

Part 2   **Directions:**   Match each definition on the right with the correct word or phrase on the left. Write the letter of the definition next to the phrase it matches. Use a dictionary if you wish.

Word or Phrase	**Definition**
_____ **5.** <u>con</u>nect two lines	**a.** cause a break between two people talking
_____ **6.** <u>in</u>terrupt	**b.** join two lines together
_____ **7.** <u>re</u>state a question	**c.** relate two ideas with each other
_____ **8.** <u>cor</u>relate two ideas	**d.** state a question again

Answers are on page 328.

Prefixes That Make Opposites

When added to a word, some prefixes change the meaning of that word to its opposite. Prefixes that often do this are those meaning "not." For example, if you take the prefix *un-* and add it to the word *healthy,* you get *unhealthy* which means "not healthy," or "the opposite of healthy."

Prefixes that change the meaning of a word to its opposite are listed in the following table.

Prefix	Meaning	Example	Definition
un-	not	unable	not able
in-	not	incorrect	not correct
im-	not	impossible	not possible
il-	not	illegal	not legal
ir-	not	irresponsible	not responsible
non-	not	nonsmoker	not a smoker
mis-	wrong	misplace	put in wrong place
dis-	not, away from	displease	not pleased
anti-	against	antiwar	against war

EXERCISE 12

Prefixes That Make Opposites

Directions: Circle the prefix in each of the words that follow. Then write the definition of the word on the blank provided. The first one is done as an example.

Word	Meaning
1. (un)kind	*not kind*
2. irresponsible	_____
3. immature	_____
4. nonviolent	_____
5. disabled	_____
6. illegitimate	_____
7. inconsiderate	_____
8. anti-inflammatory	_____
9. disappear	_____
10. uncertain	_____

Answers are on page 328.

Prefixes That Show Time

Some prefixes have meanings that are related to time. Study the following prefixes and their meanings. Notice that each of these prefixes tells when something is done. Therefore, these prefixes show time.

Prefix	Meaning	Example	Definition
ante-	before	antedate	to precede in time
pre-	before	prepare	to make ready before
post-	after	postpone	to put off until after

EXERCISE 13

Time Prefixes

Directions: Using the prefixes and their meanings, match the definitions on the right with the words or phrases they define on the left. Put the letter of each definition beside the phrase it matches. Use a dictionary if you wish.

Word or Phrase	Definition
_____ 1. antecedent	**a.** before written history
_____ 2. postpartum examination	**b.** examination after the birth of a child
_____ 3. preholiday sale	**c.** an examination after surgery
_____ 4. predetermined amount	**d.** something that went before
_____ 5. postoperative examination	**e.** after a war
_____ 6. prehistory	**f.** amount determined before
_____ 7. postwar	**g.** a sale before a holiday

Answers are on page 328.

Prefixes That Show Place

The following prefixes have meanings related to place or position. They are used to show the relationship between different people or things.

Prefix	Meaning	Example	Definition
de-	down, away	descend	to go or move down
in-, en-	in, inside	enclose	to close something in
ex-	out	exit	to go out
super-	above, over	supervise	to watch over someone's work or progress
pro-	forward	proceed	to move forward
sub-	under, below	subzero	to go below zero

EXERCISE 14

Place Prefixes

Directions: Using the prefixes and their meanings, match the definitions on the right with the correct phrases on the left. Write the letter of each definition next to the phrase it matches. You may use a dictionary if you wish.

Word or Phrase	**Definition**
_____ 1. degrade someone	a. use only outside the body (as medicine)
_____ 2. propel a boat	b. drive a boat forward
_____ 3. subterranean cave	c. a cave under the earth
_____ 4. external use only	d. to put forward an idea
_____ 5. interior use only	e. to disgrace someone or put that person down
_____ 6. detract from someone's appearance	f. use only inside (as paint)
_____ 7. to make a proposal	g. take away from someone's appearance

Answers are on page 328.

Number Prefixes

Many prefixes refer to numbers. When they are added to the beginning of words, these number prefixes tell you how many there are of something. Look at the following examples of number prefixes:

uni- means "one," so a _uniform_ is "clothing in one form"

_bi-_ means "two," so a _bicycle_ is a "vehicle with two wheels"

Study the number prefixes and their meanings in the following table.

Prefix	Meaning	Example	Definition
uni-	one	uniform	one form of clothing
mono-	one	monotone	one tone
bi-	two	bicycle	vehicle with two wheels
du-	two	duplex	a two-family house
tri-	three	trio	three people
qua-	four	quarter	one of four parts

EXERCISE 15

Number Prefixes

Directions: Using the prefixes and their meanings, match the definition on the right with the correct word or phrase on the left. Write the letter of the definition next to the word or phrase it defines. Use a dictionary if you wish.

Word or Phrase	**Definition**
_____ **1.** triplets	**a.** agreement between two sides
_____ **2.** bilateral agreement	**b.** having three angles
_____ **3.** unit	**c.** one thing
_____ **4.** triangle	**d.** three babies from the same birth
_____ **5.** quartet	**e.** musical group having four members
_____ **6.** duel	**f.** belief in one God
_____ **7.** monotheism	**g.** fight between two people

Answers are on page 328.

Suffixes

As you learned earlier, **suffixes** are syllables added to the ends of words. Most often, they are used to change a word from one part of speech into another part of speech. For example, by adding -al to a noun, you can form an adjective. Look at the following examples.

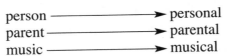

person ——————→ personal
parent ——————→ parental
music ——————→ musical

If you add –er to some verbs, you will make a noun meaning "one who does."

play ——————→ player
convey ——————→ conveyer
employ ——————→ employer

If you add –tion or –sion to some verbs, you will form a noun meaning "the result of" that action.

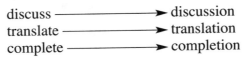

discuss ——————→ discussion
translate ——————→ translation
complete ——————→ completion

EXERCISE 16

Familiar Suffixes

Directions: Using the following table, study the suffixes and their meanings. Then match the definition on the right with the word it defines on the left. Use a dictionary if you wish.

-able, -ible	able to
-ism	belief in, practice of
-ish	like, similar to
-ology	study of
-ful	full of
-ment	process, place, result

Word

_____ 1. commercialism

_____ 2. spiteful

_____ 3. psychology

_____ 4. childish

_____ 5. legible

_____ 6. geology

_____ 7. idealism

_____ 8. agreement

Definition

a. study of the mind and behavior

b. able to be read

c. result of harmony, treaty

d. belief in ideals

e. practice of making money in business or commerce

f. like a child

g. study of the earth

h. full of spite

Answers are on page 328.

Base Words

Sometimes prefixes are attached to words that can stand alone. These words are often called **base words** because they form the base on which a new word is built.

Look at the following examples of prefixes added onto base words:

dis- similar   means   "not similar"
PREFIX BASE WORD

un- used   means   "not used"
PREFIX BASE WORD

Latin and Greek Roots

Prefixes are sometimes attached to word parts from Greek or Latin called **roots.** Some of these roots can stand alone (see base words above). However, many cannot stand on their own. Look at the following example.

pre- dict
PREFIX ROOT

The root *dict* comes from the Latin word, *dicere,* meaning "to say or tell." Therefore, *predict* means "to say or tell something before" or "to tell something that has yet to happen." Weather forecasters predict tomorrow's weather. Here's another example:

per- fect
PREFIX ROOT

The root *fect* comes from the Latin word, *facere,* meaning "to do." Therefore, the verb *perfect* means "to do something without error."

Most of us do not know Latin or Greek, so we need to learn the root and its English meaning. Some of the most common roots and their meanings are given in the following table.

Root	Meaning
fect	do
port	carry
cept, ceive	take
cred	believe, trust
fid	faith
script, scribe	write

Look at the following words. They have been divided into prefix, root or base word, and suffix. There may not always be a prefix or a suffix.

Word	Prefix	Root or Base Word	Suffix
exported	ex-	port	-ed
infecting	in-	fect	-ing
receiver	re-	ceiv	-er
except	ex-	cept	—

EXERCISE 17

Locating Roots or Base Words

<u>Part 1</u> **Directions:** Study the list of common roots in the tables. Then underline the root or base word in each of the words that follow.

1. <u>port</u>able
2. defect
3. transcript
4. inscription

5. transported
6. deceive
7. incredible
8. fidelity

9. portage
10. infect
11. infidel
12. conceive

<u>Part 2</u> **Directions:** Study the Latin and Greek roots in the table that follows. Then match the definition on the right with the phrase it defines on the left. Write the letter of each definition next to the word it matches. Use a dictionary if you wish.

graph	write
chron	time
sect	cut

Phrase

_____ 13. synchronize watches

_____ 14. bisect a line

_____ 15. photograph a person

_____ 16. biography of Abraham Lincoln

_____ 17. intersection of streets

_____ 18. chronological order

_____ 19. sectional sofa

_____ 20. a chronicle of events

Definition

a. allow light to write on film, making a picture

b. where two streets cut or cross one another

c. a piece of furniture made up of modular units

d. cut a line in two

e. a historical account of happenings

f. a written account of someone's life

g. in order by time

h. set to show the same time

Answers are on page 328.

Defining Words with Latin or Greek Roots

By understanding the meaning of Latin and Greek roots, we can understand the meanings of many English words. Take the words *portable* and *telephone*, for example.

Root	Meaning	Example	Definition
port	carry	portable	able to be carried
tele phon	distant sound	telephone	brings sound from a distance

Looking at the meaning of the Greek or Latin root can help you discover the definition of a word. Notice that from time to time you will find minor spelling changes, such as *phon* changing to *phono*. This is done so that the word will be easier to pronounce.

EXERCISE 18

Locating Greek and Latin Roots

Directions: Using the root meanings that are listed below, match each definition on the right to the word it defines on the left.

phon	sound
graph, gram	write
tele	distant
port	carry

Word

_____ **1.** telegraph

_____ **2.** portable

_____ **3.** phonograph

Definition

a. able to be carried

b. sound "written down;" instrument that reproduces sound from a disc

c. written from a distance; communication at a distance by coded signals

Answers are on page 328.

Synonyms

Synonyms are words that have very similar meanings, like the words *thin* and *slender.*

> *couch* means about the same thing as *sofa*
>
> *rock* means about the same thing as *stone*
>
> *form* means about the same thing as *shape*

EXERCISE 19

Finding Synonyms

Directions: Match each word on the left with its synonym on the right. Underline the synonym. The first one is done as an example.

1. completed   began <u>finished</u> started delayed
2. volume   write author book poem
3. foundation   concrete carpenter building base
4. courageous   brave foolish afraid cowardly
5. journey   airplane passport ticket trip
6. reasoning   talking writing thinking pausing
7. depart   arrive leave land eat
8. frequently   always never often seldom

Answers start on page 329.

Antonyms

Antonyms are words that have opposite meanings, like the words *hot* and *cold*.

> *wet* means the opposite of *dry*
>
> *tall* means the opposite of *short*

Often a sentence will include a word and its antonym. This may help you figure out the meaning of a word you don't know. For example,

Rebecca appeared very frail next to her healthy cousin.

The sentence gives you a clue. If Rebecca is frail but her cousin is healthy, *frail* must be an antonym of *healthy*.

EXERCISE 20

Finding Antonyms

Part 1 **Directions:** Match each word on the left with its antonym on the right. Underline the antonym. The first one is done as an example.

1. hot   warm   high   <u>cold</u>   wet

2. inquire   answer   ask   question   help

3. loose   lose   difficult   find   tight

4. knowledge   ignorance   learning   school   book

5. positive   decided   perfect   loud   negative

Part 2 **Directions:** As you read each of the following sentences, find the antonym of the word in **boldface type** and underline it. The first one is done as an example.

6. The **dull** finish turned <u>shiny</u> as he polished it.

7. The week after the **destruction** of the old office building, construction began on the new park and playground.

8. Although he **approved** of the ideas in the composition, he criticized the grammar and spelling.

9. Her cooking was often **spicy,** for she disliked cooking flavorless meals.

Answers are on page 329.

Chapter Review

In this chapter you have had practice in building your vocabulary. To build dictionary skills, you have reviewed alphabetizing, guide words, pronunciation, and multiple word meanings. To help understand words, you have used syllables, prefixes, suffixes, and roots or base words. You have also learned to recognize synonyms and antonyms.

EXERCISE 21

Part 1 **Directions:** As you read each of the following sentences, find the synonym of the word in **boldface type** and underline it.

1. José was so proud of his **automobile** that he polished his car every week.

2. David had **unusual** musical talent. It was rare to see such ability in one so young.

3. People who **perish** in fires often die of inhaling smoke rather than being burned.

4. The **trembling** of the earthquake was so strong that the dishes were shaking in the cupboards.

Part 2 **Directions:** Look for the word in **boldface type** in each sentence. Circle a synonym and underline an antonym for the word.

5. Heather is **slender,** so she is neither too fat nor too thin to be a model.

6. The **opening** minutes of the movie were boring, but once I got past the beginning, I was fascinated through the ending.

7. The **defective** towels were only slightly damaged but were much cheaper than those that were perfect.

8. The army **proceeded** toward the city, but it advanced only to the river before it retreated under fire.

9. No doubt the carpenter was **skilled.** His expert work only showed how incompetent others were.

Part 3   **Directions:** Use the dictionary entry below to answer the questions.

> **project**   **1.** a planned task for students   **2.** a public housing development
> **3.** a large government-supported undertaking   **4.** to plan for the future
> **5.** to protrude or jut out   **6.** to put forth for consideration

10. Circle the guide words that *project* would come between.

prologue – promote   program – prolong   profuse – progress

11. _____ Write the number of the correct meaning of *project* as used in the following sentence:

Martin's desk projects out in the hall and may be a fire hazard.

12. _____ Write the number of the correct meaning of *project* as used in the following sentence:

Our instructor assigned this project to all five of us students.

Part 4   **Directions:** Using the following table of prefixes, match the definition on the right with the word it defines on the left.

pro-	forward
il-	not
re-	back, again
tri-	three
inter-	between, among

Word	**Definition**
_____ **13.** interview	**a.** not legal
_____ **14.** regain	**b.** to move something forward
_____ **15.** illegal	**c.** to gain or possess again
_____ **16.** triplets	**d.** a talk between people
_____ **17.** propel	**e.** three born at the same time from the same mother

Part 5   **Directions:** Using the following table of suffixes, match the definition on the right with the word it defines on the left.

-logy	the study of
-ish	somewhat, similar to
-ist	one who
-ment	process, result

_____ **19.** realist	**a.** somewhat dark
_____ **20.** darkish	**b.** result of being placed
_____ **21.** biology	**c.** the study of life
_____ **22.** placement	**d.** one who deals with real life

Answers are on page 329.

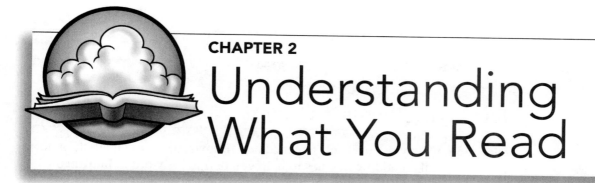

CHAPTER 2

Understanding What You Read

How well do you comprehend, or understand, what you read? In this chapter you will learn ways to improve your reading comprehension. You will study key words in sentences, key words to build main ideas, words in context, main ideas and supporting details, and summarizing and paraphrasing.

Words in Context

An important method for defining unfamiliar words is using **context clues.** The context refers to the words that surround the word you don't know. Often, the context will give you clues that help you figure out what the unfamiliar word means.

Context Clues

How do context clues work? As you read the sentences that follow, notice how the underlined words give clues to the meaning of the word in **boldface type.**

> Mr. Riley is quite **spry** for his age. <u>Every day he walks several blocks</u> to buy a newspaper, and I often see him <u>working in his garden</u>.

Since Mr. Riley is described as walking several blocks every day and working in his garden, we can guess that *spry* means *active.*

> Wilson <u>put on a heavy coat, a wool scarf, several pairs of socks inside his boots, and fur-lined gloves to protect himself</u> against the **frigid** weather.

The clues tell you that Wilson is wearing warm clothes to protect himself. You can infer that if he is wearing warm clothes for protection, the weather must be very cold. Therefore, *frigid* must mean *very cold.*

EXERCISE 1

Identifying Words in Context

Directions: As you read each sentence that follows, pay special attention to the underlined clues to help you define the word in **boldface type.** Then choose the correct definition of the word from the choices that follow.

1. Many characters in Charles Dickens's novels are **waifs.** <u>Abandoned by their parents,</u> they <u>beg for food</u> and <u>try to find shelter</u> wherever they can.

   Waif means

   (1) a homeless child
   (2) parents
   (3) a house
   (4) a beggar
   (5) a good meal

2. His **anguish** <u>over her death</u> lasted for months. Whenever he spoke of her, <u>tears welled up in his eyes</u>.

   Anguish means

   (1) happiness
   (2) beauty
   (3) pain
   (4) laughter
   (5) embarrassment

3. The doctor gave her <u>medicine</u> to **allay** <u>the pain</u>, and she <u>rested quietly</u>.

   Allay means

   (1) to increase
   (2) to relieve
   (3) to repeat
   (4) to sleep
   (5) to encourage

4. The thief had **eluded** the police by <u>hiding in the graveyard. The police could not find him.</u>

   Eluded means

   (1) been captured by
   (2) tortured by
   (3) escaped from
   (4) been arrested by
   (5) embraced by

5. <u>The king</u> had **reigned** over his peaceful little <u>kingdom</u> for twenty-five years.

    Reigned means

    (1) ruled
    (2) laughed
    (3) fought
    (4) died
    (5) lived

6. The **proprietor** of the floral <u>shop</u> told us he had <u>bought the business</u> twenty years ago.

    Proprietor means

    (1) customer
    (2) agent
    (3) worker
    (4) owner
    (5) visitor

7. Since the **polls** will be open until 7:00, I plan to <u>vote</u> on my way home from work.

    Polls means places to

    (1) sleep
    (2) talk
    (3) vote
    (4) eat
    (5) work

Answers are on page 330.

Examples Given in Context

Sometimes authors give examples that help you understand a word that is new to you. Take a look at the following sentence. Notice the examples that are underlined, and decide if they help you understand the word in **boldface type.**

> Any **tragedy,** such as <u>the death of a loved one or loss of a job,</u> can cause stress.

Although the preceding sentence doesn't actually define the word *tragedy,* the examples "the death of a loved one" and "loss of a job" give us some clues. A *tragedy* is a sad event.

Notice that the examples were introduced by the phrase *such as.* In other sentences, examples may simply be part of the sentence.

EXERCISE 2

Using Examples Given in Context

Directions: Read each of the following sentences. Look for examples that help explain the word in **boldface type.** Then circle the best definition from the choices given.

1. While in China, I was unable to read any of the **placards,** such as the railway posters, store signs, and billboards.

   Placards means

   (1) speeches
   (2) menus
   (3) newspapers
   (4) written public announcements
   (5) cartoons

2. **Bibliographies** are often placed at the end of a chapter or book to list other books in which you may find more information.

   Bibliographies are lists of

   (1) books
   (2) chapters
   (3) words
   (4) authors
   (5) mistakes

3. **Suffixes** such as *-ing, -ed, -ful,* and *-less* may cause spelling changes when added to words.

   Suffixes means

   (1) meanings of words
   (2) definitions of words
   (3) endings of words
   (4) beginnings of words
   (5) spelling of words

Answers are on page 330.

Definitions Given in Context

Sometimes authors come right out and give you the definition of a word in a sentence. For example, read the following sentence.

> **Meteorologists,** *people who study weather and weather patterns,* still have difficulty predicting the weather.

The words in *italics* actually define the term *meteorologist.*

In the previous example, the definition was set off from the rest of the sentence by commas. Sometimes the definition of a word will be preceded by the word *or,* as in the following sentence.

> **Acrophobia,** *or fear of heights,* can make life difficult for tightrope walkers who suffer from it.

EXERCISE 3

Using Definitions Given in Context

Directions: Read each sentence. Look for extra information that will help you determine what the word in **boldface type** means. Then circle the correct definition.

1. **Venison,** or deer meat, must be cooked carefully.

   (1) beef
   (2) deer
   (3) pork
   (4) lamb
   (5) fish

2. Pioneer women sometimes used a **cistern,** or tank, to catch rainwater in order to get soft water for washing.

   (1) basement for storing food
   (2) room for cooking
   (3) tank for storing milk
   (4) tank for catching rainwater
   (5) room for doing laundry

3. Tran Nguyen **emigrated** from Vietnam to the United States with his parents in 1980. It must be difficult to leave the land of your birth and settle in a new country.

   (1) moved to a new country to live
   (2) was a tourist on vacation
   (3) took a business trip
   (4) learned a new language
   (5) landed a new job

4. He had thought that brightly colored birds would be **conspicuous,** but he could not see even one amid the thick leaves of the jungle.

   (1) in a cage
   (2) very noisy
   (3) easy to see
   (4) hard to see
   (5) very pretty

5. The comedy was **hilarious.** The audience laughed loudly all through the show.

   (1) very sad
   (2) very short
   (3) very long
   (4) very funny
   (5) very scary

6. She was so **infuriated** with the salesperson who pressured her that she almost hit him.

   (1) in love
   (2) angry
   (3) happy
   (4) tough
   (5) sick

7. When the star of the soap opera was killed in a car crash, the show had to be **revised,** or rewritten, to kill the character he had played.

   (1) changed
   (2) killed
   (3) crashed
   (4) left the same
   (5) cancelled

Answers are on page 330.

Understanding Connotations

We understand words on two different levels of meaning. The first level is what the dictionary tells us a word means. We call this meaning the word's **denotation.** The second level has to do with the positive or negative feelings the word brings out in us. We call this meaning the word's **connotation.**

Words that have the same denotations can have very different connotations. When these words are used in a sentence, they give the sentence itself a connotation.

For example, read these two sentences:

Mrs. Benitez was a disciplined and fair supervisor.

Mrs. Benitez was a rigid and self-righteous boss.

Although the literal meaning (the denotation) of both sentences is similar, the connotations are quite different. The first sentence has a positive connotation because *disciplined* and *fair* are complimentary. The second sentence has a negative connotation because *rigid* and *self-righteous* are negative.

Compare the two sentences that follow. As you read them, think about what connotation, or feeling, is contained within each sentence.

She was a vision!

She was a sight!

If you were the person being described, which would you prefer to be called: a vision or a sight? You probably would rather be called a vision because the word *vision* brings out positive feelings, while the word *sight* brings out negative feelings.

Read the sentences below. Write a plus (+) next to the statement with a positive connotation, and write a minus (–) next to the statement with a negative connotation.

———— 1. Sarah has a full figure.

———— 2. Sarah is fat.

———— 3. Tom is thin.

———— 4. Tom is anorexic.

The words *full figure* in sentence 1 create a more positive image than *fat* in sentence 2. Likewise, the word *thin* in sentence 3 is more flattering than *anorexic* in sentence 4. Of course, some words are neutral; they have neither a positive nor negative connotation. For example, if someone says, "Please sit on the couch," the word *couch* is neither positive nor negative. It simply means "a piece of furniture for sitting or reclining."

EXERCISE 4

Understanding Connotations of Words and Sentences

Part 1 **Directions:** Based on their connotations, sort the following pairs of words. Put the negative word from each pair into the negative connotations box (–), and put the positive word in each pair into the positive connotations box (+). The first one is done as an example.

Pairs of Words

1. old, mature

2. jocks, athletes

3. unusual, weird

4. mob, crowd

5. firm, stubborn

6. pushy, assertive

+	–
mature	*old*

Part 2 **Directions:** Read each of the following pairs of sentences. Based on the connotations of the words in each pair, decide which sentence is positive and which sentence is negative. Mark the positive sentences with a (+) and the negative sentences with a (−).

7. _____ **a.** Mr. Jones, a famous statesman, spoke with strong conviction.

   _____ **b.** Mr. Jones, a notorious politician, proclaimed his opinions.

8. _____ **a.** My stingy aunt boasted about hoarding money.

   _____ **b.** My thrifty aunt took pride in saving money.

9. _____ **a.** I began this job with a lousy salary.

   _____ **b.** I started this position with modest wages.

Answers are on page 330.

Euphemisms

Connotations of words and sentences can cause you to feel certain emotions. Writers often deliberately use words to bring out these feelings in people. For example, connotations play an important part in euphemisms and advertising.

Euphemisms are words or phrases that are used to soften a negative event or make something sound better or less objectionable. For example, when someone dies, people often use the euphemism *passed away*. These words seem less harsh than the words *dying* and *death*.

EXERCISE 5

Translating Euphemisms

Directions: Match the euphemism in the left column to its meaning in the right column. Then write the correct letter in the space provided.

Euphemism

_____ **1.** preowned

_____ **2.** powder room

_____ **3.** garden apartment

_____ **4.** casualty

_____ **5.** sanitation engineer

_____ **6.** final resting place

_____ **7.** landfill

Meaning

a. bathroom

b. grave

c. basement apartment

d. garbage dump

e. garbage collector

f. used

g. dead person

Answers are on page 330.

Key Words in Sentences

A long sentence can be confusing, but knowing how to find the **key words** in a sentence can help you understand it better. Key words give you the basic information in a sentence. Any other words used in the sentence simply add details. To find the key words in a sentence, ask yourself, "Who (or what) did what?"

Read this short sentence:

Sentence 1: The woman walked.

Key words: The woman   walked
                 Who?   *did what?*

Now read a longer sentence:

Sentence 2: The beautiful, dark-haired woman in a red dress walked quickly around the corner and out of sight.

Key words: The woman   walked
                 Who?   *did what?*

The key words in Sentences 1 and 2 are the same. The rest of the words in Sentence 2 give you more information about the woman and her walking. However, the basic information is still "The woman walked."

Now read another sentence:

Sentence 3: The plane hit an air pocket.

Key words: The plane   hit an air pocket
                 Who or what?   *did what?*

Sentence 4: Just as the senior flight attendant began serving lunch to the passenger in seat 3–A, the plane hit an air pocket, splattering the first-class passenger with ham and potato salad.

Key words: The plane   hit an air pocket
                 Who or what?   *did what?*

Again, the key words in Sentences 3 and 4 are the same.

EXERCISE 6

Key Words in Sentences

Directions: Read the following sentences. Then answer the questions by filling in the blanks.

1. French painter Paul Gauguin, unhappy in Europe, left his family in Copenhagen to return to the South Seas, where he painted scenes of Tahiti in brilliant color.

   Who or what? _____

   Did what? _____

2. Harriet Tubman, a famous black woman, rescued thousands from slavery during the American Civil War by personally leading them north through the Underground Railroad.

   Who or what? _____

   Did what? _____

3. At a news conference today from the Oval Office, the president voiced his disappointment over recent events in the Middle East.

   Who or what? _____

   Did what? _____

Answers are on page 330.

Main Idea and Supporting Details

Key words—*who, what, when, where, how,* and *why*—help you form knowledge questions. These questions help you build details that relate to the main idea.

When reporters write stories for newspapers, they usually include the main idea in the headline. They also give information on *who* or *what* the article is about, *what* happened, *when* it happened, *where* it happened, *how* it happened, and sometimes *why* it happened. Sometimes you can learn all of this information simply by reading the first paragraph of a newspaper article.

Look at the following diagram to see how these details relate to the main idea.

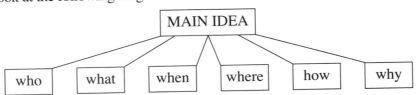

The main idea is in the top box. The boxes connected to the **main idea** contain the questions that help you identify **details** in an article. When you read, ask yourself these questions to find the most important details related to the main idea.

EXERCISE 7

Finding Main Idea in Newspaper Articles

Directions: Read the following newspaper article. Then answer the
questions. Remember that the main idea is often the headline.
Details often answer such questions as *who? what? when?*
where? how? and *why?*

New Government Agency Combines Security Efforts

In Washington, D. C. today, President George W. Bush gave
notice of a new plan for national security. The plan would put several
areas under the Department of Homeland Security. The plan would
combine border security, airline security, intelligence, and other areas.
The plan would not include the Federal Bureau of Investigation (FBI)
and the Central Intelligence Agency (CIA). Congress would have to
approve the plan by law.

—Adapted from "Bush Security Plan Requires New Powers," *Miami Herald*

1. What is the main idea of the entire article?

    (1) Homeland terror is a huge problem.
    (2) The FBI and the CIA are not part of security.
    (3) Any plan President Bush favors will work.
    (4) The Department of Homeland Security will prevent attacks.
    (5) A new plan for national security combines protection areas.

Directions: Match the details from the article in the right column with the
detail questions in the left column. Write the letter of the correct
detail next to the question it answers.

Detail Questions	**Details**
_____ **2.** Who made the announcement?	**a.** today
_____ **3.** Where was it announced?	**b.** new security plan
_____ **4.** When was it announced?	**c.** Congress
_____ **5.** What was the announcement about?	**d.** FBI and CIA
_____ **6.** What will the new agency be called?	**e.** President George W. Bush
_____ **7.** What will the agency oversee?	**f.** by law
_____ **8.** What will the plan **not** include?	**g.** Department of Homeland Security
_____ **9.** Who would have to approve?	**h.** border and airline security, intelligence, and other areas
_____ **10.** How would the plan become official?	**i.** Washington, D.C.

Answers are on page 330.

Supporting Main Idea with Details

If a friend asks about a video you've seen, you probably respond with a short statement describing what the movie is about. Such a statement gives the main idea of the movie. For example, say you've just watched the video, *Raiders of the Lost Ark*. When your friend, who has not seen it, asks you what it is about, you say, "It's about the adventures of an American archaeology professor in search of the Ark of the Covenant. It took place in the 1930s before the United States entered World War II." When you say this, you state the movie's main idea.

Just as with movies, most of what you read also has a main idea. The main idea is often stated in the title and sometimes in the first sentence of a paragraph or a passage. The main idea is supported by specific ideas, or details. These details relate to the main idea in some way.

Look at the diagram below to better understand how the main idea and details are related.

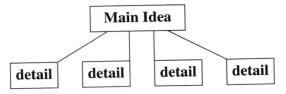

How does this diagram apply to a newspaper want ad? Read the ad that follows to see if you can identify the main idea and details.

> **Housekeeper Wanted**
> Must have own transportation.
> Be willing to work 10 hours per week.
> Be willing to take care of 4-year-old boy.
> Salary $15.00 per hour.
> Call 307-555-2345.

If we were to make the main idea and related details into a diagram, it would look something like this:

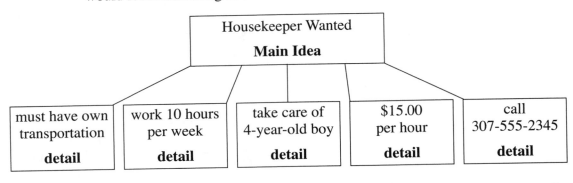

As you can see from the lines connecting each detail to the main idea, all the details are related to the idea of "housekeeper wanted." Each detail gives more specific information about the requirements of the job of housekeeper.

EXERCISE 8

Finding Main Idea in Advertisements

Directions: Read the following ad and fill in the chart that follows. First, write the main idea in the top box. Then write the details in each of the other boxes.

> ## GRAND OPENING
>
> ## PARK PLACE TOWNHOUSES
>
> **Near great schools, transportation, restaurants, and shopping mall**
>
> | | |
> |---|---|
> | **2–3 Bedrooms** | **1½ to 2½ Baths** |
> | **Air conditioning** | **Walk-in closets** |
>
> **Preconstruction Prices: $150,000 – $200,000**

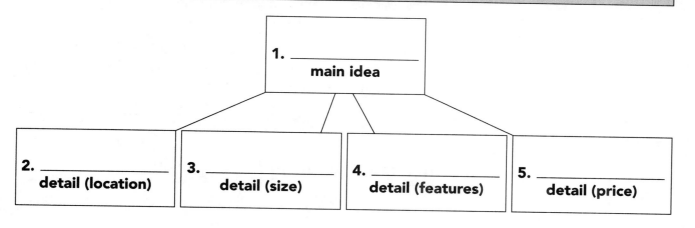

1. _____
   main idea

2. _____
   detail (location)

3. _____
   detail (size)

4. _____
   detail (features)

5. _____
   detail (price)

6. Circle the number of the statement that best explains a likely increase in price for these townhomes.

   (1) The townhouses are in a convenient location.
   (2) Like the game of Monopoly, Park Place is expensive.
   (3) Prices are labeled "Preconstruction."
   (4) Units include appliances and air conditioning.
   (5) Townhomes are near transportation.

Answers are on page 330.

Main Idea and Details in a Paragraph

The main idea in a paragraph is what the whole paragraph is about. Often, but not always, the first sentence states the main idea. The sentences that follow give details about the main idea.

As you read the following paragraph, try to locate the **main idea** sentence. Then try to identify the **supporting details**.

How Do We Prolong Life?

Your attitude about growing old is the key to a longer life, according to a new study at Yale University. Having more positive attitudes toward aging can extend a person's life by an average of 7.5 years. This is even more years than you would gain from keeping yourself in good condition. Both low blood pressure and low cholesterol are associated with a longer life span of about four years. Maintaining a healthy weight, not smoking, and exercising regularly each extend life by one to three years.

—Adapted from "Upbeat Attitude Prolongs Life, Study Says," *Chicago Sun-Times*

The main idea sentence is, "Your attitude about growing old is the key to a longer life." The other sentences are details that support the main idea.

EXERCISE 9

Main Idea and Details in a Paragraph

Directions: Read the following memo and answer the questions that follow.

Memo: Harassment Policy

Our company is committed to providing you with a work environment that is free from physical, mental, or verbal harassment. Any behavior that creates a hostile, intimidating, or offensive work environment is labeled harassment. This includes

- physical or verbal abuse
- off-color or insulting jokes
- racial, ethnic, or religious slurs
- unwelcome physical contact or sexual advances
- unfounded complaints against another employee
- unfair benefits given one employee as a result of sexual favors

It is your responsibility to be sure these activities do not take place. If you feel you are being harassed, contact Human Resources to have the problem investigated and resolved.

---

1. What is the main idea of the paragraph?

   (1) Insults are verbal harassment.
   (2) Our company wants to provide a work environment free of harassment.
   (3) Human Resources will investigate and resolve harassment charges.
   (4) Unwelcome sexual advances will not be tolerated.
   (5) Your supervisor will not harass you.

2. List four examples of harassment given in the paragraph.

   _____

   _____

   _____

   _____

Answers are on page 330.

Unstated Main Idea

In what you've read so far, the main idea has been stated directly. Sometimes, however, the main idea is not stated directly. In this case, you need to look at the details to find out how they all relate. Ask yourself the question, "What is this article mainly about?"

EXERCISE 10

Unstated Main Idea

Directions: Read the following paragraph about losing valuable papers on a train trip. Then answer the questions that follow.

I took my son to the men's room and set the briefcase down while we peed and washed our hands, and then we went to the cafeteria for breakfast. A few bites into the scrambled eggs I remembered the briefcase, went to get it and it was gone. We had an hour before the southbound arrived. We spent it looking in every trash basket in the station, outside the station, and for several blocks around. I was sure that the thief, finding nothing but manuscripts in the briefcase, would chuck it, and I kept telling him to, but he didn't chuck it where I could see it, and then our time was up and we climbed on the train. I felt so bad I didn't want to look out the window. I looked straight at the wall of our compartment, and as we rode south the two lost stories seemed funnier and funnier to me, the best work I had ever done in my life; I wept for them, and my misery somehow erased them from my mind so that when I got out a pad of paper a couple hundred miles later, I couldn't re-create even a faint outline.

—Excerpted from *Lake Wobegon Days* by Garrison Keillor

1. What would be a good title (statement of main idea) for this paragraph?

   (1) An Author and His Son Travel South
   (2) An Author Cries for the First Time
   (3) An Author Loses His Manuscripts
   (4) An Author Eats Scrambled Eggs
   (5) An Author Catches a Thief

Directions: Match the details in the right column with the detail questions in the left column. Write the letter of the detail next to the question it answers.

Detail Questions	**Details**
_____ 2. Who lost the stories?	**a.** two short stories
_____ 3. What happened?	**b.** in the men's room of a railroad station
_____ 4. Where did he leave the briefcase?	**c.** before breakfast
_____ 5. What was lost?	**d.** Garrison Keillor lost his briefcase.
_____ 6. When did he lose them?	**e.** the author, Garrison Keillor

Answers are on page 330.

Main Idea in a Passage

Passages are made up of a number of paragraphs. Each paragraph has a main idea supported by details. The passage also has a main idea which sums up the topic of the entire passage.

EXERCISE 11

Finding the Main Idea of a Passage

Directions: Read the following passage. Identify the main idea of each paragraph. Then identify the main idea of the passage.

DNA TESTS IDENTIFY CRIMINALS

(A)

DNA testing is setting a new standard for courtroom evidence. DNA structure was identified in 1953 but not used in court until 1986. DNA (deoxyribonucleic acid) is based on the molecular basis of heredity. (Heredity is the sum of all the genetic qualities a person inherits from his or her ancestors—parents and others.)

(B)

The DNA bar code is a powerful tool to solve crimes. The DNA "fingerprint" can come from the smallest sample of hair, blood, saliva, or other bodily fluids. If a DNA match is found between the DNA of a suspect and DNA at a crime scene, the suspect is likely guilty. If no match is found, the suspect can be cleared. DNA evidence also can allow some people to be set free from prison.

(C)

Most (99.9 percent) of the DNA of any two people will look alike. The key to reading the DNA genetic code is the small differences. A biologist at a university found "hiccups" in the chemical code sequence. Special patterns showed up and repeated between 50 and 10,000 times. It all depends on the person.

(D)

In the late 1990s, laboratories began to use a new method of analysis (study). It is called STR (short tandem repeats) and cuts time for analysis. Now answers can be found in just days instead of weeks.

(E)

In the past, lawyers for the defense could argue that there was a chance for error (one in 100,000). Now with the STR method, the same chance for error is much smaller (one in trillions or a quadrillion). Now crimes can be solved more quickly and with more certainty.

—Adapted from "DNA Tests Set New Standard of Criminal Identification,"
The Miami Herald

1. Write the main idea of each paragraph.

   (A) _____

   (B) _____

   (C) _____

   (D) _____

   (E) _____

2. What is the main idea of this entire passage?

   (1) Scientists and defense lawyers always disagree.
   (2) Most people in the world have the same DNA.
   (3) DNA tests set new standards for courtroom evidence.
   (4) Analysis of DNA samples now takes just days.
   (5) DNA genetic bar codes and fingerprints are alike.

Answers are on page 331.

EXERCISE 12

More Main Ideas of Passages

Directions: The following passages are part of a longer article explaining ways to save money. As you read the passages, locate the main idea of each one. Then answer the questions that follow.

Want Full Protection? Buy the Service Contract.

If you've bought a major appliance lately, chances are the salesperson tried hard to sell you a service contract, or extended warranty. Next time, before you cough up the extra cash, consider this: With most appliances, particularly electronics, defects are almost sure to show up before the original warranty expires. After that, the service contract may cost more than any needed repairs.

So why do salespeople push contracts so aggressively? Because they're very profitable. Retailers have extensive data to help them predict the average failure rate of appliances. They use that information to price service contracts to yield a handsome profit above the projected repair cost. Next time, don't fall for the pitch.

Return This Warranty Card or Else.

Remember the card that came with your last major purchase? Did you think you would lose your warranty coverage if you failed to fill out and return it? That's what manufacturers hope you'll think. In fact, you're covered whether you return the card or not.

The real reason manufacturers use these forms is to gather marketing data: your age, income bracket, how you heard about the product, where you shop. Keep in mind, though, that manufacturers need your name and address to contact you in the event of a recall. That's why I usually return these cards, but with only my name, address and the model and serial number of the product.

—Excerpted from "7 Money Rules to Break," *Reader's Digest*

1. What is the main idea of "Want Full Protection? Buy the Service Contract."?

    (1) Defects in major appliances usually show up during the warranty period.
    (2) Electronic appliances have more defects than other types.
    (3) Retailers know average failure rates of all appliances.
    (4) Retailers make profits above projected repair costs.
    (5) Service contracts for major appliances are not usually necessary.

2. What is the main idea of "Return This Warranty Card or Else."?

    (1) Warranty cards are required to be filled out.
    (2) Warranty coverage is not valid without the cards.
    (3) Manufacturers gather marketing data from warranty cards.
    (4) Manufacturers must contact you to recall products.
    (5) Warranty cards must be filled out completely.

Answers are on page 331.

Summarizing

You have learned to find the main idea and the details in both paragraphs and passages. Now you are ready to learn to summarize. To **summarize** means to include only the main idea and the important details.

Read the following example of summarizing in everyday life. Suppose a friend is telling you about a wedding she attended. She might summarize the event this way.

> The bride wore a long white gown with lace, and her bridesmaids were dressed in pale yellow. The groom and ushers wore pale gray suits with yellow ties. The bridesmaids' white and yellow bouquets matched their dresses. Afterward at the reception, there was champagne and cake for everyone. The bride and groom danced the first dance. Then everyone, young and old, danced too. When the bride and groom left, the bride threw her bouquet to a group of us single women. Guess who caught it? I did!

Note that your friend tells you something about the colors worn by the wedding party, but she does not go into detail about who the bridesmaids and ushers were or what the minister said during the ceremony. Next, she briefly describes the reception and tells you that she caught the bouquet. Like all summaries, your friend's description includes only the information she considers to be important, not everything that took place that day.

How to Summarize

To summarize a passage, you need to find the main idea and the important details. Remember, in a summary you don't include every bit of information, only what is necessary to understand what's happening. To do this, ask yourself these questions:

Who/What?   Did what?   When?   Where?   How?   Why?

To learn how this works, read the following paragraph. As you read the paragraph, ask yourself the questions *who? did what? when? where? how?* and *why?*

> We all know that the nation's psyche [mind or soul] was badly battered on September 11, 2001. But how badly? And for how long? Among the findings published in the Journal of the American Medical Association: one to two months after the attacks, 11 percent of New Yorkers had symptoms of posttraumatic stress disorder—almost three times the national average. This 11 percent included not just disaster survivors, but also those who witnessed the events on TV.

—Excerpted from "How Are We Doing?" *Newsweek*

Now read the answers to the five questions you asked yourself.

Who?	11% of New Yorkers
Did what?	suffered posttraumatic stress disorder
When?	2 months after September 11, 2001
Where?	New York
How?	witnessed events in person or on TV
Why?	a reaction to disaster (an assumption)

You can now put these answers into one sentence that summarizes the entire paragraph.

The events of September 11, 2001, may have caused 11% of New Yorkers to suffer the effects of posttraumatic stress disorder.

Sometimes, as with the following paragraph, you will not be able to answer all the questions because some information is not provided. In other cases, the answers to the questions may be given in an order different from the one that appears here.

EXERCISE 13

Summarizing a Paragraph

Directions: As you read the following passages, ask yourself the questions *who? what? when? where? how?* and *why?* Then answer the questions that follow.

Passage 1

The old lady knelt in the soft, spring earth. She was planting flowers in her garden. Her wrinkled hands dug the hole for each plant. Carefully, she placed a purple petunia in the first hole and then patted the dirt back to fill in the empty space. Then she dug the next hole.

"A red one here, I think," she said to herself.

Soon all the plants were in place. Gently she gave each one water.

"There!" she said, talking to herself again. "Even if the doc says I won't live to see it, there'll be a mass of bright color here in a few months. At least I can leave something pretty behind for other folks to enjoy."

1. On the lines that follow, write the words from the paragraph that answer each question.

   a. Who? _____

   b. What? _____

   c. When? _____

   d. Where? _____

   e. How? _____

   f. Why? _____

2. Now write your answers from question 1 as a summary statement.

_____

_____

3. Based on the information in the paragraph, choose the answer that best completes this sentence.

The old lady believes that she

(1) is too sick to do gardening
(2) needs approval from her doctor
(3) should be paid to do gardening
(4) is going to die in the next few months
(5) will enjoy the flowers next spring

Passage 2

Recently, some toy manufacturers have asked children to try out newly designed toys. One company has a special room in its factory where children may come to play for a six-week period. Toy designers then watch the children as they play. The designers want to know which toys appeal most to children, which toys are played with most often, and which toys hold up the best. They are also concerned about the safety of each toy. By watching children play, toy designers can predict which toys will be good sellers for their company.

4. a. Who? _____

   b. What? _____

   c. When? _____

   d. Where? _____

   e. How? _____

   f. Why? _____

5. Combine the information in question 4 to write one or two sentences that summarize the article.

_____

_____

_____

_____

Answers are on page 331.

Chapter Review

In order to understand what you read, you have looked at parts of comprehension. You have studied words in context, connotations, euphemisms, main ideas, supporting details, and summarizing. Context clues have included words, examples, and definitions. Main ideas have been both stated and unstated. Summarizing has been practiced in answering questions of *who, what, when, where, how,* and *why.*

EXERCISE 14

Directions: Read the following passage. As you read, look for the context clues, main idea, and supporting details. You will use these to answer questions and write a summary. The paragraphs are numbered.

(1)   "Why did you keep me from taking that place next to the window?"

(2)   Marc Seguy never considered lying. "Because you were about to sit next to someone I know."

(3)   "Someone I don't know?"

(4)   "My ex-wife."

(5)   She couldn't think of anything to say and opened her eyes wider.

(6)   "So what, darling? It'll happen again. It's not important."

(7)   The words came back to Alice and she asked, in order, the inevitable [unavoidable] questions. "Did she see you? Could she see that you saw her? Will you point her out to me?"

(8)   "Don't look now, please, she must be watching us. . . . The lady with brown hair, no hat, she must be staying in this hotel. By herself, behind those children in red."

(9)   "Yes, I see."

(10)   Hidden behind some broad-brimmed beach hats, Alice was able to look at the woman who, fifteen months ago, had still been her husband's wife.

(11)   "Incompatibility," Marc said. "Oh, I mean total incompatibility! We divorced like well-bred people, almost like friends, quietly, quickly. And then I fell in love with you, and you really wanted to be happy with me. How lucky we are that our happiness doesn't involve any guilty parties or victims!"

(12)   The woman in white, whose smooth, lustrous hair reflected the light from the sea in azure patches, was smoking a cigarette with her eyes half closed. Alice turned back toward her husband, took some shrimp and butter, and ate calmly. After a moment's silence she asked: "Why didn't you ever tell me that she had blue eyes, too?"

(13)   He kissed the hand she was extending toward the bread basket and she blushed with pleasure. Dusky and ample, she might have seemed coarse, but the changeable blue of her eyes and her wavy, golden hair made her look like a frail and sentimental blonde. She vowed overwhelming gratitude to her husband. Immodest with knowing it, everything about her bore the overly conspicuous [obvious] marks of extreme happiness.

(14)   They ate and drank heartily, and each thought the other had forgotten the woman in white. Now and then, however, Alice laughed too loudly, and Marc was careful about his posture, holding his shoulders back, his head up. They waited quite a long time for their coffee, in silence. An incandescent river, the straggled reflection of the invisible sun overhead, shifted slowly across the sea and shone with blinding brilliance.

(15)   "She's still there, you know," Alice whispered.

(16)   "Is she making you uncomfortable? Would you like to have coffee somewhere else?"

(17)   "No, not at all! She's the one who must be uncomfortable! Besides, she doesn't exactly seem to be having a wild time, if you could see her. . . ."

(18)   "I don't have to. I know that look of hers."

—Excerpted from "The Other Wife" by Collette

1. Using the context clues in paragraph 11, *well-bred people* must mean

   (1) people with controlled emotions
   (2) people who were in love
   (3) people who fought over everything
   (4) people who didn't know each other

2. Using the context clues in paragraph 12, *lustrous hair* must mean

   (1) short hair
   (2) curly hair
   (3) shiny hair
   (4) white hair

3. On the lines that follow, write words from the passage to answer each question.

   a. Who? _____

   b. What? _____

   c. Where? _____

   d. When? _____

   e. How? _____

4. Using your answers from the question above, write a summary of the passage.

_____

_____

_____

_____

_____

5. During lunch, Alice laughs "too loudly" and Marc "was careful about his posture." They wait "quite a long time for their coffee, in silence." If you synthesize, or combine, these details, how do you think the characters are feeling?

   (1) angry and bitter
   (2) happy and eager
   (3) lucky and grateful
   (4) incompatible and desperate
   (5) uncomfortable and annoyed

Answers are on page 331.

CHAPTER 3

Finding Hidden Meaning

In Chapter 2 you learned how to identify main ideas. The reading selections directly stated the main ideas and backed them up with supporting details. Sometimes, however, the writer only suggests or hints at the main idea, rather than stating it directly. To uncover an idea that is hidden, you must look for details that are stated directly and use them as clues. A good reader uses details in a passage to figure out the author's suggested message.

In this chapter, you will learn several skills that can help you uncover those hidden meanings and ideas. You will read about making inferences and predicting. You will also review study skills related to charts, outlines, and following directions.

Making Inferences

Making an inference is the process of using information stated directly to figure out an unstated or suggested message. You might think of the process of inference as similar to putting together a jigsaw puzzle. You assemble individual puzzle pieces to form a completed picture. Likewise, when you make an inference, you assemble clues to form an idea that's not directly stated.

You may not realize it, but you use inference in situations every day. For example, suppose you drop by a friend's house. He is usually happy, cheerful, and joking. Today, however, he greets you with a serious face; his voice is grim. You know from previous conversations that he has been worried about his mother's health. You also know the doctor was supposed to call him regarding some medical tests.

What can you infer from your friend's mood? You would probably infer that your friend is upset because the doctor's call brought bad news about his mother's health.

These are the clues, or direct information, that would help you make this inference:

- Your friend is usually happy; today he is serious.
- Your friend has been worried about his mother's health.
- The doctor was to call about the results of some tests.

Here's another example of using inference in everyday situations. Suppose you are driving south on a highway when the southbound traffic suddenly stops. Within a few minutes, you hear the wail of a siren. In your rearview mirror you see an ambulance, with its lights flashing, coming up behind you on the shoulder. It passes you as you wait in line. The ambulance is followed closely by a police car.

What *two* inferences might you draw from these events?

(1) The police are going to pull your car over.
(2) There has been an accident on the road ahead of you.
(3) The police car is following the ambulance too closely.
(4) The police or an ambulance may use the shoulder of the road in an emergency.
(5) Anyone may drive on the shoulder when the traffic is stopped.

You should have picked (2) and (4). These clues support inferences (2) and (4):

- Traffic suddenly stops.
- The ambulance is followed by a police car.
- The police car has its siren and flashing lights on.
- Both the police car and the ambulance are driving on the shoulder of the highway.

From these clues, you can infer that the police car and the ambulance are driving on the shoulder to reach the scene of an accident ahead.

Inference in a Cartoon

You also use inference to understand a cartoon or comic strip. There are three pieces of information you need to find in order to understand a cartoon.

- **Characters**—To fully understand a cartoon, you need to identify the characters. The characters could be famous people or people you see in your life everyday. Once you know who is represented in the cartoon, you will be able to figure out where the cartoon takes place: an office, at home, in the park.

- **Topic**—The topic of a cartoon answers the question, "What is this cartoon about?" The characters will help you figure this out. Cartoons can be about any topic. Political cartoons are often about the government or politics, while cartoons that appear in the comic section of the newspaper are usually about everyday life.

- **Opinion**—The artists of cartoons want you to learn, or understand, something about the topic. They are sending you a message through their drawing. Political cartoons either support or argue against a given topic. Comics tend to provide insight or humor about our daily lives.

Be sure to examine all the details of a cartoon and try to figure out the characters and topic represented in the cartoon. Then use those details as clues to uncover the opinion, or message, suggested by the cartoonist.

EXERCISE 1

Using Inference in a Cartoon

Directions: Look at the following cartoon and the caption beneath it. Notice the details, and think about what you might infer from them. Then answer the questions that follow.

"Go Ahead: Make Us Laugh," *Reader's Digest*

1. Which statements are clues shown directly by the cartoon? You may choose more than one.

(1) A man works in a company that requires wearing a tie.
(2) The company has a suggestion box on the wall.
(3) There is a camera above the suggestion box.
(4) The man is about to put a piece of paper in the box.
(5) The man has left the office around the corner.

2. Which of the following statements can you infer from the cartoon? You may choose more than one.

(1) The man is very unhappy with his job.
(2) Putting ideas in the suggestion box is not private.
(3) The man can run his department better than his boss.
(4) The air conditioning in the company needs repair.
(5) The company does not seem to trust its employees.

3. Based on the expression of the man in the cartoon, he is probably feeling that he should

(1) not place his ideas in the suggestion box
(2) learn more about videotaping technology
(3) come back when the office is closed
(4) use the spell-check feature on his computer
(5) get a shave and a haircut to be on camera

Answers are on page 332.

Using Details to Make an Inference

As you have learned, the clues that you've been using to make inferences are specific details that are stated directly. Read the following paragraph. Notice that the clues, or details, are in **boldface type.** You can use the clues to make an inference about the paragraph.

On Tuesday morning, Warren turned on the radio, hoping the **weather forecast** would be different from what it had been for the past six days. The announcer said **not to expect** any **cool breezes** or sunshine, so Warren grabbed a **raincoat** as he left the house. On the way to work, Warren turned on his **windshield wipers** and **headlights** and got his **umbrella** from the back seat. Everyone at work looked and felt as **damp** and **gloomy** as the weather, so as a surprise Warren arranged to have pizza delivered to the office for lunch.

What kind of day does the paragraph describe?

(1) windy
(2) sunny
(3) rainy
(4) cloudy
(5) dry

Based on the clues, you should have picked (3) rainy.

EXERCISE 2

Using Details to Make an Inference

Directions: Read the following passage. Then answer the questions that follow.

When this woman got closer to me, she looked at me hard and then she threw up her hands. She must have seen me somewhere before because she said, "It's you. And just what have you been doing lately?"

I could have said, "I have been praying not to grow any taller."

I could have said, "I have been listening carefully to my mother's words, so as to make a good imitation of a dutiful daughter."

I could have said, "A pack of dogs, tired from chasing each other all over town, slept in the moonlight."

Instead, I said, "What I have been doing lately: I was lying in bed on my back, my hands drawn up, my fingers interlaced lightly at the nape of my neck. Someone rang the doorbell. I went downstairs and opened the door but there was no one there."

—Excerpted from "What I Have Been Doing Lately" by Jamaica Kincaid

1. You can infer that the narrator is

(1) a young girl
(2) the girl's mother
(3) the woman's friend
(4) an animal trainer
(5) a student at college

2. What clues did the author state directly that helped you infer what the narrator's state of mind might be? You may choose more than one.

The narrator

(1) is very frightened of the woman approaching her
(2) says, "she looked at me hard and then she threw up her hands"
(3) has "been praying not to grow any taller"
(4) thinks about how "to make a good imitation of a dutiful daughter"
(5) chases dogs in the moonlight

3. The woman says, "And just what have you been doing lately?" The narrator thinks of several ways to answer.

This shows that the narrator

(1) is used to telling lies
(2) has a great deal to hide
(3) is mentally disturbed
(4) has a learning disability
(5) has a great imagination

Answers are on page 332.

Inference in Advertising

So far, you have learned that words can have emotional meanings or connotations. Advertisers know this and use the connotations of words to try to convince you to buy their products. The following example illustrates this.

> An exciting approach to sweaters—high-fashioned V-neck with delicate rib trimming makes you a model of fashion!

The words *exciting, high-fashioned, delicate,* and *model of fashion* have positive connotations. Advertisers count on your desire to be "high-fashioned" and "exciting" and try to convince you that buying the sweater will make you so.

Here are some other examples of wording in advertising:

1. "Essential ingredients for natural beauty"
2. "Brand-name quality at the very least cost"
3. Home installation services: "reliable, qualified professionals"
4. "Richly decorated with colors to show your pride"
5. "Gear up now for ultimate savings"

These words all have positive connotations:

1. natural beauty
2. brand-name quality
3. reliable, qualified professionals
4. richly decorated; show your pride
5. ultimate savings

EXERCISE 3

Inferring Positive and Negative Connotations from Advertisements

Part 1   **Directions:** Read the following advertisements. Then circle the words in each ad that have positive connotations.

1. A can't-go-wrong classic in silky rayon makes for on-the-go high fashion.

2. Smooth, slinky, sensual. That's what he'll think about you when you wear our newest fragrance.

3. Cozy hideaway with three bedrooms and two baths. Modern kitchen with cupboards galore. A must-see!

4. Let our experienced master mechanics diagnose your car in our modern, computerized auto clinic.

Part 2   **Directions:** Read the following advertisement. Circle the words or phrases in the ad that have positive connotations. Then reread the ad and underline all the words or phrases that have negative connotations

---

WHAT HAVE YOU GOT TO LOSE (OR GAIN)?

Are you among the more than 61% of adults who are overweight or even obese? Have you tried everything? Every diet? Every exercise program? Does nothing work for you? Is two hours of your time worth getting rid of your excess weight? 10, 50, or even 100 pounds!

**TRY OUR INSTANT WEIGHT-LOSS HYPNOSIS SEMINAR
FOR TRIED AND TRUE RESULTS.
100% GUARANTEED OR YOUR MONEY BACK.**

How long have you been smoking? 10, 20, 30, 40, or even 50 years? Are you tired of being criticized by nonsmokers? Are you tired of being told to "Take it outside!" Are you worried about your health? Does a heart attack or lung cancer scare you? Maybe it's time to *really* quit. Is two hours of your time worth kicking the habit? Take back your body! For good, and once and for all!

**TRY OUR INSTANT SMOKE-ENDERS HYPNOSIS SEMINAR
FOR TRIED AND TRUE RESULTS.
100% GUARANTEED OR YOUR MONEY BACK.**

Answers are on page 332.

EXERCISE 4

Making Inferences in Advertising

Directions: In this exercise, you will identify directly stated information and make inferences about a product in an advertisement. Read the following ad. Then answer the questions that follow.

1. Which of the following statements can you infer from the ad? You may choose more than one.

   (1) You are patriotic if you buy these bread mixes.
   (2) This is the best bread mix ever.
   (3) These are homemade breads with flavor.
   (4) Your life will be made complete with bread.
   (5) This is the only bread mix on the market.

2. What does this ad want you to believe?

   (1) These breads are low-fat for those people on diets.
   (2) Bake-Quik manufacturers are better cooks than you.
   (3) These mixes are the greatest thing since sliced bread.
   (4) During baking, the bread butters itself.
   (5) Flavorful breads will make your meals exciting.

Answers are on page 332.

Inference in Nonfiction

As you've learned in the previous exercises, you can use clues that are stated directly to infer ideas that are only suggested or hinted at. You can also use this process when you read passages like the one that follows.

> In 1972 a Pioneer 10 rocket was fired into space on a scientific mission. Because it will eventually leave the solar system, it carried a plaque with it. The plaque shows pictures of a man and a woman and a picture of the position of Earth within our solar system. The plaque was designed so that any being not of our solar system might understand what humans look like and where they live in the universe.

You could infer ideas similar to these:

Clue or Detail	What You Can Infer
1. sending a rocket on a scientific mission	Scientists believe it is important to learn more about the universe.
2. sending a plaque into space	Some scientists believe there is life somewhere else in the universe.
3. sending a picture of a man woman into space	Other beings might not resemble humans.
4. sending a picture of Earth's place in the solar system	Other beings might be able to find Earth from the picture of the solar system.

EXERCISE 5

Inferring Ideas in Passages

Directions: Read the following passage. Look for clues that will help you make inferences. Then answer the questions that follow.

A War of Symbols

Winston Churchill was Prime Minister of England during World War II when England was attacked by Germany. In the early, terrible days of the war, bombings and lost battles depressed the English people and threatened to destroy their will to fight Hitler.

Churchill knew he needed a way to cheer up the people. He knew the hated Nazi symbol, the swastika, had originally symbolized good. So Churchill invented a symbol, a *V for Victory*, that he used whenever he appeared in public. To make the *V for Victory* sign, he held his hand up, palm out, with the first two fingers raised to form a *V*.

When English people saw it, they laughed, because if the hand had been reversed, palm in, it would have made a rude English gesture. Churchill was telling the people what he really thought of Hitler. The *V for Victory* gesture soon became known worldwide as a sign of hope.

1. You can infer that Churchill's fellow citizens saw the double meaning in his gesture because the article states that

   (1) English people laughed when they saw the reversed gesture
   (2) English people were depressed with bombings and lost battles
   (3) Churchill was Prime Minister of England
   (4) the swastika had originally been a symbol for good
   (5) Churchill invented the *V for Victory* symbol

2. You can infer that without a strong leader like Churchill, England might have lost the war to Germany because the passage states that

   (1) Churchill told the English people what he really thought of Hitler
   (2) the *V for Victory* sign became known as a symbol of hope
   (3) Churchill invented a symbol for power, death, and war
   (4) bombings and lost battles had depressed the people and threatened their will to fight
   (5) Churchill was Prime Minister during World War II

3. The author of this passage would most likely agree that good leaders

   (1) use rude gestures
   (2) leave the country
   (3) never joke about war
   (4) understand the needs of the people
   (5) don't use symbols

Answers are on page 332.

Inference in Literature

Inference is most often found in literature, or fictional works. Authors often suggest ideas about the characters and events they create. The reader must infer these suggested ideas because they are not stated directly.

The next exercise provides practice at making inferences about characters and events in a fictional work.

EXERCISE 6

Drawing Inferences in Fiction

Directions: Read the following story. Then answer the questions that follow.

Let's say a guy named Roger is attracted to a woman named Elaine. He asks her out to a movie; she accepts; they have a pretty good time. A few nights later he asks her out to dinner, and again they enjoy themselves. They continue to see each other regularly, and after a while neither one of them is seeing anybody else.

And then, one evening when they're driving home, a thought occurs to Elaine, and, without really thinking, she says it aloud: "Do you realize that, as of tonight, we've been seeing each other for exactly six months?"

And then there is silence in the car. To Elaine, it seems like a very loud silence. She thinks to herself: Geez, I wonder if it bothers him that I said that. Maybe he's been feeling confined by our relationship; maybe he thinks I'm trying to push him into some kind of obligation that he doesn't want, or isn't sure of.

And Roger is thinking: Gosh. *Six months.*

And Elaine is thinking: But, hey, *I'm* not so sure I want this kind of relationship, either. Sometimes I wish *I* had a little more space, so I'd have time to think about whether I really want us to keep going the way we are, moving steadily toward . . . I mean, where *are* we going? Are we going to keep seeing each other at this level of intimacy? Are we heading toward *marriage*? Toward *children*? Toward a *lifetime* together? Am I ready for that level of commitment? Do I really even *know* this person?

And Roger is thinking: . . . so that means it was . . . let's see . . . *February* when we started going out, which was right after I had the car at the dealer's which means . . . lemme check the odometer . . . *Whoa!* I am *way* due for an oil change here.

—Excerpted from "Tips for Women: How to Have a Relationship with a Guy," in *Dave Barry's Guide to Guys*

1. Which of the ideas are directly stated in the story? You may choose more than one.

    (1) Roger is attracted to Elaine and asks her out.
    (2) Neither Roger nor Elaine is seeing anyone else.
    (3) Roger and Elaine have dated for six months.
    (4) Roger is unhappy about continuing to see Elaine.
    (5) Elaine brings up the length of their relationship.

2. Which of the following statements can you infer from the story? You may choose more than one.

    (1) Elaine is desperate for a true relationship.
    (2) Elaine has mixed feelings about Roger.
    (3) Roger is not as serious as Elaine.
    (4) Neither Elaine nor Roger is ready for commitment.
    (5) Roger is very careful and organized.

3. What can you infer is the main idea of this story?

    (1) Women talk better with other women.
    (2) Men talk better with other men.
    (3) Men communicate differently than women.
    (4) Women push men into obligations.
    (5) Men easily understand how women think.

4. With which of the following statements would the author probably agree? You may choose more than one.

    (1) Men don't understand the meaning of "relationship."
    (2) Women are usually less attentive to details.
    (3) Men and women seem to be from different planets.
    (4) Men usually try harder to make things work.
    (5) Women are usually first to reject men.

Answers are on page 332.

Making Predictions

Another skill that will help you improve your reading is **predicting.** Predicting is making a guess about what will happen next. Predicting is a skill you already have. When you see someone plant flower seeds in the spring and then water, weed, and fertilize them, you can reasonably predict that soon you'll see flowers. Predicting is something you do when you watch a movie or a television drama. Predicting what will happen next makes watching it more exciting.

Predicting Words

When reading a passage, good readers can often predict what words will come next. This ability to predict allows them to read smoothly. Readers are able to predict because language often falls into familiar patterns and often repeats ideas.

You already have some skills for predicting words. How well can you predict the missing words in the next passage? First, read the paragraph. Then go back and fill in the missing words.

    I had lost my wallet. I didn't mind losing _____ money so much, but _____ hated the idea of _____ my driver's license and credit _____.

Read the following passage with the missing words filled in, and compare your answers to these:

    I had lost my wallet. I didn't mind losing **my** money so much, but **I** hated the idea of **losing** my license and credit **cards.**

(**Note:** There may be more than one correct answer for the above blanks.)

EXERCISE 7

Predicting Words

Directions: Read the following paragraph. Then reread it, and fill in the numbered blanks with words that fit.

It was Clayton's birthday. We had planned a **(1)** _____

party for Saturday because **(2)** _____ in the family had

(3) _____ day off. Since the **(4)** _____

was warm, we decided **(5)** _____ have a barbecue

outside. **(6)** _____ brought presents and

(7) _____ cards. The party ended

(8) _____ a big birthday cake and everyone sang

(9) "_____ Birthday to You."

Answers are on page 333.

Directly Stated Predictions

Sometimes authors tell you directly what is being predicted. Read the following passage and answer the question.

> John moved hesitantly through the half-open flap of the tent.
> "Have a seat!" The fortune-teller sat at a small velvet-covered table. She motioned toward a chair opposite her.
> "Cards? Palms? Crystal ball?"
> "Uh, palms, I guess." John fumbled in his pocket for the money. She took the money and bent over his outstretched palm.
> "I see long life . . . and many children. Ah . . . but you have been unlucky in love so far. . . . Is that so?"
> John nodded.
> "Not to worry." The fortune-teller smiled. "All things in their time. You were not ready for such a love as this. But now . . . is almost time." She tossed her head, smiled at him, and looked back at his palm.
> "Ah, money, I see much money. One who waits to love you will also bring good luck for money . . . OK! Thank you! Next?"
> "Is that all?"
> "Isn't it enough?" The fortune-teller led him toward the flap. "Not many have a lucky palm like yours."

What things did the fortune-teller predict for John?

(1) a long life
(2) many children
(3) a new car
(4) a new love
(5) a lot of money

Based on the predictions, you should have chosen (1), (2), (4), and (5).

EXERCISE 8

Identifying Directly Stated Predictions

Directions: As you read the following passage, look for predictions that are made. Then answer the questions that follow.

Geyser Hill

Old Faithful erupts more frequently than any of the other big geysers, although it is not the largest or most regular geyser in the park. Its average interval between eruptions is about 92 minutes, varying from 45–120 minutes. An eruption lasts 1–1½ to 5 minutes, expels 3,700–8,400 gallons (14,000–32,000 liters) of boiling water, and reaches a height of 106–184 feet (30–55 m). Members of the Washburn Expedition of 1870 named this geyser for its consistent [regular] performance. Although its average interval [space of time] has lengthened, Old Faithful is as spectacular as it was a century ago.

—Excerpted from "Old Faithful Trail Guide," National Park Service

1. Which of the following facts about Old Faithful are stated or predicted directly in the paragraph? You may choose more than one.

   Old Faithful

   (1) erupts more frequently than other big geysers
   (2) erupts on average every 92 minutes
   (3) is the most regular geyser in Yellowstone
   (4) will still erupt a million years from now
   (5) reaches a height of 106–184 feet

2. Which two of the following statements can be predicted based on the passage?

   Old Faithful will continue to

   (1) spout over 10,000 gallons of water
   (2) erupt in a consistent way
   (3) lengthen time between eruptions
   (4) be the largest geyser in the world
   (5) erupt once every three to four hours

Answers are on page 333.

EXERCISE 9

Predicting Ideas from a Cartoon

Directions: Read the following cartoon. Think about what Earl's wife, the cartoon character, is predicting will happen. Then answer the questions that follow.

"Pickles," ©2002, The Washington Post Writers Group. Reprinted with permission.

1. Which of the following statements are stated directly in the cartoon? You may choose more than one.

   (1) Earl and his wife have an argument.
   (2) Some dogs left alone feel stressed.
   (3) Some dogs dig, chew, or scratch at doors.
   (4) Earl and his wife punish Roscoe.
   (5) Roscoe made his own "doggie door."

2. What will most likely happen next?

   (1) Roscoe will run away and hide.
   (2) The couple will keep Roscoe in a crate.
   (3) The household cat will be favored.
   (4) The couple will find other damage in the house.
   (5) Roscoe will scratch the family car.

3. Earl's wife is reading articles on dogs and stress. Which of the following can you reasonably predict in the near future?

   Earl and his wife will

   (1) look for a pet psychic to help Roscoe
   (2) give Roscoe away to a good family
   (3) punish Roscoe by taking away his food
   (4) send a videotape of Roscoe to a comedy show
   (5) reinforce all their doors with steel

Answers are on page 333.

Using Inference to Make Predictions

Sometimes authors only suggest what is going to happen. In cases like this, you have to **infer** what will happen in the story. To do this, you must use the directly stated information as a clue to help you predict the outcome of a passage.

Read how a supervisor describes Manuel, one of his employees. Make a prediction about Manuel from the information the supervisor gives you.

"I'll give this job to Manuel. Manuel may be a little slower than some of the others, but you know he'll do it right. He's dependable. He takes time to figure it out—not just any old way will do for Manuel. When he's finished, there's never a complaint from the customer!"

What does the supervisor say directly about Manuel? He mentions three characteristics:

- Manuel is slow but dependable.
- Manuel takes time to figure out the problem.
- There are no customer complaints if Manuel does the job.

From this directly stated information, you can predict what will probably happen next. Which one of the following do you predict it will be?

(1) Manuel will do the job, and the customer will be pleased.
(2) There will be complaints if Manuel does the job.
(3) Manuel will be the fastest worker.
(4) The foreman is going to fire Manuel.
(5) Manuel will be promoted to foreman.

You should have chosen (1). Based on the information you were given, you can infer that if Manuel does the job, the customer will be pleased.

EXERCISE 10

Using Inference to Make Predictions

Directions: As you read the following passage, think about what predictions you can make about reading to children. Then answer the questions that follow.

Helping Children Become Good Readers

Helping children become good readers begins early. Reading aloud is the first step. Babies even a few months old enjoy hearing Mother Goose rhymes because the little poems have rhythm, and the sounds of the language are fun to hear. Between the age of six and twelve months, babies often point to pictures in books. Parents can help by naming objects in the pictures. It's possible to buy books made of cloth, cardboard, or plastic for babies so that they can "pretend read" by turning the pages.

As they grow older, simple storybooks, such as *The Three Little Pigs* and *Little Red Riding Hood,* can be added. It's important that parents read such stories with some excitement in their voices. Then children learn that reading can be fun and can come to enjoy more picture books, ABC books, and sometimes longer stories.

At a young age, children enjoy visiting a library to pick out books. Many librarians have been specially trained to help find children's books for particular ages and interests. For birthdays and other special days, it is a good idea to give at least one book to a child to be his or her very own.

Long before formal school begins, parents, grandparents, and others can help children prepare to be good readers.

1. Which of the following sentences contain information that is directly stated in the passage?
   You may choose more than one.

   (1) Parents and others can help children become good readers.
   (2) Parents should read to babies as young as a few months.
   (3) Parents should not buy cloth books for babies.
   (4) Children enjoy simple story, picture, and ABC books.
   (5) Parents should buy books as birthday presents.

2. Which one of the following is a logical prediction? Children who have been read to as babies will

   (1) be better prepared to learn to read in school
   (2) enjoy television movies more
   (3) not want to study music
   (4) never learn their ABCs
   (5) be less likely to enjoy sports

Answers are on page 333.

Graphic Organizers and Outlines

You have learned how to read a paragraph and fill in a chart that showed the main idea and supporting details in that paragraph. In this study skill, you will be reversing that process. You will first fill in an idea map and then use it to write your own paragraph. Later, you will learn how outlines can help you write a paragraph with a main idea and supporting details.

Graphic Organizers

To learn how this is done, first look at the following partially finished **idea map.**

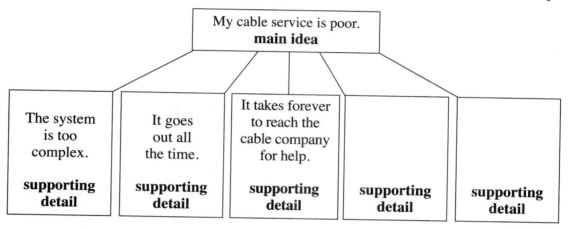

Notice that all the supporting details describe something about the main idea. Use your imagination to think of two more details that support the main idea, "My cable service is poor." Then go back and write them in the empty boxes of the idea map.

Now read the paragraph that follows. It was written by using the information in the idea map you just filled in. Complete the paragraph by writing two sentences about the supporting details you added to the idea map. The main idea is in **boldface type.**

> **My cable service is poor.** The system is too complex, and I don't understand it. The cable service goes out all the time, and I can't fix it myself. When I call the cable company for help, it takes forever to reach a technician.

_____

_____

_____

In the preceding paragraph, the main idea is in **boldface type.** The supporting ideas that follow the main idea explain it further.

EXERCISE 11

Using Graphic Organizers

Directions: Complete each of the following questions.

1. Describe something or someone you can see from where you are sitting. Do this by filling in the following idea map. Put the main idea in the top box, as shown in the previous example. Then fill in the supporting details with ideas that further describe or explain your main idea. Write as many details as you can. Consider *size*, *weight*, *shape*, *texture*, *color*, *use*, and so on.

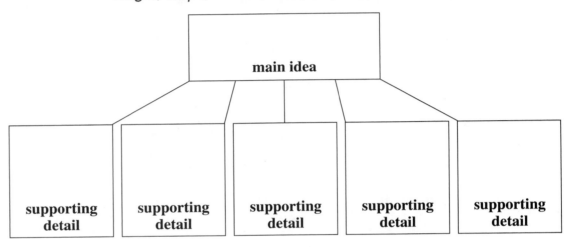

2. Now use the idea map you just created to write a paragraph. Begin with your main idea. Then put your supporting details into sentences following the main idea. If you wish, you may combine more than one detail in a sentence. Share what you have written with your teacher or with a friend.

_____

_____

_____

_____

_____

_____

_____

_____

_____

_____

Answers are on page 333.

Outlines

An **outline** can help you organize your ideas and write a paragraph. The difference between an idea map and an outline is that an idea map may organize ideas *across* the page, while an outline always organizes ideas *down* the page. However, maps and outlines contain the same information: the main idea and supporting details.

Read this example of an outline.

My teenage daughter is a great swimmer.   **main idea**

A. can swim backstroke and butterfly faster than friends
B. always placed at least third in state competitions
C. has been voted co-captain of school swim team for her ability   **supporting details**
D. swam a mile to shore after boat overturned

Notice that in this outline, the main idea is on the top line by itself. Each supporting detail has a letter of the alphabet, starting with A, in front of it.

Now read the following paragraph, which was written using the information from the outline you just read.

My teenage daughter is a great swimmer. She can swim the backstroke and the butterfly faster than any of her friends. She has always placed at least third in state swimming competitions and has been voted co-captain of her school's swim team. Her strength as a swimmer helped her swim a mile to shore after the boat she was in overturned.

Notice that the main idea in the preceding paragraph is in **boldface type.** The supporting details that follow it explain more about the main idea.

EXERCISE 12

Using Outlines

Directions: Complete each of the following exercises.

1. Consider what you would do if you won the lottery. In the outline that follows, write "If I won the lottery" on the main-idea line. Think of at least three things you might do with the money. Write those ideas on the supporting-detail lines.

   _____

   A. _____

   B. _____

   C. _____

   D. _____

   E. _____

2. Now use the outline you just created to write a paragraph. Put the main idea in the first sentence. You can reword it slightly to make it more interesting. Then add sentences for the supporting details.

_____

_____

_____

_____

_____

_____

_____

_____

_____

_____

Answers are on page 333.

Chapter Review

In this chapter, you practiced making inferences. You looked for details that were stated directly, and you figured out the message the author probably intended. You saw that inferences can be drawn from many sources, including cartoons, advertising, and literature passages in nonfiction or fiction. You worked on your skills of predicting words and ideas. Finally, you used graphic, or visual, organizers to prepare for writing a paragraph.

EXERCISE 13

Part 1 **Directions:** Following are several passages from the historical novel *Soldier's Heart* by Gary Paulsen. Read the passages and answer the questions that follow.

Passage 1

"You ain't but a boy."

"And I've got to be a man sometime. You've said it more than once yourself. Charley, you said, you've got to be a man. Well, here it is—my chance to be a man. A boy wouldn't go off to earn eleven dollars a month and wear a uniform. Only a man. So I'm going to be a man and do what a man can do."

Passage 2

"I know it ain't right," she wrote in one letter, "but you must think on coming home now. Just leave the army and walk home before they get you in a battle and shoot you apart."

Like most of the men, Charley doubted there ever would be a battle. Minnesota was mostly wild then, with Sioux and Chippewa Indians to the north and west, and there were some frontier forts on the edge of the wilderness to deal with any difficulties.

Passage 3

This can't be, he thought. I can't be here. This is all a mistake. A terrible mistake. I'm not supposed to be here.

He had forgotten to fire. The officers had marched them out into a field in perfect order and told them where to aim and fire, and he had raised his rifle and then the whole world had come at him. The Rebel soldiers were up a shallow grade a hundred yards away, behind some fallen trees, and they had opened on Charley and the others before anyone could fire.

—Excerpted from *Soldier's Heart* by Gary Paulsen

1. Which of the following details, stated directly, lead you to conclude that Charley is too young for war?
   You may choose more than one.

   (1) "You ain't but a boy." (Passage 1)
   (2) ". . . my chance to be a man" (Passage 1)
   (3) "Charley doubted there would ever be a battle." (Passage 2)
   (4) "A terrible mistake. I'm not supposed to be here."
       (Passage 3)
   (5) ". . . they had opened on Charley and the others before
       anyone could fire." (Passage 3)

2. In Passage 1, Charley's mother says, "You ain't but a boy." In Passage 2, she says, "I know it ain't right, but you must think on coming home now." How does Charley's mother feel about his being at war?

   (1) proud
   (2) angry
   (3) unconcerned
   (4) worried
   (5) scornful

3. Based on the clues in Passages 2 and 3, which war provides the setting for the novel?

   (1) Revolutionary War
   (2) American Civil War
   (3) Spanish-American War
   (4) World War I
   (5) Vietnam War

4. Reread all three passages. What has happened to Charley's feelings about war?

   (1) He is even prouder than when he enlisted.
   (2) He is very happy to contribute to the effort.
   (3) He has realized that it is a terrible mistake.
   (4) He feels that finally he is a grown man.
   (5) He wonders what the big fuss is about.

5. Based on Passage 3, what is a logical prediction about Charley's outcome?

   (1) He is promoted to captain.
   (2) He deserts the army and goes home.
   (3) He falls in love and marries.
   (4) He joins the Rebels in the South.
   (5) He is seriously injured.

Part 2 **Directions:** Use the idea map below to plan a paragraph. Put your main idea in the top box and your supporting details in the second row of boxes. Then use your idea map to write a paragraph on your own paper. Share your paragraph with your friends and your teacher.

Paragraph topic: Everyone should have (or does not need) a DVD player.

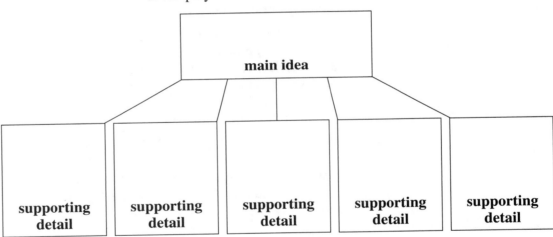

Answers are on page 333.

CHAPTER 4

Organizing Ideas

In this chapter, you will discover how authors organize their ideas. This will help you learn to read more critically. Authors use a number of different techniques to arrange information in their writing. We will examine five of these techniques:

- Fact, opinion, and generalization
- Sequence (time order)
- Comparison and contrast
- Cause and effect
- Analogies

Fact, Opinion, and Generalization

Reading critically means analyzing or questioning what you read. You do this to see whether you agree with the author's statements. To analyze an author's writing, you need to determine whether he or she is stating a fact, an opinion, or a generalization.

Facts

A **fact** is a statement that can be proved to be true. For example, the following statement is a fact:

John is six feet tall.

Anybody can measure John and find out whether this is true. Everyone can agree (or disagree) with the statement by checking the evidence—in this case, the measurement. But suppose we said the following:

John is the most handsome man in town.

This statement is not a fact because

- We can't prove that someone is the most handsome.
- We can't all agree. Some might think Ming or José is better looking.

Read the following statements and decide which of them are facts.

1. Des Moines, Iowa, is the best place to raise children.
2. Des Moines is a city in Iowa.
3. There are four quarts in a gallon.
4. John's feet are bigger than Ted's.
5. It's a fact that Sally has the greatest parties.

Did you choose statements 2, 3, and 4 as facts? These three sentences can all be proved and agreed upon. On the other hand, statement 1 is not a fact because we cannot prove which city is best, nor would we all agree. For the same reasons, statement 5 is not a fact, even though it states that it is. What makes a party "great" varies from person to person.

Opinions

An **opinion** is what a person *believes* is true. It may be true for him or her but not necessarily for others. It is a personal judgment, not a fact. Look at the following example of an opinion:

> San Francisco sourdough bread has a better flavor than any other bread on the market.

Some people feel that this bread tastes better than others, but other people may prefer a different kind of bread. Because this statement cannot be proved and all cannot agree, it is an opinion.

Read the following sentences. Then decide which statements are opinions. Remember, opinions are what a person believes to be true.

1. Mary is the kindest person in the world.
2. Mary brought home-cooked food to my family while I was in the hospital.
3. Mary needs a pet to care for.

Did you choose statements 1 and 3 as opinions? They state what someone *believes* is true. Statement 2, however, is a fact. We can check with the family to see whether Mary actually brought food daily.

EXERCISE 1

Identifying Facts and Opinions

Directions: Read each of the following statements. Write *O* in the blank if it is an opinion, something someone believes is true. Write *F* in the blank if it is a fact, something that can be proved.

_____ 1. Albert has been unemployed for one year.

_____ 2. A fire started in the basement of the house at 1801 Miller Avenue.

_____ 3. The United States should change its foreign policy regarding South American countries.

_____ 4. Fall is the most beautiful time of year with cold, crisp air and autumn leaves in colors of gold, yellow, orange, and red.

_____ 5. Abraham Lincoln was president during the Civil War.

_____ **6.** Chocolate ice cream tastes better than vanilla.

_____ **7.** Guatemala is in Central America.

_____ **8.** Guatemala has an excellent central government.

_____ **9.** A solar eclipse occurs when the moon moves between the sun and the earth.

_____ **10.** In the United States, citizens may vote at the age of eighteen.

11. Which of the following statements about opinions is true?

(1) Opinions are facts.
(2) Opinions are judgments.
(3) Opinions are always true.
(4) Opinions are always false.
(5) Opinions are never true.

Answers are on page 334.

Generalizations

A **generalization** is similar to an opinion in that it is a judgment and not a factual statement. However, it is somewhat different from an opinion because it is a statement that offers no exceptions.

A generalization is so strongly worded that it sounds like a fact. Compare the two statements that follow. One is an opinion, the other is a generalization.

Opinion: I believe students should stay in high school until they graduate.
(This statement says, "This is what I believe.")

Generalization: All students should stay in high school until they graduate.
(This statement makes no exceptions. It says that all students should stay in school.)

Notice that the generalization _sounds_ like it's a fact because it's so strongly worded. Yet, like the opinion, it can neither be proved nor agreed upon by all.

Because generalizations allow for no exceptions, and the world is full of exceptions, you need to recognize generalizations as being different from facts. Generalizations often use words such as _all, none, every, always,_ and _never._

Try identifying some generalizations. Read the two statements that follow. Mark the sentence that expresses an opinion with an *O* and the sentence that expresses a generalization with a *G*.

_____ **1.** I think Tom lied to you.

_____ **2.** Telling a lie is always wrong.

Compare your answers with these:

1. *O* At this time and given no more information, we cannot prove this statement is a fact. It is what someone *believes* to be true. Unlike a generalization, this opinion leaves room for exceptions.

2. *G* Most of us have told "white lies" or "fibs" to avoid hurting someone's feelings. We know that the word *always* in this statement provides for no exceptions, and there are exceptions to this rule for most people.

EXERCISE 2

Identifying Facts, Opinions, and Generalizations

Part 1 **Directions:** Read the statements that follow. Write an *O* in the blank provided if the statement is an opinion. Write a *G* in the blank if the statement is a generalization. Remember, you are being asked only to analyze what is being said and not to agree or disagree.

_____ **1.** All Italians are great cooks.

_____ **2.** I think Thomas was crazy to take that job.

_____ **3.** All churchgoers are good people.

_____ **4.** Republicans always know what is best for the country.

_____ **5.** I believe nuclear energy is the wave of the future.

Part 2 **Directions:** The following exercise presents opposing views of a single issue—sex education in schools. As you read each paragraph, look for facts, opinions, and generalizations used to support each side's argument. Identify each numbered sentence as a *fact*, an *opinion*, or a *generalization*. Write your answers on the lines provided.

Paragraph 1
Sex Education Should Be Taught at Home

(1) All sex education classes in school are immoral. **(2)** Only parents should teach the moral judgments that must always accompany information about sex. **(3)** For more information, you can call Mr. Vincent Bell, leader of Concerned Community Parents.

6. Sentence 1 _____

Sentence 2 _____

Sentence 3 _____

Paragraph 2
Sex Education Should Be Taught at School
(4) Sex education must be taught in our schools if we are going to stop the alarming rise in teenage pregnancy. **(5)** Trained professionals giving accurate information are always better than well-meaning but uncomfortable or ignorant parents who lack the vocabulary to discuss sex. **(6)** Mr. Leroy Miller, principal of Taylor Junior High, will speak Sunday at 7:00 P.M. in the school auditorium in support of classroom sex education.

7. Sentence 4 _____

   Sentence 5 _____

   Sentence 6 _____

8. Which two of the following are facts that could have been used in the preceding arguments?

   (1) a comparison of the pregnancy rate of teens who did or did not receive sex education
   (2) what the mayor said about the issue of sex education
   (3) interviews of pregnant teenagers and analysis of reasons for pregnancy
   (4) what the principal of the school thinks about sex education
   (5) views on morality of Concerned Community Parents

Answers are on page 334.

Sequence

Another technique that authors often use to organize their ideas is **sequencing.** Sequencing means to put things in the order in which they occur. For example, history books often discuss early historical events first. They gradually lead up through history to modern events.

Time-Line Sequencing
One way to diagram a sequence of events is to use a **time line.** A time line is a straight line that marks important events in order of the times when they occurred.

Here's an example of a time line that marks some major wars in U.S. history.

Year	1775	1812	1861	1917	1941
Event	Revolutionary War begins	War of 1812	Civil War begins	U.S. enters World War I	U.S. enters World War II

The time line records the events from left to right in the order in which they occurred. It's easy to tell from a time line how many years passed between one event and the next. For example, you can tell that 80 years passed between the beginning of the Civil War and the entry of the United States into World War II. You can figure this out by subtracting the year the Civil War began (1861) from the year the United States entered World War II (1941).

EXERCISE 3

Understanding a Time-Line Sequence

Directions: Examine the following time line of important events in the life of Angela Rodriguez. Starting at the left, read across the time line, noting the events and the dates on which they occurred. Then answer the questions that follow.

1964	1970	1982	1983	1984	1986	2001	2002
born in Memphis, Tennessee	started school	finished high school	married Carlos	daughter Carmen born	son Carlos, Jr., born	divorced Carlos	started college

1. About how old was Angela when she started school? _____

2. About how old was Angela when she finished high school? _____

3. How many years was Angela married to Carlos? _____

4. Angela returned to school

    (1) before she married Carlos
    (2) before Carlos, Jr., was born
    (3) one year before her divorce
    (4) one year after her divorce
    (5) after Carmen had graduated

Answers are on page 334.

Signal Words

Time lines can help chart the sequence of important events in a person's life. Sequencing is also important in the day-to-day events of our lives. For example, most of us follow a sequence of steps when we go about our daily activities of getting up in the morning, going to work or school, cooking, and so on.

Words such as *first, next,* and *last* are **signal words** that indicate what sequence to follow when doing something. Authors often use words like those listed below to signal the order of events to the reader.

Signal Words Showing Sequence			
first	later	since	second
then	when	third	after
last	next	before	finally

EXERCISE 4

Signal Words That Show Sequence

Directions: In the following sentences, underline the signal words that show sequence. Use the list on the previous page if you need help.

1. First, bring the water to a boil. Second, add the eggs. Third, turn down the heat. Then simmer the eggs for fifteen minutes, and last, rinse the eggs with cold water.

2. Before I met her, I was afraid I wouldn't know what to say. After meeting her in person, I found she was friendly, so I relaxed.

3. When I got on the bus, I must have had my wallet because I got my fare out of it. Later at home, I discovered my wallet was gone.

Directions: Choose the correct answer.

4. You are giving a friend three-step directions to get to a certain restaurant. In your directions, should you use the words *first, second,* and *third* for the steps, or should you use *first, next,* and *last*?

   (1) first, second, third
   (2) first, next, last
   (3) both (1) and (2) are fine because the sequence is the same

Answers are on page 334.

EXERCISE 5

Arranging Items in Correct Sequence

Directions: The following sentences describe how to wash a dog at home. Read all the sentences first and look for signal words that indicate sequence. Then go back and number the sentences in the correct sequence. Write the numbers on the lines provided.

_____ Then shampoo the dog, starting at the head. Work the shampoo well into its coat, being careful not to get soap in its eyes or nose.

_____ Next, rinse the shampoo off thoroughly.

_____ Finally, dry the dog with the towels.

_____ Before you start, gather together a large sponge, several towels, and some dog shampoo.

Answers are on page 334.

Sequence In Passages

Sequencing plays an important part in the structure of a passage. Being able to identify the correct sequence will help you understand the ideas the author presents.

EXERCISE 6

Understanding Sequence in a Story

Directions: As you read the following passages, keep track of the sequence of events. Pay special attention to signal words. Then answer the questions that follow.

Passage 1

"Twenty years ago tonight," said the man, "I dined here at Big Joe Brady's with Jimmy Wells, my best chum, and the finest chap in the world. He and I were raised here in New York, just like brothers, together. I was eighteen and Jimmy was twenty. The next morning I was to start for the West to make my fortune. You couldn't have dragged Jimmy out of New York; he thought it was the only place on earth. Well, we agreed that night that we would meet here again exactly twenty years from that date and time, no matter what our conditions might be or from what distance we might have to come. We figured that in twenty years each of us ought to have our destiny worked out and our fortunes made, whatever they were going to be."

Passage 2

"You're not Jimmy Wells," he snapped. "Twenty years is a long time, but not long enough to change a man's nose from a Roman to a pug."

"It sometimes changes a good man into a bad one," said the tall man. "You've been under arrest for ten minutes, Silky Bob. Chicago thinks you may have dropped over our way and wires us she wants to have a chat with you. Going quietly, are you? That's sensible. Now before we go to the station here's a note I was asked to hand you. You may read it here at the window. It's from Patrolman Wells."

Passage 3

Bob: I was at the appointed place on time. When you struck the match to light your cigar, I saw it was the face of the man wanted in Chicago. Somehow I couldn't do it myself, so I went around and got a plainclothes man to do the job.

—Excerpted from "After Twenty Years" by O. Henry

1. Number the events from the story in the proper sequence. The first one has been done as an example.

   _____ Jimmy and Bob made a date to meet in exactly twenty years.

   ___1___ Jimmy Wells and Bob were raised together in New York.

   _____ Bob set out for the West to make his fortune.

   _____ The best friends had dinner at Big Joe Brady's.

   _____ The policeman handed Bob a note from Patrolman Wells.

   _____ Jimmy realized that he could not arrest his old friend.

   _____ A policeman arrested Bob.

2. Given the sequence of events, what do you think might happen next to Bob?

   He will

   (1) stand trial for crimes in Chicago
   (2) shoot his way out of the restaurant
   (3) bribe his old friend to let him go
   (4) call the mayor of New York for help
   (5) reform and join the police force

3. Given the sequence of events, what do you think might happen next to Jimmy Wells?

   He will

   (1) join Silky Bob in a life of crime
   (2) ask to be assigned as a plainclothes officer
   (3) leave New York to find his fortune out West
   (4) keep doing his job as an honest policeman
   (5) have his nose changed from Roman to pug

Answers are on page 334.

EXERCISE 7

Understanding Sequence in Directions

Directions: As you read the following article, notice the sequence of steps given to solve a problem. Then answer the questions that follow.

Making Decisions

Adults must make many decisions in life. Some of those may include deciding whether or not to move, to marry, to have children, to go back to school, to change jobs, and so forth. Some people make decisions on impulse and regret their decisions later. Others just stew and worry, unable to come to any conclusion. Still others seem able to make good decisions without much hassle. How do these hassle-free decision makers do it?

One helpful way to make a decision is to sit down in a quiet place with a pencil and a sheet of paper. At the top of the paper, write the problem as a question, such as, "Should I move to New Jersey?" or "Should I marry Susan?" or "Should I return to school?" Next, fold the paper in half lengthwise. Then unfold the paper so that there are two columns. Write "Advantages" at the top of the left-hand column and write "Disadvantages" at the top of the right-hand column.

Now list all the benefits to be gained under "Advantages." Next list all the drawbacks under "Disadvantages." Last, weigh the advantages and disadvantages in your lists, and then make your decision.

1. What is the main idea of this article?

   (1) Adults make decisions on impulse and regret their decisions.
   (2) Adults worry and stew when making decisions.
   (3) Listing advantages and disadvantages can make decision making easier.
   (4) Friends and relatives can help you make decisions.
   (5) Getting married in a hurry is a mistake.

2. Number the following directions in the sequence in which they occurred in the passage.

   _____ List the benefits under "Advantages" and the drawbacks under "Disadvantages."

   _____ Weigh the advantages and disadvantages.

   _____ Write your problem in the form of a question.

   _____ Divide the paper into two columns and label one column "Advantages" and the other column "Disadvantages."

   _____ Make your decision.

Answers are on page 334.

Comparison and Contrast

Besides sequence, authors often use the comparison-and-contrast technique to help them organize their ideas. To **compare** means to see how things are **alike.** To **contrast** means to see how things are **different.** We often use these techniques to describe things in our daily lives.

Comparing Two Things

When we compare and contrast two things, we frequently use a chart to organize the comparison. In the following exercise, Lee is trying to decide which van he should buy.

EXERCISE 8

Comparing and Contrasting Information

Directions: Look at the following pictures. Then answer the questions that follow.

1. Look at the information in the following chart. Put a check in the right-hand column to indicate if the two minivans are similar or different in each factor. Then use the chart to help you answer the remaining questions.

	Honda Odyssey	Toyota Sienna	Similar	Different
Total weight	4,354 lbs	3,919 lbs		
Seating capacity	7 passengers	7 passengers		
Cargo capacity	38.1 cubic ft	26.6 cubic ft		
Length	201.2 inches	194.2 inches		
Towing capacity	3,500 lbs	3,500 lbs		
Gas use (city/highway)	18/25 MPG	19/24 MPG		
Price (dealer invoice)	$24,068	$21,514		

2. Put a check on the line next to all the statements that show how the two minivans are similar.

_____ **(1)** Both use the same amount of gas.

_____ **(2)** Both are made by the same company.

_____ **(3)** Both are seven-passenger vehicles.

_____ **(4)** Both have the same towing capacity.

_____ **(5)** Both are the same model year.

3. Put a check on the line next to all the statements that show how the two minivans are different.

_____ **(1)** One has greater cargo capacity than the other.

_____ **(2)** One is built by Honda; the other is built by Toyota.

_____ **(3)** One is heavier than the other.

_____ **(4)** One gets better gas mileage (*both* city and highway).

_____ **(5)** One is longer than the other.

4. If Lee is trying to decide which minivan to purchase, which features should he consider? Check all that apply.

———— **(1)** price

———— **(2)** seating capacity

———— **(3)** towing capacity

———— **(4)** cargo capacity

———— **(5)** garage fit (length)

Answers are on page 334.

Comparison and Contrast in a Passage

So far, you've learned how to compare and contrast two things. The next exercise will give you practice in recognizing comparison and contrast as they are used in a passage.

EXERCISE 9

Comparing and Contrasting Two People

Directions: Read the following description of the similarities and differences of two women. Then answer the questions that follow.

Hillary Clinton and Princess Diana

There's an interesting photo in a 1997 history book, *A Century of Women,* by Sheila Rowbotham. Princess Diana is shown in 1996 in the White House with Hillary Clinton. Bill Clinton was the president then, and Hillary was the first lady. Diana was married to Prince Charles, the future king of England. Does it surprise you to compare the two women? Both were strong women who spoke their own minds. Neither would stick to the traditional roles many thought they ought to play. Both tried to increase funds for charities and for health issues.

There were also differences between the two. Diana had worked as a nursery school teacher before marrying the prince in 1981. Hillary had already been a high-powered lawyer before Clinton took office. Diana may have been naïve about the life of a princess in Buckingham Palace. In contrast, Hillary was described as shrewd, ambitious, and political. Both had trouble in their marriages. Hillary chose to stay married, but Diana got a divorce. Diana died tragically in an auto accident in Paris at the age of thirty-six. Hillary was elected to the U.S. Senate from New York. We don't know what good works Diana might have accomplished if she had lived longer. On the other hand, many think Hillary will run for president someday.

—*Adapted from* A Century of Women, the History of Women in Britain and the United States *by Sheila Rowbotham*

1. Give two ways in which the women were similar.

   (1) _____

   (2) _____

2. Which of the two women was more politically-minded? What details in the passage support your answer?

   _____

   _____

3. Put a check next to four of the ways in which the women were similar. Both

   _____ (1) were strong women

   _____ (2) spoke their own minds

   _____ (3) would not stick to traditional roles

   _____ (4) did what the public wanted

   _____ (5) raised money for charities

4. Put a check next to two of the ways in which the women were different.

   _____ (1) One was a nursery school teacher; the other was a lawyer.

   _____ (2) One was unprepared for public life; the other was shrewd.

   _____ (3) One loved living in the Palace; the other loved the White House.

   _____ (4) One would talk to the media; the other one wouldn't.

   _____ (5) One was liked by the public more than the other.

5. Based on what you read, you can tell that the writer of the passage probably

   (1) likes one woman more than the other
   (2) dislikes both women
   (3) hopes Hillary will be president
   (4) supports the same charities
   (5) admires both women

Answers are on page 334.

Cause and Effect

In a **cause-and-effect** relationship, one condition or event makes another condition or event happen. Authors are not the only ones to use cause and effect. In fact, you use this relationship every day. Every time you say the word *because,* you are recognizing why something happened. This is its **cause.** The **effect** is what happened as a result of the cause. For example, look at the following sentence:

> José failed the test because he did not study.

Effect (what happened?): José failed the test
Cause (why?): because he did not study

The cause-and-effect relationship is the same regardless of the order in which ideas are stated.

Sentence 1: <u>José failed the test</u> <u>because he did not study</u>.
              effect   **cause**

or

Sentence 2: <u>Because he did not study</u>, <u>José failed the test</u>.
              cause   **effect**

We might chart a cause-and-effect relationship in this way:

| cause | — brings about → | effect |

Read the next two pairs of sentences. The sentences in each pair state the same cause-and-effect relationship, but in different orders. See if you can identify the cause and the effect in each sentence. Fill in the appropriate boxes with words from each sentence to show the cause-and-effect relationship.

1. Because Jenny hates liver, she never eats it.

    [   ] — brings about → [   ]
           cause   effect

2. Jenny never eats liver because she hates it.

    [   ] — brings about → [   ]
           cause   effect

See how your answers compare with these:

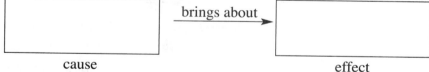

1. [Because Jenny hates liver] — brings about → [she never eats it]
        cause   effect

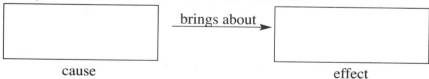

2. [because she hates it] — brings about → [Jenny never eats liver]
        cause   effect

Identifying Cause and Effect

Directions: In the following sentences, circle the words that indicate a cause, and underline the words that indicate an effect. The first one is done as an example.

1. <u>Julie fell</u> because (she did not see the hole in the sidewalk).

2. Because Carlos added salt instead of sugar, his cake tasted terrible.

3. Because Amy is allergic to bee stings, her brother rushed her to the doctor when she was stung.

4. He had a flat tire because he had run over a sharp nail.

5. Because the radio was so loud, I didn't hear the phone.

6. Pete was exhausted because he had worked overtime.

Answers are on page 335.

Understanding Signal Words

All of the cause-and-effect sentences thus far have contained the word *because*. The word *because* is called a **signal word** since it signals you that a cause is immediately following. *For* and *since* are also signal words that let you know a cause is coming next. Signal words and phrases can also introduce an effect. Some of these include *therefore* and *so*. The following sentences give examples of signal words.

> *Since* Marie ate too much, she got fat.
>   **cause** ⟶ **effect**

> Marie got fat, *for* she ate too much.
>   **effect** ⟵ **cause**

> Marie ate too much; *therefore,* she got fat.
>   **cause** ⟶ **effect**

> Marie ate too much *so* she got fat.
>   **cause** ⟶ **effect**

Read the following sentences, and see whether you can identify the cause, the effect, and the signal word. Write *cause* on the line under the part of the sentence that is the cause. Write *effect* on the line under the part of the sentence that is the effect. Then circle each signal word.

1. The rainfall was heavy; therefore, the river rose four feet.

    _____   _____

2. The rainfall was heavy, so the river rose four feet.

    _____   _____

Your answers should read:

1. The rainfall was heavy; (therefore) the river rose four feet.
   cause   **effect**

2. The rainfall was heavy, (so) the river rose four feet.
   cause   **effect**

EXERCISE 11

Identifying Cause-and-Effect Relationships

Directions: Each of the following sentences contains a cause-and-effect relationship. As you read each sentence, identify the cause and the effect. Then fill in the blank in each sentence with a signal word that indicates the proper cause-and-effect relationship. Remember to think of the relationship of the ideas.

Signal Words	
because	since
therefore	so
for	

1. _____ snakes are cold-blooded creatures and move with a crawling motion, many people find snakes unattractive.

2. Snakes are useful creatures _____ they eat mice and other small animals.

3. Some people get over their dislike of snakes; _____, they may adopt them as pets.

4. _____ snakes are very clean, they can be kept in apartments.

5. Grant lived next door; _____, I often saw him with his pet boa constrictor.

6. Boa constrictors do not eat daily, _____ Grant found that feeding his pet was cheap.

7. _____ boas need sunshine and fresh air, Grant often took his boa outside.

Answers are on page 335.

Cause-and-Effect Relationships in Paragraphs

You've learned how cause-and-effect relationships occur in sentences. Now you will learn how they occur in paragraphs. Just as you do in sentences, look for signal words in a paragraph. However, even when there are no signal words, a cause-and-effect relationship may still be present.

EXERCISE 12

Following Cause-and-Effect Relationships in Paragraphs

Directions: Read the following passages. Then answer the questions that follow.

Passage 1

What About the Forests?

Some scientists are worried about what will happen to people and animals if large forests and jungles in the world are destroyed. The trees and green plants in these forests and jungles produce oxygen, which is released into the atmosphere. Animals and people need this oxygen to breathe. If huge areas of green plants are destroyed, too little oxygen may be produced to keep people and animals alive.

1. What is the cause of some scientists' worry?

_____

2. According to the paragraph, what bad effect would occur if huge forests and jungles are destroyed?

(1) Shade trees would disappear.
(2) Oxygen in the atmosphere would be reduced.
(3) Exotic plants would die out.
(4) Less farmland would be available.
(5) Conservationists would protest.

3. A South American country wants to get rid of its forests in order to sell the lumber and to create farmland. Given the information in the paragraph you just read, what do you think scientists might advise the country's leaders to do?

(1) grow corn and rice only
(2) burn the forest down
(3) save part of the forest as it is
(4) sell the lumber for building houses
(5) go ahead and destroy the forests

Passage 2

Help for California Island Foxes

Island foxes have been in trouble in Channel Islands National Park off southern California. Here's how it started. Several islands have been overrun with pigs. The pigs can be traced to pigs that escaped from farms decades ago.

In the 1940s and 1950s pesticides wiped out bald eagles that were native to the area. Then golden eagles flew over to prey on baby pigs. These eagles also learned to kill the small island foxes.

On Santa Cruz about sixty foxes were left in 2002. The sixty foxes are being kept for breeding (producing young) to restock the island. Bald eagles, which don't prey on the foxes, are being brought back. Golden eagles are being taken back to the mainland. The pigs that began the problems are being hunted down. This will go on until Santa Cruz has no more pigs. With all these actions, island foxes will have a better chance in the future.

—Adapted from "Outfoxed by Aliens" in *National Geographic*

Directions: After reading the passage above, trace the causes and effects of this problem by filling in the blanks.

4. Cause: _____ escaped from farms decades ago.

   Effect: Later, islands were overrun by more _____.

5. Cause: _____ were used in the 1940s and 1950s.

   Effect: _____ _____ that were native to the area were wiped out.

6. Cause: _____ _____ flew over to prey on baby pigs.

   Effect: Golden eagles also learned to kill _____ _____ .

7. In Santa Cruz only 60 island foxes were left in 2002. What is being done to increase their numbers? Circle all statements that apply.

   (1) Foxes are being kept for breeding.
   (2) Bald eagles are being brought back.
   (3) Golden eagles are being taken back to the mainland.
   (4) Laws are being passed to protect the foxes.
   (5) Pigs are being hunted down.

8. What can you infer about nature by this example of the foxes?

   (1) Nature is totally unpredictable.
   (2) Pesticides are the cause of many problems.
   (3) Bald eagles are better than golden eagles.
   (4) Island foxes are not very smart.
   (5) Problems occur when the ecology of an area is upset.

Answers are on page 335.

Analogies

You have already used the technique of comparison and contrast. Next you will be comparing the relationships between words. In other words, you will determine how one pair of words is related. Then you will learn how another pair of words is related in a similar way. These comparisons of similar relationships are called **analogies.**

Finding Analogies

An analogy looks like this.

> wet : dry :: hot : cold

We translate the dots this way: One set of dots (:) means *is to*. Two sets of dots (::) mean *as*. Therefore, when we substitute words for dots in the preceding analogy, it looks like this:

> wet **is to** dry **as** hot **is to** cold

This means that *wet* is related to *dry* in the same way that *hot* is related to *cold*.

How are wet and dry and hot and cold related in the same way?

> wet : dry :: hot : cold
> *Wet* is the **opposite** of *dry,* and *hot* is the **opposite** of *cold.*

In both word pairs, the relationship of the words is that one is the opposite of the other.

Now that you know how to identify relationships between words, you can fill in a missing word in an analogy. Look at the following example:

> fat : thin :: short :_____

Since this is an analogy, you know that the relationship between *fat* and *thin* is the same as the relationship between *short* and _____. How do you fill in the blank? Follow the steps below, checking your answers as you go.

> fat : thin :: short : _____

Step 1. Translate the dots by filling in the lines below.

> fat _____ _____ thin _____ short _____ _____ _____

You should have written the following: fat **is to** thin **as** short **is to**

_____

Step 2. Now rewrite the analogy by writing the relationship between the first two words in the blank:

> fat is the _____ of *thin*

> *fat* is the **opposite** of *thin*

Step 3. Next, write the same words that express the relationship between *fat* and *thin* after the third word, *short:*

short is the _____ of _____

short is the **opposite** of _____

Step 4. Complete the analogy.

fat: thin :: short : **tall**

The word *tall* completes this analogy because it is the opposite of *short*.

So far, all the words have been opposites of each other. However, this is not always the relationship in an analogy. Next, you will work with analogies that have relationships other than opposites.

Practice completing the next analogy:

finger : hand :: toe : _____

1. finger _____ _____ hand _____ toe
    _____ _____ _____

2. finger is a _____ _____ a hand

3. toe is a _____ _____ a _____

4. finger : hand :: toe : _____

Compare your answers with these:

1. finger **is to** hand **as** toe **is to** _____

2. finger is a **part of** a hand

3. toe is a **part of** a **foot**

4. finger : hand :: toe : **foot**

Foot completes this analogy because a toe is a *part of* a foot.

EXERCISE 13

Working with Analogies

<u>Part 1</u>   **Directions:** Read each analogy. Using the steps you just learned, pick the word that best completes the analogy. Then write the letter of the word you chose in the blank provided.

1. gift : present :: plate : _____

    a. birthday
    b. dish
    c. cup
    d. holiday

2. end : finish :: start : _____

    a. motor
    b. stop
    c. begin
    d. dinner

3. leaf : tree :: petal : _____

    a. grass
    b. vase
    c. flower
    d. forest

4. see : eye :: hear : _____

    a. ear
    b. blink
    c. listen
    d. music

5. pen : write :: car : _____

    a. letter
    b. tire
    c. drive
    d. read

6. ice : cold :: fire: _____

    a. hot
    b. chilly
    c. burn
    d. fireplace

Part 2   **Directions:** Read each of the following analogies. Using the steps you learned earlier, fill in the blank with a word that completes each analogy.

  7. music : listen :: book : _____

  8. $: dollar :: % : _____

  9. glass : break :: paper : _____

10. hour : minute :: pound : _____

11. spoon : stir :: knife : _____

12. ring : finger :: belt : _____

Answers are on page 335.

Chapter Review

In this chapter you have taken a closer look at how authors organize their ideas. You've practiced five of the techniques. They are fact and opinion, generalization, sequence, comparison and contrast, cause and effect, and analogies.

EXERCISE 14

Directions: Following are four passages from the short story "Charles" by Shirley Jackson. Read the passages and answer the questions that follow.

Who Is Charles?

Passage 1

The day my son Laurie started kindergarten he renounced corduroy overalls with bibs and began wearing blue jeans with a belt; I watched him go off the first morning with the older girl next door, seeing clearly that an era of my life was ended, my sweet-voiced nursery-school tot replaced by a long-trousered, swaggering character who forgot to stop at the corner and wave good-bye to me.

Passage 2

"Why did Charles hit the teacher?" I asked quickly.

"Because she tried to make him color with red crayons," Laurie said. "Charles wanted to color with green crayons so he hit the teacher and she spanked him and said nobody play with Charles but everybody did."

Passage 3

During the third and fourth weeks it looked like a reformation in Charles; Laurie reported grimly at lunch on Thursday of the third week, "Charles was so good today the teacher gave him an apple."

"What?" I said, and my husband added warily, "You mean Charles?"

"Charles," Laurie said. "He gave the crayons around and he picked up the books afterward and the teacher said he was her helper."

Passage 4

"I've been so anxious to meet you," I said. "I'm Laurie's mother."

"We're all so interested in Laurie," she said.

"Well, he certainly likes kindergarten," I said. "He talks about it all the time."

"We had a little trouble adjusting, the first week or so," she said primly, "but now he's a fine little helper. With occasional lapses, of course."

"Laurie usually adjusts very quickly," I said. "I suppose this time it's Charles's influence."

"Charles?"

"Yes," I said, laughing, "you must have your hands full in that kindergarten, with Charles."

"Charles?" she said. "We don't have any Charles in the kindergarten."

—Excerpted from "Charles" by Shirley Jackson

1. In terms of sequence, Passage 1 is the first paragraph of the short story. Compare the mother's memory of Laurie as a tot with his first day of kindergarten.

   What is the mother feeling?

   (1) relieved at last to have some free time
   (2) excited at a new era (period in time) in her life
   (3) nostalgic (wistful or sad) for the end of an era
   (4) upset to send a child off on his own
   (5) depressed to lose close contact with Laurie

2. Based on Passage 2, why is Charles having trouble adjusting to kindergarten?

   Charles wants to

   (1) be the class clown
   (2) do things his own way
   (3) show off for his girlfriend
   (4) get his mother upset
   (5) be promoted to first grade

3. Charles's behavior in Passage 2 can be contrasted with that in Passage 3. What is the effect of this change?

   The teacher

   (1) ignores Charles
   (2) promotes Charles
   (3) calls Charles's parents
   (4) rewards Charles
   (5) sends Charles to the office

4. In Passage 4, Laurie's mother attends a school PTA meeting.

   What surprising fact does she learn?

   (1) Laurie is the smartest child in kindergarten.
   (2) Laurie has great artistic ability.
   (3) Laurie is teased for being a "teacher's pet."
   (4) Laurie and Charles are great friends.
   (5) There is no Charles in the kindergarten.

5. Reread all four passages. Then complete this analogy:

   Charles : Laurie :: fantasy : _____

Answers are on page 335.

CHAPTER 5

Understanding Fiction

The reading skills you have learned will help you when you read different types of literature passages. **Fiction** is a type of literature that describes imaginary people, places, and events. This literature may be made up or may be based on qualities of real people, places, or events. You will look mostly at prose fiction in this chapter and you will need to pay special attention to **fiction elements.** These elements are setting, tone, characterization, plot, point of view, and theme.

Prose is writing that most closely resembles everyday speech. Prose can be nonfiction or fiction. To best understand what you're reading and to make it more interesting, you need to form pictures in your mind.

Forming Pictures in Your Mind

To picture something in your mind, you take the clues an author gives you and use your imagination to picture them. When you do this, you enter the world that the author creates. You visit the places the author wants to show you and meet the people he introduces you to. You will need to combine ideas directly stated with those ideas that are implied.

Read the following sentence and think about the picture you can create from the clues.

The old gardener leaned heavily on his rake.

How do you picture the gardener? Ask yourself the following questions to help form a picture in your mind:

1. Is the gardener young or old?
2. Is the gardener standing or sitting?
3. Is the gardener energetic or tired?
4. How does the gardener's face look? Smooth or lined with wrinkles?

Compare your answers with these:

1. The gardner is old: The sentence directly states that the gardener is old.
2. He is probably standing: You can infer this since the sentence says the gardener leaned on his rake.
3. He is probably tired: You can infer this because the sentence tells you that the gardener leaned heavily on his rake.
4. His face is probably wrinkled: You can infer this since you know the gardener is old, and a person's skin tends to wrinkle as he or she ages.

EXERCISE 1

Forming Pictures in Your Mind

Directions: Read the passages that follow. Decide what kind of mental picture the details in the paragraphs help you create, and then answer the questions that follow.

Passage 1

Getting Ready for a Squall[1]

The grasses flattened. There was a hiss of wind, a sudden pungent[2] smell. Our faces looked yellow in the strange light. Caleb and I jumped over the fence and found the animals huddled by the barn. I counted the sheep to make sure they were all there, and herded them into a large stall. A few raindrops came, gentle at first, then stronger and louder, so that Caleb and I covered our ears and stared at each other without speaking. Caleb looked frightened and I tried to smile at him. Sarah carried a sack into the barn, her hair wet and streaming down her neck, Papa came behind, Lottie and Nick with him, their ears flat against their heads.

—Excerpted from *Sarah, Plain and Tall* by Patricia MacLachlan

[1]*squall:* a sudden, violent wind, often with rain or snow
[2]*pungent:* sharp or biting

1. Where are the people and animals going for safety?

   _____

2. What clues are there that a storm is brewing?

   _____

   _____

3. What details suggest color?

   _____

4. What sounds are heard?

   _____

5. How can you picture the reaction of the children (Caleb and I) to the storm?

   _____

   _____

6. How do we know that Lottie and Nick are dogs?

   _____

Passage 2

After he had gone eight miles, he came to the graveyard, which lay just at the edge of his own hay-land. There he stopped his horses and sat still on his wagon seat, looking about at the snowfall. Over yonder on the hill he could see his own house, crouching low, with the clump of orchard behind and the windmill before, and all down the gentle hill-slope the rows of pale gold cornstalks stood out against the white field. The snow was falling over the cornfield and the pasture and the hay-land, steadily, with very little wind—a nice dry snow. The graveyard had only a light wire fence about it and was all overgrown with long red grass. The fine snow, settling into this red grass and upon the few little evergreens and the headstones, looked very pretty.

—Excerpted from "Neighbour Rosicky" by Willa Cather

7. The graveyard is located

(1) in the middle of town
(2) at the edge of a field
(3) in a large city
(4) next to a lake
(5) near a mountain

8. Which one of the following is **not** in the description?

(1) a pasture
(2) a windmill
(3) a cornfield
(4) a barn
(5) a wire fence

9. The main character thinks the scene is

(1) pretty
(2) ugly
(3) funny
(4) frightening
(5) upsetting

10. At what time of year does the scene most likely take place?

(1) winter
(2) late spring
(3) early summer
(4) early fall
(5) late fall

Answers are on page 336.

Using Language to Create Mental Pictures

Authors use language in special ways to help the reader understand and create a picture of a story. Two of these special ways are the use of **comparisons and contrasts.**

Making Comparisons

Sometimes an author wants to get the reader to look at something in a different way. To do this the author will often make a comparison of one object or living thing with another, like the following:

> On his first birthday, my grandson Jack got his first Radio Flyer wagon. He looked as proud as a sixteen-year-old with the keys to his first set of wheels.

When reading such comparisons, you should ask yourself two questions:

1. What two things is the author comparing? (one-year-old grandson and a sixteen-year-old)

2. Why did the author choose that comparison? What is she trying to get you to see? (The grandson looked as proud as a sixteen-year-old with his first car.)

Now examine two more comparisons. Read the following statements. Ask yourself what comparisons are being made and for what purpose. Then fill in the blanks.

> The crowd began to depart like leaves blowing in an autumn wind.
>
> The crowd is compared with _____
>
> What is the author's purpose? _____

> I watched the light in his eyes flicker and then go out. He was dead.
>
> Being alive is compared with _____
>
> Dying is compared with _____
>
> What is the author's purpose? _____

Are your answers similar to these?

The crowd is compared with leaves blowing in an autumn wind. The author's purpose is to show people moving off in many directions, not in a straight line.

Being alive is compared with a light; dying is compared with a light flickering and then going out. The author's purpose is to show that dying can be as quick as turning off a light.

EXERCISE 2

Identifying Comparisons

Directions: Laurence Yep describes the famous San Francisco earthquake by comparing it to objects and animals. As you read the following excerpt, look for comparisons that help you form a mental picture of the events that happened. Then answer the questions that follow.

(1)   It was thirteen days after the Feast of Pure Brightness that the earthquake hit. Just a little after five A.M., demon time, I had gotten dressed and gone out to the pump to get some water. The morning was filled with that soft, gentle twilight of spring, when
(5) everything is filled with soft, dreamy colors and shapes; so when the earthquake hit, I did not believe it at first. It seemed like a nightmare where everything you take to be the rock-hard, solid basis for reality becomes unreal.

    Wood and stone and brick and the very earth became fluid-like.
(10) The pail beneath the pump jumped and rattled like a spider dancing on a hot stove. The ground deliberately seemed to slide right out from under me. I landed on my back hard enough to drive the wind from my lungs. The whole world had become unglued. Our stable and Miss Whitlaw's house and the tenements to either
(15) side heaved and bobbed up and down, riding the ground like ships on a heavy sea. Down the alley mouth, I could see the cobblestone street undulate and twist like a red-backed snake.

—Excerpted from *Dragonwings* by Laurence Yep

1. The author says, "It seemed like a nightmare . . ." in lines 6–7. What is the author comparing to a nightmare?

   (1) the morning twilight
   (2) the Feast of Pure Brightness
   (3) soft, dreamy colors and shapes
   (4) the earthquake
   (5) Miss Whitlaw's house

2. To what does the author compare the pail beneath the pump in lines 10–11?

   (1) wood and stone and brick and the very earth
   (2) the ground
   (3) a spider dancing on a hot stove
   (4) a bucket
   (5) the soft spring air

3. The author describes the movement of Miss Whitlaw's house and the tenements to either side (lines 14–16) as

   (1) tumbling down like towers of wooden blocks
   (2) riding the ground like ships on a heavy sea
   (3) twisting like a red-backed snake
   (4) coming unglued, like old wallpaper
   (5) falling like a person who has slipped on ice

4. The author compares the cobblestone street to a red-backed snake (lines 16–17) to show that the street is

(1) as dangerous as a poisonous red snake
(2) the same black color as many snakes
(3) flooded with water because of the earthquake
(4) red in color and making rippling motions
(5) shiny like a snake's skin

Answers are on page 336.

Setting and Tone

Reading becomes more interesting when you use the details given to create your own mental image about elements of a story. One element is **setting.** Setting is the time and place of a story. Often an author will describe the place and time of a story because the setting establishes the framework in which the events of a story occur.

Think of the importance of the setting to the story in movies and TV shows you have seen. For example, read the following chart:

Movie/TV Show	Place	Time
Frankenstein	a gloomy castle on a stormy night	long ago
Star Trek	inside a spacecraft and on distant planets	the future

Tone or Mood as a Part of Setting

When an author writes a story, he or she may express his or her attitude or feelings about the subject or the characters. The author may express these feelings as a part of the setting. This gives a certain **tone** or **mood** to the piece. This tone may also influence how you, the reader, feel toward the subject or characters.

Authors choose words that they think will bring out certain emotions in you. The emotions can be pleasant (such as humor, joy, or peacefulness) or unpleasant (such as fear, horror, or disgust). Nearly any emotion can be the tone of a passage.

Read the following example. What attitudes or emotions does the author feel? What words does the author use to tell you this?

The carefree child skipped along under the blossoming trees.
A playful puppy trotted after her as fast as he could.

By the use of lighthearted words such as *carefree, skipped, blossoming, playful,* and *trotted,* the author means to paint a pleasant scene that will bring out positive feelings.

In the example that follows, three people have just learned that a friend is pregnant. In the column on the left, read the reaction of each person to this news. Then match the tone from the column on the right with each statement on the left. Write the correct letter in the blank next to each statement.

Reaction   Tone

_____ **1.** "That's great! Maria is a nice   **(a)** complaining
woman. She'll be a wonderful
mother, I'm sure."   **(b)** eager

_____ **2.** "Now I suppose they'll come   **(c)** approving
crying to me for money to help
them. They always want me to bail
them out of the scrapes they
get into."

_____ **3.** "Babies are so cute and cuddly. When
is she due? Do they want a boy or
a girl? Oh, I can't wait to hold it!"

How do your answers compare with these?

1. **(c)** approving: This speaker approves of the pregnancy. The mother is "a nice woman," and she'll "be a wonderful mother."

2. **(a)** complaining: You can infer this mood or tone from the speaker's comments, "They'll come crying to me," and, "They always want me to bail them out." This speaker is concerned more about the impact of the pregnancy on his life than on anyone else's.

3. **(b)** eager: You can infer this from the words "cute and cuddly," and the phrase "Oh, I can't wait. . . ."

EXERCISE 3

Understanding Tone

Directions: As you read the following passage, picture the people and the dark scene. Pay particular attention to the words the author/narrator uses, and the emotions those words bring out in you. Then answer the questions that follow.

What Evil Act Does Montresor Commit Against Fortunato?

It was now midnight, and my task was drawing to a close. I had completed the eighth, the ninth, and the tenth tier. I had finished a portion of the last and the eleventh; there remained but a single stone to be fitted and plastered in. I struggled with its weight; I placed it partially in its destined position. But now there came from out the niche[1] a low laugh that erected the hairs upon my head. It was succeeded by a sad voice, which I had difficulty in recognizing as that of the noble Fortunato. The voice said—

"Ha! ha! ha!—he! he!—a very good joke indeed—an excellent jest. We will have many a rich laugh about it at the palazzo[2]—he! he! he!—over our wine—he! he! he!"

"The Amontillado!"[3] I said.

"He! he! he!—he! he! he!—yes, the Amontillado. But is it not getting late? Will not they be awaiting us at the palazzo, the Lady Fortunato and the rest? Let us be gone."

Yes," I said, "let us be gone."

"For the love of God, Montresor!"

"Yes," I said, "for the love of God!"

But to these words I hearkened in vain for a reply. I grew impatient. I called aloud;

"Fortunato!"

No answer. I called again.

"Fortunato!"

No answer still. I thrust a torch through the remaining aperture and let it fall within. There came forth in return only a jingling of the bells. My heart grew sick—on account of the dampness of the catacombs.[4] I plastered it up. Against the new masonry I re-erected the old rampart of bones. For the half of a century no mortal has disturbed them. *In pace requiescat!*[5]

—Excerpted from *The Cask of Amontillado* by Edgar Allen Poe

[1]*niche:* a recess in a wall
[2]*palazzo:* a large building or residence (in Italy)
[3]*Amontillado:* a fine wine
[4]*catacombs:* an underground burial place
[5]*In pace requiescat!:* "Rest in peace!"

1. What is the setting for the short story?

   (1) a beautiful palazzo
   (2) a restaurant wine cellar
   (3) the catacombs
   (4) a hospital morgue
   (5) a brick construction site

2. The narrator Montresor believed that his friend Fortunato had insulted him a thousand times. Because of this, what act does Montresor commit?

   (1) walls Fortunato in to die in the catacombs
   (2) insults the beautiful Lady Fortunato
   (3) exchanges Amontillado for lesser wine
   (4) embarrasses Fortunato in front of other noblemen
   (5) kills Fortunato with his sword

3. The author uses expressions such as "a low laugh that erected the hairs upon my head" and "Ha! ha! ha!—he! he!—." What emotion does the author want you, the reader, to feel?

   (1) happiness
   (2) excitement
   (3) anger
   (4) fear
   (5) embarrassment

4. What is the overall tone (mood) of the story?

   (1) uncomfortable
   (2) horrifying
   (3) unlucky
   (4) jolly
   (5) fantastic

Answers are on page 336.

Characterization

In addition to describing the setting and creating the tone, authors help you form a mental picture of a story by showing you what the characters are like. **Characterization** helps you understand what the people in a story are like. An author may describe the physical or personality traits of a character. The author may also reveal a character's traits by what the character says and what other characters say about him or her.

Describing a Character

As you read the following paragraph, notice the details the author gives to describe the character. Use the questions that follow to help you form a mental picture of the character.

What Does Tom Think of Work?

Tom was whitewashing [the fence] with vigor, and Aunt Polly was retiring from the field with a slipper in her hand and triumph in her eye.

But Tom's energy did not last. He began to think of the fun he had planned for this day, and his sorrows multiplied. Soon the free boys would come tripping along on all sorts of delicious expeditions, and they would make a world of fun of him for having to work—the very thought of it burnt him with fire. He got out his worldly wealth and examined it—bits of toys, marbles, and trash; enough to buy him an exchange of *work*, maybe, but not half enough to buy so much as half an hour of pure freedom.

—Excerpted from *The Adventures of Tom Sawyer* by Mark Twain

1. What is Tom doing (at first)?

2. What does Tom think about his task?

3. How does Tom imagine the other boys will react?

Compare your answers to these:

1. Tom is "whitewashing [a fence] with vigor."

2. The slipper that Aunt Polly might throw at him is a clue that Tom is working under protest. His "energy did not last." He's feeling sorry for himself, and he starts thinking about how he can get out of work.

3. Tom thinks about the "free boys" and the "world of fun" they would make of him because he has to work. That thought "burnt him like fire."

EXERCISE 4

Picturing a Character from a Description

Directions: As you read the following description, try to form a mental picture of how this person looks and acts. Then answer the questions that follow.

Is Mrs. Luella Bates Washington Jones an Easy Target?

She was a large woman with a large purse that had everything in it but a hammer and nails. It had a long strap, and she carried it slung across her shoulder. It was about eleven o'clock at night, dark, and she was walking alone, when a boy ran up behind her and tried to snatch her purse. The strap broke with the sudden single tug the boy gave it from behind. But the boy's weight and the weight of the purse combined caused him to lose his balance. Instead of taking off full blast as he had hoped, the boy fell on his back on the sidewalk and his legs flew up. The large woman simply turned around and kicked him right square in his blue-jeaned sitter. Then she reached down, picked the boy up by his shirtfront, and shook him until his teeth rattled.

—Excerpted from "Thank You, M'am" by Langston Hughes

1. The woman is described as

   (1) delicate
   (2) slender
   (3) big-boned
   (4) flabby
   (5) large

2. The woman is out alone late at night. Her reaction to the boy suggests that she is

   (1) foolish and adventurous
   (2) confident and assured
   (3) joking and cheerful
   (4) sad and depressed
   (5) friendly and warm

3. From his description of the woman, the author most likely

(1) trusts her
(2) distrusts her
(3) admires her
(4) mocks her
(5) criticizes her

Answers are on page 336.

Plot

The **plot** of a story is a series of events that leads to a believable conclusion. A plot contains these four basic elements:

Beginning ——→ Conflict ——→ Climax ——→ Conclusion

As the diagram shows, these elements are usually connected in a logical way that draws readers into the story and makes them want to know what will happen next. Being able to predict what will happen in a story adds to the suspense.

Beginning The purpose of the **beginning** is to introduce the characters and setting of the story.

Example: a boy, a girl, and the girl's father in a small town

Conflict Often people think of **conflict** as meaning a fight or argument. In stories, however, the word *conflict* means "a problem to be solved."

Example: The boy and girl are in love, but the father hates the boy. The boy and girl can't get together because of the father.

Climax The **climax** of a story serves two functions:

1. It is the most exciting part of the story.
2. It solves the problem.

Example: The girl falls into the river. → exciting
The boy saves the girl. → exciting
The father now likes the boy. → problem solved

Conclusion The **conclusion** is simply what happens at the end of the story.

Example: The girl and boy marry.

Remember that the author may not directly give all the information you need to understand the plot. Therefore, you may need to use the inference and prediction skills you learned earlier to identify the four basic elements of the plot.

Identifying Elements in Greek Myths

In the next exercise, you will have a chance to practice identifying the four elements of the plot in a Greek myth. **Myths** are stories that try to explain natural occurrences.

The ancient Greeks were great storytellers. They believed in many gods and goddesses, and in nymphs who were the spirits of trees, rivers, rocks, and other elements of nature. This myth tries to explain the reason for a flower's appearance and the cause of echoes.

EXERCISE 5

Understanding Plot

Directions: Read the myth that follows. Identify the beginning, the conflict, the climax, and the conclusion. Then answer the questions that follow.

How Did the Narcissus Flower Get Its Name?

Echo was a nymph, or spirit of nature. She was beautiful but had one problem. Because she had talked too much, one of the goddesses took away Echo's power of independent speech and allowed her only to repeat what others said.

Echo, like many of the other nymphs, fell madly in love with a handsome young man called Narcissus. Unfortunately Narcissus loved no one but himself. Echo followed him and adored him, but since she could only repeat what others said, she could not begin a conversation with him. She hoped he would notice her and speak first.

One day Narcissus came upon a clear pool. Looking down into the pool's water, he saw the image of a handsome young man.

"I love you," he said to his own reflection.

"I love you," Echo repeated, hoping he would finally look at her.

But Narcissus did not pay any attention to Echo. Instead, still longing for the handsome image in the pool, he leaned too close to the water, fell in, and drowned. After he died, a flower grew where he had sat next to the pool. The flower, called *narcissus*, always hangs its head over water so as to admire its own reflection.

Poor Echo, when she saw that Narcissus was gone, died also, leaving only her voice behind. To this day, Echo can never speak for herself but can only repeat what others say.

1. What is the conflict in the story?

   (1) Echo loves Narcissus, but he doesn't love her.
   (2) Narcissus loves Echo, but she doesn't love him.
   (3) Echo and Narcissus love each other.
   (4) Narcissus fell into the pool.
   (5) Echo and Narcissus hate each other.

2. What happens in the climax?

    (1) Echo can finally speak, not just repeat others' words.
    (2) Narcissus falls in love with Echo.
    (3) Both Narcissus and Echo die.
    (4) The other nymphs kill Narcissus.
    (5) Echo and Narcissus are married.

3. What happens at the conclusion of the story?

    (1) Narcissus and Echo get married and live happily ever after.
    (2) Narcissus drowns in the pool.
    (3) Echo and the other nymphs run away into the forest.
    (4) Narcissus becomes a flower, and Echo leaves only her voice.
    (5) Echo gives birth to her first child.

4. Like Narcissus, people who suffer from narcissism are those who

    (1) hate themselves
    (2) admire themselves too much
    (3) fall in love too often
    (4) cannot speak
    (5) are overly fond of flowers

Answers are on page 336.

Point of View

An author has choices when deciding *how* to tell a story by using a particular **point of view.** Three ways of expressing point of view are through the first person, the third person, or the third-person all-knowing.

First, the author can narrate the story in the **first person** by telling the story through the eyes or views of a **main character.** This is the character most affected by the action. When an author uses this point of view, only the thoughts of the main character are made known. The author uses the word *I,* and the narrator speaks directly to the reader. For example, read this passage from "Charles" by Shirley Jackson. The mother is the narrator identified by *I,* and Laurie is her son.

> On Monday Laurie came home late, full of news. "Charles," he shouted as he came up the hill; I was waiting anxiously on the front steps. "Charles," Laurie yelled all the way up the hill, "Charles was bad again."

Second, the author can narrate the story in the **third person.** When an author uses this point of view, someone not involved in the action tells the story, and the main character is referred to as *he* or *she* (*his* or *her*) when the character's name is not used. For example, read this passage from "Soldier's Heart" by Gary Paulsen. Notice that the description centers on *Charley* and *he.*

> He heard it all, Charley did; heard the drums and songs and slogans and knew what everybody and his rooster was crowing. There was going to be a shooting war.

Third, the author can narrate the story in the **third-person all-knowing.** In this point of view, the narrator can let the reader know what all the characters are doing, thinking, or feeling. For example, read this passage from "Thank You, M'am" by Langston Hughes. Notice that the woman's thoughts are revealed and that the boy is unaware that he is frowning.

> The woman was sitting on the daybed. After a while she said, "I were young once and I wanted things I could not get."
> There was another long pause. The boy's mouth opened. Then he frowned, not knowing he frowned.

EXERCISE 6

Identifying Point of View

Directions: Read the following short passages and match the correct point of view with each passage.

a. first person/main character	b. third person	c. third-person all-knowing

_____ **1.** Her husband caught her by passing his arm under hers. "We'll be more comfortable over there."
"There? In the middle of all those people? I'd much rather . . ."

—from "The Other Wife" by Colette

_____ **2.** Caleb and Papa and I wrote letters to Sarah, and before the ice and snow had melted from the fields, we all received answers. Mine came first.

—from *Sarah, Plain and Tall* by Patricia MacLachlan

_____ **3.** He never had so much money. It was probably enough to buy a second-hand guitar. But he felt bad, like the time he stole a dollar from the secret fold inside his older brother's wallet.

—from "The No-Guitar Blues" by Gary Soto

_____ **4.** Returning from a hunting trip, I waited at the little town of Los Piños, in New Mexico, for the south-bound train, which was one hour late. I sat on the porch of the Summit House and discussed the functions of life with Telemachus Hicks, the hotel proprietor.

—from "Telemachus, Friend" by O. Henry

Answers are on page 336.

Theme

The **theme** is the main idea, or what the story means. This is true of novels, short stories, and films. The theme is how the author gets across his or her purpose or focus. The author wants the story to have meaning for the audience.

The theme may involve an insight or understanding of the true nature of people or things. The insight may be about life, human nature, or a problem. Common themes are the loss of innocence and the struggle for survival. Other themes are the victory of good over evil and the conqueror of love over all.

Now read some examples from *Catherine, Called Birdy,* a novel by Karen Cushman. It is the year 1290 in England, and the main character Catherine is required to keep a diary. Her father is determined to find a husband for the fourteen-year-old. Write a phrase to express a theme for each example.

Example 1

5th Day of June, Feast of Saint Boniface, who wrote the first Latin grammar used in England.

I helped an ant today. She carried a burden so heavy it looked to crush her. A crumb it was, or a speck of wheat. Or a drop of honey that had hardened. She was struggling to take it back to her nest, where it would feed her fellow ants for a day or a week, as small as it was.

Theme: _____

The theme could be *respect for all living things.* Catherine is concerned with and helps a tiny ant. The theme could also be the *struggle for survival* since the ant is trying so hard.

Example 2

2nd Day of July, Feast of Saints Processus and Martinians, Roman martyrs, whose relics cure the sick, reveal perjurers, and cure lunatics.

I have been thinking about my own marriage. Once I dreamed of a handsome prince on a white horse decked in silks and bells. Now I am offered a smelly, broken-toothed old man who drinks too much. I would rather even Alf! But it occurred to me that what actually makes people married is not the church or the priest but their consent, their "I will." And I do not consent. Will never consent. "I will not."

Theme: _____

Catherine is trying to hold to her ideal for a husband. Thus, the theme could be the *search for true love.* Because she is determined not to give her consent to be married, the theme could be *being true to oneself* or *feminine independence.*

EXERCISE 7

Identifying Theme

Directions: Read the following passages and answer the questions.

Passage 1

Luis and Hector never said much at the table. It wasn't until his grandfather was finished and sitting in his favorite chair that Hector would begin asking him questions about the world, questions like, "What do Egyptians look like? Is the world really round like a ball? How come we eat chickens and they don't eat us?"

By the time Hector was nine, it was the grandfather who was asking the questions. He had become interested in real estate since he heard that by selling a house his son-in-law had made enough money to buy a brand-new car and put a brick fence around his yard.

Passage 2

There was a moment of silence. Then the woman said, "Forty-three thousand. The owners are anxious and perhaps may settle for less, maybe forty-one five."

"Wait a minute," he said to the woman. Hector looked up to his grandfather. "She says forty-three thousand."

His grandfather groaned and his dream went out like a lightbulb. He put his comb in his back pocket.

"You said thirty thousand, Son."

"I didn't know—I was guessing."

"But it's so much. *Es demasiado.*"[1]

"But you go to school and know about things."

—Exerpted from "Two Dreamers" by Gary Soto

[1]*Es demasiado:* "It's too much."

1. Who are the two dreamers identified in the story?

   _____ and _____

2. What is the one dream that both the boy and his grandfather share?

   (1) learning as scientists
   (2) being sports stars
   (3) living as politicians
   (4) travelling the world
   (5) becoming wealthy

3. In Passage 1 Hector asks a number of questions. These questions can point to a theme of pursuit (seeking) of

   (1) learning
   (2) riches
   (3) stardom
   (4) recognition
   (5) peace

4. In Passage 2 Hector asks a real estate agent about the asking price of a house for sale. When he tells his grandfather the cost of the house, the grandfather's "dream went out like a lightbulb." This reaction can point to a theme of

(1) learning from experience
(2) accepting the worst
(3) dealing with shattered dreams
(4) recognizing success
(5) never giving up

Answers are on page 336.

Chapter Review

In this chapter you have followed some of the practices of authors who write **prose fiction.** This has included forming pictures in your mind, using language to create mental pictures, and making and identifying comparisons.

You have studied main fiction elements including **setting, tone, characterization, plot, point of view,** and **theme.** You have read about how to describe a character including what the author says about the character, what the character says, and what other characters say. You have examined the four parts of plot including the beginning, the conflict, the climax, and the conclusion. You have learned that point of view is in the first person (the *I* of the main character) or the third person (he, she, they, or names). It can also be simple third person or "all-knowing" in which the author reveals additional information. You have learned that the theme, or main idea, is something you arrive at after considering the whole story.

Finally, you have learned that authors use all the elements. Authors do this to get you, the reader, to share the experience they write about.

EXERCISE 8

Directions: Read the following passages. Then answer the questions that follow.

How Is the Character, Doodle, Like the Ibis?

Passage 1

It seemed so hopeless from the beginning that it's a miracle I didn't give up. But all of us must have something or someone to be proud of, and Doodle had become mine. I did not know then that pride is a wonderful, terrible thing, a seed that bears two vines, life and death. Every day that summer we went to the pine beside the stream of Old Woman Swamp, and I put him on his feet at least a hundred times each afternoon. Occasionally I too became discouraged because it didn't seem as if he was trying, and I would say, "Doodle, don't you *want* to learn to walk?"

Passage 2

At that moment the bird began to flutter, but the wings were uncoordinated, and amid much flapping and a spray of flying feathers, it tumbled down, bumping through the limbs of the bleeding tree and landing at our feet with a thud. Its long, graceful neck jerked twice into an S, then straightened out, and the bird was still. A white veil came over the eyes and the long white beak unhinged. Its legs were crossed and its clawlike feet were delicately curved at rest. Even death did not mar its grace, for it lay on the earth like a broken vase of red flowers, and we stood around it, awed by its exotic beauty.

"It's dead, " Mama said.

"What it is?" Doodle repeated.

"Go bring me the bird book," said Daddy.

I ran into the house and brought back the bird book. As we watched, Daddy thumbed through its pages. "It's a scarlet ibis,"[1] he said, pointing to a picture. "It lives in the tropics—South America to Florida. A storm must have brought it here."

Passage 3

The knowledge that Doodle's and my plans had come to naught was bitter, and that streak of cruelty within me awakened. I ran as fast as I could, leaving him far behind me with a wall of rain dividing us. The drops stung my face like nettles, and the wind flared the wet glistening leaves of the bordering trees. Soon I could hear his voice no more.

I hadn't run too far before I became tired, and the flood of childish spite evanesced[2] as well. I stopped and waited for Doodle. The sound of rain was everywhere, but the wind had died and it fell straight down in parallel paths like ropes hanging from the sky. As I waited, I peered through the downpour, but no one came. Finally I went back and found him huddled beneath a red nightshade bush beside the road. He was sitting on the ground, his face buried in his arms, which were resting on his drawn-up knees. "Let's go, Doodle," I said.

He didn't answer, so I placed my hand on his forehead and lifted his head. Limply, he fell backwards onto the earth. He had been bleeding from the mouth, and his neck and the front of his shirt were stained a brilliant red.

"Doodle! Doodle!" I cried, shaking him, but there was no answer but the ropy rain. He lay very awkwardly, with his head thrown far back, making his vermilion[3] neck appear unusually long and slim. His little legs, bent sharply at the knees, had never before seemed so fragile, so thin.

I began to weep, and the tear-blurred vision in red before me looked very familiar. "Doodle!" I screamed above the pounding storm and threw my body to the earth above his. For a long time, it seemed forever, I lay there crying, sheltering my fallen scarlet ibis from the heresy[4] of rain.

—Excerpted from "The Scarlet Ibis" by James Hurst

[1]*ibis:* bird that wades and is related to the heron. It has a long, thin bill that curves downward.

[2]*evanesced:* vanished

[3]*vermilion:* a vivid reddish-orange color

[4]*heresy:* an opinion or practice opposite to the truth

1. Identify the places that make up parts of the setting in the story.

    a. Passage 1: _____

    b. Passage 2: _____

    c. Passage 3: _____

2. Name all the human characters mentioned in the three passages.

    a. _____

    b. _____

    c. _____

    d. _____

3. In addition, a comparison is made between one human and one nonhuman character.

    _____ is compared to _____ .

4. In Passage 1 the story is told from the point of view of

    (1) Doodle
    (2) Doodle's brother
    (3) Doodle's mother
    (4) the ibis
    (5) the all-knowing author

5. In Passage 1 you learn that Doodle cannot walk and that his brother is trying to teach him to walk. What does this reveal about the characterization of the brother? Circle all statements that apply. The brother

    (1) needs to be proud of someone or something
    (2) gets discouraged at times trying to teach Doodle to walk
    (3) is mean to birds like the scarlet ibis
    (4) is not ashamed that Doodle is crippled
    (5) is patient to try a hundred times to teach him to walk

6. In Passage 2, you read a description of the scarlet ibis. What is the key feature of the bird that is compared to Doodle in Passage 3?

    (1) uncoordinated wings
    (2) long white beak
    (3) long, slim neck
    (4) unusual cry
    (5) sturdy legs

7. In Passages 2 and 3 you learn a detail of plot that happens to both the bird and Doodle. This is that they

    (1) returned to South America
    (2) fell from a tall tree
    (3) threw themselves at the narrator's feet
    (4) died in a storm
    (5) cried after Doodle's brother

8. In Passage 3, what action of Doodle's brother shows that he sometimes had "that streak of cruelty"?

   (1) He made fun of Doodle.
   (2) He ran away from Doodle in a storm.
   (3) He threw Doodle next to a roadside bush.
   (4) He let Doodle sink in Old Woman Swamp.
   (5) He kicked Doodle in his thin, fragile legs.

9. The last line of the story is, "For a long, long time, it seemed forever, I lay there crying, sheltering my fallen scarlet ibis from the heresy of rain." In this context the "scarlet ibis" is Doodle. Why does the author say the narrator is sheltering Doodle from the "heresy of rain"?

   Rain is supposed to help

   (1) wash away dead leaves from trees
   (2) satisfy the thirst of animals and people
   (3) irrigate crops and yield a good harvest
   (4) purify the atmosphere from pollution
   (5) nourish living things but not kill them

10. The tone of the story is one of

    (1) regret
    (2) pride
    (3) joy
    (4) hope
    (5) anger

11. The theme of the story is concerned with how two feelings affect each other. These two are

    (1) anger and revenge
    (2) love and pride
    (3) hope and charity
    (4) passion and forgiveness
    (5) jealousy and rage

12. This story is set in the southern part of the United States in 1918. This was the time of World War I. The color red is important in the story. This can lead you to think of battles between

    (1) Doodle's parents
    (2) Doodle's brother and himself
    (3) Doodle and his brother
    (4) America and England
    (5) Choices (2) and (3)

Answers are on pages 336–337.

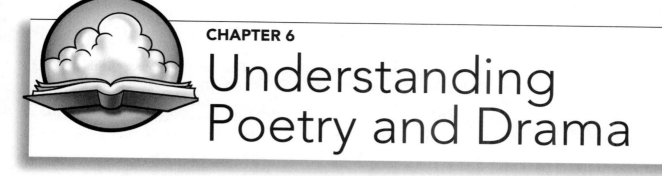

Understanding Poetry and Drama

The skills you have learned for reading prose will now be applied to reading **poetry** and **drama.** In addition, you will learn new skills and characteristics that are unique to poetry and drama.

Reading Poetry

Poetry has some unique characteristics that set it apart from prose. Poetry usually has a different format or structure than does prose. Unlike prose, poetry is traditionally written in short lines, often with a capital letter at the beginning of each line. Some poets use many periods and commas in their work, while others use few. You read poetry by the sense of the words, *not* line by line as you would read prose. It helps a great deal to read a poem silently first and then aloud. Let the rhythm and the sense of the words tell you when to start and stop.

To practice reading poetry by following the sense of the words, read the following poem first silently, then aloud. Use the letters by the words to help you decide when to begin and when to stop for a breath. *B* stands for *begin; S* stands for *stop.*

Fog
B The fog comes
on little cat feet. S
B It sits looking
over harbor and city
on silent haunches
and then moves on. S

—by Carl Sandburg

Did you notice that you only stop in two places—after *feet* and after the final *on?*

Forming a Picture

To understand prose, it's helpful to use the details the author gives. The same is true of poetry. Look again at Carl Sandburg's poem "Fog." In this poem, Sandburg creates a picture by comparing one thing to another.

Can you tell what two things the poet is comparing in "Fog"?

_____ is compared to _____.

You can tell from the title and the first line that the subject of this poem is *fog*. What does the poet tell you fog is like? In other words, to what does the poet compare the fog? In the second line, the words *little cat feet* tell you that the fog is being compared to a cat. The word *haunches* continues this image. The poet is comparing the movement of the fog to that of a cat. By doing so, Sandburg helps you "see" the fog as he does.

EXERCISE 1

Forming a Picture from a Poem

Directions: Read the following poem, silently at first and then aloud. Use the symbols by the words to tell you when to begin and when to stop. Remember, *B* stands for *begin,* and *S* stands for *stop*. As you read, try to picture in your mind what the poet is describing. Then answer the questions that follow.

>   .05
> B If i had a nickel
>   For all the women who've
>   Rejected me in my life
>   I would be the head of the
> (5) World Bank with a flunkie
>   To hold my derby as i
>   Prepared to fly chartered
>   Jet to sign a check
>   Giving India a new lease
> (10) On life S
> B If i had a nickel for
>   All the women who've loved
>   Me in my life i would be
>   The World Bank's assistant
> (15) Janitor and wouldn't need
>   To wear a derby S
> B All i'd think about would
>   Be going home S
>   —by Ishmael Reed

1. The man would be "head of the World Bank" if he had a

   (1) derby hat
   (2) chartered jet
   (3) nickel for every rejection
   (4) new lease on life
   (5) nickel for every love

2. How do you picture the head of the World Bank?

   (1) rich and famous
   (2) heartbroken and poor
   (3) ugly and unhappy
   (4) sad and lonesome
   (5) angry and scared

3. "Prepared to fly chartered / Jet to sign a check / Giving India a new lease / On life" (lines 7–10) means the man
   (1) is eager to visit India
   (2) dreams of solving India's poverty
   (3) wants a new lease for his apartment
   (4) prepares for a job as a travel agent
   (5) believes no one can solve India's problems

4. "If i had a nickel for / All the women who've loved / Me in my life i would be / The World Bank's assistant / Janitor . . ." (lines 11–15) means
   (1) women constantly fall in love with the man
   (2) people drop nickels on the street every day
   (3) the man is looking for a job
   (4) the man has not found many women who love him
   (5) the World Bank is looking for an assistant janitor

5. How do you picture the assistant janitor of the World Bank?
   (1) scholarly and wise
   (2) rich and famous
   (3) married and wealthy
   (4) ordinary and poor
   (5) confident and strong

Answers are on page 337.

Thinking About the Subjects of Poems

Poems can be about any subject. Some poems are about serious subjects such as love, beauty, courage, war, grief, or death. Other poems are about nature such as the stars, moon, sunset, clouds, mountains, garden, or seasons. Poems can also be expressions of feelings to or about a particular person, especially a loved one.

For example, one American poet who dealt with serious subjects is Emily Dickinson. Some titles of her poems are "I Died for Beauty," "My Life Closed Twice Before Its Close," and "Indian Summer." In one of her shortest poems, she deals with an important subject in just seven lines.

Not in Vain
If I can stop one heart from breaking,
I shall not live in vain:
If I can ease one life the aching,
Or cool one pain,
Or help one fainting robin
Unto his next again,
I shall not live in vain.

—by Emily Dickinson

What is the subject of the poem?

The poet is saying that she hopes to make a difference. She mentions stopping "one heart from breaking," easing "one life the aching," or helping "one fainting robin." She feels that she will not live in vain if she helps someone or some creature. Another way to say *in vain* is *without success* or *uselessly*. So you could say the subject of the poem is *having a purpose in life*. You could also say the subject is *caring or showing concern* for people and other living things.

The New England poet Robert Frost used everyday places and situations to express words of wisdom. His poem "Birches" captures the childhood experience of climbing birch trees and "riding" them to the ground. Then in the last line the poet says, "One could do worse than be a swinger of birches." This could praise someone who enjoys the simple pleasures of life. In "Stopping by Woods on a Snowy Evening," the poet describes the woods in winter. The last two lines of the poem are the same: "And miles to go before I sleep/ And miles to go before I sleep." The speaker in the poem could simply be saying that he has a long way to go to get home. He could also be saying that he has responsibilities to take care of before he stops.

EXERCISE 2

Identifying the Subjects of Poems

Directions: You might read the following poem to your child or a young relative. Read the poem and answer the questions that follow.

Three Ponies

(1) Three little ponies who didn't like their hay
Said to each other "Let's run away!"
Said the first "I will canter!"[1]
Said the second "I will trot"[2]
(5) Said the third "I will run if it's not too hot!"

And they all started off
With their tails in the air.
But they couldn't jump the fence
So they're all still there.

—by Arthur Guiterman

[1]*canter*: to move in a way that is smoother and slower than a gallop
[2]*trot*: to move at a moderately fast pace with legs moving in diagonal pairs

1. The subject of the poem deals with the reaction of the three ponies to not liking their food. They decided to canter, trot, or run away.

Each pony is probably showing too much

(1) playfulness
(2) anger
(3) disrespect for owners
(4) impatience and anxiety
(5) pride and conceit

2. Lines 8–9 say, "But they couldn't jump the fence / So they're all still there." What does this say about their ability to change their lives?

They are very

(1) upset
(2) determined
(3) serious and earnest
(4) spiritless and apathetic
(5) forgetful

Directions: Read the following poem and answer the questions that follow.

Mending Wall

(1) My apple trees will never get across
And eat the cones under his pines, I tell him.
He only says, "Good fences make good neighbors."
Spring is the mischief in me, and I wonder
(5) If I could put a notion in his head:
"Why do they make good neighbors? Isn't it
Where there are cows? But here there are no cows.
Before I built a wall I'd ask to know
What I was walling in or walling out,
(10) And to whom I was like to give offense.
Something there is that doesn't love a wall,
That wants it down." I could say "Elves" to him,
But it's not elves exactly, and I'd rather
He said it for himself. I see him there
(15) Bringing a stone grasped firmly by the top
In each hand, like an old-stone savage armed.
He moves in darkness as it seems to me,
Not of woods only and the shade of trees.
He will not go beyond his father's saying,
(20) And he likes having thought of it so well.
He says again, "Good fences make good neighbors."

—from "Mending Wall" by Robert Frost

3. Each spring the poet and his neighbor walk the fence between their properties and mend any broken sections. What is the poet's reaction to the fence? (lines 4–7)

The poet

(1) notices that apple trees have grown over the pine woods
(2) complains that cows have been running over his property
(3) questions the need to keep a fence between good neighbors
(4) believes that elves in the juniper bushes want the fence down
(5) thinks hunters have damaged the fence during the winter

4. The poet states in lines 8–9, "Before I built a wall I'd ask to know / What I was walling in or walling out." What is the subject of the poem if taken from these lines?

   (1) reasons for strict privacy
   (2) unnecessary division between people
   (3) inability to make a decision
   (4) differences of opinions
   (5) farmers and cattle ranchers

5. In line 19 the poet says, "He will not go beyond his father's saying." What does this tell you about the mindset of the neighbor?

   The neighbor

   (1) is easily convinced
   (2) argues for his point of view
   (3) is quite superstitious
   (4) is disrespectful of others
   (5) stays with tradition

6. The last line of the poem, "Good fences make good neighbors," is a key expression. If countries observed this advice, how would they act?

   Countries would

   (1) mind only their own affairs
   (2) defend their weaker allies
   (3) develop common goals
   (4) look for reasons for war
   (5) drop import and export taxes

Answers are on page 337.

Paraphrasing Poetry

Sometimes it's helpful to **paraphrase** poetic language into everyday language. That means you take the images and symbols that the poet uses and express them in more ordinary words. This technique is especially helpful when a poem is complicated. If you can paraphrase it into everyday language, you can understand its message better.

Take a look at the following poem about children. Read the poem in the left-hand column, first silently and then aloud. Then compare the poetry to the everyday language in the right-hand column.

Poem	**Paraphrase**
Your children are not your children.	Your children don't belong to you. They are part of on-going generations.
They are the sons and daughters of Life's longing for itself.	
They come through you but not from you.	They are born to you. Although they live with you, you don't own them.
And though they are with you yet they belong not to you.	
You may give them your love but not your thoughts,	You can love them, but you can't make them think as you do.
For they have their own thoughts.	
You may house their bodies but not their souls,	You can take care of their physical needs but not their ideas. This is because they will live in the future, where you cannot go.
For their souls dwell in the house of tomorrow, which you cannot visit, not even in your dreams.	
You may strive to be like them, but seek not to make them like you.	You can try to be like them, but don't ask them to be like you because they can't go backward.
For life goes not backward nor tarries with yesterday.	

—from *The Prophet* by Kahlil Gibran

Translating a poem into everyday language is also helpful in understanding poems that use symbols. In his poem "Mother to Son," Langston Hughes uses the symbol of stairs to represent life. What can you learn about life from the poet's description of stairs?

EXERCISE 3

Paraphrasing Poetry

Directions: Read the following poem, first silently and then aloud. Part of the poem has been rephrased as everyday language. Write the second part in your own words along the side of the poem. Then answer the questions that follow.

Mother to Son

(1) Well, son, I'll tell you:
Life for me ain't been no crystal stair.
It's had tacks in it,
And splinters,

(5) And boards torn up,
And places with no carpet on the floor—
Bare.
But all the time
I'se been a-climbin' on,

(10) And reachin' landin's,
And turnin' corners,
And sometimes goin' in the dark
Where there ain't been no light.
So boy, don't you turn back.

(15) Don't you set down on the steps
'Cause you finds it's kinder hard.
Don't you fall now—
For I'se still goin', honey,
I'se still climbin',

(20) And life for me ain't been no crystal stair.
—by Langston Hughes

Life for me hasn't been easy.

I've had a lot of tough problems.

_____
_____

_____
_____

_____
_____

1. This poem is mainly about a woman who is

    (1) complaining about her life
    (2) giving advice to her son
    (3) punishing her son
    (4) improving her family's situation
    (5) taking a trip with her son

2. What does she mean when she says her stair has "had tacks in it, / And splinters, / And boards torn up, / And places with no carpet on the floor—/ Bare" (lines 3–7)?

    (1) She has had problems in her life.
    (2) The stairs leading to her apartment need fixing.
    (3) She has had a very easy life.
    (4) She wants the landlord to make repairs in her building.
    (5) She has been married several times.

3. What does she mean when she says, "And sometimes goin' in the dark / Where there ain't been no light" (lines 12–13)?

    (1) The light in her apartment building needs replacing.
    (2) Sometimes she could not see how to solve her problems.
    (3) She is blind, so she can't see the stairs.
    (4) She turned out the lights to save money on electricity.
    (5) She has spent time in the hospital.

4. When she says, "Don't you set down on the steps / 'Cause you finds it's kinder hard. / Don't you fall now—" (lines 15–17), the speaker is telling her son

    (1) not to give up, even with problems
    (2) not to go up the steps
    (3) to be careful not to fall
    (4) to sit down and rest
    (5) not to sit on the hard steps

5. She says her life has not been a "crystal stair." What would her life be like if it *had* been a "crystal stair"?

    (1) full of splinters and tacks
    (2) full of landings and corners
    (3) slippery and hard to climb
    (4) smooth, bright, and easy
    (5) hard to see and hear

Answers are on page 338.

Reading Drama

When you go to a play, or **drama,** you see actors who take the roles of characters, perform the action, and speak the lines. Watching a play is much like seeing a movie or a television show because you actually see the drama unfold.

Reading a play requires some additional skills. In this section, you will learn how to read and understand a dramatic script.

Comparing Drama and Prose

In some ways, reading a play is no different from reading prose or even poetry. What makes reading drama different from reading prose is its **format.** This is the way words are arranged on the page. As you will see, a dramatic script is easy to recognize because it has a very distinctive format.

One difference in a dramatic script is that the names of the speakers in the play are shown, often in capital letters. Every time a character speaks, his or her name appears beside the lines of dialogue he or she says. In a play, **dialogue** is the conversation between characters.

Another format difference is the **stage directions,** which tell you what the characters are doing as they speak and what their tone of voice is. Stage directions are often printed in *italic type*.

Read the following passages carefully. One passage is in prose form, and the other is written in dramatic script form. These two passages are simply different versions of the same scene. John Steinbeck, the author, wrote two versions of *Of Mice and Men* so that the story could be read as a novel or performed onstage. Observe how these passages are similar and how they are different. In the play version, be sure to notice the characters' names in capital letters, the lines of dialogue, and the stage directions.

Novel Version	**Play Version**
Lennie got up on his knees and looked down at George. "Ain't we gonna have no supper?"	LENNIE: [*Gets up on his knees and looks down at GEORGE, plaintively.*[1]] Ain't we gonna have no supper?
"Sure we are, if you gather up some dead willow sticks. I got three cans of beans in my bindle.[2] You get a fire ready. I'll give you a match when you get the sticks together. Then we'll heat the beans and have supper."	GEORGE: Sure we are. You gather up some dead willow sticks. I got three cans of beans in my bindle.[2] I'll open 'em up while you get a fire ready. We'll eat 'em cold.
Lennie said, "I like beans with ketchup."	LENNIE: [*Companionably* [3]] I like beans with ketchup.
—Excerpted from the novel *Of Mice and Men* by John Steinbeck	—Excerpted from the play *Of Mice and Men* by John Steinbeck

[1]*plaintively:* sadly
[2]*bindle:* a bedroll, or sack
[3]*companionably:* in a friendly way

Answer the following questions about the play version of *Of Mice and Men.*

1. What two characters' names are in capital letters?

   _____ and _____

2. How many stage directions are there? _____

Compare your answers with these:

1. Lennie and George
2. two: [*Gets up on his knees and looks down at GEORGE, plaintively.*] and [*Companionably*]

As you probably noticed, the novel version and the play version are similar because they describe the same event: George and Lennie decide what to prepare for supper. The way this event is presented, however, is entirely different.

Novel Version

- A **narrator,** or storyteller, describes the characters' emotions and tells what they are doing.
  Example:
  Lennie got up on his knees and looked at George.

- **Dialogue** is in quotation marks.
  Example:
  Lennie said, "I like beans with ketchup."

Play Version

- **Stage directions** describe the characters' emotions and tell the actors what to do.
  Example:
  LENNIE: [*Gets up on his knees and looks down at GEORGE, plaintively.*]

- **Dialogue** appears following the name of the character who speaks.
  Example:
  LENNIE: [*Companionably*] I like beans with ketchup.

Plays are more enjoyable to read when you understand the purpose of acts and scenes, cast lists, and stage directions in scripts.

Acts and Scenes

To make their work easier to follow, playwrights divide their dramas into major sections called **acts.** If a play is long, a playwright may divide the acts into **scenes.** A scene always takes place in *one* room or place. When a new scene begins, the location, or setting, changes. The following version of *Camelot* has a typical number of two acts, but many scenes.

The entire action takes place
in England during King Arthur's reign
during the early sixth century (500s)

ACT I

PROLOGUE [1]: A Battlefield near Joyous Gard—A long time ago
Scene 1: A Hilltop near Camelot—Eight years earlier
Scene 2: Arthur's Study—Five years later
Scene 3: A Roadside near Camelot—A few months later
Scene 4: A Park near the castle—Immediately following
Scene 5: A Terrace of the castle—Two months later
Scene 6: The Jousting[2] Fields—The next day
Scene 7: The Terrace—Early evening of that day
Scene 8: The Great Hall—Immediately following

[1]*prologue:* an introduction
[2]*jousting:* fighting on horseback with steel-tipped spears

ACT II

PROLOGUE: The Castle Garden—A few years later
Scene 1: A Cloister on the castle grounds—Immediately following
Scene 2: The Terrace—A few weeks later
Scene 3: The Forest—The following day
Scene 4: The Queen's Bedchamber—Immediately following
Scene 5: Camelot—A month later
Scene 6: A Battlefield near Joyous Gard—A few weeks later

—Excerpted from *Camelot,* in *Stagebill*

On the lines below, answer questions about the play.

1. The entire action takes place in

   _____

2. How much time passes between Act One, Scene One and Act Two,

   Scene Six? _____

You responded correctly if you said that the action takes place in England, in a mythical place called Camelot. About eight years pass between Act I, Scene 1 and Act II, Scene 6. You can actually add up the years, months, and weeks, but there is no need. Act I, Scene 1 states "Eight years earlier." The other scenes proceed through years, months, and weeks of flashback. Then the final scene, Act II, Scene 6, is the same battlefield as in the beginning.

Cast of Characters

Just after the list of acts and scenes, the playwright introduces the play's characters in a **cast list.** Often, just the characters' names appear in a cast list. Sometimes, though, the playwright will include each character's age, occupation, physical traits, and personality.

Study the following cast list from the play *The Hot L Baltimore* by Lanford Wilson. As you read, notice what information the playwright provides about each character.

MR. KATZ: The hotel manager. Thirty-five, balding a little but hiding it. Firm and wary and at times more than a little weary. Dark, in an inexpensive dark suit.

MRS. OXENHAM: The day desk clerk-phone operator. Forty-five and firm; quick-speaking.

BILL LEWIS: The night clerk. Thirty, large-featured, well-built in a beefy way, a handsome but not aggressive face. He covers his difficulty in communicating his feelings for the Girl with a kind of clumsy, friendly bluster.

—Excerpted from *The Hot L Baltimore* by Lanford Wilson

Now answer the following questions about the characters.

1. How old is Mr. Katz? _____

2. What is Bill Lewis's job?

   _____

According to the cast list, Mr. Katz is thirty-five, and Bill Lewis is a night clerk.

Stage Directions

Besides describing how the stage should look, **stage directions** also tell the actors how to move around onstage as they perform. Terms like *stage right, stage left,* and *down center* are specific instructions as to where the actors should be when they speak their lines. Remember that stage directions are given from the actor's point of view as he or she faces the audience. For example, if a stage direction is *stage right,* the actor should move to his right and to the right side of the stage.

Read the following stage directions and see what information they contain.

> VERA: [*Looking fearfully at her husband and moving toward him stage right*] What do you mean, David?

1. How does Vera look at her husband? _____

2. Where should she walk as she speaks her line? _____

If you answered *fearfully* and *stage right,* you understood this stage direction correctly.

Dialogue

Drama depends mainly on **dialogue,** or conversation between characters, to gain people's interest and attention. A playwright must write dialogue that is realistic, to the point, and entertaining. In a good play, no line of dialogue is unnecessary. Every word a character says must reveal personality traits and advance the plot or story.

Sometimes a playwright uses punctuation to show an actor exactly how to speak his lines. A dash ($-$), for example, indicates a pause in a character's speech. Depending on a particular scene, such a pause can indicate hesitation, nervousness, or some sort of interruption. As you read the passages in the following exercises, use these questions to guide you:

1. Where does the scene occur? (Remember to picture the characters and setting in your mind.)
2. What information do you get from the stage directions?
3. What is the dialogue about? Does it reveal a conflict between characters?
4. How does the playwright's use of punctuation add to the dialogue?

EXERCISE 4

Practice in Reading Dialogue

Directions: Using the preceding questions as a guide, read the passage that follows from Agatha Christie's play *Verdict*. Then answer the questions.

(1) KARL: [*Moving to left of the sofa*] I have something to tell you, Inspector. I know who killed my wife. It was not Miss Koletzky.

OGDEN: [*Politely*] Who was it, then?

KARL: It was a girl called Helen Rollander. She is one of my pupils.
(5) [*He crosses and sits in the armchair*] She—she formed an unfortunate attachment to me. She was alone with my wife on the day in question, and she gave her an overdose of the heart medicine.

OGDEN: [*Moving down center*] How do you know this, Professor
(10) Hendryk?

KARL: She told me herself, this morning.

OGDEN: Indeed? Were there any witnesses?

KARL: No, but I am telling you the truth.

OGDEN: [*Thoughtfully*] Helen—Rollander. You mean the daughter
(15) of Sir William Rollander?

KARL: Yes. Her father is William Rollander. He is an important man. Does that make any difference?

OGDEN: [*Moving below the left end of the sofa*] No, it wouldn't make any difference—if your story were true.

—Excerpted from *Verdict* by Agatha Christie

1. Name the occupations of Karl and Ogden.

a. _____

b. _____

2. What are Karl and Ogden discussing? _____

3. There is a dash between *Helen* and *Rollander* in line 14 to show that

(1) Ogden speaks the name in a slow, thoughtful way
(2) someone has interrupted the conversation
(3) Ogden has trouble speaking
(4) Karl jumps as Ogden speaks the name Helen
(5) Ogden moves to the left of the sofa

4. What conflict is revealed in this passage?

(1) Karl is jealous of Ogden's feelings for Helen.
(2) Ogden does not believe Karl's explanation of the murder.
(3) Ogden is angry that Miss Koletzky has betrayed him.
(4) Helen and Miss Koletzky are jealous of one another.
(5) Helen and Ogden went to grade school together.

5. After reading the passage, you can infer that this play is probably a

    (1) comedy
    (2) musical
    (3) murder mystery
    (4) tragedy
    (5) farce

Answers are on page 338.

EXERCISE 5

Putting It All Together

This exercise is based on a passage from *The Glass Menagerie*[1] by Tennessee Williams. The main character in this play is Laura Wingfield. Laura is extremely shy and is especially self-conscious about a brace that she wears on one leg. She spends most of her time taking care of her collection of small glass animals.

In this passage, Laura and Jim talk about what Laura is doing with her life. In high school, Laura had a crush on Jim but was too shy to speak to him.

Directions: Read the passage carefully and then answer the questions that follow.

(1)   [*Jim lights a cigarette and leans indolently*[2] *back on his elbows smiling at Laura with a warmth and charm which lights her inwardly with altar candles.*[3] *She remains by the table, picks up a piece from the glass menagerie collection, and turns it in her*
(5)   *hands to cover her tumult.*[4]]

JIM: [*After several reflective*[5] *puffs on his cigarette*] What have you done since high school?

[*She seems not to hear him.*]
Huh?

(10)   [*Laura looks up.*]
I said what have you done since high school, Laura?

LAURA: Nothing much.

JIM: You must have been doing something these six long years.

LAURA: Yes.

(15)   JIM: Well, then, such as what?

LAURA: I took a business course at business college—

JIM: How did that work out?

[1]*menagerie:* a collection of many different animals
[2]*indolently:* lazily
[3]*lights her inwardly with altar candles:* she is glowing with pleasure
[4]*tumult:* confusion or agitation
[5]*reflective:* thoughtful

LAURA: Well, not very—well—I had to drop out, it gave me—indigestion—

(20)

[*Jim laughs gently.*]

JIM: What are you doing now?

LAURA: I don't do anything—much. Oh, please don't think I sit around doing nothing! My glass collection takes up a good deal of time. Glass is something you have to take good care of.

(25)

JIM: What did you say—about glass?

LAURA: Collection I said—I have one—[*She clears her throat and turns away again, acutely*[6] *shy.*]

JIM: [Abruptly[7]] You know what I judge to be the trouble with you? Inferiority complex! . . . Yep—that's what I judge

(30) to be your principal trouble. A lack of confidence in yourself as a person. You don't have the proper amount of faith in yourself. . . . For instance that clumping you thought was so awful in high school. You say that you even dreaded to walk into class. You see what you did? You dropped out of

(35) school, you gave up an education because of a clump, which as far as I know was practically non-existent! A little physical defect is what you have. Hardly noticeable even! Magnified thousands of times by imagination! You know what my strong advice to you is? Think of yourself

(40) as *superior* in some way!

—Excerpted from *The Glass Menagerie* by Tennessee Williams

[6]*acutely:* very much or extremely

[7]*abrupty:* suddenly

1. What has Laura mostly done since high school?

   (1) cared for her collection of glass animals
   (2) worked at a local department store
   (3) married her high school sweetheart and had two children
   (4) graduated from business college
   (5) cared for her sick mother

2. In lines 3–5, Laura picks up a glass animal from her collection to

   (1) prevent Jim from breaking it
   (2) hide her nervousness and confusion
   (3) show Jim how fragile the piece of glass is
   (4) hide her feelings of anger
   (5) hide the animal from her brother

3. The dashes in lines 18–19 and 26 reveal that Laura

   (1) stutters when she's nervous
   (2) is hesitant to openly talk to Jim
   (3) shares her thoughts easily with others
   (4) has a severe medical condition
   (5) has indigestion often

4. In lines 35–36 Jim says, "you gave up an education because of a clump, which as far as I know was practically non-existent!" What does Jim mean?

(1) Laura was right to drop out of high school because of her low self-image.

(2) Jim is sorry that he didn't finish high school.

(3) Laura dropped out of school because of a disability that others hardly noticed.

(4) Jim and the other students used to wonder why Laura wore the brace.

(5) Jim knows how popular he had been in high school.

Answers are on page 338.

Chapter Review: Poetry

In this chapter, you learned the differences among prose, poetry, and drama. You studied the many subjects of poetry and you paraphrased poetry into your own words.

EXERCISE 6

Directions: This poem was written by Pablo Neruda, a poet from Chile. Read the poem and answer the questions that follow.

ODE TO BICYCLES

(1) I was walking
down
a sizzling road:
the sun popped like
(5) a field of blazing maize,[1]
the
earth
was hot,
an infinite circle
(10) with an empty
blue sky overhead.

A few bicycles
passed me by,
the only
(15) insects
in
that dry
moment of summer,
silent,
(20) swift,

[1]*maize:* Indian corn

translucent;[2]
they
barely stirred
the air.

(25) Workers and girls
were riding to their
factories,
giving
their eyes
(30) to summer,
their heads to the sky,
sitting on the
hard
beetle backs
(35) of the whirling
bicycles
that whirred
as they rode by
bridges, rosebushes, brambles
(40) and midday.

I thought about evening when
the boys
wash up,
sing, eat, raise
(45) a cup
of wine
in honor
of love
and life,
(50) and waiting
at the door,
the bicycle,
stilled,
because
(55) only moving
does it have a soul,
and fallen there
it isn't
a translucent insect
(60) humming
through summer
but
a cold
skeleton
(65) that will return to
life
only
when it's needed,
when it's light,

[2]*translucent:* clear so that light can pass through

70   that is,
            with
            the resurrection[3]
            of each day.
        —by Pablo Neruda

"Ode to Bicycles," by Pablo Neruda in *Selected Odes of Pablo Neruda, III Third Book of Odes,* English translation, edited/translated by Margaret Sayers Peden. Copyright © 1990 Regents of the University of California. Also belonging to the work *Tercer Libro De Odas,* © Fundacion Pablo Neruda, 1957. Reprinted by permission of University of California Press, Agencia Literaria Carmen Balcells, and Margaret Sayers Peden.

[3]*resurrection:* the rising again or rebirth

1. Describe the setting of the poem in the first and second stanzas.

    a. What is the road like? _____

    b. What is the sun like? _____

    c. What is the sky like? _____

    d. What are the bicycles like? _____

    _____

2. Describe the workers and girls in the third stanza.

    a. What are they doing? _____

    _____

    b. What sounds are the bicycles making? _____

3. Describe the thoughts of the poet in the fourth stanza.

    a. What does he think about evening? _____

    _____

    _____

    b. What "life" does the bicycle have? _____

    _____

4. What is the main subject of this poem?

    (1) a pretty Spanish town
    (2) workers and girls going to work
    (3) the sun and the sky in summer
    (4) boys at the evening meal
    (5) the life cycle of bicycles

5. Throughout the poem, bicycles are compared to

    (1) insects like beetles
    (2) musical instruments
    (3) blazing maize
    (4) factory machines
    (5) rosebushes and brambles

Answers are on page 338.

Chapter Review: Drama

In this chapter, you learned the differences among prose, poetry, and drama. You recognized that drama has a different format that includes acts and scenes, stage directions, and dialogue.

EXERCISE 7

Directions: Read the following excerpts from the movie guide summary and screenplay of *Raiders of the Lost Ark*. Then answer the questions that follow.

MOVIE GUIDE SUMMARY

RAIDERS OF THE LOST ARK

Story [by George Lucas and Philip Kaufman] begins in 1936 as Indiana Jones (Harrison Ford), an archeologist[1] and university professor who's not above a little mercenary[2] activity on the side, plunders[3] a South American jungle tomb. He secures a priceless golden Godhead, only to have it snatched away by longtime archeological rival Paul Freeman, now employed by the Nazis.[4]

Back in the States, Jones is approached by U.S. intelligence agents who tell him the Nazis are rumored to have discovered the location of the Lost Ark of the Covenant (where the broken 10 commandments were sealed). The ark is assumed to contain an awesome destructive power.

1981: Best Art Direction, Sound, Editing, Visual Effects, Sound Effects Editing [Academy Awards]

NOMINATIONS: Best Picture, Director, Cinematography

—Excerpted from *Variety Movie Guide 2001*

[1]*archeologist:* a scientist who studies the past, including fossils, relics, and monuments
[2]*mercenary:* greedy for money
[3]*plunders:* loots or steals
[4]*Nazis:* Adolph Hitler's group in Germany during WWII

SCREENPLAY

The students stand and start to EXIT, one leaving an apple on Indy's desk.
Marcus moves in front of Indy's desk.

INDY: I had it, Marcus. I had it in my hand.

MARCUS: What happened?

INDY: Guess.

Marcus picks up the apple and polishes it on his sleeve.

MARCUS: (laughs) Belloq?

INDY: Wanna hear about it?

MARCUS: Not at all. I'm sure everything you do for the museum conforms to the International Treaty for the Protection of Antiquities.[1]

Indy begins to pace the room.

INDY: It's beautiful, Marcus. I can get it. I got it all figured out. There's only one place he can sell it, Marrakech.[2] I need two thousand dollars.

MARCUS: Listen to me, old boy.

Indy pulls some items from a drawer and shows them to Marcus.

INDY: (overlapping) Look . . .

MARCUS: I've brought some people to see you.

INDY: Look, I've got these pieces. They're good pieces, Marcus.

MARCUS: Indiana, yes, the museum will buy them as usual, no questions asked. Yes, they are nice.

Marcus takes the items.

INDY: They're worth at least the price of a ticket to Marrakech.

MARCUS: The people I brought are important. They're waiting.

INDY: What people?

MARCUS: Army Intelligence. They knew you were coming before I did. Seem to know everything. Wouldn't tell me what they wanted.

Marcus leaves the classroom and Indy follows him into the hall.

INDY: Well, what do I want to see them for? What am I, in trouble?

—Excerpted from *Raiders of the Lost Ark, The Screenplay,* by Lawrence Kasdan

From *Raiders of the Lost Ark* © 1981 Lucasfilm Ltd. &™. All rights reserved. Used under authorization. *Raiders of the Lost Ark* excerpt courtesy of Lucasfilm Ltd.

[1]*antiquities:* from ancient times, at least before the Middle Ages
[2]*Marrakech:* city in Morocco, a country on the northwest side of Africa

1. The time period of the action in *Raiders of the Lost Ark* is

   _____.

2. The movie guide summary indicated that Indiana Jones was an archeologist "who's not above a little mercenary activity on the side." What does this tell you about the character of Indiana Jones?

   He

   (1) is most interested in culture
   (2) wants to make archeology history
   (3) wants to impress the ladies
   (4) loves a life of reckless adventure
   (5) is somewhat greedy

3. The movie guide and excerpt explain the basic conflicts in the film. Circle all that apply.

   The conflicts are between

   (1) Indy and Marcus
   (2) Indy and his students
   (3) United States intelligence and the Nazis
   (4) Indy and Belloq
   (5) Indiana Jones and Paul Freeman

4. The movie guide states, "The ark is assumed to contain an awesome destructive power." What reasonable advice would you give to Indiana Jones?

   (1) Be careful, but go for it!
   (2) You only live once!
   (3) Our country needs you!
   (4) Ignore all warnings!
   (5) Forget about it!

5. The screenplay setting for the excerpt is

   (1) the Temple of Doom
   (2) the city of Marrakech
   (3) Indy's university classroom
   (4) a United States Army base
   (5) Germany in World War II

6. In the excerpt, Marcus accepts some "pieces" from Indy. Marcus says, "Indiana, yes, the museum will buy them as usual, no questions asked." This tells you that the methods the museum uses are

   (1) doubtful
   (2) lawful
   (3) aggressive
   (4) historical
   (5) reliable

7. Marcus says in the excerpt, "I'm sure everything you do for the museum conforms to the International Treaty for the Protection of Antiquities." The tone Marcus uses for this statement is probably

   (1) serious
   (2) sarcastic
   (3) angry
   (4) surprised
   (5) unconcerned

Answers are on page 338.

Answer Key

CHAPTER 1
GAINING MEANING FROM WORDS

Exercise 1: Alphabetizing (page 190)
1. broccoli, cauliflower, lettuce, peas, radish, spinach
2. Chevrolet, Dodge, Ford, Honda, Kia, Toyota
3. accept, control, free, hate, love, reject

Exercise 2: Alphabetizing Beyond the First Letter (page 190)
1. need, needle, nerd, nervous, nest
2. worm, worn, worry, wreck, wrench
3. able, about, abuse, ache, achieve

Exercise 3: Using Guide Words (page 192)
Part 1

2. after	5. after
3. before	6. after
4. before	7. same page

Part 2

8. after	12. same page
9. before	13. same page
10. after	14. before
11. after	

Exercise 4: Finding Related Forms of a Word (page 193)
2. marriage
3. quick
4. liquid
5. guardian
6. discontent
7. charge

Exercise 5: Looking Up Pronunciations (page 194)
Answers may vary because dictionaries use different symbols and key words.

Pronunciation	Key Word
2. rān	ace
3. īl	ice
4. säm	mop, mar
5. bī-əs	ice; abut
6. plāg	ace
7. plak	ash

Exercise 6: Understanding Dictionary Labels (page 195)
2. noun, verb, adjective
3. verb, noun
4. adjective, noun
5. adverb, preposition
6. noun, verb
7. adverb, adjective, preposition
8. preposition, conjunction
9. pronoun

Exercise 7: Understanding Multiple Meanings (pages 196)
The definitions in your dictionary may differ somewhat in wording from these, but the general meanings should be the same.

2. **a.** to give an account of, as for publication
   b. to present oneself, as for work
3. **a.** any of the lines of seats in a theater
   b. to propel (a boat) with oars
4. **a.** the shape of a solid item
   b. a counter, as for serving snacks or drinks
5. **a.** a factory or workshop for the manufacture of a particular product
   b. a small growing thing with leaves, stem, roots, etc.

Exercise 8: Applying the Prefix/Suffix Rule (page 198)

2. <u>sub</u>-trac-<u>tion</u>
3. <u>pre</u>-ven-<u>tion</u>
4. <u>mis</u>-spell-<u>ing</u>
5. <u>ex</u>-tend-<u>ed</u>
6. <u>re</u>-tire-<u>ment</u>
7. swift-<u>ly</u>
8. <u>pro</u>-pos-<u>al</u>

Exercise 9: Applying the VC/CV Rule (pages 199–200)

Part 1

2. rem-nant
   vc cv
3. cur-tain
   vc cv
4. ap-pen-dix
   vc cvc cv
5. bud-get
   vc cv
6. em-bas-sy
   vc cvc cv
7. con-sis-tent
   vc cvc cv
8. fil-ter
   vc cv

Part 2

10. <u>in</u>-<u>ter</u>-view-<u>er</u>
11. <u>com</u>-part-<u>ment</u>
12. <u>cor</u>-res-pond
13. or-gan-<u>ist</u>

Exercise 10: Applying the VCV Rule (page 200)

2. rē-cent
3. cab-i-net
4. tō-mā-tō
5. lī -censé
6. hū-māné
7. fē-mālé
8. lim-it

Exercise 11: Adding Prefixes (pages 201–202)

Part 1

The prefix of each word is <u>underlined</u>.

2. <u>inter</u>section
3. <u>co</u>worker
4. <u>auto</u>graph

Part 2

5. b
6. a
7. d
8. c

Exercise 12: Prefixes That Make Opposites (page 203)

2. (ir)responsible, not responsible
3. (im)mature, not mature
4. (non)violent, not violent
5. (dis)abled, not able
6. (il)legitimate, not legitimate
7. (in)considerate, not considerate
8. (anti)-inflammatory, against inflammation (swelling)
9. (dis)approve, away from sight
10. (un)certain, not sure

Exercise 13: Time Prefixes (page 204)

1. d
2. b
3. g
4. f
5. c
6. a
7. e

Exercise 14: Place Prefixes (page 205)

1. e
2. b
3. c
4. a
5. f
6. g
7. d

Exercise 15: Number Prefixes (page 206)

1. d
2. a
3. c
4. b
5. e
6. g
7. f

Exercise 16: Familiar Suffixes (page 207)

1. e
2. h
3. a
4. f
5. b
6. g
7. d
8. c

Exercise 17: Locating Roots or Base Words (page 209)

Part 1

2. de<u>fect</u>
3. tran<u>script</u>
4. in<u>script</u>ion
5. tran<u>sport</u>ed
6. de<u>ceive</u>
7. in<u>cred</u>ible
8. <u>fid</u>elity
9. <u>port</u>age
10. in<u>fect</u>
11. in<u>fid</u>el
12. con<u>ceive</u>

Part 2

13. h
14. d
15. a
16. f
17. b
18. g
19. c
20. e

Exercise 18: Locating Greek and Latin Roots (page 210)

1. c
2. a
3. b

Exercise 19: Finding Synonyms (page 211)

2. book
3. base
4. brave
5. trip
6. thinking
7. leave
8. often

Exercise 20: Finding Antonyms (page 212)

Part 1

2. answer
3. tight
4. ignorance
5. negative

Part 2

7. construction
8. criticized
9. flavorless

Exercise 21: Chapter Review (pages 213–214)

Part 1

1. car
2. rare
3. die
4. shaking

Part 2

5. *circle:* thin
   underline: fat
6. *circle:* beginning
   underline: ending
7. *circle:* damaged
   underline: perfect
8. *circle:* advanced
   underline: retreated
9. *circle:* expert
   underline: incompetent

Part 3

10. program–prolong
11. 5
12. 1

Part 4

13. d
14. c
15. a
16. e
17. b

Part 5

19. d
20. a
21. c
22. b

CHAPTER 2
UNDERSTANDING WHAT YOU READ

Exercise 1: Identifying Words in Context (pages 216–217)

1. (1) 3. (2) 5. (1) 7. (3)
2. (3) 4. (3) 6. (4)

Exercise 2: Using Examples Given in Context (page 218)

1. (4) 2. (1) 3. (3)

Exercise 3: Using Definitions Given in Context (pages 219–220)

1. (2) 3. (1) 5. (4) 7. (1)
2. (4) 4. (3) 6. (2)

Exercise 4: Understanding Connotations of Words and Sentences (pages 221–222)

Part 1

1–6.

Positive	Negative
athletes	jocks
unusual	weird
crowd	mob
firm	stubborn
assertive	pushy

Part 2

7. a. + b. –
8. a. – b. +
9. a. – b. +

Exercise 5: Translating Euphemisms (page 222)

1. f 3. c 5. e 7. d
2. a 4. g 6. b

Exercise 6: Key Words in Sentences (page 224)

Who or what?	*Did what?*
1. Paul Gauguin	left his family
2. Harriet Tubman	rescued thousands
3. the president	voiced his disappointment

Exercise 7: Finding Main Ideas in Newspaper Articles (page 225)

1. **(5)** Only choice (5) gives the main idea of the entire article. Choice (1) is an inference. Choice (2) is not true. Choices (3) and (4) are not necessarily so.
2. e 5. b 8. d
3. i 6. g 9. c
4. a 7. h 10. f

Exercise 8: Finding Main Idea in Advertisements (page 227)

1. *Main idea:* Grand Opening: Park Place Townhouses
2. *Detail (location):* near great schools, transportation, restaurants, shopping malls
3. *Detail (size):* 2–3 bedrooms
4. *Detail (features):* air conditioning; walk-in closets, 1½ to 2½ baths
5. *Detail (price)* $150,000–$200,000
6. **(3)** The prices are labeled "Preconstruction," so they will likely increase when some are built.

Exercise 9: Main Idea and Details in a Paragraph (pages 228–229)

1. **(2)** Choices (1), (3), and (4) are details. Choice (5) is not mentioned in the paragraph.
2. Your list should include four of the following: physical or verbal abuse; off-color or insulting jokes; racial, ethnic, or religious slurs; unwelcome physical contact or sexual advances; unfounded complaints against another employee; unfair benefits given an employee as a result of sexual favors.

Exercise 10: Unstated Main Idea (pages 229–230)

1. **(3)** This choice summarizes the whole paragraph.
2. e 4. b 6. c
3. d 5. a

Exercise 11: Finding the Main Idea of a Passage (pages 230–231)

1. **(A)** DNA testing is setting a new standard for courtroom evidence.
   (B) The DNA bar code is a powerful tool to solve crimes.
   (C) The key to reading the DNA genetic code is the small differences.
   (D) In the late 1990s, laboratories began to use STRs.
   (E) With the STR method, the chance for error is extremely small.

2. **(3)** This is the only statement that summarizes the whole passage. It is also the main idea of the first paragraph.

Exercise 12: More Main Ideas of Passages (page 232)

1. **(5)** The author gives several reasons for choice (5). He says, "with most appliances . . . defects are almost sure to show up before the original warranty expires." He also says, "After that, the service contract may cost more than the needed repairs." Choice (2) is not true. Choices (1), (3), and (4) are true but not the *main* idea.

2. **(3)** The real reason (and main idea) is that manufacturers want to gather information about you and your spending habits.

Exercise 13: Summarizing a Paragraph (pages 234–235)

Passage 1

1. **a.** old lady
   b. planted flowers
   c. spring
   d. in her garden
   e. carefully, thoughtfully
   f. to leave something pretty behind for others to enjoy

2. Your summary should be similar to this one: *An old lady planted flowers in her garden in the spring to leave something pretty behind for others to enjoy.*

3. **(4)** According to what the woman says her doctor has told her, you can conclude that the woman thinks that she is going to die soon.

Passage 2

4. **a.** some toy manufacturers
   b. used children to try out toys
   c. recently
   d. special room in their factory
   e. watch children as they play
   f. so that designers can test safety and predict good sellers

5. Your summary statement should be similar to this one: *Recently some toy manufacturers have asked children to try out toys in a special room in their factory so that designers can predict which toys will be good sellers and test toy safety.*

Exercise 14: Chapter Review (pages 236–238)

1. **(1)** The example given is of people who divorced "almost like friends, quietly, quickly."

2. **(3)** The clue is "reflected the light from the sea."

3. **a.** Marc Sequy and his wife Alice
   b. went to a restaurant and saw Marc's ex-wife
   c. in a restaurant by the sea
   d. probably at lunchtime because the sun is overhead (paragraph 14)
   e. by chance; the sighting makes both Marc and Alice uncomfortable

4. Your summary should be similar to this one: *Marc Seguy and his wife Alice go to a restaurant by the sea. They don't take a table by the window because Marc sees his ex-wife. Marc's new wife becomes curious about his ex-wife. Both Marc and Alice become uncomfortable and self-conscious. They try hard to ignore his ex-wife, but they are aware of her. They decide his ex-wife is the one who is uncomfortable.*

5. **(5)** Their behavior suggests that they are uncomfortable but they don't want to admit it.

CHAPTER 3
FINDING HIDDEN MEANINGS

Exercise 1: Using Inference in a Cartoon
    (page 241)
1. (2), (3), (4)
2. (2), (5)
3. (1) The man is looking up at the camera and has not yet placed his ideas in the suggestion box. He realizes he is being watched.

Exercise 2: Using Details to Make an Inference
    (pages 242–243)
1. (1) We can infer that the narrator is a young girl. The narrator says, "I have been praying not to grow any taller" and "I have been listening carefully to my mother's words."
2. (2), (3), (4) There are no clues to support choices (1) and (5).
3. (5) The narrator thinks of several different answers. The answers involve growing taller, listening carefully, and dogs sleeping in the moonlight. This shows her imagination.

Exercise 3: Inferring Positive And Negative Connotations from Advertisements
    (page 244)
Part 1
1. can't-go-wrong classic, silky, on-the-go, high fashion
2. Smooth, slinky, sensual
3. Cozy hideaway, modern, galore, must-see
4. experienced, master, modern, computerized, auto clinic

Part 2
All the words and phrases with positive connotations are shown in **boldface type.** All the words with negative connotations are shown underlined.

Are you among the more than 61% of adults who are overweight or even obese? Have you tried everything? Every diet? Every exercise program? Does nothing work for you? Is two hours of your time worth **getting rid of your excess weight**? 10, 50, or even 100 pounds!

TRY OUR **INSTANT WEIGHT-LOSS** HYPNOSIS SEMINAR FOR **TRIED AND TRUE RESULTS. 100% GUARANTEED** OR YOUR **MONEY BACK.**

How long have you been smoking? 10, 20, 30, 40, or even 50 years? Are you tired of being criticized by nonsmokers? Are you tired of being told to "Take it outside!" Are you worried about your **health**? Does a heart attack or lung cancer scare you? Maybe it's time to **really quit.** Is two hours of your time worth **kicking the habit**? **Take back your body! For good, and once and for all!**

TRY OUR **INSTANT SMOKE-ENDERS** HYPNOSIS SEMINAR FOR **TRIED AND TRUE RESULTS. 100% GUARANTEED** OR YOUR **MONEY BACK.**

Exercise 4: Making Inferences in Advertising
    (page 245)
1. (2), (3), (4)
2. (5) The ad states that flavorful breads [are] bound to bring excitement to the table.

Exercise 5: Inferring Ideas in Passages
    (pages 246–247)
1. (1) Because people laughed, they understood the double meaning and the insult to Hitler.
2. (4) The passage says that people were depressed before Churchill invented the sign.
3. (4) Churchill understood that the British people needed a morale boost, and his humorous symbol provided it.

Exercise 6: Drawing Inferences in Fiction
    (pages 248–249)
1. (1), (2), (3), and (5) are all stated directly.
2. (2), (3), (4)
3. (3)
4. (1), (3) Choices (2), (4), and (5) are not supported by the information given in the passage.

Exercise 7: Predicting Words (page 250)
1. birthday
2. everyone/everybody
3. a/the/that
4. weather/day
5. to/we'd
6. Everyone/Everybody
7. birthday/funny
8. with
9. Happy

Exercise 8: Identifying Directly Stated Predictions (page 251)
1. (1), (2), (5)
2. (2), (3)

Exercise 9: Predicting Ideas from a Cartoon (page 252)
1. (2), (3), and (5) are all shown directly in the cartoon.
2. (4) Since Roscoe made a hole in the door, he probably did other damage, too.
3. (1) Earl's wife is doing research about Roscoe's problem, so the couple may look for the help of an expert (pet psychic).

Exercise 10: Using Inference to Make Predictions (page 254)
1. (1), (2), (4), and (5) are directly stated.
2. (1)

Exercise 11: Using Graphic Organizers (page 256)
The answers in this exercise are given as examples. Your answers will be different.

1. *main idea:* our backyard
   supporting details: children, swing set, sprinkler, grill, patio
2. Here is a sample paragraph based on the answers given above.

   In the summer, there is a lot of activity in our backyard. Neighborhood children come to play on our swing set and cool off in our sprinkler. For dinner, my wife and I often cook hamburgers on the grill. When we've saved enough money, we're hoping to put in a small patio.

Exercise 12: Using Outlines (pages 257–258)
The answers in this exercise are given as examples. Your answers will be different.

1. *main idea:* **I.** If I won the lottery
   supporting: **A.** pay off all debts
   details: **B.** get gifts for family
   C. take a vacation
   D. give some money to charity
   E. put the rest in the bank
2. Here is a sample paragraph.

   I dream about winning the lottery. If I won, first I would pay off all my debts. Then I would get gifts for all my family. Next, I would go on a dream vacation, maybe even to Hawaii! Also, I would give some money to charity. Whatever is left I would put in the bank.

Exercise 13: Chapter Review (pages 258–260)
Part 1
1. (1), (2), (4) Choices (3) and (5) have nothing to do with age.
2. (4) These two quotes show that she believes he's too young and is worried about him.
3. (2) Clues are "Minnesota was mostly wild then," "Indians to the north and west," "frontier forts," and "Rebel soldiers."
4. (3) He says in Passage Three, "This is all a mistake."
5. (5) The Rebels are charging and firing, but Charley's group hasn't fired yet. The logical prediction is that Charley will be hurt.

Part 2
Share your paragraph with friends or classmates.

CHAPTER 4
ORGANIZING IDEAS

Exercise 1: Identifying Facts and Opinions (pages 262–263)

1. F   **3.** O   **5.** F   **7.** F   **9.** F
2. F   **4.** O   **6.** O   **8.** O   **10.** F

11. (2) Opinions are statements of what someone *believes* is *true*. Therefore, opinions are judgments and, unlike facts, cannot be proven.

Exercise 2: Identifying Facts, Opinions, and Generalizations (pages 264–265)

Part 1

1. G   **3.** G   **5.** O
2. O   **4.** G

Part 2

6. generalization, generalization, fact
7. opinion, generalization, fact
8. (1), (3) Both of these choices could be backed up by factual data, while choices (2), (4), and (5) are only opinions.

Exercise 3: Understanding a Time-Line Sequence (page 266)

1. about 6 years old   **3.** about 18 years
2. about 18 years old   **4.** (4)

Exercise 4: Signal Words That Show Sequence (page 267)

1. <u>First</u>, bring the water to a boil. <u>Second</u>, add the eggs. <u>Third</u>, turn down the heat. <u>Then</u> simmer the eggs for fifteen minutes, and <u>last</u>, rinse the eggs with cold water.
2. <u>Before</u> I met her, I was afraid I wouldn't know what to say. <u>After</u> meeting her in person, I found she was friendly, so I relaxed.
3. <u>When</u> I got on the bus, I must have had my wallet because I got my fare out of it. <u>Later</u>, at home, I discovered my wallet was gone.
4. (3) Choices (1) and (2) are both correct.

Exercise 5: Arranging Items in Correct Sequence (page 267)

You should have filled in the blanks in this sequence: **2, 3, 4, 1.**

Exercise 6: Understanding Sequence in a Story (pages 268–269)

1. You should have filled in the blanks in this sequence: **3, 1, 4, 2, 7, 5, 6.**
2. (1) The plainclothes man makes it clear that Bob is wanted in Chicago. He says Bob's under arrest and that he's going to the police station.
3. (4) Jimmy was not able to arrest his old friend himself. He did, however, make sure another officer did so. That shows that he does his job no matter what. He has proved that he is honest.

Exercise 7: Understanding Sequence in Directions (page 270)

1. (3) The article tells how to make decisions more easily.
2. Your directions should be numbered in this sequence: **3, 4, 1, 2,** and **5.**

Exercise 8: Comparing and Contrasting Information (pages 271–273)

1. *Similar:* seating capacity, towing capacity
Different: total weight, cargo capacity, length, gas use, price
2. (3), (4), (5)
3. (1), (2), (3), (5)
4. (1), (4), (5) Choices (2) and (3) are the same for both minivans.

Exercise 9: Comparing and Contrasting Two People (pages 273–274)

1. Your answers should include two of these three similarities: Both were strong and spoke their own minds; neither would stick to traditional women's roles; both worked to increase funds for charities and health issues.
2. Hillary was politically minded. She was a high-powered lawyer. She is a U.S. Senator from New York. She may even run for president.
3. (1), (2), (3), (5)
4. (1), (2)
5. (5) The writer calls both women "strong." The writer says both tried to increase funds for charities and health issues.

Exercise 10: Identifying Cause and Effect (page 276)

Note: The effects are underlined. The causes are in italics.

2. Because *Carlos added salt instead of sugar,* his cake tasted terrible.
3. Because *Amy is allergic to bee stings,* her brother rushed her to the doctor when she was stung.
4. He had a flat tire because *he had run over a sharp nail.*
5. Because *the radio was so loud,* I didn't hear the phone.
6. Pete was exhausted because *he had worked overtime.*

Exercise 11: Identifying Cause-and-Effect Relationships (page 277)

1. Because
2. because or since
3. therefore
4. Because or Since
5. therefore
6. so
7. Because or Since

Exercise 12: Following Cause-and-Effect Relationships in Paragraphs (pages 278–279)

Passage 1

1. The *cause* is about what will happen to people and animals if large forests and jungles in the world are destroyed.
2. **(2)** This effect is discussed throughout the paragraph.
3. **(3)** The passage states that scientists are worried about the bad effects of destroying forests. Therefore, they would probably advise national leaders to preserve at least part of the forest as it is.

Passage 2

4. *Cause:* Pigs
   Effect: pigs
5. *Cause:* Pesticides
   Effect: Bald eagles
6. *Cause:* Golden eagles
   Effect: island foxes
7. (1), (2), (3), (5)
8. (5)

Exercise 13: Working with Analogies (pages 281–282)

Part 1

1. b
2. c
3. c
4. a
5. c
6. a

Part 2

7. read
8. percent
9. tear
10. ounce
11. cut
12. waist

Exercise 14: Chapter Review (pages 283–284)

1. **(3)** She says that an era of her life has ended.
2. **(2)** Charles wanted to color with green crayons instead of red.
3. **(4)** She gives Charles an apple and calls him her helper.
4. **(5)** The teacher says, "We don't have any Charles in the kindergarten."
5. reality

CHAPTER 5
UNDERSTANDING FICTION

Exercise 1: Forming Pictures in Your Mind (pages 286–287)

Passage 1

1. inside the barn
2. Clues are "grasses flattened," "a hiss of wind," "a sudden pungent smell," and "strange light."
3. Details that suggest color are "grasses" and "Our faces looked yellow."
4. Sounds heard are "a hiss of wind," and "raindrops came, gentle at first, then stronger and louder."
5. The children covered their ears and "stared at each other without speaking." "Caleb looked frightened," and the other child is frightened, too, but tries not to show it. She "*tried* to smile at him."
6. The clue is "their ears flat against their heads."

Passage 2

7. (2) The first sentence describes the graveyard "at the edge of his own hay-land."
8. (4) There is no mention of a barn.
9. (1) In the last sentence he says it "looked very pretty."
10. (1) The description of the snow tells you that this is a description of a winter scene.

Exercise 2: Identifying Comparisons (pages 289–290)

1. (4) The author is comparing the strange effects of an earthquake to a nightmare.
2. (3) The pail "jumped and rattled like a spider dancing on a hot stove."
3. (2) They "heaved and bobbed up and down" like ships at sea.
4. (4) The street is red and twisting like a snake.

Exercise 3: Understanding Tone (pages 291–293)

1. (3) In the last paragraph the author/narrator describes the "dampness of the catacombs."
2. (1) In the first paragraph, the author/narrator describes making tiers of stone.
3. (4) Expressions such as strange laughs and "a low laugh that erected the hairs upon my head" create fear in the reader.
4. (2) The overall tone is horrifying because of the Montresor's evil act. He is leaving his friend to die.

Exercise 4: Picturing a Character from a Description (page 294–295)

1. (5) "Large" is used in the first line.
2. (2) She may be described as "confident and assured" because she fights back at the boy who tries to steal her purse.
3. (3) The author probably admires the woman because she takes care of herself. She does not allow herself to be a victim.

Exercise 5: Understanding Plot (pages 296–297)

1. (1)   2. (3)   3. (4)
4. (2) *Narcissism* comes from the name Narcissus. Therefore, you can conclude that people who suffer from narcissism think only about themselves.

Exercise 6: Identifying Point of View (page 298)

1. b. Clues are "*Her* husband" and "*his* arm."
2. a. Clues are "*I* wrote" and "*Mine* came."
3. c. Clues are "*He never*" and "But *he felt bad.*"
4. a. Clues are "*I* waited" and "*I* sat."

Exercise 7: Identifying Theme (pages 300–301)

1. Hector and his grandfather Luis
2. (5) Hector and Luis talk of real estate and money.
3. (1) The questions show a real interest in knowledge (learning).
4. (3) Luis's "dream went out like a lightbulb." He would have to deal with the shattering of his dreams.

Exercise 8: Chapter Review (page 301–304)

1. a. Old Woman Swamp
   b. outside the narrator's house
   c. beside a red nightshade bush on the road
2. a. "I" (the narrator)   c. Mama
   b. Doodle   d. Daddy
3. Doodle and the scarlet ibis
4. (2) Doodle's brother is "I."

5. (1), (2), (5) Choice 1: The narrator says, "But all of us must have something or someone to be proud of, and Doodle had become mine." Choice 2: The narrator said, "Occasionally I too became discouraged because it didn't seem as if he was trying." Choice 5: The narrator said, "I put him on his feet at least a hundred times each afternoon." There is no evidence in the passage for Choice (3). You can infer that he *is* ashamed of Doodle, so choice (4) is not true.

6. (3) In the passage, the narrator describes Doodle: "making his vermilion neck appear unusually long and slim."

7. (4) This ibis came from South America in a storm and Doodle died in a rainstorm.

8. (2) The passage says "I ran as fast as I could, leaving him far behind me with a wall of rain dividing us."

9. (5) All the other statements are true of rain, but those choices do not explain the feeling of anger with the word *heresy*.

10. (1) The narrator has let his weaker brother die in a storm, and he is crying at the end as he is sheltering Doodle.

11. (2) The narrator does love his brother, but this feeling gets mixed up with pride. He doesn't teach his crippled brother to walk just because it's the right thing to do. He does it because he's ashamed of Doodle and *needs* to feel proud of him.

12. (5) "Battles" are going on between the narrator and Doodle (Choice 3), but also within the narrator himself (Choice 2).

UNDERSTANDING POETRY AND DRAMA

Exercise 1: Forming a Picture from a Poem (pages 306–307)

1. (3) So many women have rejected the man in the poem that if he had a nickel for every rejection, he would be rich—he would be head of the World Bank.

2. (1) He would "fly chartered/Jet" and "sign a check/Giving India a new lease on life."

3. (2) If the man could give India a "new lease on life," he would solve all of India's problems, including poverty.

4. (4) If he had a nickel for every woman who has loved him, the man says, he'd be poor. So the man has not found many women who love him.

5. (4) He wouldn't "wear a derby" and would think only about "going home."

Exercise 2: Identifying the Subjects of Poems (pages 308–310)

1. (5) The ponies have an inflated view of how good their condition (hay) should be. They have *their tails in the air*.

2. (4) The ponies don't do anything to really change their lives. They have little or no interest or concern.

3. (3) The poet doesn't want to mend the fence just because that's what he and his neighbor have done year after year. He wants to at least raise the question about the need for a fence.

4. (2) He says this is an unnecessary division between people. Key words are the poet's asking what he was *walling in* or *walling out*.

5. (5) The neighbor doesn't question what his father always said. He stays with what has always been: tradition.

6. (1) If countries kept "fences" between them, they would tend to affairs only in their own "backyards." In other words, they would be isolationist.

Exercise 3: Paraphrasing Poetry (pages 312–313)

1. **(2)** In lines 14, 15, and 17 the speaker tells her boy to keep going.
2. **(1)** The mother is comparing life to a staircase. When she says her stair has had tacks and splinters, she means she has faced problems.
3. **(2)** In these lines, the mother describes times in her life that have been dark. In these times, she has not found easy solutions to her problems.
4. **(1)** The mother is telling her son not to give up.
5. **(4)** In contrast to a life filled with splinters, corners, and dark places, a crystal stair would be smooth, bright, and easy.

Exercise 4: Practice in Reading Dialogue (pages 318–319)

1. **a.** Karl is a professor.
   b. Ogden is a police inspector.
2. Karl and Ogden are discussing the murder of Karl's wife. The first lines spoken—"I have something to tell you, Inspector. I know who killed my wife."—tell you this.
3. **(1)** The stage direction on line 15 tells you that Ogden speaks his line "thoughtfully."
4. **(2)** The last line of the passage reveals this conflict.
5. **(3)** *Verdict* is probably a murder mystery. You can infer this because the two characters in this passage are discussing who murdered Karl's wife.

Exercise 5: Putting It All Together (pages 319–321)

1. **(1)** Laura describes what she has done in the middle of the selection.
2. **(2)** The stage directions say, "Laura picks up a piece . . . to cover her tumult."
3. **(2)** The dashes reveal Laura's hesitance to tell Jim what she has been doing. You can tell this because Laura is "acutely shy," and because she says, "Oh, please don't think I sit around doing nothing!"
4. **(3)** Jim wants Laura to know that her education was more important than a slight disability.

Exercise 6: Chapter Review: Poetry (pages 321–323)

Your answers to the blanks in the first three questions may vary somewhat but should be similar to these.

1. **a.** The road is sizzling (hot).
   b. The sun is very yellow: "popped like a field of blazing maize."
   c. The sky is empty (of clouds) and blue.
   d. The bicycles are like insects: "silent, swift, translucent," and barely stirring.
2. **a.** "Workers and girls were riding to their factories," paying attention to summer and the sky.
   b. The bicycles are making whirring sounds.
3. **a.** The poet is thinking about what the boys do in the evening. They wash up, eat, and drink.
   b. The bicycle only has "life" when workers, girls, and boys use it. The bicycle only has a "soul" when it is moving and needed. Otherwise, it is a "cold skeleton" until the new day.
4. **(5)** The title is a clue.
5. **(1)** Clues are: "the only insects" in the second stanza; "the hard beetle backs of the whirring bicycles" in the third stanza; and "insect humming through summer" in the fourth stanza.

Exercise 7: Chapter Review: Drama (pages 324–326)

1. World War II
2. **(5)** The key word is *mercenary* to explain the answer of *greedy*.
3. **(3), (4), (5)** There is no evidence of real conflict between Indiana Jones (Indy) and Marcus or Indy and his students.
4. **(1)** There is no real plot if Indiana Jones doesn't "go for it."
5. **(3)** At the beginning of the excerpt, students are leaving the classroom.
6. **(1)** The key phrase is "no questions asked." This means that the museum is overlooking usual moral practices.
7. **(2)** The tone is probably sarcastic because Marcus knows that Indy is somewhat mercenary. Marcus knows that Indy has been selling priceless pieces to museums. If Indy were more scrupulous, he probably wouldn't disturb priceless, religious pieces.

SOCIAL STUDIES

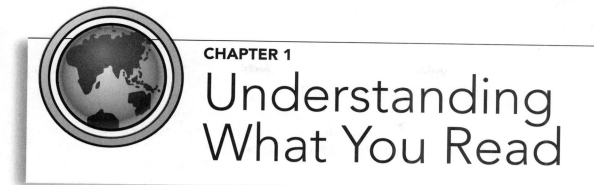

CHAPTER 1

Understanding What You Read

In order to understand social studies fully, you will need to master the skills in this section. One of the most basic reading skills is finding **facts and details**. Another basic reading skill is understanding the meaning of **unfamiliar words**. You will start work on these two skills in this chapter. Later, you will work on putting ideas in your own words by **summarizing** and restating. Then you will practice finding the **main idea**. Studying these skills will lay the groundwork for reading and understanding social studies.

Locating Facts and Details

Question Words

The first step in understanding what you read is picking out details. You should look for facts that answer six basic questions: *Who? What? Where? Why? When?* and *How?* In the following example, Judge Phillips needs to use all six questions in order to understand the case. She needs the details in order to make a decision.

JUDGE:	**Who** do you represent?
LAWYER:	My client is Elisa Canter.
JUDGE:	**Why** is she here?
LAWYER:	To sue the McWatt Shoe Company.
JUDGE:	**What** are the grounds for the suit?
LAWYER:	Manufacturing a faulty pair of boots that caused an injury.
JUDGE:	**When** did this alleged injury take place?
LAWYER:	Last March.
JUDGE:	**Where** did it happen?
LAWYER:	At Ms. Canter's home.
JUDGE:	**How** did the boots cause the injury?
LAWYER:	One of the heels broke off when she wore the boots for the first time, causing her to fall.

Finding the Information

Now practice finding information for questions asking *who, what, where, why, when,* and *how.* In the following paragraph, the speaker describes his memories of a bread line during the Great Depression of the 1930s. Try to match the correct answer with each question. Write the letter of the answer in the space provided.

> I was walking along the street at that time (1932), and you'd see the bread lines. The biggest one in New York City was owned by William Randolph Hearst. He had a big truck with several people on it, and big cauldrons of hot soup, bread. Fellows with burlap on their feet were lined up all around Columbus Circle, and went for blocks and blocks around the park, waiting.

—Excerpted from *The People's History of the United States* by Howard Zinn

1._____ Where was this bread line?

2._____ Who was waiting in the bread line?

3._____ When did this scene take place?

4._____ How did William Randolph Hearst give out food to poor people?

A. He had a big truck with several people on it.

B. in 1932

C. in New York City

D. people with burlap on their feet

Make sure you tried each question in the example above on your own before you read the following explanations. Reread the paragraph if you missed any answers.

1. C   Where: New York City.

2. D   Who: people with burlap on their feet

3. B   When: 1932

4. A   How: He had a big truck with several people on it.

EXERCISE 1

Finding Details

Directions: Read each paragraph below. Following each paragraph are detail questions. Write your answer to each question in the space provided.

In 1960, television helped elect a new president. John F. Kennedy defeated Richard M. Nixon in their famous television debates. Many political writers believe that Kennedy's good performance on television led to his narrow victory in the election.

1. Who were involved in the important televised debates of 1960?

   _____

2. According to many political writers, how did Kennedy win the 1960 presidential election?

   _____

   _____

The Swahili Coast is an 1,800-mile stretch of East African coastline between Somalia in the north and Mozambique in the south. The Swahili coast has been the site of cultural and commercial exchanges between East Africa and the outside world for many years. By the 9th century, Africans, Arabs, and Persians who lived and traded on the coast had developed the common language of Kiswahili. This language was based on the Bantu language, Sabaki, that uses Arab and Persian words. They had also developed the distinctive Swahili culture, characterized by the almost universal practice of Islam, as well as by Arabic and Asian-influenced art and architecture.

3. Where is the Swahili Coast? _____

4. When did the Swahili language and culture first develop?

   _____

5. How did the practice of Islam become a part of Swahili culture?

   _____

   _____

Directions: Read the following paragraphs. Then circle the best answer to each question that follows.

When George L. Belair was running for city council in Minneapolis, Minnesota, he gave away some Twinkies to senior citizens. Under Minnesota law, candidates for office are not allowed to give away food or drinks in order to get votes. Because of this law, Mr. Belair was arrested. He had to prove in court that he was not trying to get votes by giving away the cakes.

6. Why was Mr. Belair arrested?

(1) He tried to bribe a police officer by giving him Twinkies.
(2) It's illegal to give away a product that people usually have to pay for.
(3) He had stolen the Twinkies he was giving away.
(4) He gave free drinks to senior citizens.
(5) In Minnesota, candidates cannot give away food to get votes.

Since 1945, the human race has had to face the possibility of its own destruction. In August of that year, an American airplane named the Enola Gay dropped the first atomic bomb on Hiroshima, Japan, helping to bring World War II to an end. That single bomb destroyed the entire city. In the years since that first explosion, the United States has built enough bombs to destroy the entire world. The former Soviet Union also built enough bombs to wipe out the human race. Great Britain, France, India, Pakistan, Israel, and China also have nuclear weapons. Humanity's future now depends on countries settling their differences peacefully.

7. The first atomic bomb was dropped by

(1) the Soviet Union
(2) the United States
(3) Germany
(4) Japan
(5) China

8. What was the result when the bomb was dropped on Hiroshima?

(1) The United Nations was formed.
(2) The Soviet Union built many bombs.
(3) The entire city of Hiroshima was destroyed.
(4) The United States destroyed the entire world.
(5) An American airplane went down.

For many years, large companies fought with their workers' unions. But greater competition from overseas has forced both sides to look again at the way they work together. One example of a different approach occurred at the Chrysler Corporation. The United Auto Workers joined with the company and the government to save Chrysler. Workers accepted pay cuts while the company got back on its feet. The president of the auto workers' union became a member of the board of directors. During the crisis, management and workers tried to become partners instead of enemies.

9. Why did the union and Chrysler management decide to work together?

   (1) The government forced them to work together.
   (2) The union president joined the board of directors.
   (3) The company got tired of fighting with the union.
   (4) Greater competition from overseas threatened the company.
   (5) Workers and management wanted to become partners.

Answers are on page 487.

Understanding Unfamiliar Words

Using Context Clues

When reading, you may find words you don't know. Until you figure out the unknown words, what you read might not make sense.

You could look up these words in the dictionary. But sometimes you don't have time or a dictionary isn't handy. Sometimes the dictionary definitions are hard to understand. However, you can often figure out the meaning of a certain word by reading the words around it. This is called **using the context**. In this section, you will practice looking at the context of unfamiliar words to find their meanings.

Synonym, Definition, and Comparison Clues

Often when reading, you will find a **synonym**—another word with almost the same meaning—near an unfamiliar word. Or you might find an explanation or **definition** of what the unknown word means. Sometimes in the passage you will find a **comparison** with something you know or understand. All of these clues can help you figure out what the unknown word means.

Calvin Coolidge once said, "When more and more people are thrown out of work, unemployment results."

In this sentence, there is a definition clue. The word *unemployment* is explained directly in the sentence. Unemployment happens when "people are thrown out of work."

Now try another example. In the following passage, underline the comparison phrase that is a clue to the meaning of the word *homogeneous*.

> Like its World War II ally Germany, whose leadership all came from a similar ethnic and cultural background, Japan also had a homogeneous leadership.

Homogeneous means "similar." The comparison clue is "came from a similar ethnic and cultural background."

EXERCISE 2

Synonyms, Definitions, and Comparison Clues

Directions: In the space provided, write the meaning of the word in **boldface type.** Use the context clues in the sentences—synonyms, definitions, or comparisons—to help you.

1. Like the patent medicine sold by phony doctors to cure all kinds of illnesses, industrial growth was supposed to be a **panacea** for the nation's ills.

   panacea means _____

2. President Andrew Jackson began a questionable American political tradition, the widespread use of **patronage**—giving jobs and favors for political reasons.

   patronage means _____

3. De Beers Company created a **monopoly** in the diamond industry, controlling production and crushing its competition.

   monopoly means _____

4. Worker **productivity** has increased as new machines allow one laborer to produce much more than before.

   productivity means _____

Answers are on page 487.

Antonyms and Contrast Clues

Sometimes you can figure out the meaning of an unknown word when the nearby words have an opposite meaning. In the following sentence, what does *persist* mean?

> As the strike entered its ninth week, the workers had to decide whether to persist or to give up.

This sentence has an antonym clue. An **antonym** is a word that is the opposite of a given word. In this sentence, the workers are choosing between two choices: to persist or to give up. You can conclude that the opposite of *to persist* is *to give up*. Therefore, *to persist* means "to keep trying."

What is the meaning of *escalate* in the next sentence?

> Despite government claims that people were calming down, the violence continued to escalate.

A situation is described that is in **contrast to**, or the opposite of, another situation. In this sentence, *escalating violence* is the opposite of *people becoming calm*. You can conclude that *to escalate* means "to increase."

Clue words such as *unlike*, *despite*, and *although* may help you identify antonym and contrast clues. In the following sentence, *unlike* contrasts wealthy children in Kenwood with impoverished children in Garfield Park.

> Unlike children in wealthy Kenwood, many children in impoverished Garfield Park go hungry.

EXERCISE 3

Antonyms and Contrast Clues

Directions: The sentences below each have antonyms or contrast clues. Each sentence contains words or phrases with opposite meanings. Circle the letter of the correct answer to each question.

1. After years without restrictions on the number of immigrants allowed into the country, Congress passed the first quota law in 1921.

    A *quota* is

    (1) a person from another country
    (2) a limit, usually a number
    (3) an economic goal

2. In the late nineteenth century, new cities grew in the Northeast and Midwest. The squalor of these new industrial cities contrasted sharply with the beauty of the surrounding countryside.

    Squalor is

    (1) filth
    (2) large size
    (3) beauty

3. Despite the desire of Native Americans to live amicably with white people, treaties were broken and fighting often occurred.

   To live amicably is to

   (1) control others
   (2) be peaceful
   (3) better oneself

4. Unlike the Native American tribes, who only wanted to keep their own lands, the United States followed an expansionist policy in the nineteenth century.

   An *expansionist policy* favors

   (1) improving relations with neighbors
   (2) getting rid of foreign influence
   (3) taking over more land

Answers are on page 487.

Using the Sense of the Passage

Sometimes an important word is not defined directly. There may not be any antonyms or synonyms. In these cases, you must determine the meaning of the word by reading the entire passage. Sometimes you might be able to figure out the meaning of the unknown word by looking at examples given in the rest of the passage. Other times you will have to rely on your overall understanding of the meaning of the passage, as in the following example.

> The great American megalopolis stretches over four hundred miles from Boston to Washington, D.C. Including such cities as New York, Newark, Philadelphia, and Baltimore, it is the largest urban area in the United States.

> What is a *megalopolis*?

> **(1)** a large city and its suburbs
> **(2)** a state government
> **(3)** a group of connected cities and suburbs
> **(4)** a large lottery

The phrase *stretches over* gives you the sense of a connected or continuous area (choice 3). Since a megalopolis includes many cities, it would have to include suburban areas.

EXERCISE 4

Using the Sense of the Passage

Directions: Read each of the passages below. Then answer the questions that follow.

At the turn of the century, American life was changing rapidly. The most visible change was in transportation. Cars were beginning to be seen all over the country. In 1903, the Wright brothers made the first airplane flight. Motorized vehicles were becoming our primary way of getting around.

1. What is meant by *the turn of the century* in this passage?

   (1) around 1800
   (2) around 1900
   (3) around 2000
   (4) in 1903

Congestion in a big city can't be avoided. One experiences it everywhere. Traffic jams are a constant irritation, making one's feet the fastest way to travel most of the time. A crowded elevator and a tightly packed subway train are other reminders of congestion in the city.

2. *Congestion* means

   (1) illness
   (2) confusion
   (3) overcrowding
   (4) poverty

The United States and the United Kingdom are close allies who agree on most issues of foreign policy. However, since the United Kingdom is a sovereign nation, we cannot assume that it will automatically support all American actions.

3. *Sovereign* means

   (1) independent
   (2) important
   (3) proud
   (4) stubborn

Answers are on page 487.

Restating and Summarizing

Restating Details and Facts

In 1517, Martin Luther published his 95 Theses, which publicly condemned the selling of indulgences by the Roman Catholic Church. The 95 Theses condemning the actions of the Roman Catholic Church signaled the start Protestant Reformation.

In the above passage, the second sentence restates the facts of the first, while also explaining the significance of the details of Martin Luther's actions. Being able to restate details and facts in different words is an important step in understanding what you read.

The following passage explains the impact of World War I on African Americans.

> **(1)** The war that had exploded in Europe in 1914 had cut off the flow of immigrants from the old countries. **(2)** Northern factories, booming on war orders, were short of labor. **(3)** Manufacturers sent agents south to recruit black workers. **(4)** They came with free railroad passes in hand or offered cheap tickets to groups of migrants. **(5)** A "Northern fever" seized the Blacks of the South.
>
> —Excerpted from *The Black Americans: A History in Their Own Words*
> by Milton Meltzer

Read the following statements. If the statement is a correct restatement of the sentence or sentences indicated, write *C* in the blank and underline the part of the passage it restates. If not, write *I* for incorrect.

_____ **1.** Northern manufacturers preferred southern black workers to European immigrants. (sentences 1–2)

_____ **2.** Employers gave southern blacks assistance in moving north to work. (sentences 3–4)

Read the following explanations to see how to think through this example correctly.

1. I The passage states that the war in Europe had cut off the flow of immigrants and the factories were short of labor. It doesn't say anything about what kind of workers the manufacturers preferred.

2. C This sentence restates the information in sentence 4. The passage says that the agents of manufacturers encouraged blacks to go north to work by giving them free or cheap railroad tickets.

EXERCISE 5

Recognizing Restated Information

Directions: After reading the passage below, read the sentences that follow. If you think that the statement is a correct restatement of part of the passage, write *C* for correct. If not, write *I* for incorrect.

(1) The Han are China's largest ethnic group, constituting [including] more than 90 percent of the population. **(2)** The traditional history of China is largely the story of the Han, who emerged in what is now northern China more than 4,000 years ago.

—Excerpted from "Han Chinese Man," *Microsoft Encarta Encyclopedia 2000*

_____ **1.** The people that most Americans think of as Chinese think of themselves as the Han.

_____ **2.** Many ethnic groups played an important role in Chinese history.

Answers are on page 487.

EXERCISE 6

Restating Information in Your Own Words

Directions: Read each passage below. Then, in your own words, answer the questions that follow.

John D. Rockefeller's company, Standard Oil, managed to put a lot of other oil companies out of business. First, Rockefeller pressured railroads into lowering their freight charges for Standard Oil shipments. Then he could charge less for his products than other oil companies because his freight costs were lower. If other oil companies managed to stay in business anyway, Rockefeller had another tactic. He would lower his prices in their area until Standard Oil had lured away all the other companies' customers.

1. How did Standard Oil reduce its freight costs?

_____

_____

2. How did Standard Oil wipe out its competition?

_____

_____

The most successful of the early labor unions was the American Federation of Labor (AFL), founded in 1886 under the leadership of Samuel Gompers. The AFL was a united group of craft unions. Unlike the unsuccessful labor unions, the AFL did not sponsor its own political candidates. It also did not demand radical social change. Instead, the AFL worked toward concrete goals such as higher wages and shorter work hours.

3. What kinds of goals did the American Federation of Labor work toward?

_____

_____

4. What did the unsuccessful early labor unions do?

_____

_____

Answers are on page 488.

Summarizing Details and Facts

When you **summarize**, you make one statement that gives the main point of a group of details or facts. A summary should contain all of the important ideas. In the following example, practice finding a summary statement that pulls together all the ideas in the original sentences. Read the following three statements:

Henry Ford produced the first low-cost automobile.

Ford was able to save money through mass production of his automobile.

Millions of people were able to own a car for the first time because of the low cost.

Now place a check before the sentence that best summarizes all three of the statements.

_____ Mass production has made many products affordable.

_____ By creating the mass-produced car, Henry Ford changed America.

_____ By using mass production, Henry Ford produced a low-cost car that was bought by millions of people.

The last choice is correct. By using mass production (second statement), Ford produced a low-cost car (first statement) that was bought by millions of people (third statement). You can see that all the important ideas are covered.

EXERCISE 7

Summarizing Facts

Directions: Following each group of statements are three possible summary sentences. Circle the letter of the best summary. Make sure all the important ideas are included in the summary you choose.

1. In 1982, AT&T agreed to an end of its monopoly of long-distance service. MCI and Sprint became major long-distance telephone companies in the 1980s. AT&T had to lay off workers in order to remain competitive.

   (1) MCI and Sprint are the telephone companies of the future.
   (2) The end of the AT&T telephone monopoly led to competition and worker layoffs.
   (3) The AT&T telephone monopoly was in violation of anti-trust laws.

2. Hospital costs are higher than most people can afford. An unexpected illness can be a financial disaster for a family. Medical insurance pays for hospital costs and doctors' bills.

   (1) Medical insurance protects people from large health-care bills.
   (2) The United States should adopt national health insurance.
   (3) Medical costs are too high and should be reduced to help protect families.

Answers are on page 488.

Topic Sentences and Main Ideas

You have practiced finding and summarizing details. The next step is to start putting these details together. To get a complete picture of what the writer is talking about, you must determine the topic and the main idea.

The **topic** is the subject of a passage. The **main idea** is the point the writer wants to make about the topic. The **details** provide evidence, examples, or descriptions to explain the main idea.

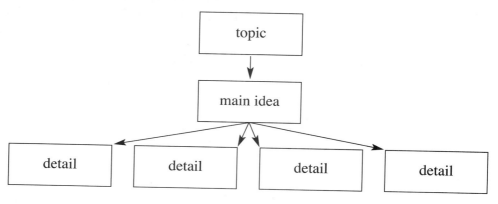

The following paragraph contains a sentence that does not belong. Read the paragraph carefully. Decide the topic of the paragraph. Then identify the sentence that is **not** about the topic.

(1) Today many people do their banking by automatic teller machine (ATM). (2) ATMs can be found in many places, including department stores and supermarkets. (3) Banks supply their customers with access cards for the machines. (4) You can pay for groceries by check at many supermarkets. (5) Most ATMs can give you money from your account, tell you your account balance, or let you make a deposit.

What is the topic of this paragraph? _____

Which sentence does not belong? _____

The topic of this paragraph is automatic teller machines. Each sentence is related to this topic except for sentence 4. Sentence 4 is about using a check, not an ATM.

EXERCISE 8

Identifying Unrelated Sentences

Directions: In each of the following paragraphs, one sentence does not belong. Read each paragraph carefully to find its topic. Then fill in the blank with the number of the sentence that does not belong.

1. _____ (1) Japanese products are popular with American consumers. (2) For many years now, Americans have been buying a wide variety of these products, including cars, stereos, and VCRs. (3) The American automobile industry is making a comeback. (4) Japanese restaurants are now becoming very popular in the United States. (5) Sushi, a Japanese dish, is almost as well known to Americans as products made by Sony.

2. _____ (1) The Consumer Price Index (CPI) measures the inflation rate. (2) The cost of housing is a major factor in the CPI. (3) Food prices often depend on the weather. (4) Food and clothing costs are also major factors in the CPI. (5) As housing, food, and clothing costs rise, so does the Consumer Price Index.

Answers are on page 488.

Finding the Main Idea

Every paragraph has a **topic**, the subject of the paragraph. And every paragraph has a **main idea**. The main idea is the most important thing, or the central point, that the writer wants to say about the topic. Practice finding the topic and the main idea in the following paragraph.

> In our free enterprise system, anyone has the right to go into business. If you see a need, you don't need government permission to try to fill it. Whether it is a new computer company or a roadside fruit stand, you have the right to try to sell your products. If you're successful, the rewards can be great.

What is the topic of this paragraph? _____

What do you think is the writer's main idea? _____

The topic is *starting a business in our free enterprise system*. Each sentence is related to this topic. The main idea is more specific than the topic. The main idea is *In our free enterprise system, anyone has the right to go into business*. This main idea tells you the central point of the rest of the sentences.

Now try another example. After the following paragraph are four choices for the main idea. Circle the letter of the best choice for the main idea.

> In past decades, most developing countries borrowed billions of dollars from large banks. Today, those loans threaten the world economy. Many developing countries, like Argentina and Brazil, have trouble repaying their loans. Since the world banking system would collapse if the loans went bad, the banks lend these nations more money to pay off their debts. Because of this cycle of borrowing, the world faces a debt crisis.

What is the main idea of this paragraph?

(1) Argentina is having trouble paying back its debts.
(2) The world economy is threatened by a debt crisis.
(3) Today, the world economy has made all countries interdependent.
(4) The United States' economy is the largest in the world.

Choice (2) sums up the central point of the paragraph. Choice (1) is too narrow because it is only a specific detail mentioned in the paragraph. Choice (3) is too broad and general. The main idea of this paragraph is more specific—debt in the world economy. Choice (4) is not mentioned in the passage at all.

EXERCISE 9

Identifying the Main Idea

Directions: Read each paragraph below. Following each paragraph are four choices for the main idea. Put *M* by the main idea. Put *N* by the choice that is too narrow. Put *B* by the choice that is too broad. Put *X* by the choice that is not in the passage.

1.   In a capitalist economy, most factories and farms are privately owned. In a socialist economy, the society as a whole owns the factories and the farms. Until recently, the Chinese had a socialist economy. But in recent years, the Chinese government has begun to experiment with private ownership. The Chinese are trying to combine the best of socialism and capitalism. In time, perhaps they will develop a completely new kind of economy.

_____ **(1)** Capitalism and socialism are the two main economic systems in the world.

_____ **(2)** China is experimenting by combining capitalism with socialism.

_____ **(3)** China has successfully controlled the growth of its population.

_____ **(4)** Most factories and farms are privately owned in a capitalist economy.

2.   One measure of a healthy economy is the savings rate. The savings rate measures how much money people deposit in savings accounts. A savings account is a cushion against hard times. It is also a source of money for investment. In the United States, the savings rate is very low. Because of the low savings rate, the United States economy has less money available for investment and less protection against hard times than a country with a higher savings rate.

_____ **(1)** The low savings rate in the United States weakens the economy.

_____ **(2)** A savings account is a cushion against hard times.

_____ **(3)** The United States faces economic hard times.

_____ **(4)** Saving rates are important.

Answers are on page 488.

Topic Sentences

The main idea of a paragraph is sometimes stated directly in one of the sentences of the paragraph. This sentence is called the **topic sentence**. The topic sentence is often at the beginning of a paragraph. However, the topic sentence may also occur at the end or in the middle of a paragraph. No matter where the topic sentence appears, all other sentences relate to it. They are supporting sentences—they support the main idea expressed in the topic sentence.

In the following paragraph, find and underline the topic sentence.

The Environmental Protection Agency (EPA) is responsible for the quality of our environment. The EPA enforces the Clean Water and Clean Air Acts. It must protect wetlands and other delicate ecosystems. In addition, toxic wastes and their disposal are the EPA's responsibility.

The first sentence states the main idea of the paragraph: the EPA is responsible for the quality of the environment. The other three sentences give examples of the EPA's responsibilities.

In the following paragraph, the topic sentence has been left out. Read the paragraph carefully and answer the two questions below the paragraph.

Only about half of all employees in the United States work a standard work week of thirty-five to forty-five hours. Almost a quarter of all employees work fewer than thirty-five hours. The rest work more than forty-five hours each week. However, experts think that these statistics don't tell the whole story. In reality, many of those thirty-five- to forty-five-hour workers may actually work much longer hours.

What is the topic? _____

What is the main idea being made about the topic?

_____

The topic is the standard work week. The main idea is that the forty-hour work week is not standard. Now write a topic sentence for the paragraph that expresses the main idea.

_____

_____

A good topic sentence for the paragraph might be: A forty-hour work week is probably not standard for most workers in the United States.

EXERCISE 10

Writing Topic Sentences

Directions: In the following paragraphs, the topic sentence has been left out.
Read each paragraph carefully and answer the questions below
each paragraph. Then write a topic sentence that introduces the
main idea of each paragraph.

1.   The Federal Deposit Insurance Corporation (FDIC) was
established in the 1930s after many people lost their life savings
when banks failed during the Great Depression. Today most bank
accounts are insured by the FDIC up to a fixed amount. As a result,
if a bank fails, the FDIC will replace money that depositors had in
accounts at the failed bank.

What is the topic? _____

What is the main point being made about the topic?

_____

Topic sentence: _____

_____

_____

2.   The civilization of Ancient Egypt first appeared beside the Nile
River about 3000 B.C. At about the same time, the Sumerian
civilization began between the Tigris and Euphrates Rivers in what
we now call Iraq. Further east, a civilization was also forming along
the Indus River in what is now Pakistan.

What is the topic? _____

What is the main point being made about the topic?

_____

Topic sentence: _____

_____

_____

Answers are on page 488.

Finding the Main Idea of a Passage

The same process is used in finding the main idea of a passage. If you find the main idea of each paragraph in a passage, you will find that they are related. They all point to one main idea for the whole passage. Read the following passage about the 1996 primary election in New Hampshire. What is the main idea of the first paragraph? the second? the third? What is the one main idea that sums up the whole passage? Write your answers on the lines below.

Before every presidential election, the Democratic and Republican parties conduct statewide primary elections to measure the popularity of candidates. The nation's first primary election, in New Hampshire, is a presidential candidate's first and probably most powerful opportunity to impress party officials and capture public attention. Successful candidates in the New Hampshire primary often do well nationwide.

Months before the New Hampshire primary, presidential candidates begin making appearances in the state. In the 1996 campaign, the Republican front-runner planned a 10-day campaign tour of New Hampshire. Another candidate hiked border-to-border across the state. Four Republican candidates all campaigned vigorously in the state.

But presidential campaigns involve more than speeches. The Republican candidates tried various strategies in New Hampshire. One candidate began airing campaign commercials months before the primary. Before dropping out of the race, another candidate selected a popular New England politician as his new national finance chairman. Another front-runner's staff conducted direct-mail campaigns and telephone surveys. Like other presidential candidates, this candidate also softened his most liberal positions to reassure conservative New Hampshire voters.

Main idea of first paragraph: _____

Main idea of second paragraph: _____

Main idea of third paragraph: _____

The main idea of the first paragraph is that doing well in the New Hampshire primary is very important to presidential candidates. The main idea of the second paragraph is that candidates all make early campaign visits to the state. The main idea of the third paragraph is that the candidates use many strategies in their New Hampshire campaigns.

Now you have looked at the main idea of each paragraph separately. But what about the passage as a whole? Write a main idea for the passage.

Main idea for the passage: _____

_____

You might have written something like this: Winning the New Hampshire primary is generally very important to presidential candidates, so they use many strategies to win votes.

Main Idea of a Passage

Directions: Read the following passage. Then choose the correct main idea for each of the three paragraphs. Finally, choose the main idea for the passage.

Paragraph (1)

The underlying causes of the Russian Revolution are rooted deep in Russia's history. For centuries, autocratic and repressive regimes ruled the country. Under the rule of the czars, most Russians lived under severe economic and social conditions. During the century prior to the 1917 Revolution, various movements of students, workers, peasants, and even the nobility tried to overthrow the oppressive government. The 1917 Revolution finally succeeded.

Paragraph (2)

There were actually two revolutions. The first revolution in February overthrew the Czar and created a Provisional Government and the Petrograd Soviet [council] of Workers' and Soldiers' Deputies. The majority of the Soviets were Mensheviks. They supported a period of capitalistic development and complete political democracy. However, they also supported Russia's continuing involvement in World War I and proved to be poor administrators as the nation fell into chaos.

Paragraph (3)

The Bolsheviks, led by Lenin, were at first a small minority. They supported the immediate seizure of all land by the peasantry, worker control in industry, an end to the war, and the transfer of all power to the Soviets. Food shortages, economic collapse, and terrible defeats in battle all discredited the Provisional Government. By October, the Bolsheviks had gained enough support and power to successfully overthrow the Provisional Government and implement their program. This was the second revolution.

1. The main idea of paragraph (1) is

   (1) The underlying causes of the Russian Revolution are rooted deeply in Russia's history.
   (2) Oppressive living conditions are a breeding ground for revolutionary activity.
   (3) The Russian Revolution of 1917 finally succeeded in overthrowing the czars.
   (4) Under the czars, most Russians lived under severe economic and social conditions.

2. The main idea of paragraph (2) is

   (1) The Russian Revolution happened in two stages in February and October 1917.

   (2) The Mensheviks were the first majority party in the Petrograd Soviet.

   (3) World War I led to major changes in many of the governments of Europe.

   (4) The first leaders of the revolution, the Mensheviks, had high ideals but ran Russia poorly.

3. The main idea of paragraph (3) is

   (1) The Bolsheviks, at first, were a small minority led by Lenin.

   (2) In October, the Bolsheviks were able to overthrow the Provisional Government.

   (3) The Bolsheviks supported a radical program to help peasants and workers.

   (4) The Bolsheviks became the Communist Party and ruled Russia for many years.

4. Using the main ideas of each individual paragraph, choose the sentence below that best summarizes the main idea of the entire passage.

   (1) In the 1917 Russian Revolution, the Bolsheviks overthrew the incompetent Provisional Government, which had thrown out the oppressive czarist regime.

   (2) Except for a feeble attempt to establish democracy, the Russian Revolution just replaced one type of tyranny with another, autocratic Communist rule.

   (3) Even when started as a noble attempt to end oppression, revolutions can quickly run out of control and have unintended negative consequences.

   (4) The revolution of 1917 changed the Russian government's war policy and resulted in Russia withdrawing from World War I.

Answers are on page 488.

Reading Between the Lines

The information in a passage is not always stated directly. Writers will often provide clues to facts or to their opinions. They will then leave it up to you to figure them out. Figuring out unstated facts and opinions is often called reading between the lines. Sometimes it's called **making an inference**.

Inferring Facts

A passage can suggest a fact by giving you clues that you can gather as you read. As you read the following paragraph, watch for clues to the time and place of the passage. What is the writer telling you that is not directly stated?

> As far as the eye could see, there were hundreds of bison grazing on the open spaces of grass. The wagon train paused to watch the huge herd and waited for it to move on.

When is this passage taking place?

(1) in the 1960s
(2) around 1900
(3) in the mid-19th century
(4) in the mid-18th century
(5) before 1500

Clues: There are several clues that this scene is taking place in the mid-19th century (choice 3). During that time period, many people traveled in wagon trains to settle the American West. By 1900, travel out West would have been by train. Before the 19th century, wagon trains did not exist. Also, bison were still abundant in the mid-19th century.

Where is this passage taking place?

(1) in Europe
(2) on the East Coast of the United States
(3) on the Great Plains of the United States
(4) in the Rocky Mountains
(5) in South America

Clue: The open spaces of grassland and the huge herd of bison are clues that this passage is taking place on the Great Plains of the United States (choice 3).

EXERCISE 12

Inferring Facts

Part A **Directions:** The following paragraph is an account of Rosa Parks in 1955. It describes one of the key events in the Civil Rights Movement in the United States. Following the passage are two inferences that can be drawn from it. List at least one clue for each inference.

Rosa Parks had worked a long day and was very tired when she finally headed home. After Ms. Parks found a seat, a white man walked up to her, expecting her to get up for him. She refused. It's the custom in many areas of the world for a man to give up his seat for a woman, but Ms. Parks was arrested for refusing to move for a white man. The black community rallied to her support, beginning the famous Montgomery, Alabama, bus boycott.

1. Inference: The incident described in the passage occurred on a bus.

   clues: _____

2. Inference: Rosa Parks is a black woman.

   clues: _____

Part B **Directions:** Read the following passages and answer the questions. The correct answers are not stated directly but can be inferred. Find at least one clue that backs up the answer you choose.

Sam's life was very hard. He was expected to be out working in the cotton fields by sunrise. No matter how hot it was, the foreman kept him working until sunset. His owner had paid $25 for him and expected to get his money's worth.

3. Sam was

   (1) a migrant farm worker
   (2) a slave
   (3) a technician
   (4) the owner of a small farm
   (5) a foreman

The following first-person account describes a situation that happened at the Triangle Shirtwaist Factory in New York City during the Industrial Revolution.

Two hundred of us were working on the floor when the fire broke out. Rolls of fabric were piled everywhere. There was barely enough room to walk between the sewing machines. Some of the other women I work with began to panic when they discovered that the fire escape door was locked. Somehow I managed to get down the stairway and out to the street. I saw women leaping from the windows. It seemed that dead bodies were everywhere.

4. The speaker in the passage was

   (1) an owner of a large mill
   (2) a New England farmer
   (3) an immigrant waiting to enter the United States
   (4) a worker at a factory
   (5) a newspaper reporter writing about a fire

When he took office, the country was in the middle of the worst economic crisis of its history. Unemployment was very high and many farms and businesses had gone bankrupt. His policies were based on a belief that government should take a more active role in helping people. He proposed programs to Congress to restore people's hope in the future and revive the economy.

5. The person described in this paragraph is

   (1) Douglas MacArthur, a general in the United States Army who served from 1918 to 1951
   (2) Woody Guthrie, a songwriter who wrote of people's hardships in the 1930s
   (3) Franklin D. Roosevelt, president of the United States from 1933 to 1945
   (4) Samuel Gompers, president of the AFL from 1886 to 1924
   (5) Andrew Carnegie, one of the men who built American industry in the 1800s

Answers are on pages 488–489.

Inferring Opinions

You have been learning to infer facts that are not stated directly in a passage. Authors can also imply opinions in their writing. You can infer opinions in the same way as facts—by looking at the evidence. As you read the following quote from Albert Einstein, the great scientist who developed much of the theory that made nuclear weapons possible, ask yourself what he might be implying about how we need to change our ways of thinking to resolve conflicts. Then answer the question that follows the passage.

> The splitting of the atom has changed everything save our modes of thinking and thus we drift toward unparalleled catastrophe. We shall require a substantially new manner of thinking if mankind is to survive.
>
> —Albert Einstein

What is most likely to be Albert Einstein's opinion regarding nuclear weapons developed from splitting the atom and conflict resolution?

(1) The best way to avoid nuclear disaster is to have huge numbers of nuclear weapons.
(2) We need to learn to resolve conflict nonviolently, since nuclear war is bad for everybody.
(3) Nuclear weapons would best be used to prevent other nations from developing them.
(4) Because our weapons are so much more powerful, we have to be prepared to use them quickly.
(5) Since we were able to develop nuclear weapons, we also know how to use them.

The correct answer is choice (2). When he wrote, "We shall require a substantially new manner of thinking if mankind is to survive," he implies that since we now have such terrible weapons, we need to learn to solve our disputes without resorting to violence. Although not stated, Einstein's opinion is clearly shown in his writing.

EXERCISE 13

Inferring Opinions

Directions: Read each passage or cartoon carefully. Answer the questions that follow each passage or cartoon, making sure you have found evidence for the answer you choose.

Franklin D. Roosevelt, president of the U.S. from 1933 to 1945, was crippled by polio. However, most Americans did not realize the extent of his handicap. FDR never discussed his health problems in public, and he was careful to show as few signs of his handicap as possible. The press also helped him by not calling attention to his physical problems. His strategy was so successful that his handicap did not prevent him from being elected president four times.

1. Why did President Roosevelt want to keep people from being very aware of his handicap?

   (1) He wanted people to believe he was healthy enough to keep up with his responsibilities.
   (2) He wanted to appear as attractive as possible and maintain his active social life.
   (3) He didn't want to be reelected because his handicap interfered with his work.
   (4) He enjoyed fooling the American public and controlling the press.
   (5) He wanted to find out how powerful the press could be in shaping public opinion.

Many economists believe that the economic boom of the 1990s was unexpected in its length. Because the economy was strong for so many years, lawmakers are failing to make the economy a priority. In the past, Congress would have passed laws to help those people who are out of work, and therefore stimulate the economy during slow economic times. Today, however, many workers in the United States have used up their unemployment benefits. Politicians in Washington, D.C. need to focus more on events at home, rather than worrying about events overseas.

2. The passage suggests that, in the past, Congress

   (1) was not able to influence the American economy
   (2) made economic downturns worse with misguided policies
   (3) was responsible for the growth of the American economy
   (4) was more interested in the economy than in other nations
   (5) was able to help improve the American economy

Questions 3 and 4 are based on the following cartoon.

Mike Keefe, *The Denver Post*

3. When the speaker says, "They run in packs and upset the ecosystem," he refers to the actions of

(1) trees
(2) wolves
(3) bad drivers
(4) people
(5) park rangers

4. It is the cartoonist's opinion that

(1) there are too many people moving into Canada
(2) Canada deserves all the problems it gets
(3) people are really more dangerous than wolves
(4) traffic at Yellowstone Park should be better regulated
(5) wolves are vicious, good-for-nothing animals

Answers are on page 489.

Expressing Opinion in Political Cartoons

A political cartoon expresses the opinion of the artist. Usually political cartoons comment on current events. To understand a political cartoon, you must determine the **characters**, **topic**, and **opinion** of the artist. One key to understanding most political cartoons is a background knowledge of what was going on in the world when the cartoon was created. In this section, you will be given background clues to the cartoons.

CARTOON TIP

One of the most commonly used symbols in political cartoons is Uncle Sam. He stands for the United States. Uncle Sam is usually a tall man with white hair and a beard. He wears clothes with stars and stripes.

Another key to understanding political cartoons is **symbols.** A symbol stands for something. For example, a dollar sign ($) stands for money. Political cartoons often use symbols.

A third key to understanding political cartoons is understanding the titles and all the labels. Always read every word on a cartoon. Notice especially when words label a particular figure or part of the cartoon.

Background clues: Since terrorists destroyed the World Trade Center on September 11, 2001, ending terrorism has been a major concern both in the United States and around the world.

Link Between Poverty and Terrorism
Theo Moudakis, *Toronto Star*

Based on the cartoon above, answer the following questions.

1. What objects, or symbols, does the cartoonist use in the cartoon?

_____

2. Why might the cartoonist have used this symbol in his cartoon?

_____

You were correct if you wrote that the cartoonist uses gears in his cartoon. He used gears because he wants to show that poverty and terrorism are linked.

The cartoonist's opinion is most likely that

(1) terrorism can lead to poverty
(2) wiping out terrorism will end poverty
(3) terrorism is evil and must be ended
(4) poverty is a cause of terrorism
(5) poverty and terrorism are unrelated

You were correct if you chose (4). Choice (5) is the opposite of the connection implied by the gears. Choice (3) does not refer to the connection between poverty and terrorism. Choices (1) and (2) both imply that terrorism is a cause of poverty, but it is more likely the cartoonist sees terrorism as a result of poverty.

EXERCISE 14

Understanding Political Cartoons

Directions: Study each cartoon and its background clues. Then answer the questions that follow.

Background clues: In 1965, the civil rights movement in the United States used nonviolent protest to end discrimination against African Americans. This cartoon is entitled "Jericho, USA." On the wall in the cartoon are the words "voting discrimination" and the people are carrying a banner that states "equal rights."

Jericho, USA.
From *The Herblock Gallery*
(Simon & Schuster, 1968). Reprinted by permission.

1. What biblical story does the cartoon refer to?

   _____

2. What are the people in the cartoon trying to do?

   _____

3. The cartoonist's opinion is that
   (1) voting discrimination is so strong, it can only be ended by force
   (2) the protesters are dreamers who cannot succeed just by protesting
   (3) like the walls of Jericho, voting discrimination will come tumbling down
   (4) to end voting discrimination, protesters need to march around the U.S. seven times
   (5) voting discrimination is necessary to protect the U.S. from outside troublemakers

Background clues: After the Civil War, New York City politics were controlled by a political organization called Tammany Hall. The boss of Tammany Hall was William Tweed.

THE "BRAINS"

"The Brains of Tammany" by Thomas Nast

4. What is drawn in place of Tweed's head?

_____

5. The cartoonist's main point is that Boss Tweed

    (1) is an honest man who works for a living
    (2) is a banker
    (3) eats too much
    (4) is corrupt
    (5) is a wealthy man

Background clues: This cartoon was published after California became the sixth state to allow women to vote. The man on the right is labeled "Corrupt Politician." The woman's hat is labeled "California."

"Now Dance!"
Robert Carter, *New York Globe*

6. There are two people in the cartoon, a man and a woman. Which one does the cartoonist appear to view more positively?

_____

7. In the opinion of this cartoonist, women voters in California

(1) will be wild and out of control, endangering innocent people
(2) will act and vote in a very similar way as male voters
(3) must be protected from corrupt and arrogant politicians
(4) will need to use handguns to defend themselves when voting
(5) will help challenge and throw out corrupt politicians

Answers are on page 489.

Chapter Review

Directions: Read the following passages and answer the questions that follow.

Questions 1–3 are based on the following passage.

The release of Daw Aung San Suu Kyi from a 19-month house arrest is welcome news for the Burmese people. It is also welcome news for concerned citizens and governments around the world that have supported her nonviolent struggle for freedom and democracy in her homeland. That support must continue.

No matter what happens in Burma (now known as Myanmar) in years to come, it will be remembered in history as yet another day on which human spirit and free will prevailed [won] against overpowering brute force.

Aung San Suu Kyi called her hard-won freedom "a new dawn" for her country. And yet she wasted no time in reminding her people—and the international community—that it may take years before the full morning arrives. It is her mission of ushering in a democratic transition that deserves the world's utmost support and active solidarity.

The recipient of the 1991 Nobel Peace Prize, Aung San Suu Kyi was instrumental in the push for democracy in the peaceful struggle against Burma's dictatorship. After spending years under house arrest as a political prisoner, she was released in 1995, with restrictions placed on her activities, and then re-arrested 19 months ago [November 2000].

The international community played a key role in Aung San Suu Kyi's release. The United States and its democratic allies, including Canada and the European Union, as well as groups like the International Labor Organization, took a strong stand against the Burmese regime by imposing various forms of punitive [punishing] measures, including economic sanctions, diplomatic pressure, and visa bans.

Similarly, grass roots "Free Burma" campaigns around the world waged successful anti-apartheid-style divestment campaigns and consumer boycotts targeting foreign investors doing business in Burma under military rule.

While Aung San Suu Kyi's release cannot be attributed to the sanctions alone, these measures helped further thwart [defeat] the regime's intention to consolidate its power.

The regime [government] appears to realize what it is up against. The economy is in shambles. AIDS is rampant. Illicit drug production and smuggling thrive on the tacit [unspoken] support of the regime. It has ruthlessly put down armed ethnic minorities, and it imprisons political dissidents for decades-long terms. The release of Aung San Suu Kyi is the clearest signal that the generals are crying for help from the very citizen whom they had devoted most of their energies and resources to get rid of.

—Excerpted from "Burma's new dawn" by Zarni, *The Progressive Media Project*

1. The topic of this passage is

   (1) key moments in the modern political history of Burma
   (2) the life of Aung San Suu Kyi, Nobel Peace Prize winner
   (3) the significance Aung San Suu Kyi's release from house arrest
   (4) the importance of the Nobel Peace Prize in resolving conflicts
   (5) the nonviolent struggle for freedom and democracy in Burma

2. It is the writer's opinion that

   (1) the Burmese generals are trying to improve life in Burma
   (2) Aung San Suu Kyi is a heroic, nonviolent freedom fighter
   (3) the generals and Aung San Suu Kyi will soon work together
   (4) Western nations have ignored the plight of the Burmese people
   (5) the rulers of Burma have decided to reform their government

3. The Burmese regime imprisoned political dissidents for decades-long terms.

   A *dissident* is

   (1) a criminal
   (2) a protester
   (3) a reporter
   (4) a soldier
   (5) a politician

Questions 4 and 5 are based on the following passage.

[In 1750] the two most important trade routes in terms of volume and financial return were controlled by British merchants: the tobacco and the sugar trades. American merchants dominated two small trades routes: the export of rice to Europe and the export of supplies from the Northern mainland to the West Indies. However, American control of these subsidiary trade routes undermined the British policy of mercantilism [colonies producing goods], which depended on raw materials from the colonies that were shipped to Great Britain and then exported as finished products. This policy discouraged any colonial trade except with Great Britain.

The colonists' participation in transatlantic trade accounted for the rise of the American port cities of Boston, New York, Newport, Philadelphia, Baltimore, and Charleston. These shipping centers gradually came to provide the commercial services, such as insurance and wholesale trade, and the small-scale industries, such as rope and sail manufacture and shipbuilding, that were necessary to sustain a merchant fleet. The independence movement began in these cities.

—Excerpted from "American Revolution," *Microsoft® Encarta® Encyclopedia 2000*

4. According to the passage, why did the independence movement begin in the port cities?

   (1) They had the most contact with the outside world.
   (2) They wanted to control the tobacco and sugar trades.
   (3) They believed in mercantilism and British economic policies.
   (4) They were developing economic independence.
   (5) They had the greatest concentration of people.

5. Americans controlled subsidiary trade routes.

   A *subsidiary* trade route would be

   (1) secret
   (2) important
   (3) dangerous
   (4) profitable
   (5) minor

Questions 6–8 are based on the following account by labor activist Mother Jones.

In the spring of 1903, I went to Kensington, Pennsylvania, where seventy-five thousand textile workers were on strike. Of this number at least ten thousand were little children. The workers were striking for more pay and shorter hours. Every day little children came into Union Headquarters, some with their hands off, some with the thumb missing, some with their fingers off at the knuckle. They were stooped little things, round-shouldered and skinny. . . .

I asked some of the parents if they would let me have their little boys and girls for a week or ten days, promising to bring them back safe and sound. . . . A few men and women went with me. . . . The children carried knapsacks on their backs in which was a knife and fork, a tin cup and plate. . . . One little fellow had a drum, and another had a fife. . . . We carried banners that said: "We want time to play."

. . . Our march had done its work. We had drawn the attention of the nation to the crime of child labor.

—Excerpted from *A People's History of the United States* by Howard Zinn

6. The children carried

    (1) eating utensils and musical instruments
    (2) knives and forks
    (3) the smaller children
    (4) money to pay the workers
    (5) a fife and drum

7. What is this passage about?

    (1) a children's march to protest child labor
    (2) an early fund-raising telethon
    (3) the right of children to play
    (4) the textile workers' strike in Kensington
    (5) the abuse and mutilation of children

8. How many textile workers were on strike in Kensington?

    (1) 10
    (2) 1,903
    (3) 7,000
    (4) 10,000
    (5) 75,000

Questions 9 and 10 are based on the following passage about Calvin Coolidge, who was president of the United States from 1923 to 1929.

The sudden thrust of the Presidential mantle about his thin shoulders staggered him for a time. He really was a timid person those first few days. He promised to carry on the Harding policies—whatever that might mean—and then lapsed into silence for a month.

During that month he was built into a myth. It was one of the greatest feats of newspaper propaganda that the modern world has seen. It really was a miracle. He said nothing. Newspapers must have copy. So we grasped at little incidents to build up human interest stories and we created a character. He kept his counsel. Therefore he was a strong and silent man. The editorial writers on newspapers which were satisfied with the status quo, the big Eastern journals, created the strong, silent man. Then, in time, as the country found out he was not a superman, neither strong nor silent, they emphasized his little witticisms, his dry wit, and we had a national character—Cal. Everybody spoke of him fondly as "Cal." He was one of us. He was the ordinary man incarnate.

—Excerpted from *The American Reader* by Paul Angle

9. Why did the newspapers make up a strong, silent image for President Coolidge?

(1) They admired his strong, silent style of leadership.
(2) They believed silence was a virtue.
(3) The real Coolidge didn't give them anything to write about.
(4) They wanted to make sure the American people understood him.
(5) They wanted to create a miracle.

10. What was the truth about the images of Coolidge?

(1) Calvin Coolidge was a master of public relations when he created his image of "Cal."
(2) The real Calvin Coolidge was different from the public image of him.
(3) Calvin Coolidge was willing to dig for the truth.
(4) Calvin Coolidge was a strong and silent man.
(5) Calvin Coolidge's inspired leadership and great sense of humor have made him one of our most remembered presidents.

Answers are on pages 489–490.

CHAPTER 2

Interpreting Graphic Materials

Tables, graphs, and maps are often used in social studies materials. It is important for you to understand illustrations. Illustrations can give detailed information without many words, so they are very helpful to both readers and writers. Understanding **tables, graphs,** and **maps** will also help you in your daily life.

Using Tables

A **table** is information organized into columns and rows. The purpose of a table is to allow you to easily locate and compare bits of information. The following example shows the major parts of a table.

EDUCATION COMPLETED, 1940–2000

Since 1940, the following percentage of Americans aged 25 or over had completed high school or college:

	High School Only	**Four or More Years of College**
1940	24.5%	4.6%
1950	34.3%	6.2%
1960	41.4%	7.7%
1970	55.2%	11.0%
1980	66.3%	16.3%
1990	77.6%	21.3%
2000	80.4%	24.4%

Source: U.S. Bureau of the Census

In the table above, the **title** gives the topic. The **subtitle** below the title gives more information about the topic. The **data**, or information, on a table is organized into **rows** and **columns**. A row of a table is all the entries on one horizontal line. In this table, each row is labeled by a year, such as 1940. A column consists of all the entries on one vertical line. The column headings are "High School Only" and "Four or More Years of College."

Understanding a Table

Just like a reading passage, every table has a topic. Look at the table below.

TABLE-READING TIP

In order to understand a table, first read the title and all the headings. Don't try to read the data until you understand what the title and headings tell you.

THE NATION'S LARGEST CITIES

2000 Rank	2000 Population	Percentage Change Since 1990
1. New York	8,008,278	9.4
2. Los Angeles	3,694,820	6.0
3. Chicago	2,896,016	4.0
4. Houston	1,953,631	19.8

Source: U.S. Census Bureau

The table tells the percent of population change in the nation's largest cities. You can figure this out by looking at the title and the headings.

EXERCISE 1

Understanding a Table

Directions: Answer the following questions.

RESULTS OF THE PRESIDENTIAL ELECTION OF 2000

Candidate	Party	Popular Vote	Electoral Vote
George W. Bush	Republican	50,459,624	271
Albert Gore, Jr.	Democratic	51,003,238	266
Ralph Nader	Green	2,882,985	0
Patrick Buchanan	Reform	449,120	0
Harry Browne	Libertarian	384,440	0
Other		232,922	1

Source: http://www.uselectionatlas.org

1. What is this table about? _____

2. What are the four headings on this table? _____

_____

Answers are on page 490.

Locating Data on a Table

In order to find specific data on a table, you must use the column and row headings to locate the information you need. The headings label the vertical and horizontal lines of data. In the following table, the column headings are 1977, 1997, and Percent Change. The row headings are the types of foods listed along the left side.

CHANGES IN FOOD CONSUMPTION, 1977–1997
(pounds per person)

	1977	**1997**	**Percent Change**
Dairy products	540.2	579.8	+7.3%
Red meat	132.3	111.0	–16.1%
Flour and cereal products	140.9	200.1	+42.0%
Fats and oils	53.3	65.6	+23.1%

Source: U.S. Department of Agriculture

TABLE-READING TIP

If you are asked to find an increase, look for numbers or percentages that become larger over time. A plus (+) sign, such as +18%, tells you there was an increase of 18%. If you are asked to find a decrease, look for numbers that become smaller over time. A minus (–) sign, such as –18%, tells you there was a decrease of 18%.

The data in the table above can be used to help us understand how the American diet changed from 1977 to 1997. Answer the following sample questions based on the table.

What was the number of pounds of red meat consumed (eaten) by the average American in 1997?

First look for the row labeled "Red Meat." Then look for the column labeled "1997." Draw imaginary lines across from "Red Meat" and down from "1997." The place where the two lines cross is the number you are looking for. The average American ate 111.0 pounds of red meat in 1997.

Of the items listed, which food had the greatest percentage change in consumption from 1977 to 1997?

You must look for the largest number in the "Percentage Change" column. That number is 42.0%. Looking across the row, you find that flour and cereal products had the greatest percentage change of the items listed.

By how many pounds did the consumption of flour and cereal products increase from 1977 to 1997?

In order to find the amount of the increase, first find the amount of consumption in 1977 and in 1997. Consumption of flour and cereal products was 140.9 pounds in 1977 and 200.1 pounds in 1997. To find the increase, you need to find the difference between the two numbers, so you subtract: 200.1 – 140.9 = 59.2 pounds.

EXERCISE 2

Finding Information on a Table

Directions: Use the information in the table to answer the questions that follow.

MEDIAN PER CAPITA INCOME IN THE U.S., 1999–2001
(per person income in U.S. dollars)

	2001	2000	1999
White Males	30,240	29,797	28,664
Black Males	21,466	21,343	20,441
Hispanic Origin Males	20,189	19,498	17,862
White Females	16,652	16,079	15,352
Black Females	16,282	15,881	14,776
Hispanic Origin Females	12,583	12,248	11,376

Source: U.S. Census Bureau

1. Another word for *capita* is _____.
2. In 1999, the median per capita income for Black Female Americans was _____.
3. Between 1999 and 2001, which group listed in the table had the largest increase in their median per capita income?

   _____

4. In 2001, which group listed in the table had the highest median per capita income? _____

Answers are on page 490.

Finding the Main Idea of a Table

TABLE-READING TIP

Because data are easier to read and compare in smaller numbers, tables that compare large numbers often use phrases such as *in thousands* in their subtitle or key. *In thousands* means that each number listed in the table is really 1,000 times that number. So, for example, the number 18 on a table that says *in thousands* actually means 18,000.

Like a reading passage, a table may illustrate a main idea. The author may want to make a central point by choosing and displaying data in a certain way. Ask yourself, "What does the table tell me and what is its purpose?" Then think of how the data could be summarized in a main idea statement.

Sometimes the main idea of a table will be stated directly in the title or subtitle. Other times you must find the main idea by looking at the headings or by studying the data.

INFANT MORTALITY RATES—1998

REGION	Deaths under age 1 per 1,000 live births
WORLD	58.2
Less Developed Countries	63.6
More Developed Countries	9.5
REGIONS: Sub-Saharan Africa	92.4
The Near East and North Africa	50.5
China	44.6
Rest of Asia and Oceania	65.7
Latin America and the Caribbean	33.2
Eastern Europe and the NIS	36.6
Rest of the World	5.8

Source: U.S. Census Bureau

Below are four choices for the main idea of the above table. Circle the number of the choice that gives the main idea for the table. (**Hint:** *mortality* means *death*)

(1) Less developed countries have higher infant mortality than the rest of the world.
(2) Infant mortality is increasing in less developed countries because of the AIDS epidemic.
(3) Infant mortality rates are inexcusably high in the less developed countries of the world.
(4) More developed countries have better health care than less developed countries.

You were correct if you circled (1). The author of the table chose to compare infant mortality in more developed countries and less developed countries by placing these two at the top of the table. The other choices do not state the main idea of this table.

EXERCISE 3

Main Idea of a Table

Directions: After each table are five choices for the main idea. Choose the one that accurately summarizes the data in the table.

EARNINGS: GENDER & OCCUPATION

For every $1,000 made by men in these occupations during 2001, women received the following amounts:

Laborers	$816	Machine operators/ inspectors	$685
Administrative assistants/ secretaries	$799	Managers	$685
Truckers/drivers	$786	Technicians	$671
Service workers	$710	Farmers, fishers	$645
Doctors and lawyers	$710	Salespeople	$613

Source: U.S. Census Bureau

1. What is the main idea of this table?

   (1) Traditionally male jobs are now being filled by women.
   (2) Women earn less than men in the same jobs.
   (3) In most jobs, men are worth more than women.
   (4) It costs more to hire a man than it does a woman.
   (5) Women's and men's salaries are finally becoming equal.

Background Clue: This chart shows how income is divided among five groups of Americans: lowest income earners through highest income earners. For example, for every dollar earned in the United States in 2000, 3.6% (or 3.6 cents) was earned by the "Lowest" group of earners, while 49.6% (or 49.6 cents) was earned by the "Highest" group of earners.

Percent of Income Received by Five Groups of Earners in the U.S.A.

Year	Lowest	Second	Third	Fourth	Highest
2000	3.6	8.9	14.8	23.0	49.6
1995	3.7	9.1	15.2	23.3	48.7
1990	3.9	9.6	15.9	24.0	46.6
1985	4.0	9.7	16.3	24.6	43.7
1980	4.3	10.3	16.9	24.9	43.2
1975	4.4	10.5	17.1	24.8	43.2

Source: U.S. Census Bureau

2. The main idea of this table is:

   (1) The lowest group of households was the poorest in America.
   (2) More tax cuts are needed to benefit the highest group.
   (3) The share of income received by each group has changed over time.
   (4) The share of the highest group increased while the rest decreased.
   (5) The third group suffered a loss of income from 1975 to 2000.

Answers are on page 490.

Reading Graphs

A **graph** allows a reader to spot trends, make comparisons, and draw conclusions from data. Being able to read graphs will help you in many practical situations as well as in social studies. This section examines four types of graphs: **pictographs, bar graphs, line graphs,** and **circle graphs.**

Finding the Topic of a Graph

Like a table, every graph has a topic. The title usually tells you the topic of the graph. Sometimes there is also a subtitle to help you out. Always read the title and check the other information on the graph, such as the labels and the data, to make sure you have an accurate idea of the topic of the graph.

GROWTH IN UNITED NATIONS MEMBERSHIP, 1945–2002

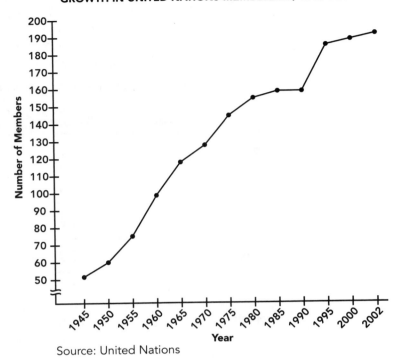

Source: United Nations

What is the topic of this graph?

This graph shows the growth in membership of the United Nations. The title of this graph tells you what the graph is about.

EXERCISE 4

Topic of a Graph

Directions: On the line below each graph, write its topic. Study the titles and other information on each graph before writing your answer.

CONSUMER PRICE INDEX FOR ALL URBAN CONSUMERS

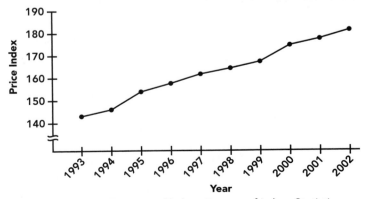

Source: U.S. Dept. of Labor, Bureau of Labor Statistics

1. Topic: _____

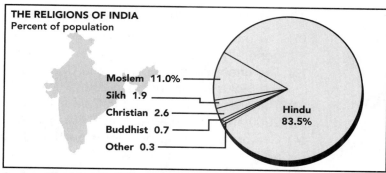

THE RELIGIONS OF INDIA
Percent of population

Moslem 11.0%
Sikh 1.9
Christian 2.6
Buddhist 0.7
Other 0.3

Hindu
83.5%

Source: *The New York Times*

2. Topic: _____

Answers are on page 490.

The Main Idea of a Graph

Graphs illustrate a point. Usually the main idea will be stated directly in the title or subtitle. To determine the main idea, read the titles and other written information and look at the data. Ask yourself, "What message is the graph giving me?" Then think of a way to summarize the information.

Read the title, scale, labels and data on the graph below. Then answer the questions.

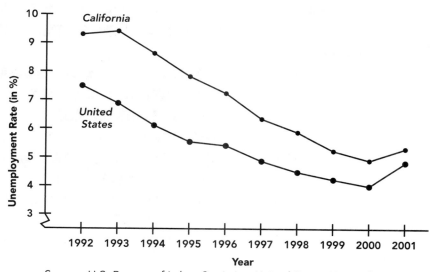

UNEMPLOYMENT RATE 1992–2001

Source: U.S. Bureau of Labor Statistics, United States Unemployment

What is the graph about?

The topic of the graph is the unemployment rates in the United States and California from 1992 to 2001. You know this by looking at the title and the boxed key that contains labels for the two lines.

Why are there two lines on the graph?

There are two lines because two things are being compared. One line stands for the United States as a whole. The other line stands for the state of California.

The main idea of this graph is

(1) The unemployment rates in California and the United States generally rose and fell together from 1992 to 2001.
(2) The unemployment rate in the United States dropped throughout the 1990s before rising in 2001.
(3) The unemployment rate in California dropped to a low of 4.9% in 2000 after being as high as 9.4% in 1993.
(4) California's unemployment is getting closer to the national average after being much worse for a decade.
(5) California had one of the highest unemployment rates in the nation throughout the 1990s before recovering.

Choice (4) is correct because it most accurately describes the relationship between the two lines. Choices (2) and (3) each deal with only one of the two lines. Choice (1) is not an accurate reading of the graph. There is not enough information for choice (5) since the graph does not show data for other states.

EXERCISE 5

The Main Idea of a Graph

Directions: Ask yourself about the message and main idea of each graph. Then answer the questions that follow.

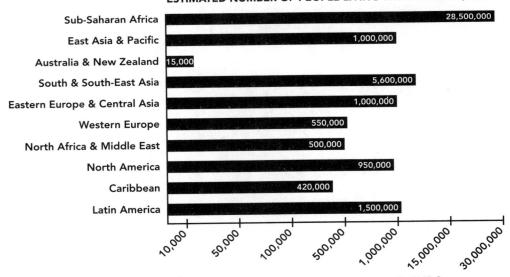

ESTIMATED NUMBER OF PEOPLE LIVING WITH HIV/AIDS, END 2001

Sub-Saharan Africa	28,500,000
East Asia & Pacific	1,000,000
Australia & New Zealand	15,000
South & South-East Asia	5,600,000
Eastern Europe & Central Asia	1,000,000
Western Europe	550,000
North Africa & Middle East	500,000
North America	950,000
Caribbean	420,000
Latin America	1,500,000

Source: Joint United Nations Program on HIV/AIDS

1. Rich countries with a strong, modern industry are considered developed, while poor countries are often described as developing. In general, are those areas with the most people living with HIV/AIDS developed or developing?

2. What is the main idea of the graph?

   (1) North America has neither the highest or lowest number of people with HIV/AIDS.
   (2) The HIV/AIDS epidemic is impacting millions of people all over the world.
   (3) Developing nations, especially in Sub-Saharan Africa, are most impacted by HIV/AIDS.
   (4) New drugs available for HIV/AIDS make it less of a global threat than the numbers might suggest.
   (5) HIV/AIDS prevention strategies should focus on the developed countries to limit the impact of the epidemic.

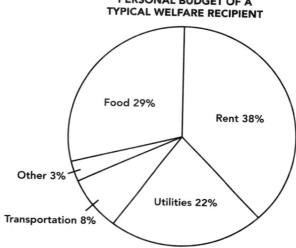

PERSONAL BUDGET OF A TYPICAL WELFARE RECIPIENT

Food 29%
Rent 38%
Other 3%
Utilities 22%
Transportation 8%

3. What is the topic of this graph? _____

4. The graph shows that, in general, welfare recipients spend most of their income on three things. What are they?

   _____

5. What is the main idea of this graph?

   (1) Because of a shortage of housing, welfare recipients spend a great deal of their income on rent.
   (2) Limiting the amount of welfare payments encourages people to find work and leave welfare.
   (3) Welfare recipients have such limited budgets, they must spend most of their money on necessities.
   (4) Because welfare recipients do not manage their money wisely, they cannot pay all their expenses.
   (5) When people have to spend most of their income on food, rent, and energy, they go on welfare.

Answers are on page 490.

Finding Information on a Pictograph

GRAPH-READING TIP

Pictographs are used to make general comparisons. The information on a pictograph is not exact.

A **pictograph** uses symbols to display information. In order to find specific details on a pictograph, you must use the **key**. A key tells you what the pictures on the graph represent. For example, look at the following pictograph. Each picture, or symbol, stands for 1 million Internet users. A pictograph is good for comparisons and approximations, but not for exact figures.

Look at the pictograph below and answer this question:

About how many people are projected to use the Internet in Italy in 2004?

PROJECTED ONLINE COUNTRIES BY POPULATION FOR 2004

KEY = 1 million people

Source: www.cyberatlas.internet.com

Find the row labeled Italy. There are approximately eight and a half symbols. The key tells you that each symbol stands for 1 million Internet users. Multiply:
$8.25 \times 1,000,000 = 8,250,000$. There will be about 8.25 million Internet users in Italy in 2004.

Look again at the pictograph and answer the following questions:

Which country is projected to have the fewest number of Internet users in 2004?

To find the country with the lowest number of Internet users, you must find the shortest row of symbols. This row is labeled The Netherlands.

Which country is expected to have the greatest number of Internet users?

The country with the greatest number of Internet users is expected to be the United States.

EXERCISE 6

Reading Pictographs

Directions: Fill in the blanks with the correct information based on the pictograph.

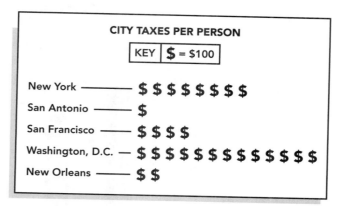

CITY TAXES PER PERSON

| KEY | $ = $100 |

New York ——— $ $ $ $ $ $ $
San Antonio ——— $
San Francisco ——— $ $ $
Washington, D.C. — $ $ $ $ $ $ $ $ $ $ $ $
New Orleans ——— $ $

1. What were the approximate taxes per person in New Orleans?

   _____

2. Which city's per-person taxes are lower, San Francisco or New York?

   _____

3. What is the main idea of the pictograph "City Taxes per Person"?

   (1) Washington, D.C. is one of the most expensive cities in the country to live.
   (2) San Antonio and New Orleans have very low city taxes.
   (3) Cities that bring in a lot of tax money are able to provide more services to the public.
   (4) Per-person city taxes in the United States can range widely.
   (5) City taxes in San Francisco are reasonable, so most people could afford to live there.

Answers are on page 490.

Reading Bar Graphs

A **bar graph** uses bars to display information. It gives you a way to compare information quickly and easily. The information is not exact, but you can make good estimates from a bar graph. In order to find specific facts on a bar graph, you must use the scale to read the height of the bars.

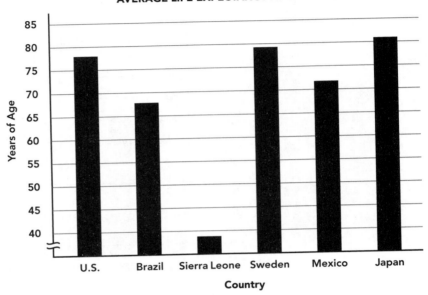

AVERAGE LIFE EXPECTANCY AT BIRTH IN 1999

Source: United Nations Development Program

What was the average life expectancy at birth in 1999 in the United States?

In order to find the average life expectancy at birth in 1999 in the United States, find the bar labeled "U.S." Now draw an imaginary horizontal line from the top end of the bar over to the scale. Read the number on the scale. If the line is between two scale entries, estimate the number. In this case, the average life expectancy at birth in 1999 in the U.S. is slightly above 75. A good estimate would be 76 or 77 years.

Use the bar graph in the example above to answer the following questions.

What nation had the shortest life expectancy at birth in 1999?

Find the shortest bar. At the bottom of the bar is the name of the country, Sierra Leone.

What was the life expectancy in the nation on the graph that had the longest life expectancy at birth in 1999?

Find the longest bar. That bar is for Japan. Now draw an imaginary horizontal line across the graph to the *y*-axis. The line is slightly above 80. A good estimate for the average life expectancy would be 81 years.

GRAPH-READING TIP

In multiple-choice questions based on graphs, you can eliminate incorrect choices. Since you are usually expected to make estimates based on graphs, there should be one answer choice that is closest to your estimate.

EXERCISE 7

Reading Bar Graphs

Directions: Fill in the blanks with the correct information from the graph. Estimate the answer if you cannot read an exact figure from the graph. (**Hint:** *Per capita* means *per person*)

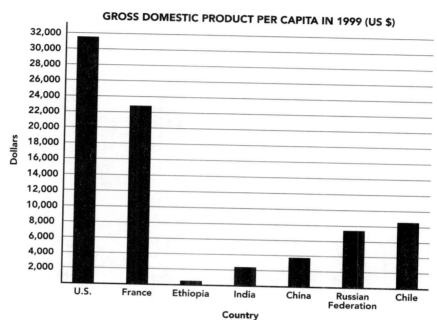

GROSS DOMESTIC PRODUCT PER CAPITA IN 1999 (US $)

Dollars / Country

Source: United Nations Development Program

1. Which nation had an average per capita Gross Domestic Product of about $23,000? _____

2. Which nation had the lowest per capita Gross Domestic Product?

   _____

3. Which of the nations in the graph had a per capita Gross Domestic Product most similar to Chile?

   _____

4. About how much more does a person in the U.S. earn than a person in China? _____

Answers are on page 491.

Reading Line Graphs

A **line graph** is similar to a bar graph in many ways. However, instead of using bars, lines connect different points, called **data points**. Line graphs are used to show trends or developments. On the side of a line graph is a vertical scale. Along the bottom of a line graph is a horizontal scale. To read a line graph, you read up from the horizontal scale and across from the vertical scale to a particular point on the line. Read the titles and other words on the graph before you try reading the data.

Use the line graph below to answer the following questions.

What was the population of London in 1800?

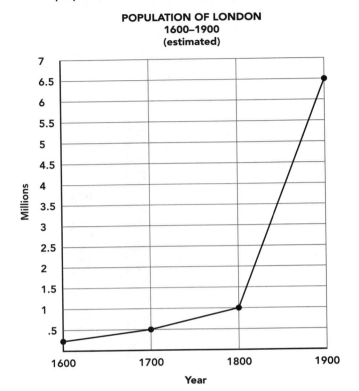

POPULATION OF LONDON
1600–1900
(estimated)

First find the year, 1800, on the horizontal scale—along the bottom of the graph. Go straight up until you reach the data point for 1800. Now go straight across to the left until you reach the vertical scale. At the height of the data point, the closest number on the vertical scale is 1. That means that the population of London in 1800 was about 1 million.

In what year shown on the graph did London have its largest population?

Look at the line and find the highest point on it. Looking down to the horizontal scale, you find the year 1900. Therefore, London had its largest population in 1900.

Between 1600 and 1900, what happened to the size of London's population?

Look at the first point on the line (the year 1600), the shape of the line, and the endpoint of the line (the year 1900). The population of London increased greatly during the period, from less than half a million people to 6.5 million.

To summarize or see a trend on a line graph, look at the whole line and get a general idea of what happened to the data over the time shown.

EXERCISE 8

Reading Line Graphs

Directions: Answer the questions based on the following graph. If you can't read an exact answer from the graph, estimate.

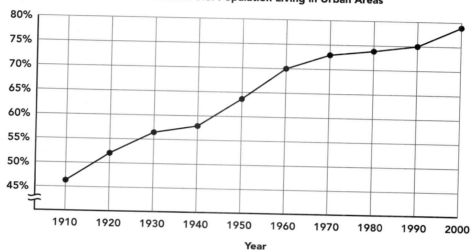

AMERICA MOVES TO THE CITIES
Percent of U.S. Population Living in Urban Areas

Source: U.S. Census Bureau American Fact Finder

1. In what year shown on the graph was the percentage of urban population the lowest? _____

2. What percentage of the population of the United States lived in urban areas in 1960? _____

3. Which of the following best describes the trend shown by this line graph?

    (1) The percentage of people living in urban areas of the United States has steadily fallen.
    (2) The percentage of people living in rural areas of the United States has steadily increased.
    (3) The percentage of people living in a few major cities in the United States has risen steadily.
    (4) In 1910, most people lived in the northeastern United States, by 1980 the population was shifting south and west.
    (5) The percentage of people living in urban areas of the United States has risen steadily.

Answers are on page 491.

Reading Circle Graphs

A **circle graph** uses parts, or segments, of a circle to display information. Think of the circle graph as a pie. The segments look like slices of the pie. The size of the segment tells how much of the whole it represents. Often circle graphs are called **pie graphs** or **pie charts**.

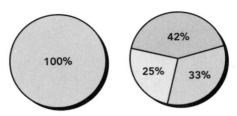

On the following graph, each segment has a label to tell you what it stands for. Find the region of the world that has the largest oil reserves.

WORLDWIDE OIL RESERVES
Measured in Millions of Barrels of Crude Per Day

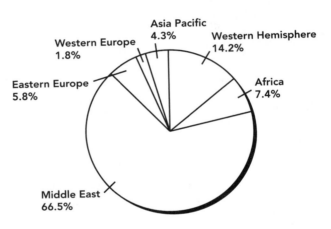

Source: Project Underground, Drillbits and Tailings

The region with the largest oil reserves is the region with the largest pie slice, the Middle East. The amount 66.5 is written just below the label of the segment, which means that the oil reserves in the Middle East are about 66,500,000 barrels of crude per day.

Sometimes in a circle graph the label and amount or percentage are written in the segment. Other times, especially when the segment is very small, they may be connected to the segment by a line.

Use the circle graph "Worldwide Oil Reserves" to answer the following question.

For many years, the Middle East has been a very important part of American foreign policy. There are those who argue that the reason for this interest is the oil in the Middle East. Does this circle graph support that claim?

Find the segment labeled Middle East. It is by far the largest segment. Therefore, the circle graph does support the argument that oil is an important reason the United States is interested in the Middle East.

EXERCISE 9

Reading Circle Graphs

Directions: Fill in the blanks with the correct information based on each graph.

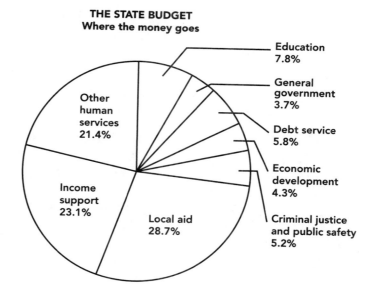

THE STATE BUDGET
Where the money goes

1. What percent of the state budget pays for education?

   _____

2. What expense uses up exactly 4.3% percent of the state budget?

   _____

3. Does the state spend more money on education or on criminal justice and public safety? _____

POPULATION BY AGE GROUP IN THE CITY OF SADDLETOP

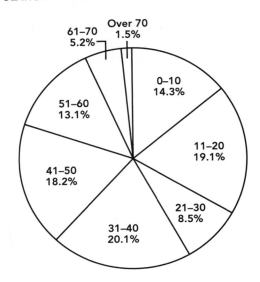

4. What age group makes up the largest percentage of Saddletop's population? _____

5. What age group below 60 makes up the smallest percentage of the population? _____

6. Which age group is larger, the 11–20 group or the 41–50 group?

_____

Answers are on page 491.

Reading Maps

A **map** is a drawing of the surface of an area. A map could represent your own neighborhood. Or it could represent a city, state, country, continent, or the world.

There are different kinds of maps for different purposes. In this chapter, you will be looking at common parts of maps, including **directions**, **distances**, **keys**, and **borders**.

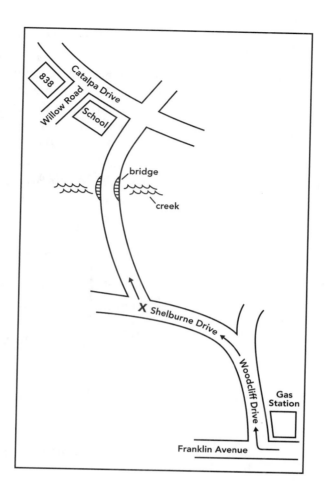

It is easier to follow directions when you use a map. Find the gas station at the corner of Franklin Avenue and Woodcliff Drive. Now follow Woodcliff Drive to where Shelburne Drive forks off from it. Continue along Shelburne Drive to another fork in the road.

Use the map to finish writing directions to 838 Catalpa Drive. Start at the X on the map and use landmarks whenever you can.

_____

_____

_____

_____

Sample Directions: Take the right fork. Go straight over a bridge above a small creek. On your left you will see a school. Turn left at the school. You will then be on Catalpa Drive. Continue on Catalpa Drive past Willow Road. On the left you'll find 838 Catalpa Drive.

Direction and Distance

Different kinds of information are found on a map. There are important symbols on a map that help orient us to it and show how the places fit together. Below is a map of the Baltimore area. The **direction symbol** in the upper right corner of the map shows that the top of the map is north. If north is toward the top of the map, south is toward the bottom. East is to the right, and west is to the left. If you know north, you can figure out the other directions.

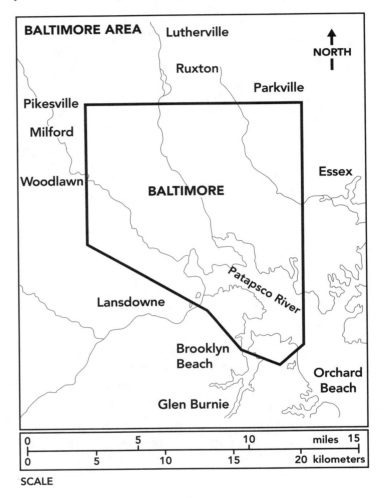

Lutherville is straight north of Baltimore. Name a town that is straight east of Baltimore. Because east is to the right, look to the right of Baltimore. The town of Essex is east of Baltimore.

At the bottom of the map is a **scale** in miles and kilometers. You can use the scale to estimate distances. The easiest way to use a scale is to mark off the distance between two places on the edge of a piece of paper. Then put the edge of the paper next to the scale to estimate the distance.

About how many miles is it from Baltimore's west boundary near Woodlawn directly across town to its east boundary?

Use the edge of a piece of paper to mark off the distance. Now line up the marking with the zero on the scale. Your marking should end at a little less than 10 miles.

Using a Map Key

Most maps have keys. A **map key** defines the various symbols used on a map. A key can define boundary lines such as international and state boundaries. It can give symbols for cities of varying sizes and for capital cities. It can identify symbols that represent vegetation, climate, population, and economic products.

The following map is of New England, a region in the northeastern United States.

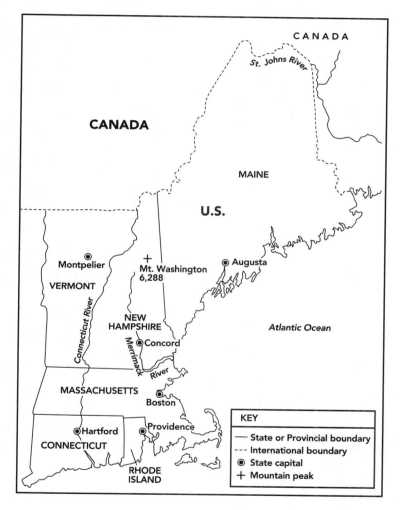

What is the state capital of Connecticut?

Look at the key to find the symbol for state capitals. Now look for the state capital symbol within the state of Connecticut. Hartford is the capital.

The only mountain peak marked on this map is Mt. Washington. In what state is Mt. Washington located?

The key tells you that the symbol for a mountain is +. Looking for the symbol, you should be able to locate Mt. Washington in the state of New Hampshire.

EXERCISE 10

Using a Map Key

Directions: Brazil is one of the largest countries in the world. It is in South America. Use the map of Brazil to answer the following questions.

KEY

— International boundary
+ Mountain peak
• City
◉ Capital

1. A major geographical feature of Brazil is a very famous river that runs across the northern part of the country. What is the name of the river? _____

2. Part of the southernmost tip of Brazil is a lake. What is the name of the lake? _____

3. The mouth of a river is where it enters the ocean. The mouth of the Amazon River is near what special line that crosses the map?

_____

4. What is the name of the highest mountain peak in Brazil?

_____

Answers are on page 491.

Historical Maps

Historical maps can help us understand the past. They can show political boundaries of a past time period. They also can be used to illustrate historical trends and events. Sometimes these maps of the past can help us make sense of the present. Look at the following map of the eastern United States before the American Revolution. What nation controlled the Great Lakes and the region around them?

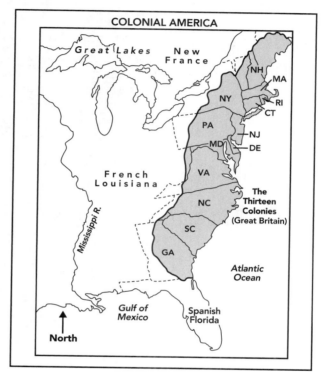

First find the Great Lakes on the map. The area north and east of the Great Lakes is called New France. The area south and west of the lakes is called French Louisiana. By reading the map you know that the whole region was controlled by France.

What nation controlled Florida?

Looking at the map, you can tell that Florida was called Spanish Florida. So you know it was controlled by Spain.

What nation controlled a large area to the west of the British colonies?

On the map, areas labeled New France and French Louisiana are west of the thirteen colonies belonging to Great Britain, so the answer is France.

EXERCISE 11

Reading Historical Maps

Directions: Answer the questions based on the following map.

NATIVE AMERICANS OF NORTH AMERICA

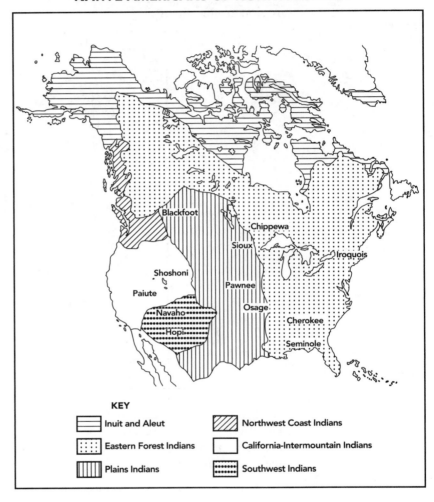

KEY

Inuit and Aleut	Northwest Coast Indians
Eastern Forest Indians	California-Intermountain Indians
Plains Indians	Southwest Indians

1. The Pawnee were part of which group of Native Americans?

   (1) Inuit and Aleut
   (2) Eastern Forests Indians
   (3) Plains Indians
   (4) Northwest Coast Indians
   (5) Southwest Indians

2. The far north of the continent was inhabited by which group?

   (1) Inuit and Aleut
   (2) Eastern Forests Indians
   (3) Plains Indians
   (4) Northwest Coast Indians
   (5) Southwest Indians

Answers are on page 491.

Chapter Review

Directions: Study each illustration carefully. Then answer the questions that follow.

Questions 1 and 2 are based on the following table.

Ten Leading Causes of Death in the U.S. (All figures are for 2000.)	
Heart Disease	710,760
Cancer	553,091
Stroke	167,661
Chronic Lower Respiratory Disease	122,009
Accidents	97,900
Diabetes	69,301
Pneumonia/Influenza	65,313
Alzheimer's Disease	49,558
Nephritis, nephrotic syndrome, and nephrosis	37,251
Septicema	31,224

Source: Centers for Disease Control

1. What was the leading cause of death in the U.S. in 2000?

   (1) heart disease
   (2) cancer
   (3) accidents
   (4) septicemia
   (5) substance abuse

2. Which of the following would have the greatest impact on the ten leading causes of death?

   (1) construction of more hospitals in underserved areas
   (2) reduced consumption of cigarettes by Americans
   (3) increasing malpractice penalties for negligent doctors and nurses
   (4) improving seat belts and air bags in automobiles
   (5) encouraging people to eat less fast food

Questions 3 and 4 are based on the following pictograph.

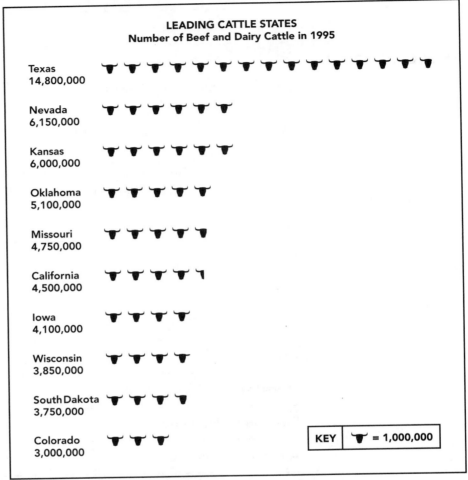

Source: Agricultural Statistics Board

3. Which state had the most beef and dairy cattle in 1995?

   (1) Texas
   (2) California
   (3) Alaska
   (4) Colorado
   (5) Nevada

4. Which state ranked third in total number of beef and dairy cattle in 1995?

   (1) Texas
   (2) California
   (3) Kansas
   (4) Wisconsin
   (5) Colorado

Questions 5 and 6 are based on the following bar graph.

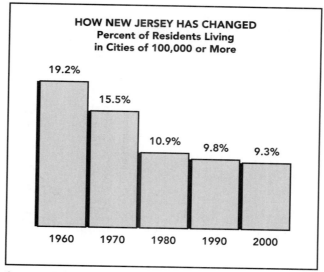

Source: U.S. Bureau of the Census

5. What is the main idea of this bar graph?

  (1) New Jersey has changed a great deal over the past forty years.
  (2) Over a forty-year period, fewer Americans lived in cities of over 100,000.
  (3) New Jersey's population declined in every decade between 1960 and 2000.
  (4) An increasing percentage of New Jersey residents live in cities of 100,000 or more.
  (5) An decreasing percentage of New Jersey residents live in cities of 100,000 or more.

6. What percent of New Jersey residents lived in cities of 100,000 or more in 1970?

  (1) 19.2%
  (2) 18.3%
  (3) 15.5%
  (4) 10.9%
  (5) 9.8%

Questions 7 and 8 are based on the following line graph.

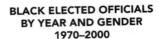

**BLACK ELECTED OFFICIALS
BY YEAR AND GENDER
1970–2000**

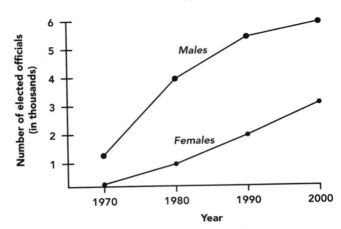

Source: Joint Center for Political and Economic Studies

7. The line graph covers the period from 1970 to 2000. What is the topic of the line graph?

   (1) black elected officials, by year and gender
   (2) the increasing importance of women in black political life
   (3) the dominance of males in black electoral politics
   (4) the enduring legacy of the Voting Rights Act
   (5) the increasing influence of black men in the Democratic Party

8. Which of the following statements **cannot** be supported by the graph?

   (1) The number of black elected officials is steadily increasing.
   (2) The gap between the number of male and female black elected officials is narrowing.
   (3) The number of elected black officials is decreasing.
   (4) In 2000, the total number of black elected officials was about 9,000.
   (5) Since 1970, there has been a six-fold increase in the number of male black elected officials.

Questions 9 and 10 are based on the following circle graph.

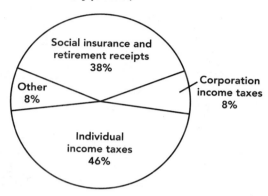

FEDERAL RECEIPTS IN 2002
(by percent)

Source: Department of the Treasury, Office of Public Affairs

9. The single most important source of receipts for the federal government in 2002 was

(1) corporation income taxes
(2) Social Security taxes
(3) Medicare receipts
(4) individual income taxes
(5) other, including excise, gift, and estate taxes

10. Which of the following percents represent social insurance and retirement receipts?

(1) 8%
(2) 16%
(3) 38%
(4) 46%
(5) 54%

Questions 11 and 12 are based on the following map.

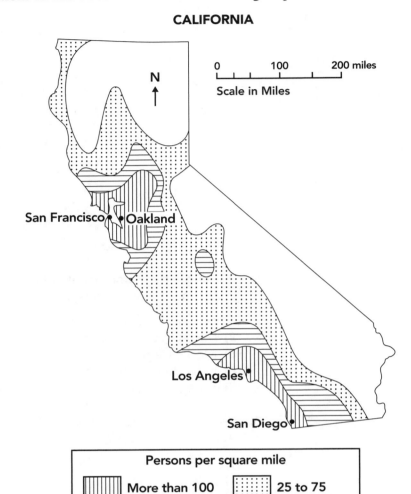

CALIFORNIA

11. What is the population density of the area within 25 miles of San Francisco?

    (1) less than 10
    (2) less than 25
    (3) 25 to 75
    (4) 75 to 100
    (5) more than 100

12. If you drove 200 miles straight north from San Diego and stopped, what would be the population density of the area you stopped in?

    (1) less than 25
    (2) 25 to 75
    (3) 75 to 100
    (4) more than 100
    (5) more than 500

Questions 13 and 14 are based on the following map.

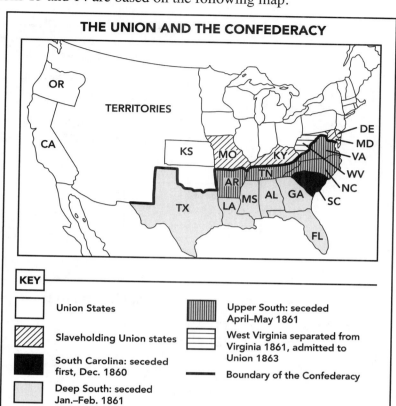

THE UNION AND THE CONFEDERACY

KEY

| | Union States | | Upper South: seceded April–May 1861 |

| | Slaveholding Union states | | West Virginia separated from Virginia 1861, admitted to Union 1863 |

| | South Carolina: seceded first, Dec. 1860 | — | Boundary of the Confederacy |

| | Deep South: seceded Jan.–Feb. 1861 | | |

13. Which of the following states was a slaveholding Union state?

(1) Kansas
(2) Kentucky
(3) Texas
(4) Arkansas
(5) California

14. What did Texas do during the Civil War?

(1) It was a Union state that banned slavery.
(2) It remained a slaveholding Union state.
(3) It seceded from the Union in December 1860.
(4) It seceded from the Union in January or February of 1861.
(5) It seceded from the Union in April or May of 1861.

Questions 15 and 16 are based on the following map.

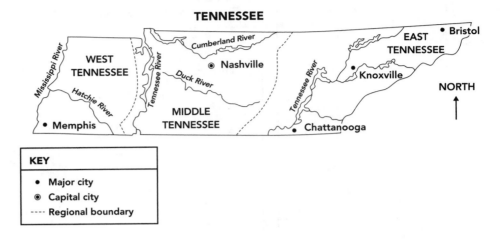

15. What major city is located in western Tennessee?

    (1) Memphis
    (2) Nashville
    (3) Bristol
    (4) Knoxville
    (5) Chattanooga

16. What major city is located on the Tennessee River directly east of the state capital?

    (1) Memphis
    (2) Nashville
    (3) Bristol
    (4) Knoxville
    (5) Chattanooga

Answers are on pages 491–492.

CHAPTER 3

Applying Information in Social Studies

Every day, you put the skills and information you have learned in your life to work for you in different situations. In this chapter, you will be applying information in a passage to new situations. You will also study practical applications of information found on maps, charts, and graphs.

Applying Information in Everyday Life

Often you read or hear information you can apply to your daily needs. You are always picking up information and using it. For example, what do you think you might do to protect your health if you read the following article?

> The total amount of energy in food is measured in calories. Most people need about 2,000 to 2,800 calories a day. Saturated fat, which is fat that is solid at room temperature, should make up less than 10% of total calories.
>
> A Ben's Burger Shack hamburger with cheese has 144 calories from saturated fat. A medium size fries adds an additional 45 calories from saturated fat. Compare this to a Rhoda's Roadside hamburger that totals 90 calories from saturated fat, with the fries adding 36 calories from saturated fat.
>
> What would you do?

You might decide to eat a hamburger and fries at Rhoda's Roadside rather than a hamburger with cheese and fries at Ben's Burger Shack because the Rhoda's Roadside meal has less saturated fat. Or you might decide to have fast-food burgers and fries less often or even not at all. You also might want to check out some other fast foods to see if they might have less saturated fat than a burger with fries.

Sometimes the news that you read or hear might influence how you respond to a situation. Information that you learn about economics or government can also have an impact on what you do. In the following exercise, you will practice applying information that you read to your life.

EXERCISE 1

Applying Information in Everyday Life

Directions: Read each passage. Then answer the questions that follow.

In October 2001, the United States was terrorized by a series of anthrax attacks. Powder containing anthrax spores was placed in envelopes and mailed to various people, the most prominent being United States Senate Majority Leader Tom Daschle. A number of people, including recipients of the letters, as well as several postal workers, came in contact with the spores. Several got anthrax, and some of them died.

Anthrax can kill in as little as three days, but can be successfully treated with antibiotics if treatment begins right away. Therefore, many experts now urge those who think they have been exposed to start treatment immediately, since waiting could be fatal.

Adapted from: *Discouraging Terrorism: Some Implications of 9/11*

1. You open a letter that contains a powder that gets on your hands. Based on the information in the passage, what would be the best thing for you to do first?

   (1) Take the letter to the police, so that they could use it in a criminal investigation.
   (2) Assume that the letter was a practical joke, unless you start feeling sick.
   (3) Send a sample of the powder to the Centers for Disease Control for analysis.
   (4) Go to a doctor immediately to get the right antibiotics and start taking them.
   (5) Alert the Post Office about the letter, so that postal workers could be protected.

Even though your vote is secret, information on whether or not you vote is not. Who votes in an election is public information. An elected official can look at who voted in previous elections. She might notice that some neighborhoods have heavy voter turnout, while other neighborhoods have very few voters. This information could influence how responsive she is to requests from various neighborhoods.

2. What might a voter be more likely to do after reading this article?

   (1) Try to vote for the person she thinks will win, since she might need help later.
   (2) Make sure she votes and encourages her neighbors to vote.
   (3) Only vote if she is either strongly for or against a particular candidate.
   (4) Encourage her neighbors to get involved in protests to fix local problems.
   (5) Give up on voting and pay more attention to her personal life.

Answers are on page 492.

Predicting an Outcome

All actions lead to outcomes, some of which you can reasonably predict. Just as you can apply your reading and reasoning skills to recognize a possible cause, you can use these skills to recognize a possible outcome.

> The manager of a supermarket advertised a sale on milk, eggs, and orange juice. Check each of the following that are likely outcomes of advertising the sale.
>
> _____ **A.** The store may sell more orange juice than usual.
>
> _____ **B.** The store may order extra milk from its supplier.
>
> _____ **C.** Business at the store may decline overall.

Did you check A and B? The store would probably sell more orange juice since the price is lower. The store probably would also order extra milk, since larger quantities might be sold at the sale price.

EXERCISE 2

Identifying Probable Outcomes

Directions: Put a check in the blank in front of each likely outcome.

1. A day-care center is starting a program where senior citizens volunteer to help care for the babies at the center.

_____ **A.** The babies may get less attention.

_____ **B.** The day-care center may have to charge more for caring for babies.

_____ **C.** The babies may be held more often.

_____ **D.** The senior citizens may feel that their help is needed.

_____ **E.** The day-care center may be able to care for more babies.

2. Sheila just got promoted from a part-time job as a receptionist to a full-time job as a customer service representative.

_____ **A.** Sheila may see her preschool children more than she did before.

_____ **B.** Sheila may learn more about working with people.

_____ **C.** Sheila may be happier about her future.

_____ **D.** Sheila may be able to buy her children new clothes.

_____ **E.** Sheila may have more time to clean her house.

Answers are on page 492.

Identifying Authors' Predictions

We cannot always be certain of the result of something. However, a writer will often try to predict the outcome of an action or a trend. In this section, you'll practice identifying predictions in a passage. In the following paragraph, look for the prediction the author is making. Answer the question that follows.

> In July of 1987 the legal drinking age rose to twenty-one. Lawmakers said that making drinking illegal for eighteen- to twenty-year-olds would help prevent accidents caused by drunken drivers. They argued that younger drinkers are more likely to take chances. They thought that if young people didn't drink, they would be involved in fewer accidents. If drinking was illegal for them, they believed that young people would not drink alcoholic beverages. However, making drinking illegal for this age group makes it more attractive and exciting to drink and actually increases drunk driving and accidents. Keeping eighteen- to twenty-year-olds out of bars only encourages them to drink elsewhere, including at house parties and right in their cars.

What does the writer predict will be the outcome of raising the drinking age to twenty-one?

(1) Accidents caused by drunk drivers will decrease.
(2) Fewer teenagers will drink any kind of alcohol.
(3) Bars will still allow eighteen- to twenty-year-olds to drink.
(4) Eighteen- to twenty-year-olds will stop drinking.
(5) More accidents will be caused by drunken drivers.

You were right if you chose (5). The author says that raising the drinking age will increase accidents caused by drunken driving.

EXERCISE 3

Identifying an Author's Prediction

Directions: Read each passage and answer the questions that follow.

> Thomas Jefferson thought that small farmers were the most valuable members of society. Jefferson would be disappointed by what's happening in agriculture today. Large farms are the most common type now, and small farms are becoming more rare. This trend is likely to continue. In the future, farms will get larger and larger, and small farms will continue to disappear.

1. The author expects that

    (1) there will be more large farms in the future
    (2) a popular movement will lead to more small farms
    (3) the number and size of farms will become stable
    (4) the government will step in to save the family farm
    (5) many large farms will fail to survive

Businesses are feeling pressure from many sides to help fill the needs of working parents. Many companies are allowing either mothers or fathers to go on leave when a new baby is born. Other companies are helping parents make child-care arrangements. A few companies are opening day-care centers in the workplace. These centers are still rare, but businesses are moving in the right direction.

2. The author predicts that

    (1) day-care centers will become more unusual in the workplace
    (2) fathers will be forbidden to take leaves when their babies are born
    (3) more mothers will stay home with their children in the future
    (4) businesses will become less concerned with the needs of working parents
    (5) there will be more day-care centers in the workplace over time

Answers are on page 492.

Predicting Based on a Passage

Many times an author gives enough information in a passage so that you can make your own predictions. Be careful to back up your predictions with evidence from the passage. Read the following passage carefully. Choose the answer to the question, basing your choice on the information that is given.

Legal segregation in the United States was abolished by 1968. However, changing the law does not always change the way people think or behave. In many cities neighborhoods are still made up of minorities. There are several key reasons that explain why these neighborhoods developed. First, realtors would not show homes to minorities if the homes were in white neighborhoods. Also, bankers would not loan money to minorities if they planned on moving into white neighborhoods. Government officials also added to segregation by creating school districts that separated minorities from whites. This was done by passing zoning laws designed to keep white children in white schools. Even today, schools often continue to be segregated. Finally, the building of suburbs increased segregation. Many white families left the cities for suburban communities. People continue to live in neighborhoods that are made up of their own race.

—Adapted from *Microsoft® Encarta® Africana Third Edition.*
© 1998–2000 Microsoft Corporation

A reasonable prediction based on information in the passage would be that

(1) the number of cities with black majorities has peaked
(2) segregation of neighborhoods in American cities will soon end
(3) segregation will continue to be a reality in many American cities
(4) practices that promote segregation will be exposed and abolished
(5) an increasing percentage of people will want to live in integrated areas

The correct answer is choice (3). The article makes clear that even though segregation is illegal, it is still a reality in much of the country. According to the information in the passage, it is reasonable to predict that segregation of neighborhoods will continue in many parts of the United States.

EXERCISE 4

Making a Prediction Based on a Passage

Directions: Read each passage and answer the questions that follow.

Haiti is, by almost any standard, in a desperate state. Brutal poverty and political terror have crippled Haiti since its independence in 1804. Many Haitians have fled to the United States to escape torture and threats of execution. Those who stay barely make a living. The average Haitian citizen earns $1,464 a year.

The biggest economic problems facing Haiti are a lack of jobs and inadequate services. According to the CIA World Fact Book 2002, there is widespread unemployment and underemployment. More than two-thirds of the labor force does not have formal jobs. This is largely because poor services make it nearly impossible to operate a business. Haitian roads are impassable. Electricity is unavailable outside the capital, and the telephone system is barely adequate. Any successful program to improve the Haitian economy must address many problems.

1. What problem would a farmer in Haiti most likely face?

(1) a lack of available farm help
(2) heavy competition from Haiti's many farmers
(3) poor quality seeds and grain
(4) transporting farm goods to market
(5) finding good farm land

2. From the information given in this passage, Haiti could be most helped by

(1) an improved electricity system
(2) an open immigration policy
(3) an increase in utility taxes
(4) bringing foreign help in to work
(5) banning the sale of foreign goods

Like many other Native American tribes, the Chukchansi of California use gambling to create jobs on their reservation. According to tribal leaders, over 60 percent of Chukchansi are currently unemployed. Leaders have asked a nonprofit organization called DreamCatchers to finance and operate a casino on their reservation. Tourists from nearby Yosemite National Park and Sierra National Forest are expected to be the primary customers. The venture will create over 600 well-paying jobs, and Native Americans will be considered first during the hiring process.

3. DreamCatchers will count on the Chukchansi people to

(1) gamble in the casino
(2) plan the casino's future
(3) work for the casino
(4) manage DreamCatcher employees
(5) invest money

Answers are on page 492.

Applying Information in a Passage

In social studies, you are often asked to apply information you read in a passage to answer a question or solve a problem. In the following example, read the passage and apply the information in the passage to make the choices.

One-hundred fifty years ago in the United States, farmers had to make the most of what they had. Typical American farm families grew their own food. They also had a variety of farm animals, perhaps including cows, horses, pigs, and sheep. Their everyday clothes might be made from materials grown on the farm, such as wool, leather, cotton, and other fibers. Their homes were made from materials they could gather—wood, stones, even earth.

However, a farm family could not provide for all its needs. Plows, tools, nails, and other metal items were made by a blacksmith. Bowls and plates were made by a potter or imported. Glass windows, storage barrels, and wagon wheels were other items that a farmer had to purchase.

Put a *P* in front of those items that a farm family could produce on its farm. Put a *B* in front of those items that a farm family had to buy.

_____ **1.** wooden spoons

_____ **2.** milk

_____ **3.** horseshoes

_____ **4.** tin lantern

You should have put a *P* in front of 1 and 2. You should have put a *B* in front of 3 and 4.

EXERCISE 5

Applying Information in a Passage

Directions: Read each passage and answer the questions that follow.

A variety of government agencies provide services to people who need help. The Department of Health and Human Services provides some benefits, including Temporary Assistance for Needy Families (TANF). Rehabilitation Services helps people with handicapping conditions get the programs and services they need. The Federal Council on Aging provides the elderly with a variety of resources.

Below are descriptions of some people and the type of assistance they need. In the blank, mark the agency each should go to for help—*H* for Department of Health and Human Services, *R* for Rehabilitation Services, and *A* for the Federal Council on Aging.

_____ **1.** A woman with two small children has been abandoned by her husband and has no job.

_____ **2.** A seventy-one-year-old woman is lonely and wants to get out and spend time with other people.

_____ **3.** A deaf man wants training in order to work with computers.

The development of the American West is limited by a shortage of water. Farmers, businesses and industry, residents, and recreational facilities all compete for water. In the future, communities will have to decide how to use their limited water supply. Will they use their water to grow more crops, to run more factories, to provide for a larger population and more homes, or to expand resorts and recreational facilities?

The city of Kerr has decided that its water will be put to best use for new homes and recreational development. The city is attractive to retired people as well as to tourists. The city council feels that construction of new homes, parks, and resorts will keep Kerr's economy strong.

Under this policy, which of the following requests for water access should the city approve? Write *YES* next to the projects the city should approve under the policy. Write *NO* next to the projects the city should not approve.

_____ **4.** St. Mary's Hospital wants to build a new, larger facility to better meet the needs of the growing elderly population.

_____ **5.** A chain of amusement parks wants to build a theme park outside Kerr and wants access to the city's water supply.

_____ **6.** A farmer wants to buy a large piece of nonirrigated land next his farm. He wants permission to extend his watering system to the nonirrigated land.

Answers are on page 492.

Applying Social Studies Concepts

On many tests, you will be given a series of concepts, facts, or ideas. You will then be asked questions in which you will apply the correct choice to a situation. Other questions might describe an example of one of the items on the list and ask you to identify which is the one being illustrated.

Thoroughly read these definitions of five types of land and then answer the questions that follow.

Tundra: an area of low-growing vegetation including shrubs, grasses, mosses, and herbs. It has a layer of permafrost, or permanently frozen subsoil, beneath the surface. It also has harsh winters, low average temperatures, little snow or rainfall, and a short summer season.

Desert: an area with little rainfall. Evaporation exceeds precipitation, so the soil has very little moisture. It has extremes of temperature.

Boreal Forest: an area dominated by coniferous trees. It is found in subarctic and alpine regions.

Grassland: an area with 10 to 30 inches of rain a year, a high rate of evaporation, and seasonal and annual droughts. The vegetation is a variety of grasses, sedges, and other forage plants, and the soil tends to be very fertile.

Rain Forest: an area of heavy rainfall and dense vegetation. The soil tends to be poor because nutrients are leached out by the heavy rains.

Wheat Belt and **Corn Belt:** regions of the United States that are among the most productive agricultural areas in the world. For the most part, fields of wheat and corn, along with human settlements such as towns and cities, have replaced the natural environment.

Of the five types of natural environments listed, which was most likely found in the area that is now the Wheat Belt and the Corn Belt?

(1) Tundra
(2) Desert
(3) Boreal Forest
(4) Grassland
(5) Rain Forest

Since wheat and corn are both grasses, they are most likely to thrive in the areas that were once grassland (4).

EXERCISE 6

Applying Social Studies Concepts

Directions: Listed below are five different methods of transporting people, goods, or information. For each of the questions that follow, identify the method of transportation that would work best.

Train: most efficient for moving large amounts of freight across land areas. Restricted to areas served by railroad tracks.

Airplane: best for moving freight and people quickly across long distances. Restricted to areas served by airports.

Ship: can move large amounts of freight across large bodies of water.

Truck: can move freight across land areas. Can go almost anywhere there are roads.

Electronic Transfer: can move information almost instantly around the world.

1. You have purchased a new refrigerator and have arranged to have it delivered to your home. It will most likely by delivered by

   (1) train
   (2) airplane
   (3) ship
   (4) truck
   (5) electronic transfer

2. Your relatives in the Dominican Republic have had their home damaged by a hurricane. You would like to help by sending them some money. The best way to deliver the money would be by

   (1) train
   (2) airplane
   (3) ship
   (4) truck
   (5) electronic transfer

3. A factory in Puerto Rico needs to have 50,000 shirts shipped to New York City. They need to arrive in New York within six weeks. The best way to deliver the shirts would be by

   (1) train
   (2) airplane
   (3) ship
   (4) truck
   (5) electronic transfer

Answers are on page 492.

Applying Map Information

You can apply the information contained on all kinds of maps to real situations and decisions. Maps that you might come across in your everyday life include road maps, subway maps, and weather maps.

One of the most common ways that you might use a map is to decide how to get from one place to another. For example, when you are trying to figure out a driving route, you look for the most direct route, the one that is closest to a straight line between the two places.

Imagine that you are a resident of Denver, Colorado. You want to drive to Los Angeles. Based on the interstate map below, describe the shortest route you could take.

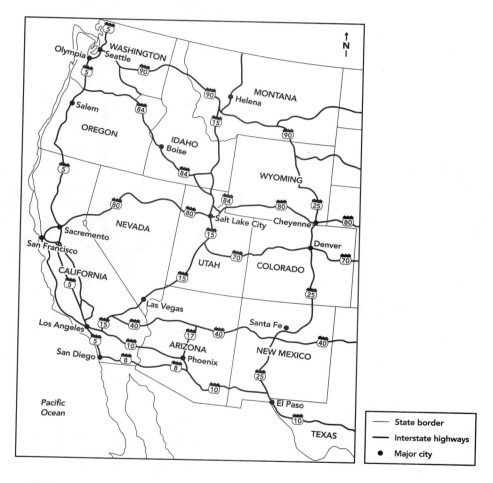

Find Denver and Los Angeles on the map. Then find the route that is closest to a straight line. You should take Route 70 west to Route 15, then south on Route 15 to Route 10, and west on Route 10 to Los Angeles.

EXERCISE 7

Applying Map Skills

Directions: Use information from the map on the previous page to answer questions 1 and 2.

1. You live in Olympia, Washington, and want to visit your brother in Cheyenne, Wyoming. What is the most direct route you could take?

_____

_____

2. You live in San Diego and want to travel to El Paso to see a rodeo. What is the shortest route you could take?

_____

_____

Questions 3 and 4 are based on the map below.

3. How do you get from the airport to North Station on the Boston subway?

_____

_____

4. A student at Harvard University wants to visit the Science Museum at Science Park. How would she get there by subway?

(1) Take the Red Line southeast.

(2) Take the Green Line north.

(3) Take the Red Line southeast to Park St. and change to the Green Line going north.

(4) Take the Blue Line southwest to Government Center and change to the Green Line going north.

(5) Take the Red Line southeast to Park St. and change to the Orange Line going north.

Answers are on pages 492–493.

Applying Data from Tables and Graphs

In social studies, you will often be asked to apply the information on tables and graphs when you need to solve a problem or understand a situation. In the following example, apply the information on the bar graph to figure out which side had the advantage in the American Civil War.

COMPARISON OF NORTH TO SOUTH
(1860)

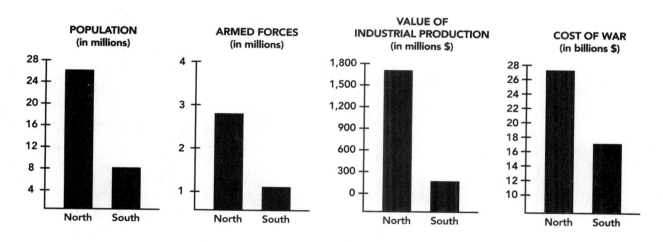

According to the information given on the bar graphs, which side had the advantage at the beginning of the Civil War?

In each of the four areas, the North had a large advantage.

Which of the four areas probably had the greatest impact on the war's outcome?

All four areas were important advantages for the North, but probably the most important was the North's enormous advantage in industrial production. The North was far more able to manufacture what its soldiers needed to win the war, including weapons, trains, ammunition, and ships.

EXERCISE 8

Applying Information from Tables and Graphs

Directions: Use the information from each table or graph to answer the questions that follow.

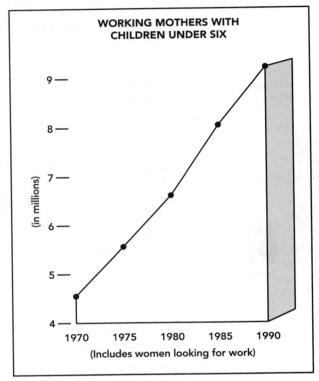

Source: U.S. Bureau of Labor Statistics

1. The number of working mothers with children under the age of six doubled between 1970 and 1990. A company that wanted to attract young women into its workforce might offer

   (1) security guards at night in areas where women work
   (2) Club Med vacations to the Caribbean
   (3) on-site day-care facilities for pre-school children
   (4) on-site athletic and swimming facilities
   (5) weekly social events in the evenings

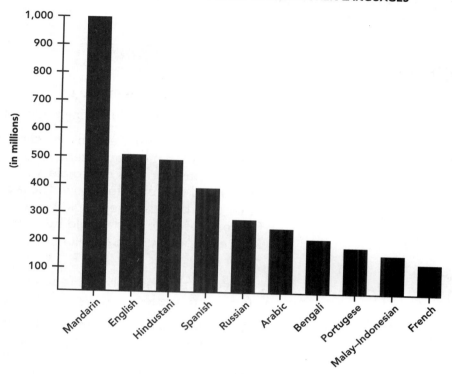

THE WORLD'S MOST WIDELY SPOKEN LANGUAGES

2. Many people around the world want to learn English. If you were producing dictionaries that translate from English to another language, what language should you target?

(1) Mandarin
(2) Arabic
(3) Hindustani
(4) Spanish
(5) French

Answers are on page 493.

Chapter Review

EXERCISE 9

Directions: Answer the questions following each passage or illustration.

Question 1 is based on the following paragraph.

In order to ensure a stable food supply for the United States, the U.S. government has an extensive farm support program. This program pays farmers not to plant some of their fields, since we don't need the food right now. These fields are not given up for other uses because they could be needed to produce food in the future. These idle fields could be planted to respond to a national food emergency, such as failure of an important crop because of major drought or disease.

1. Based on the passage, the federal government should **not** pay farmers to preserve unplanted tobacco fields because

    (1) tobacco farmers do not practice proper farm management
    (2) enough tobacco is being produced
    (3) cigarettes have been shown to cause cancer
    (4) tobacco would not be needed in a national food emergency
    (5) the tobacco lobby in Washington has been weakened by antismoking campaigns

Question 2 is based on the following passage.

Florida's Governor Jeb Bush is the brother of President George W. Bush and the son of former President George H. W. Bush. However, the family member who probably helped the governor the most in his reelection campaign was his wife, Columba Bush, who is Hispanic. His family connection, plus his fluency in Spanish and comfort with Hispanic culture, helped him connect with Hispanic voters in a way that few other Republican candidates have done. If Republicans want to be successful in future elections, they will need to follow Jeb Bush's example.

2. By following Jeb Bush's example, the author most likely means that candidates should

    (1) have relatives who are prominent politicians
    (2) marry a member of an important voting group
    (3) reach out to Hispanic and other minority voters
    (4) raise much more money than their opponents
    (5) have an important role for women in their campaigns

Questions 3 and 4 are based on the following passage and chart.

The cost of living index measures differences in the cost of six consumer goods—grocery items, housing, utilities, transportation, health care, and miscellaneous goods and services.

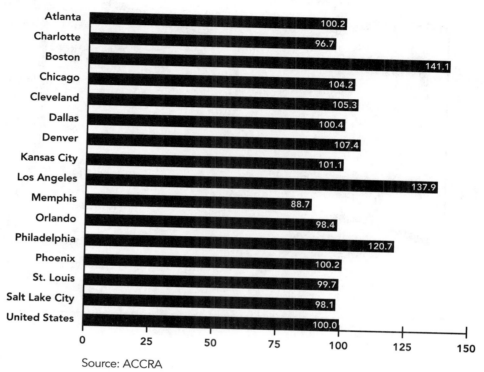

COST OF LIVING INDEX
4th QUARTER 2001

City	Index
Atlanta	100.2
Charlotte	96.7
Boston	141.1
Chicago	104.2
Cleveland	105.3
Dallas	100.4
Denver	107.4
Kansas City	101.1
Los Angeles	137.9
Memphis	88.7
Orlando	98.4
Philadelphia	120.7
Phoenix	100.2
St. Louis	99.7
Salt Lake City	98.1
United States	100.0

Source: ACCRA

3. According to the chart, the most expensive city to live in of the cities listed is

(1) Atlanta
(2) Boston
(3) Kansas City
(4) Memphis
(5) Salt Lake City

4. A small market research company has decided to relocate. The company is looking for a location in which it would be most affordable for their employees to live. According to the information in the chart, they should move to

(1) Charlotte
(2) Boston
(3) Kansas City
(4) Memphis
(5) Phoenix

Questions 5 and 6 are based on the following map.

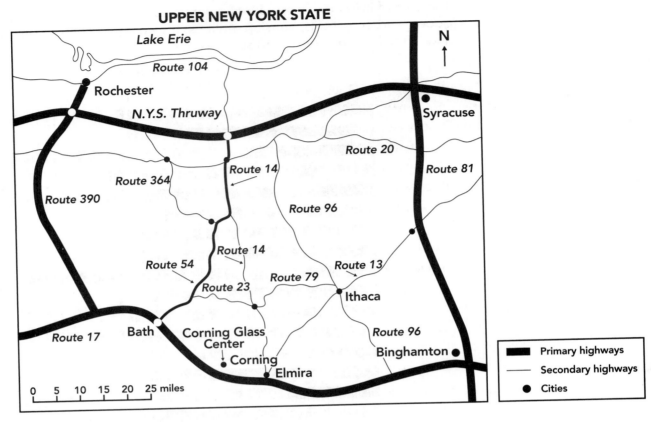

UPPER NEW YORK STATE

5. You live in Rochester and want to visit the Corning Glass Center in Corning, NY. What is the most direct route you could take?

(1) Route 390 south to NYS Thruway, east to Route 14, south to Route 17 west
(2) Route 390 south to NYS Thruway, east to Route 14, south to Route 54, south to Route 17 east
(3) Route 104 east to Route 14, south to Route 17 west
(4) Route 390 south to NYS Thruway, east to Route 81, south to Route 17 west
(5) Route 390 south to Route 17 east

6. The shortest route from the city of Syracuse to the town of Bath is

(1) NYS Thruway west to Route 14, south to Route 17 west
(2) NYS Thruway west to Route 14, south to Route 54 south
(3) NYS Thruway west to Route 390, south to Route 17 east
(4) Route 81 south to Route 17 west
(5) Route 81 south to Route 13, south to Route 17 west

Questions 7–9 are based on the first five amendments to the United States Constitution.

Amendment 1 Congress shall make no law respecting an establishment of religion, or prohibiting the free exercise thereof; or abridging the freedom of speech, or of the press, or the right of the people peaceably to assemble, and to petition the Government for a redress of grievances.

Amendment 2 A well regulated Militia, being necessary to the security of a free State, the right of the people to keep and bear Arms, shall not be infringed.

Amendment 3 No Soldier shall, in time of peace be quartered in any house, without the consent of the Owner, nor in time of war, but in a manner to be prescribed by law.

Amendment 4 The right of the people to be secure in their persons, houses, papers, and effects, against unreasonable searches and seizures, shall not be violated, and no Warrants shall issue, but upon probable cause, supported by Oath or affirmation, and particularly describing the place to be searched, and the persons or things to be seized.

Amendment 5 No person shall be held to answer for a capital, or otherwise infamous crime, unless on a presentment or indictment of a Grand Jury, except in cases arising in the land or naval forces, or in the Militia, when in actual service in time of War or public danger; nor shall any person be subject for the same offence to be twice put in jeopardy of life or limb; nor shall be compelled in any criminal case to be a witness against himself, nor be deprived of life, liberty, or property, without due process of law; nor shall private property be taken for public use, without just compensation.

7. Which of the first five amendments is **least** relevant today?

   (1) Amendment 1
   (2) Amendment 2
   (3) Amendment 3
   (4) Amendment 4
   (5) Amendment 5

8. In response to the terrorist attacks of September 11, 2001, the United States detained terrorist suspects at its Naval Base at Guantanamo Bay, Cuba, without bringing specific charges against the detainees. Which of the listed amendments is most relevant to this situation?

   (1) Amendment 1
   (2) Amendment 2
   (3) Amendment 3
   (4) Amendment 4
   (5) Amendment 5

9. Some Native American cultures in the Southwest use peyote in religious rituals. Peyote, as well as other substances, are illegal under U.S. law. What amendment is most relevant to this situation?

   (1) Amendment 1
   (2) Amendment 2
   (3) Amendment 3
   (4) Amendment 4
   (5) Amendment 5

Question 10 is based on the following passage.

Rickerton Park residents are disgusted with mudslinging in Timothy Ayers's city council campaign. Everyone expected a civilized reelection of Democrat Vanessa Alexander; however, Ayers appears determined to humiliate his opponent. He has questioned her sanity, attacked her family, and personally defaced Alexander's campaign posters. These dirty tactics have failed miserably, winning only a 10-point drop for Ayers in the pre-election public opinion polls.

10. Based on the information in the passage, it is reasonable to expect that

   (1) Timothy Ayers will win the election for city council
   (2) Timothy Ayers will be arrested for breaking the law
   (3) Vanessa Alexander will win the election for city council
   (4) Vanessa Alexander will withdraw from the race
   (5) Vanessa Alexander will do more mudslinging in her next campaign

Answers are on page 493.

CHAPTER 4

Analyzing Social Studies Materials

In this chapter, you will learn three skills that will help you recognize patterns in social studies materials. These skills are **sequence**, or getting things in the right order; **cause and effect**, or understanding what happened and why; and **comparison and contrast**, or looking at how things and events are the same and how they are different. Later in the chapter, you will practice the following analysis skills: **distinguishing fact from opinion**—or being able to figure out whether or not something can be proved—and **developing a hypothesis**—or coming up with a proposed explanation of why certain things happen. These skills will help you to analyze written material, time lines, graphs, maps, tables, cartoons, and illustrations.

Recognizing Sequence

Using a Time Line

SEQUENCE TIP

Words, as well as dates, can help you identify sequence. When putting events in time order, look for words like *soon, before, after, later, then,* and *while.*

Sequence is the organization of events in time order. Most passages present information in time order. In order to make time sequence clear, you can place events on a time line. In this book, you will be using time lines that look like this:

earlier

later

The following passage shows how to use this kind of time line.

> The nineteenth century was America's Age of Invention. People like Samuel Morse, Alexander Graham Bell, and Thomas Edison developed devices that changed people's daily lives. "What hath God wrought?" were the immortal words tapped out by Samuel Morse on his telegraph key in 1837.
>
> "Mr. Watson, come here; I want you," was the first sentence ever spoken on a telephone by its inventor, Alexander Graham Bell, in 1876.
>
> "Mary had a little lamb," were the words recorded by Thomas Edison on his gramophone in 1887.

The three events described in the passage give information about three inventions: the telegraph in 1837, the telephone in 1876, and the gramophone (record player) in 1887. You can use the years to list the three events in order.

1837—telegraph (Morse)
1876—telephone (Bell)
1887—gramophone (Edison)

You could then describe the events on a time line:

earlier
├── Samuel Morse introduced the telegraph in 1837.
├── Alexander Graham Bell introduced the telephone in 1876.
├── Thomas Edison introduced the gramophone in 1887.
later

Now read another passage.

On October 8, 1871, a kerosene lamp fell over and started the Great Chicago Fire. In a few hours, the fire spread through the West Side and then jumped the South Branch of the Chicago River. The city was in flames.

Twenty-four hours after it started, the fire was finally put out. Food, clothing, and money began pouring in from all over the world to help the destroyed city.

Make a list of the events in the passage. Then fill in the events on the following time line.

earlier

later

Your completed time line should look like this:

earlier
├── A kerosene lamp fell over.
├── Fire spread through the West Side.
├── The fire jumped the Chicago River.
├── The fire was put out.
├── Food, clothing and money began pouring in.
later

EXERCISE 1

Putting Events in Sequence

Directions: Read the following passage. Number the events listed at the end
of the passage in the correct time order and then write them on
the time line below.

On January 24, 1848, while building a sawmill for John Sutter,
James Marshall found some small stones that he thought might
contain gold. About a week later, he went to see Sutter at the local
fort to show him the stones. Sutter and Marshall tested the stones
and found that they were pure gold. Despite their desire to keep
their discovery quiet, word spread fast. Soon groups of men were
appearing at the mill, looking for gold. Trying to get rid of them,
Marshall then sent them off in all directions. To his surprise, many of
them found gold. The California Gold Rush had begun.

_____ Marshall sends gold seekers off to look for gold.

_____ Marshall and Sutter test the stones to see if they are gold.

_____ Groups of men discover gold in the places where Marshall
sent them.

_____ Marshall discovers gold at Sutter's Mill.

earlier

later

Answers are on page 493.

Sequence Not in Time Order

Passages often present events in an order different from the order in which
they occurred. In those cases, you must use clues in the passage to figure out
the correct time order. Often you can use dates to help you put events in
order, as in the following passage.

Representing the American colonists, Thomas Jefferson drafted
the Declaration of Independence, which was approved in
Philadelphia on July 4, 1776. The colonists wanted independence
from Great Britain because of many conflicts with England.

For example, the British parliament issued the Proclamation of
1763. The proclamation stated that no colonists would be allowed
to settle west of the Allegheny Mountains. This angered many
colonists who had hoped to move west.

Then the Sugar Act of 1764 and the Stamp Act of 1765 forced the colonists to pay taxes to England. Colonists throughout the thirteen colonies opposed these actions. Ten years later, in 1775, the opposition had grown so strong that fighting broke out between the British and the colonists of Massachusetts. It was only a matter of time before the colonies would become an independent nation.

Number the following events in correct time order, using clues from the passage.

_____ The Declaration of Independence is approved.

_____ British ban the colonists from moving west of the Allegheny Mountains.

_____ Fighting breaks out between the British and the colonists of Massachusetts.

_____ The British force the colonists to pay taxes.

The correct order is 4, 1, 3, 2. Now place the events in order on the time line below.

earlier

later

In this passage, the writer presents events out of time order so as to emphasize the main point. The main idea, that the Declaration of Independence was the result of a long series of conflicts, is made in the second sentence. The description of events in the second paragraph supports that main idea. Even though the approval of the Declaration of Independence happened after the other events, the author mentions it first in order to make his main idea clear. Your completed timeline should look like this:

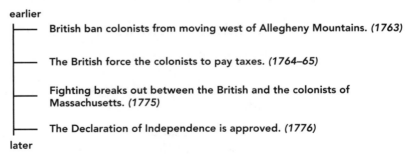

earlier

British ban colonists from moving west of Allegheny Mountains. *(1763)*

The British force the colonists to pay taxes. *(1764–65)*

Fighting breaks out between the British and the colonists of Massachusetts. *(1775)*

The Declaration of Independence is approved. *(1776)*

later

EXERCISE 2

Using Dates to Identify Sequence

Directions: After this passage is a list of the events described in the passage. Number the events in the order in which they occurred, and place them in order on the time line.

Following the European discovery of America by Christopher Columbus in 1492, other nations sent explorers and settlers to North America. The Spanish were ruthless and bloodthirsty. One Spanish explorer, Hernando De Soto, marched through the southeastern United States from 1539 to 1542. He used torture to force the Native Americans to lead him to gold. Since there was almost no gold to be found, he killed several thousand Native Americans at the settlement of Mabila on the Alabama River.

The French also sent explorers to North America, but they treated the Native Americans well and traded with them. When Jacques Cartier discovered the mouth of the St. Lawrence River in 1534, he opened up Canada to French exploration. From 1603 to 1615, Samuel de Champlain explored parts of southern Canada and northern New York. He also established the fur trade with the Native Americans. Over fifty years later, Marquette and Joliet traveled down the Mississippi River as far as Arkansas, establishing French claims to the entire Mississippi valley.

_____ Columbus discovers America.

_____ De Soto murders thousands of Native Americans at Mabila.

_____ Cartier discovers the mouth of the St. Lawrence River.

_____ Marquette and Joliet travel down the Mississippi River.

_____ Champlain establishes the fur trade with the Native Americans.

earlier

later

Answers are on page 493.

Sequence in Graphs

A line graph is well suited to showing a trend over time. By showing how something changes over time, a graph illustrates a sequence very clearly. The following line graph traces the approximate path of world income per capita—how much each person earns in one year—from the beginnings of agriculture and the appearance of the first towns through the year 2000. Study the graph. Then answer the question following the graph by circling the correct choice.

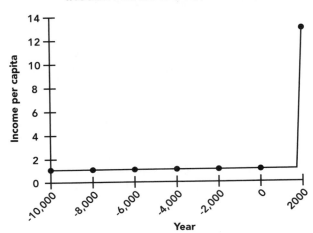

INCOME PER CAPITA, 10,000 B.C. – 2,000 A.D.

Source: *The Secret History of the Industrial Revolution*, Gregory Clark

The trend on the graph can be best described as

(1) a steady increase in income per capita from 10,000 B.C. to 2000
(2) an increase in the income gap between rich and poor since 10,000 B.C.
(3) after years of stability, a rapid increase in per capita income during the past century
(4) major changes throughout history, with the past century seeing the greatest change
(5) workers being underpaid and exploited throughout history to 2000

You were correct if you circled choice (3). The line is horizontal from 10,000 B.C. to about 100 years ago, meaning that per capita income was somewhat steady over all these centuries. Then it turns sharply up. There is no information in the graph about choice (2) the gap between rich and poor or about choice (5) workers being underpaid or exploited. Choices (1) and (4) do not correctly describe the sequence of events recorded by the graph.

EXERCISE 3

Sequence in Graphs

Directions: Study the following graph. Then answer the questions that follow.

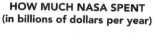

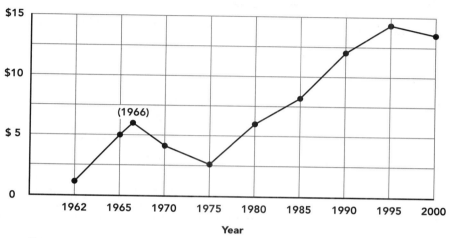

Source: U.S. Census Bureau American Fact Finder

1. Between 1965 and 1970, NASA spending

   (1) rose and then fell
   (2) dropped steadily
   (3) rose slightly
   (4) remained constant
   (5) dropped and then rose

2. Which of the following best describes the pattern of NASA spending between 1962 and 1990?

   (1) It rose steadily throughout the time from 1962 to 1990.
   (2) After rising at first, it then fell for the rest of the period.
   (3) After reaching a low in 1975, it rose steadily until 1990.
   (4) It rose until 1966, then it fell until 1975, then rose again.
   (5) It rose, then it fell, then it rose again, and finally fell slightly.

Answers are on page 493.

Sequence on Expedition Maps

Maps can depict a chain of events or changes over time. For example, the route of an explorer or an army can be traced on a map. Study the following example to learn how examining the route of the explorers Lewis and Clark can help us understand their journey.

LEWIS AND CLARK EXPEDITION

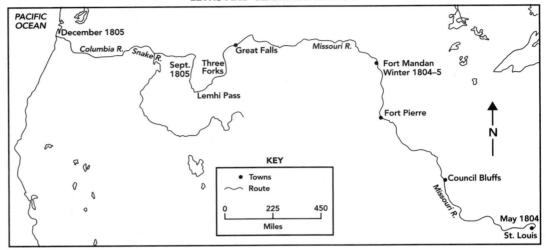

When did Lewis and Clark leave St. Louis?

Trace along the line that represents the route of Lewis and Clark until you find St. Louis at the eastern end of their route. The date of *May 1804* is written next to the city. That is the date that Lewis and Clark left St. Louis.

Where did Lewis and Clark spend the winter of 1804–5?

Trace the route of the expedition until you find *Winter 1804–5* written below Fort Mandan. Therefore, they spent the winter at Fort Mandan.

When did Lewis and Clark reach the Pacific Ocean?

Trace the route of the expedition until it reaches the Pacific Ocean. Find the date *December 1805*, which is when the expedition reached the Pacific Ocean.

EXERCISE 4

Sequence on Expedition Maps

Directions: This map shows the route of an explorer through what is now the southeastern United States. Answer the questions that follow.

DE SOTO'S MARCH 1539–1543

1. Where did friendly Native Americans supply food to De Soto?

   (1) Tampa Bay
   (2) Quizquiz
   (3) Guaxulle
   (4) Mabila
   (5) Ocale

2. When did De Soto die?

   (1) September 1539
   (2) October 1540
   (3) June 1541
   (4) May 1542
   (5) September 1543

3. What important event happened at Quizquiz?

   (1) Several thousand Native Americans were killed.
   (2) De Soto died.
   (3) Friendly Native Americans supplied food.
   (4) A bison was caught.
   (5) The Mississippi River was discovered.

Answers are on page 494.

Sequence on Maps of Historical Change

Maps can illustrate a trend over time of either growth or decline of an area. The changing boundaries of nations, areas of settlement, or areas of production of a product can all be shown on maps. The map below shows the pattern of settlement of the thirteen original U.S. colonies over time.

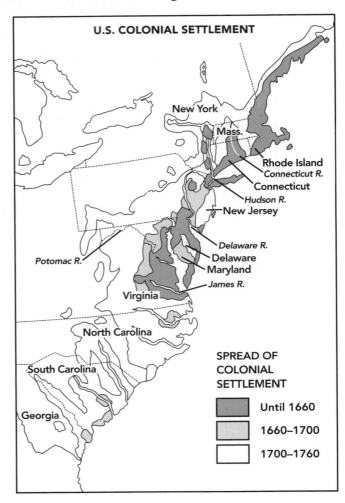

U.S. COLONIAL SETTLEMENT

SPREAD OF COLONIAL SETTLEMENT

- Until 1660
- 1660–1700
- 1700–1760

Until 1660, most settlement was along the coast of the Atlantic Ocean. True or False?

You were right if you thought the statement was true. Find the areas that match the key for the areas settled before 1660. These areas are mainly along the coast, as well as along the James, Hudson, and Connecticut Rivers.

In general, most of the early colonists settled south of Virginia, with settlement spreading north in later years. True or False?

You were right if you thought the statement was false. Just the opposite is true. The early settlement was in the northern part of the continent from Maine to Virginia. Settlement then spread south through the Carolinas and Georgia.

EXERCISE 5

Reading Maps of Historical Change

Directions: This map shows how the United States expanded into its current 48 connected states. After studying the map, mark each statement *T* if it is true or *F* if it is false.

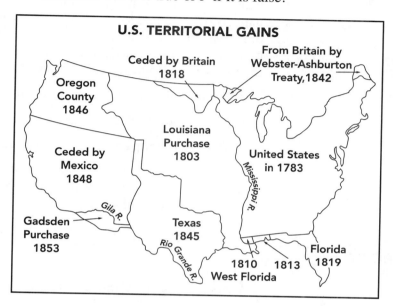

_____ **1.** The Southwest was ceded by Mexico after the Oregon Country was already under United States control.

_____ **2.** The Louisiana Purchase was the first major territorial gain for the United States after 1783.

_____ **3.** After the Mexican cession in 1848, the United States had all the land that would become the connected 48 states.

Answers are on page 494.

Recognizing Cause and Effect

Identifying Cause and Effect

In order to function in your daily life, you have to understand **cause and effect**. For example, if your family didn't pay the rent or mortgage every month, you would be evicted from your home. The cause would be not paying the rent or mortgage. The effect would be eviction.

CAUSE: ⎯⎯⎯⎯⎯⎯⎯⎯⟶ **EFFECT:**
not paying rent   eviction or
or mortgage   forclosure

CAUSE-AND-EFFECT TIP

In your reading, watch for cause-and-effect clue words and phrases like *because* and *as a result of*. *Before* and *after* can also function as cause-and-effect clue words.

Sometimes cause and effect can be very clear. A sixteen-year-old student cuts school sixty-eight days. The effect is that she does not get passing grades. Much of political debate is about causes and effects. One politician says, "If we raise taxes, the economy will improve." At the same time, another says, "If we lower taxes, the economy will improve."

In order to understand cause and effect, you should ask yourself, "What happened?" and "Why did it happen?" When you answer the question "What happened?" you understand the effect. When you answer the question "Why did it happen?" you understand the cause. Your reading will often contain clues that can help you decide what is the cause and what is the effect. Read the following sentence. Decide what happened and why it happened.

Because of poor management, the company went bankrupt.

What happened? _____

Why did it happen? _____

You should have written, "the company went bankrupt" as the answer to the first question and "because of poor management" as the answer to the second. *Because* is a clue word for the cause, or the answer to "Why did it happen?"

EXERCISE 6

Identifying Cause and Effect

Directions: For each sentence, decide what happened—the effect—and why it happened—the cause.

1. Because the wholesale price of coffee had dropped 25%, Colombia found itself in financial trouble.

   What happened? _____

   Why did it happen? _____

2. The American West developed rapidly after the Civil War because of the railroads.

   What happened? _____

   Why did it happen? _____

3. Oil prices increased dramatically as a result of the formation of the OPEC oil cartel in 1973.

   What happened? _____

   Why did it happen? _____

4. NASA conducted an investigation after the space shuttle Columbia broke apart on re-entry.

   What happened? _____

   Why did it happen? _____

Answers are on page 494.

Identifying Cause and Effect in a Passage

You cannot depend on a cause and effect always being in the same sentence or being clearly pointed out. In the paragraph below, underline the cause and circle the effect.

About 6000 B.C., agriculture and animal breeding helped to improve the diets of people living in Mesopotamia. Mesopotamians began to eat different types of meat, such as beef, mutton, and pork. They also started to grow lentils, peas, wheat, and barley. This variety of meats, grains, and legumes resulted in improved health and increased life expectancies.

The key word *resulted* can help you find what happened (the effect): improved health and increased life expectancies. The second and third sentences explain why it happened (the cause): Mesopotamians began to eat beef, mutton, and pork, and grow lentils, peas, wheat, and barley.

EXERCISE 7

Cause and Effect in a Passage

Directions: Following each passage are questions about cause and effect.

North America is named for one of the greatest frauds of all time, Amerigo Vespucci. Vespucci published an account of a voyage he had led in 1497. This voyage never took place. After reading Vespucci's false account, the king of Portugal asked him to accompany the Portuguese explorer Coelho and write about the voyage. Vespucci went on two voyages commanded by Coelho. In his writings, he took full credit for both voyages and never mentioned Coelho.

Vespucci's writings were read by many people because he included stories of native customs. In 1507, a young professor of geography in France placed the name America, a variation of Amerigo, on a map of what we now call South America. By the time people agreed that Columbus had really discovered the New World, it was too late. The name America had been given to the New World.

1. What was the effect of Vespucci's false account of his voyage to the New World in 1497?

   (1) Vespucci became the first explorer to discover America.
   (2) The King of Portugal forced Vespucci to leave Portugal.
   (3) The King of Portugal asked Vespucci to accompany Coelho.
   (4) Coelho gave Vespucci credit for Coelho's expeditions.
   (5) Coelho came to value Vespucci's great knowledge of America.

2. Why were Vespucci's accounts read by so many people?

   (1) He wrote about native customs.
   (2) Vespucci made Coelho famous.
   (3) The whole world focused on the daring Portuguese explorers.
   (4) A French professor had his students study Vespucci's work.
   (5) Vespucci discovered America.

Poverty has been reduced in India since independence, although in 1994, 35.04 percent of the population still lived below the poverty line. Industrialization [the building of factories] has created jobs in the cities, and rural workers have been able to diversify their sources of income. Urban workers at entry level [jobs], however, are usually forced to live in appalling [terrible] conditions in slums.

Modern water supply and sanitation arrangements are rare in the poor areas of most towns and cities and are lacking entirely in most villages. As a result, many Indians suffer and even die from diarrhea, malaria, typhoid, and cholera. India has succeeded in eradicating smallpox and has brought down the overall death rate, in significant part by investing in a health care system that includes hospitals, clinics, and drug manufacture and distribution.

—Excerpted from: "India," *Microsoft® Encarta® Encyclopedia 2000*

3. A major cause of disease in India is

   (1) the building of polluting factories in cities
   (2) the building of new hospitals and clinics
   (3) the preference of Indian families for male children
   (4) the decrease in the size of the average family
   (5) the lack of clean water and waste disposal

4. One negative effect of industrialization in India is

   (1) a reduction in the poverty rate to 35.04 percent
   (2) the growth of terrible slums in many cities
   (3) lack of a modern water supply in most villages
   (4) a better health care system
   (5) the creation of many new job in the cities

Answers are on page 494.

Applying Cause and Effect

Government has a strong effect on our lives as Americans. American blacks are one group whose lives have been affected, for good and bad, by the actions of the government. In the next exercise, you will be asked to match four actions of government with the effect each action might have had on an individual person.

EXERCISE 8

Applying Cause and Effect

Directions: Three documents are listed below that greatly influenced the conditions for black Americans. Following the documents are quotes that describe the effect of each of these documents. Write the letter of each government action on the line before the quote it made possible.

A. Supreme Court separate-but-equal decision—1896
Segregation of public facilities, such as schools, was declared legal by the Supreme Court.

B. Voting Rights Act—1965
Laws preventing black people from voting were banned by Congress.

C. Civil Rights Act—1964
Discrimination in public places was banned by Congress.

_____ **1.** "As our first black mayor, I pledge to serve all the people."

_____ **2.** "I remember when I had to sit in the back of the bus. Now I can sit where I please."

_____ **3.** "I have to go to a separate school from white people. Some people say it is just as good, but I don't believe them."

Answers are on page 494.

Recognizing Comparison and Contrast

Looking at Similarities

Despite the great differences among human societies, anthropologists have found an institution they all share. All societies, regardless of their geographic location, religious beliefs, customs, tradition, or values, have some form of marriage.

The above paragraph compares the societies of the world. Marriage is the similarity shared by all. A **comparison** can show how two or more things are alike. Read the following paragraph. As you read, look for ways in which Buddhism and Christianity are similar.

Despite great differences in philosophy and practice, Buddhism and Christianity have much in common. Each religion was created by a founder who left no surviving written teachings. Both Siddhartha Gautama Buddha and Jesus Christ had loyal disciples who accompanied them and spread their teachings. In both cases, all surviving accounts of their life were written years after their deaths by idealizing followers. Also in both cases, those accounts have inspired millions of followers. Today, there are approximately 2 billion Christians and 360 million Buddhists.

How are Buddhism and Christianity similar?

A number of similarities are given in the passage. Both religions have a single founder who had loyal disciples. Both Jesus and Buddha left no written teachings, and all surviving accounts were written years after their deaths by idealizing followers. Both religions have millions of followers. However, one difference is that today Christianity has far more followers than Buddhism.

EXERCISE 9

Identifying Similarities

Directions: In your own words, answer the questions following each passage.

The West African nations of Sierra Leone and Liberia were shaped and influenced by similar forces. In the 17th and 18th centuries, both areas were active in the slave trade. In the early 19th century, both became sites for resettling former slaves. Sierra Leone became a British colony and a destination for freed British slaves, while Liberia became the first independent republic in sub-Saharan Africa. Liberia was protected by the U.S. government and settled by freed American slaves. Tensions continued for many years between the descendants of the freed slaves and the indigenous people. In recent years, both countries have been ravaged by brutal civil wars.

1. What are some of the historical similarities between Sierra Leone and Liberia?

_____

_____

_____

2. What was the dominant force that shaped both Sierra Leone and Liberia?

_____

_____

The United Kingdom and Japan have much in common. Both are large island nations separated from the mainland by narrow bodies of water. At one time, both controlled vast amounts of land and millions of people. While the Industrial Revolution began in the United Kingdom and only reached Japan years later, each nation developed powerful economies and international influence that was far greater than their actual area.

3. How is the geography of the United Kingdom and Japan similar?

_____

_____

4. How is the history of the United Kingdom and Japan similar?

_____

_____

Answers are on page 494.

Looking at Differences

When you **contrast** two things, you concentrate on how they are different. Examining differences as well as similarities helps you get a better picture of what you are studying. Read the following passage. Then use the information in the passage to fill in the chart.

During the past 200 years, technology has changed our lives. For example, while our ancestors depended on horses to travel long distances, today we travel from coast to coast in a few hours by airplane. When we want to get around town, we may drive a car or take a train or bus.

Another dramatic change we have experienced has been in communication. It once took weeks for the news to travel by boat from England to the United States. Today, through television and the Internet, we have instant access to world events. In addition, world leaders can talk on the telephone even though they may be separated by an ocean.

CONTRAST: 200 YEARS AGO AND TODAY		
	200 Years Ago	Today
travel		
overseas communication		

Your chart might look something like the one below. Did you show how different things are today than they were 200 years ago?

CONTRAST: 200 YEARS AGO AND TODAY		
	200 Years Ago	**Today**
travel	depended on horses, so long-distance travel was very slow	can get around town or even coast to coast very fast
overseas communication	messages had to travel by boat across the ocean	now can talk on phone or e-mail; hear radio and TV news the same day something happens

Comparison and Contrast in Illustrations

Maps, charts, and graphs can be used to illustrate comparison and contrast. For example, the map below compares and contrasts black voting rights in Southern states during the early years of the civil rights movement. Answer the question based on the map.

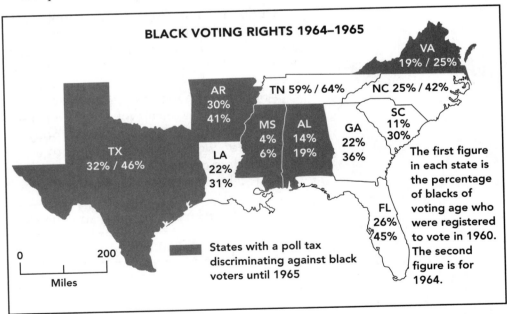

BLACK VOTING RIGHTS 1964–1965

VA 19% / 25%

AR 30% 41%

TN 59% / 64%   NC 25% / 42%

SC 11% 30%

MS 4% 6%   AL 14% 19%   GA 22% 36%

TX 32% / 46%

LA 22% 31%

FL 26% 45%

The first figure in each state is the percentage of blacks of voting age who were registered to vote in 1960. The second figure is for 1964.

0 — 200 Miles

States with a poll tax discriminating against black voters until 1965

Which states used a poll tax to discriminate against blacks until 1965?

You were right if you listed Texas, Arkansas, Mississippi, Alabama, and Virginia. These states are all shaded on the map, showing that they used a poll tax.

EXERCISE 10

Comparison and Contrast in Illustrations

Directions: Mark each statement *T* if it is true or *F* if it is false.

Questions 1 and 2 are based on the "Black Voting Rights" map on the previous page.

_____ **1.** Of all the states shown, Mississippi showed the smallest increase in black voter registration—only 2% between 1964 and 1965.

_____ **2.** In 1965, Texas had the highest percentage of any southern state of eligible blacks registered, with 46%.

Questions 3–5 are based on the following line graph.

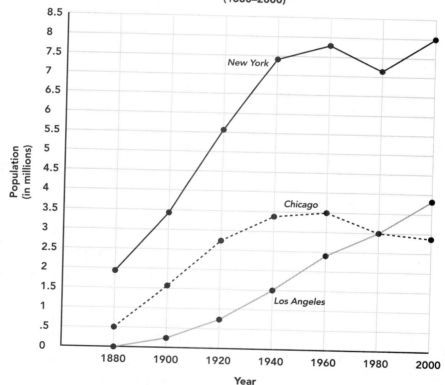

**THE THREE LARGEST CITIES IN 2000 AND THEIR
POPULATIONS IN EARLIER YEARS
(1880–2000)**

Source: U.S. Bureau of the Census

_____ **3.** New York and Chicago have always had about the same population.

_____ **4.** In 1980, Chicago and Los Angeles had about the same population.

_____ **5.** When the population of Chicago was decreasing, the population of Los Angeles was also decreasing.

Answers are on page 495.

Distinguishing Between Fact and Opinion

A **fact** is a statement that can be proven. An **opinion** is a belief that cannot be proven. If you believe that something is true, it still has to be proven to be a fact. When you read social studies material, notice whether a statement you read is fact or opinion. Can a statement be proven? Or is it something the author believes but cannot prove?

Of the following two statements, one is a fact and one is an opinion. Write *F* in the blank before the fact and *O* in the blank before the opinion.

_____ The U.S. Constitution is the greatest political document ever written.

_____ In 1995, there were twenty-six amendments to the U.S. Constitution.

You were right if you thought the first statement was an opinion. The word *greatest* gives the opinion of the writer. The second statement is a fact that can be checked by looking at a copy of the U.S. Constitution.

EXERCISE 11

Fact Or Opinion?

Directions: In the blank preceding each sentence, write *F* if the sentence is a fact and *O* if it is an opinion.

_____ 1. The United States is a democracy in which people elect their government officials.

_____ 2. Democracy is the best form of government.

_____ 3. Local governments mismanage their responsibilities of police and fire protection.

_____ 4. Local governments have responsibility for the public schools.

_____ 5. The vice president has the most unimportant job in the entire federal government.

_____ 6. If the president dies in office, the vice president becomes the new president.

Answers are on page 495.

FACT VS. OPINION TIP

Phrases like *I think, I believe,* and *we should* tell you that the writer is expressing an opinion.

Facts and Opinions in a Passage

Writers often tell you facts and express their opinions in the same piece of writing. They use the facts as evidence to back up their opinions. In the following example, read how the author uses facts to support his opinion. Read the paragraph and underline the sentences that contain facts. Circle the sentences that contain opinions.

The United States is a member of the North Atlantic Treaty Organization (NATO). The members of NATO coordinate their military activity in Europe through the NATO military command. Because we have to work through the NATO chain of command, NATO restricts our ability to act on our own. We should withdraw from NATO because our military needs to be able to work freely in Europe.

The first two sentences are facts. The writer can prove that the United States is a member of NATO and that NATO has a military command that coordinates the activity of member nations. The second two sentences are opinions. It is his opinion that membership in NATO restricts our ability to act on our own.

EXERCISE 12

Facts and Opinions in a Passage

Directions: For each sentence in the following passages, write *F* if the sentence is a fact and *O* if the sentence is an opinion.

Passage 1

(1) The best political system ever developed is the two-party system of the United States. (2) Since the Civil War, no third party has been able to threaten the political power of either the Democratic Party or the Republican Party. (3) Every president of the last one hundred years has been a member of one of these two parties. (4) No third party has been able to gain control of either house of Congress. (5) The country has been spared the chaos that results when there are more than two parties. (6) Additionally, the people have not had to endure the tyranny of one-party rule.

1. _____   3. _____   5. _____

2. _____   4. _____   6. _____

Passage 2

(7) The book *The Hard Times of Mortimer Mitchell* should not be on the shelves of our high school library. (8) First, the characters take drugs. (9) Second, there are three scenes in the book in which sexual activity between unmarried people is described in detail. (10) Third, the main character murders another character and then goes unpunished. (11) This is not the kind of book that the children in our community should read. (12) A parents' committee should be formed to help the school librarian choose good reading material for our teens.

7. _____   9. _____   11. _____

8. _____   10. _____   12. _____

Answers are on page 495.

Developing Hypotheses

Distinguishing Fact from Hypothesis

Sometimes an author gives the cause of an event or a trend as a statement of fact, as in the following example:

> Women in the United States were guaranteed the right to vote by the ratification of the 19th Amendment to the Constitution in 1920.

Effect: Women were guaranteed the right to vote.

Cause (fact): the ratification of the 19th Amendment in 1920

Sometimes, however, a writer is not sure of the cause of an event. He or she may make an educated guess, or **hypothesis.** The writer in the following passage gives a hypothesis for why something happened.

> Nearly a century after women received the right to vote, the vast majority of elected mayors and governors are still men. An important reason for this might be that most voters believe a woman would not be as tough on crime as a man.

Effect: The majority of elected mayors and governors are still men.

Possible Cause (hypothesis): Most voters believe that a woman would not be as tough on crime as a man.

EXERCISE 13

Distinguishing Fact from Hypothesis

Directions: Each of the following sentences describes a cause-and-effect relationship. Write *F* in the blank if the cause is stated as a fact. Write *H* in the blank if the cause is stated as a hypothesis.

_____ 1. The cause of the Air India crash was the explosion of a terrorist bomb.

_____ 2. As a result of six months of intensive counseling, the Martins decided not to file for divorce.

_____ 3. Qualified candidates choose not to run for office probably because they don't have enough money.

_____ 4. Research suggests that brain damage in criminals may be a cause of violent crime.

Answers are on page 495.

Identifying a Hypothesis

In a social studies passage, an author will often state a cause as a possibility, or hypothesis, rather than as a fact. It is important to recognize when authors are stating facts and when they are suggesting a hypothesis. In the following passage, notice that the author does not know for sure why leaders are supporting basic education. But she does give you a possible explanation.

> All over the country, both labor and business leaders are supporting efforts to provide basic education to adults. These leaders may feel that workers will need this basic education in order to get and keep jobs in the future.

According to the passage, what is the most likely cause of the efforts of labor and business leaders to educate adults?

(1) They feel a new spirit of charity.
(2) They want workers to be able to vote in union elections.
(3) In the future, workers will need to have a basic education.
(4) They recognize that labor and business must work together.
(5) They are concerned about a lack of workers for unskilled jobs.

You were right if you chose (3). The author says, "These leaders may feel that workers will need this basic education in order to get and keep jobs in the future."

EXERCISE 14

Finding the Author's Hypothesis

Directions: Read each passage and answer the questions that follow.

> To middle-class Americans, the main purpose of a house is not simply protection from the weather. Instead, a house is an investment. To many, the most important feature of a house is its possible resale value. The focus on resale value has brought about changes in houses. For example, in 1900, only the richest families had two bathrooms in their houses. Now two- and three-bathroom houses are common because the extra bathrooms increase the resale value of a house.

1. Why does the author think that two- and three-bathroom houses are now common in the United States?

(1) Many families have more servants.
(2) Many families are larger and need more than one bathroom.
(3) Extra bathrooms increase the resale value of a home.
(4) Americans have settled down and now have enough time to make additions to their homes.
(5) The homes are designed to house more than one family.

Economics is the study of how people produce, distribute, and consume goods and services. In other words, how people make things, ship them, sell them, and use them. While each town, city, and country has an economy, the world's economy is quickly becoming linked.

You may have noticed that information from stock markets around the world is reported on your local news. You may read in the newspaper about changes in stock prices if a war is about to start, or if a natural disaster has created problems in a given country. The world's economy can change in an instant due to events anywhere.

Because of the ability of world events to impact people locally, governments need to work together to prevent economic catastrophes like the one that hit Asia during the 1990s. Governments need to create laws that protect nations, businesses, and individuals from the effects of economic crises.

2. The author's main hypothesis is

   (1) Economies that produced the Asian financial crisis still exist.
   (2) Free markets are the best way to encourage a nation's growth.
   (3) A global safety net needs to be created to protect weak economies.
   (4) Global markets need to be controlled by professionals.
   (5) The global economy needs to be more cautious and prevent crises.

Answers are on page 495.

Developing a Hypothesis

Sometimes a writer leaves it up to the reader to figure something out. The writer might describe an event or a trend without explaining why it happened. You can often use the evidence in the passage along with your common sense to develop a hypothesis that explains something. Read the following passage and answer the question that follows.

Bantu-speaking people originated in present-day eastern Nigeria and Southern Cameroon. Approximately 4,000 years ago, they grew yams and oil palms while they spread across the tropical rainforests and savannahs, displacing the hunting-and-gathering Pygmies, who today survive in scattered bands in the forest. By 1000 B.C., the Bantu knew how to make iron and had adopted new crops like the grain millet and bananas. They spread rapidly east and south, displacing the hunting, gathering, Khoisan-speaking people who had previously lived in those areas. Eventually, Bantu speakers were dominant across much of sub-Saharan Africa.

A possible cause of the rapid spread of Bantu-speaking people is

(1) they had developed a more effective language than other groups
(2) they were better hunters and gatherers than the original inhabitants
(3) they were more aggressive and warlike than the original inhabitants
(4) they adopted agriculture and iron which allowed them to be more productive
(5) they had stronger and more effective leaders who planned their expansion

You were correct if you chose (4). The passage suggests this explanation in several ways. During the Bantus' first period of expansion, they adopted agriculture and displaced people who were hunters and gatherers. During the second period of expansion, they adopted iron and new crops and displaced other hunters and gatherers. There's no evidence in the passage for the other choices.

EXERCISE 15

Making a Reasonable Hypothesis

Directions: Read each passage and answer the questions that follow.

At the end of World War II, the Allies had totally defeated the Axis powers of Germany and Japan. Germany had been mercilessly bombed by Allied planes, while Japan had been attacked by the first, and only, nuclear bombs to be used in warfare. But after their unconditional surrenders, the leader of the Allies, the United States, decided against humiliating them further. Instead, the United States tried to help both nations rebuild their economies and establish thriving democracies. By the end of the twentieth century, Japan and Germany had the second and third largest economies in the world as well as stable democratic governments. Instead of enemies, they were among the United States' closest and most trusted friends.

1. Which of the following is the most likely hypothesis why Japan and Germany, once enemies of the United States, are now our close allies and friends?

(1) The destruction of war was so great, they decided it was safer to be our friends.
(2) By helping them instead of humiliating them, the United States gained their trust.
(3) All democracies are friends of the United States, and they are now democracies.
(4) Along with the United States, they are now the world's largest economies.
(5) The people of Germany and Japan were grateful that the Allies defeated them.

In 1967, the Field Foundation paid a group of doctors to study hunger and malnutrition in certain areas of the United States. These doctors found that many people in the United States were going hungry.

Ten years later, the foundation sent another group of doctors to the same areas. The second group of doctors reported that food aid programs—such as food stamps—had helped people in those regions. In 1967, the doctors had seen many children with swollen stomachs, dull eyes, and open wounds. In 1977, they saw fewer signs of hunger and its related illnesses.

2. In 1967, what was the probable cause of the poor physical condition of many children?

(1) They were too dependent on handouts.
(2) They were being neglected by their parents.
(3) They lived in unsanitary conditions.
(4) They did not have enough good food.
(5) There were not enough doctors.

Answers are on page 495.

Chapter Review

EXERCISE 16

Directions: Answer the questions following each passage or illustration.

Questions 1 and 2 are based on the following map.

SPREAD OF THE COTTON KINGDOM

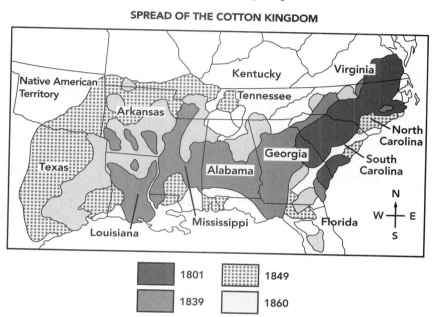

1. In 1801, the Cotton Kingdom was centered in the Carolinas, Georgia, and Virginia. From 1801 to 1860, the Cotton Kingdom spread to

   (1) the north and east
   (2) the south and west
   (3) the east
   (4) Illinois
   (5) the Atlantic coast

2. The areas that had the greatest growth from 1801 to 1839 in land devoted to cotton were

   (1) Texas, Native American Territory, and Arkansas
   (2) the Carolinas, Georgia, and Virginia
   (3) Georgia, Alabama, Mississippi, and Louisiana
   (4) Florida and Texas
   (5) Tennessee, Kentucky, and North Carolina

Questions 3 and 4 are based on the following passage and map.

Otto von Bismarck, chief minister of Prussia, was the architect of German unification. By maneuvering the German states into three wars, all of which they won, he was able to dramatically increase the size of the territory under his control. In 1871, all the newly gained territory was unified by Bismarck and William I as the German Empire.

GERMAN UNIFICATION

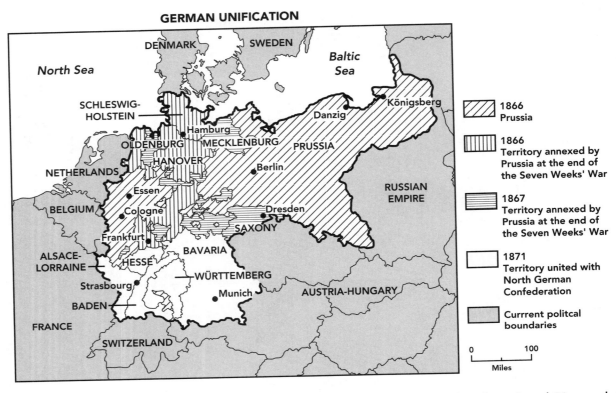

3. German states came under the control of William I and Bismarck in which order?

   (1) Prussia, Bavaria, Saxony, Hanover
   (2) Prussia, Saxony, Hanover, Bavaria
   (3) Prussia, Hanover, Bavaria, Saxony
   (4) Prussia, Saxony, Bavaria, Hanover
   (5) Prussia, Hanover, Saxony, Bavaria

4. Based on the information given in the passage and the map, which is the most likely hypothesis for German unification?

   (1) The military superiority of Prussia led to German unification.
   (2) The rapid industrialization of German land led to unification.
   (3) It was the right time for Prussia to lead German unification.
   (4) Germans united in order to defend themselves from outside threats.
   (5) The other nations of Europe wanted German unification.

Questions 5–8 are based on the following passage.

When high-tech industries are struggling, the next high-tech boom may be getting started. When laid-off executives and scientists don't have enough to do, they dream of running their own companies or building new products. So they start new companies offering those new products.

Thus, while the giant companies suffer through hard times, dozens of new companies are quietly setting up shop. Often these new firms create the new products of the next boom. When these breakthrough products capture the public's imagination, the new boom explodes. Old and new firms rush to copy the product. The industry shoots into a period of frantic growth that may last two years or more.

Then the public's love affair with the product ends, or a giant company takes over the whole market. Then the boom is over. The industry slumps back into the next recession. This bust-boom-bust cycle has happened over and over in high technology: in the late 1960s with minicomputers, in the mid-'70s with video games, in the early '80s with personal computers and VCRs, and in the early '90s with video camcorders and cellular phones, and in the mid '90s with the Internet and dot coms.

5. How were the high-tech booms of the late 1960s, the mid-'70s, the early '80s, and the early and mid '90s similar?

(1) They all got started when new firms introduced new products.
(2) They were all dominated by the entertainment industry.
(3) They all ended when one giant company took over the market.
(4) They all began during times of prosperity and growth.
(5) They were all dominated by the Japanese and Koreans.

6. How were the high-tech booms of the late 1960s, the mid-'70s, the early '80s, and the early and mid '90s different?

(1) Their patterns of boom and decline are different.
(2) Only in the mid-'70s did firms rush to copy the new product.
(3) Only in the early '80s was there a major new breakthrough product.
(4) Different innovative products and services led each boom.
(5) Economic conditions varied while the new companies were getting started.

7. What is the correct sequence of each high-tech boom cycle?

(1) large companies develop new product, new market booms, industry slumps
(2) development during previous boom, short recession, new boom
(3) development of new product during slow period, boom, industry slumps
(4) company mergers, development of new product, booming new market, leveling off
(5) mass advertising campaign, booming sales, new firms created, period of stability

8. According to the passage, which of the following might cause a high-tech boom to end?

(1) scientists developing a new product
(2) the public losing interest in the new product
(3) other firms copying the product
(4) computers becoming obsolete
(5) executives getting laid off

Questions 9 and 10 are based on the following line graph.

INDUSTRIAL PRODUCTION

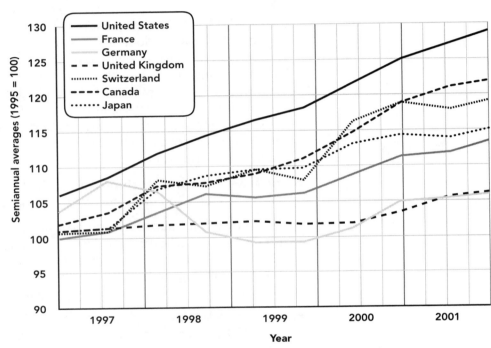

Source: International Monetary Fund, *International Financial Statistics*

9. According to the graph, which nation had the strongest consistent industrial growth from 1997 to 2001?

(1) United States
(2) France
(3) Germany
(4) Canada
(5) Japan

10. Which nation was suffering the most from an industrial slowdown in 1999?

(1) United States
(2) France
(3) United Kingdom
(4) Switzerland
(5) Japan

Questions 11 and 12 are based on the following cartoon.

Background clues: As part of its efforts to combat terrorism, the George W. Bush administration proposed an Office of Information Awareness that would gather data on all Americans. It recommended that John Poindexter be in charge of the new office.

"YES, THERE'S A DEFINITE PATTERN HERE...SPEAKING FREELY, WEAPONS POSSESSION, SENSITIVITY TO SEARCHES, REFUSING TO ANSWER QUESTIONS ABOUT HIMSELF... ...HE'S OBVIOUSLY A THREAT... HAVE SOMEONE PICK UP THIS MR. **BILL O. RIGHTS.**"

11. Speaking freely, possessing weapons, protection from unreasonable searches, and the right to refuse to answer questions about yourself are part of what American document?

    (1) The Declaration of Independence
    (2) The United States Constitution
    (3) The Civil Rights Act of 1964
    (4) The Emancipation Proclamation
    (5) The Articles of Confederation

12. What is the cartoonist's opinion of the Office of Information Awareness?

    (1) We need the new office to protect us from the attacks of terrorists.
    (2) We can trust the government to use the information it gathers wisely.
    (3) The Bill of Rights has become outdated in this new age of terrorism.
    (4) The new office is more a threat to civil liberties than it is to terrorists.
    (5) The Office of Information Awareness will benefit all Americans.

Question 13 is based on the following passage.

Mel Fisher first heard about two treasure ships that sank in 1622 in a book called *The Treasure Hunter's Guide.* In 1970, Fisher began a sixteen-year search of the ocean floor near Florida looking for the ships. Fisher had to raise money from 1,200 investors to pay for the costly search. He finally found one of the ships, the *Atocha,* in 1986. It held a treasure of over $400 million worth of jewels and precious metals.

13. Which of the following hypotheses best explains why Mel Fisher was looking for the ships?

    (1) He wanted to know how ships were built in the 1600s.
    (2) He wanted to publish a book on the dangers of shipping in the 1600s.
    (3) He wanted the valuable treasure from the ships.
    (4) He was doing research for his book, *The Treasure Hunter's Guide.*
    (5) He was working for a group of investors.

Question 14 is based on the following passage.

In 1940, only 8 percent of black men earned more money than the average white man. By 1980, 29 percent of employed black men earned more money than the average white man.

What brought about this dramatic change? One study examined several major factors: education, the migration of blacks from the South to the North, blacks moving from rural areas into cities, welfare programs, and affirmative action programs. The study concluded that when blacks moved to cities they had better opportunities. However, education enabled blacks to take advantage of these opportunities. Education was the key factor that allowed blacks to succeed.

14. What do the authors of the study believe is the best way to improve the standard of living of black people?

    (1) provide educational opportunities
    (2) encourage relocation in the South
    (3) maintain affirmative action programs
    (4) ensure that there is good medical care
    (5) encourage migration to urban areas

Answers are on pages 495–496.

CHAPTER 5

Evaluating Social Studies Materials

In this chapter, you will learn to **evaluate** what you read. When you evaluate, you ask yourself whether something is logical. You will also practice judging whether you **have enough information** to answer a question or solve a problem and whether the information you have is what you need. Then, you will learn to **identify errors in reasoning**, and **recognize the values** that have an effect on beliefs, decision making, and action. Finally, you'll learn what **propaganda** is and how to recognize it.

Having Enough Information

Using the Information in a Passage

Every day you evaluate whether you **have enough information** to solve a problem or answer someone's question. Sometimes you evaluate information to make a decision. You also need to evaluate the social studies materials you read. You need to be able to decide whether the information provided is enough for you to reach a particular conclusion. Read the paragraph below carefully and then decide whether you have enough information to prove the following statements.

> Ancient Athens is considered the world's first democracy. It was the first place in which citizens elected their own leaders. But this democracy was far from perfect. Women were not allowed to vote, nor were slaves or men not born in Athens. In fact, out of a population of 200,000, only 50,000 had the right to vote.

Put a check (√) in front of each statement that the passage gives you enough information to prove.

_____ **1.** Ancient Athens created an entirely new form of government.

_____ **2.** Women were unsuccessful in their struggle to be able to vote in Ancient Athens.

_____ **3.** Only a minority of the population of Athens had the right to vote.

You should have checked statement 1. There is enough information: the first sentence states that Athens is considered the world's first democracy. The second sentence says it was the first place where citizens elected their own leaders. You should not have checked statement 2. There is not enough information. While the passage states that women did not have the right to vote, it made no mention whether or not they ever struggled to get the right to vote. You should have checked statement 3. There is enough information. 50,000 is less than half of 200,000. Therefore, only a minority of the population had the right to vote.

EXERCISE 1

Is There Enough Information?

Directions: Following each passage are three statements. In the blank before each statement, put a check (√) if it can be proven by using the information in the passage.

All but one of the sixteen southern states allow the death penalty. In 1992 in those states, there was a total of 1,488 prisoners waiting for execution. Of the thirty-four states outside the South, twenty-one allow the death penalty. In 1992, those states had 1,106 prisoners on death row.

_____ 1. In 1992, there were more prisoners on death row in the sixteen southern states than in all thirty-four other states.

_____ 2. Murder is increasing in the southern United States.

_____ 3. A person convicted of murder in any southern state might not be given the death penalty.

When people talk about the "heartland" of America, they usually mean the Midwest. Some researchers have decided that the "typical American voter" lives in Dayton, a service and manufacturing city on the Miami River in southwestern Ohio. This typical American voter is a housewife whose husband is a machinist—perhaps with General Motors or Delco—and whose brother-in-law is a policeman. She considers herself a Democrat but often votes Republican.

Companies that want to find out what products people will buy also believe that the Midwest is typical. Columbus, Ohio, boasts that companies like to test-market new products there because it offers such a good cross section of the country.

_____ 4. Many companies believe that if a new product is successful in Columbus it will be successful in the nation as a whole.

_____ 5. The "typical American voter" lives in a city.

_____ 6. Ohio will always be the home of the typical American voter.

Answers are on page 496.

Using the Information on a Map

A map might not always have all the information you need to answer a question. See what information you can get from the following map.

Does the map of Vermont provide enough information to prove these statements? Put a check (√) in front of the statement you can prove.

_____ **1.** The capital of Vermont is Montpelier.

_____ **2.** Potatoes are produced in Vermont.

You should not have put a check in front of the first statement. The map shows a few cities, but not Montpelier. You should have put a check in front of the second statement. Scanning the map, you will see several spots where potatoes are produced.

EXERCISE 2

Using Information on a Map

Directions: Following each map are three statements. In the blank before each statement, put a check (√) if there is enough information on the map to prove the statement true.

Questions 1–3 are based on the Vermont map above.

_____ **1.** Vermont's forest products are more important than its potatoes.

_____ **2.** Dairy products are Vermont's major source of farm income.

_____ **3.** Maple syrup is produced in Vermont.

Questions 4–6 are based on the following map.

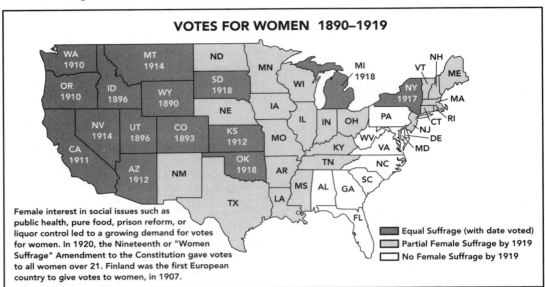

VOTES FOR WOMEN 1890–1919

Female interest in social issues such as public health, pure food, prison reform, or liquor control led to a growing demand for votes for women. In 1920, the Nineteenth or "Women Suffrage" Amendment to the Constitution gave votes to all women over 21. Finland was the first European country to give votes to women, in 1907.

Equal Suffrage (with date voted)
Partial Female Suffrage by 1919
No Female Suffrage by 1919

_____ **4.** In general, the western states gave equal suffrage to women before the rest of the country.

_____ **5.** Pennsylvania (PA) did not allow any female suffrage by 1919.

_____ **6.** More women lived in New York in 1917 than in any other state.

Answers are on page 496.

Looking for the Right Information

Doreen is a feminist—a supporter of women's rights. When she went to vote in the primary for state senator, she found that Marie Home was running against Tom Taylor. Doreen voted for Marie because she was a woman. She later found out that it was Tom, not Marie, who supported the women's issues that were important to her.

Doreen used the wrong information to make an important decision. She wanted a state senator who would support women's issues. She thought that all she needed to know was which candidate was a woman. Unfortunately, her choice went against her desire to have a state senator who would support women's rights.

Irrelevant Information

Irrelevant information isn't really related to the subject being talked about. Sometimes writers try to persuade you to do something by giving you irrelevant but appealing information. Study the following advertisement. Think about what the advertiser wants you to do and what reasons you are given to do it.

What does the advertiser want you to do?

What irrelevant reasons are given for doing it?

The purpose of the ad is to convince you to buy magazines. However, two facts are irrelevant: "the largest sweepstakes of its kind in America" and "Ed McMahon will hand you your winning check." Both are poor reasons to buy the magazines. However, getting your favorite magazine at the lowest price is a good reason to buy the magazines.

EXERCISE 3

Identifying Irrelevant Information

Directions: Read the following letter. First, figure out what the writer wants you to do. Then answer the questions that follow.

Dear Editor,

I want to urge your readers to vote for Gil Cohen for mayor. Everyone agrees that he is more attractive than his opponent. He has years of administrative experience, much more than the other candidate. He has promised to increase the police budget in order to control crime. Finally, people should vote for him because he has spent over $100,000 of his own money to get elected.

Sincerely,
Bernice Cohen

1. What does the writer want her readers to do?

   _____

2. What irrelevant reasons for doing this does she give?

   _____

3. What relevant question should be asked about the author of the letter? _____

Answers are on page 496.

EXERCISE 4

Using Information Correctly

Directions: Read each passage. Then answer the questions that follow.

Many people outside the United States think of Americans as self-centered and selfish. Yet there is evidence for quite a different view. In 1985, Americans responded to the record "We Are the World" and the Live Aid concert by contributing millions of dollars to famine relief in Africa. A year later, Americans participated in Hands Across America, an event in which millions of people joined hands to raise millions of dollars more to feed hungry Americans.

1. Hands Across America was

- **(1)** a concert to benefit starving people in Africa
- **(2)** a record that featured America's most famous singers
- **(3)** an event that raised millions of dollars to feed hungry Americans
- **(4)** an event that proved that Americans were self-centered
- **(5)** an event that proved that Americans were willing to help needy people from other countries

2. There is enough proof in the passage to show that

- **(1)** the U.S. government is concerned with world hunger
- **(2)** Africa is successfully coping with its food problems
- **(3)** all musicians are concerned with helping others
- **(4)** Americans are becoming more self-centered
- **(5)** Americans can show generosity

In recent years, the United States has been divided sharply over the concept of affirmative action. For many years, minorities and women were kept out of jobs and schools because of their race or gender. Affirmative action programs try to correct past prejudice. Schools and employers using these programs search for qualified women and minorities to fill their openings.

Many Americans believe that hiring should not be influenced by race, gender, or religion. They insist that affirmative action is the wrong way of dealing with prejudice because it is prejudice working in reverse. This topic continues to be argued by politicians today.

3. There is enough information to determine that

- **(1)** affirmative action programs have made up for past prejudice and are no longer needed
- **(2)** affirmative action is not fair to white males
- **(3)** affirmative action will not result in more black people in important jobs
- **(4)** affirmative action is an attempt to make up for past prejudice
- **(5)** affirmative action will be a major issue of the 2000s

The kibbutz is a type of cooperative community found in Israel. In a kibbutz, most things are owned by everyone as a group. The kibbutz owns the land, all farm animals and equipment, and all crops. Sometimes it owns its own factories. In some kibbutzim, even the houses are owned by the community.

4. A kibbutz is a community in which

- **(1)** everybody must learn Hebrew, the language of Israel
- **(2)** new members must be over thirty-five years old
- **(3)** most things are owned in common
- **(4)** children cannot live with their parents
- **(5)** factories are owned by the richest people

Answers are on page 497.

Finding Errors in Reasoning

In this part of the chapter, you will practice recognizing other errors in reasoning, such as

- substituting personal beliefs, desires, or experience for facts:
  "I have never been given a parking ticket on this street; therefore, it must be legal to park here."

- making general statements based on one example:
  "All those TV offers are rip-offs. My sister sent in $25 for a set of knives, and she never got it."

- backward reasoning:
  "If all American voters are people over eighteen years old, then all people over eighteen years old are American voters."

Below are two reasons for a certain action. Put a check (√) in front of the one that shows good reasoning.

_____ **1.** The staff will get more work done if new computer equipment is purchased and used.

_____ **2.** Cali, the office manager, thinks the office should have the latest and fanciest computer equipment.

You should have put a check in front of the first statement. A good reason for purchasing new equipment is to improve productivity. The second statement is an example of substituting a personal desire for good reasons.

EXERCISE 5

Recognizing Errors in Reasoning

Directions: Below each statement are two reasons for making a choice or taking an action. Put a check (√) in the blank before the choice that shows good reasoning.

1. Mel's Auto Body Shop is in financial trouble.

_____ **(1)** Since Mel's business has had an excellent financial record for thirty years, Mel is confident his bank will help him.

_____ **(2)** Since the government bailed out the Chrysler Corporation when it was in financial trouble, it will help out Mel's Auto Body Shop.

2. The Lightstone neighborhood decided not to work with the Froston Redevelopment Authority to improve the neighborhood.

———— **(1)** The Froston Redevelopment Authority wiped out the West End neighborhood thirty years ago. Therefore, the same thing will happen to the Lightstone neighborhood.

———— **(2)** For over thirty years, the Froston Redevelopment Authority has constantly ignored the wishes of Froston's neighborhoods. Instead, it has listened to wealthy developers. Therefore, it is risky to work with them.

Answers are on page 497.

What Is the Problem Here?

It is important to be able to explain why reasoning is correct or why it is flawed. In the following exercise, you'll practice identifying and explaining reasoning problems. Try answering the questions based on the cartoon.

Background clues: In 2002, President George W. Bush proposed that the United States use preemptive strikes to attack a nation that might be preparing to attack us. This would be a major change from the previous American policy of only going to war in response to an attack from another nation.

According to the cartoonist, what is the reasoning error of the doctrine of preemption or striking first?

What does the cartoonist most likely mean by naming his cartoon "No Exit"?

According to the artist, if an enemy thinks that it might be attacked first, it is more likely to try to attack the United States first. So instead of making us safer, preemption makes us less safe. By "No Exit" the cartoonist means that being willing to strike first will result in an endless cycle of war from which there is no escape.

Read the following passage. Then answer the questions that follow.

In 1763, after the British defeated France in the French and Indian War, British leaders thought it was reasonable for the American colonies to pay taxes to cover the debts from the war and to pay British troops stationed in the colonies for protection. They also thought that the American colonies should help pay for the costs of running the British Empire. As a result, the British Parliament passed a series of laws, including the Stamp Act, the Townshend Acts, and the Tea Act, which were vigorously opposed in the colonies. The colonists saw the laws as "taxation without representation," since they were not allowed to vote in the British Parliament.

What was the reasoning of the British?

What is the problem with that reasoning?

The British thought that since the American colonists had benefited from the protection of the British during the French and Indian War and afterwards, they should pay for that protection. The flaw in the reasoning is that the British Parliament imposed the taxes on the colonists, and the colonists could not vote in the Parliament. Therefore, the colonists thought that the taxes were unfair.

EXERCISE 6

Errors in Reasoning

Directions: Read each passage. Then answer the questions that follow.

In 1980, Ronald Reagan was running for president against President Jimmy Carter. He asked the voters if they were better off than they were four years before. He suggested that, if they were worse off, they should vote for him to replace President Carter.

I had had a hard year in 1980. My wife died, and my children dropped out of school. I started drinking and got fired from my job. I was doing much worse than four years before. Therefore, I voted for Ronald Reagan for president.

1. The writer of the passage decided to vote for Ronald Reagan because

    (1) he supported Reagan's economic policies
    (2) his life was going badly
    (3) he did not like Jimmy Carter
    (4) he felt that it was time for a change
    (5) he thought Reagan was a great speaker

2. What is the problem with this man's reasoning? _____

_____

_____

     Prior to the beginning of World War II, the United States and the United Kingdom had the largest commercial and consumer economies in the world. The Germans and Japanese were both ruled by militaristic dictatorships. Germany reasoned that the British would not have the stomach or the strength to oppose them as they conquered continental Europe and bombed British cities, including London. Japan believed that the Americans would be no match for their military forces. The Japanese leaders thought that if they could destroy most of the American Pacific fleet at Pearl Harbor, the Americans would not have the will or the power to fight against them. The reasoning of the German and Japanese leaders turned out to be fatally flawed.

3. Both the German and Japanese leadership reasoned that the United Kingdom and the United States would not oppose them for long because

    (1) they had smaller and weaker economies than Germany and Japan

    (2) they had inferior military equipment compared to Germany and Japan

    (3) their leadership was not as skilled as the leaders of Germany and Japan

    (4) they had been spoiled by their prosperity and would not be tough enough to fight

    (5) they felt safe since they were separated from Germany and Japan by bodies of water

4. What was the problem with the reasoning of Germany's and Japan's leaders?

_____

_____

_____

During the twentieth century, many companies grew by purchasing other companies. The Radio Corporation of America (RCA) was a pioneer in electronics, beginning with radio. In the 1920s, it developed the first national radio network, the National Broadcasting Corporation (NBC). By the 1950s, RCA had expanded into records and television. In the 1960s, it was involved in space exploration. By the 1970s, the company had decided to diversify and developed into a huge conglomerate by purchasing companies such as Random House Publishing and Hertz Corporation, the leading car rental company. These newer acquisitions did not have anything to do with electronics, RCA's core business. The leadership of RCA had no idea how to run these companies. In addition, the effort it took to run these companies took time, energy, and funding away the electronics side of the company. By the time RCA decided to sell its non-electronic subsidiaries, it was too late to save the company, which was bought by General Electric.

5. What was the reason that RCA purchased Random House and Hertz Corporation?

    (1) The more businesses it controlled the stronger the company would be.
    (2) It would be a humbling experience for its executives to learn new businesses.
    (3) There was a natural connection between radios, television, books, and car rentals.
    (4) They mistakenly thought that the companies were involved in electronics.
    (5) They expected to be able to sell the companies for a profit a few years later.

6. What was the problem with the reasoning of RCA? _____

_____

_____

Answers are on page 497.

Recognizing Values

Everybody has **values**, those things that they consider important. We often think of the United States as a nation shaped by values. Many of the early settlers from Europe came to America for religious freedom.

It is important to be able to recognize the values of an author or of the people an author writes about. Some people have values that you may think are noble, such as consideration for others or the importance of honesty. Other values can include wanting to make money, getting what you want no matter who gets hurt, concern for world peace, and patriotism.

Try to identify the values being expressed in the cartoon below.

Background clues: The National Rifle Association (NRA) opposes all gun control laws. They believe that all law-abiding Americans have the right to own and use guns.

OF COURSE WE SELL ARMOR-PIERCING BULLETS... WHO KNOWS WHEN YOU'LL SEE A DEER DRIVING A SHERMAN TANK?

What value is being expressed by the shop owner in the cartoon?

(1) patriotism
(2) world peace
(3) human rights
(4) freedom to carry weapons
(5) consideration for others

The correct answer is choice (4), freedom to carry weapons. The caption shows that he will sell dangerous ammunition that is clearly not meant to be used against deer. The cartoon does not suggest choice (1). His willingness to sell something so dangerous eliminates choices (2), (3), and (5).

EXERCISE 7

Recognizing Values

Directions: Study each passage or cartoon. Then answer the questions.

Conversations about politically correct speech have been taking place at college campuses across the nation. Some school officials, alarmed by incidents of racial and sexual harassment, have adopted speech codes prohibiting hateful language in classrooms and dormitories. They hope to protect minority students from prejudice. Opponents argue that the codes restrict students' and teachers' First Amendment right to free speech.

1. What value did colleges hope to preserve by adopting speech codes?

   (1) quiet study areas for students
   (2) fair treatment of all people
   (3) access to education for all Americans
   (4) support of the U.S. government
   (5) separation of the sexes in schools

2. What value did opponents of the codes hope to preserve?

   (1) equality among races
   (2) pursuit of money
   (3) freedom to express ideas
   (4) racial hatred
   (5) the right to sue

Background clues: Throughout history each U.S. president has developed a special relationship with the press. The cartoon below refers to the First Amendment to the U.S. Constitution, which protects the freedom of the press to operate without government interference.

"I propose we reword the First Amendment and make it FREEDOM FROM THE PRESS."

3. According to the cartoonist, which value was most important to the president?

    (1) freedom of the press
    (2) making money
    (3) power of the president
    (4) solving America's problems
    (5) human rights

4. Based on this cartoon, what value seems to be most important to the cartoonist?

    (1) freedom of the press
    (2) making money
    (3) power of the presidency
    (4) solving America's problems
    (5) human rights

    The New England town meeting has been called the purest form of democracy. At the meetings, every voter has the opportunity to "stand up and be counted" on issues that are important to the town. Any group coming to a town meeting has the chance to appeal to the voters by speaking directly to them. One town's preservation society thought they had an issue that couldn't lose at the town meeting. They wanted the town to buy an old farm and save the land for recreation and education.

    Everybody on the purchase committee wanted a chance to speak to the voters. Despite a poll of voters that showed them strongly in favor of saving open land, the proposed purchase of the farm was badly defeated.

5. What value of the voters did the town preservation society try to appeal to?

    (1) the need for efficiency
    (2) conservation of open land
    (3) the desire for lower taxes
    (4) the importance of communication
    (5) the spirit of fair play

Answers are on page 497.

Recognizing Propaganda

Propaganda presents a person, a product, or an idea as good or bad. Its purpose is to convince you. You see examples of propaganda every day. The most common example of propaganda is advertising. Does the following example look familiar?

NEW MEDICAL BREAKTHROUGH!!!

Lose up to 50 Pounds Without Dieting

EAT ALL YOUR FAVORITE FOODS AND STILL LOSE WEIGHT

All of us have seen these kinds of ads before. They pull at our emotions and desires. They tell only the good side of their products and leave out any possible harmful side effects. They are a form of propaganda.

Propaganda uses information to convince a reader. It uses ideas, facts, or accusations to help or hurt a cause. It generally tries to promote a single point of view and is one-sided. Propaganda often distorts facts. Advertisers use a variety of propaganda techniques to convince us to buy their products.

How is this advertiser trying to convince you to buy the product?

TRAIN YOUR VOICE FOR SUCCESS!

Never again will you be overanxious or fearful when meeting new people or speaking in public. You will be absolutely self-confident knowing that your voice can have the resonance of a James Earl Jones, the controlled charm of a Courtney Cox, the poise of a Tom Brokaw, or the seductive power of a Julia Roberts!

Order Your Voice-Training Cassette Today!

This ad tries to convince you to buy the cassette by claiming that

(1) it can make you speak as well as some famous people
(2) you can become a famous actor if you use it
(3) most people you know have benefited from it already
(4) people who use it get better jobs
(5) you don't need to improve your public speaking skills

The correct answer is choice (1). This is an example of a very common propaganda technique, the "famous or respected person" technique. It uses the names of famous people. The ad tries to get you to think that you'll learn the same techniques that have made these people so successful.

Other common propaganda techniques include:

- **Glittering generalities**—using vague positive words and images
"Our salon's secret techniques will bring out the timeless beauty in you. Our experts think age and elegance go hand in hand."

- **Name calling**—connecting a negative image to an idea, a product, a person, or a group
"Stop using dirty, smelly, smoky oil. Change to clean electric heat."

- **Bandwagon**—everybody is doing it
"Four out of five people surveyed use Shine Toothpaste."

- **Card stacking**—mentioning only the favorable facts and ignoring the negative facts
"Top Choice Chewing Tobacco gives you that real tobacco flavor without smoke. For real tobacco satisfaction, use Top Choice." (Not mentioned in the ad are the dangers of smokeless tobacco.)

EXERCISE 8

Propaganda and Advertising

Directions: Read each advertisement. Then answer the questions that follow.

1. According to the ad, you should eat Chocorich because

   (1) everybody eats Chocorich
   (2) famous people eat Chocorich
   (3) eating Chocorich will make you popular
   (4) more people eat Chocorich than any other candy
   (5) other candy makers use lower-quality chocolate and sugar

2. The ad gives only reasons why you should eat Chocorich. Can you

   think of a reason not to eat Chocorich? _____

3. This ad appeals to people who believe that

   (1) attractive men have large muscles
   (2) it is a good idea to keep your weight down
   (3) it is important to be healthy
   (4) women like intelligent men
   (5) it is important to be considerate of others

4. Women will be attracted to this ad because

   (1) they look like the woman in the drawing
   (2) they are tired of the summer and want to look ahead to fall
   (3) they are looking for a bargain
   (4) they want to think of themselves as sophisticated
   (5) they do not want to attract attention to themselves

Answers are on page 498.

Political Propaganda

Propaganda has been used frequently in the political world. A lot of **political propaganda** consists of advertisements for political candidates.

In addition, governments and political candidates use propaganda to convince people to support a cause. Political propaganda is also used to turn public opinion against other people or other countries, as in the following example.

> Englishmen cannot understand great ideas; they lack any real intelligence. They only care about material things and comforts.

These ideas are an example of Italian propaganda at the beginning of World War II.

What did the Italian government want its people to believe about the English?

(1) The English were a dangerous enemy who must be feared.
(2) The English were evil people who wanted to destroy the world.
(3) The English were small-minded and could be defeated easily.
(4) The English had a powerful economy that had to be destroyed.
(5) The English were a noble people who should be copied.

The correct answer is choice (3). The writer says that the English lacked real intelligence. The Italian government insulted the English so that the Italian people would be more supportive of the war against the English.

EXERCISE 9

Political Propaganda

Directions: Read each passage or study the illustration. Then answer the questions that follow.

> Following a disastrous defeat of the Germans by the Soviets at Stalingrad, Goebbels, Hitler's propaganda chief, spoke to the German people. He said that the 300,000 Germans killed in the battle were all heroes. They had slowed down six Soviet armies, which otherwise would be rampaging toward Germany. He claimed that the Germans had been "purified" by the defeat at Stalingrad. It had given them the new strength they required for victory.

1. List two reasons that, according to Goebbels, the defeat at Stalingrad was good for the Germans.

_____

_____

2. Why would Goebbels have described the terrible outcome of the Battle of Stalingrad as he did?

    (1) He believed that military defeats were good for the German spirit.
    (2) He thought the Russians might retreat.
    (3) He wanted the Americans and British to break their alliance with the USSR.
    (4) He didn't want people to realize what a disaster it was.
    (5) He wanted Germany to surrender to the Russians.

INTEREST IN HOLISTIC HEALING SKYROCKETS!

Americans nationwide are choosing holistic medicine over traditional treatment.

You, too, can experience the benefits of holistic healing!

---

3. According to this advertisement, you should try holistic medical treatment because

    (1) it works faster than traditional medical treatments
    (2) everybody is trying holistic medicine
    (3) traditional drugs have unhealthy side effects
    (4) a lot of research has gone into the development of holistic medicine
    (5) holistic medicines are much cheaper than other treatments

Answers are on page 498.

Chapter Review

EXERCISE 10

Directions: Read each passage or study each illustration. Then answer the questions that follow.

Questions 1 and 2 are based on the following map.

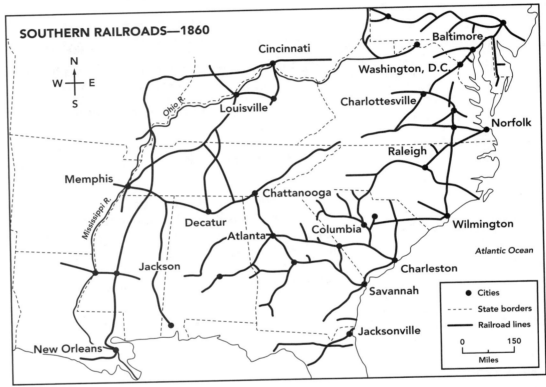

1. According to the map, in 1860 it was impossible to travel by train from

   (1) Jackson to New Orleans
   (2) Atlanta to Columbia
   (3) Atlanta to Chattanooga
   (4) Raleigh to Charlottesville
   (5) Jacksonville to Savannah

2. There is enough information on the map to determine that

   (1) the North would win the Civil War by using the rail system to transport the troops
   (2) Atlanta was the largest city in the South because it was an important railroad junction
   (3) Savannah was the main shipping port for cotton because all cotton grown across the South could be shipped there by train
   (4) the western frontier could not be reached from the South by train
   (5) the South was mostly farmland and, therefore, did not need an extensive rail network

Questions 3 and 4 are based on the following passage.

Amnesty International is a very special organization. It does not support any one form of government or economic system. It does, however, watch out for human rights throughout the world, working on thousands of cases of political imprisonment, torture, and murder. As a result of this work, many people put in prison or tortured for their beliefs have been freed. Governments have been pressured to end their abuse of people who disagree with them. In recognition of its work, Amnesty International was awarded the Nobel Peace Prize in 1977.

3. Amnesty International's purpose is

 (1) the defeat of conservative politicians
 (2) the protection of human rights
 (3) the growth of democracy
 (4) to win major awards
 (5) to raise money through contributions

4. To decide if Amnesty International has been effective, you would want to know

 (1) how many awards it has won
 (2) whether it has the support of the United States government
 (3) if it has helped make governments more respectful of human rights
 (4) whether it has fought against imperialism
 (5) whether it has been able to raise more money than other human rights groups

Questions 5 and 6 are based on the following passage.

The United Nations was founded after World War II to help nations solve their differences peacefully. While there has not been another world war, the past fifty years have been far from peaceful. For example, in the 1950s, the United Nations sent troops to fight in the Korean War. In addition, there has been conflict in Southeast Asia and the Middle East for over half a century. And, even though the United Nations sent peace-keeping forces to the Balkans, horrible ethnic wars continued to rage.

Both the Security Council and the General Assembly of the United Nations were supposed to be places where nations could talk about their differences and solve them without violence. Unfortunately, nations have, at times, used these forums to attack each other verbally rather than to settle disputes.

5. From the passage, it is clear that

(1) the United Nations has failed and should be abolished
(2) the United Nations should be given more money
(3) the United Nations has promoted war rather than prevented it
(4) the United Nations still needs to develop ways to solve disputes peacefully
(5) the United Nations should follow American foreign policy

6. A guiding principle of the United Nations is

(1) only the strong survive
(2) the meek shall inherit the earth
(3) if you have the votes, you have the power
(4) people should be free to live as they choose
(5) conflicts should be settled peacefully

Question 7 is based on the following ad.

KEEP AMERICA STRONG!

VOTE FOR

VITO AMORELLI

FOR U.S. CONGRESS

7. As a voter, what reasonable response might you have to this ad?

(1) to vote for Vito because you want America to be strong
(2) to vote against Vito because you want America to be weak
(3) to not vote at all because it does not matter who is elected
(4) find out how Vito proposes to keep America strong
(5) to run for Congress yourself

8. "Equal pay for equal work" has become a rallying cry for women's groups. On the average, women are paid only two-thirds of what a man receives for either the same job or a job of equal difficulty and responsibility. What might be a good reason for a particular man to be paid more than a particular woman for a similar job?

(1) He needs to be paid more because he must support a family.
(2) Men are more important than women.
(3) He has more years of experience than the woman.
(4) He must save for retirement.
(5) His pride would be hurt if a woman made as much as he.

Answers are on page 498.

Answer Key

CHAPTER 1
UNDERSTANDING WHAT YOU READ

Exercise 1: Finding Details (pages 343–345)
Your wording may vary, but your answers should contain the same information as the answers below.

1. John F. Kennedy and Richard M. Nixon
2. Kennedy's good performance in the televised debates got him the extra votes he needed.
3. The Swahili Coast is in East Africa.
4. The Swahili language and culture first developed by around the 9th century.
5. Arabs and Persians practiced Islam by the ninth century. When they moved to the Swahili Coast, they probably brought Islam with them.
6. **(5)** The second sentence tells you about a law against giving away food or drinks. The third sentence says Mr. Belair was arrested because of this law.
7. **(2)** The second sentence states that an American plane dropped the first atomic bomb.
8. **(3)** The third sentence states that the bomb destroyed the entire city.
9. **(4)** The second sentence states that competition from overseas forced both sides to look at the way they work together. While the other statements could be true, only (4) is stated directly in the passage as the cause of cooperation.

Exercise 2: Synonyms, Definitions, and Comparison Clues (page 346)
Your wording may vary, but your answers should contain the same information as the answers below.

1. phony cure-all or phony medicine
2. giving jobs and favors for political reasons
3. a company that controls production of a product and has no competition
4. amount of goods produced

Exercise 3: Antonyms and Contrast Clues (pages 347–348)
1. **(2)** The contrast clue is "After years without restrictions on the number of immigrants."
2. **(1)** The clue is "contrasted sharply with the beauty."
3. **(2)** The contrast clue is "fighting broke out."
4. **(3)** The contrast clue is "unlike the Native American tribes, who only wanted to keep their own lands."

Exercise 4: Using the Sense of the Passage (page 349)
1. **(2)** The Wright brothers' flight in 1903 gives you a clue that it must be around 1900. In addition, the paragraph presents changes taking place over time, so the answer shouldn't be a specific year.
2. **(3)** The paragraph is full of examples of overcrowding—traffic jams, crowded elevators, and crowded subway trains.
3. **(1)** An independent nation has the authority to make its own decisions. Even though the United Kingdom agrees with the U.S. on most issues, it can still act independently.

Exercise 5: Recognizing Restated Information (page 351)
1. **C** Sentence (1) states that more than 90 percent of the people of China are ethnic Han. Most Americans refer to members of this ethnic group as Chinese.
2. **I** Sentence (2) states that Chinese history is mostly the story of the Han, playing down the importance of other ethnic groups in Chinese history.

Exercise 6: Restating Information in Your Own Words (pages 351–352)

Your wording may vary, but your answers should contain the same information as the answers below.

1. Rockefeller forced the railroads to charge him low freight costs on his oil shipments.
2. Rockefeller would cut prices for his oil in areas where he had competitors.
3. The AFL promoted clear-cut issues such as higher pay and shorter workday.
4. The unsuccessful unions put up candidates for political office and asked for major changes in American society.

Exercise 7: Summarizing Facts (page 353)

In this exercise, the correct summary is always the choice that contains all the important ideas from the three original statements.

1. **(2)**
2. **(1)**

Exercise 8: Identifying Unrelated Sentences (page 354)

1. **(3)** The other sentences talk about American interest in Japanese products.
2. **(3)** The topic of the other four sentences is the Consumer Price Index.

Exercise 9: Identifying the Main Idea (page 356)

In this exercise, the main idea choice (M) is supported or explained by the details in the rest of the paragraph. The other choices are either too broad (B), too narrow (N), or not mentioned in the passage (X).

1. **(1)** B This idea is too broad.
   (2) M This is the main idea of the passage.
   (3) X This is not in the passage.
   (4) N This idea is too narrow.
2. **(1)** M This is the main idea of the passage.
   (2) N This idea is too narrow.
   (3) X This is not in the passage.
   (4) B This idea is too broad.

Exercise 10: Writing Topic Sentences (page 358)

Your wording may vary, but your answers should contain the same information as the answers below.

1. Topic: FDIC
   Main Point: The FDIC protects people who deposit in a bank.
   Topic Sentence: The purpose of the Federal Deposit Insurance Corporation is to protect people against bank failure.
2. Topic: ancient civilizations
   Main Point: The first civilizations began about 5000 years ago near rivers.
   Topic Sentence: About 5000 years ago, the first civilizations began near major rivers.

Exercise 11: Main Idea of a Passage (pages 360–361)

1. **(1)** Choice (2) is too broad to be the main idea since the paragraph focuses on Russia. Choices (3) and (4) are details that tell you more about the main idea.
2. **(4)** Choices (1) and (2) are details. Choice (3) is not discussed in the paragraph.
3. **(2)** Choices (1) and (3) are details. Choice (4) is not discussed in the paragraph.
4. **(1)** Choice (2) is not discussed in the passage. Choice (3) is too broad, since the passage focuses on the Russian Revolution. Choice (4) is a detail.

Exercise 12: Inferring Facts (page 363–364)
Part A

Check to make sure you have the following information in your answers.

1. The paragraph talks about seats, and the last sentence mentions a bus boycott.
2. The paragraph says that the black community rallied to her support and points out that in most parts of the world, a man gives up his seat to a woman; so you can infer that she is a black woman.

Part B

3. (2) The clues that Sam had an owner and was bought for $25 tell you that Sam was a slave.

4. (4) The speaker says, "Two hundred of us were working . . ." A factory would have that many workers. By using the pronoun *us*, she tells you she was one of the workers, rather than a reporter.

5. (3) The passage states "When he took office . . . ," and it says that he proposed programs to Congress, implying that he was president of the United States. Franklin Roosevelt became president during the Great Depression.

Exercise 13: Inferring Opinions (pages 366–367)

1. (1) The passage describes how careful Roosevelt was to keep the public eye off his handicap. The last sentence of the passage says that this was a deliberate strategy. You can infer that Roosevelt was making sure that people thought he was healthy and able.

2. (5) The passage states that lawmakers seem to have forgotten that they can do something about the economy. This implies that they were able to help the economy in the past.

3. (4) The speaker is a wolf, so "they" must be the people he is watching.

4. (3) The cartoon suggests that people, rather than wolves, should be sent away to protect the ecosystem.

Exercise 14: Understanding Political Cartoons (pages 369–371)

Your wording may vary from the sample answers below. Check to be sure you have the right information in your answer.

1. The cartoon refers to the biblical story of the conquest of Jericho.

2. They are trying to bring down the wall of voting discrimination by marching around it.

3. (3) The Israelites peacefully marched around Jericho, and the walls collapsed. In a similar way the civil rights movement used nonviolent protest to bring down the walls of voting discrimination.

4. a bag of money

5. (4) The cartoonist is saying that Boss Tweed controlled New York with money instead of intelligence.

6. The woman is viewed more positively. She is young, attractive, and dressed in a stylish cowgirl outfit. The man looks overweight and is dressed in rich man's clothes, both of which contribute to the impression that he is corrupt.

7. (5) The caption, "Now, Dance!" refers to women voters making life difficult for corrupt politicians.

Exercise 15: Chapter Review (pages 372–376)

1. (3) The passage concentrates on the importance of Aung San Suu Kyi's release from house arrest. The other choices are all too broad to describe the topic of the passage.

2. (2) The writer calls Aung San Suu Kyi's release "welcome news." She appears to greatly admire Suu Kyi and consider her very important.

3. (2) Since dissidents are imprisoned for long terms, it is most likely that they are opposed to the regime, or current government. While they might be politicians or reporters, there are politicians and reporters who are not dissidents.

4. (4) The passage describes how the port cities first developed economic independence by supporting American traders. Economic independence led to an interest in political independence.

5. (5) A subsidiary trade route would be minor. The British reserved the most important and profitable trade routes for themselves.

6. (1) You summarize the items listed in the second paragraph: knife, fork, cup, plate, drum, fife. These are all eating utensils and musical instruments.

7. (1) The final paragraph makes the topic clear: ". . . Our march had done its work. We had drawn the attention of the nation to the crime of child labor."

8. (5) This number is given in the first sentence.

9. (3) The passage states, "He said nothing. Newspapers must have copy." You can infer that the newspapers started making things up about Coolidge because he gave them nothing else to write about.

10. (2) The passage implies that the real Calvin Coolidge did not reveal himself to the public. All the country had to go on was "his little witticisms, his dry wit"—not enough to get to know the real Coolidge.

CHAPTER 2
INTERPRETING GRAPHIC MATERIALS

Exercise 1: Understanding a Table (page 378)

1. The table is about the United States Presidential Election of 2000.
2. Candidate, Party, Popular Vote, Electoral Vote

Exercise 2: Finding Information on a Table (page 380)

1. person or individual
2. $14,776
3. Hispanic males had the largest increase, $2,327, increasing from $17,862 in 1999 to $20,189 in 2001.
4. In 2001, white males had the highest median per capita income, $30,240.

Exercise 3: Main Idea of a Table (pages 382–383)

1. **(2)** In every occupation shown on the table, women earn less than men. None of the other answer choices is based on the table.
2. **(4)** The data in the table shows that every group except the highest lost a percentage of its share of total national income. While choices (1) and (5) are supported by the graph, they are not as inclusive as choice (4). Choice (2) is contradicted by the data on the graph. While choice (3) is supported by the graph, it is more general and not as specific a match to the data as choice (4).

Exercise 4: Topic of a Graph (pages 384–385)

1. Graph 1 topic is about the changes in the Consumer Price Index for all urban consumers from 1993 to 2002.
2. Graph 2 topic is about the percent of Indian people who practice each of India's religions.

Exercise 5: The Main Idea of a Graph (pages 386–387)

Your wording may vary, but your answers should contain the same information as the answers below.

1. The longest bars are for Sub-Saharan Africa and South and South-East Asia, all of which are developing areas.
2. **(3)** Choice (3) is the best choice since the bars for the developing nations, especially in Sub-Saharan Africa, are longer than the bars for the developed nations. Choice (1) is a detail. Choice (2) is true, and would be a good choice for main idea if the bars were closer in size to each other. Choices (4) and (5) are not based on the graph at all.
3. This graph gives a general idea of how people on welfare spend their money.
4. Food, rent, and utilities. These items are the largest parts of the graph.
5. **(3)** Food, rent, and utilities are necessities. Most of the graph is taken up by these items. Choice (1) is true, but it is only a detail. Choices (2), (4), and (5) are not based on the graph.

Exercise 6: Reading Pictographs (page 389)

1. $200   Each of the symbols stands for $100.
2. San Francisco   Comparing the rows for the two cities, you can see that San Francisco has the shorter row.
3. **(4)** This choice pulls together all the information on the graph. Choice (2) is a detail. Choices (1), (3), and (5) cannot be proven by the graph.

Exercise 7: Reading Bar Graphs (page 391)

1. France   The bar for France is the only bar that stops between $22,000 and $24,000.
2. Ethiopia   It has the shortest bar.
3. Russian Federation   Of all the bars in the graph, it is the closest in height to Chile.
4. about $28,000   Given the degree of precision of this graph, answers between $27,000 and $29,000 are acceptable.

Exercise 8: Reading Line Graphs (page 393)

1. 1910   The lowest point on the graph is at the year 1910.
2. 70%   At 1960 on the horizontal scale, the data point is at 70% on the vertical scale.
3. (5)   The percentage has risen every decade.

Exercise 9: Reading Circle Graphs (pages 395–396)

1. 7.8%   The label for the Education segment is at the top right corner.
2. Economic development   Scanning the labels and percentages, you should pick out 4.3%.
3. Education   The education segment is 7.8% of the total. The criminal justice and public safety segment is smaller, 5.2%.
4. 31–40   This is the largest segment, 20.1% of the population.
5. 21–30   Among the age groups under 60 years of age, 21-30 is the smallest segment, 8.5%.
6. 11–20   Because these segments are almost the same size, you must read the percentages to answer the question correctly.

Exercise 10: Using a Map Key (page 400)

1. the Amazon River   This is the only river shown on the map in the northern part of Brazil.
2. Lake Mirini   It is at the bottom of the map, in the southernmost portion of Brazil.
3. the Equator   The mouth of the Amazon is on the northern coast of Brazil at the Equator.
4. Picó da Neblina   Two high mountains are marked on the map with the + symbol. Picó da Neblina has the higher elevation.

Exercise 11: Reading Historical Maps (page 402)

1. (3)   The Pawnee were in the region cutting through the center of the map. The key shows that the Plains Indians lived in this region.
2. (1)   The farthest northern parts of the map match the Inuit and Aleut section of the key.

Exercise 12: Chapter Review (pages 403–410)

1. (1)   With 710,760 deaths, heart disease was the leading cause of death in the U.S. in 2000.
2. (2)   Reducing the use of cigarettes would lower deaths from the four top causes. None of the other choices would have as great an impact.
3. (1)   The row of symbols for Texas is the longest row.
4. (3)   Although Nevada and Kansas have the same number of symbols, the actual numbers show Nevada with 6,150,000 and Kansas with 6,000,000.
5. (5)   The percentage of New Jersey residents living in cities of 100,000 or more dropped for each decade shown on the graph. The other choices cannot be proven by the graph.
6. (3)   The second bar is for 1970. The percent for that bar is 15.5%.
7. (1)   The topic is stated in the title.
8. (3)   The number of black elected officials is not declining. All the other statements can be supported by the graph.
9. (4)   The single most important source of income would be the largest of the slices, which is individual income taxes.
10. (3)   Find the slice marked "Social insurance and retirement receipts." It represents 38%.
11. (5)   The area around San Francisco matches the key for more than 100 persons per square mile.
12. (1)   Measure off 200 miles going straight up the map from San Diego. The area there matches the key for less than 25 persons per square mile.
13. (2)   Find the part of the key for slaveholding Union states. Then check each of the states that matches that part of the key. Only Kentucky is among the answer choices.

14. (4) Find Texas on the map. Then find the part of the key that matches Texas. That part of the key says "seceded Jan.-Feb. 1861."

15. (1) Find the regional boundary for west Tennessee. The only city shown in west Tennessee is Memphis.

16. (4) Find Nashville and look to the east. Knoxville is directly east of Nashville and is located on the Tennessee River.

CHAPTER 3
APPLYING INFORMATION IN SOCIAL STUDIES

Exercise 1: Applying Information in Everyday Life (page 412)

1. (4) The passage states that although anthrax can kill within three days, it can be successfully treated with antibiotics if they are started right away.

2. (2) The passage says that even though who she votes for will be secret, it will be known whether or not she and her neighbors vote. And if more of them vote, they will be more likely to be listened to by elected officials.

Exercise 2: Identifying Probable Outcomes (page 413)

1. (C), (D), (E)

2. (B), (C), (D)

Exercise 3: Identifying an Author's Prediction (pages 414–415)

1. (1) The author states that farms will get larger and larger and that small farms will continue to disappear.

2. (5) In the last sentence, the writer states that day-care centers in the workplace will become more common in the future.

Exercise 4: Making a Prediction Based on a Passage (pages 416–417)

1. (4) According to the passage, Haiti's roads are impassable, so they couldn't be used to transport farm goods.

2. (1) An improved electrical system would help Haitian businesses grow, especially outside the capital. Then the businesses could give more people jobs.

3. (3) DreamCatchers will be operating the casino, so DreamCatchers will manage employees, invest profits, and plan the casino's future. That leaves mostly service jobs for the Chukchansi.

Exercise 5: Applying Information in a Passage (page 418)

1. H The woman should go to the Department of Health and Human Services.

2. A The woman should go to the Federal Council on Aging.

3. R The man should find Rehabilitation Services.

4. yes The city should approve this project.

5. yes The city should approve this project.

6. no The city should not approve this project.

Exercise 6: Applying Social Studies Concepts (page 420)

1. (4) A truck would be the best way to deliver an appliance to a home since it is able to get to almost any home in America.

2. (5) An electronic transfer would be the best way to get money to family who live far away, since they would get the help almost instantly.

3. (3) Since Puerto Rico is an island and New York City is on the Atlantic Coast, either airplane or ship would be an option. Since six weeks is plenty of time for a ship to go from Puerto Rico to New York, a ship is the best choice.

Exercise 7: Applying Map Skills (page 422)

1. Take Route 5 south to Route 84, Route 84 east to Route 80, and Route 80 east.

2. Take Route 8 east to Route 10 and Route 10 east to El Paso.

3. The airport is on the Blue Line. North Station is on the Orange Line. Take the Blue Line to State and change to the Orange Line going north.

4. **(3)** Harvard is on the Red Line. The Science Museum is on the Green Line. The two lines intersect at Park St.

Exercise 8: Applying Information from Tables and Graphs (pages 424–425)

1. **(3)** The graph shows many women with children under six in the workforce. Day-care at their workplace is likely to appeal to these women.

2. **(1)** Since Mandarin is by far the most widely spoken language in the world, an English-Mandarin dictionary would have the potential to have the greatest number of sales.

Exercise 9: Chapter Review (pages 426–430)

1. **(4)** The passage says that the fields are preserved in case they are needed for food production in the future. Tobacco is not a food.

2. **(3)** The passage is referring to Governor Jeb Bush's command of Spanish and his willingness and ability to reach out to Hispanic voters. These are actions that any candidate can do.

3. **(2)** Boston, with the longest bar on the chart, is the most expensive of the cities listed.

4. **(4)** Memphis has the lowest cost of living of the cities listed, making it the most affordable of the cities.

5. **(5)** First find Rochester and Corning on the map. Then find the route that is closest to a straight line.

6. **(2)** First find Syracuse and Bath on the map. Then find the route that is closest to a straight line.

7. **(3)** Amendment 3 is the least relevant today. The United States government has never tried to house soldiers in private homes.

8. **(5)** Amendment 5 is the most relevant in this case since it deals with the general prohibition against holding someone without charges and the situations in which there are exceptions to this rule.

9. **(1)** Amendment 1 guarantees freedom of religion. The legal question then becomes whether or not the use of peyote is a religious practice.

10. **(3)** Vanessa Alexander was popular in Rickerton Park, and her opponent's campaign has only angered voters. It is reasonable to expect that she will win the election.

CHAPTER 4
ANALYZING SOCIAL STUDIES MATERIALS

Exercise 1: Putting Events in Sequence (page 433)
The correct order is 3, 2, 4, 1.

earlier
- Marshall discovers gold at Sutter's Mill.
- Marshall and Sutter test the stones to see if they are gold.
- Marshall sends gold seekers off to look for gold.
- Groups of men discover gold in the places where Marshall sent them.

later

Exercise 2: Using Dates to Identify Sequence (page 435)
The correct order is 1, 3, 2, 5, 4.

earlier
- Columbus discovers America.
- Cartier discovers the mouth of the St. Lawrence River.
- De Soto murders thousands of Native Americans at Mabila.
- Champlain establishes the fur trade with the Native Americans.
- Marquette and Joliet travel down the Mississippi River.

later

Exercise 3: Sequence in Graphs (page 437)

1. **(1)** Looking at the graph between 1965 and 1970 on the horizontal scale, you can see that the line goes up and then goes down.

2. **(4)** Choice (4) represents the pattern shown on the graph from 1962 to 1990. Choice (5) represents the pattern of the entire graph from 1962 to 2000 but the question is for the period 1962 to 1990.

Exercise 4: Sequence on Expedition Maps (page 439)

1. **(3)** Trace De Soto's route and look for a box that tells you where friendly Native Americans supplied food. That box is labeled 7 and it is connected by a line to the dot labeled Guaxulle.

2. **(4)** Continue to trace De Soto's route, looking for his death. Box 13, dated 21 May 1542, tells of De Soto's death.

3. **(5)** Scan the map to find the circle labeled Quizquiz. It is just below box 10, which tells you that De Soto discovered the Mississippi River there.

Exercise 5: Reading Maps of Historical Change (page 441)

1. T The Oregon Country became part of the United States in 1846. Mexico ceded most of the Southwest in 1848.

2. T The first major purchase shown on the map is the Louisiana Purchase in 1803. All the other new territories were added in later years.

3. F The Gadsden Purchase (1853) followed the Mexican Cession.

Exercise 6: Identifying Cause and Effect (page 442)

1. What happened? Colombia found itself in financial trouble
   Why did it happen? the wholesale price of coffee had dropped 25%

2. What happened? the American West developed rapidly after the Civil War
   Why did it happen? because of the railroads

3. What happened? oil prices increased dramatically
   Why did it happen? the OPEC oil cartel was formed in 1973

4. What happened? NASA conducted an investigation
   Why did it happen? the space shuttle Columbia broke apart on re-entry

Exercise 7: Cause and Effect in a Passage (pages 443–444)

1. **(3)** The third sentence of the first paragraph says that the king of Portugal asked Vespucci to go after reading Vespucci's false story.

2. **(1)** The first sentence of the second paragraph tells you this. The clue word *because* makes the cause-and-effect relationship very clear.

3. **(5)** Poor modern water supply and sanitation arrangements are blamed for many of the deadly diseases that are present in India.

4. **(2)** Slums is the only negative effect of industrialization described.

Exercise 8: Applying Cause and Effect (page 445)

1. B Laws banning discrimination against black voters led to a surge in the election of black officials.

2. C Under the Civil Rights Act, blacks and whites had to be treated the same in public places.

3. A Based on this decision, black and white children were segregated into different schools.

Exercise 9: Identifying Similarities (pages 446–447)

Your wording may vary, but your answers should contain the same information as the answers below.

1. They were both sites for slave trade and for the settlement of freed slaves. There is tension between the descendants of the freed slaves and the indigenous people, and they both have had brutal civil wars in recent years.

2. The slave trade was the dominant force that shaped both Sierra Leone and Liberia.

3. They are large islands, located not far off the coast of a major continent.

4. They both developed powerful economies and extensive international influence.

Exercise 10: Comparison and Contrast in Illustrations (page 449)

1. **T** To make sure this statement is true, you must check all the states to make sure none had an increase of less than 2%.
2. **F** Tennessee had a higher percentage, 64%.
3. **F** New York has always been much larger than Chicago.
4. **T** Both cities had about 3 million people.
5. **F** Chicago's population decreased between 1960 and 2000. Los Angeles gained population between 1960 and 2000.

Exercise 11: Fact or Opinion? (page 450)

1. **F** This statement is a fact that can be proven.
2. **O** The word *best* is a clue word that this statement is an opinion that cannot be proven.
3. **O** This statement is an opinion that cannot be proven.
4. **F** This statement is a fact that can be proven.
5. **O** This statement is an opinion that cannot be proven.
6. **F** This statement is a fact that can be proven.

Exercise 12: Facts and Opinions in a Passage (page 451)

1. **O** The word *best* is a clue word that this statement is an opinion that cannot be proven.
2. **F** This statement is a fact that can be proven.
3. **F** This statement is a fact that can be proven.
4. **F** This statement is a fact that can be proven.
5. **O** "Has been spared the chaos" makes this statement an opinion.
6. **O** "Have not had to endure the tyranny" makes this an opinion.
7. **O** The words *should not* are a clue word that this statement is an opinion that cannot be proven.
8. **F** This statement is a fact that can be proven.
9. **F** This statement is a fact that can be proven.
10. **F** This statement is a fact that can be proven.
11. **O** This statement is an opinion that cannot be proven.
12. **O** The word *should* is a clue word that this statement is an opinion that cannot be proven.

Exercise 13: Distinguishing Fact from Hypothesis (page 452)

1. **F** This statement is a fact that can be proven.
2. **F** This statement is a fact that can be proven.
3. **H** This statement is a hypothesis. Note that it says "probably because."
4. **H** This statement is a hypothesis. Note that it says "may be a cause."

Exercise 14: Finding the Author's Hypothesis (pages 453–454)

1. **(3)** In the last sentence, the author states that two- and three-bathroom houses are common because the extra bathrooms increase the resale value of a house.
2. **(5)** In the final sentence, the author states his hypothesis that governments need to protect the people who live in the world.

Exercise 15: Making a Reasonable Hypothesis (pages 455–456)

1. **(2)** The most plausible explanation is that the United States gained their trust by helping them rebuild their economies and establish democratic government, instead of using its victory to further humiliate them.
2. **(4)** In 1967, the doctors found that many people were hungry. The symptoms of the children probably occurred because they were not getting enough to eat.

Exercise 16: Chapter Review (pages 457–462)

1. **(2)** As the years passed, more cotton was grown in areas to the south and west (below and to the left) of the 1801 cotton-growing area.
2. **(3)** The area that matches the key for 1839 shows the growth in cotton land between 1801 and 1839. Large portions of these four states are in this area.
3. **(5)** Prussia (before 1866), Hanover (1866), Saxony (1867), Bavaria (1871)
4. **(1)** The passage states that Bismarck maneuvered the German states into three wars, all of which they won. This supports the hypothesis of military superiority. The other hypotheses are not supported by information given.

5. (1) The first paragraph tells you that a high-tech boom gets started by new companies offering new products. The last sentence of the passage tells you that the pattern described in the passage applies to all three high-tech booms.

6. (4) The last sentence of the passage lists the different products that created each boom.

7. (3) The three paragraphs describe these steps in order. The first paragraph talks about a new product being created when thinkers don't have enough to do in a slow period. The second paragraph describes the industry boom that follows. The third paragraph describes the industry going into a slump.

8. (2) In the last paragraph, the writer states, "Then the public's love affair with the product ends. . . . Then the boom is over."

9. (1) The line for the United States is the highest of all the countries for the entire period, and it increased the most during the period.

10. (4) In 1999, the line for Switzerland declined the most of all the countries listed.

11. (2) All the rights mentioned are in the American Bill of Rights, the first 10 Amendments to the United States Constitution.

12. (4) The cartoonist sees the new office as more of a threat to our civil liberties than to terrorists. He thinks that the office would undermine the Bill of Rights.

13. (3) Fisher heard about the ships by reading *The Treasure Hunter's Guide*. He put an extraordinary amount of time and money into his search. The evidence suggests that he was hoping it would pay off in valuable treasure.

14. (1) In the last two sentences, the author states that education was the key to success.

CHAPTER 5
EVALUATING SOCIAL STUDIES MATERIALS

Exercise 1: Is There Enough Information?
(page 464)

1. √ This statement can be proven by the information in the passage.
2. This statement cannot be proven.
3. This statement cannot be proven.
4. √ This statement can be proven by the information in the passage.
5. √ This statement can be proven by the information in the passage.
6. This statement cannot be proven.

Exercise 2: Using Information on a Map
(pages 465–466)

1. This statement cannot be proven.
2. This statement cannot be proven.
3. √ This statement can be proven by the information on the map.
4. √ This statement can be proven by the information on the map.
5. √ This statement can be proven by the information on the map.
6. This statement cannot be proven.

Exercise 3: Identifying Irrelevant Information
(page 468)
Your wording may vary, but your answers should contain the same information as the answers below.

1. The writer wants people to vote for Gil Cohen for mayor.
2. The irrelevant reasons are (1) he is more attractive than his opponent, and (2) he has spent over $100,000 of his own money to get elected.
3. The author of the letter has the same last name as the candidate she is endorsing. Voters should question if the author is a relative of the candidate.

Exercise 4: Using Information Correctly (pages 468–469)

1. **(3)** The last sentence tells you that this event raised millions of dollars to feed hungry Americans.

2. **(5)** The passage gives examples of Americans raising money for charitable causes.

3. **(4)** The third sentence of the passage tells you that affirmative action programs try to correct past prejudice. The passage does not contain enough information to prove any of the other choices.

4. **(3)** The second sentence tells you that in a kibbutz most things are owned by everyone as a group. The other choices are not mentioned in the passage.

Exercise 5: Recognizing Errors in Reasoning (pages 470–471)

1. Choice (1) shows good reasoning.
   Choice (2) shows an error in reasoning. There is no reason to believe that the government will help Mel's Auto Body Shop.

2. Choice (1) shows an error in reasoning. There is no link between the events of thirty years ago and now.
   Choice (2) shows good reasoning.

Exercise 6: Errors in Reasoning (pages 472–474)

Your wording may vary, but your answers should contain the same information as the answers below.

1. **(2)** The writer says he was doing much worse than he had been four years before, so he voted for Reagan.

2. The reasons he was doing badly—his wife dying, his children dropping out of school, his drinking, and losing his job—had nothing to do with the president or the government. These factors should not have influenced his vote.

3. **(4)** The passage states that the Germans thought that the British would not have the stomach to oppose them and the Japanese thought that the Americans would not have the will to fight.

4. Both Germany and Japan assumed that since both the United States and the United Kingdom valued economic prosperity over militarism, they would not respond when attacked and would be no match for their fighters. In both cases they were wrong. The British and the Americans both fought far better than Germany and Japan had expected.

5. **(1)** RCA appeared to think that the more different companies it owned the stronger it would be.

6. The problem with RCA's reasoning is that they bought businesses that were not related to their core business of electronics. RCA could not run the new businesses well, and the new businesses distracted RCA from its core business of electronics.

Exercise 7: Recognizing Values (pages 476–477)

1. **(2)** The passage says the codes were meant to protect students from prejudice, which in this case means unfair treatment on the basis of race or sex.

2. **(3)** The passage says that opponents think the codes violate the right to free speech, which is the right to express ideas.

3. **(3)** The caption of the cartoon tells you that the president would like to be free from the press, which would mean he would not be criticized by reporters and news writers. This would add greatly to his power.

4. **(1)** The cartoonist makes the president and his advisors look sinister as they talk about not liking the press. Since the cartoonist is part of the press, it is likely that he would value freedom of the press.

5. **(2)** The purpose of buying the old farm would be to save the land for education and recreation.

Exercise 8: Propaganda and Advertising (pages 479–481)

1. **(5)** The ad says that Chocorich is America's highest-quality candy, using only the finest chocolate and sugar. It implies that other candies are made from lower-quality ingredients.
2. Answers will vary.
3. **(1)** The ad implies that you will look like the muscle man in the "After" picture if you use this program. Men who want to look like a muscle man would be attracted to the ad.
4. **(4)** The ad implies that if you shop at Leslie's, you will look sophisticated.

Exercise 9: Political Propaganda (pages 482–483)

Your wording may vary, but your answer should contain the same information as the answer below.

1. They had slowed down six Soviet armies, and they had been "purified" by the defeat.
2. **(4)** Goebbels didn't want the Germans to think they were losing the war. If the real extent of the disaster were known, people might become angry with the German government and military leaders.
3. **(2)** The only thing the ad tells you about holistic medicine is that Americans across the country are trying it, and interest in it is rising. So the ad is arguing that you should use it simply because it's popular.

Exercise 10: Chapter Review (pages 484–486)

1. **(5)** There is no dark line from Jacksonville to Savannah, so there was no railroad. The other cities are connected, although some are not directly connected.
2. **(4)** All the train lines end just beyond the Mississippi. Anyone wanting to go farther west would have to travel another way.
3. **(2)** The passage says that Amnesty International watches out for human rights throughout the world.
4. **(3)** Since the purpose of the organization is to promote human rights, you would want to know if it was accomplishing that purpose. The other choices would not tell you whether it was.
5. **(4)** The passage describes the violent conflicts that rage in the world despite the efforts of the United Nations to keep the peace. The passage does not support the other choices.
6. **(5)** The first sentence tells you that the United Nations was founded to help nations solve their differences peacefully.
7. **(4)** The ad does not tell you much about Mr. Amorelli's ideas. You would want to find out more before you decide whom to vote for.
8. **(3)** Experience usually helps to determine what a person's work is worth. The other choices do not relate to what a person's work is worth.

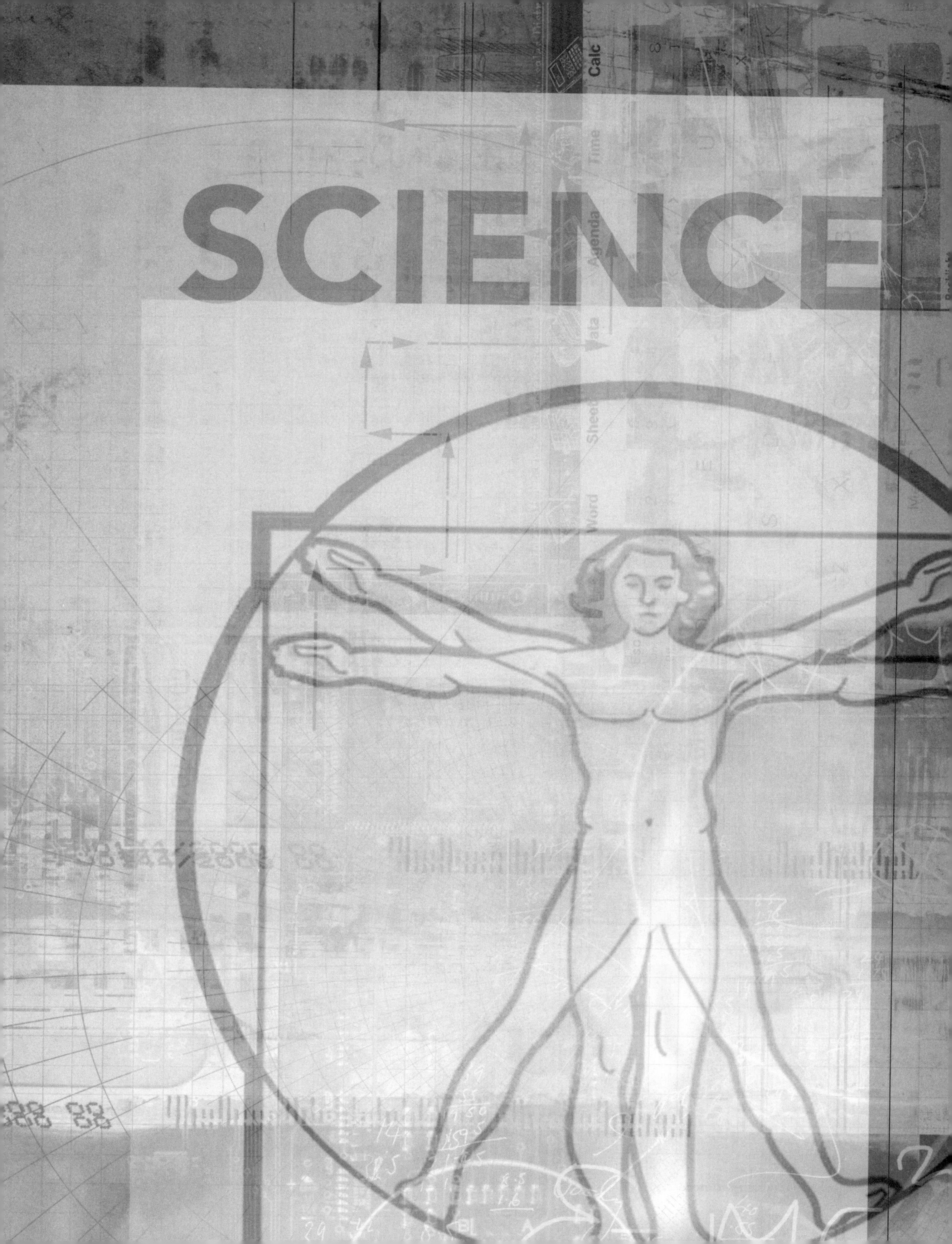
SCIENCE
Calc
Time
Agenda
Word

Science Knowledge and Skills

Meanings of Scientific Words

Scientists use a lot of big words, but most of them are made of smaller parts. If you understand the parts, you can often figure out the meaning of a word. Sometimes the way a word is used in a sentence is a clue to its meaning.

Compound Words

The easiest words to figure out are **compound words.** Compound words are made by combining two words. *Grassland*, *freshwater*, and *wildlife* are all commonly used compound words in science. A *heartbeat* is one beat of a heart. A *landfill* is low-lying land that is filled with garbage and then covered with more land.

EXERCISE 1

Compound Words

Directions: Read each definition. Then write the word it describes on the blank. Some words will not be used.

sunspot	horsepower	earthquake	rattlesnake
lifetime	spaceship	catfish	wavelength

1. The power of one horse in pulling an item: _____

2. A ship that travels in outer space: _____

3. A spot on the surface of the sun: _____

4. A shaking or trembling of the ground: _____

5. The length of a wave of light or sound: _____

6. A fish with "whiskers" like a cat: _____

Answers are on page 641.

Before and After: Roots, Prefixes, and Suffixes

Scientific words are often made from several word parts put together. The main part of a word is the **root**. A word part attached to the beginning of a root is a **prefix**. A word part attached to the end of a root is a **suffix**. Prefixes and suffixes change the meaning of the root. For example, the prefix *inter-*, meaning "among or between," can be added to the root *ocean*. The word *interocean* means "between oceans." The suffix *-logy*, meaning "the study of," can be added to the root *ocean*. *Oceanology* means "the study of oceans."

Roots, prefixes, and suffixes often come from Latin or Greek words or word parts. The following chart contains the meanings of some common word parts used in science and everyday English. Study the chart carefully.

Prefixes	Roots	Suffixes
anti- (against)	bio (life, living)	-al (having to do with)
di-, bi- (two, double)	cardio (heart)	-er, -or, -ist (person who does something)
inter- (among, between)	derm (skin)	-full (full of)
mal- (bad, ill)	hydro (water)	-itis (disease or inflammation of)
multi- (many)	graph, gram (writing)	-less (without)
post- (after)	meter (measure)	-log, -logue (talk, to speak)
pre- (before)	mono (one, single)	-logy (the study of)
re- (back, again)	micro (very tiny)	
tri- (three)	neur (nerves)	
un- (not)	nuclear (central, atomic)	
	therm (heat)	

You have learned that word parts can be put together to make whole words. In addition, the same word part can be put together with many different parts. For example, the root *bio* means "life" or "living." When a word contains the root *bio*, you know that the word has something to do with life or living things. *Biology* is the study of living things. *Biochemistry* is the chemistry of living things. A *biography* is a true story written about the life of another person. Similarly, the prefix *re-* means "back or again." The word *redo* means "to do over," and an *instant replay* shows a sports play over again.

Knowing the meanings of common word parts can help you figure out many new words. For example, what might an article about antinuclear protesters be about? The chart shows that *anti-* means "against" and *nuclear* can mean "atomic." *Antinuclear protesters* are probably people protesting against the use of atomic weapons. The chart can also help you figure out the meaning of the word *neuritis*. Since the root *neuro* means "nerves" and the suffix *-itis* means "disease," *neuritis* must be a disease of the nerves.

EXERCISE 2

Word Parts

Directions: Read each pair of sentences. Then use the chart of prefixes, roots, and suffixes, as well as words you already know, to figure out which word belongs in each sentence. Write the word that is missing on the line. Do not use a dictionary.

-logy (study of)—dermatology, hydrology, neurology

1. The study of the skin is called _____.

2. _____ is the study of the nervous system.

therm (heat)—thermometer, thermonuclear, biothermal

3. _____ is heat energy that comes from living things.

4. A _____ is an instrument that measures heat.

tri- (three)—trimonthly, tricycle, trifocals

5. A _____ magazine is published quarterly (every three months).

6. Glasses that focus at three different distances are _____.

cardio (heart)—cardiologist, cardiogram, cardiac

7. A written record of your heartbeat is a _____.

8. A doctor specializing in heart disease is a _____.

micro (tiny)—micrometer, microbiology, microfilm

9. The study of very tiny living things is called _____.

10. A _____ is used to measure very small distances.

Answers are on page 641.

Context Clues

Often you can figure out the meaning of a new word by looking for **context clues.** Context refers to the words and sentences around the unfamiliar word. Using context is easiest when the meaning of a new word is clearly stated. The following sentences, for example, tell the meanings of new words:

> Ichthyologists, scientists who study fish, may find the next solution to the world's hunger problem.

> One of the worst childhood diseases, scarlet fever, can now be controlled by antibiotics.

The first sentence explains that *ichthyologists* are scientists who study fish. The second sentence states that *scarlet fever* is a disease that children used to get. Notice that each explanation of a new word is separated from the rest of the sentence by commas. Sometimes the sentence does not give a complete definition. Even so, there may be **context clues** that suggest at least part of the meaning. Read the following sentence:

> She poured the mixture into the crucible and put it on the burner.

From this sentence you can tell that a *crucible* is a container in which things are heated.

EXERCISE 3

Using Context Clues

Directions: Read each sentence. Use context clues to figure out the meaning of the word in **boldface type**. Then write what you think the word means on the line. Do not look up the words in a dictionary.

1. The astronomer used her **astrolabe** to measure the distance between the two stars.

   An *astrolabe* might be _____.

2. Information sent into **cyberspace** can be viewed by computer operators around the world.

   Cyberspace might be _____.

3. Most plastics are only one color, but this one was **polychromatic**.

   Polychromatic probably means _____.

4. Cats, wolves, and dogs are all **carnivores**, but mice, rabbits, and horses prefer to eat grasses and grains.

   Carnivores are probably animals that eat _____.

5. **Hydroponic** farming makes it possible to grow vegetables in areas with no fertile soil.

   Hydroponic might be farming _____.

Answers are on page 641.

Understanding Scientific Language

Don't be discouraged if a science passage doesn't make sense at first. You may have to read it several times. You may need to figure out the meanings of scientific words, reread tough sentences, and put all of the ideas together. Read the following chart.

Steps for Reading Difficult Passages

1. Read until you come to a sentence that doesn't make sense.

2. Read that sentence again more slowly. Sometimes it helps to read it out loud quietly.

3. Look for words you don't know. Try to figure out their meanings using word parts and context clues. If necessary, look up words in a dictionary.

4. Look at the next few sentences for clues about the sentence you are working on. Only read as far ahead as needed for you to understand the confusing sentence.

5. Finally, read the sentence again. Use simpler words to be sure you understand the sentence.

6. Reread the whole passage once more at regular speed. This will help you to put all the ideas together.

Restating Ideas

One of the key steps in understanding a difficult sentence is being able to break the sentence into smaller parts and use simpler words. Read the following example:

> In considering the experimental results, it would not be wise to take too optimistic a view of the eventual usefulness of the new drug in the treatment of cardiac diseases.

First, define any words that are new to you, such as *optimistic, eventual*, and *cardiac. Optimistic* means "always expecting the best thing to happen." *Eventual* means "at the end" or "in the long run." The root in *cardiac* tells you that the word has something to do with the heart. Next, read the sentence piece by piece.

Original	Simpler Version
In considering the experimental results,	When you look at the results of the experiments,
it would not be wise to	you shouldn't
take too optimistic a view of the	expect too much
eventual usefulness of	in the future from using
the new drug in the treatment	the new drug to help people
of cardiac diseases.	with heart disease.

Finally, put the simpler version all together.

> When you look at the results of the experiments, you shouldn't expect too much in the future from using the new drug to help people with heart disease.

Put even more simply:

> The experiments don't prove that the new drug will help people with heart disease.

EXERCISE 4

Understanding Scientific Language

Directions: Rewrite the following sentences using simpler words. Use your knowledge of context clues and word parts and look up words in a dictionary as needed.

1. The effects of atmospheric pollution are among the most seriously adverse.

   _____

   _____

2. The generation of hydroelectric power was the primary development necessary to provide inexpensive residential electricity.

   _____

   _____

3. Children whose playthings provide intellectual as well as recreational experiences may be better adapted for scientific inquiry.

   _____

   _____

Answers are on page 641.

Using the Scientific Method

Emily is in a sound sleep, enjoying a recurring dream from her childhood. Suddenly, she is awakened by a shrill, piercing sound. Alertly recognizing the sound of a smoke alarm, she rolls out of bed and onto the floor. She instantly checks for signs of fire, but doesn't smell any smoke or see any flames flickering through the open door. Turning on the overhead light, Emily grabs her shoes and heads out. She searches the rest of the house for smoke or fire and is thankful to find neither. She checks outside the house but still finds nothing unusual.

From these facts, Emily guesses that the battery in the smoke alarm has run low. She finds a new battery and replaces the old one. The alarm itself remains silent, and the red indicator light signals that the alarm is working properly. Emily knows that she has solved the problem with the smoke alarm.

This example shows that an everyday person like Emily and a scientist have a lot in common. They both solve problems, and they do it mostly in the same way. First, both an everyday person and a scientist identify the problem. Then both collect all the facts that they can. Next, they make a careful guess, based on those facts, about what is really happening. Then they test the guess. Finally, they draw a conclusion from the results and decide whether the guess was right or wrong. The way a person and a scientist solve problems is the same. A scientist's way, however, has a special name—**the scientific method.**

The following chart shows the five steps Emily followed and the five steps of the scientific method. You can see how solving a problem is a lot like using the scientific method.

Solving the Mystery	The Scientific Method
1. Emily hears a smoke alarm and wonders if there's a fire.	1. Deciding the question
2. Emily searches the house for smoke or flames.	2. Finding the facts
3. Emily guesses that the battery in the alarm has run low.	3. Forming a hypothesis
4. Emily puts a new battery in the smoke alarm.	4. Testing the hypothesis
5. Emily concludes that her guess is right: The old battery had run low.	5. Deciding on a theory

Step One: Deciding the Question

Scientists usually decide what problems they want to work on; there are thousands of questions in our universe waiting for answers. People, on the other hand, usually try to find answers to problems as they occur.

It is important to read a question very carefully before you try to answer it. Read through a sample question and figure out what kind of answer the person is looking for.

Question 1. What is the average yearly snowfall in Nebraska?

1. Will the answer to this question be a word, a number, a place, or somebody's name?

_____

2. What unit of measure (inches, gallons, pounds, or whatever) will this answer probably be in?

_____

3. Where do you think you could find the answer to this question?

_____

For question 1, you should have figured out that the answer is a number. We know that snowfall is usually measured in inches. If you didn't know this, listening to the radio weather reports would help to answer question 2. You could probably find the answer for question 3 in a reading passage, a graph, or a chart—maybe in a newspaper or an encyclopedia. This is not the kind of information you would be expected to know on your own.

Now read another question.

Question 2. What would probably happen to people if all the green plants on Earth died?

1. Will this answer probably be in words or numbers?

_____

2. Where would you expect to find the answer to this question?

_____

The answer to question 1 will probably be in words. The question doesn't ask for a number. If you have studied science, you know how important green plants are, and you will be able to figure out the answer for question 2. You might also find information in a science reading passage.

Step Two: Finding the Facts

Have you ever assumed that something you heard or read was a **fact** but later learned it wasn't? A fact is something that can be proved with evidence. In science, evidence can be obtained by making an **observation**, or noting what you hear, feel, smell, taste, or see. Some observations are recorded in the form of a **measurement**, using a tool such as a ruler, a scale, or a thermometer.

FACT VS. OPINION TIP

Phrases such as *I think,* *I believe,* and *we should* are clues that an opinion is being expressed.

Sometimes what we think is a fact is really an **opinion**. An opinion is something a person *believes* to be true. Opinions often are based on a person's values, or personal beliefs about how to live one's life. Our values are things that we care about very much, but values cannot be proved right or wrong.

Read the following examples of opinions:

- Pizza tastes horrible.
- Women should work in any job they like.
- Blue is the best color.

You may agree or disagree strongly with some of these statements. You cannot, however, prove them right or wrong because they are opinions, not facts.

EXERCISE 5

Fact and Opinion

Directions: Write *F* before the statements that are facts—those that could be proved by observation or measurement. Write *O* before the statements that are opinions—those that are based on someone's values. Then write three sentences of your own and indicate if they are facts or opinions.

_____ **1.** Vancouver is a better place to live than Chicago.

_____ **2.** New York is ninety-two miles away from Philadelphia.

_____ **3.** Everyone should try to earn a high school diploma or a GED certificate.

_____ **4.** Eighty percent of employers surveyed said they would hire a job applicant with a diploma or GED certificate before hiring an applicant without one.

_____ **5.** Listening to loud music can damage a person's ears.

_____ **6.** Nuclear power plants ought to be shut down for the next five years.

_____ **7.** There have been several accidents at nuclear power plants in the past five years.

_____ **8.** _____

_____ **9.** _____

_____ **10.** _____

Answers are on page 641.

Step Three: Forming a Hypothesis

After scientists have collected all the facts they can find about a particular problem, they use those facts to make a careful guess about the solution. This guess is called a **hypothesis.** Two or more guesses are called **hypotheses.**

Scientists are not the only people who make hypotheses. We all make careful guesses, or hypotheses, about things every day. For instance, what might you **hypothesize**—or guess—if your child came home from school soaking wet? Read the following chart.

Fact: Your child came home from school soaking wet.

Hypothesis 1: It is raining outside.

Hypothesis 2: Your child walked through a sprinkler.

Hypothesis 3: Your child played with water balloons on the way home.

Every hypothesis is a best guess based on all the facts available. Make one hypothesis for the following situation:

Your washing machine won't work, and the light over your laundry table won't go on. What do you think has happened?

_____

_____

Would you be correct to guess that the washing machine is broken? No, because that doesn't explain why the light won't go on either. Your first hypothesis might be that something is wrong with the electricity.

EXERCISE 6

Everyday Hypotheses

Directions: Practice making hypotheses with these everyday situations. Write your hypothesis in the space provided.

1. During a big thunderstorm, your lights go off suddenly.

   Your hypothesis: _____

   _____

2. Bill, who works for you, has been asking for time off during hunting season, but you have had to turn him down. On the first day of the season, Bill's wife calls and says that Bill is too sick to come to work.

   Your hypothesis: _____

   _____

3. Your crew leader at work has left his job, and you have a good chance to be promoted to his position. Your boss calls you into her office, saying she has some good news for you.

Your hypothesis: _____

Answers are on page 641.

Fitting All the Facts

Most scientific hypotheses are based on more than one or two facts. Your doctor bases her diagnosis—her hypothesis about why you are sick—on many facts. She considers your temperature, your appearance, any symptoms, and your medical history.

A good hypothesis must fit all the facts available. A careful scientist never ignores a fact just because it doesn't fit her first ideas. Instead, she changes her ideas to fit all the facts.

EXERCISE 7

Choosing Hypotheses

Directions: Choose the hypothesis that best fits each set of facts.

1. A scientist had twelve identical green plants. He put three plants on a windowsill inside a room. He put three plants in a closet without a light. He put three plants outside on the ground. He put the last three plants outside in paper bags with air holes.

All the plants were given good soil and enough water. The plants on the windowsill and the plants outside in the open grew well. The plants outside in the bags turned yellow and grew poorly. The plants in the closet died. What hypothesis can be made?

(1) Green plants turn yellow due to disease.
(2) Green plants don't live for very long.
(3) Green plants need light to grow.
(4) Green plants cannot grow inside.
(5) Green plants grow well in closets.

2. Louis Pasteur, a famous scientist in the 1800s, made an important hypothesis about bacteria. He noticed that bacteria grew quickly in open jars of liquid, such as soup. Bacteria also grew in jars of soup that were sealed tightly so that no air could get in. However, bacteria didn't grow in jars that were sealed tightly, then boiled and kept sealed after they cooled. What was Pasteur's correct hypothesis?

(1) Bacteria cannot grow in jars.
(2) Bacteria must have air to survive.
(3) Bacteria grow only in soup.
(4) Bacteria can be killed by boiling.
(5) Bacteria can live in boiling liquids.

3. Janet kept track of the weather and the fuel oil used in her house. She made the following chart showing the facts.

Month	Average Temperature	Weather	Oil Used
September	45	Mostly rainy	60 gal
October	39	Sunny, some snow	90 gal
November	23	Rainy and snowy	140 gal
December	26	Mostly snowy	125 gal
January	20	Mostly sunny	160 gal

What did Janet discover about the amount of oil she burned?

(1) More oil was burned when it was not sunny.
(2) More oil was burned when temperatures were lower.
(3) More oil was burned each month as winter went on.
(4) More oil was burned whenever it snowed.
(5) More oil was burned during the holidays.

Answers are on page 641.

EXERCISE 8

Forming Hypotheses

Directions: Write a scientific hypothesis to fit each of the following situations.

1. Tests prove that a river is polluted with lead, mercury, and detergent. Upstream, past a town, the water shows signs of lead and mercury, but no detergent. Further upstream, past a factory, the water is clean and not polluted. Knowing that water flows downstream, write a hypothesis about where the detergent is coming from.

2. Carl had a two-inch magnet. He did an experiment to see what it would pick up. The results are listed below.

Picked up	**Not picked up**
1-inch steel paper clip	1-inch goldfish
wet iron nail	2-inch copper wire
3-inch steel wire	wet dollar bill

What kind of items can Carl's magnet pick up?

Answers are on page 642.

Step Four: Testing the Hypothesis

Once a scientist has made a hypothesis, he tries to test it—to check it out. This is the fourth step of the scientific method. The most common way for a scientist to check a hypothesis is to do an **experiment**.

In an experiment scientists work with groups of things, called **subjects**. He puts them in an artificial situation where everything is the same except the **variable**. A variable is the one thing he wants to test. He usually leaves at least one subject in its natural state. This natural subject is called his **control**. Then he records the results of his experiment. He checks to see if the results prove his hypothesis correct or not. It's easier to understand the parts of an experiment when we review an example from everyday life.

Imagine that a house painter has just learned about a new type of paint. He hypothesizes that it will keep its color better than the paint he usually uses.

He takes ten pieces of wood to test his hypothesis. These are his subjects. He paints five pieces of wood with the new paint and five with the old paint. The new paint is the variable. The pieces of wood with the old paint are the control group.

The painter leaves all of the boards together in his backyard for a month. When he brings the boards back in, he notices that the boards painted with the old paint have faded more than the boards with the new paint. These are the results of the experiment. The painter's hypothesis is correct: The new paint fades less.

In order to really prove his hypothesis, the painter must repeat the experiment with two new sets of boards to see if the results are the same. It would be even better if he had someone else repeat the experiment. Scientists will not accept the results of an experiment unless it is reproducible—that is, unless it can be repeated with the same results. This shows that the first results were not just a coincidence.

Below are the parts of the painter's experiment.

- subjects: the ten pieces of wood
- variable: the type of paint
- control group: the boards painted with old paint
- results: the boards with new paint faded less

Read the requirements for a good experiment.

- The subjects need to be similar, and there should be more than one subject in each group.

- All the conditions of the experiment should be the same except for the variable being tested.

- There should be a control group.

- The results should be reproducible.

If an experiment does not meet these requirements, the results are not **valid** and **reliable**. *Valid* means getting true results. *Reliable* means getting the same results when the experiment is repeated. When the results are not valid and reliable, the experiment is not very useful. You can see this for yourself by reading the following experiment. Can you figure out what is wrong with it?

A chef wanted to find out if egg whites could make his piecrust flakier. He made three pies using egg whites in the crusts and three pies without egg whites. As they baked, he noticed that the pies with the egg whites browned more quickly, so he took them out ten minutes early, leaving the other pies in for the full amount of time. When he served the pies, everyone said that the crusts of the first three pies were flakier. The chef decided that using egg whites will make his piecrusts better.

What's wrong with the chef's results? _____

_____

_____

The problem with the chef's experiment is that he didn't keep all the conditions the same. The variable he wanted to test was the use of egg whites, but he also used different cooking times for the two groups. Maybe it was the egg whites that made the crust of the first group of pies flakier; maybe it was the shorter cooking time. He can't be sure, so his experiment is not valid or reliable.

EXERCISE 9

Errors in Experiments

Directions: Explain what is wrong with each experiment. Choose from the list below and write your answer on the line.

- not enough subjects
- subjects not similar
- conditions of experiment not kept the same
- experiment not reproduced

1. A gardener wanted to know if Acme's new fertilizer would be good for his vegetables. He fertilized all his bean plants with Acme fertilizer but didn't put any fertilizer on his pepper plants. His beans didn't do well at all, but he got a good crop of peppers. He concluded that Acme fertilizer was no good.

2. A molding machine in a factory was not working very well. About a third of the time, the plastic squirt guns that it produced came out with a flaw in the handle. The repair mechanic adjusted the stamping pressure. Then she ran one gun through. It came out just fine, so the mechanic figured she had solved the problem.

Answers are on page 642.

Step Five: Deciding on a Theory

After a scientist has chosen a problem, collected the facts, formed a hypothesis, and tested it with several experiments, he is ready to decide if his correct hypothesis is a theory. A **scientific theory** is an idea or explanation based on the available facts and experimentation. Scientists are never absolutely sure about any of their theories because new facts discovered later can contradict the old theories. *To contradict* something means *to prove the opposite* of it.

Here are two scientific theories that were later contradicted.

Example 1   **Scientific theory:** Years ago scientists proved that the atom was one solid particle that could not be split.

Contradiction: Later, Einstein and others discovered two new facts: atoms can be split, and the splitting of atoms releases atomic energy.

Example 2   **Scientific theory:** Many years ago chemical companies proved that the pesticide DDT was perfectly safe.

Contradiction: Later, it was discovered that DDT caused the death of fish, birds, and some people. Now DDT is prohibited from use in this country.

Making Decisions

You already use the scientific method to solve problems in your life. When you have an important decision to make, for instance, you collect all the facts you can. Then you look at possible solutions—or hypotheses.

You try out these solutions one by one. Sometimes you just try them out in your head, saying to yourself, "What would probably happen if I did this? Or this? Or maybe that?" You might ask some friends for their opinions. If possible, you try out a solution in real life to see what will happen. Finally, you make your decision, but you don't know right away whether you have decided correctly. Just as in science, in real life there are very few guarantees.

You can use a variation of the scientific method when you take a test. After reading the test question, collect facts by reading the passage and studying any illustrations. Then read *every* possible answer. Consider each answer carefully to determine which one makes the most sense.

Chapter Review

EXERCISE 10

Review of the Scientific Method

Directions: Read this real-life example. Then answer the questions about each step in the scientific method.

Smallpox is a terrible disease that once killed thousands of people every year. By 1980 doctors around the world considered smallpox a disease of the past. This is mostly because of the work of an English doctor named Edward Jenner, who lived from 1749 to 1823.

When Jenner was a young doctor, an epidemic—a sudden spread of a disease—of smallpox broke out. He worked hard to save his patients, but many of them died. He noticed that milkmaids—the women who milked the cows on dairy farms—didn't seem to catch the disease. He decided to find out why.

1. As the first step in his process, what question do you think Jenner asked himself?

   _____

   _____

   Jenner talked to many milkmaids. He discovered that the women often caught a disease called cowpox from the cows. This disease caused spots like smallpox, but the spots were only on the women's hands. The disease wasn't very serious. No one ever died of cowpox. The remarkable thing was that no one who had had cowpox ever seemed to catch smallpox.

2. What facts did Jenner collect?

   _____

   _____

3. What hypothesis would you make if you were Jenner?

   _____

   _____

   _____

Jenner guessed that having cowpox somehow protected people against smallpox for the rest of their lives.

4. How do you think Jenner decided to test his hypothesis?

_____

_____

_____

_____

Jenner decided to check his hypothesis by putting cowpox germs on a needle and deliberately injecting them into people. After these people got over the cowpox, he watched to see if any of them got smallpox. He did this to several people, and none of them got smallpox.

Jenner's idea of deliberately giving people a mild disease to protect them from a serious disease was the beginning of modern vaccinations. At the time, though, many people did not like Jenner's idea. But when it became clear that many lives were being saved, more and more people came to get vaccinated, and Jenner became famous.

5. Based on the results of Jenner's experiment, what can you conclude about cowpox? Write your theory below.

_____

_____

_____

_____

_____

Answers are on page 642.

CHAPTER 2

Living Things

Restating and Summarizing

Many people have trouble understanding the kind of technical writing often found in science textbooks. This chapter will help you develop three reading techniques that can help you understand what you read: restating facts, summarizing, and finding the main idea.

Restating Facts

One way to check your understanding of what you have read is to **restate** it— to say the same thing in different words. You will often be asked to do this on tests. For example, a sentence from a reading passage might read as follows:

> **Sentence:** Researchers have found that your chances of getting heart disease may be lower if you eat fish oil.

If a test question asked you to choose a restatement of the sentence, you might choose the following:

> **Restatement:** Studies show that eating fish oil could help protect you against heart disease.

Notice that the sentence and the restatement mean the same thing, but they do not use exactly the same words. Therefore, in a test situation be sure to look for a restatement with the same meaning as the sentence in the passage.

To find out if you understand this idea, write the numbers from Group One before their restatements in Group Two.

Group One Sentences	Group Two Restatements
1. Luther Burbank was a very famous plant breeder.	_____ His plants helped to improve many people's diets.
2. He was one of the first people to breed hybrid plants.	_____ He was one of the most well-known plant breeders of his time.
3. He developed many of the plants that farmers grow today.	_____ Many important food plants were bred by Luther Burbank.
4. Many people eat better today because of Luther Burbank.	_____ He was one of the discoverers of hybrid plants.

The correct answers are *4, 1, 3, 2.*

EXERCISE 1

Restating Facts

Directions: Write a new sentence that says the same thing in different words.

1. If you don't smoke, you have less chance of getting lung cancer.

2. Many GED graduates are successful businessmen and businesswomen.

3. Nuclear energy is a powerful tool and a dangerous weapon.

4. Learning is often easier as you get older because you have more experience.

Answers are on page 642.

Summarizing

Another type of test question might ask you to **summarize** a passage. To summarize something is to put all the important points together in one short statement. The following facts are the important points from a passage:

- John decided to start his science experiment.
- He spilled the chemicals he was mixing.
- The Bunsen burner wouldn't light.
- When he finally turned in his results, they were all wrong.

Here is one way to summarize the facts:

Everything went wrong for John when he tried to do the science experiment.

Now you try summarizing. Read the following facts:

- Most snakes are not poisonous.
- Snakes eat many insects, mice, and rats that otherwise would destroy farmers' crops.
- We need snakes, just as we need other living things, to keep the natural balance of our world.

Which of the following is the best summary of the facts?

(1) Snakes eat insects, mice, and rats.
(2) Most snakes do more good than harm.
(3) Snakes drink milk and strangle small animals.
(4) Only farmers need snakes.
(5) Some snakes are poisonous.

The best summary is (2) because it covers all of the facts. According to the facts listed, (3) and (4) are not true. Both (1) and (5) are true, but they each deal with only one fact.

EXERCISE 2

Summarizing

Directions: Read each group of facts carefully. Then circle the letter of the correct answer.

- Florence Nightingale was one of the first people to understand that nursing had to be a professional job.
- When she went to nurse soldiers wounded in the Crimean War, she was shocked by the poor conditions.
- Most of the people working as nurses had no training.
- Florence Nightingale taught them basic ideas of cleanliness and nursing.
- Later, she went on to start one of the first real nursing schools.

1. Which of the following is the best summary of the facts?

   (1) Crimean War nurses had little training.
   (2) Soldiers need the best nursing care.
   (3) Florence Nightingale was a famous woman.
   (4) Crimean War hospitals were very bad.
   (5) Florence Nightingale made a big improvement in nursing.

- Aspirin can help stop minor pains such as headaches.
- Aspirin reduces the swelling in joint injuries such as sprains and can even ease the pain of arthritis.
- Because aspirin makes blood less likely to clot, it can sometimes be used to prevent heart attacks and strokes.

2. Which of the following is the best summary of the facts?

   (1) Aspirin has been used for a long time.
   (2) Everyone should use more aspirin.
   (3) Aspirin has many uses in modern medicine.
   (4) Aspirin is good for headaches.
   (5) Aspirin can prevent all heart attacks.

Answers are on page 642.

Finding the Main Idea

Have you ever read something interesting and then told a friend about it? If so, you probably described the writer's most important idea. The most important idea in a paragraph is called the **main idea**. Every **paragraph** is a group of related sentences. One of those sentences usually states the main idea. The other sentences in the paragraph are **details** that explain or prove the main idea. Read the following example:

> **Albert Einstein was a slow learner who turned out to be a true genius.** He didn't learn to talk until he was almost three. Later, he did very poorly in school, especially in mathematics. One teacher even said he was mentally disabled! But when he grew up, he developed the theory of relativity, which is the main scientific theory about nuclear energy. He became known as one of the greatest scientists of all time.

The main idea of this paragraph is the first sentence: *Albert Einstein was a slow learner who turned out to be a true genius.* The other sentences contain details that explain how this happened.

In many paragraphs the main idea will be the first sentence. However, sometimes the writer builds up the details and then puts the main idea at the end of the paragraph. Read the following example:

> Nancy kept watching the hands on the clock, but they never seemed to move. She hated the sound of the drill and the sight of the other equipment. The numbness in her mouth was beginning to feel uncomfortable. **Nancy could hardly wait for her dentist to finish her root canal.**

This time the main idea is the last sentence.

At other times, the main idea is a sentence in the middle of the paragraph. Read the following example:

> Women are working as doctors, veterinarians, and laboratory technicians. Some of the most respected science professors at large universities are women. **More and more women are working at scientific jobs that people used to think were only for men.** Several women have even become astronauts and flown in space.

Probably the most difficult type of paragraph is one in which the main idea is never really stated. The author just implies—or hints at—an idea by using details.

> She held her breath as the top of the skull came into sight. She knew it could be more than two million years old! Very carefully she brushed away the sand until she could lift the skull out. Her hands trembled as she realized that she was holding the oldest human bone she had ever seen.

The main idea of this paragraph is that *the woman was very excited about the old skull she had found.* The author never really states it, but the details that the woman held her breath, that she thought about the age of the skull, and that her hands trembled show you her excitement.

When you are asked to find the main idea, be careful to choose the most important idea about the whole paragraph.

EXERCISE 3

Finding the Main Idea of a Paragraph

Directions: In each of the next three paragraphs, underline the sentence that contains the main idea.

1. Cactuses are remarkable plants that live in one of nature's harshest environments. In place of regular leaves, they have needles that also serve as a good defense against hungry animals. Their stems are full of hollow cells that can store enough water to last for months. They can survive the great heat of the desert sun at noon and the cold of some desert nights.

2. What do all passenger cars have in common? They all are powered by an engine. Most car engines have round tubes called cylinders, and each cylinder contains a piston that is connected by a rod to a crankshaft. When gasoline burns in the cylinders, the gasoline explodes, causing the pistons to move back and forth. The motion of the pistons moves the rods, which turn the crankshaft. The rotating crankshaft is connected to a drive shaft that turns the car's wheels.

3. Allen has red eyes and a runny nose. He is sneezing and coughing, and his skin is all broken out in big, red, itchy patches. Does Allen have some horrible disease? No. In fact, Allen doesn't have a disease at all. He has an allergy. When you have an allergy, your body's defenses react strongly to something that is normally harmless, like dog hair or ragweed pollen. Allergies can be mild or very serious. Some people have even died from severe allergic reactions. Even though it is simply a reaction of your own body, an allergy can really make you miserable!

Answers are on page 642.

The Main Idea of a Passage

Test questions often ask you to find the main idea of a passage that contains more than one paragraph. Questions that ask you for the **best title** for a passage are also asking for the main idea.

You can use the same skills to find the main idea of a passage as you use to find the main idea of a paragraph. In a passage, each paragraph supports the main idea of the passage. To find the main idea of the passage, first find the main idea of each paragraph. These ideas will all be related and will point toward one overall idea for the entire passage.

Use the method described above to find the main idea of each paragraph that follows and then of the entire passage. Beneath each paragraph, write the main idea of that paragraph.

Many animals in Australia belong to a very old group of mammals called marsupials. Marsupials are unusual in that they raise their young differently than other mammals. Most marsupials give birth when their young are still very undeveloped. These tiny babies are often blind and hairless. They do not have fully developed arms or legs. They must live in their mother's pouch until they are ready to survive in the outside world. This way of raising young is not as safe as that of other mammals where the baby is carried inside the mother until it is ready to be born.

Main Idea: _____

Most marsupials are found only in Australia. These ancient animals were able to survive there because they didn't have the usual competition from more developed animals. Long ago, the ocean cut Australia off from the main part of Asia. After this separation, the more developed animals that evolved in Asia were unable to get to Australia because of the great distance across the ocean.

Main Idea: _____

In recent times, many new animals, like rabbits, pigs, and sheep have been brought to Australia. These animals are pushing out the marsupials. If we do not take action to save the marsupials, we may lose some of these interesting animals forever.

Main Idea: _____

The first paragraph explains that *many animals in Australia are marsupials: animals that give birth to babies that are very undeveloped.* The second paragraph states that *most marsupials are found only in Australia and have been able to survive there because other more developed animals could not get to Australia.* The main idea of the last paragraph is that *marsupials are now threatened by animals recently brought to Australia.*

Now put all these ideas together. Which of the following tells the main idea of the whole passage?

(1) All unusual animals need to be protected.
(2) Marsupials are unusual because of the way they raise their young.
(3) Many people want to save the marsupials.
(4) Marsupials can survive without any help from us.
(5) Marsupials, a unique group of animals, are now in danger.

If you chose (5), you are correct. This sentence covers all of the ideas in the passage. Choice (1) is too broad; the passage is not about all unusual animals, just marsupials. Choice (2) is too narrow; the passage does say that marsupials raise their young in an unusual way, but that is not all it says. Choice (3) is probably true, but it is not mentioned in the passage. Choice (4) is false, according to the passage.

EXERCISE 4

Finding the Main Idea of a Passage

Directions: Practice choosing the main idea of a passage. Circle the number of the best answer. Be careful not to choose an answer that is too broad or one that covers only part of the passage.

About 900,000 children in the United States are suffering from lead poisoning. Why are the numbers so high? Years ago, before the dangers of lead were known, paint manufacturers used lead in their paints. People used the leaded paint to cover the walls, doors, and windows in their homes. Today, every time someone opens a painted window or door in an old house, a fine dust of lead scrapes away, flies through the air, and settles onto other surfaces. This puts people, especially children, in danger of getting lead poisoning. Children crawl around on the floors, grasp windowsills and other surfaces, and then put their fingers and hands in their mouths.

Lead is highly toxic when eaten or inhaled. It is absorbed by the red blood cells and carried to all parts of the body. It builds up in soft tissues such as the liver and kidneys. Even worse, it attacks the central nervous system. Lead slows down the development of nerves. It harms parts of the brain related to memory, movement, thought, and reasoning. Lead can also cause anemia, hearing loss, spasms, coma, and death. People living in old houses and apartments need to be aware of the dangers of lead poisoning.

1. This passage is mainly about

   (1) the number of children suffering from lead poisoning
   (2) the problems with opening and closing windows
   (3) why paint manufacturers put lead in their paint
   (4) some causes and dangers of lead poisoning
   (5) how lead attacks the central nervous system

2. The best title for this passage would be

   (1) Warning Your Children About Lead
   (2) Keep Your Children's Hands Clean
   (3) What You Should Know About Lead
   (4) How to Paint Old Houses
   (5) Four Memory Tips That Work

Answers are on page 643.

Plant and Animal Cells

We share Earth with millions of other living things, from the smallest bacteria to the huge blue whale. Many of these creatures affect our lives directly. All of them have some of the same needs as human beings: to find food, to escape enemies, and to reproduce. When we learn about other living things, we also learn something about ourselves.

Cells

Did you know that you are made of millions of tiny units called **cells**? In fact, every living thing is made of cells. Cells are so small that you can see them only through a microscope; there are tens of thousands of cells in the tip of your little finger alone. Some cells make up large, multicellular beings like yourself. Other cells live on their own as one-celled creatures.

There are many different types of cells. A nerve cell in your brain is very different from a muscle cell in your arm. A human cell is even more different from a cell in the trunk of an oak tree. Still, there are some things that are alike in all cells.

Animal Cells

The diagram below shows an animal cell. Every cell—both animal and plant—has a **nucleus**, which looks like a dark spot, usually near the center of the cell. The nucleus is like the brain of the cell. It controls most of what happens inside the cell. Inside the nucleus are **chromosomes** that carry the directions—or blueprints—for making new cells.

ANIMAL CELL

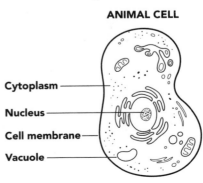

Cytoplasm

Nucleus

Cell membrane

Vacuole

The **cell membrane** is a thin wrapping around the outside of the cell. The cell membrane holds the cell together. It keeps out many things that could harm the cell, while letting in things the cell needs, such as food and oxygen. The inside of the cell is filled with **cytoplasm**, a clear, jelly-like liquid. The open space in the cytoplasm is called a **vacuole**. Vacuoles store water and food for the cell.

Plant Cells

A plant cell is similar to an animal cell, but there are some important differences. All plant cells have a **cell wall** around the outside of the cell membrane. This wall is made of **cellulose**, a stiff material that helps plants keep their shape. Also in plant cells, a large vacuole often takes up much of the space inside the cell.

PLANT CELL

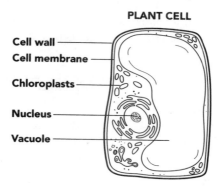

Cell wall
Cell membrane
Chloroplasts
Nucleus
Vacuole

In most plant cells there are also small oval objects called **chloroplasts**. The chloroplasts contain a green chemical called **chlorophyll**, which is the chemical that helps green plants make their own food. Animal cells do not have cell walls or chloroplasts, and no animal can make its own food.

EXERCISE 5

Cells

Directions: Match the word with its definition.

_____ **1.** cell membrane   **a.** contain chlorophyll

_____ **2.** cell wall   **b.** jelly-like liquid inside cells

_____ **3.** cellulose   **c.** carry blueprints for new cells

_____ **4.** chloroplasts   **d.** directs most cell activities

_____ **5.** chlorophyll   **e.** stores food and water for the cell

_____ **6.** chromosomes   **f.** holds animal cells together

_____ **7.** cytoplasm   **g.** stiff material in cell walls

_____ **8.** nucleus   **h.** chemical that helps plants make food

_____ **9.** vacuole   **i.** stiff structure around plant cells

10. Which of the following describes a difference between plant and animal cells?

    (1) Plant cells have cell walls; animal cells don't.
    (2) Plant cells can't move; animal cells can.
    (3) Plant cells live in water; animal cells don't.
    (4) Plant cells have a nucleus; animal cells don't.
    (5) Plant cells have vacuoles; animal cells don't.

Answers are on page 643.

Viruses and Bacteria

Infectious diseases—diseases caught from someone else—are caused by microbes. A **microbe** is a living thing that is too small to be seen without a microscope. Some types of microbes invade your body and make you sick.

Three Main Types of Microbes

Virus

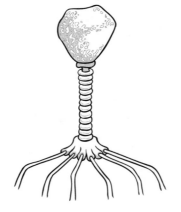

A **virus** is the smallest of the three main types of microbes. Unlike the other types, a virus is not a cell. A virus lives by getting inside a cell in your body and forcing that cell to make hundreds of copies of the virus. Eventually, all the copies burst out of the cell and go looking for other cells to invade. Colds, the flu, and the measles are a few diseases caused by different types of viruses. Some scientists think that viruses may even cause some kinds of cancer.

Viruses cannot be killed by antibiotics or other medicines. If you go to the doctor with a bad cold, he can't give you an antibiotic to make it go away faster.

Bacteria

Bacteria are microbes that consist of one cell. Different kinds of bacteria cause different diseases, such as strep throat, tetanus, and tuberculosis. Today, many bacteria can be killed by penicillin and other antibiotics. With antibiotics, many diseases that were once very serious can now be cured.

Not all bacteria cause diseases. Some bacteria are actually helpful. Bacteria are needed to break down dead plants and animals in nature. There is even one kind of bacterium that lives in your intestines and helps your body produce certain vitamins.

Protozoan

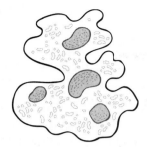

A **protozoan** is a microbe that consists of a single cell. A protozoan is larger than a bacterium cell. If you have looked at a drop of pond water through a microscope, you have probably seen protozoans, such as amoebas and paramecia, swimming around in it. Although most protozoans are harmless, malaria and some forms of diarrhea are caused by more dangerous types of protozoans.

Viruses, bacteria, and protozoans are all around us, so why aren't we sick all the time? One reason is that a person's body builds immunity to a disease by creating defenses against microbes it has fought before. One way to build immunity to a disease is to catch it. A better way is to get a shot, called an **immunization** or a **vaccination**, from your doctor. The doctor puts a small number of dead or weakened germs into you. This makes your body create the same defenses it would if you had the real disease, but you don't really get sick. It is very important to make sure children get all of their immunization shots because those shots protect them from many diseases.

EXERCISE 6

Viruses and Bacteria

Directions: Write the word that best completes each sentence.

microbes	immunity	viruses
bacteria	vaccination	protozoans
immunization		

1. Diseases can be caused by problems inside your body or by

   (a) _____ invading from outside of your body.

   Three types of microscopic living things are **(b)** _____,

   (c) _____ , and **(d)** _____ . Your

   body builds up some protection, called **(e)** _____,

   to diseases it has fought before. A shot that causes your body to

   build up protection against a disease is called an **(f)** _____

   or a **(g)** _____ .

2. Which of the following is the main idea of the passage that follows
   the chart?

   (1) Doctors have medicines to cure disease.
   (2) Immunizations can be given by your doctor.
   (3) Many diseases can be prevented.
   (4) People should get immunized to protect against disease.
   (5) Immunizations will make you sick.

Answers are on page 643.

Photosynthesis

Unlike animals, plants have the ability to make their own food. Without plants, there would be no food on Earth. Since animals cannot make their own food, they must eat plants or other animals to survive.

Plants make food using a process called **photosynthesis**. They use energy from the Sun to change carbon dioxide and water into food. Carbon dioxide is a gas taken from the air, while the water that plants use. comes from the soil. Plants carrying out photosynthesis also give off oxygen, which all animals, including people, need to breathe.

Photosynthesis takes place only in green plants. These plants contain cells that have a green substance called **chlorophyll**. Scientists have not been able to figure out how to perform photosynthesis in a laboratory. It takes place only in living, green plants.

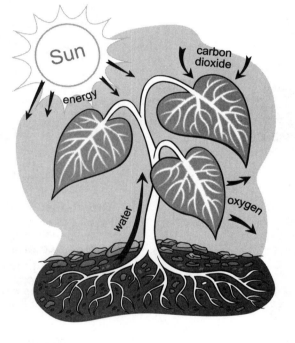

The most advanced plants are members of either the fern family or the seed-bearing plant family. Plants in both of these families use chlorophyll to make their own food.

Less advanced plants called **fungi** cannot make their own food because they have no chlorophyll in their cells. They must live off other living things—often things that are dead or decaying. Molds, mildews, and mushrooms are all types of fungi. Some fungi are helpful to people, like the yeast that makes bread rise. Other fungi, like the fungus that causes athlete's foot or the molds that spoil food, are harmful.

The simplest plants are called **algae**. Some algae have only one cell; others have more than one cell. Algae live in water and contain chlorophyll so they can make their own food.

Fungi

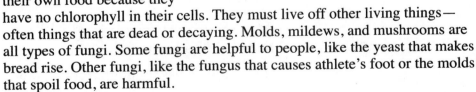

Algae

EXERCISE 7

Photosynthesis

Directions: Read each of the following statements. Circle *T* if the statement is true or *F* if the statement is false.

T F **1.** All fungi are harmful to people.

T F **2.** Oxygen is given off during photosynthesis.

Directions: Choose the best answer for each question.

3. Which of the following do green plants need for photosynthesis?

  (1) energy, water, and carbon dioxide
  (2) water, carbon dioxide, and oxygen
  (3) energy, water, and soil
  (4) energy, carbon dioxide, and oxygen
  (5) energy, water, and oxygen

4. Which of the following best summarizes the passage about plants?

  (1) Some plants make food spoil.
  (2) Plants get or make their food in different ways.
  (3) There are many types of one-celled plants.
  (4) Animals get their food by eating plants and other animals.
  (5) The oxygen released during photosynthesis fights air pollution.

Answers are on page 643.

Classification of Animals

Scientists believe that when Earth was formed, it was a ball of hot, molten—or melted—rock and gases. As Earth began to cool, clouds formed and the first rain fell. The low spots on Earth filled with water and became oceans.

Fossils, the preserved remains of dead animals and plants, helped scientists develop the idea of **evolution**. Evolution is a theory that explains how complex forms of life develop from simpler forms. Fossils started to be formed billions of years ago when simple plants and animals were trapped or died in mud or sand. Over the centuries the mud or sand turned to rock, and the remains were preserved.

Fossils show that life began in the oceans, about 3½ billion years ago. The first living things were very simple beings such as viruses and bacteria. About 3 billion years ago the first true plants developed. These were one-celled algae that could carry out photosynthesis. Much later, about 1 billion years ago, simple one-celled animals developed and fed on the plants. Gradually these single-celled creatures grouped together in colonies. These became the first many-celled plants and animals. Fossils of these more developed plants and animals have been found in rock and tar, as well as in amber, which is ancient tree sap that has hardened to stone.

Early Animals

The first many-celled animals lived in the sea. They were all **invertebrates**—animals without backbones. There are many invertebrates still living today, such as insects, worms, crabs, and jellyfish. The first **vertebrates**—animals with backbones—were fish, which appeared about 550 million years ago. All other vertebrates are descended from fish.

About 400 million years ago, the first descendants of fish crawled out of the water and onto land. These were early **amphibians**. The amphibians had to stay close to the water because they laid their eggs in water. The eggs hatched into tiny creatures that swam with fins and breathed underwater with gills just like fish. When they grew older, these creatures lost their fins and gills, grew legs and lungs, and went out onto the land. You can watch the same thing happening today when tadpoles change into toads or frogs.

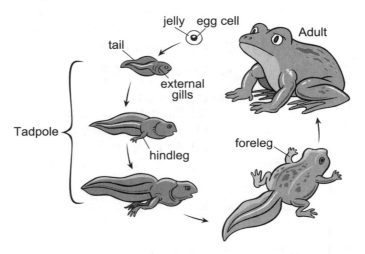

The next animals to develop, more than 250 million years ago, were **reptiles**. Some of the most amazing reptiles that ever lived were the giant **dinosaurs**. There were so many dinosaurs and other reptiles on Earth during this time that we call this period the **Age of Reptiles**.

Snakes, turtles, and alligators are all reptiles that are alive today. Reptiles look similar to amphibians, but they have scales instead of smooth skin, and they lay their eggs on land rather than in water. Reptiles are **cold-blooded**. This means that they need the sun's heat to keep their bodies warm. A reptile **embryo**—the not-yet-born form of an animal—develops inside the egg. The egg has a tough outer covering to preserve moisture. A reptile does not have gills during any stage of its life. Instead, reptiles breathe through lungs.

Birds and Mammals

During the last part of the Age of Reptiles, while dinosaurs still existed, two new types of animals began to be seen. **Birds** developed from some of the smaller two-legged dinosaurs. **Mammals** were small creatures similar to mice that developed from reptiles that lived before the dinosaurs. Birds and mammals had an advantage over the reptiles; they were **warm-blooded**. This meant that their bodies stayed at a constant temperature. To help their bodies do this, birds developed feathers, while mammals developed hair. Both of these are much better insulators than scales. This meant that birds and mammals could survive in a colder climate than reptiles.

Like reptiles, birds lay eggs with shells that are tough enough to protect the developing embryo inside. Mammals developed a whole new way of reproducing. The female mammal carries the embryo inside her body until it has grown enough to survive in the outside world. After giving birth, she feeds her young on milk that she makes in her own body. This way of reproducing is safer than laying eggs because the young are better protected.

About 70 million years ago, the dinosaurs and most of their relatives suddenly died out. No one knows exactly why, but some scientists think the cause was a change to cooler, drier weather over most of Earth. Only a few families of reptiles survived, and the **Age of Mammals** began.

The first mammals changed and developed into many of the animals we see today. Every animal that gives live birth and feeds its young with milk is a member of the class of mammals.

The final part of the story began only about 2 million years ago with the coming of the first human. **Humans** are mammals, since we give birth to live young and feed them with milk. We belong to the primate **order** in the **class** of mammals, along with monkeys and apes. Order and class are two ways scientists classify all living things. To understand better how humans are related to other animals, look at the part of our family tree below.

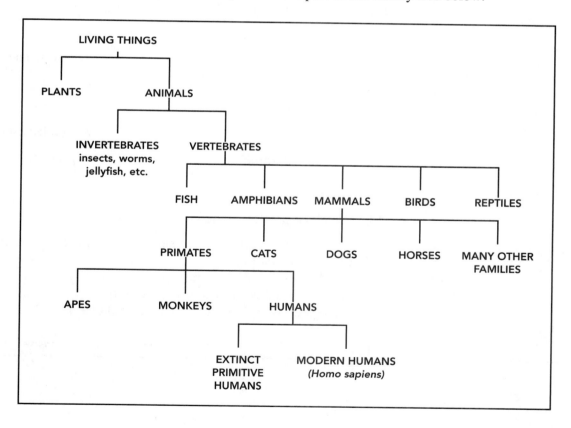

EXERCISE 8

Types of Animals

Directions: Match each word with its definition.

_____	1.	animals that feed their young with milk
_____	2.	animals that live first in water, then on land
_____	3.	animals without backbones
_____	4.	animals with scales that lay eggs on land
_____	5.	animals that breathe with gills
_____	6.	animals with backbones
_____	7.	animals with feathers

a. invertebrates

b. vertebrates

c. fish

d. amphibians

e. reptiles

f. birds

g. mammals

Directions: Match each animal with the group to which it belongs.

_____	8.	invertebrate
_____	9.	fish
_____	10.	amphibian
_____	11.	reptile
_____	12.	bird
_____	13.	mammal

a. cow

b. rattlesnake

c. robin

d. guppy

e. bumblebee

f. bullfrog

Directions: Circle the number of the best answer.

14. Which of the following describes evolution?

(1) the development from simple to complex living things
(2) a very fast process
(3) the growth of an embryo
(4) an animal with gills instead of lungs
(5) a process scientists no longer believe in

Answers are on page 643.

Genetics

We all know that children tend to look like their parents, but why? The science that studies this question is called **genetics.** It is the study of how traits are **inherited**—or passed along—from parents to children.

Every cell in your body contains a kind of blueprint of the plans for your whole body. Inside the nucleus of each cell are tiny threadlike structures called **chromosomes.** The chromosomes are made of **genes** strung together like beads. Each pair of genes carries the code for a certain trait. **Traits** are things such as the color of your hair or eyes and the size and general shape of your body.

The simplest one-celled plants and animals **reproduce** by splitting. For example, each chromosome in a bacterium's nucleus splits into two identical copies. Then the nucleus splits, with one copy of each chromosome going into each new nucleus. Finally, the whole cell splits into two bacteria. Both bacteria start growing again until each of them is the same size as the original cell. This is called **asexual reproduction.** The diagram below illustrates the stages of asexual reproduction.

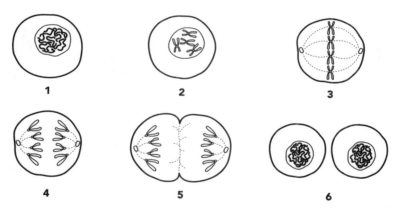

More advanced plants and animals, such as humans, reproduce sexually. A male cell and a female cell must combine to form the first cell of the new being. This new being gets half its chromosomes from each parent. This is called **sexual reproduction.** Sexual reproduction allows for more variety. This is because the new being will inherit characteristics from both its father and its mother. It will not be an exact copy of either parent.

An early genetic experiment was done by Gregor Mendel who first investigated the basic facts of genetics. He crossed a tall pea plant with a dwarf pea plant. Each of the **offspring**—the new plants—received a gene for tallness from one parent and a gene for shortness from the other. Plants with mixed parents like this are called **hybrid** plants. This diagram shows the results of Mendel's experiment.

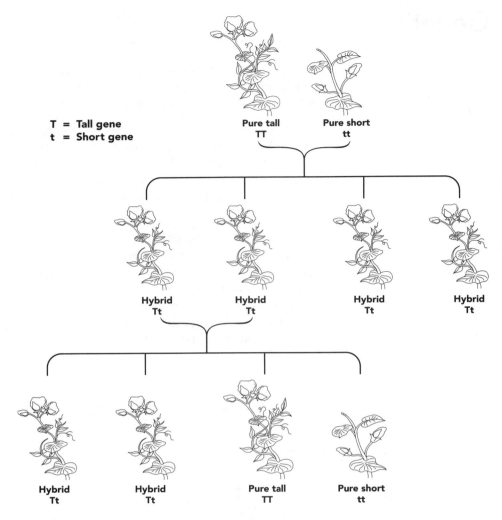

T = Tall gene
t = Short gene

Pure tall TT   Pure short tt

Hybrid Tt   Hybrid Tt   Hybrid Tt   Hybrid Tt

Hybrid Tt   Hybrid Tt   Pure tall TT   Pure short tt

Strangely enough, the entire first generation of new plants looked tall, even though each plant had one gene for shortness. The gene for tallness is **dominant**. This means that the gene for tallness will always override the gene for shortness. The gene that is not dominant, in this case the gene for shortness, is called **recessive**.

As you can see in the diagram, if two of the hybrid plants are crossed, one-fourth of the offspring will be pure short (tt). This is because they have inherited two genes for shortness, one from each parent. Half of the offspring will be tall but carry a hidden gene for shortness (hybrid Tt). The last fourth will be pure tall plants (TT)—plants that carry both genes for tallness.

Inheritance in people works the same way, although it is more complicated. Sometimes more than one set of genes controls a certain trait, such as skin color.

In humans, many inherited diseases, such as juvenile diabetes and Tay-Sachs disease, are the result of recessive genes. This means that a person could be healthy yet carry a dangerous gene. If that person marries another person with the same recessive gene, one or more of their children could get both recessive genes. Therefore, their children could have the disease. People whose families show any of these diseases often have their genes checked before they have children. This is called **genetic counseling**.

EXERCISE 9

Genetics

Directions: In hamsters, dark eye color is dominant and light eye color is recessive. First, fill in the following gene chart showing what happens when a dark-eyed hamster with two (DD) genes mates with a light-eyed hamster with two (dd) genes. Then answer the questions that follow.

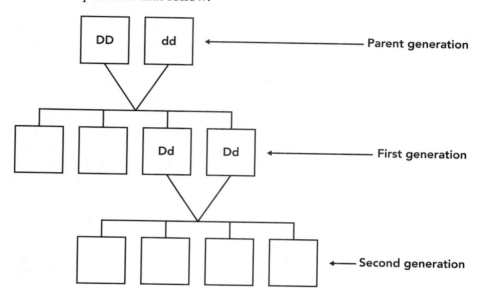

1. In the first generation of hamsters, how many would likely have dark eyes?

   _____

2. In the first generation, how many hamsters would carry one recessive gene for light eyes?

   _____

3. Two of the first-generation hamsters mate with each other. How many of the offspring out of every four would likely have light eyes, and how many would have dark eyes?

   _____

4. The second-generation hamsters that have dark eyes carry the dominant gene. How many of these second-generation dark-eyed hamsters would carry a gene for light eyes?

   _____

Answers are on page 643.

Chapter Review

Directions: Read each passage carefully. Then circle the letter of the best answer to each question.

Questions 1 and 2 are based on the following passage.

Vaccines play an important role in keeping children healthy. However, some people are questioning whether the pertussis—known as whooping cough—vaccine, which is part of the standard DPT shot given to babies, is being used safely. A group called **D**issatisfied **P**arents **T**ogether claims that too many children are permanently hurt by reactions to this shot. The American Medical Association admits that pertussis vaccine can cause bad reactions, but it says that the risk of a bad reaction is very small. Many people would like to see the government investigate this problem. In fact, some drug companies are working to make a safer vaccine. In the meantime, some doctors say that if a child has a severe reaction to a DPT shot, the child probably shouldn't be given any more pertussis vaccinations.

1. Which of the following would be a safe and effective way for the government to investigate this problem?

   (1) Test the vaccine on different groups of babies.
   (2) Ask the companies that make the vaccine if it is safe.
   (3) Require doctors to keep records of all reactions to the vaccine.
   (4) Stop the shots and see how many children get sick.
   (5) Take an opinion poll to see how many people think the shots are dangerous.

2. Which of the following do some doctors recommend if a child has a bad reaction to a DPT shot?

   (1) The child should delay getting the next shot.
   (2) The child should not get any more pertussis vaccine.
   (3) The child should get the next shot earlier than usual.
   (4) The child should not receive shots of any kind.
   (5) The child should continue the shots on schedule.

Questions 3 and 4 are based on the following passage.

The word *dinosaur* comes from two Greek words, *deinos* (terrible) and *sauros* (lizard). During the long Age of Reptiles dinosaurs dominated Earth. There were many dinosaurs that lived in swamps and ate plants. One of these, the huge apatosaurus, was over 90 feet long and weighed 70,000 pounds. There were terrifying meat-eating dinosaurs, such as the allosaurus—50 feet long, 16,000 pounds—and its even larger cousin, the tyrannosaurus—50 feet long, 20,000 pounds. There were dinosaurs that glided through the air, like the pterosaurs, and dinosaurs that swam in the ocean. There were even small 3-foot-long dinosaurs that ran around on two legs. They probably lived by eating the eggs of their larger relations.

3. Which of the following is the largest dinosaur mentioned in the passage?

(1) apatosaurus
(2) allosaurus
(3) tyrannosaurus rex
(4) pterosaur
(5) archaeopteryx

4. Which of the following is **not** true according to the passage?

(1) Dinosaurs were reptiles.
(2) Dinosaurs lived during the Age of Reptiles.
(3) Some dinosaurs could swim.
(4) Some dinosaurs were smaller than people.
(5) Dinosaurs ate only meat.

Questions 5 and 6 are based on the following passage.

Some genetic problems are caused by mutations. A mutation happens when radiation, chemicals, or chance causes a sudden change in a gene. The offspring inheriting that gene will be different from its parents in some way. Some mutations are harmful, like the one that causes some horses to be born with one short leg. When a mutation is life-threatening, the mutated creature will probably not survive to breed, so the damaged gene will not be passed on. Once in a while, a mutation is helpful—for example, one mutation made a hen lay stronger eggshells than normal. A helpful mutation makes a creature more likely to survive and have offspring that will inherit the new gene. This is called natural selection, and it is one of the ways evolution takes place.

5. Why is a harmful mutation **not** usually passed on in animals?

(1) The animal doesn't want to pass it on.
(2) The animal lays stronger eggs.
(3) The animal has a shorter leg.
(4) The animal is chosen by natural selection.
(5) The animal probably will not survive to breed.

6. Which of the following describes the idea that successful creatures will have more offspring and pass on their good genes?

   (1) mutation
   (2) radiation
   (3) survival
   (4) natural selection
   (5) breeding

Questions 7 and 8 are based on the following passage.

After a plant is grown, photosynthesis enables the plant to make its own food. But how does a green plant grow from a seed that is planted in soil? A seed contains a young plant called an embryo. Stored food is also inside a seed. The embryo is inactive, but if placed in a warm, moist environment, the embryo will germinate, or start to grow. The germinating embryo gets the energy it needs for growth from the food stored inside the seed. When the stem of the plant grows green leaves, the plant can start making its own food through photosynthesis.

7. Which of the following states the main idea of this passage?

   (1) Green plants make their own food through photosynthesis.
   (2) Seeds can be planted in a warm, moist environment.
   (3) A seed develops into a green plant that can make its own food.
   (4) A germinating embryo needs sunlight and water.
   (5) Seeds contain food stored inside them.

8. Which of the following describes the growth of a seed into a green plant?

   (1) photosynthesis
   (2) embryo
   (3) germination
   (4) warm, moist environment
   (5) stored food

Answers are on page 644.

CHAPTER 3

Human Biology

Reading Graphic Information

"A picture is worth a thousand words." That old saying can be true even when you're reading a textbook. Sometimes a picture can give you information more quickly and easily than any number of words. Many textbooks and tests use special pictures called diagrams, charts, and graphs. Understanding these special illustrations is a very important reading skill.

Diagrams

The science topics in this chapter are about your body, some of its many parts, and how they work. Many of the reading passages will have **diagrams** to go with them. A diagram is a drawing that shows the parts of something or how a process works. Look at the diagram below.

AREAS OF THE BRAIN

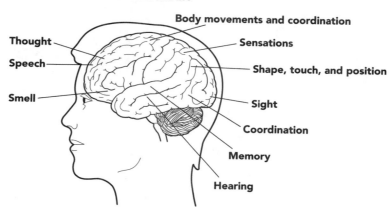

Always look at the **title** of a diagram first. The title tells you what the diagram is about. The title "Areas of the Brain" explains that the diagram is showing you different parts of the brain.

Now look at the drawing. It is a drawing of the inside of a person's head. It is not a realistic drawing. Like most diagrams, this drawing has been simplified to get the main point across.

Finally, look at the **labels**. The labels are words that identify important parts of the drawing. In this diagram, the words show what different parts of the brain do. For example, the part that gets messages from the eyes is at the back of the brain. An injury to the back of the head may cause a person to lose sight. The part that directs body movements is at the top of the brain. An injury in this area may prevent a person from being able to move well.

> **DIAGRAM-READING TIP**
>
> To understand a diagram, first read the title. Next, look at the drawing itself. Finally, read all the labels.

You can use the diagram to figure things out. For instance, what might happen to a person who is injured at the forehead?

If you decided the person might have trouble speaking, you were right. You used information from the diagram to draw that conclusion.

Diagrams

Directions: Look at the diagram below and answer the questions.

The Human Eye

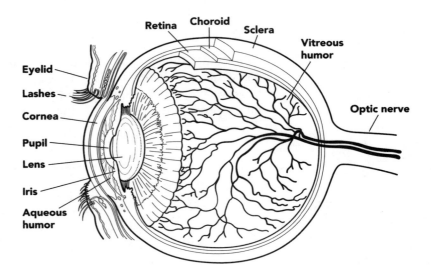

1. What is the opening in front of the lens called?

   _____

2. What fills the inside of the eye? _____

3. What is the innermost layer on the back of the eyeball called?

   _____

4. What is the name of the nerve that runs out the back of the eye?

   _____

5. When a person gets a cataract, the cornea of the eye becomes clouded. Why would this make it difficult for a person to see?

   _____

Answers are on page 644.

Comparing Diagrams

Sometimes a diagram will have more than one drawing. You should carefully compare the drawings to see how they are alike and how they are different.

Look at this diagram with three drawings. Try to answer the questions that follow. Then read on to see if your answers were correct.

- Read the title. What is this diagram about?

  _____

- What is the difference in shape between the normal eye and the nearsighted eye?

  _____

  _____

- What is the difference in shape between the normal eye and the farsighted eye?

  _____

  _____

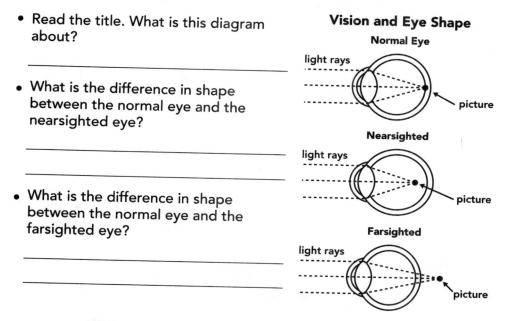

Vision and Eye Shape

The title explains that the diagram is about the relationship between vision and eye shape. The nearsighted eyeball is longer than the normal one; the farsighted eyeball is shorter; the normal eye looks perfectly round.

When you see something, a picture forms where the light rays focus—or come together—in your eye. In a normal eye, the light rays focus on the retina to create a clear picture.

- Where does a picture form in a nearsighted eye?

  _____

- Where does a picture form in a farsighted eye?

  _____

- Why do you think that nearsighted and farsighted people have trouble seeing clearly?

  _____

Because a nearsighted eye is longer, light rays focus in front of the retina to create a picture. In a farsighted eye, light rays focus behind the retina to create a picture. In both cases, the picture is blurry because light rays are not focused exactly on the retina.

EXERCISE 2

Comparing Diagrams

Directions: Look at this diagram. Then answer the following questions.

GROWTH OF THE FETUS DURING EARLY PREGNANCY

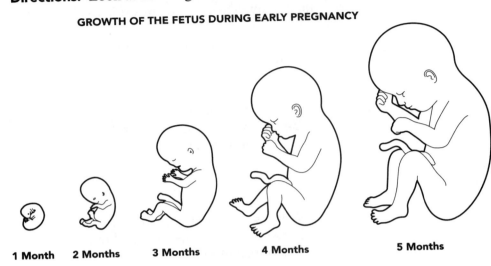

1 Month   2 Months   3 Months   4 Months   5 Months

1. What does this diagram show? _____

2. When does the fetus first show toes? _____

3. From the title and the diagram, what do you think the word *fetus* means? Circle the best answer.

    (1) a baby
    (2) a deformed head
    (3) a young boy
    (4) an unborn child
    (5) a new drug

Answers are on page 644.

Charts

CHART-READING TIP

To understand a chart, first read the title of the chart. Then read the heading of each column. Be sure you understand what the chart is about before you try to get specific information from it.

You can also gather information from charts. Charts are very useful for organizing facts into categories. You can read facts from top to bottom in **columns** and from left to right in **rows**.

Read the **title** of the following chart. The title explains that the chart is about blood types and transfusions. To understand the chart, you need to know that people have different **blood types**. There are four main blood types called *O, A, B,* and *AB.* If a person gets blood from someone else in a **transfusion**, it has to be the right blood type. The wrong type of blood could kill someone.

Blood Types and Transfusions

Blood Type	Can Take Blood From	Can Give Blood To
O	O	O, A, B, AB
A	O, A	A, AB
B	O, B	B, AB
AB	O, A, B, AB	AB

Each column of a chart has a **heading**. The three headings on this chart are "Blood Type," "Can Take Blood From," and "Can Give Blood To." Each heading describes the information you will find in that column.

Now read across the rows of the chart. For example, look in the first column for blood type O. Read across the row to the second column. You can see that someone with blood type O can take blood only from someone else with type O. Now read across the row to the third column. You can see that a person with blood type O can safely give blood to people having type O, A, B, and AB blood.

Now you try it. Find blood type B on the chart.

- A person with blood type B can take blood from what types?

  _____

- Type B people can give blood to what types?

  _____

According to the chart, type B people can take type O or type B blood. Type B people can give blood to type B or type AB.

EXERCISE 3

Charts

Directions: Use this chart to answer the following questions.

Vitamins	Source	Vitamin's Use in the Body
A	Fish, butter, eggs, liver, yellow vegetables	Keeps eyes and skin healthy; helps digestion and breathing
C	Leafy vegetables, tomatoes, citrus fruits such as lemons and oranges	Prevents a gum disease called scurvy
D	Sunshine, fish oils, liver	Helps to build strong bones and teeth
E	Vegetable and animal oils	Protects the nervous system and the reproductive system

B Group Vitamins		
B1 (thiamine)	Yeast, liver, nuts, grains, lean pork	Protects the nervous system; prevents a disease of the nerves, digestive system, and heart called beriberi
B2 (riboflavin)	Yeast, wheat germ, liver, meat, eggs	Affects entire body; prevents skin and mouth diseases
Niacin	Vegetables, meat, yeast, milk	Prevents skin disorders such as pellagra
B12	Vegetables, liver	Prevents anemia

1. What eight vitamins does this chart include? _____

_____

2. What disease does vitamin C prevent? _____

3. What two vitamins can be found in fish? _____

4. What three vitamins might a doctor recommend for a skin

   problem? _____

Answers are on page 644.

Line Graphs

Sometimes a chart is not the best way to show information. For example, Jack wanted to find out how he could make his tomatoes grow bigger, so he did an experiment. He put a different amount of fertilizer on each of nine rows of plants. Then he recorded how many pounds of tomatoes he harvested from each row. He entered his results on a chart.

Tomato Experiment

Row	Fertilizer Used	Tomatoes Harvested
1	2 oz	4 lb
2	4 oz	10 lb
3	6 oz	16 lb
4	8 oz	20 lb
5	10 oz	23 lb
6	12 oz	26 lb
7	14 oz	28 lb
8	16 oz	20 lb
9	18 oz	13 lb

Groups of numbers, such as those on Jack's chart, can more clearly be shown on a **graph**. Jack decided to use the numbers to draw a **line graph**. A line graph has a title, a horizontal axis (goes across), a vertical axis (goes upward), and a graph line.

Examine each part in the line graph that follows. First, read the title of the graph. What is the line graph about? If you said that the graph shows how fertilizer affects the growth of tomatoes, you're right!

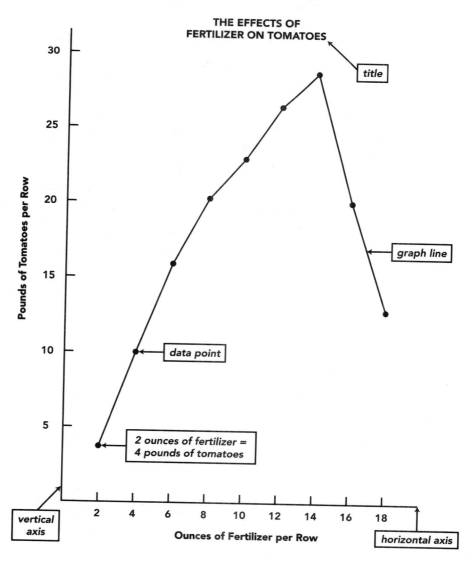

Reading Each Axis

Look at each axis. The axis that runs from left to right is called the **horizontal axis**. The axis that runs upward is called the **vertical axis**. Each axis has a scale of numbers or measurements on it and a label that explains what the axis shows. Always read the label on each axis carefully. In the graph on the previous page, the horizontal axis shows how many ounces of fertilizer Jack used in each row. What does the vertical axis show? If you said the vertical axis shows how many pounds of tomatoes grew in each row, you're right again!

It's also important to read the **scale** on each axis carefully. Notice that each step on a scale in this graph stands for more than one unit. For instance, each step on the vertical axis is equal to five pounds. What does each step on the horizontal axis equal? You should have determined that each horizontal step equals two ounces.

Reading the Graph Line

Now look at the **graph line**. A graph line helps you to easily find and compare specific facts. Many graph lines have dots on them, called **data points**, to help you find particular points on the graph. If a point lies between two steps on the scale, you must **estimate** the measurement for that point. You might want to use something straight, such as a ruler or the edge of a sheet of paper, to line up the point with the scale on the axis.

Now find out how many pounds of tomatoes grew with 6 ounces of fertilizer. Point to 6 ounces on the horizontal axis. Move your finger straight up to the data point above 6 ounces. Then move your finger to the left—or use a straight edge—until you reach the vertical axis. Your finger should be slightly above 15 pounds on the scale. You can estimate that about 16 pounds of tomatoes grew with 6 ounces of fertilizer.

The overall shape, or **trend**, of a graph line can help you draw conclusions about the subject of the graph. For example, the shape of Jack's graph line shows that more fertilizer is not always better for tomatoes. The amount of tomatoes harvested peaked with 14 ounces of fertilizer. Jack may conclude that he would get the greatest harvest of tomatoes from his garden next year by using 14 ounces of fertilizer on each row.

Look at the graph that follows. Then answer the questions.

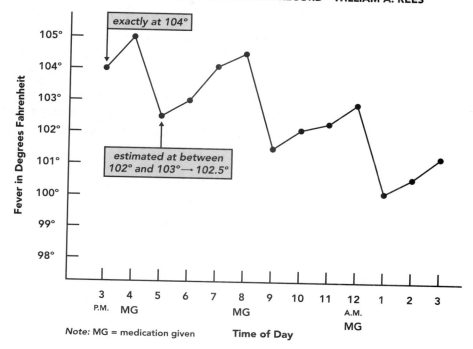

TWELVE-HOUR TEMPERATURE RECORD—WILLIAM A. REES

exactly at 104°

estimated at between 102° and 103°→ 102.5°

Note: MG = medication given **Time of Day**

LINE GRAPH TIP

When a data point on a graph falls between two values, you need to estimate. For example, in the temperature line graph, the data point for 5:00 P.M. falls about halfway between 102°F and 103°F on the vertical scale. An estimate of that the data point is about 102.5°F.

1. What is the title of the graph? _____

    The title is *Twelve-Hour Temperature Record—William A. Rees*. From this title, we might guess that Mr. Rees is sick, because someone is keeping careful track of his temperature.

2. What does the horizontal axis measure? _____

    It measures time, in hours.

3. What does the vertical axis measure? _____

    It measures Mr. Rees's fever on the Fahrenheit scale. This is the same temperature scale we use daily. People in other countries often use a different scale, called the Celsius scale.

Now look at the graph line and answer these questions.

4. When was Mr. Rees's temperature first recorded? _____

5. What was his temperature at 6:00 P.M.? _____

6. For which one-hour period did his fever remain nearly the same?

_____

7. On the whole, does Mr. Rees seem to be getting better? Explain.

_____

    Here are the correct answers: *3:00 P.M., 103°F, 10:00 P.M. to 11:00 P.M., On the whole, he seems to be getting better because his fever is getting lower with each cycle of medication.*

EXERCISE 4

Line Graphs

Directions: Read the passage and look at the graph carefully. Then circle the best answer for each of the following questions.

Sarah was prying rocks out of the lawn at her cabin in the mountains. She noticed that she had to use different-sized crowbars to move different rocks. She did some experimenting with this idea and plotted her results in the graph below.

CROWBARS AND ROCKS

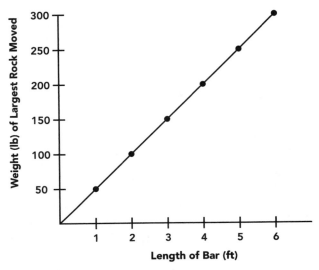

1. What length crowbar helped Sarah move the heaviest rock?

   (1) 2 feet
   (2) 3 feet
   (3) 4 feet
   (4) 5 feet
   (5) 6 feet

2. Which of the following hypotheses could be based on this graph?

   (1) Sarah is an extremely strong person.
   (2) To move a heavy rock, you should use a thick crowbar.
   (3) Sarah had no rocks weighing less than 50 pounds.
   (4) The longer the crowbar, the heavier the rock that can be moved.
   (5) Everyone needs a 5-foot crowbar to move a 250-pound rock.

3. Which of the following titles would be more accurate for this graph?

   (1) Lengths of Crowbars Needed to Move Different Rocks
   (2) How Sarah Cleared Her Cabin Lawn
   (3) Weights of Rocks That Can Be Moved
   (4) Lengths of Crowbars Commonly Available
   (5) Weights of Rocks on a Mountain Cabin Lawn

Answers are on page 644.

Bar Graphs

BAR GRAPH TIP

On some bar graphs, the bars extend across from the vertical axis. To read this type of bar graph, read down from the bar to the value given on the horizontal axis.

Some groups of numbers are better shown on a **bar graph**. A bar graph uses bars instead of lines to display data. The bars usually rise up from the horizontal axis. You read the graph by determining the heights of the bars on the scale of the vertical axis. Look at the example that follows.

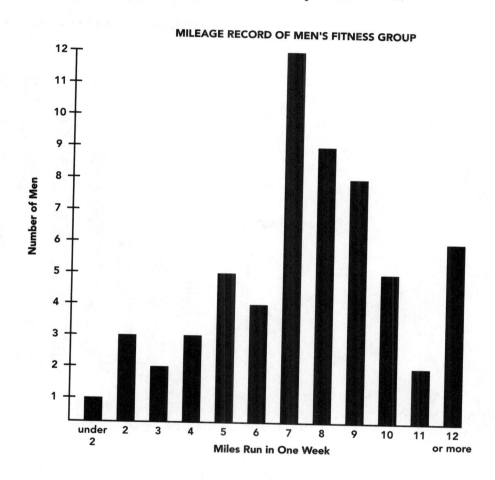

MILEAGE RECORD OF MEN'S FITNESS GROUP

Number of Men

Miles Run in One Week

To read this graph, look at the bars rising up from the horizontal axis. Use a straight edge, such as a sheet of paper, to line up the top of each bar with the vertical scale.

1. How many men ran only two miles? _____

2. What distance was run by eight men? _____

3. What distance was run by the greatest number of men?

    _____

Your answers should be as follows: *3 men*, *9 miles*, and *6 miles*.

EXERCISE 5

Bar Graphs

Directions: Look at this bar graph carefully. Then answer each of the following questions.

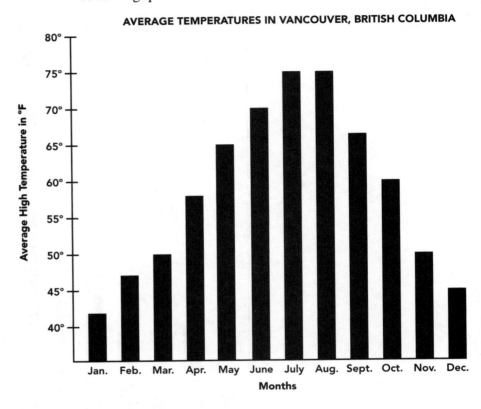

AVERAGE TEMPERATURES IN VANCOUVER, BRITISH COLUMBIA

1. Based on the title, what information do you expect to find on this graph? _____

2. What does the horizontal axis show? _____

3. What does the vertical axis measure? _____

4. How big is each step on the vertical axis? _____

5. What is the average high temperature in November? _____

6. Which two months are the warmest? _____

7. Do you think it often gets below freezing in Vancouver? Explain.

Answers are on page 644.

Human Body Systems

To get the most out of modern medical care, you need to know something about the way your body works. It also helps to know some of the special scientific words used to describe the human body.

Your body is made of many different kinds of **cells**. Similar kinds of cells are grouped together into **tissues**. For example, groups of nerve cells make up nerve tissue, and groups of muscle cells make up muscle tissue. Groups of tissues that work together for a specific purpose form an **organ**. For example, muscle tissue and skin tissue form an organ called the stomach. These tissues work together so the stomach can digest food. Groups of organs that work together for a specific purpose form a **system**. For example, your mouth, stomach, intestines, and many other organs work together to digest food as parts of the **digestive system**.

The Skeletal System

All the strength in your body comes from two systems: the **skeletal system**, which is made of the bones and their connecting tissues, and the **muscular system**, which is made of all the muscles in your body. There are 206 separate bones in an adult body! Some bones are large, such as the leg bones. Others are small, such as the delicate bones in the ear. The diagram of a skeleton shows some of the most important bones.

THE HUMAN SKELETON

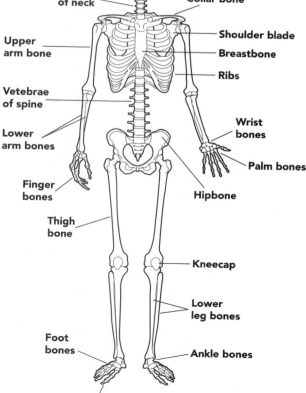

The skeleton does three important things. First, it supports the body. Without your skeleton you would be shapeless, like a jellyfish. You wouldn't be able to move, breathe, or even live. Second, some bones of the skeleton protect organs of the body. Your hard skull bones protect your brain. Your ribs protect your heart and lungs. Third, inside some of your bones is a soft substance called **marrow**. New blood cells are made in bone marrow.

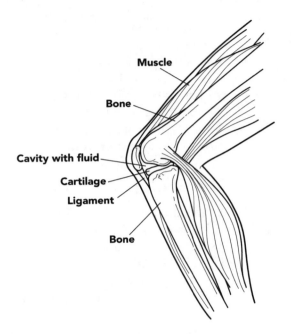

The skeletal system contains two other kinds of tissue, called cartilage and ligaments. **Cartilage** is a tough but flexible tissue that is softer than bone. Your nose and the outside of your ears are made of cartilage. Children's bones are said to be "soft." That is because young children's bones have much more cartilage in them. The cartilage hardens up into real bone as they get older.

A **joint** is the place where two bones come together. Most joints are padded with cartilage to prevent the bones from rubbing together and damaging their ends. Bones are held together at the joints by very tough bands of tissue called **ligaments**. When a doctor says that you have sprained your ankle, you have actually stretched or torn some ligaments.

A common problem with the skeleton is **osteoporosis**, which makes a person's bones become very brittle and breakable. One of its causes is not having enough calcium in the diet. Osteoporosis is particularly common among older women, which is why women are advised to get plenty of calcium throughout their lives.

The Muscular System

Muscles are made of special cells that contract to get shorter and relax to get longer. That is how muscles move. Muscles that are attached to bones are called **skeletal muscles**. These muscles are attached to bones by strong, fibrous tissues called **tendons**. The diagram shows what happens when you tighten an arm muscle: every cell in the arm muscle contracts. The shortened muscle pulls on the tendon attached to the arm bone, and the arm moves.

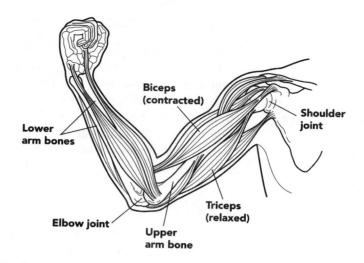

Skeletal muscles are **voluntary**, which means that you can control their movement. Two other kinds of muscles are mostly **involuntary**—you have no control over their movement. **Smooth muscles** are the kind in your stomach, lungs, bladder, and intestines. They expand and contract in rhythm, which helps to digest your food and keep it moving through the digestive system. **Cardiac muscles** are found only in the heart. These muscles are especially strong and reliable, which is important in keeping this organ working.

EXERCISE 6

The Skeletal and Muscular Systems

Directions: Circle *T* if the statement is true and *F* if it is false.

T F **1.** There are more than 200 bones in the human body.

T F **2.** Bones support and protect the body.

T F **3.** Cartilage is harder than bone.

T F **4.** Ligaments attach one bone to another.

T F **5.** Osteoporosis is caused partly by a lack of calcium.

T F **6.** You have no control over your voluntary muscles.

T F **7.** The cardiac muscles of the heart are involuntary.

Directions: Circle the best answer.

8. Look at the diagram of a skeleton in this section. What are the bones in your backbone and neck called?

    (1) ribs
    (2) hip bones
    (3) collarbones
    (4) vertebrae
    (5) shoulder blades

Answers are on page 645.

The Respiratory and Circulatory Systems

Television shows about hospital emergency rooms often portray hectic scenes of doctors and nurses working frantically on a patient who has stopped breathing or whose heart has stopped beating. Why is it important to treat these patients quickly and properly? A person's breathing and blood circulation involve two systems of the body—the **respiratory system** for breathing and the **circulatory system** for blood circulation. These two systems work together, and if a major part of either system stops working, the patient's life becomes critical within minutes.

Breathing

When you breathe in, the **diaphragm**—a thin, flat muscle that lies under the lungs—pulls downward. The chest muscles pull up and out. This causes suction inside the chest, which pulls in air and makes the **lungs** expand. The lungs are the main organs of the respiratory system.

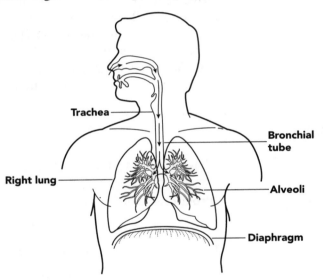

Air enters the body through the **nose** or **mouth** and flows down the **trachea**, or windpipe. From the trachea, the air goes down two **bronchial tubes** that lead into the lungs. Inside the lungs, the air flows through thousands of little tubes to tiny air sacs called **alveoli**. The alveoli are surrounded by very small blood vessels called **capillaries**. Blood picks up oxygen from air in the alveoli and drops off carbon dioxide, a waste product of the body's cells.

When you exhale, the diaphragm and chest muscles relax, putting pressure on the lungs. The air in the alveoli, which now contains carbon dioxide, starts the return trip out of the body. The air flows from the alveoli, through the little tubes, into the bronchial tubes, up the trachea, and back out the nose or mouth. Then the breathing cycle starts all over again.

Smoking can cause diseases of the respiratory system. When a person smokes, tars and other chemicals in the smoke build up in the alveoli. These air sacs become stiff and are less able to pull in or push out air. This disease is called **emphysema**. People with emphysema cannot breathe deeply and therefore are unable to exercise. Eventually, they cannot breathe at all.

The Circulatory System

The **circulatory system** is the body's transport system. It carries food, nutrients, antibodies, and oxygen to all parts of the body. The center of the circulatory system is the heart. The heart is an amazing muscle that contracts and relaxes sixty to eighty times every minute. It pumps blood through almost 60,000 miles of **blood vessels** in the body. Blood vessels going away from the heart are called **arteries.** Blood vessels going toward the heart are called **veins**.

As blood circulates through parts of the body, it releases oxygen to the cells and picks up carbon dioxide. Blood then flows through veins back to the heart. From the heart the blood is pumped through arteries to the lungs. In the lungs, blood releases carbon dioxide and picks up oxygen. Then the lungs send the oxygen-rich blood back to the heart in veins. Next, the heart pumps the oxygen-rich blood through arteries to all parts of the body.

Blood contains three different types of cells: **red blood cells, white blood cells,** and **platelets.** The following chart describes the purpose of each type of cell.

Blood Cells

Type of cell	Purpose
Red blood cell	Carries oxygen to all cells of the body
White blood cell	Fights disease by attacking harmful bacteria and viruses in the body
Platelet	Clots the blood by sealing off cuts in blood vessels

You can do a lot to keep your heart and circulatory system healthy. By eating a balanced diet, not smoking, getting regular exercise, and learning to manage tension, you may avoid two of the main causes of death among Americans—high blood pressure and heart attacks.

EXERCISE 7

The Respiratory and Circulatory Systems

Directions: Summarize the information about breathing and blood cells by filling in the blanks in the following paragraphs. Choose words from the list.

white blood cells	alveoli	nose
carbon dioxide	lungs	mouth
bronchial tubes	trachea	platelets
red blood cells	oxygen	

The **(1)** _____ are the main organs in the respiratory system. Air enters the body through the

(2) _____ or **(3)** _____ and goes

down the **(4)** _____. From there it goes into two

(5) _____ and then into small tubes in the lungs

that lead to tiny air sacs called **(6)** _____. Tiny

blood vessels pick up **(7)** _____ from the air in

these sacs and give off **(8)** _____.

The **(9)** _____ in your blood carry oxygen to all

cells in the body. The **(10)** _____ help the body to

fight disease. When blood vessels are cut, **(11)** _____

seal off the wound and cause the blood to clot.

Answers are on page 645.

The Digestive System

The food you eat goes through a long journey and many changes before it is ready to be used by your body. The process of breaking down food into simpler chemicals that the body can use is called **digestion**. The place where this process happens is the **digestive system**.

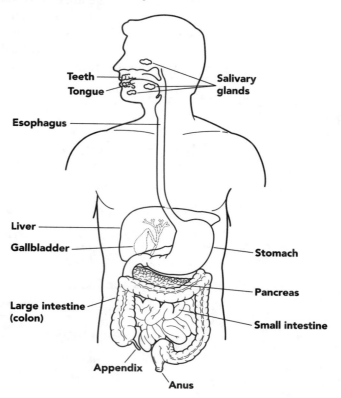

The digestive system begins with your **mouth**. Here food is taken in and ground down into small pieces by the **teeth**. It is mixed with **saliva**, which is produced by **salivary glands** that lie next to your mouth. Saliva moistens the food and starts to break it down. The smaller pieces of food then slide easily down the long tube of your **esophagus** into the **stomach.** The stomach is a muscular sac that turns and squeezes the food, mixing it with a little acid and some enzymes. **Enzymes** are special chemicals that help break down foods. An enzyme in saliva breaks down starches, and two enzymes in your stomach break down proteins.

After the stomach mixes and mashes the food into liquid, it goes into the **small intestine**. The small intestine is about twenty feet long. At its beginning, enzymes from the **liver, gallbladder,** and **pancreas** are mixed with the food. These enzymes help to digest fats and to complete the digestion of proteins. As the digested food moves through the small intestine, the nutrients your body needs are **absorbed**—or soaked up—into the bloodstream. This leaves only the waste materials and water. These pass into the **large intestine**, which is wider than the small intestine but only about five feet long. There most of the water is absorbed by the body. The waste materials pass out of the body through the **anus**.

EXERCISE 8

The Digestive System

Directions: Match the words with their definitions.

_____ **1.** mouth

_____ **2.** saliva

_____ **3.** salivary glands

_____ **4.** esophagus

_____ **5.** stomach

_____ **6.** small intestine

_____ **7.** liver, pancreas, and gallbladder

_____ **8.** large intestine

a. organ in which water is absorbed

b. tube that runs from mouth to stomach

c. organ in which nutrients are absorbed into the bloodstream

d. glands that produce saliva

e. organs that dump enzymes into the small intestine

f. liquid that moistens food in the mouth

g. place where food enters the body

h. organ that mixes food with acid and enzymes

Directions: Circle the best answer.

9. The order in which food moves through the digestive system is

(1) stomach, esophagus, small intestine, large intestine
(2) large intestine, small intestine, stomach, esophagus
(3) stomach, large intestine, esophagus, small intestine
(4) esophagus, stomach, small intestine, large intestine
(5) esophagus, small intestine, stomach, large intestine

Answers are on page 645.

The Nervous System

The **nervous system** is the communication network of your body. The **brain** is the center of the system. It is like a computer that runs your body, only it is much more amazing than any computer.

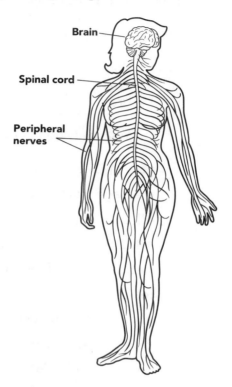

The **spinal cord** is the main link between the brain and the rest of the body. Most of the nerves in the body connect into the spinal cord. Only some nerves in the head connect directly to the brain. The spinal cord runs down the middle of the vertebrae in the backbone. The brain and the spinal cord together are called the central nervous system.

Two kinds of nerves run throughout the rest of the body. **Motor nerves** carry messages from the brain and spinal cord to other parts of the body. These messages tell the body to do things, such as to move an arm or wink an eye. **Sensory nerves** carry messages to the brain and spinal cord from the body. These nerves send messages to the brain about changes in the environment around you. The messages include sights, sounds, tastes, smells, pain, heat, and pressure. There are many sensory nerves in the head, coming from the eyes, nose, mouth, and ears. There also are sensory nerves all over the skin, such as those in the fingertips, and even some inside the body. The messages that travel through nerves are called **nerve impulses**. These impulses travel very quickly through the body—at a rate of more than 300 feet per second!

EXERCISE 9

The Nervous System

Directions: Trace the path of the following messages through your nervous system by filling in the blanks. Choose words from the list. The first one is done as an example.

skin	hand	spinal cord
brain	motor	nerve impulses
brain	sensory	

You are lying in bed on a cold winter night. The nerve endings in

your **(1)** _____*skin*_____ feel the air getting colder. This

message travels up a **(2)** _____ nerve to your

(3) _____ and then up to your

(4) _____. Your **(5)** _____

decides to do something about the cold. It sends a message down a

(6) _____ nerve, through your spinal cord, down

your arm to your **(7)** _____, telling it to pull up the

blankets. All this happens before you even realize it, because of the

speed at which **(8)** _____ _____

travel.

Answers are on page 645.

Health and Nutrition

Nutrition is the study of the foods, or **nutrients**, that the human body needs to live and grow. Poor nutrition can cause serious health problems, including severe depression, high blood pressure, and premature births. Poor nutrition can also weaken the systems of the body so that we are more likely to catch colds, the flu, and other illnesses.

Your body needs six types of nutrients: **proteins, carbohydrates, fats, vitamins, minerals,** and **water.** The following chart describes what each nutrient does and lists some good sources of each nutrient.

Nutrients

Nutrient	Purpose	Some Good Food Sources
Proteins	Provide building material for new cells	Meat, fish, eggs, tofu, milk products, beans, peanuts
Carbohydrates (starches and sugars)	Provide energy	Whole-grain breads, tortillas, rice, corn, pasta, fruits
Fats	Provide concentrated energy needed for body chemistry	Meat, butter, whole grains, milk, olives, avocado, vegetable oils, cheese
Vitamins	Needed for enzymes and other body chemistry	Fruits, vegetables, liver, whole grains, eggs, milk, tuna
Minerals	Make strong bones and teeth	Milk products, green leafy vegetables
	Iron is needed for blood for body chemistry.	Seafood, liver, beans, oranges, meat
Water	Needed by all parts of the body, which is about 70% water	Water, milk, fruit juices

It is important to eat a variety of different foods to obtain the nutrients you need. **Nutritionists**—people who study nutrition—have set up a food guide pyramid that shows the types and amounts of foods that an adult should eat each day. Children, teenagers, pregnant or nursing women, and athletes have slightly different needs.

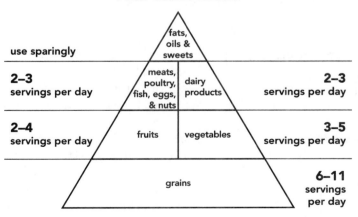

FOOD GUIDE PYRAMID

EXERCISE 10

Nutrition

Directions: Circle the best answer.

1. According to the nutrients chart you just read, which of the following is the main purpose of carbohydrates?

   (1) to build new cells
   (2) to provide energy
   (3) to make enzymes
   (4) to provide liquid
   (5) to keep bones healthy

2. Which of the following is an opinion, not a fact?

   (1) It is important to eat a variety of foods.
   (2) Some vitamins are destroyed by cooking.
   (3) Poor nutrition can cause health problems.
   (4) Everyone should take vitamin pills.
   (5) Cheese and meat provide protein.

Answers are on page 645.

Health

How well you live—and for how long—is mostly in your hands. If you maintain your body now, chances are good that you will live a long and healthy life. To make sure you're on the right track, check out the tips in the chart below.

Tips for Living a Long and Healthy Life	
Get enough rest.	Research has shown that most people need eight hours of sleep each day. Sleep keeps the systems in your body healthy. It prevents illnesses, such as colds and flu. It rests your mind and prevents depression. It keeps you alert so you can deal with problems that arise during daytime.
Eat a nutritious diet.	How well your body works depends on how much energy it gets from the food you eat. A balanced diet that includes the proper amounts of vitamins, minerals, proteins, carbohydrates, fats, and water will ensure that your body is healthy.
Manage stress.	Some stress in life is normal and healthy. Too much stress, however, puts a heavy demand on your physical and mental energy. If you suffer from headaches, tense muscles, anxiety, dizziness, rapid heartbeats, high blood pressure, or insomnia, you may be under too much stress. A change in lifestyle, relaxation techniques, physical exercise, deep breathing, soothing music, and massage therapy can help you to manage stress in your life.

Get enough exercise.	Regular exercise—just twenty to thirty minutes of exercise each day—strengthens the muscles and bones in your body and keeps all of the organs healthy. Exercise also reduces stress, increases your energy level, improves mental alertness and memory, makes you more productive, lowers high blood pressure and increases the good cholesterol, improves sleep, reduces the feeling of depression, and improves your overall well-being.
Don't smoke.	Smoking causes mouth, esophagus, lung, stomach, and bladder cancers; respiratory infections, bronchitis, and emphysema; stomach ulcers; heart disease; and strokes. By stopping smoking, you will reverse the damage already done to your body.
Reduce alcohol intake.	Alcohol affects your brain by interfering with speech, thinking, memory, judgment, and coordination. It also increases the heartbeat and slows breathing. Too much alcohol over a long period of time damages the liver; leads to cancers of the mouth, esophagus, and liver; causes high blood pressure and depression; leads to malnutrition; and can seriously harm the unborn fetus of a pregnant mother. By reducing alcohol intake, you can slow or prevent many of the long-term effects of alcohol.
Keep up with medical news.	Doctors and scientists release the results of studies almost daily. By keeping abreast of health news, you can change your lifestyle as needed to ensure that you are doing all that you can for a healthy and long life.

EXERCISE 11

Health

Directions: Circle the number of the best answer.

1. According to the chart, which of the following tips could be taken care of through regular exercise?

   (1) get enough rest and don't smoke
   (2) manage stress and lower cholesterol
   (3) improve sleep and reduce stress
   (4) eat a nutritious diet and keep up with medical news
   (5) manage stress and don't smoke

2. Which of the following is the best reason for keeping up with medical news?

   (1) The results of a new study may contradict an earlier guideline.
   (2) A new study may provide information about the best doctors.
   (3) Medical advances are slow to occur, so you wouldn't have to pay attention too often.
   (4) A change in lifestyle is a great way to reduce stress in your life.
   (5) The news media creates information overload and, thus, stress.

Answers are on page 645.

Chapter Review

Directions: Read each passage carefully. Then circle the number of the best answer to each question.

Questions 1 and 2 are based on the following passage and diagram.

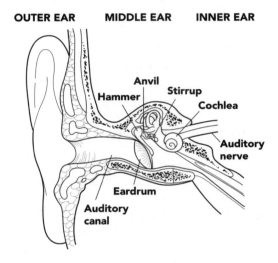

OUTER EAR   MIDDLE EAR   INNER EAR

Look at the diagram of the ear. Sound enters the **outer ear** and travels down the **auditory canal** to the **eardrum**. The sound causes the eardrum to vibrate. The vibrations of the eardrum move three little bones called the **hammer**, the **anvil**, and the **stirrup**. These three bones transfer the vibrations to the **inner ear**, which contains the **cochlea**. The cochlea is a coiled tube filled with liquid. The vibrations in this liquid are changed to nerve impulses, or messages, that travel along the **auditory nerve** to the brain.

1. According to the diagram, which part of the ear contains the hammer, anvil, and stirrup bones?

   (1) outer ear
   (2) auditory canal
   (3) middle ear
   (4) inner ear
   (5) auditory nerve

2. When a person gets an ear infection, the middle ear fills with fluid. Which hypothesis best explains why someone with an ear infection can't hear as well as usual?

   (1) The fluid prevents the eardrum from vibrating easily.
   (2) The pain makes it hard to hear.
   (3) The fluid makes the inner ear too cold for nerve impulses.
   (4) The fluid helps the sound travel better.
   (5) The pain keeps the person from paying attention.

Questions 3 and 4 are based on the following chart.

Recommended Energy Intake for Average-Sized People

Category	Age (years)	Energy Needs (calories)
Children	1–3	900–1,800
	4–6	1,300–2,300
	7–10	1,650–3,300
Males	11–14	2,000–3,700
	15–18	2,100–3,900
	19–22	2,500–3,300
	23–50	2,300–3,100
	51–75	2,000–2,800
	76+	1,650–2,450
Females	11–14	1,500–3,000
	15–18	1,200–3,000
	19–22	1,700–2,500
	23–50	1,600–2,400
	51–75	1,400–2,200
	76+	1,200–2,000

3. According to the chart, about how many calories does a 45-year-old man need?

(1) 1,400–2,200
(2) 1,600–2,400
(3) 2,000–2,800
(4) 2,000–3,700
(5) 2,300–3,100

4. Which of these statements is true, according to the information on the chart?

(1) The older you get, the more calories you need.
(2) All men need more calories than all women.
(3) Men need more calories than women of the same age.
(4) Girls need more calories than boys.
(5) Children need more calories than teenagers.

Question 5 is based on the following passage.

People used to believe that an unborn baby—called a fetus—was protected from most things that happened to its mother. Now doctors know that the fetus is affected by many things.

If a pregnant woman catches German measles or certain other diseases, her baby might have a birth defect. When the baby is born, something could be wrong with its brain or body. Some medicines taken by the mother can also cause birth defects. Even some of the most common drugs, such as aspirin and sleeping pills, can cause trouble for a fetus. Almost all illegal drugs can cause birth defects. Alcohol, even just beer and wine, may hurt a baby and cause it to be mentally disabled.

Regular smoking can cause a baby to be born too small or too early. Some problems with fetuses happen for unknown reasons. However, if a pregnant woman follows her doctor's advice and takes good care of herself, she is giving her baby the best possible chance.

5. Which of the following is the main idea of the passage?

   (1) A fetus is protected from most things that happen to its mother.
   (2) German measles can cause a birth defect.
   (3) A woman who is healthy throughout pregnancy is likely to give birth to a healthy baby.
   (4) Medicines taken by a pregnant woman can cause birth defects.
   (5) Smoking can cause a baby to be born early and underweight.

Questions 6 and 7 are based on the following graph.

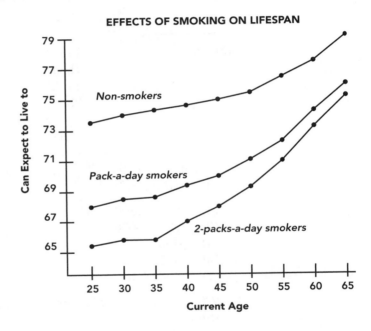

EFFECTS OF SMOKING ON LIFESPAN

6. An average 45-year-old nonsmoker can expect to live about how many years longer than an average 45-year-old who smokes two packs a day?

   (1) 2 years
   (2) 5 years
   (3) 7 years
   (4) 68 years
   (5) 75 years

7. What is one reasonable hypothesis you could form from the information on this graph?

   (1) It doesn't matter whether you smoke one or two packs daily.
   (2) On the average, the less you smoke, the longer you may live.
   (3) Women tend to smoke less than men do, so they live longer.
   (4) Young people smoke less than older people.
   (5) Not smoking is the most important thing you can do.

Answers are on page 645.

CHAPTER 4

Physics

Understanding Sequence

A major goal in science—and in life—should be to go beyond a basic understanding of things you read and hear. You should carefully examine the ideas presented and form opinions about them. You should make judgments based on the ideas and your own prior experiences. You should also decide whether the ideas presented are logical and sensible. By analyzing ideas, both in life and specifically in science, you will gain a better appreciation for the vast world in which you live.

In science it is important to know the **sequence**, or time order, of things that happen. For example, to track down the source of a computer problem, a technician will want to know which keys you pressed on the keyboard and the order in which you pressed them. Also, questions you will encounter on different tests often refer to the order of events in a passage.

Read the following examples:

Before he did the experiment, he got all his equipment together.

You will see a flash of lightning **first**; a few seconds **later** you will hear the thunder.

Next the warm air begins to rise **after** the cool air moves down and pushes it up.

Notice in the previous examples that the first event written in a sentence is not always the first event to happen. By paying attention to the sequence words in each sentence, you can determine the order of events.

Now read the following examples. Underline the sequence words in the sentences and answer the questions.

1. Sir Isaac Newton developed the law of gravity after he developed his famous laws of motion.

   Which did he work on first, the laws of motion or the law of gravity?

   _____

In this sentence, *after* gives a clue about the order of events. It tells you that Newton's work on the laws of motion came first, and the law of gravity came after that.

SEQUENCE TIP
Watch for these sequence words in sentences and passages.

first	before
second	after
third	next
then	afterward
finally	in the meantime
later	today
until	when
that day	

2. Before Newton's work, some people believed that angels kept the Moon moving around Earth.

   Did people believe that angels moved the Moon before or after Newton did his work?

   _____

Before is the sequence word here. It tells you that some people had unusual ideas about how the planets moved before Newton's work with gravity.

Now try your sequence skills on this paragraph. As you read this passage, underline the sequence words and answer the questions that follow.

Why is it that after you put a pot of water on the burner of a stove, the handle of the pot becomes hot even though it is not directly on the burner? First, particles that make up the bottom of the pot absorb heat from the burner. Next, this heat energy causes the particles to vibrate faster and collide with each other. When the particles collide, the heat energy transfers from particle to particle. Finally, even the particles in the very end of the handle are colliding and transferring heat. This way of transferring energy through the collisions of particles is called conduction.

1. What do particles in the bottom of the pot do before they begin to

   vibrate faster? _____

2. What happens after the particles vibrate faster?

   _____

3. What is important about the collisions of particles?

   _____

4. What part of the pot is the last place to which heat is conducted?

   _____

Now check your answers. You should have underlined the following sequence words in the paragraph: *after, First, Next, When,* and *Finally.* Here are the answers to the four questions above:

1. They absorb heat.
2. They collide with other particles.
3. Heat energy is transferred from particle to particle.
4. The end of the handle is the last part to which heat is conducted.

EXERCISE 1

Sequencing

Directions: Read the following passage. Then order the events from earliest to latest by numbering them from 1 to 4. You may want to underline the sequence words as you read.

Sir Isaac Newton is known today as the "Father of Modern Physics." He is best known for his theory of gravitation. As a boy, he was more interested in building mechanical things than in studying. He was considered a poor student. At fourteen, he had to leave school to help his mother manage the farm. But later, he went back to school. He graduated from Trinity College at Cambridge University in 1665.

Some accounts of Newton's life state that during the same year, Newton was sitting in his backyard drinking tea when he saw an apple fall from a tree. According to the story, the falling apple gave him the idea of gravity, the idea that all objects in the universe pull toward each other. Objects that are close together pull harder than objects that are far apart. Objects that are heavier pull harder than light objects.

Newton did some of his work on gravitation in 1665 and 1666, but he was not satisfied with it and put it away. More than twenty years later, after he was already a professor and a well-known scientist, a friend persuaded him to publish his theory. After it was published, Newton received many honors.

_____ **a.** Newton published his theory of gravitation.

_____ **b.** Newton dropped out of school.

_____ **c.** Newton started work on his theory of gravitation.

_____ **d.** Newton became a professor.

Answers are on page 646.

Common Sense

Sometimes a passage does not contain sequence words that show the order of events. You can often tell the order using your own common sense. For example, which of the following two events happened first?

a. The owner laid insulation in the attic to reduce the heat loss.

b. Most of the heat lost from the house went out through the roof.

If you said *b* came before *a*, you used good logic. Before the insulation was laid in the attic, most of the heat was lost through the roof.

Now try to put these three statements in logical order.

a. Jamie catches the rebounding ball.

b. Jamie throws a ball at a wall.

c. The wall exerts an opposite force on the ball, causing it to bounce off.

The logical order is *b, c, a*. First Jamie throws the ball at the wall, then the wall exerts a force in the opposite direction on the ball, and finally Jamie catches the rebounding ball.

EXERCISE 2

Logical Sequence

Directions: List these groups of events in logical order.

1. **a.** Steam locomotives pulled the first trains.

   b. The steam engine was invented.

   Logical order: _____

   _____

2. **a.** Benjamin Franklin discovered that lightning is a form of electricity.

   b. People believed that lightning was a weapon of the gods.

   c. Franklin invented lightning rods to keep buildings safe.

   Logical order: _____

   _____

   _____

Answers are on page 646.

Understanding Cause and Effect

What causes potholes in roads? Why does gold conduct electricity so well? What happens if a nuclear power plant leaks radioactivity into the environment? Science is concerned with many questions like these, questions about cause and effect.

Why Did It Happen?

A **cause** is whatever makes something happen. An **effect** is what happens as a result of the cause. Sometimes a passage will contain clue words such as *because, since, as a result, so,* and *therefore.* Other times you must use logic to identify the cause and effect.

Label each of the following statements as a *cause* or an *effect.*

_____ Many drivers bought radar detectors.

_____ Police started to use radar to catch speeders.

If you said that because police started to use radar to catch speeders (cause), many drivers bought radar detectors (effect), you're right.

Sometimes a single cause may have more than one effect. For instance, imagine that Lester woke up late this morning. Because he got up late, he missed the bus, forgot to pack his lunch, and had a headache all morning. Getting up late caused three separate effects.

Try writing two different effects for the given cause.

Cause: Birth control methods were invented.

Effect: _____

Effect: _____

The invention of birth control methods might have led to lower birthrates, smaller families, and other effects.

Likewise, a single effect can have several causes. For example, a great scientific discovery may have been caused by one scientist's curiosity, another scientist's lucky accident, and a conference that brought the two scientists together.

Now write two different causes for the given effect.

Cause: _____

Cause: _____

Effect: May Chen grew a huge crop of lettuce in her garden.

Did you say that good weather, the use of fertilizers, and careful weeding are possible causes of May's bumper crop of lettuce? If so, you're right! These and other causes may have resulted in May's large crop.

EXERCISE 3

Causes and Effects

Directions: Read each paragraph. Then write the missing cause or effect.

Uranium ore must be refined and purified before it can be used in nuclear power plants. The pure uranium is shipped to fuel fabrication plants. There it is put into fuel rods that fit into the cores of nuclear power reactors. In the power plant, a chain reaction, which is a series of tiny atomic explosions, is kept under careful control. If the chain reaction goes very fast, the whole plant could blow up. If the reaction is slowed down too much, not enough heat will be released.

1. **Cause:** _____

   Effect: The power plant could blow up.

2. **Cause:** The chain reaction goes too slowly.

   Effect: _____

   The heat from the chain reaction is used to boil water. The steam that is formed is used to turn giant generators that make electricity. Electricity from nuclear power plants is used by many communities across the country.

3. **Cause:** The chain reaction makes heat.

   Effect: _____

4. **Cause:** _____

   Effect: Electricity is made.

Answers are on page 646.

Drawing False Conclusions

When identifying cause-and-effect relationships, you need to think carefully about the events. Ask yourself questions such as the following: How are the events related? Does one event actually cause the other? Could something else have caused the effect? Is there enough evidence to draw a conclusion? Faulty thinking sometimes leads to a false conclusion such as in the following example:

Whenever I flip the switch on the wall, electricity flows in a circuit and turns on the lamp on my table. I flipped the switch on the wall, but the lamp on the table did not turn on. Something must be wrong with the electric circuit.

Do you recognize the faulty thinking in the example? While it is possible that there may be a break in the circuit, it is also possible that the light bulb in the lamp has burned out, that the lamp is not plugged in, or that there's a problem with the wiring in the lamp. There is not enough evidence to support the conclusion drawn in the example. Therefore, the conclusion is false.

For practice in recognizing false conclusions, read the following examples. Draw a line through those that draw false conclusions.

1. The temperature was thirty-five degrees below zero last night. My car didn't start this morning. The car's battery and fuel line are probably frozen.

2. John forgot to take his vitamins yesterday. Today he has a cold. If John had taken his vitamins yesterday, he wouldn't have a cold today.

3. Emily was pumping air into her bike tire. The tire exploded. The air pressure inside the tire must have been more than the tire could hold.

4. Helen wore boots with plastic soles instead of rubber soles. She slipped and fell on the ice. If Helen had worn boots with rubber soles, she wouldn't have fallen.

Did you draw a line through numbers 2 and 4? The conclusions in these examples are false. Example 2 is false because there is no relationship given in the example between vitamins and colds. Example 4 is false because there may be another cause for Helen's fall; perhaps she is clumsy and falls frequently.

EXERCISE 4

Finding Causes and Effects

Directions: Read the passage and circle the best answer to each question.

What led to Albert Einstein's success as the most important physicist of the twentieth century? As a child he hated the way students merely repeated everything said by a teacher. Einstein liked to think creatively. He was curious about things in his world. He wanted to know about the invisible forces that pointed his compass arrow to the north. He wondered about the relationship between matter and energy. He questioned long-standing ideas about the world. Most importantly, he set out to find the answers himself.

Other scientists thought Einstein's ideas were a bit strange. He didn't let that stop him. He was determined to prove his ideas to be true. Sometimes he would go for months without finding answers. Not giving up, he kept reading, questioning, and learning until he proved his ideas. These traits helped Einstein to become one of the greatest scientists of all time.

1. Which of the following is **not** a cause for Einstein's fame?

   (1) his curious nature
   (2) his love of school
   (3) his creativity
   (4) his imagination
   (5) his determination

2. Which of the following is the best conclusion that can be drawn from the passage?

   (1) Einstein was the most important physicist of the twentieth century.
   (2) Teaching methods have changed a great deal since Einstein's time.
   (3) Einstein is famous for his theory of relativity.
   (4) Einstein was curious about the magnetic forces in a compass.
   (5) Scientific discoveries result from creativity, imagination, and determination.

Answers are on page 646.

Making Inferences

Sometimes writers do not directly state information. Instead, they **imply**, or hint at, some things in their writing. Read the following example:

> After reading his home's gas bill, Juan wished he had made use of solar energy in his heating system.

Consider all that is implied by this one sentence. Juan is questioning his choice of home heating systems. He uses natural gas to heat his home. His gas bill is high. At some point he made a choice not to use solar energy in his heating system. None of these things are said directly, but you can tell that they are all true.

When a writer implies things without stating them directly, you have to **infer**—or figure out—the writer's meaning. The skill of figuring out what a writer is implying is called **making inferences**. You might think of making inferences as "reading between the lines." Let's look at another example.

> The study had shown that natural gas is the cheapest energy source for home heating systems. Of course, the study was conducted by a company that sells natural gas.

What do you think the writer is implying? _____

The writer is implying that the company might have rigged the results of the study so that it could sell more natural gas.

EXERCISE 5

Making Inferences

Directions: Read the following statements. Then write your inferences on the lines provided. Some statements imply more than one thing.

1. Burying nuclear waste deep in the mountains of Nevada is a popular solution for people who don't live in or near the state.

   What does the writer imply about the people of Nevada?

   _____

2. Technologies that followed the invention of electricity, such as the light bulb, radio, TV, and computers, have increased the quality of people's lives.

    a. What does the writer imply that the technologies rely on?

    _____

    b. What does the writer imply about people's lives before electricity?

    _____

3. People in the United States still rely mostly on fossil fuels as an energy source, even though scientists warn of the limited supply of these fuels.

    a. What does the writer imply about people in the United States?

    _____

    b. What does the writer imply that people in the United States should do?

    _____

Answers are on page 646.

Simple Machines

The universe is made of matter and energy. **Matter** is anything that takes up space. A brick, a person, water, the Sun, and air are all matter. They all take up space. **Energy** is the ability to do work. Common forms of energy are electricity, gravity, heat, and light. **Physics** is the branch of science that studies matter and energy and the relationship between them.

When you think of machines, you probably think of such things as hair dryers, electric drills, and bulldozers. These machines get power from electricity and gasoline. But some machines, such as crowbars and screwdrivers, use human muscle power. These are called **simple machines**.

Work

A **machine** is anything that makes work easier. Scientists say that **work** is done whenever something is moved by a force. **Force** is the push or pull that moves something. To figure how much work is done, multiply the amount of force (F) by the distance (D) the object moves. For example, if you lift a box weighing 20 pounds onto a shelf that is 5 feet above the ground, you have done 100 **foot-pounds** of work.

Work = F × D

Work = 20 pounds × 5 feet

Work = 100 foot-pounds

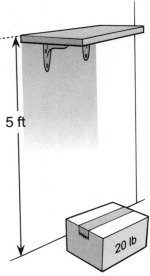

5 ft

20 lb

Now figure the amount of work done in the following cases. Label your answers in foot-pounds.

1. A 10-pound fish is lifted 3 feet into a boat. _____

The force is 10 pounds; the distance is 3 feet. 10 × 3 = 30 foot-pounds of work.

2. A 200-pound man climbs an 8-foot ladder. _____

The force is 200 pounds; the distance is 8 feet. 200 × 8 = 1,600 foot-pounds of work.

Have you ever wanted to move something that required more force than your muscles could give? **Simple machines**, like all machines, make work easier. One type of simple machine is called a **lever**. For example, a crowbar is a lever. A lever decreases the amount of effort you apply to one end of the lever to move an object at the other end. You are able to apply less force because you move the end of the lever over a longer distance.

An **inclined plane**, a slanted surface or ramp, is another type of simple machine. As with all simple machines, the work you put into a machine equals the work done by the machine. In other words,

work put in = work done

F × D = F × D

You can use this equation to figure the force you must put into a machine to get the work done. For example, imagine that you want to load a 300-pound motorcycle onto the tailgate of a pickup, which is two feet off the ground. You can't just lift 300 pounds, so you use a ramp, a type of inclined plane. Let's say the ramp is 12 feet long.

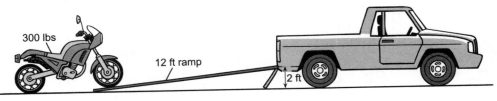

300 lbs

12 ft ramp

2 ft

First, figure the amount of work that must be done by the inclined plane. The force is 300 pounds, the weight of the motorcycle. The distance the motorcycle must be lifted is 2 feet. Therefore, the **work to be done** is 300 pounds times 2 feet, or 600 foot-pounds.

work put in = **work done**

$$F \times D = \textbf{F} \times \textbf{D}$$

$$F \times D = \textbf{300 pounds} \times \textbf{2 feet}$$

$$F \times D = \textbf{600 foot-pounds}$$

Since the work you put in must equal the work done, you know that the **work put in** will also equal 600 foot-pounds. Recall that the ramp is 12 feet long. Now figure the effort force you need to put in. Substitute 12 feet for distance. Then divide 600 foot-pounds by 12 feet to find the answer.

work put in = work done

$$\textbf{F} \times \textbf{D} = 600 \text{ foot-pounds}$$

$$\textbf{F} \times \textbf{12 feet} = 600 \text{ foot-pounds} (600 \div 12 = 50)$$

$$\textbf{50 pounds} \times \textbf{12 feet} = 600 \text{ foot-pounds}$$

You need to apply a force of 50 pounds to push the motorcycle up a ramp that is 12 feet long.

Now suppose your ramp is only 6 feet long. How much effort force would you need to push the same motorcycle up the ramp? The work done is the same as in the previous example.

work put in = work done

$$F \times D = 600 \text{ foot-pounds}$$

$$F \times 6 \text{ feet} = 600 \text{ foot-pounds} (600 \div 6 = 100)$$

$$100 \text{ pounds} \times 6 \text{ feet} = 600 \text{ foot-pounds}$$

You would need to apply 100 pounds of force to move the motorcycle up a ramp that is 6 feet long. Notice that the shorter the inclined plane, the more effort you need to apply.

EXERCISE 6

Simple Machines

Directions: Fill in the blanks with the appropriate words.

| amount | effort | foot-pounds | simple machines |

1. Crowbars, screwdrivers, and inclined planes are all types of

(a) _____ _____.

Force is the (b) _____ of _____ that moves something.

The amount of work is measured in (c) _____.

Directions: A hill is also a type of inclined plane. Question 2 refers to the following diagram.

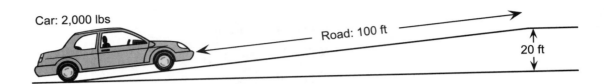

Car: 2,000 lbs

Road: 100 ft

20 ft

2. How much work is done when the car is driven up the road to the top of the hill?

   (1) 20 foot-pounds
   (2) 2,000 foot-pounds
   (3) 4,000 foot-pounds
   (4) 40,000 foot-pounds
   (5) 200,000 foot-pounds

Answers are on page 646.

Newton's Laws of Motion

In the seventeenth century, Isaac Newton became curious about moving bodies. What causes an object to move? Why does an object stop moving? What causes an object to change speed or direction? Why isn't it possible to move all objects? Newton spent much of his life searching for answers to questions like these. His findings are known as **Newton's Three Laws of Motion**.

Newton's First Law

THE FIRST LAW OF MOTION
Matter tends to stay at rest or in motion unless acted on by an outside force.

Newton noticed that an object doesn't move unless a force is applied to it. From this he thought—and proved—that an object would keep moving unless a force caused it to stop. This property of matter is called **inertia**. Every object has inertia.

The first part of the law of inertia is easy to understand. You know that a book, for instance, will stay at rest on a desk until you or something else applies a force to make it move. You experience the second part of the law of inertia when you ride in a car. If the car is in motion, you and everything in the car also are in motion. If the car's brakes are applied quickly, you feel your body continue to move forward until the seatbelt holds you back. This tendency of your moving body to continue moving explains the second part of the law of inertia.

Newton's Second Law

THE SECOND LAW OF MOTION

A change in motion depends on the **mass**, or amount of matter in an object, and the amount of force acting on the object.

Newton also noticed that an object moves with speed according to the amount of force applied. If you give a ball a gentle push, for example, the ball will move slightly. If you give the same ball a hard push, the ball will move with greater speed and for a greater distance.

The size of the object also affects its motion. If you push a toy car with the same amount of force that you use to push a full-size car, the toy car will move fast and far whereas the full-size car may hardly move at all. The opposite is also true: More force is needed to stop the full-size car than is needed to stop the toy car.

Newton's Third Law

THE THIRD LAW OF MOTION

For every action there is an equal but opposite reaction force.

Finally, Newton noticed that when one object exerts a force on a second object, the second object reacts by exerting an equal force in the opposite direction. For example, imagine that you are jumping on a trampoline. When you jump down onto the trampoline, the trampoline exerts the same amount of force in the opposite direction, which pushes you upward into the air. The harder you jump, the higher you bounce into the air. The more lightly you jump, the lower you bounce.

EXERCISE 7

Motion

Directions: Read each case below. Then write *1st, 2nd,* or *3rd* to identify the law of motion it shows.

_____ 1. A person sitting at a desk on a desk chair pushes against the desk. The chair rolls backwards.

_____ 2. A leaf lies on the grass until the wind catches it and blows it into the air.

_____ 3. A child throws a baseball and then a 16-inch softball with the same amount of force. The baseball moves faster and farther than the softball.

_____ 4. A bobsledder takes a running start, pushing the sled as she runs, before climbing on board.

_____ 5. When a person jumps from a boat to a dock, the boat moves away from the dock.

_____ 6. While standing in the aisle of a train, a person is thrown off balance when the engineer quickly applies the brakes.

Answers are on page 646.

Electricity and Magnetism

Imagine a world with no telephones, no refrigerators, no TVs, and no washing machines. A little over a hundred years ago, this was the world that everyone lived in. Then, in 1882, Thomas Edison built the first electric power station in New York City. Now power companies supply electricity to almost every location in the United States.

Electricity

What is electricity? All matter is made of tiny **atoms.** An atom has electrically charged particles called **electrons** that whirl around the **nucleus,** or center, of the atom. Because the electrons are always moving, some of them can easily be rubbed off. These electrons move from one atom to another. The movement of electrons from one place to another is called **electricity.** Friction, magnetism, heat, or an outside source can start the electrons flowing from one atom to another. This flow is called an **electric current.**

Substances that electricity flows through easily are called **conductors.** Gold, copper, steel, and silver are examples of good conductors. Materials that electricity does not easily flow through are called **insulators.** Rubber, glass, plastic, and most fabrics are insulators. The wires that carry electricity in your home are made of copper or aluminum. They are surrounded by insulation made of plastic, rubber, or fabric.

TYPICAL HOUSEHOLD CIRCUIT

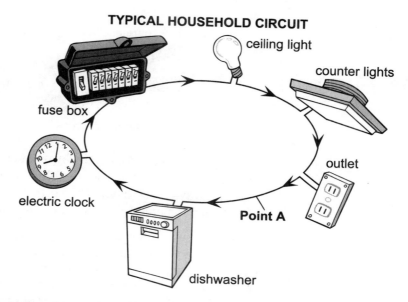

Electricity always flows in a **circuit**. A circuit must be a complete circle or electricity will not flow. For example, there is electric wiring on each side of the wall sockets in your house. When you plug in and turn on a toaster, the metal prongs of the plug complete the circuit. Electricity flows through the toaster. A light switch works the same way. When you turn it on, you complete the circuit and allow electricity to flow through the light.

Sometimes a wire wears through its insulation, a connection becomes loose, or a break occurs in the circuit. In these cases, the current tries to find a short cut, or **short circuit**. The wire touches some other conductor, and the electricity flows along a path different from its usual path. An electric current in the wrong place can cause things to get very hot and may even start a fire.

In older homes, each electric circuit has a **fuse**. A fuse is a small strip of metal designed to burn out if too much electricity flows through it. If the wiring in your house has a short circuit or if you use too many appliances on one circuit, the fuse will blow and the circuit will be broken. No more electricity will flow in that circuit until you find the problem or replace the fuse. Modern electrical systems have **circuit breakers** instead of fuses. A circuit breaker is a switch that turns off whenever too much electricity flows through it.

Magnetism

Electricity and magnetism are closely related. In fact, each can be used to make the other. The electrons in many atoms move in pairs. In some atoms, however, the electrons are not paired. The atoms of iron, cobalt, and nickel, for example, have electrons that are not paired. These electrons act like little magnets. A **magnet** has two **poles**, or regions, where the magnetic force is very strong. One pole always points to the north when the magnet is allowed to swing freely. This pole is called the north pole. The other pole is called the south pole. The area around a magnet is called a **magnetic field**. The magnetic field produces lines of force going out of a magnet from its north pole and returning into the magnet at its south pole.

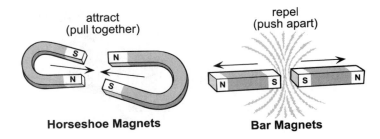

attract
(pull together)

S N
N S

Horseshoe Magnets

repel
(push apart)

N S S N

Bar Magnets

Opposite poles of a magnet **attract** each other. The north pole of one magnet is attracted to the south pole of a second magnet. Like poles **repel**—or push away—each other. The north pole of one magnet repels the north pole of a second magnet. Likewise, the south poles repel each other.

Only a few things have a strong magnetic force that can be put to good use in the world. Fortunately, electricity produces a magnetic field. We can use electricity to build temporary magnets that are very powerful. An **electromagnet** is a temporary magnet that can be made by flowing an electric current through a coil of wire. An electromagnet loses its magnetic force when the electric current stops.

ELECTROMAGNET

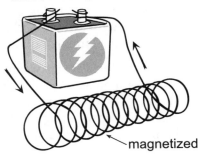

magnetized

EXERCISE 8

Electricity and Magnetism

Directions: Look at the electric circuit diagram. Show the flow of electricity through each item in the circuit, starting at the fuse box.

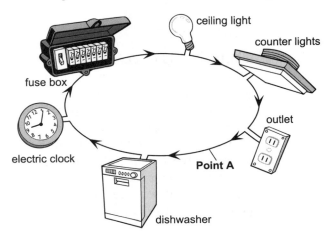

ceiling light

counter lights

fuse box

outlet

electric clock

Point A

dishwasher

Electricity starts at the fuse box and flows to

1. _____

2. _____

3. _____

4. _____

5. _____

The circuit is complete when electricity returns to the fuse box.

Directions: Question 6 refers to the diagram of an electric circuit. Circle the number of the best answer.

6. What would happen if the wire in the diagram broke at Point A?

   (1) The ceiling light, counter lights, and outlet would still work, but the dishwasher and clock wouldn't.
   (2) The lights would still work because they draw so little electricity.
   (3) The dishwasher and the electric clock would work, but nothing else would.
   (4) Everything would still work.
   (5) Nothing would work.

Directions: Match the words on the left with their descriptions on the right. Write the correct letter on the line.

_____ 7. attracts

_____ 8. electromagnet

_____ 9. magnet

_____ 10. magnetic field

_____ 11. north pole

_____ 12. repels

a. a temporary magnet that works when electricity flows through it

b. lines of force going out of a magnet from the north pole and returning into the south pole

c. an object that has two poles and attracts iron and a few other elements

d. the part of a magnet that points north

e. what happens when a north pole and a south pole are near each other

f. what happens when two south poles are near each other

Answers are on page 647.

Nuclear Power

Like every new discovery, nuclear power has advantages and disadvantages. The two speeches that follow discuss some of the pros and cons of nuclear power.

Speaker A

America needs nuclear power. Fossil fuels such as coal, natural gas, and oil are becoming more expensive and harder to find. Air pollution laws have also made fossil fuels expensive to burn, due to multimillion-dollar antipollution devices that are now required. In addition, dependence on fossil fuels means depending on foreign countries for much of our energy needs. This limits our political options and ruins our balance of trade.

Radical environmental groups say that nuclear energy is too dangerous to use. They are ignoring the excellent safety record of nuclear power in the United States. American nuclear power plants are now built with so many safeguards that it is virtually impossible for a serious accident to occur.

In the long run, nuclear power will save money for consumers. The small amount of fuel needed to run a nuclear power plant is much less expensive than the barrels of oil or tons of coal needed to fuel regular power plants. The environment will benefit too, since nuclear power plants release no acid smoke or filthy discharge.

Speaker B

Nuclear power is just not worth the risks involved. These risks associated with nuclear power can be divided into three main areas.

First, there is the direct risk of accident. Every year, accidents happen at nuclear power plants, and small amounts of radiation leak into the environment. The accident at Chernobyl showed the damage that can be caused by a major accident. Chances are that sooner or later there will be an accident in the United States that cannot be stopped.

Second, there is the constant risk of pollution. Nuclear power plants release large amounts of heated water from their cooling devices. This water increases the growth of algae, killing off some types of fish. This water also carries slight amounts of radiation. The authorities assure us that these amounts are too small to be dangerous, but how can they be sure? The solid nuclear waste produced by nuclear power plants is especially polluting. If just small amounts of it got into our water system, many people would die. No one has yet solved the problem of what to do with these wastes.

Third, there is the danger of terrorist attacks and sabotage. There are many power plants around the country and uranium is shipped regularly to these facilities. Nuclear power plants probably don't have tight enough security to stop a terrorist from getting in and maybe causing a major accident. The risks associated with nuclear power are simply too large.

EXERCISE 9

Nuclear Power

Directions: Read the following statements. Put an *A* in front of the ones that you think Speaker A would agree with. Put a *B* in front of the statements that Speaker B would agree with.

_____ **1.** Security checks at nuclear power plants should be tougher.

_____ **2.** Scientists don't know enough about the effects of small doses of radiation.

_____ **3.** Some people exaggerate the dangers of nuclear energy.

Directions: Circle the number of the best answer.

4. Which of the following is a fact from Speaker B's speech?

 (1) Other nations are going full speed ahead to develop nuclear power.
 (2) It would be fairly easy for a group of terrorists to steal uranium.
 (3) America needs nuclear power.
 (4) The United States would be better off developing solar and wind power and forgetting about nuclear power.
 (5) Every year accidents happen at nuclear power plants.

5. Which of the following is most likely to be Speaker A?

 (1) a doctor studying the effects of radiation
 (2) a public relations person for a utility company
 (3) a member of an environmental protection group
 (4) a scientist doing research on solar energy
 (5) an engineer working for an oil company

Answers are on page 647.

Light and Sound Waves

You are familiar with light waves and sound waves. Without these waves you would not see or hear. **Light** and **sound** are types of energy that travel as waves from one place to another. A **wave** is a periodic disturbance that carries energy from point to point through space or matter.

Light Waves

Light travels very fast, about 186,000 *miles per second*. That means light can travel to the Moon and back in less than three seconds. Nothing else in the universe is that fast.

The Sun is our main source of light, and most of us think of sunlight as **white light**. That white light, however, is really a mixture of all different colors of light. You can see the different colors when light passes through a **prism**, a triangular piece of glass. The light splits into a band of different colors. You see the same thing when drops of water in the air split sunlight to make a rainbow.

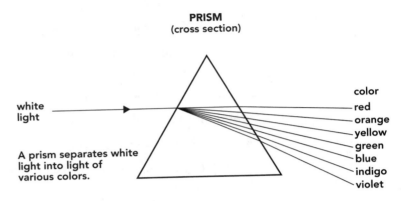

PRISM
(cross section)

white light

A prism separates white light into light of various colors.

color
red
orange
yellow
green
blue
indigo
violet

Light waves move in a straight line. So when light strikes an object, three things can happen. The object can either absorb the light, reflect the light, or let the light pass through. If the light goes through easily, we say the object is **transparent**. Glass, water, and air are mostly transparent. Light rays bend a little when they go through a transparent object. This is how eyeglasses work. The lenses bend the light rays to focus them correctly for your eyes.

Light that doesn't pass through an object is either **reflected**—bounced back—or **absorbed**. Most things reflect some colors of light while absorbing others. The reflected colors are what we see. For example, a blue sofa reflects blue light but absorbs all the other colors. The darker something is, the more light it absorbs. If something absorbs all light, it looks black.

Sound

Sound is caused by the vibration of molecules. For example, when someone plucks a guitar string, the molecules in the string **vibrate** by moving quickly back and forth. The vibrating string hits the molecules of air around it, making them vibrate. These molecules hit other molecules, until eventually the vibration comes to your ear. The vibrating air moves against your eardrum making it vibrate too. A nerve carries a message about the vibration from your eardrum to your brain, and you say, "That's great music!"

Like light, sound moves as a wave. Sound waves, however, move much more slowly than light waves do. Sound travels at a speed of about 1,088 *feet per second* in air. If there is a thunderstorm nearby, you will see the lightning before you hear the thunder. The more time between the flash of light and the sound of thunder, the farther away the storm.

Sound travels in waves of different lengths. Shorter sound waves make higher tones, while longer waves make lower tones. Mixed-up combinations of waves just sound like noise. Unlike light, sound can travel best through solid objects. This is because the molecules are closer together in solid things.

Parts of a Wave

Every wave shares the same parts. The **crest** of a wave is the top of the wave. Wave energy is greatest at the crest. The **trough** is the bottom or lowest point of a wave. Wave energy is lowest at the trough. The **wavelength** is the distance between waves. Wavelengths can be measured from the crest of one wave to the crest of the next wave, from the trough of one wave to the trough of the next, or from any point on one wave to the same point on the next wave. The **amplitude** is the distance a wave rises or falls from its resting position. A wave's amplitude depends on the amount of energy in the wave. The more energy in a wave, the greater the amplitude.

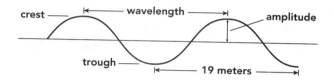

EXERCISE 10

Light and Sound Waves

Directions: Circle *T* if the sentence is true; circle *F* if it is false.

T   F   **1.** Light and sound both travel as waves.

T   F   **2.** Sound travels faster than light.

T   F   **3.** There is no color in white light.

T   F   **4.** A lens is used to bend light.

T   F   **5.** You hear sound when your eardrums vibrate.

T   F   **6.** Sound travels best through air.

T   F   **7.** A wavelength is the distance from one crest to the next.

T   F   **8.** A wave that rises just a little has little energy.

Answers are on page 647.

Chapter Review

Directions: Read each passage and study each diagram carefully. Then circle the number of the best answer to each question.

As you know, a lever is one type of simple machine. A basic lever is just a straight object, such as a bar or a board, that moves freely around a fixed point called the fulcrum. Each part of the bar, on either side of the fulcrum, can be called an arm. A seesaw is one type of lever.

To check whether or not a lever is balanced, we can use the following equation:

$$\underset{\text{Force} \times \text{Distance}}{\text{left arm}} = \underset{\text{Force} \times \text{Distance}}{\text{right arm}}$$

When this equation is used with levers, the force is equal to the weight on each arm. The distance is the length of each arm to the fulcrum. Look at the following diagram of a lever in balance:

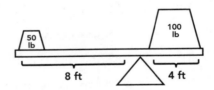

Substitute the numbers for this lever into the equation.

left arm   right arm
50 lb × 8 ft = 100 lb × 4 ft
            or
      400 = 400

The lever is balanced.

Question 1 refers to the following diagrams.

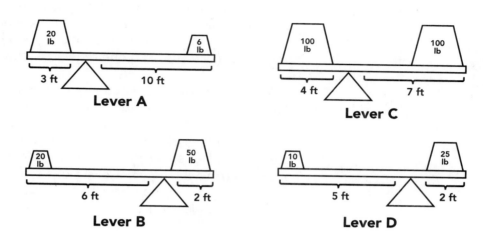

1. Which of the levers above are balanced?

   (1) lever A only
   (2) lever B only
   (3) levers B and C only
   (4) levers A and D only
   (5) levers B and D only

2. Look at the following drawing of a balanced lever. What will happen if a one-pound weight is added to side A?

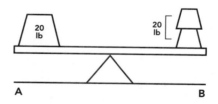

   (1) The lever will stay balanced because there are two weights on each side.
   (2) Side B will go down because the weight on top is heavier.
   (3) Side A will go up because it is heavier.
   (4) Neither end will go up or down because one pound isn't enough to make any difference.
   (5) Side A will go down because it is heavier.

Questions 3 and 4 refer to the following passage and diagram.

You have learned that electricity is a flow of electrons in a circuit and that a circuit must be a complete circle or electricity will not flow. One way to keep the electrons moving is to use a device that pumps the electrons from one object to another. A battery is such a device.

A battery generates electricity by pumping electrons between its negative and positive terminals. Electrons always flow from an area with more electrons to an area with fewer electrons. The negative terminal of a battery has a surplus of electrons. So when a battery is part of an electric circuit, the electrons flow out of the negative terminal. The electrons move to parts of the circuit that need electricity and then back to the battery's positive terminal, which has few electrons.

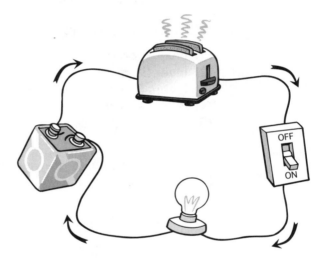

3. This circuit contains a switch. When the switch is on, the electrons flow through the circuit. Which of the following would not work if the switch were off?

   (1) the toaster
   (2) the light
   (3) the battery
   (4) the toaster and the light
   (5) the toaster, the light, and the battery

4. Which of the following can you infer if the battery is dead?

   (1) More electrons are in the negative terminal than in the positive terminal.
   (2) More electrons are in the positive terminal than in the negative terminal.
   (3) The electrons in the negative terminal need more power.
   (4) The electrons in the positive terminal need more power.
   (5) The positive and negative terminals have an equal amount of electrons.

Questions 5 and 6 refer to the following passage.

Some people heat their homes with energy from the Sun in a process called solar heating. When sunlight hits an object, some of the light rays are absorbed and changed into heat. This is why the Sun feels so good on a chilly day. Your body absorbs some of the Sun's rays and warms up.

The simplest kind of solar heating uses a basic principle. The darker an object, the more light it will absorb and change to heat. Large windows can be placed on the south side of a house—the side where the most sunlight comes in. If the floors under those windows are covered in dark carpeting—absorbing the sunlight—heat will be released into the room. This type of solar heating, using no special machines or instruments, is called passive solar heating.

Active solar heating systems use special heat collectors lined with black material. Light is often concentrated in these collectors by reflecting metal foils or mirrors. Small electric motors pass air or liquid over the heated metal. This heated air or liquid is then pumped into the heating system of the house.

5. Which of the following explains why heat collectors use black material?

(1) Black is cheaper than other colors.
(2) Black material reflects light the best.
(3) Black material absorbs light the best.
(4) It is traditional to use black.
(5) Black cannot be stained by the liquid.

6. What is one problem with solar heat?

(1) Solar heat collectors are hard to find.
(2) Solar heat can be collected only when the Sun shines.
(3) Most people don't like dark carpeting.
(4) Solar heat is less polluting than other heat sources.
(5) Large windows are expensive to install.

Questions 7 and 8 refer to the following passage and chart.

Sound travels in waves. The more sound energy in a wave, the more pressure it puts on our eardrums and the louder the sound seems to us.

The strength of a sound wave is measured in decibels (dB). On the decibel scale, each increase of 10 units means a sound 10 times louder. Therefore, a noise rated at 80 decibels is 10 **times** louder than one at 70 dB. A noise at 90 dB is 100 times louder than one at 70 dB. Repeated exposure to levels of 90 to 115 dB can cause permanent hearing loss. Lower levels of continuous noise may not damage hearing, but they add to stress and stress-related diseases.

Sound Rating	
Ordinary conversation	60 dB
Busy street traffic	75 dB
Office adding machines	80 dB
20 feet from a subway train	90 dB
Can manufacturing plant	100 dB
Newspaper printing press	102 to 108 dB
Caterpillar tractor, idling	104 dB
Circular saw	105 to 116 dB
Drills, shovels, trucks operating	108 dB

7. The sound of office adding machines is how many times the sound of ordinary conversation?

   (1) 2
   (2) 10
   (3) 20
   (4) 100
   (5) 200

8. Which of these workers may suffer the worst job-related hearing loss?

   (1) a heavy-equipment operator
   (2) a worker in a can factory
   (3) a teacher
   (4) a traffic cop
   (5) a printing press operator

Answers are on page 647.

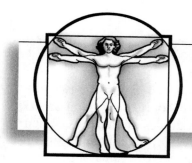

CHAPTER 5
Chemistry

Chemistry is the branch of science that studies matter and how matter changes. Matter makes up everything around you. The chair you're sitting in, the book you're reading, the clothes you're wearing, and you yourself are all examples of matter. **Matter** is anything that occupies space and has **mass**, or an amount of material in it. Matter can exist in four different states. It can be a **solid**, such as a desk; a **liquid**, such as water; a **gas**, such as air; or **plasma**, the gas-like substances that make up the Sun and other stars.

The work of many **chemists** involves the development of new elements and compounds that are not found in nature. These new chemicals are used to make new products, such as synthetic fibers, plastics, medical supplies, construction materials, and many other things. Other chemists investigate the chemistry that goes on in living things. These chemists are responsible for many new medicines and medical treatments.

Atoms and Molecules

All matter is made of tiny particles called **atoms**. They are too small to be seen, even with the most powerful microscope. Even so, scientists have been able to learn a great deal about atoms by doing experiments.

Each atom is like a tiny sun surrounded by planets. In the center of the atom is the **nucleus**. The nucleus contains **protons**, which have a positive electrical charge, and **neutrons**, which have no electrical charge. **Electrons** circle the nucleus like little planets. Electrons have a negative electrical charge and spin freely in energy levels called **shells**. The model of an aluminum atom below shows the parts of an atom.

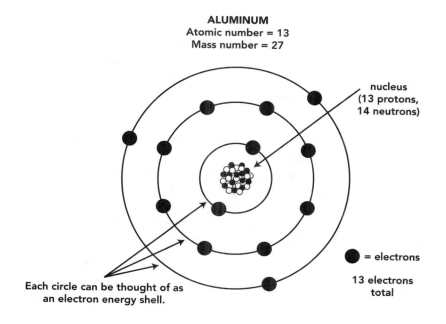

ALUMINUM
Atomic number = 13
Mass number = 27

nucleus
(13 protons,
14 neutrons)

= electrons

13 electrons
total

Each circle can be thought of as
an electron energy shell.

Scientists have found ninety-two different atoms and have made twenty other atoms in laboratories. A substance that contains only one kind of atom is called an **element**. Gold, silver, and oxygen are examples of elements. When two or more atoms combine, they form a **molecule**. Air, for example, contains oxygen molecules. Each oxygen molecule contains two oxygen atoms. Oxygen gas does not exist in air as an individual oxygen atom.

Oxygen molecule

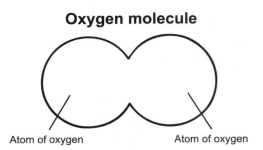

Atom of oxygen   Atom of oxygen

Most matter is made of more than one type of atom. A molecule of water, for instance, is made of two hydrogen atoms and one oxygen atom. That's why we say water is H_2O.

Water molecule

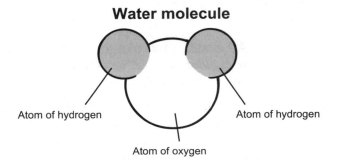

Atom of hydrogen   Atom of hydrogen

Atom of oxygen

There are millions of different ways that the atoms of elements can combine. That is why there are so many different substances in the universe.

Atomic Energy

The most powerful kind of energy in the universe is the energy that holds together the nucleus of an atom. This energy is called **atomic energy**. Another name for it is **nuclear energy**. When the nucleus of an atom is blown apart, an enormous amount of energy is released.

Some elements with many protons in the nucleus, such as radium and uranium, give off particles from the nucleus all the time, not just when there is an atomic explosion. We call these elements **radioactive**. Other elements may become radioactive if they have a large number of extra neutrons. Radioactive substances are dangerous because they damage or destroy living cells. The damaged cells cause cancer, birth defects, and other illnesses.

Atoms and Molecules

Directions: Match the words with their definitions.

———— **1.** atoms

———— **2.** electron

———— **3.** element

———— **4.** molecule

———— **5.** neutron

———— **6.** nucleus

———— **7.** proton

———— **8.** radioactive

———— **9.** shell

a. the center of an atom

b. positively charged particle in the nucleus

c. tiny particles that make up all matter

d. substance that contains one kind of atom

e. an energy level in which electrons orbit

f. atoms that give off particles from the nucleus

g. two or more combined atoms

h. negatively charged particle that orbits the nucleus

i. neutral particle in the nucleus of an atom

Answers are on page 648.

Mixtures, Solutions, and Compounds

As you know, there are many different substances in the universe. How those substances are formed depends on how their particles combine. Some particles are attracted to each other and join easily. Other particles are more selective about how they combine. A few particles won't combine with anything. Particles of matter can combine in mixtures, solutions, and chemical compounds.

Simple Mixtures

The simplest way particles of matter combine is as a **mixture**. A mixture contains two or more substances that are mixed together. The substances in a mixture are not changed. They don't join to form something new. The substances can usually be separated out of the mixture by picking them out, by evaporation, or by pouring. The amount of each substance in a mixture may differ. There may be more of one substance than another.

For example, a salad is a mixture of different vegetables. All the vegetables are combined in the same salad bowl, but you can still separate the tomatoes from the lettuce and the peppers from the onions. Plus, the mixture may contain more lettuce than tomatoes, peppers, and onions. The amount of each vegetable differs and none of the vegetables have changed; they have simply been put together.

Solutions

A **solution** is a special mixture in which one substance dissolves in another. The substance being dissolved is the **solute**. The substance in which the solute dissolves is the **solvent**. A salt-water solution is an example of salt (solute) being dissolved in water (solvent).

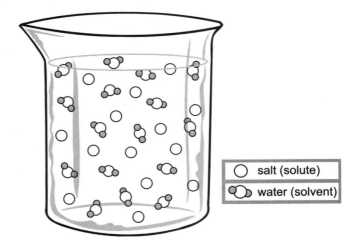

| ○ | salt (solute) |
| ○◐ | water (solvent) |

Most solutions are formed when a solid dissolves in a liquid. In a salt-water solution, for example, salt is a solid being dissolved in liquid water. Other solutions are formed through different combinations of solids, liquids, and gases. For example, air is a solution of the gases oxygen, argon, carbon dioxide, and water vapor dissolved in another gas, nitrogen. Antifreeze is a solution of a liquid, ethylene glycol, dissolved in a liquid, water.

A solvent can dissolve only a given amount of a solute. For instance, when you continue to add salt to a glass of water, you eventually see the salt collecting on the bottom of the glass. The water has reached a point where it cannot dissolve any more salt. We say that the salt solution is **saturated**. The salt on the bottom of the glass will not dissolve into the solution.

How does a solution differ from a simple mixture? For one thing, the substances in a solution are **homogenous**. That is, they spread out evenly throughout the solution. In a salt-water solution, the salt molecules spread evenly throughout the water molecules. If you tasted samples of the solution from the bottom, middle, and top of the glass, they all would taste the same. Another difference between a solution and a mixture is that a solution cannot be separated by **filtration**. This means that the solute will not separate from the solvent if you try to filter them through a screen or filter paper.

Compounds

A chemical **compound** is very different from a mixture or a solution. In mixtures and solutions, the original substances are still there. In a salad mixture, for instance, the lettuce, tomatoes, peppers, and onions don't change into something new. In a salt-water solution, even though you can't see the salt, the taste tells you the salt is still there, basically unchanged. But when two or more substances combine chemically, they form something totally different from the original substances.

For example, hydrogen and oxygen are both invisible gases in the air you breathe. When they combine chemically, they make the compound water. As you know, water is a liquid you can easily see but certainly cannot breathe. Carbon is an element that occurs naturally on Earth as a solid. Coal, for example, is carbon in its pure form. Carbon can combine chemically with hydrogen and oxygen to form sugar—something very different from coal, oxygen, or hydrogen! Compounds are formed when atoms of two or more elements bond, or join, to form a single molecule.

	SIMPLE MIXTURE Example: a bag of coins	SOLUTION Example: salt & water	COMPOUND Example: water (hydrogen & oxygen)
Can you see the separate parts?	Yes. You can easily see the separate pennies, nickels, dimes, and quarters.	No. You can't see the molecules of salt at all.	No. Water does not look like hydrogen or oxygen.
Is it homogenous?	No. The mixture may have more pennies and dimes at the top of the bag than at the bottom.	Yes. The solution is the same all the way through. The salt molecules spread evenly throughout the water molecules.	Yes. Water is the same all the way through.
Can you separate it by sifting or filtering?	Yes. The coins can be separated by hand or by sorting them in a coin machine.	No. The salt molecules will slip through even the finest filter paper along with the water.	No. You cannot separate water into the gases hydrogen and oxygen by sifting or filtering it.
Is the result a totally new substance?	No. The pennies are still pennies, the nickels are still nickels, and so on. No new substance is formed.	No. It is still water and salt. Even though you can't see the salt, you know it is there because you can taste it.	Yes. Water is completely different from hydrogen and oxygen. You can see and drink water, but you can't breathe it.

EXERCISE 2

Mixtures, Solutions, and Compounds

Directions: Write *M* if the substance is a mixture, *S* if the substance is a solution, or *C* if the substance is a compound.

_____ **1.** popcorn balls made from popcorn and caramel

_____ **2.** carbon dioxide gas made from carbon and oxygen

_____ **3.** sugar stirred into hot coffee

_____ **4.** different types of candies in a dish

_____ **5.** oxygen and nitrogen gas making nitrate fertilizer

_____ **6.** hot cocoa made from chocolate powder and hot milk

Directions: Circle the best answer.

7. Chlorine is a poisonous gas. When chlorine joins with sodium, it forms a white solid called salt, which people eat every day. Which of the following describes salt?

(1) simple mixture
(2) poison
(3) compound
(4) solution
(5) solvent

Answers are on page 648.

Naming Compounds

In our everyday lives we know many compounds by their common names, such as water, bleach, alcohol, and cleaning fluid. People in other countries often have different names for the same substances. In the world of science, however, it is important for scientists in one part of the world to know exactly what substances their colleagues in another part of the world are referring to. So scientists around the world use **chemical names** for compounds.

A chemical name uses part or all of the names of the elements in the compound as root words. It may also add prefixes and/or suffixes to give more clues about the compound. Prefixes attached to a root indicate the number of atoms of that element. Some common prefixes are *mono-* meaning one, *di-* meaning two, *tri-* meaning three, *tetra-* meaning four, and *pent-* meaning five. For example, the chemical name *carbon dioxide* contains the root words *carbon* and *oxygen*. The prefix *di-* in *dioxide* indicates that there are two atoms of oxygen in the compound.

Suffixes also give clues about a compound. For example, the chemical name for rust is *iron oxide*. From the root word clues in this name we know that the compound contains the elements *iron* and *oxygen*. The suffix *-ide* gives another clue. It tells us that only the elements named by the roots are in the compound. However, a chemical name containing the suffixes *-ite* and *-ate* means that oxygen is also part of the compound. For instance, the root words in the chemical name *hydrogen sulfate* indicate that hydrogen and sulfur are in the compound. The suffix *-ate* indicates that oxygen is also part of the compound.

Examine the following chemical names for clues about the elements that make up the compounds.

Chemical name	Root word clues	Prefix or suffix clue	Elements in the compound
carbon monoxide	*carbon, ox*	*mono-* meaning one atom of oxygen	carbon and oxygen
nitrogen pentoxide	*nitrogen, ox*	*pent-* meaning five atoms of oxygen	nitrogen and oxygen
sodium hydroxide	*sodium, hydr, ox*	*-ide*, meaning only the named elements are in the compound	sodium, hydrogen, and oxygen
aluminum sulfate	*aluminum, sulf*	*-ate*, meaning oxygen is also in the compound	aluminum, sulfur, and oxygen
calcium nitrate	*calcium, nitr*	*-ate*, meaning oxygen is also in the compound	calcium, nitrogen, and oxygen

Chemical Symbols and Formulas

Scientists have a shorthand way of naming elements and compounds. Scientists use **symbols** to name the elements. Every element has a different symbol of one or two letters taken from the name of the element. The first letter is a capital letter. The second letter, if there is one, is lower case.

The following table contains some common elements that you should know. You may want to memorize the symbols for these elements.

Common Elements

Name	Symbol
Hydrogen	H
Carbon	C
Nitrogen	N
Oxygen	O
Sodium	Na
Sulfur	S
Chlorine	Cl
Calcium	Ca
Iron	Fe

Scientists use a combination of symbols and numbers to write the names of compounds. A **formula** shows the type and number of atoms in one molecule of the compound. If a symbol is not followed by a small number, there is only one atom of that element. For instance, the formula for the compound hydrogen chloride is HCl. Since there are no small numbers following the symbols, we know that a molecule of hydrogen chloride contains one atom of hydrogen and one atom of chlorine. The formula for water is H_2O. One molecule of water contains two atoms of hydrogen and one atom of oxygen.

A full-size number in front of a formula indicates that more than one molecule is represented. For example, two molecules of water would be written $2H_2O$. Notice that two molecules of water contain four atoms of hydrogen ($2 \times 2 = 4$) and two atoms of oxygen ($2 \times 1 = 2$).

EXERCISE 3

Chemical Names and Formulas

Directions: From the list below, write the correct formula after each chemical name. Look back at the chart of symbols if you need to.

CaO	$CaCl_2$	CO
HNO_2	H_2S	$NaSO_4$

1. calcium chloride _____

2. calcium oxide _____

3. hydrogen sulfide _____

4. sodium sulfate _____

5. carbon monoxide _____

6. hydrogen nitrite _____

Directions: Circle the best answer.

7. Carbon tetrachloride is the chemical name for a common cleaning fluid. *Tetra-* is a prefix meaning *four*. Which of the following formulas correctly describes one molecule of carbon tetrachloride?

(1) CCl
(2) $CaCl_2$
(3) $4CO_2$
(4) C_4Cl
(5) CCl_4

Answers are on page 648.

Acids and Bases

We use chemistry in our lives every day. Cooking and cleaning are two areas in which chemistry plays a major role. Many foods and cleaning products, for example, contain a group of chemicals called **acids**. An acid is a substance that has a sour taste, such as lemon juice or vinegar. The chart below lists some acids used in everyday life. The examples on the chart indicate that the chemical formula for an acid usually begins with an *H* for hydrogen. Read the chart to find out where these acids are found and how they are used.

Acid	Formula	Where it is found	How it is used
Acetic acid	$HC_2H_3O_2$	Vinegar	For pickling and in salad dressings; for cleaning glass and china
Citric acid	$H_3C_6H_5O_7$	Oranges, lemons, grapefruits	As a preservative in many canned foods
Lactic acid	$HC_3H_5O_3$	Sour milk	In the production of cheese; in the manufacture of drugs and plastics
Boric acid	H_3BO_3	Eyewash	As an eye rinse; as a soil fertilizer; as a mild disinfectant; as a flame retardant
Sulfuric acid	H_2SO_4	Batteries, acid rain	For cleaning corroded metals

Bases are another group of chemicals found in some foods and in many cleaning products. Most drain cleaners contain sodium hydroxide ($NaOH$), a very strong base that is commonly known as lye. Washing soda ($NaCO_3$) and baking soda ($NaHCO_3$) are both bases. Ammonia (NH_3) is a base that is used in many kinds of household cleaners. Magnesium hydroxide $Mg(OH)_2$, commonly known as milk of magnesia, and aluminum hydroxide $Al(OH)_2$ are both bases used in common antacid medicines.

Most bases are bitter tasting and have a slippery feel to them. The chemical formula for many bases shows an (OH) group on the end, as in sodium hydroxide ($NaOH$).

Both acids and bases are very **reactive**; that is, they react easily with other chemicals. Being reactive makes acids and bases good cleaners because they will react with dirt and grease. But being reactive also makes acids and bases very dangerous. A strong acid or base can burn a person very badly because it reacts with the water and other chemicals in skin. Acids and bases also react very easily with each other. If an acid and a base are combined, they will react together to form water and a type of salt. When this happens, the acid and the base have **neutralized** each other.

Because some acids and bases are so dangerous, chemists test for them using **litmus paper**. Litmus paper is a strip of red or blue paper that is dipped into a solution. If the paper turns red, the solution is an acid. If the paper turns blue, the solution is a base.

EXERCISE 4

Acids and Bases

Directions: Complete this review by filling in the blanks.

acids	oranges	red	drain cleaner
acids	bitter	lemons	litmus paper
bases	ammonia	sour	washing soda
bases	grapefruit	blue	

(1) _____ and (2) _____ are two common groups of chemicals that are very reactive.

(3) _____, (4) _____, and (5) _____ are examples of foods that contain acids.

Three cleaners that are bases include (6) _____, (7) _____, and (8) _____.

There are many ways to tell an acid from a base. Acids taste (9) _____, while bases taste (10) _____.

(11) _____ feel slippery to the touch, but (12) _____ don't. Scientists test acids and bases using (13) _____ _____. This special paper turns (14) _____ when it touches an acid and (15) _____ when it touches a base.

Answers are on page 648.

Poisons

Children under five are the most common victims of poison. Young children do not know what is food and what isn't. They taste everything they find. Many poisons are so strong that even a taste can be very dangerous.

People are often surprised at the number of **toxic**—or poisonous—chemicals that are contained in many common household items. Bleach, drain cleaner, floor polish, and most cleaning supplies can all be deadly. Children can also be poisoned by consuming relatively small amounts of ordinary medicines such as cough syrups, laxatives, and pain relievers. Cosmetics, such as eye shadow, face cream, and lipstick, also can be toxic when eaten. Vitamins often look like candy to children, but an **overdose** of vitamins can also be toxic.

Adults, too, can become poison victims. The most common cause of adult poisoning is drug overdose. Most drug overdoses are accidental. Some people take extra doses of prescription medicines, thinking that if a little medicine is good, a lot will be even better. This is simply not true!

Some adults become poison victims while working around the house. They may breathe toxic fumes or gases from insecticides, paints, or solvents. They may unknowingly make and breathe a dangerous chlorine gas by mixing ammonia with bleach or other chlorine-based cleaners. Some adults even siphon gasoline by mouth. Siphoning gasoline is extremely risky because just a few drops of gasoline in the lungs can kill a person.

Safety Precautions

An accident with poison can be a real tragedy. You can help prevent poisonings in your own home by following these basic safety precautions.

Home Safety Checklist

Storing chemicals

✓ Store all chemicals, cleaners, cosmetics, and medicines in high cabinets.

✓ Add childproof locks and hooks on all cabinets.

✓ Return chemicals, cleaners, cosmetics, and medicines to these cabinets immediately after use; never leave them out on a countertop or table.

✓ Never store cleaning fluids, oils, or other chemicals in discarded food containers, such as empty beverage bottles and milk cartons.

Using warning labels

✓ Put warning stickers on all poisons. These stickers are available free from your local hospital or poison control center.

✓ Read the labels on containers of all household products. Follow the advice on these labels.

✓ Read the labels on medicines every time you take or give a dose. Use only the amount prescribed on the label.

Protecting children

✓ Don't coax children to take medicine by telling them that it is candy.

✓ Never encourage a child to take "just a sip" of an alcoholic drink.

✓ Remove tobacco, ashes, and alcoholic drinks from rooms where young children may be alone.

Using chemicals with fumes

✓ Use cleaners and other chemicals with strong fumes only in well-ventilated areas.

✓ If you start to feel sick from fumes, go out into the fresh air. If you still feel ill, call a doctor or a hospital emergency room.

Reacting in an emergency

✓ Keep a list near your telephone of phone numbers for your local hospital emergency room and the nearest poison control center.

✓ Buy a bottle of syrup of ipecac from your drugstore and store it with your other medicines. Syrup of ipecac will cause a person to vomit— or throw up. Sometimes vomiting will help; sometimes it will make things worse. *Do not use ipecac until told to by a health professional.*

Chemicals That Cause Disease

Modern chemistry has made our lives longer, fuller, and more comfortable. Without chemistry, for instance, we would not have plastic, nylon, rayon, polyester, detergents, photographs, and contact lenses. For many people, medicines are very important chemicals. Before 1940, people died from infected wounds and from common diseases such as strep throat and pneumonia. Today our doctors give us an antibiotic, and we feel fine in a few days. People with heart disease, high blood pressure, and many other diseases depend on modern medicines to help them lead normal lives. But chemicals can be harmful as well as helpful.

Terrible chemical weapons, such as nerve gas and napalm, have been used in wars since World War I. Often innocent civilians are harmed by such chemicals. Many times a chemical used during war is later found to cause serious side effects.

Medicines are tested before being approved for public use. Unfortunately, these tests cannot check every possible use of the drug and predict every possible outcome. For example, doctors used to think that aspirin was good for treating children with the flu. Now doctors believe that aspirin may cause children to have a reaction called **Reye's syndrome**. This disease may cause convulsions, coma, permanent brain damage, or death.

Asbestos is another chemical that was once thought to be beneficial. This chemical was used widely in construction because it is fireproof, makes good insulation, and strengthens other materials such as concrete and plastic. Millions of tons of asbestos were used to build schools, homes, and stores. Now scientists have discovered that asbestos can cause cancer, and asbestos is being carefully removed from buildings. For people who got cancer from asbestos, however, the damage is already done.

Chemicals in Food

Food additives, or chemicals that are added to foods, have made a great variety of foods available to us in easy-to-prepare forms. Almost all prepackaged foods, and many other canned and frozen foods, contain food additives. Preservatives, for instance, help keep foods from spoiling or going stale. Artificial flavors and flavor enhancers make foods taste better. Artificial colors make foods more attractive and appealing. Now scientists are discovering that some additives can be dangerous to our health.

Manufacturers of artificial sweeteners have often found themselves in a sticky mess. According to some tests, cyclamates and saccharin, two popular artificial sweeteners, may cause cancer. Another sweetener called aspartame—often used as a sugar substitute—was carefully tested before it was used, but some people still say that it gives them headaches and other problems.

Sodium nitrite is a preservative that keeps meat from spoiling and prevents people from getting food poisoning. Meats such as hot dogs, salami, and bacon contain sodium nitrite. Recent experiments show that sodium nitrite can cause cancer in lab animals. Now some people are demanding that manufacturers ban the use of sodium nitrite as a preservative.

Many people think we need to be more careful about the chemicals we use. This can be accomplished through the cooperation of concerned individuals, manufacturers, and government agencies such as the Food and Drug Administration (FDA) and the Environmental Protection Agency (EPA).

EXERCISE 5

Decisions About Chemicals

Directions: Write your answers to questions 1 and 2 on a separate sheet of paper. State your opinions and support your opinions with reasons. There are no right or wrong answers to these questions.

1. Should people be allowed to buy artificial sweeteners, even though they may cause cancer?

2. In the mid-1980s, the budgets of agencies such as the EPA (Environmental Protection Agency) and FDA (Food and Drug Administration) were cut. At the same time, more and more money was spent on the military. Was this a wise way to spend money?

Directions: Circle the best answer.

3. Which of the following is an opinion, not a fact, from the passage?

   (1) Some tests show that saccharin may cause cancer.
   (2) Manufacturers should work to make sure that chemicals are safe.
   (3) Artificial colors are intended to make food more appealing.
   (4) Chemistry has been important in the construction business.
   (5) Sodium nitrite can cause cancer in animals.

Answers are on page 648.

Chapter Review

EXERCISE 6

Directions: Using the information given, circle the best answer.

Questions 1 and 2 refer to the chart below.

Some Elements and Their Chemical Symbols		
Cl—Chlorine	N—Nitrogen	Ag—Silver
Si—Silicon	O—Oxygen	Cu—Copper

1. How many of these compounds contain silver?

   $AgNO_3$ Cu_2O Ag_2O Ag_2S Au_2O

   (1) one
   (2) two
   (3) three
   (4) four
   (5) five

2. Which of the following is the correct name for CuCl?

    (1) silver calcite
    (2) chlorine sulfate
    (3) copper oxide
    (4) silver chloride
    (5) copper chloride

Questions 3 and 4 are based on the label below.

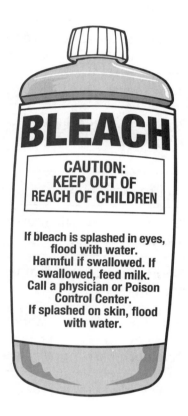

3. According to this label, laundry bleach can be harmful to which parts of the body?

    (1) eyes
    (2) stomach
    (3) skin
    (4) all of the above
    (5) none of the above

4. Which of the following should you do if someone swallows bleach?

    (1) Flood the person with water.
    (2) Have the person drink milk.
    (3) Have the person drink water.
    (4) Rinse the person's eyes with water.
    (5) Rinse the person's eyes with milk.

Questions 5 and 6 are based on the information in the chart below.

Many people are exposed to materials on the job that are dangerous to their health. The following chart lists some symptoms and possible causes.

Area Affected	Symptoms	Common Cause(s)
Head	Headache, dizziness	Excessive noise
Nose and throat	Coughing, sneezing, sore throat	Ozone, solvents, ammonia, caustic soda, dusts
	Nasal cancer	Hardwood dusts and resins
Chest and lungs	Dry cough, wheezing, congestion	Cotton dust, detergent enzymes, beryllium, solvents, TDI (an isocyanate found in polyurethane)
	Flu-like symptoms	Metal oxides from welding
	Shortness of breath after mild exercise	Long-term exposure to asbestos
Ears	Ringing, temporary deafness, hearing loss	Excessive noise
Eyes	Irritation, redness, watering	Gases, fumes, smoke, metal dust, acids
	"Welder's flash," grainy feeling	Ultraviolet radiation
Skin	Itching, dryness, redness	Epoxies, solvents, oil, fiberglass, nickel, caustic soda
	Ulcers, skin cancer	Arsenic, pitch, tar, mineral oils, radiation
Nervous system	Nervousness, irritability, stress, tremors, sleeplessness, speech changes	Noise, metal poisoning (mercury, lead)
Reproductive system	Irregularities in menstruation	Polystyrene production, xylene, solvents
	Miscarriage	Pesticides, radiation, lead, anesthetic gas
	Damage to chromosomes or fetus sterilization	Lead, mercury, radiation, benzene

5. Betty works in a chemical factory. She has been having problems with her nervous system. According to this chart, what is one possible cause?

   (1) solvents
   (2) metal poisoning
   (3) ozone
   (4) acid fumes
   (5) radiation

6. Workers in another plant are exposed to many different kinds of dust. According to the chart, which of the following problems is probably not caused by dust?

   (1) irritated eyes
   (2) sore throat
   (3) dry cough
   (4) sneezing
   (5) headache and dizziness

Questions 7 and 8 are based on the following opinions.

Speaker A

   Some people are calling for a ban on food additives. This would be a big mistake. If food additives were banned, most foods would spoil on the way to markets that often are thousands of miles away from where they were grown or manufactured. Food would become scarce in parts of the United States and in other countries where we export food. Vitamins and minerals are additives in foods such as milk, flour, cereal, and margarine. Without these additives, many people's diets would lack the nutrients their bodies need. Although some studies have shown that food additives cause cancer in test animals, the quantities of additives given to those animals far exceed the amount humans eat in foods. So, it does not make sense that humans will get cancer from additives in their foods.

Speaker B

   There have been many news stories lately about a link between food additives and cancer. Experiments have shown that some food additives cause cancer in test animals. It logically follows that those same food additives are likely to cause cancer in humans. The FDA says that there is no connection because the amount of additives given to the animals is much more than humans get in foods. But one source says that Americans eat their weight in food additives each year. This can add up to 100 pounds or more of additives each year for an adult. Eating such a large amount of food additives every year probably can and does cause cancer in humans. If people are going to eat that much of something, it should at least be food, not chemicals—especially chemicals that have no right being in food.

7. Which of the following statements would Speaker B probably agree with?

   (1) The chances of getting cancer from food additives are slim.
   (2) Governments should not allow chemicals to be added to foods.
   (3) People who call for a ban on food additives probably grow their own foods already.
   (4) Vitamins are important food additives that should not be banned from foods.
   (5) A ban on food additives would starve more people to death than would be killed by cancer.

8. Both of these articles are mostly opinion. What is one fact mentioned by Speaker A?

   (1) It does not follow that humans will get cancer from food additives.
   (2) Banning food additives would be a big mistake.
   (3) If food additives were banned, food would become scarce around the world.
   (4) People should stop thinking about themselves and do what is right for the majority of people in the world.
   (5) The quantities of additives given to test animals far exceed the amounts eaten by humans.

Answers are on page 648.

CHAPTER 6

Earth and Space Science

Evaluating Ideas

Scientific discoveries allow us to do things we have never done before. Scientific progress, however, brings questions and problems along with the benefits.

Should businesses be required to protect the environment, even if that means jobs will be lost and prices will rise?

Should new medicines that might cure diseases such as AIDS be put on the market right away, or should they first go through a five-year testing program to make certain they are useful and safe?

Should the government spend millions of dollars to put astronauts in space, or should it spend that money on health care for the elderly?

Should human cloning be allowed by the government or banned, even if it could save lives?

Questions such as these cannot be answered by scientists alone. There is no scientific answer to the question, "What is the right thing to do?" Science only provides facts. What we do with those facts is a question of values and beliefs.

Values and Beliefs

Each person has his or her own **value system**, a set of beliefs about what is important and what is right and wrong. We develop these values as we grow. They are shaped by our family, culture, religion, and life experience. We rely on our values every time we make a decision.

Sometimes our values are conflicted. Often the conflict is between a short-term value and a long-term value. A **short-term value** is something that will make us feel good right now. A **long-term value** is something that we think is important in the long run. For example, should a city build an inexpensive sewage treatment plant that will save the taxpayers money now but will likely pollute the local drinking water within ten years? Or should the city raise taxes now to pay for a more expensive plant that is better for the environment?

Sometimes conflicts arise between important long-term values. For instance, doctors take an oath to do no harm to a patient, yet most people believe they should be able to die with dignity. These opposite issues raise difficult questions. Should patients be allowed to refuse medical treatment and die in peace? Should doctors always try to keep patients alive as long as possible?

Some conflicts come about because of limited money, time, and manpower. Should we spend money on weapons to defend our country or on programs for education and food stamps? Should we increase Medicare benefits for senior citizens or provide more nutritious hot lunches in schools? Different groups of people will have different ideas about what is most important and what should be done.

Consider the following case:

A certain town uses chemical herbicides—weed killers—along the sides of the roads. Some people want to stop the town from doing this because the chemicals pollute the environment and a few children have become very sick from the herbicides. The mayor says that if the town can't use herbicides, she will have to hire extra workers to mow the roadsides. That means higher taxes. The mayor also says that the town has been using these chemicals for years, and no one has really been hurt. If the weeds are not destroyed by herbicides or by mowing, people with allergies will suffer more.

If you were voting on this issue, would you vote for or against the use of herbicides? Here are some questions you might consider.

1. Which is more important to you, a cleaner environment or lower taxes?

2. Should everyone have to pay more just because a few children are sensitive to these chemicals?

3. Is the mayor right that no one has been hurt?

4. Should everyone have to pay more to benefit only those people with allergies?

Now check how you would vote and list your reasons for voting that way.

_____ use herbicides   _____ do not use herbicides

Reason A: _____

Reason B: _____

Reason C: _____

Do you think your answer would be different if you had a brother or sister who was sensitive to herbicides? What if you had severe allergic reactions to pollen from weeds? How about if your family had a low income and you were afraid of losing your home because of higher taxes? To make fair decisions, we have to look at what is best for us personally and what is best for our community.

EXERCISE 1

You Decide

Directions: Read each pair of opposing opinions on a current issue involving the use of science. Put a check next to the opinion you agree with. Then write three reasons that support your opinion.

1. _____ Scientists should control the genes of unborn children so that the next generation is stronger and smarter.

   _____ Scientists should not try to control the genes of unborn children.

   Reasons that support your opinion:

   a. _____

   b. _____

   c. _____

2. _____ Some areas of government land—national parks, for example—should be closed to all people so that the wilderness can be preserved.

   _____ All government lands should be open to tourists and to careful mining, ranching, and lumbering.

   Reasons that support your opinion:

   a. _____

   b. _____

   c. _____

3. _____ Employers should have the right to test workers to find out if they are using drugs.

   _____ Employers should not have the right to do drug testing.

   Reasons that support your opinion:

   a. _____

   b. _____

   c. _____

Answers are on page 649.

Critical Reading

Advertisers want you to buy their products. Politicians want you to vote for them. Even your family and friends try to persuade you to see and do things their way. To help yourself understand important issues and make good decisions about them, ask yourself these two questions: Am I getting all the facts? If not, where can I get more information?

Many times someone will try to persuade you to think or do something without giving you all the facts. For example, an advertiser will say, "Strike detergent is new and improved. Buy some today!" However, the ad doesn't say how Strike is new or how it is improved. Does it clean better, cost less, or just smell nicer? You need more information before you can decide if Strike is the detergent you want to buy.

Read this statement from a medicine company. Then list at least two questions you would want answered before deciding whether to buy Sager aspirin.

"Ninety percent of people surveyed prefer Sager aspirin."

1. _____

2. _____

You may have listed many different questions, including the following:

How many people were surveyed? If only ten people were surveyed, the results don't mean as much as if thousands were surveyed.

How was the survey done? Were people chosen at random, or were only people who bought Sager questioned?

Who conducted the survey? Was it done by an independent company or the Sager company itself?

Why did the people prefer Sager? Was it cheaper? Did it work best for headaches or perhaps for arthritis?

EXERCISE 2

The Whole Story

Directions: Read the following persuasive statements. Write at least one question that you would need answered in order to have all the facts.

1. Move to California; we have the best weather in the nation.

   _____

   _____

2. Take vitamins to improve your health.

   _____

   _____

3. Stop your taxes from going up by voting against the new park.

_____

_____

4. We must build more roads; we can't stand in the way of progress.

_____

_____

5. Chemical X must be banned because it causes cancer in mice.

_____

_____

Answers are on page 649.

Where to Go Next

It is important to find accurate information on a subject from **reliable sources**, such as books, journals, encyclopedias, and experts. The sources you choose should have special knowledge about the subject. It is important that the source is not **biased**—prejudiced toward one side of an issue. For example, if you wanted to know which brand of stereo needs the fewest repairs, you wouldn't just ask the salesperson. After all, he probably makes more money if he sells you a more expensive product. Instead, you could check in a magazine such as _Consumer Reports_ for the results of independent testing.

There are several good places to look for information: the Internet, a public library, your local government. The Internet contains valuable information from news organizations, researchers, government organizations, individual experts, and universities. The Internet, however, also contains sites that may not offer legitimate information and useful opinions. It is important to consider the sources of the sites you visit. Choose sites that are associated with a reputable organization. Distinguish facts from opinions, and double-check all facts with another source.

Public libraries have a wealth of information in books, magazines, encyclopedias, technical manuals, films, videos, and recorded interviews. Don't be afraid to ask a librarian for assistance if you are not sure where to find information. Librarians are happy to help people find the information they want.

A good source for local questions about new laws or government programs is your city, town, county, or state government. A phone call, e-mail, or letter to local politicians or members of Congress will often result in helpful information. Citizens' groups may also provide information. These groups deal with many different issues, from wildlife preservation to the prevention of birth defects, and they are usually more than happy to provide information on their areas of interest.

EXERCISE 3

Information, Please

Directions: Circle the numbers of the **two best sources** of information for each of the following questions.

1. Is the factory in my town polluting our river?

    (1) a publicity release from the factory
    (2) the town health department
    (3) Citizens for a Better Environment
    (4) a friend who fishes on the river all the time

2. If a child has a fever of 101°F, does the child need to see a doctor?

    (1) a doctor
    (2) the child's grandmother
    (3) a neighbor whose child had a similar fever last week
    (4) the hospital emergency room

3. Are health foods really better for you than regular foods?

    (1) books on nutrition from the library
    (2) the county health department
    (3) your brother, who is always on a diet
    (4) a clerk at your local health food store

Answers are on page 649.

Geology

People have lived on Earth for hundreds of thousands of years, and we have always been curious about the things around us. Our curiosity has led to the discovery of countless facts about our amazing planet. Yet there always seems to be something new to discover. We continue to investigate those hard-to-reach places, such as the depths of the oceans. Scientists continue to discover plants and animals that are still unnamed. Our curiosity has even sent us on fact-finding missions to the other planets and their moons, the stars, comets, meteors, and asteroids. Human curiosity encompasses the entire universe.

THE STRUCTURE OF THE EARTH

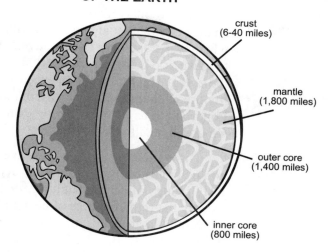

crust (6-40 miles)

mantle (1,800 miles)

outer core (1,400 miles)

inner core (800 miles)

Geology is the study of Earth—what it is made of and how it is organized. **Geologists** learn about Earth and its history by studying its mountains, oceans, mineral deposits, rocks, and atmosphere. Geologists have learned that the structure of Earth is a bit like an apple. Earth has a thin outer layer like a peel, an inner layer, and a core. The thin outer layer of Earth is called the **crust**. It is very irregular, bumping up into mountains and flattening out in plains. The thickest part of the crust is only about forty miles thick, but it provides everything we need for life.

Below the crust is a thick layer called the **mantle**. No one has ever drilled down into the mantle or the layers beneath it. From studying the way vibrations pass through this layer, geologists believe the mantle is made of solid rock.

Inside the mantle are the **outer core** and the **inner core**. Both cores are probably made of a mixture of iron and nickel. It is very hot inside the cores, up to 9,000°F. The outer core is molten—or liquid. The enormous pressures on the inner core at the center of Earth, however, have forced the iron and nickel located there into a solid state.

Buried Treasure

You know that people dig mines into Earth's crust in search of substances such as diamonds, iron, copper, coal, limestone, and uranium. These substances are **minerals**—natural elements and compounds. We use minerals to make things, from cars and buildings to plastics and jewelry.

Metals are minerals that are usually found mixed with other elements in mineral compounds called **ores**. The iron we use to make steel for buildings and machinery, the copper we use to make electric wires, the aluminum we use to make aircraft and kitchen devices, the gold and silver we use to make coins and jewelry, and the uranium we use in atomic power plants all come from ores.

Oil, coal, and natural gas, called **fossil fuels**, are minerals formed from the remains of plants that lived millions of years ago. These plants died and were buried in layers deep within Earth, where heat and pressure gradually changed them to coal and oil. During this process, they gave off natural gas, which was trapped in Earth's layers. Fossil fuels, which took millions of years to make, are being used up very quickly. We burn fossil fuels to get most of the energy for our cars, homes, and industry. We also use them to make many important chemical products, from medicines to plastics. Fossil fuels are so important to us that many people are worried about what will happen when we use them all up.

Throughout history, people have valued jewels, such as diamonds, rubies, and emeralds because of their beauty and rarity. Strangely enough, jewels are just ordinary minerals that have been changed into clear and colorful gems by exactly the right amounts of heat and pressure within Earth. Rubies are made of aluminum and oxygen, while diamonds are pure carbon, the same material as in black coal. Besides being used for jewelry, gemstones are used in industry. Diamonds, which are the hardest natural material, are used in drills and cutting tools, and rubies are used to focus laser beams.

EXERCISE 4

Geology

Directions: List two things you use that are made from these minerals.

1. copper: _____

2. iron: _____

3. aluminum: _____

4. fossil fuels: _____

Directions: Circle the number of the best answer.

5. Look again at the passage under the diagram, "Earth's Interior." How do scientists learn about the layers under Earth's crust?

   (1) by drilling down under the crust
   (2) by reading science fiction
   (3) by going down into the center of Earth
   (4) by measuring vibrations that pass through Earth
   (5) by studying the material that comes out of volcanoes

Answers are on page 649.

Soil Conservation

When pioneers first settled our country, a farmer needed a strong back and lots of energy. Today a successful farmer also needs plenty of scientific knowledge. New machines and chemicals have changed the way people farm. Successful farmers have learned to maintain their land through soil conservation.

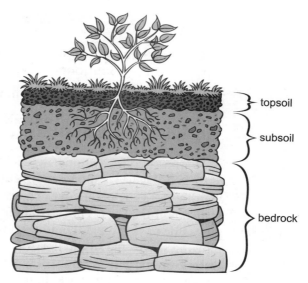

topsoil

subsoil

bedrock

Soil is the loose material found on the top of Earth's crust. Plants get most of their nutrients—the materials they need for growth—from the soil. Most of the available nutrients are found in the upper layer of the soil called the **topsoil**. Topsoil is a mixture of sand, clay, and humus. **Humus** is material from decaying plants and animals. Humus provides many nutrients and keeps the soil spongy so it can hold air and water. **Sand** makes the soil loose, which allows water and air to get in and plant roots to grow easily. **Clay** helps the soil hold water and provides some necessary minerals. All three materials are needed for good topsoil.

Beneath the topsoil is the **subsoil**, which may be sand, clay, gravel, or a mixture of all three. Since subsoil has no humus in it, most plants cannot grow in it directly. Some plants, however, have very deep roots that allow them to get some of their minerals from the subsoil. Both the topsoil and the subsoil rest on the **bedrock** that makes up Earth's crust.

Soil Damage

Soil can become damaged if the ground is left bare of grass and plants. Wind and running water carry away the topsoil in a process called **erosion**. Water erosion is more likely on hilly land, while wind erosion happens most often on flat land that has no hedges or windbreaks. Fall plowing adds to wind erosion because the ground is left bare. Crops such as corn and cotton that grow in rows, leaving the soil bare between the plants, also cause erosion.

All plants damage the soil by taking in minerals. Minerals are used up faster if the same crops are grown every year because more and more of the same minerals are taken from the soil. If minerals aren't returned to the soil, the soil will no longer be able to grow healthy plants.

Keeping Soil Healthy

Soil conservation means that farmers must use the soil with as little waste as possible. Through soil conservation, farmers hope to leave an adequate supply of fertile soil for future generations. The chart shows some of the goals of soil conservation.

Goals of Soil Conservation

1. Decrease the rate of erosion so it is less than the rate of soil formation—about one to five tons per acre per year.

2. Keep the levels of nutrients in the soil at appropriate levels.

3. Replenish the soil with organic matter and nutrients.

Farmers do many things to decrease the rate of erosion. They plant lines of trees or bushes, called **windbreaks**, to slow down the wind as it crosses their fields. They plant **cover crops** to hold down the soil after the main crop is taken off the land. They avoid plowing in the fall. Farmers with hilly land plow sideways around the hills—a process called **contour plowing**. Contour plowing leaves the soil in horizontal ridges that catch water, preventing the water from running straight downhill. Some farmers use **conservation tillage**, which leaves plant material in the top layer of soil. All of these things help keep valuable topsoil from being blown or washed away.

To preserve the minerals in the soil, farmers sometimes let a field lie **fallow**—resting for a year without crops. Farmers also **rotate** their crops, growing different crops on the same piece of land each year. A crop such as corn, which takes a lot of minerals from the soil, may be followed by clover or alfalfa—crops that help replace some minerals.

Farmers add **fertilizer** to their soil to replace the minerals used by plants. **Inorganic fertilizers** are chemicals made in a laboratory that can be added to the soil. Some commonly added chemicals are nitrogen, phosphorus, and potassium. **Organic fertilizer** comes from living things such as compost, manure from farm animals, and waste material from crops. Organic fertilizer can be more expensive, and its chemical content is harder to measure exactly. However, only organic fertilizer contains humus, which is necessary for healthy soil.

EXERCISE 5

Soil Conservation

Directions: Read the following list of farming practices. On the line with each farming practice, write whether the practice **harms** or **helps** the soil. The first one is done for you.

1. Using fertilizer _____ *helps* _____ the soil.

2. Planting the same crop every year _____ the soil.

3. Letting a field lie fallow _____ the soil.

4. Plowing straight up and down hills _____ the soil.

5. Planting cover crops _____ the soil.

6. Rotating crops _____ the soil.

7. Contour plowing _____ the soil.

Directions: Circle the number of the best answer.

8. Which of the following best describes how to improve a garden whose soil is sandy and worn-out?

   (1) Plant only easy-to-grow things, such as radishes and beans.
   (2) Add lots of dried manure for fertilizer.
   (3) Plow it well before planting.
   (4) Leave it bare all winter to soak up water.
   (5) Spread pure nitrogen fertilizer on it.

Answers are on page 649.

Ecosystems

As you know, plants and animals interact with each other for food, water, sunlight, living space, mates, and shelter. The area in which these living and nonliving things interact is called an **ecosystem**. An ecosystem may be big, like an ocean or a forest, or small, like a drop of water or a flower. Scientists have learned that the balance of nature in an ecosystem is very fragile. Through **ecology**—the study of the balance of nature—ecologists have examined how living things relate to each other and to their **environment**—the world around them. Ecologists have learned that living things depend on their environment and on each other in very complex patterns.

One pattern that ecologists study is called a **food web**. A food web is the path that energy, in the form of food, follows as it moves through an ecosystem. Examine the meadow food web shown below.

MEADOW FOOD WEB

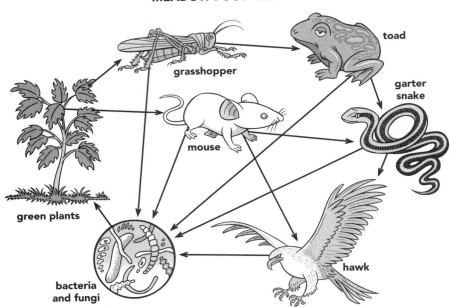

A food web starts with green plants. Green plants are called **producers** because they make their own food using energy from the Sun. Green plants are the source of food for every other living thing in the ecosystem. Things that eat the producers are called **consumers**. All animals are consumers. Animals that eat plants, such as the grasshopper and mouse in the meadow food web, are called **primary consumers**. Animals that eat other animals, such as the toad, snake, and hawk, are called **secondary consumers.** When plants and animals die, **decomposers** such as bacteria and fungi break them down and return their nutrients to the soil. The nutrients then are reused by living plants and animals.

If just one link in a food web is disturbed, all the other parts are affected. Take another look at the meadow food web and think about the effect of the following events.

- If a sudden dry spell prevented the toads from breeding, there would be fewer toads to eat grasshoppers.

- Millions more grasshoppers would survive, so farmers' crops in the area would be under attack from the hungry grasshoppers.

- Snakes would not do well either because there wouldn't be very many toads for them to eat.

- Because there would be fewer snakes, there would probably be fewer hawks too.

People and the Environment

The previous example of the meadow food web shows how a natural change, such as a change in weather, can affect the food web. Humans also upset the balance of nature. To obtain lumber for building and paper for reading materials, we cut down forests that are the source of food and shelter for many animals and plants. To obtain electricity and water, we dam rivers that are home to various fish, plants, and animals. To obtain meat—whether for food or for sport—we kill animals. To heat our homes in winter and cool them in summer, we burn fossil fuels that release harmful chemicals into the environment. People rely on the environment to provide the things we need or want. However, every time we take something from the environment, move something from one place to another in the environment, or put something into the environment, we affect the ecosystem.

Air, water, and soil pollution as well as the conservation of natural resources are only some of the problems we must address to keep our natural environment safe. Read the following chart to learn how human activities affect an ecosystem.

How Humans Upset an Ecosystem	
We use up the natural resources.	**Natural resources** include the air, water, food, trees, and oil that we take from the environment. Some of these resources are **renewable** and can be replaced. Other resources, such as soil, coal, and oil, are **nonrenewable**.
We pollute the air.	When we burn fuels in our homes, factories, and cars, chemicals are released into the air. **Air pollution** is caused by these harmful chemicals. **Smog** over a city is air pollution that you can see.
We pollute the water.	**Water pollution** results when substances are not disposed of properly and they end up in our streams, rivers, lakes, and oceans. Fertilizers and pesticides can seep into our water. Sewage often ends up in rivers and lakes. Oil spills from tankers release oil into the oceans.

EXERCISE 6

A Forest Ecosystem

Directions: The diagram shows a food web in a forest ecosystem. Answer the following questions. Notice that the arrows in the food web point to consumers.

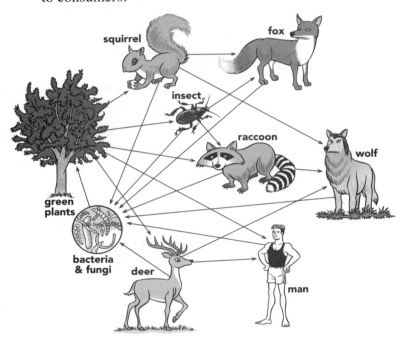

Note: All dead organisms are decomposed by bacteria and fungi; their nutrients are returned to the soil to be used by plants.

1. What are the producers in this food web? _____

2. What are the primary consumers? _____

3. What are the secondary consumers? _____

4. What are the decomposers? _____

Directions: Circle the number of the best answer.

5. When hazardous wastes, such as fertilizers and pesticides, seep into the soil in the forest ecosystem, which of the following in the food web is affected?

   A. green plants
   B. the squirrel, insect, raccoon, and deer
   C. the fox, wolf, and man

   (1) A only
   (2) B only
   (3) C only
   (4) B and C only
   (5) A, B, and C

Weather

How does weather affect your everyday life? Many people think the weather determines only the clothes they wear and the activities they participate in. But weather also affects many other things, such as the food we grow, the roads and buildings we construct, the places where we vacation, and the way we travel or ship goods. Ultimately, the weather affects every country's economy and way of life.

Because weather is so important in our lives, it is included in a major branch of science called **meteorology**. Meteorology is the study of Earth's **atmosphere**, the blanket of air that surrounds Earth. A main goal of meteorologists is to study the changes in the atmosphere that cause weather. The data that is collected about air pressures, winds, temperatures, and moisture in the atmosphere helps **meteorologists** to predict weather conditions.

Air Pressure

Because we move through air so easily, we don't usually think of it as having weight. But the atmosphere extends for hundreds of miles above us. Like everything else on Earth, gravity pulls the atmosphere's air toward Earth. The atmosphere presses on us with a force of about fourteen pounds per square inch. We don't usually notice this pressure, called **air pressure**, unless it suddenly changes. But we notice changes in air pressure before a storm and when we fly up and down in an airplane. A change in air pressure can make our ears pop and gives some people a headache.

The amount of pressure that air exerts depends on the temperature of the air. Warm air is lighter than cold air and creates less pressure than cold air. To help predict the weather, forecasters measure air pressure with an instrument called a **barometer**. When the **barometric pressure** rises, good weather may occur. When the air pressure falls, bad weather may be on the way.

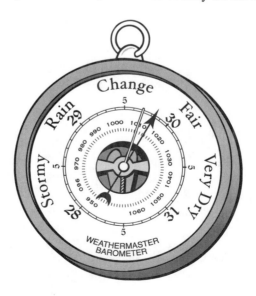

Wind

Wind is moving air. When air is warm, it becomes lighter and rises. Colder, heavier air moves in close to the ground to take the place of the warm air. This movement of air causes wind. A light wind feels good on a hot day, but strong winds, as in tornadoes and hurricanes, can be very destructive.

Large masses of air move in predictable patterns around Earth due to Earth's **rotation**—or spinning. Weather patterns in the United States, for example, generally move from west to east. Small masses of air, however, can move in different directions because of differences in temperature.

Clouds

Clouds are part of the natural water cycle. They are formed when water evaporates into warm air. As the warm air rises, it cools, and tiny droplets of water form. These droplets are so small and light that they just hang in the air, forming a cloud.

Clouds come in many sizes and shapes. **Cirrus** clouds are thin, feathery-looking clouds that are usually high up in the atmosphere. **Cumulus** clouds are the familiar soft, puffy clouds that look like pieces of cotton wool. Light, white cumulus clouds are usually a sign of good weather. Cumulus clouds with dark, heavy-looking bottoms mean rain or snow is probably on the way. **Stratus** clouds are low, flat clouds that often cover the whole sky.

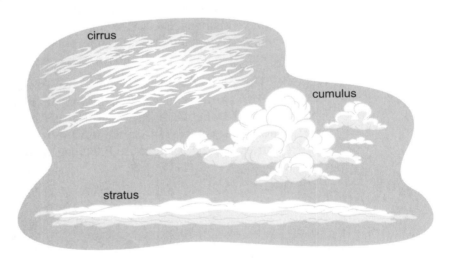

Precipitation

Precipitation is water that falls from the sky in the form of rain, snow, sleet, or hail. Each type of precipitation is formed under different conditions. **Raindrops** are formed when water droplets in a cloud combine into larger and larger drops. When the drops of water get heavy enough, they fall to the ground as rain. If the air cools very quickly, the water droplets freeze before they can combine and precipitation falls as **snow**. If already-formed raindrops go through a very cold air layer on their way to the ground, they freeze into hard little pellets called **sleet**. **Hail** develops when raindrops are blown up and down between layers of warm and cold air, freezing, melting, and refreezing. Strong winds can hold hailstones up in the clouds until they are the size of golf balls or even larger.

EXERCISE 7

Weather

Directions: Write *T* for each true statement and *F* for each false statement. Make each false statement true by changing the underlined word. Write the correct word on the line after each statement.

_____ 1. <u>Water</u> pressure is also known as barometric pressure.

_____

_____ 2. Weather in the United States usually moves from <u>west</u> to <u>east</u>. _____

_____ 3. <u>Cirrus</u> clouds are soft-looking, puffy clouds.

_____

_____ 4. Rain, snow, sleet, and hail are all forms of <u>precipitation</u>.

_____

_____ 5. <u>Snow</u> is formed when frozen raindrops are blown up and down between layers of warm and cold air.

_____

Directions: The diagram shows why, on a warm day, you can often find a cool breeze blowing from a lake or an ocean. Use the diagram to answer the question.

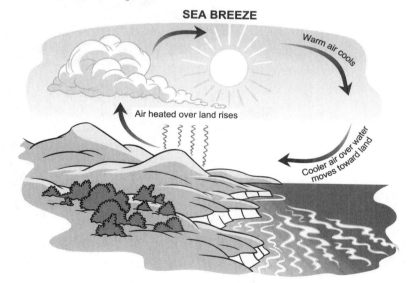

SEA BREEZE

Warm air cools

Air heated over land rises

Cooler air over water moves toward land

6. Which of the following best explains why air rises over the land?

(1) The Sun draws it up by gravity.
(2) The water is warmer than the land.
(3) The shade from the cloud makes the air cooler.
(4) The Sun heats the land and the air over it.
(5) The strong wind causes friction.

Our Galaxy and Solar System

When you look up at the night sky, you may see the Moon, stars, and a few planets. The night sky reveals only part of the **universe**. The universe is the biggest thing we know. It includes all matter and all space, everywhere. No one knows where the edge of the universe is located. Some **astronomers**— scientists who study the stars and other bodies in the universe—think that the universe is expanding, meaning it may just go on forever.

The Milky Way Galaxy

A **galaxy** is a group of stars in the universe. Our galaxy is called the Milky Way. It contains about 200 billion stars grouped in a giant spiral pattern that is about 100,000 light-years across. A **light-year**—the distance that light travels in one year—is the unit used to measure distance in space. One light-year is equal to almost 6 trillion miles, a distance too large for anyone to really imagine.

Stars are enormous balls of very hot gases in which nuclear reactions continually occur. These nuclear reactions produce heat and light, which are given off into space.

Stars may be different sizes and colors. Our **Sun** is a yellow star more than halfway out from the center of our galaxy. The Sun is only a medium-sized star, although it looks much bigger to us because it is so much closer than any other star. Nine known **planets** orbit—or go around—our Sun; one of these planets is Earth. Astronomers think that other suns may have planets, but those stars are too far away for us to see any of their planets.

Our Solar System

The Sun, its nine major planets and their moons, and various other bodies, such as comets and asteroids, make up the **solar system**.

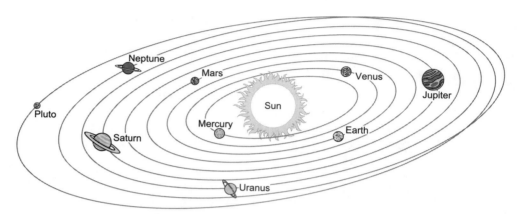

Mercury is the planet closest to the Sun. Mercury rotates very slowly, taking almost fifty-nine Earth days to spin around once. Because of this, one side of Mercury gets very hot while the other side, away from the Sun, gets very cold.

Venus is about the same size as Earth, nearly 8,000 miles in **diameter**— the distance across, going through the center. Venus is always covered with clouds, so only a few space probes have allowed us to see its surface.

Earth is the only planet known to have life. This may be because the Sun warms Earth at just the right temperature range. It is neither too hot like Venus, nor too cold like Mars. Therefore, Earth can support life as we know it.

Mars is about one-half the diameter of Earth. One theory is that there may once have been life on Mars before the planets cooled off. Some even think there might still be life. Others say that life is impossible because the atmosphere is too thin and cold. Space probes sent to Mars did not find any life.

Jupiter is more than eleven times the diameter of Earth and more than 300 times its mass. The atmosphere of Jupiter is very thick and heavy, made up mostly of hydrogen, methane, and ammonia gases. Jupiter has several moons that scientists study.

Saturn is slightly smaller than Jupiter, and it is known mostly for its beautiful rings. There are three main bands of rings around Saturn, each made up of many small icy particles that orbit around Saturn and sparkle brightly from reflected sunlight.

Uranus and **Neptune** are the seventh and eighth planets. They are both very far from the Sun and very cold. They are about the same size, with diameters approximately $3\frac{1}{2}$ times that of Earth. The *Voyager* space probes discovered that both planets have small rings and many small moons.

For most of its orbit, **Pluto** is the farthest planet from the Sun. At times, however, its orbit brings it closer to the Sun than Neptune. Because Pluto is so far away—about $3\frac{1}{2}$ billion miles from the Sun—it was not discovered until 1930. Although the Hubble Space Telescope has provided images of Pluto, little is known about the smallest planet in the solar system.

At least seven of the planets have **moons** orbiting around them. Jupiter has thirty-nine known moons, and more are likely to be discovered. Even though Earth has only one moon, it is large, about one-fourth the diameter of Earth. Most moons are smaller. Only four of Jupiter's and one of Saturn's moons are as big as, or larger than, our moon.

Asteroids are small chunks of rock that orbit the Sun in a belt between Mars and Jupiter. They range in size from the largest, Ceres, which is about 580 miles across, down to tiny particles of rock dust. Some scientists believe that the asteroids are matter that never grouped together to form a planet. Others think that they might be the remains of a planet that blew up.

Meteors are small chunks of rock and ice that fall toward Earth. Most of them burn up in the atmosphere. When we see meteors burning up in the atmosphere, we call them shooting stars. A chunk of meteor that survives its fall and hits the ground is called a **meteorite**.

Comets are good-sized balls of dust and ice. They have very strange orbits. One end of the orbit comes very near the Sun, while the other end swings out far beyond Pluto's orbit. When a comet's orbit brings it near the Sun, the ice in it begins to melt and then boils away. The gas from the boiling ice reflects the sunlight and looks like a long white tail. Halley's Comet is the most famous of the comets that pass by Earth. One complete orbit of Halley's Comet takes approximately 76 years. The last time it passed near Earth was in 1986 and it won't be near Earth again until 2061.

EXERCISE 8

Orbiting Bodies

Directions: Write the correct word in front of each definition.

_____ **1.** largest planet in the solar system

_____ **2.** huge balls of hot gases giving off light and heat

_____ **3.** chunks of rock orbiting between Mars and Jupiter

_____ **4.** group of stars in the universe

_____ **5.** planet with thick layer of clouds

_____ **6.** the Sun, its nine planets, moons, and other bodies

_____ **7.** ball of ice and dust with a long, gaseous tail

Directions: Circle the number of the best answer.

8. Consider how the term *solar system* is used in this passage. Which phrase best defines the word *solar*?

(1) very hot
(2) having to do with Earth
(3) far apart
(4) having to do with the Sun
(5) related to comets

Answers are on page 650.

A Solar Eclipse

A **solar eclipse** is not magic, although people used to believe it was. A solar eclipse happens when the Moon comes between Earth and the Sun. Study the diagram below.

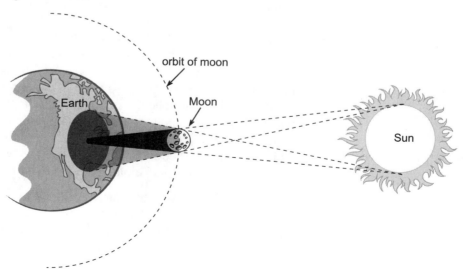

When the Moon is directly between Earth and the Sun, the Sun's rays cannot reach a small part of Earth—a circular area 169 miles in diameter. If you are standing in this area where the Moon's shadow falls, it will seem as if the Sun has disappeared. Actually, the Moon is blocking your view of the Sun. It is important, however, to avoid looking at the Sun during an eclipse because doing so may cause permanent damage to your eyes.

If you are near the shadow area, but not directly in it, only part of the Sun will be blocked. This is called a **partial eclipse**. Total solar eclipses are rare. When there is one, scientists from around the world travel to the region to study the eclipse.

EXERCISE 9

An Eclipse

Directions: On a separate sheet of paper, answer the following question in a few sentences.

1. Imagine that you had never heard about eclipses, and suddenly you saw the Sun start to disappear. What might you think, feel, and do?

Directions: Circle the number of the best answer.

2. Which of the following can you infer from the eclipse diagram?

   (1) During a solar eclipse, some people on Earth can't see the Sun or the Moon.
   (2) Earth is almost as big as the Sun.
   (3) Most of Earth is dark during a solar eclipse.
   (4) Solar eclipses happen mostly at night.
   (5) The Moon is closer to the Sun than to Earth.

Answers are on page 650.

Studying the Universe

Scientific ideas are based on experiments and observations. The first humans to study the universe, however, were unable to conduct experiments in space. Instead they made observations about objects in the sky. Then they used what they knew about things on Earth to form ideas about objects in space. As early as 4000 B.C., people noticed that the Sun and the Moon moved in regular paths. From about 2950 B.C. to 1600 B.C., people in England built a stone structure called Stonehenge in three separate phases. The final phase, which was built of stone and still stands today, probably was a type of astronomical observatory for keeping track of the Sun and the Moon. By 350 B.C. the Chinese had recorded more than 800 stars as well as many other objects in the sky, such as comets, sunspots, meteorites, and novas.

Eventually **telescopes** were developed to help astronomers see distant objects more clearly. These instruments increase the amount of light collected from space. With more light, astronomers can see the colors of objects in space. The colors help scientists to determine what each object is made of and its temperature.

When **satellites**—or unmanned spacecraft—were launched into space in the 1950s, instruments on board conducted the first experiments in space. These experiments provided information about such things as weightlessness, cosmic rays, temperature, and meteorite collisions. But it wasn't until the first **astronauts** landed on the Moon in 1969 that people finally studied an object in space up close. Now both manned and unmanned space missions play a major role in how we study and learn about the universe.

Space Travel

Space travel today includes both manned and unmanned missions whose goals are to carry out detailed studies of our universe. Some studies deal with the origin, evolution, and distribution of life in the universe. Other studies involve the exploration of distant planets, stars, and other space objects. Experimental data and information are gathered through the space shuttle, the International Space Station, the Hubble Space Telescope, and satellites such as Galileo, Voyager, and Magellan.

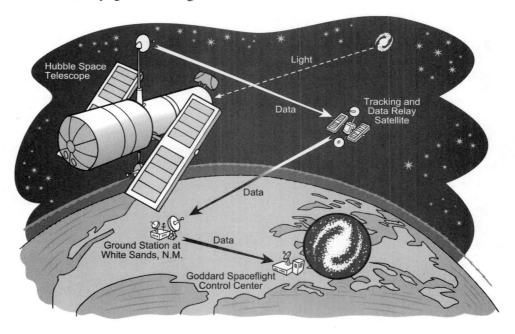

Have you ever dreamed of rocketing into space to conduct your own informal study of the universe? If so, you're not alone. Several space tourists have already paid tens of millions of dollars for the opportunity to travel beyond Earth's atmosphere. Experts predict that affordable tourism into space is less than twenty years away. Who knows, maybe you will be one of the millions of people who will become space tourists in the near future!

EXERCISE 10

Studying the Universe

Directions: Write short answers to the following questions.

1. According to the section titled "Studying the Universe," what are three ways in which humans have studied the universe from Earth?

    a. _____

    b. _____

    c. _____

2. Do you think space tourism should be promoted? Give at least three reasons in support of your answer.

    a. _____

    b. _____

    c. _____

Directions: Circle the number of the best answer.

3. With which of the following statements would the author of this passage most likely agree?

    (1) Scientific ideas based only on observations are not valid.
    (2) Information gathered by spacecraft is more valuable than information gathered by using telescopes.
    (3) People who lived long ago were not very smart because they noticed only that the Sun and the Moon move in regular paths.
    (4) The expense of space exploration is not worth the small amount of information that we obtain from it.
    (5) Through experimental and observational evidence, logical thinking, and technology, humans will continue to learn about the universe.

Answers are on page 650.

Chapter Review

EXERCISE 11

Directions: Read each passage carefully. Then circle the number of the best answer to each question.

Questions 1 and 2 are based on the following passage.

There are over 2,000 types of minerals found in Earth's crust, but they can all be classified in three basic groups. The first type is igneous rock. Igneous rock is formed when hot, liquid rock from the center of Earth pushes up through cracks and then cools and hardens. Since the whole crust of Earth was once liquid, most of the crust is made of igneous rock.

Sedimentary rock is often formed under water. For example, some types of sedimentary rock are formed as a layer of sand, mud, small rocks, and shells drifts to the bottom of the ocean each year. As the layers pile up, more and more pressure is put on the bottom layers. As they are pressed together, they gradually turn into rock.

Metamorphic rock is rock that has been changed. If an igneous or sedimentary rock gets buried deeply under other rocks, sometimes the heat and pressure will cause the rock to change its form. For example, marble is a metamorphic rock made from limestone.

1. Which of the following explains why most of Earth's crust is made of igneous rock?

   (1) There are many volcanoes in the world.
   (2) Metamorphic rock is changed to igneous rock.
   (3) Sedimentary rock is found only where oceans have been.
   (4) Granite is a kind of igneous rock.
   (5) Earth's crust was once all hot, liquid rock.

2. Limestone contains small shells and bits of fish skeletons. Limestone must be what type of rock?

   (1) metamorphic
   (2) sedimentary
   (3) igneous
   (4) useless
   (5) expensive

Questions 3 and 4 are based on the following passage and diagrams.

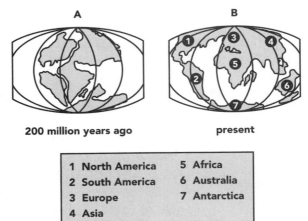

200 million years ago   present

1 North America	5 Africa
2 South America	6 Australia
3 Europe	7 Antarctica
4 Asia	

One of the most interesting ideas in science is the theory of continental drift. Scientists who hold this theory believe that at one time all seven continents formed one giant land mass. Gradually, over millions of years, the continents broke apart and shifted to the places where they are today.

There is a good bit of evidence supporting this theory. In the above diagrams, you can see how the western edges of Europe and Africa seem to fit into the eastern edges of North and South America. Also, similar fossil plants and animals have been found on widely separated continents, such as Africa and South America. It is hard to believe that those once living plants and animals somehow crossed a wide ocean to reach land on the other side. The finding is easier to explain if, at one time, Africa and South America lay next to each other.

Underwater exploration has offered further proof of the drift theory. Scientists have seen rifts in the ocean floor where two plates—continent-sized sections of Earth's crust—are moving apart and molten rock is flowing out, adding new areas of sea floor.

3. Which of the following is a way to test the idea of continental drift?

   (1) Watch the continents from a spacecraft.
   (2) Try to push a continent with many large ships.
   (3) Keep careful records of the positions of the continents over hundreds of years.
   (4) Measure very carefully to see if the continental edges would still fit together exactly.
   (5) Find out if ancient scientists believed in continental drift.

4. Fossils of a certain animal have been found in both Africa and South America. If the continental drift theory is true, when did that animal probably exist?

   (1) recently
   (2) about 1,000 years ago
   (3) only after the continents drifted apart
   (4) before the continents drifted apart
   (5) before Earth's crust began to cool

Questions 5 and 6 are based on the following passage.

Early explorers in Africa and South America wrote about the endless jungle—the tropical rain forest, dark and tangled and teeming with life. Today, however, the jungle is disappearing. Within twenty years there may not be any tropical rain forests left outside of a few parks and reserves.

People are destroying the rain forests. Every year thousands of acres of rain forests are cut down by lumber companies that take only the largest trees and destroy the rest in the process. Other people clear many more acres to make farms and ranches. Towns and even cities are springing up in areas that used to be primitive forests.

Why should we care if the rain forests eventually disappear from Earth? One reason is that unusual rain forest plants provide us with many medicines, dyes, and other chemicals. Even more importantly, the rain forests are a major part of the air renewal system of this planet. All the millions of green plants in the rain forests put out enormous amounts of oxygen every day. Without the rain forests, some scientists think there might not be enough green plants on Earth to maintain the oxygen level.

Scientists are concerned about the destruction of the rain forests and what that destruction might do to our planet. We need to listen to their concerns and take steps now to preserve and protect one of our most important natural resources, the tropical rain forests.

5. What is the main idea of the third paragraph of this passage?

   (1) Rain forests are beautiful.
   (2) Rain forests are valuable to us.
   (3) Rain forests are being destroyed.
   (4) Rain forests are difficult to travel in.
   (5) Rain forests are useless and unnecessary.

6. Which of the following is the best source of information about the destruction of the rain forests?

   (1) a pamphlet put out by a lumber company
   (2) your hometown daily newspaper
   (3) a high school chemistry textbook
   (4) articles in an ecology journal
   (5) advertisements for real estate in tropical countries

Questions 7 and 8 are based on the graph below.

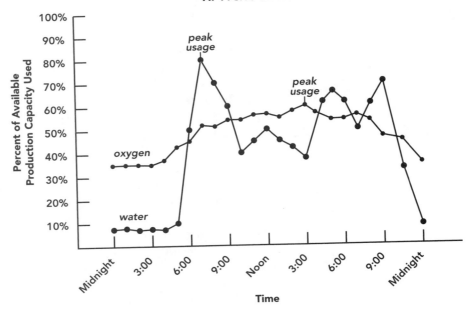

7. Which of the following can you conclude from the graph?

   (1) Water and oxygen show exactly the same pattern of usage.
   (2) Oxygen use changes more during the day than water use.
   (3) The lowest usage of water and oxygen occur at the same time.
   (4) Oxygen is more necessary than water.
   (5) Water and oxygen use both peak at the same time.

8. Which question cannot be answered from the information in the graph?

   (1) When is the most oxygen used during a 24-hour period?
   (2) Who uses more water, male or female crew members?
   (3) When is water use the highest?
   (4) Do crew members use less oxygen when asleep?
   (5) Does the crew use all of the water that can be produced?

Answers are on page 650.

CHAPTER 1
SCIENCE KNOWLEDGE AND SKILLS

Exercise 1: Compound Words (page 501)
1. horsepower
2. spaceship
3. sunspot
4. earthquake
5. wavelength
6. catfish

Exercise 2: Word Parts (page 503)
1. dermatology
2. Neurology
3. Biothermal
4. thermometer
5. trimonthly
6. trifocals
7. cardiogram
8. cardiologist
9. microbiology
10. micrometer

Exercise 3: Using Context Clues (page 504)
Your answers should be similar to these answers. If you are not sure whether your answer is correct, check with your teacher.

1. An *astrolabe* might be an instrument for measuring stars.
2. *Cyberspace* might be a kind of space that is controlled by computers.
3. *Polychromatic* probably means many-colored.
4. *Carnivores* are probably animals that eat meat.
5. *Hydroponic* might be farming in something other than soil.

Exercise 4: Understanding Scientific Language (page 506)
There are many ways to simplify these sentences. Here are some sample answers. If you are not sure whether your answer is correct, check with your teacher.

1. Air pollution can have very bad effects.
2. Learning how to use water power to make electricity was necessary in order to make cheap electric power.
3. Children who play with educational toys may learn to question things, a skill that is good in science.

Exercise 5: Fact and Opinion (page 509)
1. O   That Vancouver is nicer is a matter of opinion.
2. F   You could prove this by measuring the distance.
3. O   Statements about what people *should* do can never be proven; they are always opinions.
4. F   You could prove this by taking a survey.
5. F   You could prove this by measuring the hearing of people who listen to a lot of very loud music.
6. O   Statements about what should or ought to be done are usually opinions.
7. F   You could prove this by looking at the records of nuclear power plants.
8–10.   Answers will vary.

Exercise 6: Everyday Hypotheses (page 510)
Your answers should be similar to these answers.

1. The storm has caused a power outage.
2. Bill isn't sick; he's out hunting.
3. You are going to be promoted.

Exercise 7: Choosing Hypotheses (page 511)
1. (3)   The plants without light died, and the plants with little light did not grow well. Therefore, you can hypothesize that green plants need light to grow and live.
2. (4)   The bacteria in the jars were killed by the boiling temperatures. Choice (2) is wrong because bacteria grew in a sealed jar with no air.
3. (2)   The amount of oil burned is directly related to the average temperature. Choices (1), (4), and (5) are not correct because the most oil was burned in January, when it was sunny, not snowy, and not the holiday season. Less oil was burned in December than in November, so choice (3) is not correct.

Exercise 8: Forming Hypotheses (page 512)

Your answers should be similar to these answers. If you are not sure whether your answer is correct, check with your teacher.

1. The detergent is coming from the town. Upstream from the town there was no detergent in the river.
2. Carl's magnet, like all magnets, only picks up things made of iron or steel. It makes no difference how big the object is or whether or not it is wet.

Exercise 9: Errors in Experiments (page 515)

Your answers should be similar to these answers.

1. **subjects not similar** OR **conditions of experiment not kept the same**
   The gardener used pepper plants for one group and beans for the other, so his subjects were not all similar. He couldn't tell if the beans didn't grow because of the fertilizer, because the seeds were bad, because it was a bad year for beans, or for some other reason.
2. **not enough subjects** OR **experiment not reproduced**
   The mechanic tried only one squirt gun, so she didn't have enough subjects in her test group. Since the machine was having trouble only a third of the time, maybe the next gun or the one after that would have been flawed. The mechanic needs to reproduce the experiment.

Exercise 10: Chapter Review (pages 517–518)

Your answers should be similar to these answers.

1. Why didn't the milkmaids catch smallpox?
2. Milkmaids contracted cowpox. They didn't catch smallpox.
3. Getting cowpox keeps you from catching smallpox.
4. He tested his hypothesis by giving people cowpox and seeing if it protected them against smallpox.
5. Cowpox helped prevent people from getting smallpox.

CHAPTER 2
LIVING THINGS

Exercise 1: Restating Facts (page 520)

Your answers should be similar to these answers.

1. Nonsmokers are less likely to get lung cancer.
2. Many people who pass the GED Test go on to do well in business.
3. Nuclear energy is very powerful, but it can also do horrible damage.
4. Older people's experiences help them to learn more easily than they might have as children.

Exercise 2: Summarizing (page 521)

1. **(5)** This is the best summary. Choices (1) and (4) are too narrow; each covers only one of the facts given. Choice (3) is too broad, and choice (2) is not even mentioned.
2. **(3)** This is the best summary. Choices (1) and (2) are not given as facts. Choice (4) is too narrow; it covers only one of the facts given. Choice (5) is not a true statement.

Exercise 3: Finding the Main Idea of a Paragraph (page 523)

1. The main idea is "Cactuses are remarkable plants made to live in one of nature's harshest environments." The rest of the paragraph gives you details on how they are able to survive harsh conditions.
2. The main idea is "They all are powered by an engine." The rest of the paragraph gives details about the parts of an engine and how the parts work together to produce power and motion.
3. The main idea is "Even though it is only a reaction of your own body, an allergy can really make you miserable!" The rest of the paragraph explains how an allergy is a reaction and just how miserable it can be.

Exercise 4: Finding the Main Idea of a Passage (page 525)

1. (4) The passage describes the causes and dangers of lead poisoning. Choices (1), (2), (3), and (5) are details.

2. (3) The passage explains what people need to know about lead. Choice (1) is not mentioned in the passage, choice (2) is too narrow, and choices (4) and (5) are not mentioned in the passage.

Exercise 5: Cells (page 527)

1. f   **4.** a   **7.** b
2. i   **5.** h   **8.** d
3. g   **6.** c   **9.** e
10. (1) The last sentence under the heading "Plant Cells" states "Animal cells do not have cell walls."

Exercise 6: Viruses and Bacteria (page 529)

1. a. microbes   **e.** immunity
   b. viruses   **f.** immunization
   c. bacteria   **g.** vaccination
   d. protozoans

2. (4) The passage talks about how important it is to get immunized. Choices (1), (2), and (3) are too narrow, covering only one part of the paragraph. Choice (5) is not true according to the passage.

Exercise 7: Photosynthesis (page 531)

1. F   Some fungi, such as yeast, are helpful.
2. T   This is stated in the second paragraph of the text.
3. (1) This is stated in the second paragraph of the text.
4. (2) Choice (2) is the best summary. Choices (1), (3), and (4) are too narrow. Choice (5) is not mentioned.

Exercise 8: Types of Animals (page 534)

1. g   **4.** e   **6.** b
2. d   **5.** c   **7.** f
3. a

8. e   A bumblebee has no backbone.
9. d   A guppy has a backbone and breathes all its life with gills.
10. f   A bullfrog first lives in water as a tadpole, then changes and lives on land.
11. b   A rattlesnake has scales, is cold-blooded, and lays eggs on land.
12. c   A robin has feathers and is warm-blooded.
13. a   A cow gives milk and gives birth to its young.
14. (1) This is the main idea of the first section of this passage.

Exercise 9: Genetics (page 537)

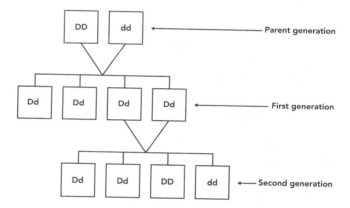

1. All the hamsters would have dark eyes because they all would inherit one dominant gene for dark eyes from one parent.

2. All of them would carry one recessive gene for light eyes from the other parent.

3. One hamster out of four would probably have light eyes; it would probably have received a recessive gene from each parent. Three would have dark eyes.

4. Two out of three of the dark-eyed second-generation offspring would carry a light-eye recessive gene.

Exercise 10: Chapter Review (pages 538–540)

1. **(3)** The risk of a bad reaction may be small compared with the risk of disease. Doctors would want to keep giving the vaccine but record all reactions. Choices (1) and (4) are too dangerous. Choices (2) and (5) are just ways of getting opinions, not scientific proof.

2. **(2)** This is stated in the last sentence of the passage.

3. **(1)** The size and weight of the apatosaurus are the largest given. The dinosaurs in choices (2) and (3) are both smaller. The pterosaur's size is not given, so (4) is wrong. Choice (5) is not mentioned in the passage.

4. **(5)** The passage mentions that some dinosaurs ate plants.

5. **(5)** A mutated animal usually does not survive to breed.

6. **(4)** Read the last two sentences of the passage for this definition.

7. **(3)** A seed develops into a green plant that can make its own food. Choices (1), (2), and (5) are too narrow. Choice (4) is false.

8. **(3)** A germinating embryo grows into a plant. Choice (1) is described in the first sentence in the paragraph. Choice (2) is described in the third sentence of the paragraph. Choices (4) and (5) are needed for germination to occur but are not the process itself.

CHAPTER 3
HUMAN BIOLOGY

Exercise 1: Diagrams (page 542)

1. the pupil
2. vitreous humor
3. the retina
4. the optic nerve
5. If the cornea becomes clouded, light cannot pass through it to the pupil and into the eye.

Exercise 2: Comparing Diagrams (page 544)

1. It shows drawings of a fetus for the first five months of pregnancy.
2. at four months
3. **(4)** Choices (1) and (3) are not right because the title says that this child hasn't been born yet. Choice (2) is wrong; the head looks different because it hasn't grown yet. Choice (5) has nothing to do with the diagram.

Exercise 3: Charts (page 546)

1. vitamins A, C, D, E, B1, B2, niacin, and B12
2. scurvy
3. vitamins A and D
4. vitamins A, B2, and niacin

Exercise 4: Line Graphs (page 550)

1. **(5)** The heaviest rock (300 pounds) is the top data point on the graph line and corresponds to 6 feet.

2. **(4)** The graph line shows that longer crowbars move heavier rocks. Choice (2) is wrong because the graph shows the length of the crowbar, not the thickness. Not enough information is given to conclude choice (1) or (3). Choice (5) is a generalization.

3. **(1)** The main idea of the graph is to show how long a crowbar must be to move rocks of different weights. Choice (3) is not true; some rocks weighing more than 300 pounds can be moved by other methods. Information for choices (2) and (4) is not given in the graph. Choice (5) is not complete.

Exercise 5: Bar Graphs (page 552)

1. You expect to find information about the average temperatures in Vancouver.
2. It shows the months of the year.
3. It shows the average high temperatures in degrees Fahrenheit.
4. 5°F
5. 50°F
6. July and August
7. No, it probably doesn't get below freezing very often because the lowest temperature is only 42°F.

Exercise 6: The Skeletal and Muscular Systems (page 555)

1. T There are 206 bones.
2. T These are two of the main functions of bones.
3. F Cartilage is softer than bone.
4. T Ligaments are tough bands of tissue that hold bones together at the joints.
5. T One possible cause of osteoporosis is not getting enough calcium.
6. F Voluntary muscles are controlled by you.
7. T You have no control over involuntary muscles. Cardiac muscle is involuntary; you do not control the movement of the heart muscles.
8. (4) The diagram shows "vertebrae of neck," or neck bones, and "vertebrae of spine," or backbone.

Exercise 7: The Respiratory and Circulatory Systems (page 558)

1. lungs
2. nose/mouth
3. mouth/nose
4. trachea
5. bronchial tubes
6. alveoli
7. oxygen
8. carbon dioxide
9. red blood cells
10. white blood cells
11. platelets

Exercise 8: The Digestive System (page 560)

1. g
2. f
3. d
4. b
5. h
6. c
7. e
8. a

9. (4) This order is given in the last two paragraphs of the passage.

Exercise 9: The Nervous System (page 562)

1. skin
2. sensory
3. spinal cord
4. brain
5. brain
6. motor
7. hand
8. nerve impulses

Exercise 10: Nutrition (page 564)

1. (2) See the chart. Find carbohydrates in the "Nutrient" column. Then look to the right under "Purpose."
2. (4) A statement about what someone *should* do is always an opinion. All the other choices are facts.

Exercise 11: Health (page 565)

1. (3) The chart states that two of the many benefits of regular exercise are that it reduces stress and improves sleep. Choices (1), (2), (4), and (5) are wrong because the explanation for getting enough exercise does not mention smoking, alcohol, nutrition, or medical news.
2. (1) As the results of new studies are released, doctors and scientists revise their guidelines. Staying current with medical news will ensure you are following the most recent and best advice available. Choices (2), (4), and (5) may be true, but each is too specific and not the best reason. Choice (3) has nothing to do with keeping up with medical news.

Exercise 12: Chapter Review (pages 566–568)

1. (3) The diagram shows that these three bones are located in the middle ear.
2. (1) If the eardrum cannot vibrate, the person's hearing is affected. Choices (2) and (5) are wrong because we have no evidence about the effect of pain on hearing. Choice (3) is wrong because the fluid would be at body temperature, not cold. Choice (4) is wrong because if the sound traveled better, the person would hear better, not worse.
3. (5) See the chart, across from "Males, 23–50."
4. (3) This is true for men and women of all ages. Choice (1) is not true because after age 23, people need fewer calories. Choice (2) is wrong because a 19- to 22-year-old woman needs more calories than a 76-year-old man. Choices (4) and (5) are not right according to the chart.
5. (3) The passage describes things that a pregnant mother can do or diseases she may contract that could affect a fetus. Choice (1) is false according to the passage. Choices (2), (4), and (5) are in the passage, but they are only details.

6. (3) The graph shows that a 45-year-old nonsmoker can expect to live until age 75, while a 2-packs-a-day smoker of the same age can expect to live only until age 68. The difference is 7 years.

7. (2) The graph shows that people who smoke less tend to live longer. This can be concluded by comparing the life spans of smokers and nonsmokers. Choice (1) is false. Information about women in choice (3) and young people in choice (4) is not given in the graph. Choice (5) may be true but is not supported by details in the graph.

CHAPTER 4
PHYSICS

Exercise 1: Sequencing (page 571)
a. 4   **b.** 1   **c.** 2   **d.** 3

Exercise 2: Logical Sequence (page 572)
1. b, a   Steam engines had to be invented before they could be put into locomotives.
2. b, a, c   Before Franklin discovered what lightning really was, some people believed it was a weapon of the gods. Franklin had to discover what lightning was before he could invent lightning rods.

Exercise 3: Causes and Effects (page 574)
Your answers should be similar to these answers. If you are not sure, check with your teacher.

1. *Cause:* The chain reaction goes very fast.
2. *Effect:* Not enough heat will be released.
3. *Effect:* The water boils.
4. *Cause:* The steam turns giant generators.

Exercise 4: Finding Causes and Effects (page 575)
1. (2) He hated the teaching methods of schools in that time. Choices (1), (3), (4), and (5) are mentioned in the passage as traits that led to Einstein's success.
2. (5) Scientific discoveries will result only if people think creatively about the world and pursue answers to their questions. Choice (1) is stated but is not the best conclusion for the passage. Choices (2), (3), and (4) are true but are only individual details.

Exercise 5: Making Inferences (page 576)
Your answers should be similar to these answers. If you are not sure, check with your teacher.

1. The people of Nevada oppose the burying of nuclear waste in their state.
2. a. They rely on electricity.
   b. They were not as easy or satisfying as they are now.
3. a. They disregard warnings from scientists with knowledge about fossil fuels.
   b. They should develop alternate fuels before the supply of fossil fuels runs out.

Exercise 6: Simple Machines (page 579)
1. a.   simple machines
   b.   amount, effort
   c.   foot-pounds
2. (4) Work = force × distance; Work = 2,000 pounds (weight of the car) × 20 feet (height of the hill); Work = 40,000 foot-pounds

Exercise 7: Motion (page 582)
1. This shows the 3rd law of motion. The person pushes against the desk. The desk exerts an equal force in the opposite direction.
2. This shows the 1st law of motion. The leaf stays at rest until the force of the wind causes it to move.
3. This shows the 2nd law of motion. The baseball has a smaller mass than the softball and can be thrown farther and faster than the softball.
4. This shows the 2nd law of motion. The sled will move faster and farther when it is pushed harder.
5. This shows the 3rd law of motion. The person pushes against the boat. The boat exerts an equal force in the opposite direction—away from the dock.
6. This shows the 1st law of motion. The person is moving with the train. When the train slows suddenly, the person continues moving forward and is thrown off balance.

Exercise 8: Electricity and Magnetism (page 584)

1. ceiling light
2. counter lights
3. outlet
4. dishwasher
5. electric clock
6. (5) Nothing would work because there must be a complete circuit for the electricity to flow.
7. e Opposite poles attract each other.
8. a An electromagnet works only when electricity flows through it.
9. c A magnet has a north pole and a south pole, each of which is magnetically attracted to elements such as iron, cobalt, and nickel.
10. b A magnetic field is the area around a magnet, extending from the north pole to the south pole.
11. d The north pole of a magnet always points north when the magnet swings freely.
12. f Like poles repel each other.

Exercise 9: Nuclear Power (page 587)

1. B Speaker B is worried about security not being able to stop terrorists.
2. B Speaker B asks, "How can they be sure?"
3. A Speaker A says the groups worried about nuclear power are radical.
4. (5) This fact is given in the second paragraph. Choice (1) is a fact from selection A, not B. Choice (2) is an opinion from B, not a fact. Choice (3) is an opinion, not a fact, from A.
5. (2) Obviously Speaker A is in favor of nuclear power. Utility companies are the companies that own and operate nuclear and other types of power plants. Choice (3) would be against nuclear power. Choices (1), (4), and (5) would not necessarily be interested in nuclear power plants at all.

Exercise 10: Light and Sound Waves (page 589)

1. T The first paragraph indicates this is true.
2. F Light is faster than sound. Light travels 186,000 miles per second; sound travels about 1/5 mile per second in air.
3. F White light is a combination of all colors.
4. T The last sentence in paragraph 4 proves this.
5. T Paragraph 6 explains this.
6. F Sound travels best through solid things.
7. T Read the last paragraph in this section.
8. T Read the last paragraph in this section.

Exercise 11: Chapter Review (pages 590–594)

1. (4) Only levers A and D are balanced. Check this by multiplying the force by the distance on each side of the fulcrum.
2. (5) Side A will go down because the heavier side always goes down, even if the difference is only a pound. It does not matter how *many* weights are on each side, but rather how *much* the total weight is on each.
3. (4) The passage states that electricity flows through a circuit only if the circuit is a complete circle. If the switch is off, the circuit is no longer complete. Neither the toaster nor the light will work. Choices (3) and (5) are wrong because the battery is the source of energy, not a user of energy.
4. (5) The passage states that electrons flow from an area with more electrons to an area with fewer electrons. When the number of electrons in both terminals is the same, the flow of electricity stops, or the battery is dead. Choices (1) and (2) are wrong because of the previous explanation. Choices (3) and (4) don't make sense because electrons have no power; they only carry a negative charge.
5. (3) This is implied in the sentence "The darker the object, the more light it will absorb and change to heat." Choice (2) is incorrect because of the same sentence. Choices (1), (4), and (5) are not mentioned in the passage.
6. (2) Solar heat is defined in the passage as heat from sunlight. Choices (1), (3), and (5) are not indicated in any way in the passage. Choice (4) is true, but it is not a problem; it is an advantage.
7. (4) As in the example in the passage, a sound 20 decibels higher is actually 100 times louder than the softer sound, because each 10-decibel jump means 10 times as much sound. $10 \times 10 = 100$
8. (1) According to the chart, drills, shovels, and trucks put out the most decibels of sound, so a person working with them would have the greatest chance of job-related hearing damage.

CHAPTER 5
CHEMISTRY

Exercise 1: Atoms and Molecules (page 597)

1. c	**4.** g	**7.** b
2. h	**5.** i	**8.** f
3. d	**6.** a	**9.** e

Exercise 2: Mixtures, Solutions, and Compounds (page 600)

1. M	**3.** S	**5.** C
2. C	**4.** M	**6.** S

Items 1 and 4 are simple mixtures because they could be separated into their original substances by physical means. Items 2 and 5 are compounds because two substances join together to make completely different substances. Items 3 and 6 are solutions because the original substances could not be separated by sorting or filtering.

7. (3) Salt is a compound, rather than a mixture or a solution, because it is an entirely different substance from its original parts. It can't be a poison, since people eat it every day.

Exercise 3: Chemical Names and Formulas (page 602)

1. $CaCl_2$	**4.** $NaSO_4$
2. CaO	**5.** CO
3. H_2S	**6.** HNO_2

7. (5) The compound contains one carbon atom and four chlorine atoms. Choices (1) and (4) have the wrong number of chlorine atoms. Choices (2) and (3) have the wrong elements.

Exercise 4: Acids and Bases (page 604)

1–2. These may appear in either order: acids, bases

3–5. oranges, lemons, grapefruit

6–8. drain cleaner, washing soda, ammonia

9. sour

10. bitter

11. Bases

12. acids

13. litmus paper

14. red

15. blue

Exercise 5: Decisions About Chemicals (page 608)

1–2. Answers will vary. Opinions should be supported with reasons.

3. (2) An opinion is a statement that tells people what they *should* do. The other choices are facts from the passage.

Exercise 6: Chapter Review (pages 608–612)

1. (3) Three of the listed compounds contain Ag, the symbol for silver.

2. (5) CuCl contains copper and chlorine. None of the other chemicals named has these two elements.

3. (4) All three body parts are listed as possible places of damage.

4. (2) See line 3 of the instructions.

5. (2) Metal poisoning is the only choice given that is listed as causing problems with the nervous system.

6. (5) Dust is not listed as one of the causes of headaches and dizziness.

7. (2) Speaker B would disagree with the other choices because he or she is arguing against the ban on food additives.

8. (5) You could compare the amount given to test animals with the amount eaten by humans each year. Choices (1), (2), and (3) are opinions because no one can prove them at this time. Choice (4) is an opinion because it talks about what people *should* do.

CHAPTER 6
EARTH AND SPACE SCIENCE

Exercise 1: You Decide (page 615)
1–3. Answers will vary.

Exercise 2: The Whole Story (page 616)
Answers will vary. The following are some possibilities:

1. How hot or cold does it get in California? Is there much rain?
2. How do vitamins improve one's health? Which vitamins should be taken? How much of each do I need? What specific health problems will each vitamin solve?
3. How much would taxes go up because of the park? What will the park include?
4. Why are new roads needed? What does the speaker mean by "progress"?
5. How many mice were tested in the study? What quantities of chemical X did the mice receive? What is the evidence that chemical X causes cancer in humans?

Exercise 3: Information, Please (page 618)
1. **(2), (3)** Choice (1) is not a good source because the factory would be biased toward persuading you that it is not polluting the river. Choice (4) is not the best source because the friend is probably not as knowledgeable as the health department or Citizens for a Better Environment.
2. **(1), (4)** Neither (2) nor (3) is as knowledgeable, unless one of them happens to be a health care provider.
3. **(1), (2)** Choice (3), your brother, is probably not as knowledgeable, and choice (4), the health food store clerk, may be biased since his job depends on people buying health foods.

Exercise 4: Geology (page 620)
Answers will vary. Here are some possibilities.

1. copper—electrical wires, kitchen pans, jewelry
2. iron—cars, stainless steel and cast-iron kitchen utensils, wood stoves, steel beams, wrought-iron railings, many tools
3. aluminum—kitchen utensils, foil, electrical wires
4. fossil fuels—gasoline, natural gas, heating oil, polyester clothes, draperies and upholstery
5. **(4)** This is stated in the second paragraph.

Exercise 5: Soil Conservation (page 623)
1. helps
2. harms
3. helps
4. harms
5. helps
6. helps
7. helps

8. **(2)** The text says that manure is organic fertilizer. Organic fertilizer has humus, which is needed for healthy soil. Choice (5) is incorrect because soil needs more than just nitrogen. Choices (1) and (3) wouldn't improve the soil. Choice (4) would cause erosion.

Exercise 6: A Forest Ecosystem (page 626)
1. The producers are green plants—the tree, the bush, and the grass. Only green plants can produce food.
2. The primary consumers are the squirrel, insects, deer, raccoon, and man because they all eat plants.
3. The secondary consumers are the fox, wolf, raccoon, and man because they eat other animals.
4. Bacteria and fungi are the decomposers.
5. **(5)** Everything in the food web is affected. The roots of green plants absorb the chemicals. When the green plants are eaten, the chemicals are eaten as well. When the primary consumers are eaten, the chemicals are passed along to the secondary consumers.

Exercise 7: Weather (page 629)

1. F   **Air** pressure is also known as barometric pressure.
2. T
3. F   **Cumulus** clouds are soft-looking, puffy clouds.
4. T
5. F   **Hail** is formed when frozen raindrops are blown up and down between layers of warm and cold air.
6. (4)   Warm air rises. Choice (1) is wrong because the Sun's gravity causes an equal—but very small—pull on *all* air on Earth. Choices (2) and (3) are not true according to the diagram. Choice (5) is not mentioned in the diagram.

Exercise 8: Orbiting Bodies (page 633)

1. Jupiter
2. stars
3. asteroids
4. galaxy
5. Venus
6. solar system
7. comet
8. (4)   The Sun is the center of the solar system.

Exercise 9: An Eclipse (page 634)

1. Answers will vary.
2. (1)   Both the Sun and the Moon are on one side of Earth, so people on the other side of Earth can't see them.

Exercise 10: Studying the Universe (page 636)

1. using only their eyes, using telescopes, and using satellites
2. Answers will vary.
3. (5)   This is the main idea of the passage. Choices (1), (2), and (3) are not supported by anything in the passage. Choice (4) is not mentioned in the passage.

Exercise 11: Chapter Review (pages 637–640)

1. (5)   See the first paragraph of the passage.
2. (2)   Since limestone contains small pieces of sea creatures, it must have formed under the ocean; therefore, it is sedimentary.
3. (3)   This method would show whether or not the continents were shifting. Choices (1), (2), and (4) are not practical. Choice (5) is incorrect because ancient scientists weren't always right.
4. (4)   The animal must have existed before the continents split apart in order to be found on both sides of the ocean. That eliminates answers (1), (2), and (3). Choice (5) is impossible; no animals lived on land before the crust cooled.
5. (2)   The paragraph lists many examples of how the rain forests are valuable. Choices (1), (3), and (4) are all details. Choice (5) is untrue.
6. (4)   The journal would be a good source of information on conservation issues. Sources (1) and (5) would probably be biased. Source (2) might have some information, but it would not be as complete as articles in a specialized journal. Choice (3) would contain information about chemistry, not about ecology issues.
7. (3)   Lowest usage of both water and oxygen occur from midnight to 3:00 A.M., presumably because the crew members are all asleep. Choices (1), (2), and (5) are false according to the information on the graph. There is no information on the graph about choice (4).
8. (2)   There is nothing on the graph to show which members of the crew are using the water.

MATHEMATICS

CHAPTER 1

Whole Numbers

Understanding Place Value

Whole numbers are written as one or more **digits** (0 through 9) arranged in a particular order. Whole numbers include the number 0 and all the **counting numbers** 1, 2, 3, 4, ... 999, and so on. There is no greatest whole number.

The **value** of a digit is determined by its place in a number.

Most numbers you will use have four or fewer digits. The number 2,905 is a four-digit number.

- A comma is often used to separate the thousands place from the hundreds place. In a four-digit number, though, the comma is not always written. For example, the number 2,905 can also be written 2905.

- Zero (0) is used as a **placeholder** to show that there are no ones, tens, or hundreds.

> **MATH FACT**
>
> A comma is **not** used when writing a date or an address.
>
> **Examples:**
> Year: 1176
> Address: 2942 Pine St.

THE FIRST FOUR PLACE VALUES

thousands	hundreds	tens	ones
2	**9**	**0**	**5**

2 thousands ⌐
9 hundreds ⌐
0 tens ⌐
5 ones ⌐

EXERCISE 1

<u>Part A</u> **Directions:** Fill in each blank with the correct digit.

1. **a.** 17 has _____ tens and _____ ones.

   b. 28 has _____ tens and _____ ones.

2. **a.** 30 has _____ tens and _____ ones.

   b. 90 has _____ tens and _____ ones.

3. 283 has _____ hundreds _____ tens and _____ ones.

4. 509 has _____ hundreds _____ tens and _____ ones.

5. 7,056 has _____ thousands _____ hundreds _____ tens and _____ ones.

6. 9,840 has _____ thousands _____ hundreds _____ tens and _____ ones.

Part B **Directions:** Write the value of each underlined digit. The first one is done as an example.

7. a. 5<u>4</u>7 _____4 tens_____   b. <u>2</u>70 _____
8. a. <u>9</u>6 _____   b. 8<u>3</u> _____
9. a. <u>1</u>43 _____   b. 7<u>8</u>9 _____
10. a. 4<u>0</u>5 _____   b. <u>6</u>30 _____
11. a. 2,32<u>5</u> _____   b. <u>1</u>,923 _____
12. a. <u>4</u>,270 _____   b. 9,0<u>5</u>0 _____

Larger Numbers In larger numbers, commas separate digits into groups of three. Notice the pattern of hundreds, tens, and ones in each three-digit group.

LARGER NUMBERS								
Millions			Thousands			Ones		
3	4	5 ,	8	0	5 ,	7	1	9
100s	10s	1s	100s	10s	1s	100s	10s	1s

Part C **Directions:** Write the value of each underlined digit. Several are done as examples.

13. a. 2<u>4</u>,150 _4 thousands_   b. 1<u>5</u>,398 _____
14. a. <u>1</u>7,000 _____   b. 32,1<u>4</u>7 _____
15. a. 7<u>5</u>,350 _____   b. 51,<u>3</u>00 _____
16. a. <u>8</u>2,625 _____   b. 1<u>9</u>,432 _____
17. <u>1</u>64,290 _____
18. <u>7</u>64,000 _____
19. 2,<u>3</u>74,500 _3 hundred thousands_
20. 3,<u>5</u>25,000 _____
21. 1<u>4</u>,830,000 _____
22. <u>2</u>3,175,800 _2 ten millions_
23. <u>2</u>50,000,000 _____
24. <u>3</u>75,600,000 _____

Answers are on page 819.

Reading and Writing Whole Numbers

To read or write a whole number, think about each group of digits separately: millions group, thousands group, and ones group.

Examples

MATH FACT

Infinity (∞) is **not** a number. It is a concept that refers to anything that has no upper limit.

If you think of ∞ as a number, then answer this question: What is ∞ + 1?

Ones Group

| 63 | sixty-three |
| 489 | four hundred eighty-nine |

} The group name *ones* is not said.

Thousands Group and Ones Group

5,427	five thousand, four hundred twenty-seven
35,600	thirty-five thousand, six hundred
143,256	one hundred forty-three thousand, two hundred fifty-six

Millions Group, Thousands Group, and Ones Group

| 2,750,008 | two million, seven hundred fifty thousand, eight |
| 138,900,000 | one hundred thirty-eight million, nine hundred thousand |

Notice how these rules are followed in the examples above:

- When writing a number, place a hyphen in compound words. For example, twenty-one and ninety-nine.

- Do not use the word *and* when writing or saying whole numbers.

- The group name *ones* (for numbers between 1 and 999) is not said.

- Place a comma after the word *million* and after the word *thousand*, but not after the word *hundred*.

EXERCISE 2

Part A **Directions:** Write a number that has these digits.

1. 8 tens, 6 ones _____

2. 4 hundreds, 9 tens, 6 ones _____

3. 5 thousands, 4 hundreds, 7 tens, 2 ones _____

4. 27 thousands, 6 hundreds, 3 tens, 4 ones _____

5. 329 thousands, 4 hundreds, 8 tens, 0 ones _____

6. 6 millions, 418 thousands, 6 hundreds, 2 tens, 4 ones _____

7. 75 millions, 200 thousands, 1 hundred, 7 tens, 5 ones _____

8. 250 millions, 500 thousands, 4 hundreds, 0 tens, 0 ones _____

Part B **Directions:** Match each number with its word meaning.

	Number		Word Meaning
_____	**9.** 407,000	**a.**	four million, seven thousand
_____	**10.** 4,700,000	**b.**	forty-seven million
_____	**11.** 47,000,000	**c.**	four million, seven hundred thousand
_____	**12.** 4,007,000	**d.**	forty million, seventy thousand
_____	**13.** 470,000	**e.**	four hundred seven thousand
_____	**14.** 40,070,000	**f.**	four hundred seventy thousand

MATH REMINDER

1,000	1 thousand
10,000	10 thousand
100,000	100 thousand
1,000,000	1 million
10,000,000	10 million
100,000,000	100 million

Part C **Directions:** Write each number using digits.

15. four thousand, six hundred twenty _____

16. twelve thousand, two hundred seventy-seven _____

17. one hundred thirty thousand, eight hundred fifty-nine _____

18. two million, three hundred ninety thousand, one hundred sixty _____

19. twenty-five million, fifty thousand, one hundred sixty-five _____

20. four hundred twenty-five million, six hundred thousand, five hundred _____

Part D **Directions:** Write each number in words.

21. speed of sound in air: 1,088 feet per second _____

22. speed of light in air: 186,000 miles per second _____

23. distance from Moon to Earth: 237,300 miles _____

24. distance from Sun to Earth: 92,900,000 miles _____

25. diameter of Earth: 7,926 miles _____

26. distance around Earth at equator: 24,850 miles _____

27. average number of human heartbeats per day for an average person: 103,680 _____

Answers are on page 819.

Adding Whole Numbers

To **add** is to combine two or more numbers.

- Addition is indicated by the **plus** (+) sign.
- Numbers being added are called **addends**.
- The answer to an addition problem is called the **sum**.

Example 1 Numbers with two or more digits are added one column at a time. Move from right to left, starting in the ones column. Continue until you have added every column.

ADDITION FACTS

Changing the order of addends does not change the sum.

$8 + 6 = 6 + 8$
$24 + 9 = 9 + 24$

Adding 0 does not change a number's value.

$12 + 0 = 12$
$0 + 3 = 3$

$$\begin{array}{r} 5241 \\ + 1230 \\ \hline 1 \end{array}$$

Add ones

$$\begin{array}{r} 5241 \\ + 1230 \\ \hline 71 \end{array}$$

Add tens

$$\begin{array}{r} 5241 \\ + 1230 \\ \hline 471 \end{array}$$

Add hundreds

$$\begin{array}{r} 5241 \\ + 1230 \\ \hline 6471 \end{array}$$

Add thousands

Adding two-digit or larger numbers often involves **regrouping** (also called **carrying**). To **regroup** means to take a digit from the sum of one column and place it at the top of the next column to the left.

Example 2 When the sum of digits in the ones column is greater than 10, move the tens digit to the top of the tens column.

STEP 1 Add the ones: $6 + 7 = 13$
Write the 3; move the 1.

STEP 2 Add the tens: $1 + 4 + 2$
Answer: 73

Move the 1 ten to the top of the tens column.

$$\begin{array}{r} \overset{1}{4}6 \\ + 27 \\ \hline 73 \end{array}$$

Write the 3 ones in the ones column.

Write 7 $(1 + 4 + 2)$ in the tens column.

Example 3 When the sum of digits in the tens column is greater than 10, move the 1 to the top of the hundreds column.

STEP 1 Add the ones: $5 + 3 = 8$

STEP 2 Add the tens: $7 + 5 = 12$
Write the 2; move the 1.

STEP 3 Add the hundreds:
$1 + 6 + 2 = 9$
Answer: 928

$$\begin{array}{r} \overset{1}{6}75 \\ + 253 \\ \hline 928 \end{array}$$

Write 8 in the ones column.

Write 2 $(7 + 5 = 12)$ in the tens column. Move 1 to the top of the hundreds column.

Write 9 $(1 + 6 + 2)$ in the hundreds column.

EXERCISE 3

Part A **Directions:** Add. No regrouping is needed.

1. $\begin{array}{r} 25 \\ + 13 \end{array}$ $\begin{array}{r} 61 \\ + 27 \end{array}$ $\begin{array}{r} 70 \\ + 14 \end{array}$ $\begin{array}{r} 84 \\ + 12 \end{array}$ $\begin{array}{r} 35 \\ + 20 \end{array}$ $\begin{array}{r} 18 \\ + 11 \end{array}$

2. $\begin{array}{r} 568 \\ + 200 \end{array}$ $\begin{array}{r} 314 \\ + 405 \end{array}$ $\begin{array}{r} 701 \\ + 231 \end{array}$ $\begin{array}{r} 327 \\ + 112 \end{array}$ $\begin{array}{r} 700 \\ + 238 \end{array}$ $\begin{array}{r} 483 \\ + 106 \end{array}$

Part B **Directions:** Add. Regrouping is needed.

3. $\begin{array}{r} 48 \\ + 7 \end{array}$ $\begin{array}{r} 63 \\ + 9 \end{array}$ $\begin{array}{r} 52 \\ + 8 \end{array}$ $\begin{array}{r} 68 \\ + 36 \end{array}$ $\begin{array}{r} 77 \\ + 48 \end{array}$ $\begin{array}{r} 35 \\ + 29 \end{array}$

4. $\begin{array}{r} 274 \\ + 62 \end{array}$ $\begin{array}{r} 883 \\ + 95 \end{array}$ $\begin{array}{r} 497 \\ + 31 \end{array}$ $\begin{array}{r} 273 \\ + 236 \end{array}$ $\begin{array}{r} 928 \\ + 590 \end{array}$ $\begin{array}{r} 742 \\ + 385 \end{array}$

5. $\begin{array}{r} 674 \\ + 87 \end{array}$ $\begin{array}{r} 458 \\ + 46 \end{array}$ $\begin{array}{r} 117 \\ + 85 \end{array}$ $\begin{array}{r} 573 \\ + 89 \end{array}$ $\begin{array}{r} 263 \\ + 49 \end{array}$ $\begin{array}{r} 489 \\ + 37 \end{array}$

6. $\begin{array}{r} 858 \\ + 475 \end{array}$ $\begin{array}{r} 765 \\ + 737 \end{array}$ $\begin{array}{r} 894 \\ + 379 \end{array}$ $\begin{array}{r} 637 \\ + 563 \end{array}$ $\begin{array}{r} 759 \\ + 748 \end{array}$ $\begin{array}{r} 946 \\ + 164 \end{array}$

Part C **Directions:** Solve each word problem by adding.

7. If a class contains 23 men and 16 women, how many students are in the class?

8. If it is now 19 minutes past 8 o'clock, what time will it be in 26 minutes?

9. 2,385 people attended the Huskies' first basketball game and 1,749 people attended the second. What is the total attendance for both games?

10. What is the total of John's three bills: rent for $405, telephone for $39, and electricity for $165?

Answers are on page 820.

Subtracting Whole Numbers

To **subtract** is to take one number away from another.

- Subtraction is indicated by the **minus** (–) sign.
- The number being subtracted is called the **minuend**; the number being subtracted from is called the **subtrahend**.
- The answer to an subtraction problem is called the **difference**.

<u>**Example 1**</u>   Numbers with two or more digits are subtracted one column at a time. Move from right to left, starting in the ones column. Continue until you have subtracted every column.

SUBTRACTION FACTS
Changing the order of numbers in a subtraction problem changes the difference.
10 – 5 is **not** the same as 5 – 10.
Subtracting 0 does **not** change a number's value.
9 – 0 = 9

```
  8429         8429         8429         8429
– 5124       – 5124       – 5124       – 5124
─────        ─────        ─────        ─────
    5           05          305         3305
```
Subtract ones   Subtract tens   Subtract hundreds   Subtract thousands

Subtracting two-digit or larger numbers often involves **regrouping** (also called **borrowing**). To regroup in subtraction means to take a 1 from one column and move it to the top of the next column to the right.

<u>**Example 2**</u>   When the ones digit of the minuend (bottom number) is larger than the ones digit of the subtrahend (top number), regroup by moving 1 ten from the tens column to the ones column.

STEP 1   You cannot subtract 7 from 2. So regroup the 6 tens, moving 1 ten to the ones column. Cross out the 6 and write a 5 above it.

```
      5 10
      6 2
   –  3 7
```
Replace 6 with 5. Move 1 ten.

STEP 2   Add the regrouped 10 to the 2 in the ones column. Think of this as putting 12 ones in the ones column. (10 + 2 = 12 ones)

```
   5 12
    6 2
 –  3 7
```
Add the moved 10 to the ones column to give a total of 12 ones.

STEP 3   Subtract the ones column: 12 – 7 = 5
Subtract the tens column: 5 – 3 = 2

```
   5 12
    6 2
 –  3 7
   ───
    2 5
```
You can now subtract each column.

Answer: 25

EXERCISE 4

Part A **Directions:** Subtract. No regrouping is needed.

1.	26 − 14	53 − 22	44 − 10	79 − 29	98 − 35	51 − 20

2.	280 − 160	746 − 432	482 − 270	703 − 502	928 − 317	274 − 163

Part B **Directions:** Subtract by **regrouping the tens** column.

3.	47 − 9	20 − 6	62 − 5	42 − 25	197 − 58	472 − 107

Part C **Directions:** Subtract by **regrouping the hundreds** column.

To subtract the tens column, you may need to regroup the hundreds column and move 10 tens (1 hundred) to the tens column.

Example
$$\overset{2\ 17}{\cancel{3}\cancel{7}4}$$
$$-\ 182$$
$$\overline{192}$$

4.	148 − 92	347 − 73	426 − 84	310 − 60	953 − 82	846 − 75

Part D **Directions:** Subtract by **regrouping the thousands** column.

To subtract the hundreds column, you may need to regroup the thousands column and move 10 hundreds (1 thousand) to the hundreds column.

Example
$$\overset{1\ 13}{2{,}\cancel{3}94}$$
$$-\ \ \ 482$$
$$\overline{1{,}912}$$

5.	5,486 − 675	4,583 − 720	3,572 − 722	7,484 − 943	1,373 − 650	2,437 − 525

Part E **Directions:** Subtract by **regrouping both the tens and hundreds** columns.

6.	654 − 96	845 − 79	637 − 38	320 − 267	762 − 175	555 − 367

Answers are on page 820.

Subtracting from Zero

Subtraction problems often have one or more 0s in the top number. Because you can't subtract from 0, you must regroup. The example below shows how to regroup the hundreds column when there is a 0 in the tens column.

Example   Subtract: 503
                             − 238

Solution: $\overset{9}{\overset{4\ \cancel{10}\ 13}{\cancel{5}\cancel{0}\cancel{3}}}$
              − 238
              265

STEP 1   Because you can't subtract 8 from 3, you must borrow. But you can't borrow from the 0 in the tens column. You must borrow from the 5. Here's how to do it:
- Cross out the 5 and write a 4 above it.
- Write the borrowed 1 hundred as 10 tens, and place the 10 above the 0 in the tens column.

$\overset{4\ \cancel{10}}{\cancel{5}0\cancel{3}}$
− 238

STEP 2   Now borrow from the tens column. Cross out the 10 and write 9 above it. Write the borrowed 1 ten above the ones column. This puts 13 ones in the ones column.

$\overset{9}{\overset{4\ \cancel{10}\ 13}{\cancel{5}\cancel{0}\cancel{3}}}$
− 238

STEP 3   Subtract each column:
    Ones column: 13 − 8 = 5
    Tens column: 9 − 3 = 6
    Hundreds column: 4 − 2 = 2

$\overset{9}{\overset{4\ \cancel{10}\ 13}{\cancel{5}\cancel{0}\cancel{3}}}$
− 238
265

Answer: 265

EXERCISE 5

Directions: Subtract. The first row is partially completed.

1. $\overset{9}{\overset{3\ 10\ 13}{\cancel{4}\cancel{0}\cancel{3}}}$ $\overset{9}{\overset{4\ 10\ 11}{\cancel{5}\cancel{0}\cancel{1}}}$ $\overset{9}{\overset{1\ 10\ 16}{\cancel{2}\cancel{0}\cancel{6}}}$ $\overset{9}{\overset{7\ 10\ 13}{\cancel{8}\cancel{0}\cancel{3}}}$ $\overset{9}{\overset{3\ 10\ 15}{\cancel{4}\cancel{0}\cancel{5}}}$ $\overset{9}{\overset{4\ 10\ 13}{\cancel{5}\cancel{0}\cancel{3}}}$
      − 47   − 39   − 167   − 549   − 278   − 289

2. 506   105   230   305   701   460
      − 47   − 68   − 98   − 149   − 318   − 236

3. 504   902   850   701   900   800
      − 427   − 335   − 239   − 243   − 264   − 367

Answers are on page 820.

Adding and Subtracting Money

To add or subtract dollars and cents, line up the decimal points and then add or subtract the columns. Line up the decimal points by placing one directly below another.

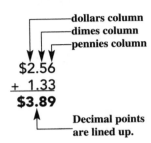

Example 1   Add $2.56 and $1.33

MATH FACT

Only one dollar sign ($) is written in a problem and one in an answer.

STEP 1   Write the numbers in a column. Line up the decimal points.

STEP 2   From right to left, add.
pennies column: 6 + 3 = 9
dimes column: 5 + 3 = 8
dollars column: 2 + 1 = 3

dollars column
dimes column
pennies column

$2.56
+ 1.33
$3.89

Decimal points are lined up.

Example 2   Subtract 87¢ from $7.35

STEP 1   Write 87¢ as a decimal: $0.87.

STEP 2   Write the numbers in a column. Line up the decimal points.

STEP 3   Regroup to allow subtraction.

STEP 4   From right to left, subtract.
pennies column: 15 − 7 = 8
dimes column: 12 − 8 = 4
dollars column: 6 − 0 = 6

Borrow 1 dime from the 3, replacing the 3 with a 2. The 5 pennies become 15 pennies.

Next, borrow 1 dollar from the 7, replacing the 7 with a 6. The 2 dimes now become 12 dimes.

  12
6 2 15
$7.35
− 0.87
$6.48

EXERCISE 6

Directions: Add or subtract as indicated. Two problems are partially completed.

1. $5.23	$5.89	$6.50	$1.75	$9.08	$0.86
+ 2.35	− 3.25	+ 1.25	− 1.50	+ 0.71	− 0.60
2. $8.95	$3.45	$9.77	$6.09	$14.37	$5.24
+ 1.57	− 1.28	+ 3.89	− 2.19	+ 12.74	− 2.37
3. $5.00	$5.00	$8.00	$10.00	$20.00	$50.00
− 3.85	− 2.18	− 5.60	− 6.49	− 12.83	− 27.98

Answers are on page 820.

Multiplying Whole Numbers

MATH FACTS

Changing the order of factors does not change the product:
$7 \times 5 = 5 \times 7$

Multiplying any number by 0 gives a product of 0:
$12 \times 0 = 0$

Multiplying any number by 1 gives the same number:
$26 \times 1 = 26$

To **multiply** is to use a shortcut that takes the place of repeated addition.

- Multiplication is indicated by the **times (×)** sign.
- Numbers being multiplied are called **factors**.
- The answer to a multiplication problem is called the **product**.

Multiplying Single Digits

In this lesson you'll practice multiplying single-digit numbers. The **multiplication facts**, shown on the table below, are the basis of all multiplication. The table does not include 0.

Remember: The product of any number times 0 is 0. Example: $5 \times 0 = 0$

	1	2	3	4	5	6	7	8	9
1	1	2	3	4	5	6	7	8	9
2	2	4	6	8	10	12	14	16	18
3	3	6	9	12	15	18	21	24	27
4	4	8	12	16	20	24	28	32	36
5	5	10	15	20	25	30	35	40	45
6	6	12	18	24	30	36	42	48	54
7	7	14	21	28	35	42	49	56	63
8	8	16	24	32	40	48	56	64	72
9	9	18	27	36	45	54	63	72	81

Example 1

Multiply: 7
          × 6
          ———
           42

Find 7 in the indicated row.
Find 6 in the indicated column.

The square at the intersection of the row and the column shows the product (answer).

Answer: 42

Example 2

Multiply: 3
          × 9
          ———
           27

Find the "3" row.
Find the "9" column.

The square at the intersection of the row and the column gives the product.

Answer: 27

EXERCISE 7

Part A **Directions:** Multiply. Practice until you can do each problem with confidence.

1. 6	8	1	9	4	3	7	5
× 3	× 7	× 9	× 0	× 2	× 6	× 8	× 1

2. 7	3	9	2	6	0	9	6
× 0	× 2	× 5	× 8	× 5	× 2	× 7	× 9

3. 4	6	4	7	7	9	8	5
× 3	× 7	× 9	× 0	× 2	× 6	× 8	× 1

4. 2	4	8	3	7	9	8	3
× 2	× 5	× 4	× 7	× 9	× 8	× 3	× 5

5. 6	5	2	6	7	8	9	9
× 2	× 8	× 8	× 3	× 6	× 2	× 5	× 2

6. 5	3	1	2	7	8	4	4
× 6	× 9	× 9	× 5	× 2	× 6	× 3	× 4

7. 9	2	7	6	5	8	5	5
× 3	× 3	× 7	× 7	× 9	× 8	× 3	× 7

8. 8	3	5	8	7	4	6	9
× 5	× 3	× 4	× 7	× 2	× 9	× 8	× 1

Part B **Directions:** Write each word phrase in symbols and then solve. The first one is done as an example.

9. five times six   seven times three

$5 \times 6 = 30$

nine times eight   zero times four

10. five multiplied by nine   the product of eight and seven   six multiplied by seven

Answers are on page 820.

Multiplying by One-Digit Numbers

Numbers with two or more digits are multiplied one digit at a time. Move from right to left, starting with the ones digit. Continue until you have multiplied every digit.

- Write the product of the ones digits in the ones column.
- Write the product of the tens digit in the tens column.
- Write the product of the hundreds digit in the hundreds column.

Example 1

$$
\begin{array}{r}
134 \\
\times\ \ 2 \\
\hline
268
\end{array}
$$

Multiply the ones: $2 \times 4 = 8$
Multiply the tens: $2 \times 3 = 6$
Multiply the hundreds: $2 \times 1 = 2$

Answer: 268

Example 2

$$
\begin{array}{r}
512 \\
\times\ \ 3 \\
\hline
1{,}536
\end{array}
$$

Multiply the ones: $3 \times 2 = 6$
Multiply the tens: $3 \times 1 = 3$
Multiply the hundreds: $3 \times 5 = 15$

Answer: 1,536

EXERCISE 8

Part A **Directions:** Multiply.

1.
$$
\begin{array}{r} 21 \\ \times\ 3 \\ \hline \end{array} \quad
\begin{array}{r} 32 \\ \times\ 2 \\ \hline \end{array} \quad
\begin{array}{r} 11 \\ \times\ 8 \\ \hline \end{array} \quad
\begin{array}{r} 34 \\ \times\ 2 \\ \hline \end{array} \quad
\begin{array}{r} 13 \\ \times\ 3 \\ \hline \end{array} \quad
\begin{array}{r} 20 \\ \times\ 4 \\ \hline \end{array} \quad
\begin{array}{r} 12 \\ \times\ 3 \\ \hline \end{array}
$$

2.
$$
\begin{array}{r} 41 \\ \times\ 8 \\ \hline \end{array} \quad
\begin{array}{r} 94 \\ \times\ 2 \\ \hline \end{array} \quad
\begin{array}{r} 32 \\ \times\ 4 \\ \hline \end{array} \quad
\begin{array}{r} 71 \\ \times\ 6 \\ \hline \end{array} \quad
\begin{array}{r} 80 \\ \times\ 9 \\ \hline \end{array} \quad
\begin{array}{r} 83 \\ \times\ 3 \\ \hline \end{array} \quad
\begin{array}{r} 81 \\ \times\ 7 \\ \hline \end{array}
$$

Part B **Directions:** Multiply.

3.
$$
\begin{array}{r} 312 \\ \times\ 3 \\ \hline \end{array} \quad
\begin{array}{r} 141 \\ \times\ 2 \\ \hline \end{array} \quad
\begin{array}{r} 232 \\ \times\ 3 \\ \hline \end{array} \quad
\begin{array}{r} 403 \\ \times\ 2 \\ \hline \end{array} \quad
\begin{array}{r} 213 \\ \times\ 3 \\ \hline \end{array} \quad
\begin{array}{r} 324 \\ \times\ 2 \\ \hline \end{array} \quad
\begin{array}{r} 240 \\ \times\ 2 \\ \hline \end{array}
$$

4.
$$
\begin{array}{r} 431 \\ \times\ 3 \\ \hline \end{array} \quad
\begin{array}{r} 723 \\ \times\ 3 \\ \hline \end{array} \quad
\begin{array}{r} 804 \\ \times\ 2 \\ \hline \end{array} \quad
\begin{array}{r} 721 \\ \times\ 4 \\ \hline \end{array} \quad
\begin{array}{r} 432 \\ \times\ 3 \\ \hline \end{array} \quad
\begin{array}{r} 911 \\ \times\ 8 \\ \hline \end{array} \quad
\begin{array}{r} 630 \\ \times\ 3 \\ \hline \end{array}
$$

Answers are on page 820.

Multiplying by Two-Digit Numbers

To multiply by a two-digit number, multiply the top number by each digit of the bottom number.

- When multiplying by the ones digit, start the answer in the ones column.

- When multiplying by the tens digit, start the answer in the tens column.

The answer to each step of multiplication is called a **partial product**. The answer to the problem is found by adding the partial products.

Example Multiply: 42
           × 13

Solution:
```
      42
    × 13
     126   partial products
      42  ← Treat this blank
     ---    space as a 0.
     546
      ↑
     tens column
```

STEP 1 Multiply 42 by 3, the ones digit: 42 × 3 = 126
Write 126, with the 6 in the ones column.

STEP 2 Multiply 42 by 1, the tens digit: 42 × 1 = 42
Write 42, with the 2 in the tens column. This second partial product is written in the tens and hundreds columns. It does **not** start in the ones column.

STEP 3 Add the partial products.

Answer: 546

EXERCISE 9

Part A **Directions:** Write the second partial products where needed. Add the partial products to find the answer.

1.
```
   31      30      40      52      420     521     422
 × 22    × 23    × 12    × 23    × 34    × 24    × 43
   62      90      80     156    1680    2084    1266
   62      60     ___     ___    1260    ___     ___
```

Part B **Directions:** Multiply.

2.
```
   32      24      31      40      41      421     512
 × 12    × 22    × 11    × 21    × 37    × 43    × 32
```

Answers are on page 820.

Multiplying and Regrouping

When the product of two digits is 10 or more, regroup as in addition. Move a digit from a product and place it at the top of the column to the left. Example 1 shows how to regroup 35 in the ones column, moving 3 tens to the tens column.

Example 1 Multiply: $\begin{array}{r} 45 \\ \times\ 7 \\ \hline \end{array}$ Solution: $\begin{array}{r} \overset{3}{4}5 \\ \times\ 7 \\ \hline \mathbf{315} \end{array}$

STEP 1 Multiply the ones digit: $7 \times 5 = 35$
Think of 35 as 3 tens and 5 ones.
Place the 5 in the ones column.

$\begin{array}{r} \overset{3}{4}5 \\ \times\ 7 \\ \hline 315 \end{array}$ **Write the 3 tens at the top of the tens column.**

STEP 2 Move the 3 to the top of the tens column.

Place 5 in the ones column.

STEP 3 Multiply the tens digit: $7 \times 4 = 28$
Add the regrouped 3 to 28: $28 + 3 = 31$
Write 31 in the tens and hundreds columns.

Remember: Multiply the tens digit before adding the regrouped digit.

Example 2 Multiply: $\begin{array}{r} 507 \\ \times\ 3 \\ \hline \end{array}$ Solution: $\begin{array}{r} 5\overset{2}{0}7 \\ \times\ 3 \\ \hline \mathbf{1{,}521} \end{array}$ **When multiplying the tens digit, first multiply 3×0. Then, add 2 to the product $(2 + 0)$.**

When multiplying 0s, remember these two rules:

- The product of any number times 0 is 0.

- Multiply the 0 first, then add the regrouped digit.

Example 3 shows how a regrouped digit from the product of the tens digit is moved to the hundreds column.

Example 3 Multiply: $\begin{array}{r} 291 \\ \times\ 6 \\ \hline \end{array}$ Solution: $\begin{array}{r} \overset{5}{2}91 \\ \times\ 6 \\ \hline \mathbf{1{,}746} \end{array}$

STEP 1 Ones digit: $6 \times 1 = 6$ Write 6 in ones column.

STEP 2 Tens digit: $6 \times 9 = 54$ Write 4 in tens column.
Place 5 at the top of hundreds column.

STEP 3 Hundreds digit: $6 \times 2 = 12$ Add 5 to 12: $12 + 5 = 17$
Write 17, placing the 7 in the hundreds column.

EXERCISE 10

<u>**Part A**</u> **Directions:** Multiply.

1.
$$\begin{array}{r} 17 \\ \times\ 2 \\ \hline \end{array} \qquad \begin{array}{r} 15 \\ \times\ 5 \\ \hline \end{array} \qquad \begin{array}{r} 24 \\ \times\ 4 \\ \hline \end{array} \qquad \begin{array}{r} 36 \\ \times\ 3 \\ \hline \end{array} \qquad \begin{array}{r} 47 \\ \times\ 2 \\ \hline \end{array} \qquad \begin{array}{r} 29 \\ \times\ 3 \\ \hline \end{array}$$

2.
$$\begin{array}{r} 54 \\ \times\ 7 \\ \hline \end{array} \qquad \begin{array}{r} 37 \\ \times\ 6 \\ \hline \end{array} \qquad \begin{array}{r} 42 \\ \times\ 9 \\ \hline \end{array} \qquad \begin{array}{r} 75 \\ \times\ 6 \\ \hline \end{array} \qquad \begin{array}{r} 38 \\ \times\ 9 \\ \hline \end{array} \qquad \begin{array}{r} 37 \\ \times\ 5 \\ \hline \end{array}$$

<u>**Part B**</u> **Directions:** Multiply.

3.
$$\begin{array}{r} 107 \\ \times\ 5 \\ \hline \end{array} \qquad \begin{array}{r} 206 \\ \times\ 4 \\ \hline \end{array} \qquad \begin{array}{r} 307 \\ \times\ 3 \\ \hline \end{array} \qquad \begin{array}{r} 706 \\ \times\ 7 \\ \hline \end{array} \qquad \begin{array}{r} 803 \\ \times\ 9 \\ \hline \end{array} \qquad \begin{array}{r} 609 \\ \times\ 6 \\ \hline \end{array}$$

4.
$$\begin{array}{r} 308 \\ \times\ 6 \\ \hline \end{array} \qquad \begin{array}{r} 702 \\ \times\ 9 \\ \hline \end{array} \qquad \begin{array}{r} 403 \\ \times\ 5 \\ \hline \end{array} \qquad \begin{array}{r} 909 \\ \times\ 8 \\ \hline \end{array} \qquad \begin{array}{r} 608 \\ \times\ 4 \\ \hline \end{array} \qquad \begin{array}{r} 507 \\ \times\ 3 \\ \hline \end{array}$$

<u>**Part C**</u> **Directions:** Multiply.

5.
$$\begin{array}{r} 271 \\ \times\ 3 \\ \hline \end{array} \qquad \begin{array}{r} 152 \\ \times\ 4 \\ \hline \end{array} \qquad \begin{array}{r} 370 \\ \times\ 3 \\ \hline \end{array} \qquad \begin{array}{r} 192 \\ \times\ 4 \\ \hline \end{array} \qquad \begin{array}{r} 251 \\ \times\ 3 \\ \hline \end{array} \qquad \begin{array}{r} 284 \\ \times\ 2 \\ \hline \end{array}$$

6.
$$\begin{array}{r} 482 \\ \times\ 4 \\ \hline \end{array} \qquad \begin{array}{r} 571 \\ \times\ 2 \\ \hline \end{array} \qquad \begin{array}{r} 620 \\ \times\ 9 \\ \hline \end{array} \qquad \begin{array}{r} 461 \\ \times\ 7 \\ \hline \end{array} \qquad \begin{array}{r} 580 \\ \times\ 6 \\ \hline \end{array} \qquad \begin{array}{r} 281 \\ \times\ 5 \\ \hline \end{array}$$

<u>**Part D**</u> **Directions:** Solve.

7. Jayne's car gets 28 miles to the gallon. How many miles can Jayne expect to drive on the remaining 9 gallons of gas in her tank?

8. Each day, Monday through Friday of last week, Terrence ate a Big Sam Burger—a sandwich with a total of 394 calories. How many calories did Terrence eat last week just from these sandwiches?

Answers are on page 820.

Multiplying Larger Numbers

When you are multiplying larger numbers, more than one regrouping may be needed to find each partial product.

MATH FACTS

Each partial product has its own regrouped digits. It is a good idea to write regrouped digits lightly in pencil. You can erase them after you compute each partial product.

Example   Multiply: 247
                              × 38

Solution: 247
            × 38
            1 976
            7 41
            9,386

STEP 1   Multiply 247 by 8:
            (3 and 5 are the
            regrouped digits)

$$\overset{3\,5}{247}$$
× 38
1976

STEP 2   Multiply 247 by 3:
            (1 and 2 are the
            regrouped digits)

$$\overset{1\,2}{247}$$
× 38
1976
741

STEP 3   Add the partial products.

Answer: 9,386

EXERCISE 11

Part A   **Directions:** Complete the second partial products as needed. Add the partial products to find the answer.

1.

86	52	95	753	846	937
× 22	× 47	× 82	× 38	× 29	× 43
172	364	190	6024	7614	2811
172	____	____	2259	____	____

Part B   **Directions:** Multiply.

2.

64	83	49	79	53	75
× 37	× 54	× 28	× 48	× 29	× 64

Answers are on page 821.

Multiplying by 10, 100, and 1,000

There are three easy rules to follow when multiplying by 10, 100, or 1,000.

RULE 1   To multiply a number by 10, place one 0 to the right of the number.

Examples

$$\begin{array}{r} 35 \\ \times\ 10 \\ \hline 350 \end{array} \qquad \begin{array}{r} 278 \\ \times\ 10 \\ \hline 2{,}780 \end{array} \qquad \begin{array}{r} 10 \\ \times\ 9 \\ \hline 90 \end{array}$$

RULE 2   To multiply a number by 100, place two 0s to the right of the number.

Examples

$$\begin{array}{r} 463 \\ \times\ 100 \\ \hline 46{,}300 \end{array} \qquad \begin{array}{r} 3{,}647 \\ \times\ 100 \\ \hline 364{,}700 \end{array} \qquad \begin{array}{r} 100 \\ \times\ 87 \\ \hline 8{,}700 \end{array}$$

RULE 3   To multiply a number by 1000, place three 0s to the right of the number.

Examples

$$\begin{array}{r} 81 \\ \times\ 1000 \\ \hline 81{,}000 \end{array} \qquad \begin{array}{r} 195 \\ \times\ 1000 \\ \hline 195{,}000 \end{array} \qquad \begin{array}{r} 1000 \\ \times\ 6 \\ \hline 6{,}000 \end{array}$$

EXERCISE 12

Part A   **Directions:** Multiply.

1. $\begin{array}{r} 83 \\ \times 10 \end{array}$ $\begin{array}{r} 100 \\ \times 24 \end{array}$ $\begin{array}{r} 1000 \\ \times 9 \end{array}$ $\begin{array}{r} 10 \\ \times 7 \end{array}$ $\begin{array}{r} 100 \\ \times 18 \end{array}$ $\begin{array}{r} 1000 \\ \times 36 \end{array}$

2. $\begin{array}{r} 100 \\ \times 28 \end{array}$ $\begin{array}{r} 10 \\ \times 26 \end{array}$ $\begin{array}{r} 71 \\ \times 100 \end{array}$ $\begin{array}{r} 4216 \\ \times 1000 \end{array}$ $\begin{array}{r} 330 \\ \times 10 \end{array}$ $\begin{array}{r} 100 \\ \times 85 \end{array}$

Part B   **Directions:** Multiply.

3. $\begin{array}{r} 74 \\ \times 28 \end{array}$ $\begin{array}{r} 100 \\ \times 33 \end{array}$ $\begin{array}{r} 84 \\ \times 67 \end{array}$ $\begin{array}{r} 27 \\ \times 10 \end{array}$ $\begin{array}{r} 1000 \\ \times 42 \end{array}$ $\begin{array}{r} 45 \\ \times 36 \end{array}$

4. $\begin{array}{r} 59 \\ \times 10 \end{array}$ $\begin{array}{r} 100 \\ \times 68 \end{array}$ $\begin{array}{r} 36 \\ \times 32 \end{array}$ $\begin{array}{r} 1000 \\ \times 25 \end{array}$ $\begin{array}{r} 89 \\ \times 75 \end{array}$ $\begin{array}{r} 10 \\ \times 47 \end{array}$

Answers are on page 821.

Dividing Whole Numbers

To **divide** is to find how many times one number will **go into** a second number. For example, because there are nine 4s in 36, 4 divided into 36 is 9.

- Division is indicated by the **division sign** ÷, or by a **division bracket** $\overline{)}$

- The number being divided into is called the **dividend**.

- The number being divided by is called the **divisor**.

- The answer to a division problem is called the **quotient**.

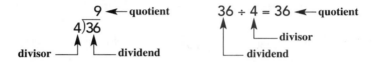

To divide, ask, "How many times does the divisor go into the dividend?" Look at the following examples.

Example 1	**Example 2**	**Example 3**
$\dfrac{6}{3\overline{)18}}$	$\dfrac{34}{2\overline{)68}}$	$\dfrac{20}{4\overline{)80}}$
	1st: Divide 2 into 6. 2nd: Divide 2 into 8.	1st: Divide 4 into 8. 2nd: Divide 4 into 0.

Remember: As Example 3 shows, 0 divided by any number is 0.

A **remainder** is a number left over in division. For example, if you divide 9 cookies among 4 students, each student gets 2 cookies (2 × 4 = 8). One cookie is left over (9 − 8 = 1).

Remainders are common in division.

Example 4

```
  2 r 1
4)9
 -8  ←  4 divides into 9 only 2 times.
  1     Write 2 × 4 = 8 below the 9.
        Subtract 8 from 9 to find out
        how much is left over.
```

Example 5

```
   5 r 2
3)17
 -15  ←  17 ÷ 3 = 5 plus a remainder.
   2     Write 5 × 3 = 15 below 17.
         Subtract: 17 − 15 = 2
```

EXERCISE 13

<u>Part A</u> **Directions:** Divide. These one-step problems are a review of division facts.

1. $3\overline{)27}$ $8\overline{)56}$ $5\overline{)35}$ $4\overline{)24}$ $9\overline{)72}$ $8\overline{)64}$

2. $6\overline{)42}$ $7\overline{)56}$ $9\overline{)45}$ $8\overline{)40}$ $7\overline{)49}$ $5\overline{)30}$

3. $2\overline{)18}$ $8\overline{)48}$ $9\overline{)63}$ $7\overline{)28}$ $9\overline{)54}$ $5\overline{)40}$

Part B **Directions:** Divide. There are no remainders in these problems.

4. 4)484   3)639   2)120   7)350   6)612   7)714

5. 2)612   3)927   5)510   6)636   7)749   9)918

Part C **Directions:** Divide. There is a remainder in each problem.

6. 4)7   5)9   3)7   2)5   4)9   6)11

7. 5)23   4)18   7)41   9)61   3)22   6)27

8. 12)30   10)67   11)48   15)34   14)72   13)64

Part D

9. Adam and 6 friends are going to evenly share a bag of 50 marbles.

   a. How many marbles does each person get?

   b. How many marbles are left over?

10. Kelli is going to cut a 75-inch board into 8 pieces of equal length.

    a. What is the greatest length each piece can be?

    b. If Kelli cuts each piece the greatest length possible, what length of board will be left over?

Answers are on page 821.

Using Long Division

Long division is a four-step process you use for most division problems. Long division is used when a remainder occurs before all the digits are divided.

Example 1   Divide: 4)92

Step 1	Step 2	Step 3	Step 4
2	2	2	2
4)92	4)92	4)92	4)92
	8	−8	−8
		1	12

STEP 1   Divide 4 into 9. Write 2 above the 9.

STEP 2   Multiply: 2 × 4 = 8 and write 8 below the 9.

STEP 3   Subtract: 9 − 8 = 1 and write the remainder 1 below the 8.

STEP 4   Bring down the 2 and place it next to the remainder 1.

Now repeat this four-step process. Start by dividing 4 into 12.

STEP 1 Divide 4 into 12. Write 3 above the 2.

STEP 2 Multiply: $3 \times 4 = 12$ and write 12 below the 12.

STEP 3 Subtract: $12 - 12 = 0$ and write 0 below the 12.

STEP 4 There is no other digit to bring down, and there is no remainder. The problem is finished.

$$
\begin{array}{r}
23 \\
4\overline{)92} \\
-8 \\
\hline
12 \\
-12 \\
\hline
0
\end{array}
$$

Answer: 23

Answers With Remainders

As the examples below show, many long-division problems also have a remainder as part of the quotient. When you have **brought down** all the numbers and have finished dividing, you may still have a remainder.

Example 2

$$
\begin{array}{r}
13\ r\ 2 \\
5\overline{)67} \\
-5 \\
\hline
17 \\
-15 \\
\hline
2
\end{array}
$$

Example 3

$$
\begin{array}{r}
52\ r\ 1 \\
7\overline{)365} \\
-35 \\
\hline
15 \\
-14 \\
\hline
1
\end{array}
$$

Example 4

$$
\begin{array}{r}
89\ r\ 1 \\
3\overline{)268} \\
-24 \\
\hline
28 \\
-27 \\
\hline
1
\end{array}
$$

EXERCISE 14

Part A **Directions:** Divide. There are no remainders.

1. $3\overline{)42}$ $\quad$ $5\overline{)85}$ $\quad$ $4\overline{)96}$ $\quad$ $7\overline{)119}$ $\quad$ $4\overline{)92}$ $\quad$ $5\overline{)435}$

2. $2\overline{)36}$ $\quad$ $4\overline{)60}$ $\quad$ $6\overline{)78}$ $\quad$ $3\overline{)51}$ $\quad$ $8\overline{)96}$ $\quad$ $5\overline{)75}$

3. $4\overline{)136}$ $\quad$ $5\overline{)465}$ $\quad$ $3\overline{)237}$ $\quad$ $4\overline{)236}$ $\quad$ $7\overline{)434}$ $\quad$ $8\overline{)704}$

Part B **Directions:** Divide. There are remainders.

4. $4\overline{)75}$ $\quad$ $5\overline{)67}$ $\quad$ $8\overline{)93}$ $\quad$ $6\overline{)157}$ $\quad$ $7\overline{)365}$ $\quad$ $3\overline{)268}$

5. $5\overline{)62}$ $\quad$ $7\overline{)89}$ $\quad$ $4\overline{)75}$ $\quad$ $8\overline{)95}$ $\quad$ $2\overline{)57}$ $\quad$ $3\overline{)83}$

6. $5\overline{)474}$ $\quad$ $6\overline{)523}$ $\quad$ $3\overline{)137}$ $\quad$ $7\overline{)692}$ $\quad$ $4\overline{)339}$ $\quad$ $2\overline{)175}$

Answers are on page 821.

Multiplying and Dividing Money

When multiplying or dividing dollars and cents, remember to place the decimal point and dollar sign in the answer.

Example 1   Multiply:

$$\begin{array}{r} \$5.24 \\ \times\ \ \ 6 \\ \hline \$31.44 \end{array}$$

STEP 1   Multiply the numbers: $524 \times 6 = 3144$

STEP 2   Place the decimal point and dollar sign in the product.

Answer: $31.44

Example 2   Divide:

$$\begin{array}{r} \$1.32 \\ 7)\overline{\$9.24} \\ -7\ \ \ \ \ \\ \hline 2\,2\ \ \\ -2\,1\ \ \\ \hline 14 \\ -14 \\ \hline 00 \end{array}$$

STEP 1   Divide the numbers: $924 \div 7 = 132$

STEP 2   Place the decimal point and dollar sign in the quotient.

Answer: $1.32

EXERCISE 15

Part A   **Directions:** Multiply.

1.
$$\begin{array}{r}\$2.21\\\times\ \ \ 4\\\hline\end{array} \quad \begin{array}{r}\$3.00\\\times\ \ \ 6\\\hline\end{array} \quad \begin{array}{r}\$5.85\\\times\ \ \ 9\\\hline\end{array} \quad \begin{array}{r}\$10.00\\\times\ \ \ \ 8\\\hline\end{array} \quad \begin{array}{r}\$12.50\\\times\ \ \ \ 7\\\hline\end{array} \quad \begin{array}{r}\$24.75\\\times\ \ \ \ 5\\\hline\end{array}$$

2.
$$\begin{array}{r}\$1.25\\\times\ \ 13\\\hline\end{array} \quad \begin{array}{r}\$2.30\\\times\ \ 11\\\hline\end{array} \quad \begin{array}{r}\$4.50\\\times\ \ 15\\\hline\end{array} \quad \begin{array}{r}\$30.00\\\times\ \ 25\\\hline\end{array} \quad \begin{array}{r}\$8.94\\\times\ \ 17\\\hline\end{array} \quad \begin{array}{r}\$9.85\\\times\ \ 25\\\hline\end{array}$$

Part B   **Directions:** Divide.

3. $5)\overline{\$13.45}$ $8)\overline{\$12.40}$ $6)\overline{\$3.60}$ $4)\overline{\$8.84}$ $7)\overline{\$22.40}$ $3)\overline{\$13.02}$

4. $4)\overline{\$1.08}$ $5)\overline{\$5.25}$ $3)\overline{\$6.09}$ $4)\overline{\$12.24}$ $9)\overline{\$18.18}$ $7)\overline{\$31.50}$

Answers are on page 821.

Multiplication and Division Word Problems

EXERCISE 16

Directions: Solve each word problem using multiplication or division.

1. On his new diet, Jeremy plans to lose 75 pounds. If he loses 4 pounds each month, how many pounds can Jeremy expect to lose in one year?

2. When green onions are selling for three bunches for $2.37, what price would you pay for a single bunch?

3. To find the area of a rectangle, you multiply the length times the width. What is the area of a rectangle (in square feet) that measures 25 feet long and 13 feet wide?

4. Farmer Murphy's cows produce 672 quarts of milk each day. How many gallons of milk is this? **Hint**: To change quarts to gallons, divide by 4.

5. The Men's Store sold 21 shirts during a Saturday sale. If the shirts sold for $24.95 each, how much money was taken in from the sale of these shirts?

6. Lin makes and sells clay statues in her pottery shop. If she uses 6 pounds of clay for each statue, how many complete statues can she make with 44 pounds of clay?

7. Julia works 38 hours each week as an administrative assistant. For this work, she earns $12.50 per hour. How much does Julia earn each week?

8. Carlos brought a microwave oven for $239.58. He agreed to pay for it in 6 equal monthly payments. What amount will Carlos pay each month?

9. Shelly puts $42 each month in a savings account for her infant son. At this rate, how much can she save in 18 months?

10. Shaun is paid a $24 commission on each piece of furniture he sells. During April, Shaun earned a commission of $576. How many pieces of furniture did Shaun sell during April?

11. At an average highway speed of 52 miles per hour, how far can Alondo travel in his car in 9 hours?

12. If Grace can type 65 words per minute, how many minutes will it take her to type a 2,990-word report?

Answers are on page 821.

Rounding Whole Numbers

Often it is useful to **estimate**—to give a number that is almost equal to an accurate amount. One way to estimate is to use rounded numbers.

To round a number, replace one or more of its digits with a 0.

A sports reporter says that 800 people attended a high school football game. Actually, 792 were there. The number 800 is called a **rounded number**.

- To the nearest ten, 792 rounds to 790.

- To the nearest hundred, 792 rounds to 800.

- To the nearest thousand, 792 rounds to 1,000.

You most often round whole numbers to the nearest 10, 100, or 1,000.

- Round up when a number is halfway or more between two rounded numbers.

- Round down when a number is less than halfway between two rounded numbers.

Nearest Ten	**Nearest Hundred**	**Nearest Thousand**
25 rounds to 30	137 rounds to 100	3,650 rounds to 4,000

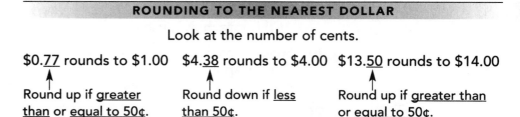

25 is halfway between 20 and 30. 25 rounds up to 30.	137 is less than halfway between 100 and 200. 137 rounds down to 100.	3,650 is more than halfway between 3,000 and 4,000. 3,650 rounds up to 4,000.

You most often round money to the nearest $1.00 or $10.00.

ROUNDING TO THE NEAREST DOLLAR

Look at the number of cents.

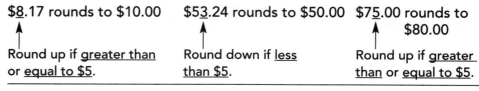

$0.<u>77</u> rounds to $1.00 $4.<u>38</u> rounds to $4.00 $13.<u>50</u> rounds to $14.00

Round up if <u>greater than</u> or <u>equal to 50¢</u>. Round down if <u>less than 50¢</u>. Round up if <u>greater than</u> or <u>equal to 50¢</u>.

ROUNDING TO THE NEAREST TEN DOLLARS

Look at the number of dollars.

$<u>8</u>.17 rounds to $10.00 $5<u>3</u>.24 rounds to $50.00 $7<u>5</u>.00 rounds to $80.00

Round up if <u>greater than</u> or <u>equal to $5</u>. Round down if <u>less than $5</u>. Round up if <u>greater than</u> or <u>equal to $5</u>.

EXERCISE 17

Part A   **Directions:** Round each number. Circle each answer choice.

> The symbol ≈ means *is approximately equal to*. This symbol is often used when rounding and estimating.

To the nearest ten	To the nearest hundred	To the nearest thousand
1. 63: 60 or 70	165: 100 or 200	2,350: 2,000 or 3,000
2. 87: 80 or 90	450: 400 or 500	5,824: 5,000 or 6,000

Part B   **Directions:** Round each number to the nearest ten.

   3. 65 ≈   83 ≈   17 ≈   44 ≈   98 ≈

Directions: Round each number to the nearest hundred.

   4. 118 ≈   271 ≈   192 ≈   321 ≈   950 ≈

Directions: Round each number to the nearest thousand.

   5. 1,285 ≈   3,400 ≈   4,500 ≈   8,375 ≈   950 ≈

Part C   **Directions:** Round each purchase to the nearest dollar.

6.

$2.29 ≈ $24.79 ≈ $12.29 ≈ $7.38 ≈

Directions: Round each purchase to the nearest ten dollars.

7.

$34.95 ≈ $87.25 ≈ $168.50 ≈ $123.75 ≈

Answers are on page 821.

Estimating with Whole Numbers

CLUE WORDS FOR ESTIMATION

about
approximately
close to
estimate
guess
on average

Sometimes you may need to find an exact numerical answer. For example, you will do this when giving change to a customer at a cash register.

Other times, you may want to **estimate**—to find an approximate answer. An estimate is a number or amount that is **about equal to** the exact answer. You can use estimation in several ways:

- to give an approximate answer when an exact answer is not needed
- to check the accuracy of your math when doing an exact calculation
- to help choose among answer choices on a multiple-choice test
- to check a calculator answer

Rounding numbers before doing a calculation is a good way to estimate.

Example 1   What is the approximate sum of 823, 489, and 214?

STEP 1   Round each number to the nearest 100.

$$823 \approx 800 \quad 489 \approx 500 \quad 214 \approx 200$$

STEP 2   Add the rounded numbers.

$$
\begin{array}{r}
800 \\
500 \\
+\ 200 \\
\hline
1{,}500
\end{array}
$$

Answer: 1,500. The exact sum is 1,526.

Example 2   You are busy shopping, and you suddenly remember that you have only $10 in your wallet. Do you have enough money to pay for the items in your cart?

Instead of adding the exact prices, you estimate:

		Estimate
cereal	$3.89	about $4.00
bread	$1.09	about $1.00
juice	$1.98	about $2.00
soap	$0.89	about $1.00
	Total:	about $8.00

Answer: Your estimate tells you that $10 is enough money. The exact total is $7.85.

EXERCISE 18

Part A **Directions:** Estimate an answer. Any reasonable estimate is acceptable.

	Estimate		**Estimate**		**Estimate**
1.	62		138		$9.25
	47		96		3.89
	+ 39		+ 47		+ 1.17

	Estimate		**Estimate**		**Estimate**
2.	$12.84		983		1,025
	− 4.79		− 407		− 498

	Estimate		**Estimate**		**Estimate**
3.	38		189		$3.08
	× 11		× 23		× 19

	Estimate		**Estimate**		**Estimate**
4.	9)88		11)295		21)399

Part B **Directions:** Estimate an answer. Then use your estimate to circle the exact answer.

5. At a price of $1.89 each, what is the total cost of 315 floor tiles?

    a. $286.55   **b.** $334.85   **c.** $422.25   **d.** $595.35   **e.** $698.15

    Estimate _____

6. What is the total cost of the following four items: shoes $48.50; shirt $21.95; jacket $62.75; umbrella $12.25?

    a. $118.75   **b.** $145.45   **c.** $183.65   **d.** $203.35   **e.** $211.95

    Estimate _____

7. The Blakelys drove 194 miles of the 406 miles they need to drive. How many more miles must they drive to reach Salem?

    a. 112   **b.** 161   **c.** 212   **d.** 248   **e.** 307

    Estimate _____

8. Meagan wants to divide 319 counters among the 29 students in class. How many counters should Meagan give to each student?

    a. 4   **b.** 6   **c.** 8   **d.** 11   **e.** 15

    Estimate _____

Answers are on pages 821–822.

Whole Numbers Review

EXERCISE 19

Part A **Directions:** Fill in each blank with the correct digit.

1. 4,509 has _____ thousands _____ hundreds

   _____ tens and _____ ones.

2. 7,640 has _____ thousands _____ hundreds

   _____ tens and _____ ones.

Part B **Directions:** Write the value of each underlined digit.

3. 7<u>9</u>3 _____

4. <u>2</u>86 _____

5. <u>3</u>,410 _____

6. <u>1</u>1,650 _____

Directions: Write a number that has these digits.

7. 3 thousands, 8 hundreds, 3 tens, 0 ones _____

8. 32 thousands, 5 hundreds, 7 tens, 5 ones _____

Directions: Write each number in words.

9. diameter of the Moon: 3,480 miles _____

   _____

10. land area of New York: 53,989 square miles _____

   _____

Part C **Directions:** Add.

11. 32   53   19   26 $0.45 $7.60
    + 6   + 14   + 7   + 9   + 0.29   + 3.80

12. 135   247   364   288 $3.47 $53.80
    + 53   + 48   + 46   + 93   + 1.90   + 27.50

Part D **Directions:** Subtract.

13. 19   28   17   35 $0.73 $1.32
    – 8   – 14   – 9   – 17   – 0.26   – 0.79

14. 174   247   738   160   500 $6.00
    – 89   – 168   – 539   – 93   – 182   – 3.42

Part E **Directions:** Multiply.

15. 9   12   74   43 $5.82 $6.05
    × 5   × 4   × 2   × 6   × 9   × 8

16. 41   53   367   74   48   516
    × 36   × 22   × 5   × 19   × 37   × 84

Part F **Directions:** Divide.

17. $5\overline{)35}$ $8\overline{)56}$ $3\overline{)936}$ $4\overline{)808}$ $6\overline{)\$3.30}$ $7\overline{)\$5.04}$

18. $11\overline{)40}$ $5\overline{)325}$ $4\overline{)75}$ $8\overline{)347}$ $9\overline{)\$8.10}$ $7\overline{)\$46.34}$

Part G **Directions:** Round each number to the nearest ten.

19. 73 ≈   45 ≈   13 ≈   92 ≈   36 ≈

Directions: Round each number to the nearest hundred.

20. 189 ≈   203 ≈   484 ≈   363 ≈   882 ≈

Directions: Round each number to the nearest thousand.

21. 1,446 ≈   2,700 ≈   3,500 ≈   9,125 ≈   870 ≈

Part H **Directions:** Estimate an answer for each problem below. Any reasonable estimate is acceptable.

	Estimate	**Estimate**	**Estimate**	**Estimate**
22.	107 92 + 48	816 − 392	79 × 21	9)674

Answers are on page 822.

CHAPTER 2

Using a Calculator

Basic Calculator Skills

Being able to work with a calculator is an important mathematics skill. Although many calculators are similar, the GED Mathematics Test permits use of only the Casio *fx-260SOLAR* calculator shown below. On the next few pages, you will have a chance to practice basic calculator skills. Check with your instructor about which calculator you should use while studying this book.

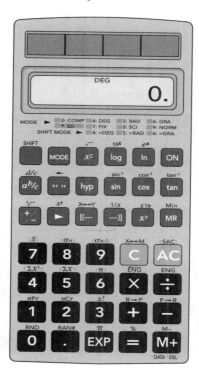

As a first step in every calculation, press $\boxed{\text{ON}}$. This clears the display and lets you start a new problem.

When referring to a calculator, the word *clear* means to erase. When a correction key clears the display or parts of a calculation, it replaces each number with a 0 and ignores the last operation key pressed. The Casio *fx-260SOLAR* has two specialized clear keys.

All Clear Key $\boxed{\text{AC}}$ is used to clear the display and to clear all parts of a calculation.

Clear Key $\boxed{\text{C}}$ is used to clear the display only. The clear key does not clear parts of a calculation.

Using the Calculator with Whole Numbers

Adding Whole Numbers

Example   1,635 + 846 + 78 =

Keys	Display	
ON	0.	
1 6 3 5	1635.	← A decimal point appears at the right of a whole number. There is no comma key, and no comma appears in the display.
+	1635.	
8 4 6	846.	
+	2481.	← A subtotal is displayed each time you press the add key + .
7 8	78.	
=	2559.	← The sum is displayed when you press the equals key = .

Answer: 2,559

EXERCISE 1

Part A **Directions:** Add.

1. 8 + 6 =   7 + 9 =   8 + 7 + 5 = $9 + $7 + $6 =

2. 38 + 24 =   75 + 59 =   24 + 19 + 16 = $36 + $21+ $8 =

3. 673 + 275 =   4,359 + 2,425 =   3,640 + 1,038 + 742 =

4. $842 + $349 = $1,582 + $829 = $2,500 + $1,900 + $750 =

Part B **Directions:** Add.

5. On the first three days of her vacation, Jodi drove 246 miles, 178 miles, and 341 miles. What total number of miles did Jodi drive on these three days?

6. Attendance figures for three basketball games were: Thursday 2,368; Friday 3,490; Saturday 3,435. How many tickets were sold for the three games?

Answers are on page 822.

Subtracting Whole Numbers

Example   147 − 63 − 9 =

ON	0.	More than one number can be subtracted during a calculation.
1 4 7	147.	
−	147.	
6 3	63.	
−	84.	← A subtotal is displayed each time you press the subtract key −.
9	9.	
=	75.	← The difference is displayed when you press the equals key =.

Answer: 75

EXERCISE 2

Part A   **Directions:** Subtract.

1. 9 − 2 =   17 − 9 =   15 − 3 − 7 = $19 − $11 − $3 =

2. 75 − 49 =   93 − 36 =   84 − 49 − 17 = $78 − $52 − $19 =

3. 839 − 457 =   2,682 − 1,375 =   4,562 − 3,150 − 898 =

4. $783 − $254 = $2,350 − $1,775 = $5,647 − $3,500 − $1,736 =

Part B   **Directions:** Subtract.

5. Juan is taking a trip to San Francisco, a distance of 872 miles from his home. How far will Juan have left to drive after driving 589 miles of this distance?

6. Naomi cut a 34-inch length of ribbon from a piece of ribbon that was 127 inches long. She then cut a 26-inch piece from the original ribbon. What length of the original ribbon remains?

Answers are on page 822.

Multiplying Whole Numbers

Example   79 × 43 =

ON		0.	**Numbers can be multiplied in either order without changing the product.**
7 9		79.	
×		79.	
4 3		43.	
=		3397.	← The product is displayed after you press the equals key = .

Answer: 3,397

EXERCISE 3

Part A   **Directions:** Multiply.

1. 4 × 0 =   12 × 1 =   8 × 5 =   9 × 7 =

2. 72 × 10 =   52 × 9 =   89 × 57 =   48 × 36 =

3. 325 × 32 =   870 × 25 =   25 × 14 × 10 =   75 × 49 × 12 =

4. $3.75 × 6 = $45.65 × 16 = $124.50 × 9 = $368.70 × 34 =

Part B   **Directions:** Multiply.

5. As a fast-food cook, Rebecca is able to cook 126 hamburgers each hour during a busy day. At this rate, how many hamburgers can Rebecca cook during a busy 8-hour shift?

6. What is the total price of 19 gallons of gasoline at a price of $1.49 per gallon?

7. When the half-cup size of Yummy Yogurt went on sale for $0.49, Maria bought all 31 cartons on the shelf. What total amount did Maria pay for all this yogurt? Write your answer in dollars and cents.

Answers are on page 822.

Dividing Whole Numbers

Example   646 ÷ 19 =

Keys	Display	
ON	0.	The dividend (number divided into) must be entered first.
6 4 6	646.	
÷	646.	
1 9	19.	
=	34.	← The quotient is displayed after you press the equals key = .

Answer: 34

EXERCISE 4

Part A   **Directions:** Divide.

1. 12 ÷ 3 =   27 ÷ 9 =   88 ÷ 8 =   0 ÷ 15 =

2. 136 ÷ 8 =   625 ÷ 5 =   0 ÷ 136 =   406 ÷ 7 =

3. 4,200 ÷ 10 =   4,200 ÷ 100 =   3,942 ÷ 27 =   8,124 ÷ 6 =

4. $4.88 ÷ 4 = $38.76 ÷ 6 = $54.36 ÷ 12 = $975.75 ÷ 25 =

Part B   **Directions:** Divide.

5. On a trip to Chicago, Charlie drove 276 miles in 6 hours. On average, how many miles did he drive each hour?

6. When a deck of 52 cards is dealt to 4 people, how many cards does each person receive?

7. Irene worked 9 hours on Saturday at a part-time job. If she earned $63.90, how much was she paid for each hour of work?

8. During the past 15 years, Manuel paid a total of $160,200 in mortgage payments. During this time, he made 180 equal monthly payments. How much did Manuel pay each month?

Answers are on page 822.

Calculator Review

Part A   **Directions:** Add.

1. $89 + 27 =$ $125 + 78 =$ $2,490 + 945 + 325 =$

2. $\$14.65 + \$3.25 =$ $\$57.48 + \$24.63 =$ $\$3,500 + \$1,900 + \$750 =$

Part B   **Directions:** Subtract.

3. $74 - 59 =$ $341 - 167 =$ $562 - 238 - 117 =$

4. $\$25.68 - \$9.15 =$ $\$20.00 - \$14.79 =$ $\$10.00 - \$4.29 - \$2.88 =$

Part C   **Directions:** Multiply.

5. $19 \times 7 =$ $35 \times 16 =$ $42 \times 10 \times 2 =$ $162 \times 18 \times 3 =$

6. $\$2.47 \times 5 =$ $\$16.80 \times 8 =$ $\$35.60 \times 8 =$ $\$264.75 \times 10 =$

Part D   **Directions:** Divide.

7. $3,560 \div 10 =$ $7,700 \div 100 =$ $4,632 \div 8 =$ $1,764 \div 21 =$

8. $\$8.90 \div 2 =$ $\$46.06 \div 7 =$ $\$125.30 \div 14 =$ $\$825.70 \div 10 =$

Part E   **Directions:** Solve.

9. At the Huskies' first game of the season, 23,450 people showed up. The second game drew 26,780; the third game drew 25,750. What was the total attendance for these first three games?

10. Out of her monthly check of $1,840, Darlene pays $735 for rent and $145 for utilities. How much does Darlene have remaining after making these two payments?

11. During a sale, Uptown Music shipped 1,238 boxes of compact discs. If each box holds 13 CDs, how many CDs were shipped?

12. A 234-page book contains 72,072 words. On the average, how many words are written on a single page?

Answers are on page 823.

CHAPTER 3

Solving Word Problems

A **word problem** is a short story that asks a question or tells you to find something. Using the information that is given, you are asked to solve a problem.

In this chapter, you will learn five steps for solving a word problem.

FIVE STEPS FOR SOLVING A WORD PROBLEM

1. **Understand the Question.** Know what you are being asked to find.

2. **Choose Necessary Information.** Decide which numbers you will need to use.

3. **Plan the Math.** Decide which operations you need to use: addition, subtraction, multiplication, or division.

4. **Do the Math.** Estimate the answer and then perform each operation as it is needed.
   - One-step problems are solved in one step using one operation.
   - Multistep problems are solved in two or more steps using two or more operations.

5. **Think About Your Anwer.** Make sure your answer makes sense. Ask yourself, "Does this answer sound reasonable to me? Is the answer about what I had expected it to be?" Compare your answer with your estimate.

Step 1: Understand the Question

Word problems may be written as a single sentence or as several sentences. In each type of problem, the first step is to identify the question and to understand what you are being asked to find.

Example 1 How much does a 3-pound package of chicken cost if the price per pound is $1.48?

Asked to Find: cost of 3 pounds of chicken

Example 2 JiNin bought a blouse for $14 and a skirt for $24. She also bought shoes for $24.95. What total amount did JiNin pay for the blouse and skirt?

Asked to Find: total cost of blouse and skirt

EXERCISE 1

Directions: Circle the words within the parentheses that tell what you are asked to find.

1. If Sarah pays $450 each month for rent, how much rent does she pay for one year?

    (weekly rent, monthly rent, yearly rent)

2. A gallon of milk weighs about 9 pounds. How much does 3 gallons of milk weigh?

    (weight of 3 gallons of milk, cost of 3 gallons of milk, weight of 27 gallons of milk)

3. This year, Manuel paid $1,350 in federal income tax, $426 in state income tax, and $460 in property tax. Find the amount that Manuel paid in state and federal taxes.

    (total of property and state tax, total of federal and state tax, total of all taxes)

4. June bought the following items at the store: 1 can of soda for $0.75, 1 gallon of milk for $2.79, 2 tubes of toothpaste for $3.29. How many items did June buy?

    (cost of all items, total number of items, total number of food items)

5. The driving distance between Salem and Eugene is 67 miles. From Eugene to Oak Ridge is 42 miles. If you are driving through Eugene, what is the distance from Oak Ridge to Salem?

    (mileage from Salem to Eugene, mileage from Salem to Oak Ridge, mileage from Eugene to Oak Ridge)

6. If 9 cats, 14 dogs, and 6 other animals are in the Pet Parade, how many pets are in the parade?

    (number of cats, number of dogs, number of pets)

7. Donnelle teaches kindergarten. Her class contains 14 girls and 11 boys. How many children are in Donnelle's class?

    (number of girls and boys, number of girls, number of boys)

8. Carin bowls each Thursday night. She pays $1.75 for shoe rental and $1.35 for each game she bowls. This Thursday, Carin bowled 4 games. What total amount did she pay for her bowling evening?

    (cost of shoe rental, cost of shoe rental plus cost of bowling 1 game, cost of shoe rental plus cost of bowling 4 games)

Answers are on page 823.

Step 2: Choose Necessary Information

Word problems often contain more information than is needed to answer the question. For these problems, you must decide what information is important.

Necessary information is numbers that are needed to answer the question.

Extra information is numbers that are **not** needed to answer the question.

<table>
<tr><td style="background:black; color:white">MATH FACT</td></tr>
<tr><td>Tables, graphs, maps, and schedules almost always contain much more information than you need.</td></tr>
</table>

Example 1 Martina had $40.00 in cash. She bought a sweater for $21.95 and a pair of gloves for $14.75. How much did she spend in all?

Asked to find: cost of sweater and gloves

Necessary information: $21.95, $14.75

Extra information: $40.00

Example 2 On Monday, Wednesday, and Friday of each week, Kevin jogs 4 miles. Each Saturday, he rides his bike 10 miles. How many miles does Kevin jog each week?

Asked to find: miles Kevin jogs each week

Necessary information: 3 days each week, 4 miles each day

Extra information: 10 miles of biking on Saturday

Example 3 Refer to the table below. How many grams of protein are in 16 ounces (1 pound) of dark meat chicken?

Nutrition Information		
	Protein (grams per ounce)	Fat (grams per ounce)
Chicken: Light Meat	9	1
Chicken: Dark Meat	8	2

Asked to find: grams of protein in 16 ounces of dark meat chicken

Necessary information: 16 ounces per pound, 8 grams per ounce

Extra information: 9 grams per ounce, 1 gram per ounce, 2 grams per ounce

EXERCISE 2

Directions: On the line below each problem, write the information that is needed to solve the problem. The first one is done as an example.

1. Brianna lost 13 pounds on her diet. Her weight dropped from 167 pounds to 154 pounds. If she still wants to lose 14 more pounds, what weight is Brianna trying to attain?

   154 pounds and 14 pounds

2. At Jeffrey's Market, a gallon of milk costs $2.39, a loaf of rye bread costs $1.79, and green seedless grapes are on sale for $1.09 per pound. What is the total cost of 5 pounds of green seedless grapes?

   _____

3. What was the total rainfall during the first three days of the week, during the week shown in the table at right?

   _____

4. Amelie earned a total of $294.50 last week. During the week, she baby-sat for 8 hours, earning $4 per hour. She also worked 35 hours as a cook, earning $7.50 per hour. How much money did she earn last week baby-sitting?

   _____

Weekly Rainfall	
Monday	2 inches
Tuesday	3 inches
Wednesday	3 inches
Thursday	1 inch
Friday	4 inches

5. Bradley bowled 3 games Tuesday night. His scores were 147, 172, and 165. These scores were well below his league average of 182. Find the sum of his Tuesday night scores.

   _____

6. In Marysville there are 127,560 registered voters. Of these, 62,483 are men and 65,077 are women. During the November election, 26,394 men and 31,425 women voted. How many people voted in the November election?

   _____

7. At Huang's market, apples are on sale for $0.59 per pound. These apples normally sell for $0.79 per pound. What is the total price of a 7-pound bag of apples on sale?

   _____

Answers are on page 823.

Step 3: Plan the Math

Most math problems are solved by doing one operation (+, −, ×, or ÷) with two numbers. Examples: $12.50 + $3.75; 246 − 132; $8.25 × 3; and 351 ÷ 3. Problems that involve only one operation are called **one-step problems.**

Often, the hardest part of a one-step problem is deciding which operation to use! Should you add, subtract, multiply, or divide? One way to decide is to look for words that give clues. These words are called **key words**. Some key words or phrases are listed below.

Addition	Subtraction	Multiplication	Division
add	subtract	multiply	divide
sum	difference	product	quotient
total	change	total	each
altogether	more than	times	average
combined	less than	twice (× 2)	split
increased by	decreased by	when finding several of a given amount	when given an amount and finding one part
in all	farther than		
when combining different amounts	when comparing one amount with another	when given the part and finding the whole	when sharing, cutting, or splitting

Example 1 How much change did Virginia receive when she paid a $26.45 grocery bill with a check for $40.00?

Key word: change

Operation: subtraction ($40.00 − $26.45)

Example 2 Kerry and three friends are splitting the cost of a large pizza. If the price of the pizza is $16.80, what is each person's share?

Key word: split

Operation: division ($16.80 ÷ 4)

EXERCISE 3

Directions: Underline the key word or phrase in each problem below. Then, circle the operation that would be used to solve each problem. You do **not** need to solve these problems.

1. While driving to San Francisco, Gerardo passed a sign that read "San Francisco 187 miles." After he drives another 75 miles, how far will Gerardo be from San Francisco?

   Operation: + − × ÷

2. A case of 24 cans of dog food costs $36.72. What is the price of each can?

   Operation: + − × ÷

3. To save energy, Erin lowered her thermostat setting from 73 degrees to 68 degrees. By how many degrees did Erin reduce the temperature?

   Operation: + − × ÷

4. The Wilsons' rent of $575 per month is being increased to $635 per month. By how much is the Wilsons' monthly rent increasing?

   Operation: + − × ÷

5. Three roommates are dividing their monthly rent. Each plans to pay the same amount of the $1,245 total. What will be each roommate's share?

   Operation: + − × ÷

6. Jerry's restaurant sold 284 small sodas on Saturday. Each small cup holds 8 ounces of soda. Find the total ounces of soda that the restaurant sold on Saturday.

   Operation: + − × ÷

7. Kaitlan bought a pair of shoes for $18.75, a skirt for $23.50, and a blouse for $32.00. How much did Kaitlan spend in all for these three items?

   Operation: + − × ÷

8. Linda's car gets 21 miles per gallon. How many miles can Linda expect to drive on a total of 18 gallons?

   Operation: + − × ÷

9. Peter weighs 97 pounds more than his wife, Paula. If Paula weighs 136 pounds, how much does Peter weigh?

   Operation: + − × ÷

10. Four salesmen sold a total of $26,400 worth of furniture during May. On the average, how much did each salesman sell during this month?

    Operation: + − × ÷

Answers are on page 823.

Step 4: Do the Math

Once you understand the question and choose the correct operation, it is a good idea to make an **estimate** before actually doing the math. To estimate is to use round numbers to find out approximately what the answer should be. First you round the numbers in the problem and then you do the correct math using the rounded numbers.

Example 1   Jocelyn paid $20.00 for a book that costs $11.29. How much change should Jocelyn receive?

Estimate: $20 – $11 = **$9**

MATH TIP

For both an estimate and an exact answer, it is a good idea to write all numbers neatly in columns. Then it is easy to check to see that you did each computation step correctly.

After you have estimated the answer, solve the problem exactly: $20.00 – $11.29 = $8.71. The estimate of $9 is close to the exact answer of $8.71. Comparing an exact answer with an estimate gives you confidence you did the math correctly—either by pencil and paper or by calculator.

On a **multiple-choice test,** estimating first may save you the trouble of actually finding an exact answer. Your estimate may be all you need.

Example 2   Chicken salad is on sale at Benji's Deli for $1.94 per pound. How much does 6.2 pounds cost? Circle your answer.

(1) $8.24   **(2)** $11.15   **(3)** $12.03   **(4)** $13.98   **(5)** $14.85

Estimate: $2 × 6 = **$12**

The estimate of $12 enables you to quickly choose (3) $12.03 as the correct answer. On this problem, you do not need to find an exact answer.

EXERCISE 4

Directions: For each problem below, estimate and then find the exact answer.

1. If Stacey saves $19 each week, how long will it take her to save $589?

   Estimate: _____

   Exact Answer: _____

2. The owner of a grocery store bought 53 loaves of bread for $0.94 per loaf. How much did the owner pay for all of the bread?

   Estimate: _____

   Exact Answer: _____

3. Sonja types at the rate of 48 words per minute. How long will it take Sonja to type a report that contains 1,968 words?

   Estimate: _____

   Exact Answer: _____

4. How many calories are in a meal of one hamburger with 403 calories, one cola drink with 189 calories, and fries with 296 calories?

Estimate: _____

Exact Answer: _____

5. Melinda's car gets 32 miles per gallon when she drives in the city. How many miles of city driving can she expect to do on a full tank of 19 gallons?

Estimate: _____

Exact Answer: _____

6. What is the total price of 19 gallons of gas at a cost of $1.59 per gallon?

Estimate: _____

Exact Answer: _____

7. Nine people won a lottery that has a value of $7,642,980. If they split the prize equally, what is each person's share?

Estimate: _____

Exact Answer: _____

8. After Robbie's monthly wages were reduced by $102.75, his take-home pay was $1,589.25 per month. What was Robbie's monthly salary before the pay reduction?

Estimate: _____

Exact Answer: _____

9. On Monday, Alyce drove 349 miles. On Tuesday, she drove 497 miles. How far did Alyce drive on these two days?

Estimate: _____

Exact Answer: _____

10. Jon bought a pair of sweatpants for $23.89. He paid the clerk with a $10 bill and a $20 bill. How much change did Jon receive?

Estimate: _____

Exact Answer: _____

Answers are on page 823.

Step 5: Think About Your Answer

The final step in any problem is to take a moment and think about your answer.

- Does the answer make sense?

- Is the answer about what you think it should be?

- Did you do the math correctly?

Without thinking about your answer, you may do what seems to be a good job in solving a problem and still get the wrong answer.

Example

Brandon and Meredith read the following problem.

Lauren bought a new blouse for $14.95. The sales tax was $0.90. Lauren paid for the blouse with a $20 bill. Including tax, how much did Lauren pay for the blouse?

(1) $4.15   **(2)** $8.45   **(3)** $12.65   **(4)** $15.85   **(5)** $20.90

> **Math Fact**
>
> In the example, a reasonable estimate is $15 + $1 = $16, which tells you that the correct answer is **(4)** $15.85.

Brandon chose **(1)** $4.15 as the answer. He estimated that the change would be less than $5.00. Answer **(1)** is the only answer that is less than $5.00, so Brandon thought he was correct.

Meredith chose **(5)** $20.90 as the answer. She added $0.90 to $20.00. She checked the total, $20.90, with her estimate of $21.00 ($20 + $1). Meredith's answer was one of the answer choices, so she thought she was correct.

What is Brandon's mistake?

Brandon's reasoning is correct, but he is **not** answering the question that is asked! Brandon's answer, $4.15, tells the correct amount of change Lauren should receive. However, this is not what Brandon is asked to find.

What is Meredith's mistake?

Meredith added $0.90 to $20.00. Although she added correctly and made a good estimate, her answer is not correct. She did **not** add the right numbers! The correct solution is to add $0.90 to $14.95. Meredith should have realized that the correct answer would be less than $20!

Brandon and Meredith both would have seen their mistakes if they had thought for a moment about their chosen answers.

Remember: Follow these steps when thinking about your answer:

- Make sure you understand the question that is asked.

- Make sure you are using the right numbers for that question.

- Think: "Does my estimate make sense?"

- Compare your exact answer with your estimate. If your exact answer is close to your estimate, you can be confident that you have done the math correctly. If you used a calculator, you can be confident that you didn't make a keying error.

EXERCISE 5

Directions: In each problem below, a student circled an incorrect answer choice.

- Write the mistake that the student made.
- Write an estimate of the correct answer.
- Write the correct answer.

1. Carlos bought running shoes for $39.95, sweat socks for $4.95, and a sweatshirt for $12.50. He paid the clerk with three $20 bills. Not counting the sales tax of $3.44, how much did Carlos spend in all?

   (1) $2.60   **(2)** $16.61   **(3)** $20.05   **(4)** $57.40   **(5)** $60.00

   What mistake did the student make? _____

   _____

   Estimate: _____   **Correct answer:** _____

2. Each day, Monday through Saturday, Antonio delivers a newspaper to each of the 78 homes on his paper route. On Sunday, he delivers a total of 93 papers. How many papers does Antonio deliver Monday through Saturday?

   (1) 171   **(2)** 375   **(3)** 375   **(4)** 468   **(5)** 561

   What mistake did the student make? _____

   _____

   Estimate: _____   **Correct answer:** _____

3. For his car tune-up business, Kerry bought 15 cases of oil. Each case holds 24 quarts of oil. Each quart of oil costs Kerry $0.68. How much does Kerry pay for each case of oil?

   (1) $8.92   **(2)** $9.45   **(3)** $10.20   **(4)** $16.32   **(5)** $244.80

   What mistake did the student make? _____

   _____

   Estimate: _____   **Correct answer:** _____

Answers are on page 823.

Multistep Problems

Many word problems cannot be solved in one step. These problems, called **multistep problems**, may require two or more steps before you reach a solution.

A multistep problem is solved by breaking it down into two or more one-step problems. Each step is solved by a single operation.

Writing a **solution sentence** is often a good way to begin a multistep problem. A solution sentence consists of brief words, phrases, and numbers to state a problem's solution as simply as possible.

Example 1   Raphael planned to spend $50.00 at Gene's Men Store. After buying a shirt for $29.95 and a tie for $12.45, how much did Raphael have left?

Here's a solution sentence for this problem:

amount left = $50 **minus** cost of shirt and tie together
                                   missing information

The total cost of shirt and tie together is not given as a single number. Because it isn't, this amount is called **missing information.** Finding missing information is the first step in a multistep problem.

missing information = cost of shirt and tie together

= $29.95 + $12.45

= **$42.40**

Knowing the missing information, you can easily find the amount left.

amount left = $50.00 − $42.40 = **$7.60**

In Example 2, there are two items of missing information.

Example 2   Lynn bought 2 sweaters for $18.99 each. She also bought 3 skirts for $16.50 each. How much did Lynn pay for all these clothes?

cost of clothes = cost of sweaters **plus** cost of skirts
                         missing information   *missing information*

Each item of missing information is found separately:

cost of sweaters = $18.99 × 2 = **$37.98**

cost of skirts = $16.50 × 3 = **$49.50**

Place the missing information numbers in the solution sentence and add.

cost of clothes = $37.98 + $49.50 = **$87.48**

EXERCISE 6

<u>Part A</u> **Directions:** Solve each problem. For each problem, a solution sentence is written as a hint.

1. At Richie's Market, Jason bought hamburger for $3.58, a gallon of milk for $2.19, and a box of cereal for $2.89. If he paid the clerk with a $20 bill, how much change did Jason receive?

   change = $20 minus total cost of groceries

2. Each day Monday through Friday, Frieda delivers a newspaper to each of 121 customers. Last weekend she delivered a total of 257 papers. What total number of papers did Frieda deliver during the entire week?

   total papers = total papers Monday through Friday plus 257

3. Flora baked cookies for her son's first grade class. From the 84 cookies she baked, she kept 12 at home for her family. She took the rest to school. If there are 24 students in the class, how many cookies can each child have at snack time?

   cookies per child = cookies taken to class divided by 24

4. Five friends agree to split the cost of dinner. Together they have a pizza for $16.75, soft drinks for $6.75, and salads for $8.75. What is each person's share of the bill?

   each share = total cost of meal items divided by 5

5. Shelley made 23 gift packages for children attending her church. Each package contains $0.79 worth of candy, a $1.98 toy, and a balloon that costs $0.35. How much did Shelley spend for all the items in all 23 packages?

   total cost of all items = cost of items in one package times 23

6. George bought 15 cases of oil to use in his car tune-up business. Each case contains 24 quarts. George uses 5 quarts of oil for each tune-up. How many tune-ups can George do before he needs to buy more oil?

   total number of tune-ups = total quarts purchased divided by 5

Part B **Directions:** Solve each problem below. As your first step, complete each solution sentence below the problem.

7. Holly, a plumber, fixed the sink at Mark's house. She charged Mark a total of $87.40. The cost of new parts included $28.50 for a new faucet, $13.65 for tubing, and $1.50 for washers. How much did Holly charge for her labor?

   Solution Sentence: labor cost =

   Answer:

8. In his pickup Dion can carry 8 large boxes. He can also carry 16 more boxes in a trailer attached to the pickup. How many boxes can Dion move in 8 trips if he using both pickup and trailer?

   Solution Sentence: total number of boxes =

   Answer:

9. Three clubs rented Town Hall for a celebration dance. The rent was $185, the cost of the band was $294, and the refreshments cost $142. If the 3 clubs split the costs evenly, what was each club's total share?

   Solution Sentence: each club's share =

   Answer:

10. As part of a sales idea, Bobbie gave away 55 balloons every day during the 30 days in April. At the end of the month, she still had 245 balloons left over. Knowing this, figure out how many balloons Bobbie started with.

    Solution Sentence: total number of balloons =

    Answer:

11. Marie bought 3 dresses during the Spring Clearance Sale. One dress cost $34.95, one cost $27.50, and the other cost $19.95. If she paid for the dresses with a $100 bill, how much change should Marie receive?

    Solution Sentence: total change =

    Answer:

12. For the first meeting of his first aid class, Bill bought 17 manuals. Each manual cost $8.49. He also bought a first aid kit for $27.50. Find the total cost of Bill's supplies.

    Solution Sentence: total cost of supplies =

    Answer:

Part C **Directions:** Solve each problem below. As your first step, write a solution sentence below the problem.

13. Working as a waitress Monday through Thursday, Lita serves about 95 people each day. On Saturday she serves about 165. During the 5 days that Lita works, about how many people does she serve?

    Solution Sentence:

    Answer:

14. Jon and his two brothers split the cost of renting a small mobile home for a hunting trip. Daily rental cost is $44.60. If they keep the home for 6 days, how much is each brother's share of the total rental cost?

    Solution Sentence:

    Answer:

15. Angie traded in her old Ford for a newer Toyota. The Ford had 167,825 miles on it. The Toyota had only 32,540 miles. During the next year, Angie drove the Toyota an average of 1,350 miles each month. At the end of the year, how many miles were on the Toyota's mileage indicator?

    Solution Sentence:

    Answer:

16. Heather bought a tube of toothpaste for $2.89, a hairbrush for $4.98, and bathroom tissue for $1.29. Although she had a $10 bill in her pocket, Heather decided to pay by check. For how much should she write the check if she wants $5 in change?

    Solution Sentence:

    Answer:

17. In Lewisville there are 26,840 registered voters. During the fall election, 14,730 people voted for Measure #4. Of those who voted, 6,538 were Republicans and 7,521 were Democrats. How many people who voted were neither Republicans nor Democrats?

    Solution Sentence:

    Answer:

Answers are on page 824.

Using a Number Grid

A few problems on the GED Math Test will ask you to mark your answers on a **number grid**. Each grid has five blanks across the top to write your answer on. Below each blank is a column of numbers and symbols where you color your answer on the circles.

Example   Find the sum of 569 and 225. Then round your answer to the nearest ten and mark the rounded sum on the answer grid.

STEP 1   Add.
$$\begin{array}{r} 569 \\ +\ 225 \\ \hline 794 \end{array}$$

STEP 2   Round 794 to the nearest ten.
The answer is 790.

To answer the question on a number grid, write the correct answer in the blank boxes at the top of each column. Use a separate column for each digit. Then fill in one circle below each column that corresponds to the digit that you wrote on top.

Below are three **correctly** filled in grids with the answer 790. The first answer starts at the left side of the grid. The second answer is centered. The third answer finishes at the right side of the grid.

Correct Answers

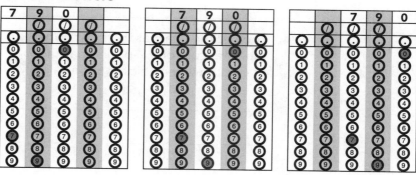

Be careful when you fill in a number grid. Below are two **incorrectly** filled in grids for the last example. On the first grid, the circles were not filled in. On the second grid, all the circles were filled in using only the first column.

Incorrect Answers

Word Problem Review

Part A   **Directions:** Circle the words within the parentheses that tell what you are asked to find.

1. Children brought 9 cats and 14 dogs to the First Grade Pet Parade. Fifty-eight parents and 4 teachers showed up. How many pets did the children bring?

   (number of children, number of cats and dogs, number of adults)

2. During one week, Janelle worked a 35-hour shift, earning $11.50 per hour. She also worked 4 hours of overtime, earning $17.25 per hour. How much overtime pay did Janelle receive during this week?

   (total pay for the week, total hours worked during the week, total overtime pay for the week)

Part B   **Directions:** Write the necessary information below each problem.

3. Michael bowled three games Tuesday night. His scores were 147, 172, and 165. These scores were well below his league average of 192. Find the sum of his Tuesday scores.

   _____

4. Look at the chart at the right. What is the total cost of a 7-pound package of chicken when chicken is on sale?

   _____

   _____

Deli Prices (per pound)		
	Regular	Sale
Beef	$3.29	$2.79
Chicken	$2.89	$2.39
Turkey	$4.49	$3.79

Part C **Directions:** Underline the key word in each problem. Then circle the operation that solves each problem.

5. Jocelyn has two packages to mail. Postage for the smaller package is $2.57. Postage for the larger package is $3.74. What total postage will Jocelyn be charged?

Operation: + − × ÷

6. If Tony received $4.81 in change after paying the clerk with a $20 bill, what was the cost of his purchase?

Operation: + − × ÷

7. Georgia packs and ships music CDs. She is able to pack 6 CDs in a single mailing box. Divide to determine how many boxes Georgia needs in order to ship out 24 CDs.

Operation: + − × ÷

Part D **Directions:** For each problem below, estimate and then find the exact answer.

8. Attendance figures for the first three basketball games were 4,891; 3,250; and 5,780. What was the total attendance at these three games?

Estimate:

Exact Answer:

9. During the past 32 months, Holly's weight has dropped from 198 to 139. How many pounds has Holly lost during this time?

Estimate:

Exact Answer:

10. Carole took a 9-minute typing test. During this time, she typed a total of 648 words. On the average, how many words did Carole type each minute?

Estimate:

Exact Answer:

11. Stan makes a monthly rent payment of $675. How much rent does Stan pay each year?

Estimate:

Exact Answer:

<u>**Part E**</u> **Directions:** Solve each problem.

12. Juan and his two brothers split the cost of renting a small car. Daily rental cost is $48.75. If they keep the car for 5 days, what is each person's share of the rental cost?

13. As part of a sales promotion, Bob gave away 55 pens every day for 30 days. At the end of this time he still had 142 pens left. Knowing this, figure out how many pens Bob started with.

<u>**Part F**</u> **Directions:** For each problem below, circle the answer that makes the most sense. Each listed answer is obtained by performing the operation indicated.

14. The time in Seattle is 3 hours earlier than the time in New York City. What time is it in New York when it is 8:00 A.M. in Seattle?

    (1) addition: 11:00 A.M.   **(2)** subtraction: 5:00 P.M.

15. Wilma buys 5 cans of dog food. Each can costs $0.75 and weighs 15 ounces. How much does Wilma pay per ounce for this dog food?

    (1) multiplication: $11.25   **(2)** division: $0.05

16. At 5:00 A.M. the temperature in Chicago was a cool 26°F. By 11:00 A.M., the sun had warmed the air by 13 degrees. What was the temperature at 11:00 A.M.?

    (1) addition: 39°F   **(2)** subtraction: 13°F

Answers are on page 824.

CHAPTER 4

Decimals

Understanding the Decimal System

Numbers, money, and metric measurement are based on the **decimal system**—a system in which each unit is divided into ten equal parts.

- 1 hundred = 10 tens

- 1 ten = 10 ones

- 1 one = 10 tenths

- 1 tenth = 10 hundredths, and so on

Writing Dollars and Cents as Decimals

When writing dollars and cents, we think of a dollar as being divided into dimes (tenths of a dollar) and pennies (hundredths of a dollar).

25¢

1 dollar = **10 dimes** = **100 pennies**

10¢

A decimal point separates whole dollars from parts of a dollar.

$3.27

3 whole dollars ⎯⎯⎯⎯⎯⎯ 7 pennies [7 hundredths of a dollar]
2 dimes [2 tenths of a dollar]

5¢

We often write the value of a coin as a decimal part of a dollar.

- One quarter is $0.25 — 25 parts out of 100

- One dime is $0.10 — 10 parts out of 100

- One nickel is $0.05 — 5 parts out of 100

1¢

- One penny is $0.01 — 1 part out of 100

EXERCISE 1

Directions: Write each amount using a dollar sign. The first one is done.

1. _____ $0.35 _____

3. _____

2. _____

4. _____

Answers are on page 824.

Reading and Writing Familiar Decimals

Decimals that represent part of a whole are written as one or more digits to the right of the decimal point (.).

- When writing money, you write cents as the first two decimal places.

- Most other decimals you will ever use will have three or fewer digits.

The first three decimal places are **tenths**, **hundredths**, and **thousandths**.

The First Three Decimal Places

MATH TIP	
Decimal	**Meaning**
0.1	1 of 10
0.01	1 of 100
0.001	1 of 1000

↑ leading 0

A **leading 0** is usually written to the left of the decimal point if there is no whole number.

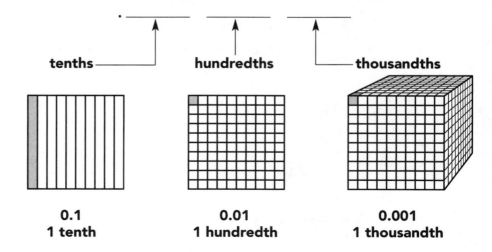

tenths ——→ hundredths ——→ thousandths

0.1 — 1 tenth 0.01 — 1 hundredth 0.001 — 1 thousandth

Rules for Reading Decimals
- To read a decimal, first read the number. Then say the place value of the right-most digit to the right of the decimal point.

Examples: Read 0.4 as *four tenths.*
Read 0.07 as *7 hundredths.*
Read 0.125 as *125 thousandths.*

- Read the decimal point as the word *and.*

Examples: Read 3.4 as *3 and 4 tenths.*
Read $2.75 as *2 dollars and 75 cents.*

EXERCISE 2

Part A   **Directions:** Write the decimal that describes the shaded part of each figure.

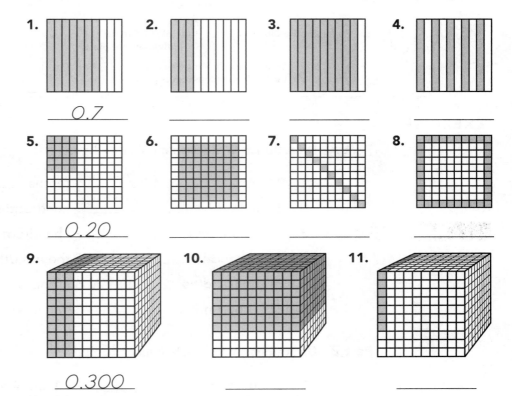

1. ___*0.7*___   2. _____   3. _____   4. _____

5. ___*0.20*___   6. _____   7. _____   8. _____

9. ___*0.300*___   10. _____   11. _____

Part B   **Directions:** Tell how each number is read in words.

12. 0.5 ___*5 tenths*___   0.8 _____

13. 0.09 _____   0.04 _____

14. 0.25 _____   0.41 _____

15. 0.005 ___*5 thousandths*___   0.086 _____

16. 2.235 _____   3.126 _____

17. $0.08 _____ $0.04 _____

Rules for Writing Decimals
- Identify the place value of the right-most digit.
- Write the number so that the right-most digit is in its proper place.
- Then write 0s as placeholders when necessary.

Example 1   Write 34 hundredths as a decimal.

Write 34 so that the 4 is in the hundredths place.

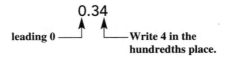

Example 2   Write 65 thousandths as a decimal.

Write 65 so that the 5 is in the thousandths place.

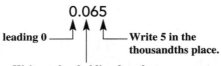

EXERCISE 3

Part A **Directions:** Write each number as digits.

1. 9 tenths _____ *0.9* _____ 5 tenths _____

2. 2 hundredths _____ *0.02* _____ 7 hundredths _____

3. 31 hundredths _____ 29 hundredths _____

4. 3 thousandths _____ *0.003* _____ 5 thousandths _____

5. 24 thousandths _____ 65 thousandths _____

6. 227 thousandths _____ 375 thousandths _____

Part B **Directions:** Write each number as digits.

7. 2 and 3 tenths _____ *2.3* _____ 1 and 4 tenths _____

8. 5 and 7 hundredths _____ *5.07* _____ 3 and 8 hundredths _____

9. 6 and 25 hundredths _____ 12 and 15 hundredths _____

10. 1 and 6 thousandths _____ *1.006* _____ 3 and 7 thousandths _____

11. 3 and 65 thousandths _____ 7 and 89 thousandths _____

12. 9 and 625 thousandths _____ 20 and 750 thousandths _____

Answers are on page 825.

Necessary and Unnecessary 0s

The digit 0 has no value, but as you've seen, 0 can be used as a **placeholder**.

- Placed between the decimal point and a digit, zero changes the value of a decimal fraction.

- Placed at the far right of a decimal, zero changes the way the decimal is read but does not change its value.

Example 1 0.6 differs from 0.06 because of the 0 in the tenths place.

This 0 holds the 6
in the hundredths place.

0.6 = 6 tenths   0.06 = 6 hundredths

0.6   **0.06**

SAME VALUES
0.9 = 0.90
0.9 = 0.900
0.25 = 0.250
3.6 = 3.600
8 = 8.00

DIFFERENT VALUES
0.9 and 0.09
0.9 and 0.009
0.25 and 0.025
3.6 and 0.036
8 and 0.08

A **necessary 0** is a 0 that comes anywhere between the decimal point and the last non-zero digit to the right of the decimal point.

A necessary 0 **cannot** be removed without changing a decimal's value.

Examples of necessary 0s: 0.0̲4   0.30̲7   2.0̲40   0.00̲7

Example 2 0.5 and 0.50 differ in the way they are read, but they have the same value. This is similar to the fact that 5 dimes has the same value as 50 pennies.

0.5   **0.50**

0.5 = 5 tenths   0.50 = 50 hundredths

This 0 changes the way the decimal
is read but does not change its value.

An **unnecessary 0** is a 0 that is placed at the far right of a decimal.

An unnecessary 0 **does not** change the value of a decimal.

Examples of unnecessary 0s: 0.70̲   0.030̲   3.500̲   0.250̲

EXERCISE 4

Directions: Underline each necessary 0. Ignore leading 0s.

1. 0.08   0.150   0.009   5.600   7.750

2. 0.204   0.025   6.020   0.405   6.008

3. 5.000   0.625   0.070   1.904   3.006

Answers are on page 825.

Comparing Decimals

Decimals are easily compared when they have the same number of digits to the right of the decimal point.

To compare decimals:

- Add one or more 0s to give the decimals the same number of digits to the right of the decimal point.

- Compare the decimals digit by digit, starting with the tenths digit.

Remember, writing a 0 at the right-hand end of a decimal does not change the value of the decimal.

REMINDER
> means *is greater than*
< means *is less than*
= means *is equal to*

Example 1

Compare 0.42 and 0.26.

0.42

0.26

↑
different tenths digits

4 > 2, so **0.42 > 0.26**

Example 2

Compare 0.27 and 0.273.

0.270 ← Add a 0 to give both decimals the same number of digits.

0.273

↑ **different thousandths digits**

3 > 0, so **0.273 > 0.270**
or **0.273 > 0.27**

EXERCISE 5

Part A **Directions:** Write >, <, or = to compare each pair of decimals.

1. 0.4 _____ 0.7   0.5 _____ 0.8   0.26 _____ 0.28

2. 2.4 _____ 2.06   3.80 _____ 3.8   0.456 _____ 0.45

3. 0.2 _____ 0.189   0.46 _____ 0.5   1.73 _____ 0.89

4. 1.9 _____ 1.999   2.06 _____ 2.095   5.41 _____ 5.410

Part B **Directions:** List the swimmers in order of finish. **Hint:** The least amount of time wins the race.

5. Sheena 38.795 seconds   1st _____

6. Brianne 38.49 seconds   2nd _____

7. Maria 39.56 seconds   3rd _____

8. Cathy 39.098 seconds   4th _____

9. Nadine 38.8 seconds   5th _____

Answers are on page 825.

Rounding Decimals

So far you have worked with the first three decimal place values: tenths, hundredths, and thousandths.

Decimal place values continue beyond thousandths.

MATH FACT

You will rarely work with place values to the right of the thousandths place.

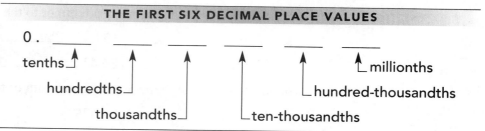

THE FIRST SIX DECIMAL PLACE VALUES

0 . _____ _____ _____ _____ _____ _____

tenths
hundredths
thousandths
ten-thousandths
hundred-thousandths
millionths

To simplify a number (or answer), decimals are often rounded to the nearest whole number, nearest tenth, or nearest hundredth. To **round a decimal** to a chosen place value, look at the digit to the right of that chosen place value.

- If the digit is greater than or equal to 5, **round up**. Drop all digits to the right of the chosen place value.

- If the digit is less than 5, **round down**. Leave the digit in the chosen place value **unchanged** and drop all digits to the right.

Rounding to a Whole Number (nearest one)

Check the digit in the tenths place.

REMEMBER

The symbol ≈ means *is approximately equal to.*

8.7 ≈ 9

greater than 5,
so round up

3.27 ≈ 3

less than 5,
so round down

16.535 ≈ 17

equal to 5,
so round up

Rounding to the Tenths Place (nearest tenth)

Check the digit in the hundredths place.

0.25 ≈ 0.3

equal to 5,
so round up

7.63 ≈ 7.6

less than 5,
so round down

9.281 ≈ 9.3

greater than 5,
so round up

Rounding to the Hundredths Place (nearest hundredth)

Check the digit in the thousandths place.

0.378 ≈ 0.38

greater than 5,
so round up

1.392 ≈ 1.39

less than 5,
so round down

4.245 ≈ 4.25

equal to 5,
so round up

EXERCISE 6

Part A **Directions:** Round each decimal to the nearest whole number or to the nearest dollar.

1. 4.4 m ≈ _____ $6.92 ≈ _____   9.75 cm ≈ _____

2. $31.25 ≈ _____   12.6 kg ≈ _____   23.5 mpg ≈ _____

Round each decimal to the nearest tenth or to the nearest dime.

3. 18.36 m ≈ _____ $5.84 ≈ _____   35.75 km ≈ _____

4. $16.53 ≈ _____   20.41 kg ≈ _____ $9.75 ≈ _____

Round each decimal to the nearest hundredth or to the nearest penny.

5. 6.543 m ≈ _____ $1.479 ≈ _____   8.625 m ≈ _____

6. 83.5¢ ≈ _____   10.495 m ≈ _____   0.4528 in. ≈ _____

Part B **Directions:** Round each decimal as indicated.

	Nearest Whole	Nearest Tenth	Nearest Hundredth
7. 7.362	_____	_____	_____
8. 2.098	_____	_____	_____
9. 5.625	_____	_____	_____

Part C

10. Emily, a grocery clerk, used a calculator to find the selling price of each product listed below. Round each calculator answer to the nearest cent.

	Weight (lb)		Price ($ per lb)		Calculator Answer	Selling Price
Cheese	1.77	×	$4.29	=	7.5933	_____
Chicken	4.56	×	$2.98	=	13.5888	_____
Fruit salad	2.4	×	$1.89	=	4.536	_____
Sliced meat	1.2	×	$4.79	=	5.748	_____

Answers are on page 825.

Estimating with Decimals

As with whole numbers, rounding decimals is very useful when you want to estimate an answer instead of working out a problem exactly. Estimating is a good way to check a calculator answer. On a test, estimating may help you choose a correct answer from a group of answer choices.

To estimate with decimals, round each number **before** you add, subtract, multiply, or divide.

Example 1 Estimate the sum: 8.64 + 5.4

STEP 1 Round each decimal to $8.64 \approx 9$ $5.4 \approx 5$
the nearest whole number.

STEP 2 Add the whole numbers. $9 + 5 = 14$

Answer: 8.64 + 5.4 ≈ 14

Example 2 Estimate the product: 12.3 × 4.7

STEP 1 Round each decimal to $12.3 \approx 12$ $4.7 \approx 5$
the nearest whole number.

STEP 2 Multiply the whole numbers. $12 \times 5 = 60$

Answer: 12.3 × 4.7 ≈ 60

EXERCISE 7

Part A **Directions:** Estimate an answer for each problem below.

	Estimate		**Estimate**		**Estimate**
1. $6.89 + 3.16		**2.** 9.1 − 5.975		**3.** $11.14 × 9.8	

Part B **Directions:** Estimate an answer. Then use your estimate to circle the exact answer.

4. At a price of $2.89 per pound, what is the total cost of 3.1 pounds of flank steak?

a. $8.12   **b.** $8.96   **c.** $9.78   **d.** $11.18   **e.** $12.34

Estimate _____

5. A ribbon is 4.9 meters long. If Paula wants to cut off a piece that is 1.96 meters long, how long will the remaining piece be?

    a. 2.18 m   **b.** 2.48 m   **c.** 2.82 m   **d.** 2.94m   **e.** 3.14 m

Estimate _____

6. What is the total price of four items that cost $4.87, $6.09, $12.78, and $8.25?

    a. $25.49   **b.** $27.19   **c.** $31.99   **d.** $34.49   **e.** $37.29

Estimate _____

Answers are on page 825.

Basic Arithmetic with Decimals

Adding Decimals

To add decimals:

- Write the numbers in a column and line up the decimal points.

- Use placeholding 0s as needed to give all numbers the same number of decimal points.

- Add the columns.

- Place a decimal point in the answer directly below the decimal points of the numbers being added.

Example 1   Add: 12.4 + 4.68 + 0.375

                        Line up the decimal points.

	MATH FACT

A whole number is understood to have a decimal point to the right of the ones digit.

    12.400 ◄—— Write two placeholding 0s.
     4.680 ◄—— Write one placeholding 0.
  + 0.375
    17.455 ◄—— Add the columns.

                Place a decimal point in the answer.

Answer: 17.455

Example 2   Add: 6 + 2.45

                Place a decimal point to the right of 6. Add two placeholding 0s.

    6.00
  + 2.45
    8.45

Answer: 8.45

Calculator Solution of Example 1

 `C` `1` `2` `•` `4` `+` `4` `•` `6` `8` `+` `•` `3` `7` `5` `=` `17.455`

Calculator Solution of Example 2

 `C` `6` `+` `2` `•` `4` `5` `=` `8.45`

EXERCISE 8

Directions: Add. Use 0s as placeholders where needed.

1. $\begin{array}{r} 0.8 \\ + 0.5 \end{array}$ $\begin{array}{r} 0.65 \\ + 0.37 \end{array}$ $\begin{array}{r} 3.2 \\ + 2.9 \end{array}$ $\begin{array}{r} \$0.64 \\ + 0.34 \end{array}$ $\begin{array}{r} \$3.59 \\ + 2.48 \end{array}$

2. $\begin{array}{r} 4 \\ 2.6 \\ + 0.125 \end{array}$ $\begin{array}{r} 2.5 \\ 1.74 \\ + 0.53 \end{array}$ $\begin{array}{r} 4.78 \\ 3 \\ + 2.147 \end{array}$ $\begin{array}{r} 3 \\ 1.15 \\ + 2.392 \end{array}$ $\begin{array}{r} 3.15 \\ 2 \\ + 1.074 \end{array}$

3. $7.325 + 5.7 + 2.50 =$ $6 + 3.625 + 2.5 =$

Answers are on page 825.

Subtracting Decimals

To subtract decimals:

- Write the numbers in a column and line up the decimal points.
- Use placeholding 0s as needed to give all numbers the same number of decimal points.
- Subtract the columns just as you would whole numbers.
- Place a decimal point in the answer directly below the decimal points of the numbers being subtracted.

Example   Subtract: $7 - 2.483$

    Place a decimal point to the right of 7. Line up the decimal points.
$\begin{array}{r} 7.000 \\ - 2.483 \\ \hline 4.517 \end{array}$ ← **Write three placeholding 0s.**

     ← **Subtract the columns.**

     Place a decimal point in the answer.

Answer: 4.517

Calculator Solution

 $\boxed{C}\ \boxed{7}\ \boxed{-}\ \boxed{2}\ \boxed{\bullet}\ \boxed{4}\ \boxed{8}\ \boxed{3}\ \boxed{=}\ \boxed{4.517}$

EXERCISE 9

Directions: Subtract. Use 0s as placeholders where needed.

1. $\begin{array}{r} 0.9 \\ - 0.3 \end{array}$ $\begin{array}{r} 0.78 \\ - 0.49 \end{array}$ $\begin{array}{r} 0.34 \\ - 0.125 \end{array}$ $\begin{array}{r} 5.784 \\ - 2.3 \end{array}$ $\begin{array}{r} \$12.34 \\ - 5.82 \end{array}$

2. $4.75 - 3.8 =$ $5 - 3.08 =$ $1 - 0.006 =$

Answers are on page 825.

Multiplying Decimals

MATH FACT

The number of decimal places is the number of digits to the right of the decimal point. A whole number has zero decimal places.

To multiply decimals:

- Multiply the numbers as you would whole numbers.

- Count the number of decimal places in each of the numbers you are multiplying. This tells you the number of decimal places in the product (answer).

- Place a decimal point in the answer.

Example 1   Multiply: 3.24 × 4

3.24 ◄——— 2 decimal places
×   4 ◄——— + 0 decimal places
12.96   2 decimal places

—— Place the decimal point so that the answer has 2 decimal places.

Answer: 12.96

Example 2   Multiply: 1.37 × 2.6

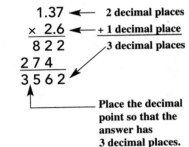

1.37 ◄——— 2 decimal places
× 2.6 ◄——— + 1 decimal place
8 2 2   3 decimal places
2 7 4
3 5 6 2

—— Place the decimal point so that the answer has 3 decimal places.

Answer: 3.562

Calculator Solution of Example 2

C   1   •   3   7   ×   2   •   6   =   3.562

EXERCISE 10

Directions: Multiply. Use estimation or a calculator to check each answer.

1.   3.5   5.4   12.7 $0.45 $2.76
      × 4   × 3   × 2   × 6   × 8

2.   7.8   8.2   6.94 $5.60 $3.80
      × 2.5   × 1.6   × 0.45   × 2.5   × 0.75

3. 2.65 × 7 =   2.84 × 3.4 =   7.68 × 0.25 =

Answers are on page 825.

Dividing Decimals

To divide decimals:

- Move the decimal point in the divisor to the right.
- Move the decimal point in the dividend (the number being divided into) an equal number of places to the right, adding placeholding 0s if needed.
- Divide the numbers.
- Place a decimal point in the quotient (answer) directly above the new decimal point in the dividend.

Example Divide $1.4\overline{)4.48}$

STEP 1 Change the divisor (1.4) to a whole number. Do this by moving the decimal point one place to the right. Then move the decimal point in the dividend (4.48) one place to the right.

$$1.4\overline{)4.48}$$

$$\begin{array}{r} 3.2 \\ 14.\overline{)44.8} \end{array}$$

STEP 2 Divide the whole number 14 into the new dividend 44.8.

$$\begin{array}{r} -42 \\ \hline 2\,8 \\ -2\,8 \end{array}$$

REMEMBER

Moving the decimal point an equal number of places in both divisor and dividend makes sure that the decimal point is placed correctly in the answer.

Answer: 3.2

Calculator Solution

$\boxed{C}\,\boxed{4}\,\boxed{\bullet}\,\boxed{4}\,\boxed{8}\,\boxed{\div}\,\boxed{1}\,\boxed{\bullet}\,\boxed{4}\,\boxed{=}\,\boxed{3.2}$

EXERCISE 11

Directions: Divide.

1. $3\overline{)6.3}$ $7\overline{)4.97}$ $2\overline{)0.842}$ $5\overline{)3.05}$ $6\overline{)0.612}$

2. $0.02\overline{)1.6}$ $0.12\overline{)0.48}$ $0.07\overline{)49.14}$ $0.04\overline{)3.108}$ $2.3\overline{)0.529}$

3. $0.06\overline{)12}$ $1.5\overline{)30}$ $0.003\overline{)6}$ $2.5\overline{)50}$ $0.04\overline{)24}$

Answers are on page 825.

Decimal Word Problems

EXERCISE 12

Directions: Solve the following word problems.

1. When she had the flu, Leng's temperature went from 98.6∞F to 103.2°F. By how many degrees did Leng's temperature rise?

2. The area of the United States is 3.62 million square miles. The area of Mexico is 0.76 million square miles. How many square miles is the combined area of the United States and Mexico?

3. A dining table has three removable center boards. Two boards are each 22.6 centimeters wide. The third board is 26.5 centimeters wide. Without the boards in place the table is 139.25 centimeters wide. How wide is the table with all three boards in place?

4. In Saturday's race, Wilma ran the 100-meter dash in 11.45 seconds. How much slower did she run than the school record of 11.365 seconds?

5. Aaron earns time and a half for each hour of overtime he works. His overtime pay rate is found by multiplying his regular pay rate by 1.5. What is Aaron's overtime pay rate if his regular hourly rate is $8.76?

6. In the metric system, small weight is measured in grams, a unit much smaller than the ounce. It takes 28.4 grams to equal 1 ounce.

    a. What is the weight in grams of a 6-ounce can of tuna fish?

    b. To the nearest gram, how many grams are equal to 1 pound? Remember: 1 pound = 16 ounces.

7. For his jewelry-making business, Jason uses small pieces of solid gold wire. To make several rings, Jason wants to divide a piece of wire that is 23.4 centimeters long into 6 equal pieces. How long should he cut each piece?

8. Myrna works parttime for Betty's Word Processing Service. Betty charges customers $24.50 per hour for word processing. Myrna is paid $10.50 per hour. How much does Myrna earn during a day in which she works 8 hours?

Answers are on page 826.

Decimals Review

EXERCISE 13

Part A **Directions:** Write each amount using a dollar sign.

1. _____

3. _____

2. _____

4. _____

Part B **Directions:** Tell how each number is read in words.

5. 0.8 _____ 0.008 _____

6. 0.12 _____ 0.012 _____

Write each number as digits.

7. 7 tenths _____ 7 hundredths _____

8. 15 hundredths _____ 15 thousandths _____

9. 4 thousandths _____ 40 thousandths _____

Part C **Directions:** Write >, <, or = to compare each pair of decimals.

10. 0.5 _____ 0.15   0.4 _____ 0.40   0.27 _____ 0.72

11. 3.2 _____ 2.93   2.73 _____ 2.5   0.598 _____ 0.589

Part D **Directions:** Round each decimal as indicated.

	Nearest Whole	Nearest Tenth	Nearest Hundredth
12. 4.639	_____	_____	_____
13. 12.485	_____	_____	_____

Part E **Directions:** Estimate an answer for each problem below.

14.

$$\begin{array}{r} 12.9 \\ + \; 8.93 \\ \hline \end{array}$$

$$\begin{array}{r} 10 \\ - \; 7.98 \\ \hline \end{array}$$

$$\begin{array}{r} 14.86 \\ \times \quad 19 \\ \hline \end{array}$$

$$8.4\overline{)121.75}$$

Part F **Directions:** Solve each problem below.

15.
6	5.08	8	7.265	1.84
3.1	1.9	2.49	2.14	1.2
+ 1.625	+ 0.75	+ 1.005	+ 1.3	+ 0.007

16.
1.2	4.3	8.45	0.94	62.7
− 0.8	− 2.4	− 5.9	− 0.09	− 12.625

17.
8.2	6.04	13.5	0.625	0.325
× 5	× 4	× 15	× 4	× 12

18. 0.4)3.6   0.02)0.72   3.4)74.8   0.12)3.612   1.3)26.52

Part G **Directions:** Estimate an answer to each problem. Then find each exact answer.

19.
$12.89	$15.00	$21.75	
7.25	− 8.78	× 8	4)$78.84
+ 3.97			

Answers are on page 826.

CHAPTER 5

Fractions

Understanding Fractions

A **proper fraction** such as $\frac{1}{2}$ represents a number less than 1.

- The top number (**numerator**) tells the number of parts you are describing.

- The bottom number (**denominator**) tells the number of parts into which the whole is divided.

The whole may be a single object or a group of objects.

Example 1 How much of the circle is shaded?

$\frac{2}{3}$ ← numerator
  ← denominator

2 parts out of 3 total parts are shaded.

Read $\frac{2}{3}$ as *two thirds*.

Example 2 What fraction of the group of circles is shaded?

3 out of 4 circles are shaded.

$\frac{3}{4}$ ← circles shaded
  ← total circles

EXERCISE 1

Part A   **Directions:** Write a fraction to show how much of each figure or group is shaded.

1.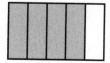

_____

2.

_____

3.

_____

4.

_____

<u>**Part B**</u> **Directions:** Shade the figures below.

5. Shade $\frac{4}{6}$ of the group of squares below.

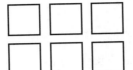

6. Shade $\frac{7}{10}$ of the distance between 0 and 1.

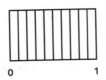

7. Shade $\frac{1}{3}$ of the circle below.

Answers are on page 826.

Equivalent Fractions

There is more than one way to write a fraction to represent a given amount. For example, the two cups contain equal amounts of milk.

Equal Amounts

- The cup at the left is divided into 8 equal measuring units.

- The cup at the right is divided into 4 equal measuring units.

The fractions $\frac{3}{4}$ and $\frac{6}{8}$ represent the same amount. The two fractions are called **equivalent fractions**.

$\frac{6}{8}$ full $= \frac{3}{4}$ full

Equivalent Fractions

To find equivalent fractions, multiply the numerator and denominator of a fraction by the same number.

Examples $\dfrac{3 \times 2}{4 \times 2} = \dfrac{6}{8}$ $\dfrac{1 \times 4}{2 \times 4} = \dfrac{4}{8}$ $\dfrac{3 \times 3}{5 \times 3} = \dfrac{9}{15}$

EXERCISE 2

<u>Part A</u> **Directions:** Write equivalent fractions for each pair of figures as indicated.

1. the shaded fraction of each circle

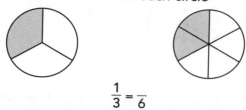

$$\frac{1}{3} = \frac{}{6}$$

2. the shaded fraction of each group

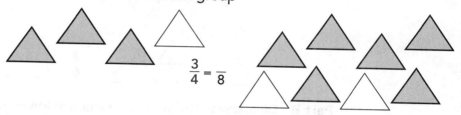

$$\frac{3}{4} = \frac{}{8}$$

<u>Part B</u> **Directions:** Write an equivalent fraction as indicated.

3. $\frac{2}{3} \times \frac{3}{3} = \frac{}{9}$ $\frac{5}{7} \times \frac{2}{2} = \frac{}{14}$ $\frac{3}{4} \times \frac{3}{3} = \frac{}{12}$ $\frac{1}{2} \times \frac{4}{4} = \frac{}{8}$

4. $\frac{1}{3} = \frac{}{9}$ $\frac{2}{3} = \frac{}{6}$ $\frac{3}{4} = \frac{}{16}$ $\frac{1}{2} = \frac{}{12}$

Answers are on page 826.

Reducing Fractions to Lowest Terms

To **reduce a fraction to lowest terms** is to write the fraction as an equivalent fraction using the lowest numbers possible.

<u>Examples</u> $\frac{4}{8}$ reduces to $\frac{1}{2}$ $\frac{6}{9}$ reduces to $\frac{2}{3}$ $\frac{4}{16}$ reduces to $\frac{1}{4}$

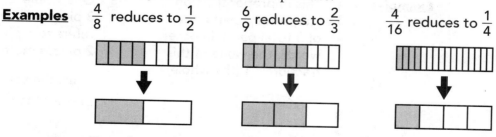

To reduce a fraction to lowest terms, divide both numerator and denominator by the greatest number that divides evenly into both.

<u>Examples</u> $\frac{4}{8} \div \frac{4}{4} = \frac{1}{2}$ $\frac{6}{9} \div \frac{3}{3} = \frac{2}{3}$ $\frac{4}{16} \div \frac{4}{4} = \frac{1}{4}$

EXERCISE 3

<u>Part A</u> **Directions:** Reduce each fraction to lowest terms as indicated.

1. the shaded fraction of each circle

$$\frac{4}{6} = \frac{}{3}$$

2. the shaded fraction of each group

$$\frac{3}{6} = \frac{}{2}$$

<u>Part B</u> **Directions:** Reduce each fraction to lowest terms as indicated.

3. $\dfrac{6}{8} \div \dfrac{2}{2} = \dfrac{}{4}$ $\dfrac{8}{12} \div \dfrac{4}{4} = \dfrac{}{3}$ $\dfrac{2}{4} \div \dfrac{2}{2} = \dfrac{1}{2}$ $\dfrac{14}{16} \div \dfrac{2}{2} = \dfrac{}{8}$

4. $\dfrac{4}{6} = \dfrac{2}{3}$ $\dfrac{8}{10} = \dfrac{4}{5}$ $\dfrac{9}{12} = \dfrac{3}{4}$ $\dfrac{4}{8} = \dfrac{2}{4} \quad \dfrac{1}{2}$

Answers are on page 826.

Improper Fractions and Mixed Numbers

An **improper fraction** is a fraction in which the numerator is equal to or greater than the denominator.

Examples

$\dfrac{3}{3}$ This improper fraction stands for 3 parts out of 3 total parts. In other words, the value of this fraction is 1 (the whole).

$\dfrac{3}{3}$

$\dfrac{5}{3}$ One whole is divided into 3 pieces. The numerator 5 refers to 5 pieces. This is 2 pieces more than 1 whole.

Thus, the value of $\dfrac{5}{3}$ is 2 pieces greater than 1 whole.

$\dfrac{5}{3}$

A **mixed number** such as $1\frac{2}{3}$ is a whole number together with a fraction.

- The number 1 stands for 1 whole object.
- $\frac{2}{3}$ stands for part of a second object.

Notice that $\frac{5}{3}$ and $1\frac{2}{3}$ represent the same amount. An amount greater than 1 can be written as either an improper fraction or a mixed number.

$1\frac{2}{3}$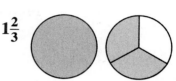

EXERCISE 4

Part A **Directions:** Write the improper fraction represented by each drawing below.

1. _____ 2. _____ 3. _____

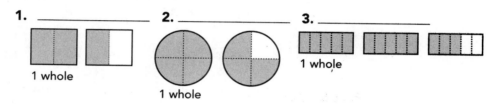

1 whole   1 whole   1 whole

Part B **Directions:** Write the mixed number represented by each drawing below.

4. _____ 5. _____ 6. _____

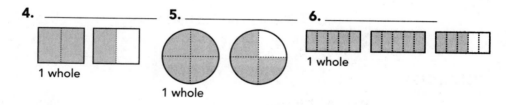

1 whole   1 whole   1 whole

Answers are on page 826.

Comparing Fractions

To compare **like fractions**, compare the numerators. The fraction with the greater numerator is the greater fraction.

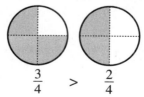

$$\frac{3}{4} \quad > \quad \frac{2}{4}$$

$\frac{3}{4}$ is greater than $\frac{2}{4}$ because 3 is greater than 2.

To compare **unlike fractions**, write them as like fractions. First, choose a **common denominator**—the same denominator for both fractions. Next, write each fraction in terms of the common denominator. The lowest possible common denominator is called the **least common denominator** (LCD).

To find the LCD for two fractions such as $\frac{2}{3}$ and $\frac{3}{4}$, use the method of **comparing multiples**. The example shows how to do this.

<u>Example</u>   Compare the fractions $\frac{2}{3}$ and $\frac{3}{4}$.

STEP 1   Write several multiples for each of the two denominators: 3 and 4.

multiples of 3:   3   6   9   12   15

multiples of 4:   4   8   12   16   20

STEP 2   Circle the smallest number that is written on <u>both</u> lists.

The least common denominator is **12.**

STEP 3   Rewrite each fraction as an equivalent fraction that has a denominator of 12.

$$\frac{2}{3} = \frac{2 \times 4}{3 \times 4} = \frac{8}{12} \quad \text{and} \quad \frac{3}{4} = \frac{3 \times 3}{4 \times 3} = \frac{9}{12}$$

STEP 4   Compare the like fractions; then compare the original fractions.

$\frac{9}{12}$ is greater than $\frac{8}{12}$.

So $\frac{3}{4}$ is greater than $\frac{2}{3}$.

Do you notice that $\frac{3}{4}$ is $\frac{1}{12}$ greater than $\frac{2}{3}$?

EXERCISE 5

<u>Part A</u>   **Directions:** Write >, <, or = to compare each pair of fractions.

1. $\frac{5}{8}$ —— $\frac{6}{8}$ $\frac{3}{4}$ —— $\frac{2}{4}$ $\frac{10}{12}$ —— $\frac{11}{12}$ $\frac{1}{2}$ —— $\frac{2}{4}$

<u>Part B</u>   **Directions:** Write each fraction as an equivalent fraction as indicated.

2. $\frac{3}{8} = \frac{}{16}$ $\frac{3}{4} = \frac{}{12}$ $\frac{2}{5} = \frac{}{10}$ $\frac{5}{8} = \frac{}{24}$

<u>Part C</u>   **Directions:** Write the first five multiples of each number below. The first one is done as an example.

3.   2: _2, 4, 6, 8, 10_   3: _____   4: _____

4.   6: _____   8: _____   10: _____

Part D **Directions:** Use the method of comparing multiples to find the LCD for each pair of fractions. The first one is done as an example.

5. $\frac{1}{4}$ and $\frac{1}{3}$ $\frac{7}{10}$ and $\frac{4}{5}$

4: 4 8 (12) 16

3: 3 6 9 (12)

_____

$\frac{5}{8}$ and $\frac{2}{3}$ $\frac{6}{8}$ and $\frac{5}{6}$

_____   _____

_____   _____

Part E **Directions:** Write >, <, or = to compare each pair of fractions. As a first step, write each pair using a common denominator. Use the common denominators found in Part D for these same pairs of fractions.

6. $\frac{1}{4}$ ____ $\frac{1}{3}$ $\frac{7}{10}$ ____ $\frac{4}{5}$ $\frac{5}{8}$ ____ $\frac{2}{3}$ $\frac{6}{8}$ ____ $\frac{5}{6}$

Answers are on pages 826–827.

Adding and Subtracting Fractions and Mixed Numbers

Adding and Subtracting Like Fractions

Like fractions are fractions that have the same denominator.

Examples $\frac{5}{8}$ and $\frac{1}{8}$ $\frac{7}{16}$ and $\frac{3}{16}$

- To **add** like fractions, add the numerators and write the sum over the denominator. Reduce the answer to lowest terms.

- To **subtract** like fractions, subtract one numerator from the other. Write the difference over the denominator. Reduce the answer to lowest terms.

Example 1   Add: $\frac{5}{8} + \frac{1}{8}$

STEP 1   Add the numerators: $5 + 1 = 6$

STEP 2   Place the sum 6 over the denominator 8: $\frac{6}{8}$

STEP 3   Reduce $\frac{6}{8}$ to lowest terms.

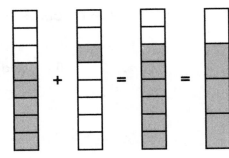

$$\frac{6}{8} \div \frac{2}{2} = \frac{3}{4}$$

$$\frac{5}{8} + \frac{1}{8} = \frac{6}{8} = \frac{3}{4}$$

CALCULATOR FACT

The Casio *fx-260* has a fraction key that looks like this:

The examples show how to use this key to solve fraction problems.

Answer: $\frac{3}{4}$

Calculator Solution

 C 5 a⅟c 8 + 1 a⅟c 8 = 3⌐4

Example 2   Subtract: $\frac{11}{12} - \frac{7}{12}$

STEP 1   Subtract the numerators: $11 - 7 = 4$

STEP 2   Place the difference 4 over the denominator 12: $\frac{4}{12}$

STEP 3   Reduce $\frac{4}{12}$ to lowest terms.

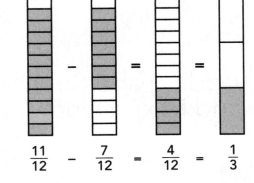

$$\frac{4}{12} \div \frac{4}{4} = \frac{1}{3}$$

$$\frac{11}{12} - \frac{7}{12} = \frac{4}{12} = \frac{1}{3}$$

Answer: $\frac{1}{3}$

Calculator Solution

 C 1 1 a⅟c 1 2 − 7 a⅟c 1 2 = 1⌐3

EXERCISE 6

<u>Part A</u> **Directions:** For each figure, indicate the addition or subtraction that is represented.

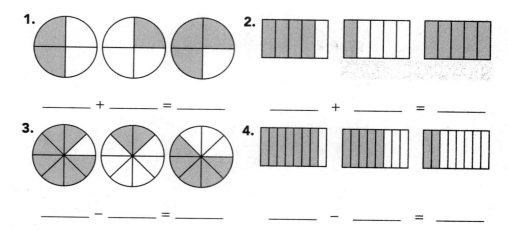

1. _____ + _____ = _____

2. _____ + _____ = _____

3. _____ − _____ = _____

4. _____ − _____ = _____

<u>Part B</u> **Directions:** Add or subtract each pair of fractions as indicated.

5. $\dfrac{2}{4} + \dfrac{1}{4} =$ $\dfrac{7}{10} - \dfrac{4}{10} =$ $\dfrac{5}{8} + \dfrac{2}{8} =$ $\dfrac{6}{8} - \dfrac{5}{8} =$

<u>Part C</u> **Directions:** Add each pair of fractions. The first one is done as an example.

6. $\dfrac{2}{4} + \dfrac{2}{4} = \dfrac{4}{4} = 1$ $\dfrac{3}{8} + \dfrac{5}{8} =$ $\dfrac{2}{3} + \dfrac{1}{3} =$ $\dfrac{3}{5} + \dfrac{2}{5} =$

<u>Part D</u> **Directions:** Add each pair of fractions. Write each answer as a mixed number. The first one is done as an example.

7. $\dfrac{3}{4} + \dfrac{2}{4} = \dfrac{5}{4} = 1\dfrac{1}{4}$ $\dfrac{4}{5} + \dfrac{2}{5} =$ $\dfrac{7}{8} + \dfrac{4}{8} =$ $\dfrac{3}{4} + \dfrac{3}{4} =$

<u>Part E</u> **Directions:** Subtract as indicated. The first one is done as an example.

8. $\dfrac{5}{4} - \dfrac{3}{4} = \dfrac{2}{4} = \dfrac{1}{2}$ $\dfrac{9}{8} - \dfrac{3}{8} =$ $\dfrac{7}{5} - \dfrac{3}{5} =$ $\dfrac{4}{3} - \dfrac{2}{3} =$

Answers are on page 827.

Adding and Subtracting Unlike Fractions

Unlike fractions are fractions that do **not** have the same denominator.

<u>Examples</u> $\dfrac{1}{2}$ and $\dfrac{1}{4}$ $\dfrac{5}{6}$ and $\dfrac{1}{3}$

Follow the same procedure with adding and subtracting unlike fractions as you used when comparing unlike fractions, earlier in this chapter.

To add or subtract unlike fractions:

- First, choose a common denominator.
- Second, write each fraction as an equivalent fraction that has the common denominator.
- Add or subtract numerators and write the sum or difference over the denominator.

Example 1 Add: $\frac{1}{2} + \frac{1}{4}$

STEP 1 Change $\frac{1}{2}$ to $\frac{2}{4}$

$$\frac{1}{2} = \frac{2}{4}$$

STEP 2 Add: $\frac{2}{4} + \frac{1}{4} = \frac{3}{4}$

Answer: $\frac{3}{4}$

Example 2 Subtract: $\frac{5}{6} - \frac{1}{3}$

STEP 1 Change $\frac{1}{3}$ to $\frac{2}{6}$

$$\frac{1}{3} = \frac{2}{6}$$

STEP 2 Subtract: $\frac{5}{6} - \frac{2}{6} = \frac{3}{6}$

STEP 3 Reduce $\frac{3}{6}$ to lowest terms.

$$\frac{3}{6} = \frac{1}{2}$$

Answer: $\frac{1}{2}$

Calculator Solution of Example 1

 C 1 $a^b/_c$ 2 + 1 $a^b/_c$ 4 = 3⌐4

Calculator Solution of Example 2

 C 5 $a^b/_c$ 6 − 1 $a^b/_c$ 3 = 1⌐2

EXERCISE 7

Part A Directions: For each figure, indicate the addition or subtraction that is represented.

1.
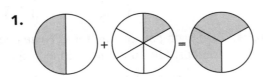

_____ + _____ = _____

2.
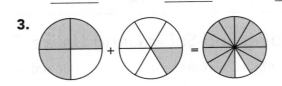

_____ − _____ = _____

3.

_____ + _____ = _____

4.

_____ − _____ = _____

Part B **Directions:** Write the missing numerators. Then find the sum or difference as indicated. Reduce all answers to lowest terms.

5. $\dfrac{1}{2} = \dfrac{}{4}$ $\dfrac{1}{3} = \dfrac{}{6}$ $\dfrac{7}{8} = \dfrac{7}{8}$ $\dfrac{5}{6} = \dfrac{5}{6}$ $\dfrac{11}{16} = \dfrac{11}{16}$

$+\dfrac{1}{4} = \dfrac{1}{4}$ $+\dfrac{1}{6} = \dfrac{1}{6}$ $-\dfrac{1}{4} = \dfrac{}{8}$ $-\dfrac{1}{2} = \dfrac{}{6}$ $+\dfrac{1}{4} = \dfrac{}{16}$

6. $\dfrac{1}{3} = \dfrac{}{12}$ $\dfrac{4}{5} = \dfrac{}{15}$ $\dfrac{1}{2} = \dfrac{}{6}$ $\dfrac{3}{4} = \dfrac{}{20}$ $\dfrac{1}{2} = \dfrac{}{14}$

$+\dfrac{1}{4} = \dfrac{}{12}$ $-\dfrac{2}{3} = \dfrac{}{15}$ $-\dfrac{1}{3} = \dfrac{}{6}$ $-\dfrac{2}{5} = \dfrac{}{20}$ $+\dfrac{1}{7} = \dfrac{}{14}$

Part C **Directions:** Add or subtract as indicated. Reduce to lowest terms.

7. $\dfrac{1}{2}$ $\dfrac{1}{2}$ $\dfrac{3}{4}$ $\dfrac{9}{10}$ $\dfrac{5}{8}$

$-\dfrac{1}{4}$ $+\dfrac{1}{3}$ $-\dfrac{1}{3}$ $+\dfrac{3}{5}$ $+\dfrac{1}{4}$

8. $\dfrac{1}{2}$ $\dfrac{3}{4}$ $\dfrac{3}{4}$ $\dfrac{1}{5}$ $\dfrac{7}{8}$

$-\dfrac{2}{5}$ $+\dfrac{1}{5}$ $-\dfrac{1}{2}$ $+\dfrac{1}{6}$ $-\dfrac{1}{2}$

Answers are on page 827.

Adding and Subtracting Mixed Numbers

To add mixed numbers:

- Add the fractions and the whole numbers separately; if the sum of the fractions is an improper fraction (greater than 1), change the improper fraction to a mixed number.

- Add the two whole numbers and write the new proper fraction.

Example 1 Add: $2\dfrac{2}{3} = 2\dfrac{4}{6}$

$+1\dfrac{1}{2} = 1\dfrac{3}{6}$

$3\dfrac{7}{6} = 3 + (1 + \dfrac{1}{6}) = \mathbf{4\dfrac{1}{6}}$

The improper fraction $\dfrac{7}{6}$ is changed to $1\dfrac{1}{6}$. The 1 is added to 3 to give 4.

Answer: $\mathbf{4\dfrac{1}{6}}$

Calculator Solution

 $\boxed{\text{C}}\ \boxed{2}\ \boxed{a^{b}/_{c}}\ \boxed{2}\ \boxed{a^{b}/_{c}}\ \boxed{3}\ \boxed{+}\ \boxed{1}\ \boxed{a^{b}/_{c}}\ \boxed{1}\ \boxed{a^{b}/_{c}}\ \boxed{2}\ \boxed{=}\ \boxed{4 \rfloor 1 \rfloor 6}$

To subtract mixed numbers:
- Subtract the fractions; if the fraction being subtracted is the greater fraction, then regroup the top mixed number and change the top fraction to an improper fraction.

- Subtract the fractions and whole numbers.

Example 2   Subtract: $6\frac{1}{4} = 6\frac{1}{4}$ Notice that $6\frac{1}{4}$ must be regrouped because $\frac{2}{4}$ is greater than $\frac{1}{4}$.

$-3\frac{1}{2} = 3\frac{2}{4}$

Write $6\frac{1}{4} = \underbrace{5 + 1}_{\text{6 regrouped}} + \frac{1}{4} = 5 + \frac{4}{4} + \frac{1}{4} = 5 + \frac{5}{4} = 5\frac{5}{4}$

The subtraction problem becomes:

$6\frac{1}{4} = 5\frac{5}{4}$

$-3\frac{1}{2} = 3\frac{2}{4}$

$2\frac{3}{4}$

After the regrouping, the top fraction is greater than the bottom fraction. The fractions can now be subtracted. Regrouping with fractions is very similar to regrouping with whole numbers.

Answer: $2\frac{3}{4}$

Calculator Solution

 C 6 a^b/$_c$ 1 a^b/$_c$ 4 − 3 a^b/$_c$ 1 a^b/$_c$ 2 = 2⌐3⌐4

EXERCISE 8

Part A   Directions: Add or subtract as indicated.

1. $2\frac{1}{2}$ $4\frac{2}{3}$ $3\frac{3}{4}$ $4\frac{7}{8}$ $6\frac{3}{4}$
    $+1\frac{1}{2}$ $+2\frac{2}{3}$ $+1\frac{1}{2}$ $+2\frac{3}{4}$ $+1\frac{2}{3}$

2. $3\frac{1}{3}$ $5\frac{1}{4}$ $6\frac{1}{2}$ $4\frac{1}{4}$ $5\frac{3}{8}$
    $-1\frac{2}{3}$ $-1\frac{3}{4}$ $-2\frac{3}{4}$ $-1\frac{1}{3}$ $-2\frac{3}{4}$

Part B **Directions:** Solve each problem.

3. Zander ordered carpet that is $\frac{11}{16}$ inch thick. The pad underneath it is $\frac{5}{8}$ inch thick. How thick are the carpet and pad together?

4. On Saturday, $\frac{5}{6}$ inch of rain fell. On Sunday, $\frac{3}{4}$ inch of rain fell. How much more rain fell on Saturday than on Sunday?

5. Last month Bertina lost $3\frac{7}{8}$ pounds on her diet. This month she plans to lose another $2\frac{1}{2}$ pounds. If she succeeds, how much weight will Bertina have lost in these two months?

6. A cookie recipe calls for $3\frac{1}{2}$ cups of flour. If Lanna has only $2\frac{5}{8}$ cups, how much more flour does she need?

7. Kate ran $2\frac{3}{4}$ miles on Monday. On Wednesday she ran $3\frac{5}{8}$ miles. How many miles did she run on these two days?

8. To make a large fruit salad, Miguel mixed $2\frac{1}{2}$ pounds of grapes, $4\frac{2}{3}$ pounds of strawberries, and $6\frac{1}{4}$ pounds of apples. How many pounds of salad does Miguel have?

9. Jessica grew $1\frac{1}{4}$ inches last year. This is $\frac{5}{16}$ of an inch more than she grew the previous year. How much did Jessica grow the previous year?

Answers are on page 827.

Multiplying Fractions

Multiplying a Fraction by a Fraction

To **multiply a fraction by a fraction** is to find part of a part.

For example, the drawings below show three fraction products:

$\frac{1}{2}$ of $\frac{1}{2}$ $\qquad$ $\frac{1}{2}$ of $\frac{1}{4}$ $\qquad$ $\frac{1}{3}$ of $\frac{1}{4}$

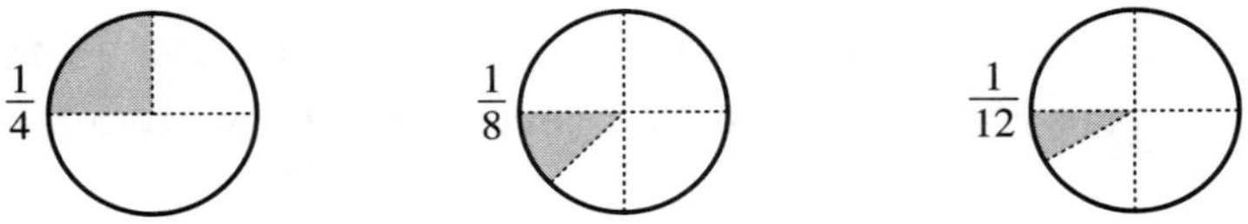

$\frac{1}{2} \times \frac{1}{2} = \frac{1}{4}$ $\qquad$ $\frac{1}{2} \times \frac{1}{4} = \frac{1}{8}$ $\qquad$ $\frac{1}{3} \times \frac{1}{4} = \frac{1}{12}$

Multiplying fractions is the same for both like fractions and unlike fractions.

- Multiply the numerators to find the numerator of the answer.
- Multiply the denominators to find the denominator of the answer.

Example 1 Multiply: $\frac{1}{2} \times \frac{1}{2}$

STEP 1 Multiply the numerators. $\frac{1}{2} \times \frac{1}{2} = \frac{1}{}$

STEP 2 Multiply the denominators. $\frac{1}{2} \times \frac{1}{2} = \frac{1}{4}$

Answer: $\mathbf{\frac{1}{4}}$

Calculator Solution

[C] [1] [a b/c] [2] [×] [1] [a b/c] [2] [=] [1⌋4]

Example 2 Multiply: $\frac{2}{3} \times \frac{3}{4}$

STEP 1 Multiply the numerators. $\frac{2}{3} \times \frac{3}{4} = \frac{6}{}$

STEP 2 Multiply the denominators. $\frac{2}{3} \times \frac{3}{4} = \frac{6}{12}$, reduces to $\frac{1}{2}$

Answer: $\mathbf{\frac{6}{12}}$ **or** $\mathbf{\frac{1}{2}}$

Calculator Solution

[C] [2] [a b/c] [3] [×] [3] [a b/c] [4] [=] [1⌋2]

EXERCISE 9

Part A **Directions:** Multiply each pair of fractions. The first one in each row is done as an example.

1. $\frac{1}{2} \times \frac{3}{4} = \frac{3}{8}$ $\frac{1}{3} \times \frac{1}{2} =$ $\frac{1}{4} \times \frac{3}{4} =$ $\frac{2}{5} \times \frac{1}{3} =$

2. $\frac{1}{5} \times \frac{1}{3} = \frac{1}{15}$ $\frac{5}{7} \times \frac{1}{2} =$ $\frac{2}{3} \times \frac{2}{5} =$ $\frac{3}{4} \times \frac{1}{2} =$

Part B **Directions:** Multiply each pair of fractions. Reduce each answer to lowest terms. The first one in each row is done as an example.

3. $\frac{1}{2} \times \frac{2}{3} = \frac{2}{6} = \frac{1}{3}$ $\frac{1}{3} \times \frac{3}{4} =$ $\frac{2}{5} \times \frac{5}{8} =$ $\frac{1}{4} \times \frac{2}{5} =$

4. $\frac{3}{4} \times \frac{1}{3} = \frac{3}{12} = \frac{1}{4}$ $\frac{2}{3} \times \frac{3}{5} =$ $\frac{4}{7} \times \frac{1}{2} =$ $\frac{3}{4} \times \frac{2}{3} =$

Part C **Directions:** Solve each problem.

5. Carlina eats $\frac{1}{4}$ of a piece of chocolate that weighs $\frac{5}{8}$ pound. What weight of chocolate does Carlina eat?

6. Emmitt Paving Company has $\frac{7}{8}$ of a mile of road left to pave. They plan to finish $\frac{1}{3}$ of this job by the end of the week. What fraction of a mile does Emmitt Paving plan to finish by the end of the week?

7. A cookie recipe calls for $\frac{3}{4}$ pound of butter. Alyce plans to use only $\frac{2}{3}$ of the amount of butter recommended by the recipe. What fraction of a pound of butter should Alyce use?

Answers are on page 827.

Multiplying Fractions, Whole Numbers, and Mixed Numbers

To multiply any combination of fractions, whole numbers, or mixed numbers, the first step is to change each whole number or mixed number to an improper fraction. Then multiply as usual.

Example 1   Multiply: $\frac{3}{4} \times 8$

STEP 1   Rewrite 8 as $\frac{8}{1}$.

STEP 2   Multiply the fractions. $\frac{3}{4} \times \frac{8}{1} = \frac{24}{4} = 6$

Answer: 6

Calculator Solution

 $\boxed{C}\ \boxed{3}\ \boxed{a^{b}\!/_{c}}\ \boxed{4}\ \boxed{\times}\ \boxed{8}\ \boxed{=}\ \boxed{6}$

Example 2   Multiply: $3\frac{1}{2} \times \frac{1}{4}$

STEP 1   Rewrite $3\frac{1}{2}$ as an improper fraction.

　　　a. Change 3 to an improper fraction
　　　with a denominator of 2.　　　　　$3 = \frac{6}{2}$

　　　b. Combine $\frac{6}{2}$ and $\frac{1}{2}$.　　　　$\frac{6}{2} + \frac{1}{2} = \frac{7}{2}$

STEP 2   Multiply the fractions.　　　$\frac{7}{2} \times \frac{1}{4} = \frac{7}{8}$

Answer: $\frac{7}{8}$

Calculator Solution

 $\boxed{C}\ \boxed{3}\ \boxed{a^{b}\!/_{c}}\ \boxed{1}\ \boxed{a^{b}\!/_{c}}\ \boxed{2}\ \boxed{\times}\ \boxed{1}\ \boxed{a^{b}\!/_{c}}\ \boxed{4}\ \boxed{=}\ \boxed{7 \lrcorner 8}$

EXERCISE 10

<u>Part A</u> **Directions:** Multiply each pair of fractions. The first problem in each row is done as an example.

1. $\dfrac{1}{3} \times \dfrac{4}{1} = \dfrac{4}{3} = 1\dfrac{1}{3}$ $\dfrac{1}{2} \times \dfrac{5}{1} =$ $\dfrac{3}{4} \times \dfrac{6}{1} =$ $\dfrac{9}{10} \times \dfrac{2}{1} =$

2. $\dfrac{7}{2} \times \dfrac{1}{3} = \dfrac{7}{6} = 1\dfrac{1}{6}$ $\dfrac{5}{2} \times \dfrac{1}{2} =$ $\dfrac{4}{3} \times \dfrac{3}{4} =$ $\dfrac{3}{2} \times \dfrac{5}{2} =$

<u>Part B</u> **Directions:** Multiply each fraction and whole number. As a first step, write the whole number as an improper fraction—the whole number over the number 1. The first one in each row is done as an example.

3. $\dfrac{1}{5} \times 3 = \dfrac{1}{5} \times \dfrac{3}{1}$ $\dfrac{1}{3} \times 2 =$ $\dfrac{5}{8} \times 7 =$ $\dfrac{3}{4} \times 5 =$
   $= \dfrac{3}{5}$

4. $3 \times \dfrac{3}{4} = \dfrac{3}{1} \times \dfrac{3}{4}$ $5 \times \dfrac{2}{3} =$ $2 \times \dfrac{3}{8} =$ $8 \times \dfrac{3}{4} =$
   $= \dfrac{9}{4} = 2\dfrac{1}{4}$

<u>Part C</u> **Directions:** Multiply each fraction and mixed number. As a first step, write the mixed number as an improper fraction. The first one in each row is done as an example.

5. $\dfrac{1}{2} \times 1\dfrac{1}{3} = \dfrac{1}{2} \times \dfrac{4}{3}$ $\dfrac{1}{3} \times 1\dfrac{1}{2} =$ $\dfrac{3}{4} \times 2\dfrac{1}{3} =$ $\dfrac{2}{3} \times 2\dfrac{1}{2} =$
   $= \dfrac{4}{6} = \dfrac{2}{3}$

6. $2\dfrac{1}{4} \times \dfrac{3}{4} = \dfrac{9}{4} \times \dfrac{3}{4}$ $1\dfrac{1}{2} \times \dfrac{3}{4} =$ $2\dfrac{1}{4} \times \dfrac{3}{8} =$ $1\dfrac{3}{4} \times \dfrac{1}{2} =$
   $= \dfrac{27}{16} = 1\dfrac{11}{16}$

<u>Part D</u> **Directions:** Solve each problem.

7. If lean hamburger is $\dfrac{1}{5}$ fat, how many ounces of fat are in 72 ounces (6 pounds) of hamburger?

8. Danny mixes $\dfrac{5}{6}$ pint of coloring into each gallon of paint he uses. How many pints of coloring will Danny need to complete a job that requires 18 gallons of paint?

Dividing Fractions

To divide is to find out how many times one number is contained in a second number. This is also true with fractions.

Example 1   To find how many $\frac{1}{8}$-inch wide washers must be placed next to each other to span a distance of $\frac{3}{4}$ inch, divide $\frac{3}{4}$ by $\frac{1}{8}$.

$$\frac{3}{4} \div \frac{1}{8} = ?$$

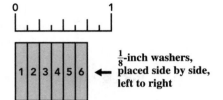

As shown in the drawing, the answer is 6.

$\frac{1}{8}$-inch washers, placed side by side, left to right

Dividing fractions involves one more step than multiplying fractions:

- First, invert the divisor (the number you are dividing by).

- Second, change the division sign to a multiplication sign.

- Third, multiply the two fractions.

To **invert the divisor** means to turn a fraction upside down—interchange the numerator and denominator. In other words, you switch the top and bottom numbers.

Example 2   Divide: $\frac{3}{4} \div \frac{1}{8}$

STEP 1   Invert the divisor: $\frac{1}{8}$ inverted is $\frac{8}{1}$.

STEP 2   Change the division sign to a multiplication sign and multiply.

$$\frac{3}{4} \div \frac{1}{8} = \frac{3}{4} \times \frac{8}{1} = \frac{24}{4} = 6$$

Answer: 6

Calculator Solution

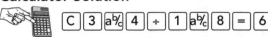

EXERCISE 11

Directions: Divide. The first one is done as an example.

1. $\frac{3}{4} \div \frac{1}{2} = \frac{3}{4} \times \frac{2}{1} = \frac{6}{4} = 1\frac{1}{2}$ $\qquad$ $\frac{2}{3} \div \frac{3}{4} =$

2. $\frac{5}{8} \div \frac{1}{3} =$ $\qquad$ $\frac{3}{5} \div \frac{1}{10} =$

Answers are on page 828.

Dividing Fractions, Whole Numbers, and Mixed Numbers

To divide fractions and whole numbers or mixed numbers:

- Change a whole number divisor to a fraction by placing the whole number over 1.

- Change a mixed number divisor to an improper fraction.

- Invert the divisor.

- Change the division sign to a multiplication sign.

- Multiply the fractions.

Type of Divisor	Example	Write the Divisor as a Fraction	Invert the Divisor and Change the Sign
proper fraction	$\frac{3}{4} \div \frac{7}{8}$	$\frac{3}{4} \div \frac{7}{8}$	$\frac{3}{4} \times \frac{8}{7}$
improper fraction	$\frac{2}{3} \div \frac{4}{3}$	$\frac{2}{3} \div \frac{4}{3}$	$\frac{2}{3} \times \frac{3}{4}$
whole number	$\frac{1}{2} \div 3$	$\frac{1}{2} \div \frac{3}{1}$	$\frac{1}{2} \times \frac{1}{3}$
mixed number	$\frac{1}{4} \div 1\frac{1}{2}$	$\frac{1}{4} \div \frac{3}{2}$	$\frac{1}{4} \times \frac{2}{3}$

Example   Divide: $\frac{1}{4} \div 1\frac{1}{2}$

STEP 1   Rewrite $1\frac{1}{2}$ as $\frac{3}{2}$.

STEP 2   Invert the divisor: $\frac{3}{2}$ inverted is $\frac{2}{3}$.

STEP 3   Change the sign and multiply. $\frac{1}{4} \times \frac{2}{3} = \frac{2}{12}$, reduces to $\frac{1}{6}$

          Answer: $\frac{1}{6}$

Calculator Solution

 $\boxed{C}$ $\boxed{1}$ $\boxed{a^{b/c}}$ $\boxed{4}$ $\boxed{\div}$ $\boxed{1}$ $\boxed{a^{b/c}}$ $\boxed{1}$ $\boxed{a^{b/c}}$ $\boxed{2}$ $\boxed{=}$ $\boxed{1 \lrcorner 6}$

EXERCISE 12

<u>Part A</u> **Directions:** Invert each number below.

1. $\frac{1}{2} =$ $\frac{3}{4} =$ $\frac{5}{8} =$ $\frac{2}{3} =$ $\frac{1}{4} =$

2. $\frac{5}{4} =$ $\frac{7}{3} =$ $\frac{3}{2} =$ $\frac{5}{3} =$ $\frac{8}{5} =$

3. $3 =$ $8 =$ $5 =$ $2 =$ $4 =$

4. $1\frac{3}{4} =$ $2\frac{1}{2} =$ $1\frac{1}{3} =$ $3\frac{1}{4} =$ $2\frac{1}{3} =$

<u>Part B</u> **Directions:** Divide. Reduce fraction answers if possible. The first one in each row is done as an example.

5. $\frac{3}{4} \div \frac{2}{3} = \frac{3}{4} \times \frac{3}{2}$ $\frac{2}{3} \div \frac{1}{2} =$ $\frac{4}{5} \div \frac{3}{10} =$ $\frac{7}{8} \div \frac{1}{4} =$
$\qquad = \frac{9}{8} = 1\frac{1}{8}$

6. $\frac{1}{4} \div \frac{5}{2} = \frac{1}{4} \times \frac{2}{5}$ $\frac{1}{2} \div \frac{4}{3} =$ $\frac{5}{8} \div \frac{3}{2} =$ $\frac{1}{5} \div \frac{5}{2} =$
$\qquad = \frac{2}{20} = \frac{1}{10}$

7. $\frac{3}{8} \div 2 = \frac{3}{8} \times \frac{1}{2}$ $\frac{3}{5} \div 3 =$ $\frac{1}{2} \div 4 =$ $\frac{3}{5} \div 5 =$
$\qquad = \frac{3}{16}$

8. $1\frac{1}{2} \div \frac{3}{4} = \frac{3}{2} \times \frac{4}{3}$ $1\frac{1}{4} \div \frac{2}{3} =$ $\frac{5}{8} \div 2\frac{1}{3} =$ $\frac{1}{2} \div 1\frac{1}{2} =$
$\qquad = \frac{12}{6} = 2$

<u>Part C</u> **Directions:** Solve each problem.

9. For a barbecue, Emily bought $4\frac{1}{2}$ pounds of hamburger. If she divides this into patties that each weigh $\frac{1}{4}$ pound, how many patties can she make?

10. Randy has $1\frac{7}{8}$ cubic yards of wet concrete left in his truck. He is going to pour this concrete into a number of foundation forms that each will hold $\frac{1}{8}$ cubic yard. How many forms can he fill?

11. A skateboard team race covers a total of $3\frac{3}{4}$ miles. How many people are needed on each team if each person skates $\frac{3}{8}$ mile?

12. Janette wants to lose $3\frac{3}{4}$ pounds. If, on the average, she loses $\frac{1}{8}$ pound each day, how many days will it take Janette to reach her goal?

13. How many washers, each $\frac{1}{16}$-inch thick, does it take to span a space that measures $\frac{3}{8}$ inch?

14. Each month, Aaron adds about $\frac{3}{4}$ quart of oil to his car engine. If Aaron has $5\frac{1}{4}$ quarts of oil in his garage, how many more times can he fill his car engine before he runs out of oil?

Answers are on page 828.

Fractions Review

EXERCISE 13

<u>Part A</u> **Directions:** Write a fraction to show how much of each figure or group is shaded.

1.   2.   3.   4.

_____   _____   _____   _____

Write an equivalent fraction for each pair of fractions as indicated.

5. the shaded fraction of each circle

6. the shaded fraction of each group

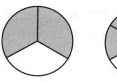   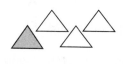

$\overline{3} = \overline{6}$ $\overline{4} = \overline{8}$

Reduce each fraction to lowest terms.

7. $\frac{4}{8} = $ — $\frac{4}{6} = $ — $\frac{6}{10} = $ — $\frac{4}{12} = $ —

Write the improper fraction represented in each drawing below.

8. _____   9. _____   10. _____

         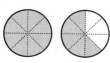   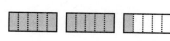

Part B **Directions:** Write > (is greater than) or < (is less than) to compare each pair of fractions.

11. $\dfrac{2}{4}$ —— $\dfrac{3}{4}$ $\dfrac{7}{8}$ —— $\dfrac{3}{4}$ $\dfrac{3}{4}$ —— $\dfrac{2}{3}$ $\dfrac{5}{6}$ —— $\dfrac{2}{3}$

Part C **Directions:** Solve each problem below.

12.
$$\begin{array}{c}\dfrac{1}{2}\\[4pt]+\dfrac{1}{2}\\\hline\end{array}\qquad\begin{array}{c}\dfrac{2}{4}\\[4pt]+\dfrac{1}{4}\\\hline\end{array}\qquad\begin{array}{c}\dfrac{2}{3}\\[4pt]+\dfrac{2}{3}\\\hline\end{array}\qquad\begin{array}{c}\dfrac{3}{4}\\[4pt]+\dfrac{2}{3}\\\hline\end{array}\qquad\begin{array}{c}4\dfrac{5}{8}\\[4pt]+1\dfrac{1}{2}\\\hline\end{array}$$

13.
$$\begin{array}{c}\dfrac{7}{8}\\[4pt]-\dfrac{3}{8}\\\hline\end{array}\qquad\begin{array}{c}1\dfrac{1}{4}\\[4pt]-\dfrac{3}{4}\\\hline\end{array}\qquad\begin{array}{c}3\dfrac{3}{8}\\[4pt]-1\dfrac{7}{8}\\\hline\end{array}\qquad\begin{array}{c}6\dfrac{1}{3}\\[4pt]-2\dfrac{1}{2}\\\hline\end{array}\qquad\begin{array}{c}5\dfrac{3}{4}\\[4pt]-2\dfrac{7}{8}\\\hline\end{array}$$

14. $\dfrac{1}{2}\times\dfrac{2}{3}=$ $\dfrac{3}{4}\times\dfrac{1}{2}=$ $\dfrac{3}{8}\times\dfrac{1}{3}=$ $\dfrac{4}{5}\times\dfrac{3}{4}=$

15. $1\dfrac{1}{4}\times\dfrac{3}{4}=$ $2\dfrac{1}{2}\times\dfrac{3}{8}=$ $\dfrac{3}{4}\times1\dfrac{3}{8}=$ $\dfrac{1}{2}\times2\dfrac{1}{2}=$

16. $\dfrac{1}{2}\div\dfrac{3}{4}=$ $\dfrac{1}{3}\div\dfrac{1}{2}=$ $\dfrac{3}{4}\div\dfrac{3}{8}=$ $\dfrac{3}{5}\div\dfrac{1}{2}=$

17. $1\dfrac{1}{4}\div\dfrac{1}{2}=$ $2\dfrac{1}{2}\div\dfrac{3}{8}=$ $\dfrac{3}{4}\div1\dfrac{1}{2}=$ $\dfrac{7}{8}\div2\dfrac{1}{2}=$

Part D **Directions:** Solve each problem below.

18. A cookbook recommends $\dfrac{1}{3}$ hour of cooking per pound of roast. For how long should an $8\dfrac{1}{2}$-pound roast be cooked?

19. Laslo, a jewelry maker, uses $\dfrac{3}{16}$ ounce of gold for each bracelet he makes. How many bracelets can Laslo make when his gold supply is down to 4 ounces?

Answers are on page 828.

CHAPTER 6

Ratio and Proportion

Understanding Ratios

A **ratio** is a comparison of two numbers. If there are 8 women and 5 men in your class, the ratio of women to men is 8 to 5; the ratio of men to women is 5 to 8. There are three ways to write the ratio 8 to 5, but each is read as *8 to 5*:

using the word *to*	**writing a fraction**	**using a colon**
8 to 5	$\dfrac{8}{5}$	8:5

In a ratio, the order in which numbers are written is very important. The ratio 8 to 5 is **not** the same as the ratio 5 to 8.

RULES FOR WRITING A RATIO

1. Reduce a ratio to lowest terms. Reduce a ratio in the same way you reduce a fraction.

   $6 \text{ to } 12 = \dfrac{6}{12} = \dfrac{1}{2}$

2. Leave an improper-fraction ratio as an improper fraction.

   $9 \text{ to } 6 = \dfrac{9}{6} = \dfrac{3}{2}$

3. Write a whole-number ratio as an improper fraction.

   $8 \text{ to } 2 = \dfrac{8}{2} = \dfrac{4}{1}$

A ratio problem may involve two steps.

<u>**Example**</u>   Of the 16 games they played this season, the Huskies won 12. What is the ratio of the games the Huskies won to the games they lost?

STEP 1   Determine how many games the Huskies lost.

$16 - 12 = 4$

STEP 2   Write a ratio of games won to games lost.

$\dfrac{\text{games won}}{\text{games lost}} = \dfrac{12}{4} = \dfrac{3}{1}$

Answer: 3 to 1

EXERCISE 1

Part A **Directions:** Simplify each ratio by reducing it to lowest terms. The first one is done as an example.

1. 2 to 8 = _1 to 4_   3 to 9 = _____   9 to 12 = _____

2. 8 to 4 = _____   12 to 3 = _____   8 to 6 = _____

Part B **Directions:** Solve each problem.

3. Amanda's basketball team won 8 games and lost 10.

   a. What is the ratio of games won to games lost?

   b. What is the ratio of games lost to games won?

4. In Willard's swimming class, there are 14 boys and 10 girls.

   a. What is the ratio of boys to girls?

   b. What is the ratio of girls to boys?

Part C **Directions:** Solve each problem.

5. A fruit punch recipe calls for 4 cans of water to each 3 cans of punch concentrate.

   a. What is the ratio of punch concentrate to water?

   b. What is the ratio of punch concentrate to the whole mixture?

6. Juanita takes home $1,800 each month. Her employer withholds $600 each month for taxes and other withholdings.

   a. What is the ratio of the amount that is withheld from Juanita's salary to her take-home pay?

   b. What is the ratio of the amount that is withheld from Juanita's salary to her total monthly earnings?

7. There are 24 students in Sheena's art class: 16 women and 8 men.

   a. What is the ratio of men to women?

   b. What is the ratio of men to total number of students?

8. There are 30 students in Angelica's math class. Only 14 of these students are women.

   a. What is the ratio of men to women?

   b. What is the ratio of women to total number of students?

9. Keri's bowling team won 9 of 16 matches during league play. What is the ratio of matches won to matches lost?

Answers are on page 828.

Working with Rates

A **rate** is a ratio that compares two measurements, such as miles and hours or dollars and pounds. A **unit rate** is the rate for one unit of a quantity, such as miles per hour or dollars per pound. To find a unit rate, divide the two numbers in the ratio. The word *per* is often used with rates. *Per* means *for each*.

Example 1   A car drives 120 miles in 3 hours.

COMMON RATES

miles per hour
cents per ounce
dollars per pound
cost per container
words per minute
calories per ounce
miles per gallon
beats per minute
pages per hour
pages per minute

a. What is the car's speed in miles per hour (mph)?

Write the ratio of miles to hours. This ratio is a rate called *speed*.

$$\text{speed} = \frac{120 \text{ miles}}{3 \text{ hours}} = \frac{40 \text{ miles}}{1 \text{ hour}} \text{ or } \textbf{40 miles } \textit{per} \textbf{ hour (40 mph)}$$

rate given
in problem ⟶   ⟵ unit rate

b. At this rate, how far will this car travel in 6 hours?

distance in 6 hours = 40 mph × 6 = **240 miles**

Example 2   The price of yogurt is $1.96 for 4 small containers.

a. What is the price per container?

Write the ratio of cost to number of containers. Divide to find unit (container) cost.

$$\text{price per container} = \frac{\$1.96}{4} = \frac{\$0.49}{1} = \textbf{\$0.49}$$

b. At this same rate, how much would 7 containers cost?

cost of 7 containers = $0.49 × 7 = **$3.43**

EXERCISE 2

Part A   **Directions:** Write each unit price.

1. 3 pounds of chicken for $4.17   _____

2. 7 pencils for $0.98   _____

3. 6 bottles of soda for $2.88   _____

4. 10 ounces of mixed nuts for $2.84 _____

Part B   **Directions:** Solve each problem.

MATH FACT

A rate may be a whole number, a mixed number, or a fraction.

5. Ramona earns $300 each week for 40 hours of work.

   a. What is Ramona's pay rate in dollars per hour?

   b. At this same rate, how much does Ramona earn for 25 hours of work?

6. Quan walks 14 miles in 4 hours.

   a. What is Quan's walking rate in miles per hour?

   b. At this rate, how far can Quan walk in 15 hours?

7. Stacey measured her heart rate. She counted 132 beats in 2 minutes.

   a. What is Stacey's heart rate in beats per minute?

   b. At this rate, how many times does Stacey's heart beat each hour?

8. A 12-ounce soda contains 240 calories of food energy.

   a. What is the calorie content of this soda in calories per ounce?

   b. How many calories are in a 40-ounce serving of this soda?

9. Daniel read 80 pages of a western novel in 120 minutes. The novel has an average of 250 words per page.

   a. About how many total words does the 80 pages contain?

   b. What is Daniel's reading rate in words per minute?

   c. At this rate, how long would it take Daniel to read a novel that contains 240,000 words?

Answers are on page 829.

Understanding Proportions

A **proportion** is made up of two equal ratios. You write a proportion as a pair of **equivalent fractions**.

Example 1 Suppose you add 1 cup of punch concentrate to 3 cups of water. The ratio of concentrate to water is 1 to 3. You get the same flavor of punch if you add 2 cups of punch concentrate to 6 cups of water. These two mixtures form a proportion.

written as equivalent fractions: $\frac{1}{3} = \frac{2}{6}$

You read a proportion as two equal ratios connected by the word *as.*

$\frac{1}{3} = \frac{2}{6}$ is read *1 is to 3 as 2 is to 6*

In a proportion, the **cross products** are equal. To find cross products, multiply each numerator by the opposite denominator.

Cross Multiplication

$$\frac{1}{3} \diagdown\diagup \frac{2}{6}$$

Equal Cross Products

$$1 \times 6 = 3 \times 2$$
$$6 = 6$$

Finding a Missing Number in a Proportion

Sometimes you are asked to find a **missing number** in a proportion. **To find the missing number,** follow these steps:

- Write *n* (or some other letter) to stand for the missing number.

- Write equal cross products. Notice that one cross product contains *n*.

- To find *n*, divide the complete cross product by the number that multiplies *n*.

Example 2 Find the value of n: $\frac{n}{4} = \frac{9}{12}$

STEP 1 Cross multiply: $12n = 36$

STEP 2 To find n, divide 36 by 12.

Answer: $n = \frac{36}{12} = 3$

Proportion: $\frac{3}{4} = \frac{9}{12}$

Example 3 Find the value of x: $\frac{2}{x} = \frac{10}{15}$

STEP 1 Cross multiply: $10x = 30$

STEP 2 To find x, divide 30 by 10.

Answer: $x = \frac{30}{10} = 3$

Proportion: $\frac{2}{3} = \frac{10}{15}$

EXERCISE 3

Part A **Directions:** Circle *Yes* if each pair of fractions forms a proportion; circle *No* if it does not. Remember, in a proportion, cross products must be equal.

1. $\frac{2}{4} \overset{?}{=} \frac{2}{3}$ Yes   No $\frac{3}{4} \overset{?}{=} \frac{6}{8}$ Yes   No $\frac{2}{3} \overset{?}{=} \frac{3}{5}$ Yes   No

2. $\frac{8}{12} \overset{?}{=} \frac{2}{3}$ Yes   No $\frac{3}{6} \overset{?}{=} \frac{5}{8}$ Yes   No $\frac{3}{8} \overset{?}{=} \frac{9}{24}$ Yes   No

Part B **Directions:** Write equal cross products for each proportion. The first one is done as an example.

3. $\frac{n}{4} = \frac{6}{8}$ $\frac{4}{n} = \frac{16}{24}$ $\frac{2}{x} = \frac{8}{12}$ $\frac{21}{9} = \frac{n}{3}$

   $8n = 24$

4. $\frac{x}{8} = \frac{1}{4}$ $\frac{3}{x} = \frac{18}{12}$ $\frac{2}{3} = \frac{n}{9}$ $\frac{28}{12} = \frac{7}{x}$

Part C **Directions:** Write equal cross products for each proportion. Then divide to find the correct value of *n* or *x*.

5. $\frac{2}{4} = \frac{n}{24}$ $\frac{x}{2} = \frac{15}{10}$ $\frac{n}{3} = \frac{25}{15}$ $\frac{4}{n} = \frac{16}{24}$

6. $\frac{x}{8} = \frac{10}{16}$ $\frac{2}{3} = \frac{n}{18}$ $\frac{3}{x} = \frac{18}{12}$ $\frac{30}{24} = \frac{5}{n}$

Answers are on page 829.

Proportions with Word Problems

Proportions can be used to solve word problems that involve comparisons. Remember to write the terms of each ratio in the correct order.

Example 1   A punch recipe calls for 5 parts juice to 2 parts ginger ale. To make this punch, how much ginger ale should be added to 15 cups of juice?

STEP 1   Write a proportion where each ratio is $\dfrac{\text{cups of ginger ale}}{\text{cups of juice}}$

Let *n* stand for the unknown cups of ginger ale. $\dfrac{n}{15} = \dfrac{2}{5}$

STEP 2   Write cross products. $5n = 15 \times 2 = 30$

STEP 3   To find *n*, divide 30 by 5. $n = \dfrac{30}{5} = 6$

Answer: *n* = 6 cups of ginger ale

Example 2 On Saturday, Keisha drove 440 miles in 8 hours. At this same speed, how far can Keisha drive in 11 hours.

STEP 1 Write a proportion where each ratio is $\dfrac{\text{number of miles}}{\text{number of hours}}$

Let n stand for the unknown number of miles.

$$\dfrac{n}{11} = \dfrac{440}{8}$$

STEP 2 Write cross products.

$$8n = 11 \times 440 = 4{,}840$$

STEP 3 To find n, divide 4,840 by 8.

$$n = \dfrac{4840}{8} = \mathbf{605}$$

Answer: n = 605 miles

EXERCISE 4

Part A Directions: Choose the correct proportion that can be used to solve each problem.

1. A recipe calls for 2 cups of cream for 12 servings of dessert. Which proportion can be used to find the number of cups of cream needed to make 8 servings?

   a. $\dfrac{n}{12} = \dfrac{2}{8}$ **b.** $\dfrac{n}{2} = \dfrac{12}{8}$ **c.** $\dfrac{n}{8} = \dfrac{2}{12}$

2. At McGill Publishing Company, 5 out of every 8 editors are women. Which proportion can be used to find how many of the 72 editors who work at McGill are women?

   a. $\dfrac{n}{5} = \dfrac{8}{72}$ **b.** $\dfrac{n}{72} = \dfrac{5}{8}$ **c.** $\dfrac{n}{8} = \dfrac{72}{5}$

3. Of the 32 teachers at Highland Middle School, 14 are women. Suppose this same ratio is true for all 140 middle-school teachers in the school district. Which proportion can be used to find the total number of **male** middle-school teachers in this district?

   a. $\dfrac{n}{140} = \dfrac{18}{32}$ **b.** $\dfrac{n}{140} = \dfrac{14}{32}$ **c.** $\dfrac{n}{16} = \dfrac{14}{32}$

Part B Directions: Use a proportion to solve each problem.

4. Carlos was paid $118.80 for 12 hours of work. At this rate, how much will Carlos earn for working 31 hours?

5. In a survey of 250 voters, 3 out of 5 voters said they planned to vote for a proposed new county library.

   a. How many of these voters plan to vote for the library?

   b. How many are **not** planning to vote for the library?

Answers are on page 829.

Ratio and Proportion Review

EXERCISE 5

Part A **Directions:** Solve each ratio problem.

1. Each night, Lauren sleeps for 8 hours. She is awake for 16 hours each day. What is the ratio of the hours that Lauren sleeps to the hours she is awake?

2. During January, 18 of 31 days had snow. No snow fell on 13 days. What is the ratio of days on which snow fell to total days in the month?

3. In the local high-school election, Alan received 300 votes of 1,200 votes cast. What is the ratio of votes Alan received to the votes he did not receive?

4. Beverly takes home $1,800 each month. Of this, she saves $400 and spends the rest. What is the ratio of the amount of money Beverly saves to the amount of money she spends?

Part B **Directions:** Write each unit price.

5. 4 pounds of seedless grapes for $5.16

6. 3 bottles of shampoo for $8.67

Part C **Directions:** Solve the following rate problem.

7. Joyclyn earns $350 each week for 40 hours of work.

 a. What is Joyclyn's pay rate in dollars per hour?

 b. At this same rate, how much does Joyclyn earn in 55 hours?

Part D **Directions:** Write equal cross products for each proportion. Then divide to find the correct value of *n* or *x*.

8. $\dfrac{3}{4} = \dfrac{n}{16}$ $\qquad$ $\dfrac{x}{3} = \dfrac{12}{18}$ $\qquad$ $\dfrac{n}{2} = \dfrac{7}{14}$ $\qquad$ $\dfrac{6}{n} = \dfrac{24}{20}$

Part E **Directions:** Use a proportion to solve each problem.

9. Melons are on sale for 3 for $1.89. How much would 8 melons cost?

10. Allyna rode her bike a total of 52 miles in 4 hours. Riding at this same rate, how far can Allyna ride in 7 hours?

11. Maxi-Strength Epoxy is supposed to be mixed in the ratio of 3 parts hardener to 7 parts base. About how many drops of hardener should be mixed with 50 drops of base?

Answers are on page 829.

CHAPTER 7

Percent

Understanding Percent

Percent is another way to write part of a whole.

Percent refers to the **number of parts out of 100 equal parts**. The symbol % is used to indicate percent.

- 5 percent means 5 parts out of 100 equal parts.

- 5 percent is written 5%.

Examples   One dollar is equal to 100 cents. Coins can be thought of as a percent of a dollar.

REMEMBER
100¢ = $1.00
1¢ = 1% of $1.00
5¢ = 5% of $1.00
10¢ = 10% of $1.00
25¢ = 25% of $1.00

 = 1% of   = 10% of

 = 5% of   = 25% of

Dividing a large square into 100 equal parts is another way to visualize percent.

Each large square is divided into 100 smaller squares.

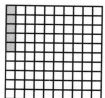      

5% of the large square is shaded.   40% of the large square is shaded.   75% of the large square is shaded.

What is 100%?

100% stands for a whole object.

At the right, 80% of the large square is shaded; 20% is unshaded.

80% + 20% = 100%

shaded + unshaded = whole square

753

EXERCISE 1

Part A **Directions:** What percent of $1.00 is each group of coins?

1. _____   2. _____   3. _____

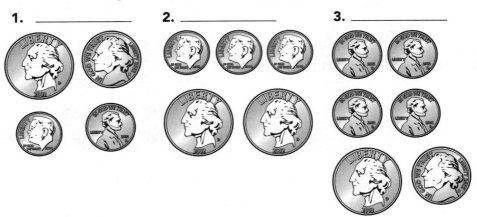

Part B **Directions:** Write the percent of each square that is shaded, and write the percent of each square that is unshaded. For each square, write the total of the two percents.

4. % shaded _____

   % unshaded _____

   total % _____

5. % shaded _____

   % unshaded _____

   total % _____

6. % shaded _____

   % unshaded _____

   total % _____

7. % shaded _____

   % unshaded _____

   total % _____

<u>**Part C**</u> **Directions:** Answer each question.

8. One hundred students attend classes at Sheldon Community Center. Eighty-nine students showed up for classes on Thursday.

   a. What percent of students came to class Thursday?

   b. What percent of students did not come to class?

9. A meter is a metric unit of length that is a little longer than a yard. A meter is divided into 100 smaller units called centimeters.

   a. What percent of 1 meter is a length of 47 centimeters?

   b. What percent of 100 meters is a length of 72 meters?

Answers are on page 829.

Relating Decimals, Fractions, and Percents

MATH FACT

Every number less than 1 can be written in three equal ways:
- a fraction
- a decimal
- a percent

When calculating with percents, the first step is to change the percent to a decimal or a fraction.

- A percent has the same value as a two-place decimal.

43% is equal to 0.43.

- A percent has the same value as a fraction that has a denominator of 100.

43% = $\frac{43}{100}$

The fractions $\frac{1}{3}$ and $\frac{2}{3}$ are **special fractions** because they are commonly used, and their decimal and percent forms include a fraction.

$$\frac{1}{3} = 0.33\frac{1}{3} = 33\frac{1}{3}\% \qquad \text{and} \qquad \frac{2}{3} = 0.66\frac{2}{3} = 0.66\frac{2}{3}\%$$

Because these fractions often appear in word problems, you should memorize the three forms of each.

EXERCISE 2

Part A **Directions:** Write each percent as a decimal.

1. 25%   62%   84%   37% $33\frac{1}{3}$%

Part B **Directions:** Write each percent as a whole number. The first one is done as an example.

2. 300%   500%   100%   800%   600%

    $3.00 = 3$

Part C **Directions:** Write each percent as a fraction. Reduce the fraction to lowest terms if possible.

3. 50%   25%   40%   75% $66\frac{2}{3}$%

Part D **Directions:** Write the shaded part of each large square as a percent, a decimal, and a fraction.

MEMORY AID
To write a percent as a decimal, let the two 0s in the % sign remind you of two decimal places.
To write a percent as a fraction, let the two 0s in % remind you of two 0s in the denominator.

4.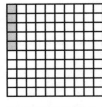

percent _____

decimal _____

fraction _____

5.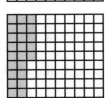

percent _____

decimal _____

fraction _____

Part E **Directions:** Answer each of the following questions. Reduce fractions to lowest terms.

6. Amanda has completed $\frac{1}{3}$ of a novel.

    a. What percent of the novel has Amanda completed?

    b. Expressed as a decimal, what part of the novel has Amanda completed?

    c. What percent of the novel has she **not** yet completed?

7. Brandon has completed 45 miles of a 100-mile bike trip.

    a. What fraction of the trip has Brandon completed?

    b. What percent of the trip has Brandon **not** yet completed?

    c. Expressed as a decimal, what part of the trip has Brandon **not** yet completed?

8. A kilometer (about 0.6 mile) is a metric length unit that is equal to 1,000 meters.

   a. What fraction of a kilometer is a distance of 300 meters?

   b. What decimal part of a kilometer is a distance of 300 meters?

   c. What percent of a kilometer is a distance of 300 meters?

Part F **Directions:** The table below includes commonly used percents, fractions, and decimals. For review, complete this table.

Fraction	Percent	Decimal
9. $\frac{1}{8}$		
10. $\frac{1}{4}$		
11. $\frac{1}{3}$		
12. $\frac{1}{2}$		
13. $\frac{2}{3}$		
14. $\frac{3}{4}$		
15.	75%	
16.	50%	
17.	$66\frac{2}{3}\%$	
18.	25%	
19.	$33\frac{1}{3}\%$	
20.	12.5%	
21.		0.25
22.		0.125
23.		$0.33\frac{1}{3} (= 0.33 \ldots = 0.\overline{3})$
24.		0.75
25.		$0.66\frac{2}{3} (= 0.66 \ldots = 0.\overline{6})$
26.		0.5

Answers are on pages 829–830.

Identifying Numbers in a Percent Problem

A percent problem contains three important numbers: the **percent**, the **whole**, and the **part**.

Examples

25%	of	200	is	50.
↑		↑		↑
percent		whole		part

75%	of	$24	is	$18.
↑		↑		↑
percent		whole		part

A percent problem asks you to find one of these three numbers when you know the other two.

- Find the **part** when you know the percent and the whole.

  What is 30% of $40?

  percent = 30%, whole = $40, part = ?

- Find the **percent** when you know the whole and the part.

  What percent of 60 is 12?

  whole = 60, part = 12, percent = ?

- Find the **whole** when you know the percent and the part.

  If 50% of a number is 80, what is the number?

  percent = 50%, part = 80, whole = ?

EXERCISE 3

Part A **Directions:** Identify the percent, the whole, and the part in each statement.

1. 30% of 50 is 15.

   a. percent = _____

   b. whole = _____

   c. part = _____

2. $9.00 is 75% of $12.00.

   a. percent = _____

   b. whole = _____

   c. part = _____

Part B **Directions:** Circle the word that represents what you are asked to find.

3. 40% of what number is 60?

   You are asked to find the . . .

   percent   whole   part

4. 25 is what percent of 150?

   You are asked to find the . . .

   percent   whole   part

Answers are on page 830.

MEMORY AID

P = % × W
part percent whole

Finding the Part

Finding the part: To find the part, multiply the percent times the whole.

How to do it: Change the percent to a decimal or a fraction; then multiply.

Example   A $65 jacket is on sale for 30% off. How much can you save by buying this jacket on sale?

Think: You save 30% of $65.

Method 1

STEP 1   Change 30% to a decimal.

30% = 0.30 = 0.3

STEP 2   Multiply $65 by 0.3.

$$\begin{array}{r} \$65 \\ \times\ 0.3 \\ \hline 19.5 = \$19.50 \end{array}$$

Answer: $19.50

Method 2

STEP 1   Change 30% to a fraction.

$30\% = \dfrac{30}{100} = \dfrac{3}{10}$

STEP 2   Multiply $65 by $\dfrac{3}{10}$.

$$\frac{65}{1} \times \frac{3}{10} = \frac{195}{10}$$

$$\frac{195}{10} = 19.5$$

Answer: $19.50

Calculator Solution

C 6 5 × 3 0 [SHIFT] [%] = 19.5

EXERCISE 4

Part A   **Directions:** Find each part.

1. 30% of 90   25% of 180   50% of 276 $33\frac{1}{3}$% of 27

2. 8% of $25   6% of $12   9% of $46   5% of $350

3. 5.5% of $18   6.5% of $8   7.5% of $20   12.5% of 200

Part B **Directions:** Answer each question.

4. A $190 television set is on sale for 40% off.

   a. How much can be saved by buying the television at this sale price?

   b. What is the sale price of the set?

   Hint: sale price = original price − savings

5. A sweater sells for $45.

   a. In a state with a 6% sales tax, what sales tax must be paid on the sweater?

   b. Including sales tax, what will be the total cost of the sweater?

   Hint: total cost = selling price + sales tax

6. Chiana's property tax bill is increasing by 5% this year. Last year her property tax was $1,400.

   a. By how much is her property tax increasing?

   b. What will Chiana's property tax be this year?

7. Jake's Sweat Shoppe is offering a 25% discount on all sweatshirts in stock. Shelley chooses a sweatshirt that normally sells for $32.

   a. How much can Shelley save by buying this sweatshirt at the sale price?

   b. What will be the sale price of this sweatshirt?

   c. If Shelley must pay a 7% sales tax, what will be her total cost for the sweater?

8. Only 35% of the employees at BMN Electronics are women.

   a. How many of BMN's 240 employees are women?

   b. What percent of BMN's employees are men?

   c. How many of BMN's employees are men?

Answers are on page 830.

Finding the Percent

MEMORY AID

$$\% = \frac{P}{W}$$

Finding the percent: To find the percent, divide the part by the whole.

How to do it: Write the fraction $\frac{\text{part}}{\text{whole}}$. Reduce this fraction if possible. Then change the fraction to a percent. One way to change a fraction to a percent is to multiply the fraction by 100%.

Example   Out of his salary of $2,000 per month, Miguel has $400 withheld for taxes and health insurance. What percent of Miguel's income is withheld?

STEP 1   Write the fraction: $\frac{\text{part}}{\text{whole}} = \frac{400}{2000}$

STEP 2   Reduce the fraction: $\frac{400}{2000} = \frac{4}{20} = \frac{1}{5}$

STEP 3   Change the fraction to a percent by multiplying the fraction by 100%. $\frac{1}{5} \times 100\% = \frac{100\%}{5} = 20\%$

Answer: 20%

Calculator Solution

$$\boxed{C}\ \boxed{4}\ \boxed{0}\ \boxed{0}\ \boxed{\div}\ \boxed{2}\ \boxed{0}\ \boxed{0}\ \boxed{0}\ \boxed{\underset{\text{SHIFT}}{\ }\underset{\%}{\ }}\ \boxed{=}\ \boxed{20}$$

EXERCISE 5

Part A   **Directions:** Find each percent.

1. What percent of 30 is 6?

2. $12 is what percent of $48?

3. What percent of 40 pounds is 8 pounds?

4. 27 inches is what percent of 1 yard? (1 yard = 36 inches)

Part B   **Directions:** Solve each problem.

5. In Sandy's dance class, 12 of the 16 students are men.

    a. How many of the dance students are women?

    b. What percent of the dance students are women?

6. A gallon contains 4 quarts.

    a. How many quarts are in 8 gallons?

    b. What percent of 8 gallons is 16 quarts?

7. On her math test, Alycia got 40 out of 50 questions correct.

    a. What percent of questions did Alycia get correct?

    b. What percent of questions did Alycia get incorrect?

8. Out of Vida's monthly paycheck of $1,600, her employer withholds $250. To the nearest percent, what percent of Vida's check is withheld?

9. A sport coat that normally sells for $80 is on sale for $48.

    What percent discount is this?

    Hint: percent discount = $\frac{\text{amount of discount}}{\text{original price}}$ written as a percent

10. Carlos has driven 250 of the 800-mile distance to Chicago.

    a. What percent of the total distance to Chicago has Carlos driven?

    b. What percent of the total distance to Chicago does Carlos still have left?

Answers are on page 830.

Finding the Whole

MEMORY AID

$$W = \frac{P}{\%}$$

Finding the whole: To find the whole, divide the part by the percent.

How to do it: Change the percent to a decimal or a fraction; then divide.

Example   40% of the students in Gail's writing group are men. If 12 men are in the group, how many people (men and women) are in the group? In other words, 12 is 40% of what number?

Method 1

    STEP 1   Change 40% to a decimal.

               40% = 0.40 = 0.4

    STEP 2   Divide 12 by 0.4.

$$0.4\overline{)12.0} \quad \frac{3\ 0}{}$$

Answer: 30

Calculator Solution

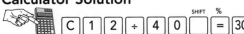

Method 2

    STEP 1   Change 40% to a fraction.

               40% = $\frac{40}{100}$ = $\frac{4}{10}$ = $\frac{2}{5}$

    STEP 2   Divide 12 by $\frac{2}{5}$.

$$12 \div \frac{2}{5} = \frac{12}{1} \times \frac{5}{2} = \frac{60}{2} = 30$$

Answer: 30

MATH FACT

In most problems, Method 1 is easier.

Method 2 is easier when the percent is either

$33\frac{1}{3}\%$ or $66\frac{2}{3}\%$ $\left(\frac{1}{3}\text{ or }\frac{2}{3}\right)$.

EXERCISE 6

<u>**Part A**</u> **Directions:** Using any method you choose, answer these questions.

1. 25% of what number is 33?

2. $14 is 20% of what number?

3. 16 pounds is $66\frac{2}{3}$% of what weight?   **Hint:** $66\frac{2}{3}\% = \frac{2}{3}$

4. $33\frac{1}{3}$% of what number is 80? **Hint:** $33\frac{1}{3}\% = \frac{1}{3}$

<u>**Part B**</u> **Directions:** Solve each problem below.

5. When he bought a new stove, Meyer made a $146 down payment. If this down payment is 25% of the purchase price, what is the cost of the stove?

6. Twenty percent of Julian's monthly paycheck is withheld for taxes. If his employer withholds $480 each month, what is Julian's monthly income?

7. According to the evening newspaper, only 4% of the residents of Glenwood ride the bus more than once each week. If 1,200 Glenwood residents ride the bus more than once each week, how many people live in Glenwood?

8. At Central Community College, 25% of students come from foreign countries. If the number of foreign students is 3,400, how many students in all attend Central?

9. On his credit card this month, Alonzo paid an interest fee of $9.00. This fee is 1.5% of Alonzo's unpaid total charges. Use this information to determine the amount of unpaid charges on Alonzo's card.

10. When she bought a used car, Kylie made a down payment of $750. If the $750 is 15% of the purchase price, what is the purchase price?

11. During the November special election, only 35% of registered voters in Blaine went to the ballot box. If 15,400 votes were cast, how many registered voters live in Blaine?

12. At a going-out-of-business sale, Wendy bought a blouse for $16.20. The blouse was marked 70% off.

    a. What percent of the original price is $16.20?

    b. What was the original price of the blouse?

Answers are on page 831.

Solving Percent Problems by Using Proportions

REMINDER

To review proportions, see Chapter 6.

Another way to remember how to solve each type of percent problem is to write a proportion. The proportion below is easy to remember because when you're working with percents, you can always think of the whole as being divided into 100 equal pieces. Then the ratio of *part to whole* equals the ratio of *percent to 100*.

$$\frac{\text{part}}{\text{whole}} = \frac{\%}{100}$$

Example 1   Find 20% of 34.

    STEP 1   Identify the part, the whole, and the percent.

        part: not given   **whole**: 34   **percent**: 20%

    STEP 2   Write the known values in the proportion. $\dfrac{n}{34} = \dfrac{20}{100}$

        (*n* stands for the unknown **part**)

    STEP 3   Solve the proportion. $100n = 20 \times 34$ or $n = \dfrac{20 \times 34}{100} = 6.8$

    Answer: 6.8

Example 2   What percent of 45 is 18?

    STEP 1   Identify the part, the whole, and the percent.

        part: 18   **whole**: 45   **percent**: not given

    STEP 2   Write the known values in the proportion. $\dfrac{18}{45} = \dfrac{n}{100}$

        (*n* stands for the unknown **percent**)

    STEP 3   Solve the proportion. $45n = 18 \times 100$ or $n = \dfrac{18 \times 100}{45} = 40$

    Answer: 40%

Example 3   75% of what number is 27?

    STEP 1   Identify the part, the whole, and the percent.

        part: 27   **whole**: not given   **percent**: 75%

    STEP 2   Write the known values in the proportion. $\dfrac{27}{n} = \dfrac{75}{100}$

        (*n* stands for the unknown **whole**)

    STEP 3   Solve the proportion. $75n = 27 \times 100$ or $n = \dfrac{27 \times 100}{75} = 36$

    Answer: 36

EXERCISE 7

Directions: Solve each problem below. Use any method you wish.

1. Jordan bought a rug on sale for $156. If this price is 75% of the original price, what was the cost of the rug before the sale?

2. During the month of December, 42% of the babies born at St. Mary's Hospital were girls. If 150 babies were born there during December, how many were girls?

3. Out of Jeffrey's monthly salary of $2,480, his employer withholds $198.40 for state income tax. What percent of Jeffrey's salary is withheld for this tax?

4. During a snowstorm, only 36% of the employees of Amer Electronics Company were able to get to work. If only 90 employees reported to work, how many people work for this company?

5. Grace paid $21.00 for a sweater that normally sells for $35.00.

    a. How much did Grace save by buying this sweater on sale?

    b. What percent of the original price did Grace save?

6. Martina pays $360 each month in rent. However, if she pays on the first of each month, she is given a 3% discount.

    a. How much does Martina save each month by paying on the first of the month?

    b. For how much should Martina write the month's rent check if she pays by the first of the month?

Answers are on page 831.

Percent Review

EXERCISE 8

<u>**Part A**</u> **Directions:** Answer the following questions.

1. Write the percent of the square that is shaded, the percent that is unshaded, and the total of the two percents.

    % shaded _____

    % unshaded _____

    total % _____

2. What percent of $1.00 is the group of coins shown below?

Part B **Directions:** Write each percent as a decimal.

3. 50% _____   82% _____ $66\frac{2}{3}$% _____

Write each percent as a fraction.

4. 40% _____   75% _____ $33\frac{1}{3}$% _____

Part C **Directions:** Find each part.

5. 40% of 60 _____   85% of 200 _____ $66\frac{2}{3}$% of 36 _____

6. In a state with a 7% sales tax, how much sales tax must be paid on a jacket that sells for $64?

7. 32% of the registered voters in Benton County voted to raise property taxes. How many of the 29,000 registered voters in Benton County voted to raise property taxes?

Part D **Directions:** Find each percent.

8. What percent of 80 is 20? _____ What percent of $40 is $15? _____

9. In Antonio's GED class there are 8 men and 12 women. What percent of all the students are men?

10. A suit that normally sells for $300 is on sale for $225. By what percent has the price of the suit been lowered?

Part E **Directions:** Find each whole.

11. 5% of what amount is $2.50?   33 ounces is 75% of what weight?

12. 80% of the students at Roosevelt Elementary School have had chicken pox. If 400 students at Roosevelt have had chicken pox, how many students attend this school?

13. Lam made a down payment of $300 on a new dining room set. This down payment is 40% of the total price. What is the total price?

Answers are on page 831.

CHAPTER 8

Data and Probability

Finding Mean, Median, and Mode

Data is information that is presented in an organized way. Data may be written in a list or table or displayed as a graph, most often a bar graph, a circle graph, or a line graph.

Two characteristics of data are its **typical value** and its **spread**. Typical value can be described by three different measures: **mean**, **median**, and **mode**. The spread in data is described by the **range** of the data.

- The **mean** is the average value of a set of data.
  To find the mean (or average), follow these two steps:

  1) Add the numbers in the set.

  2) Divide the sum by the amount of numbers in the set.

- The **median** is the middle value of a set of numbers put in order.

- The **mode** is the number that occurs most often in a set of data.

- The **range** is the difference between the greatest and least numbers in a set of data.

Examples 1 through 4 are based on the prices shown on the chart below.

Example 1   What is the **mean** (or average) price of a large pepperoni pizza?

STEP 1   Add the five pizza prices:

$16.50
16.00
19.50
18.00
+ 16.00
———
$86.00

Large Pepperoni Pizza Prices	
Luigi's	$16.50
Mia's	$16.00
Pizza Pie	$19.50
Toby R's	$18.00
Pizza Ria	$16.00

STEP 2   Divide the sum by 5.

$17.20 ◄—— mean
5)$86.00 ◄—— sum
▲
└—number in set

Answer: $17.20

Example 2 What is the **median** price of a large pepperoni pizza?

STEP 1 Write the prices in order from least to greatest.

$16.00 $16.00   ($16.50) $18.00 $19.50

STEP 2 Circle the middle price.

Answer: $16.50

Example 3 What is the **mode** of the large pepperoni pizza prices?

Answer = $16.00, the only price that appears more than once

Example 4 What is the **range** of prices of large pepperoni pizzas?

To find the range, subtract the least price from the greatest.

Answer = $19.50 – $16.00 = $3.50

MATH FACT

Not all sets of data have a mode.

Sometimes a set of data may have two or more modes.

EXERCISE 1

<u>Part A</u> **Directions:** Find the mean, median, mode (if there is one), and range in each set of data below.

1.

Soda Sizes	
Small	8 fl oz
Medium	12 fl oz
Large	16 fl oz

Mean: _____

Median: _____

Mode: _____

Range: _____

2.

Student Ages	
Jerry	6
Nicholle	8
Susan	5
Amy	8
Blake	7

Mean: _____

Median: _____

Mode: _____

Range: _____

3.

Popcorn Prices	
Small	$1.00
Medium	$1.50
Large	$2.50
X-Large	$3.50
Tub	$5.00

Mean: _____

Median: _____

Mode: _____

Range: _____

Part B **Directions:** When there is an even number of data values, the median is the average of the two middle values.

4. What is the median of the following four numbers: 3, 4, 5, and 6?

5. What is the median of the following six car prices: $4,000, $5,000, $9,000, $10,500, $12,000, and $14,500?

Part C

Martina kept a tally of the number of students who signed up for an art class each month.

6. What is the mean number of monthly students?

7. What is the median number of monthly students?

March	April	May	June
ЖЖ ЖЖ	ЖЖ ЖЖ	ЖЖ ЖЖ	ЖЖ ЖЖ
ЖЖ IIII	ЖЖ	ЖЖ ЖЖ	ЖЖ ЖЖ
		ЖЖ I	

Answers are on page 831.

Reading a Table

A **table** displays data in labeled **rows** and **columns**.

A row is read from left to right.

Row $1.75 $2.56 $7.50

Read across. ⟶

A column is read from top to bottom.

Column

240   Read
           down.
193

486   ↓

205

MATH FACT

Information is often found in charts and schedules.

Charts are most often used to compare values.

Example: nutrition chart

Schedules are most often used to list the times of events.

Example: train schedule

Below is a nutrition chart for several grains. This chart contains a **title** (Nutrition Values of Selected Grains). Each column has a **label** (Calories, P, C, F). Each row has a label also (Barley, Brown rice, and so on).

Nutritional Values of Selected Grains

Protein (P), Carbohydrate (C), and Fat (F) content of one cup of selected grains. All amounts are given in grams.

	Calories	P	C	F
Barley	936	26	170	5.7
Brown rice	667	14	140	4.3
Millet	660	20	150	5.9
Rye berries	591	21	130	3.9
Wheat berries	578	24	120	4.7

Example 1

How many grams of carbohydrates are contained in one cup of rye berries?

The answer is found at the intersection of the row labeled *Rye berries* and the column labeled *C*.

<u>C</u>

. |Read
. |down.

150↓

Rye berries . . . . 21 ➞ 130

Answer: 130 grams

Example 2

Which of the listed grains has the highest fat content?

Scan down the column labeled *F*. Find the greatest value and read the row label for that value.

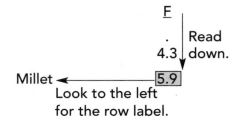

<u>F</u>

. | Read
4.3 ↓ down.

Millet ⟵ 5.9

Look to the left
for the row label.

Answer: Millet

EXERCISE 2

<u>Part A</u> **Directions:** For questions 1–4, refer to the nutrition chart on the previous page.

1. How many carbohydrates are in 1 cup of wheat berries?

2. How many carbohydrates are in 2.5 cups of brown rice?

3. Which of the listed grains has the greatest number of calories?

4. What is the median number of calories per cup for the grains listed?

5. What is the mean (average) number of grams of protein per cup for the grains listed?

<u>Part B</u> **Directions:** Questions 6–10 are based on the chart below.

Nutritional Values of Selected Meats
(Each value is for a six-ounce serving.)

MEAT	Calories (nearest 10)	Protein (g) (nearest 1)	Fat (g) (nearest 1)	Iron (mg) (nearest 0.1)
BEEF				
lean ground	370	47	19	6.0
round steak	440	48	26	5.9
CHICKEN (skinned)				
light meat	280	54	6	2.2
dark meat	300	48	11	2.9
HAM (lean)	460	40	52	5.2
LAMB (lean)	480	43	32	2.9

6. How many milligrams of iron are contained in a six-ounce serving of round steak?

7. How many more grams of fat are contained in six ounces of chicken dark meat than in chicken light meat?

8. What is the median number of calories for six ounces of the meats listed?

9. What is the ratio of the number of calories in lean ham to the number of calories in chicken dark meat?

10. What is the mean (average) number of grams of protein for the six-ounce servings of the meats listed?

Answers are on page 831.

Reading Graphs

Bar Graph

A **bar graph** gets its name from the bars that it uses to show data values. Data bars may be drawn vertically (up and down) or horizontally (across).

The bar graph below has a **title** and **labels** along each **axis**—the side of a graph along which words or numbers are listed. Data value is represented by the height of each bar.

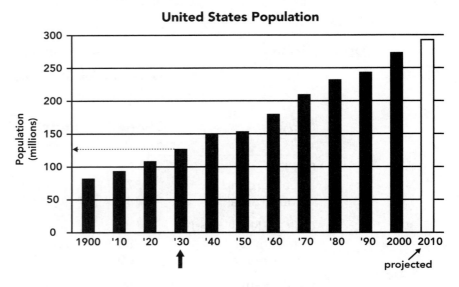

United States Population

Example 1	What was the population of the United States in 1930?
	First, locate the bar that is above the year 1930. A vertical arrow has been drawn to help you.
	Then, from the top of the bar, look to the left until you reach the numbers on the vertical axis. The dotted line on the graph has been drawn to help you.
	As read on this axis, the value of the 1930 population is about halfway between 100 and 150, or about 125 million.
	Answer: About 125 million
Example 2	What is the approximate ratio of the 1960 population of the United States to its population in 1900?
	To compute this ratio, divide the approximate population in 1960 (175) by the approximate population in 1900 (75).

$$\frac{1960 \text{ population}}{1900 \text{ population}} = \frac{175}{75} = \frac{7}{3}$$

Answer $= \frac{7}{3}$ **(7 to 3)**

EXERCISE 3

<u>**Part A**</u> **Directions:** Questions 1–4 refer to the graph on the previous page.

1. By about how many people did the population of the United States increase between the years 1980 and 2000?

2. What is the approximate ratio of the population of the United States in 2000 to the population of the United States in 1900?

3. By about how many people did the population of the United States change each decade (10 years) between 1900 and 2000?

4. What is the population of the United States estimated to become by the year 2010?

<u>**Part B**</u> **Directions:** Questions 5–8 refer to the graph below.

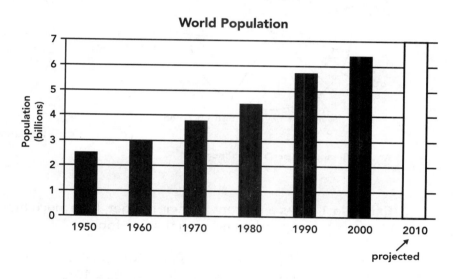

5. By about how many people did the world population increase between the years 1980 and 2000?

6. What is the approximate ratio of the world population in 2000 to the world's population in 1960?

7. What is the median value of the world population for the 6 years shown between 1950 and 2000?

8. What is the world population estimated to become by the year 2010?

Answers are on page 832.

Circle Graph

A **circle graph** displays data as sections (parts) of a divided circle. A circle graph shows how a whole amount is made up of several parts.

Circle graphs usually show data in one of two ways:

- **percents**, where the whole equals 100%
- **cents per dollar,** where the whole equals $1.00

The circle graphs below each have a **title** and a **label** for each section.

Graph A
Johnson Family Budget

clothing 9%
medical care 12%
food 20%
housing 30%
other 8%
savings 6%
transportation 15%

Breakdown per $1.00 of budget

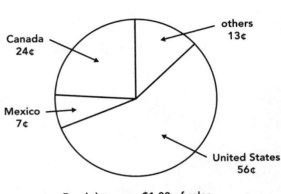

Graph B
Apene Corporation Sales
(total sales: $750,000)

Canada 24¢
others 13¢
Mexico 7¢
United States 56¢

Breakdown per $1.00 of sales

Example 1   As a percent of their budget, how much more do the Johnsons spend on housing than on food?

The answer is found by subtracting the food percent from the housing percent: 30% – 20% = 10%.

Answer: 10%

Example 2   If the Johnson family monthly income is $3,800, what dollar amount do they pay for housing?

The answer is found by computing 30% of $3,800. [0.3 × $3,800]

Answer: $1,140

Example 3 What percent of Apene's sales was made in Canada?

See the segment labeled *Canada*. $0.24 out of each sales dollar means that 24% of all sales were made in Canada.

Answer: 24%

Example 4 What dollar amount of sales was made in Canada?

The dollar amount is obtained by calculating 24% of $750,000—the total sales amount. [0.24 × $750,000]

Answer: $180,000

EXERCISE 4

Part A Directions: Questions 1–2 refer to Graph A on the previous page; questions 3–4 refer to Graph B.

1. As a percent of their budget, how much more do the Johnsons spend on food than on medical care?

2. If the Johnson family monthly income is $3,800, what dollar amount do they pay for medical care?

3. What percent of Apene's sales was made in Mexico?

4. What dollar amount of Apene's sales was made in the United States?

Part B Directions: Questions 5–10 refer to the graph below.

5. According to the graph title, what is the Pyuns' monthly income?

6. Out of each $1.00 of monthly income, how many cents does the Pyun family spend on housing?

7. What percent of their monthly income does the Pyun family spend on housing?

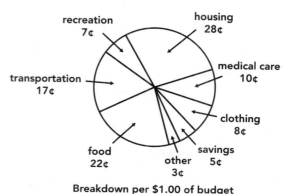

Pyun Family Budget
(monthly income: $3,400)

recreation 7¢
housing 28¢
transportation 17¢
medical care 10¢
clothing 8¢
food 22¢
other 3¢
savings 5¢

Breakdown per $1.00 of budget

8. What total dollar amount does the Pyun family spend on housing each month?

9. What is the ratio of the amount the Pyun family spends on recreation to the amount they spend on medical care?

10. Each month, the Pyun family donates 1.5% of their monthly income to their church. What dollar amount is this each month?

Answers are on page 832.

Line Graph

A **line graph** gets its name from the thin line that is used to connect data points. Because every point on the line has a value, a line graph shows how data changes in a continuous way.

The line graph below has a **title**, **labels** along each **axis**, and 21 **data points**. The value of each point on the line is read as two numbers, one taken from each axis. This graph shows how the height of an average-size girl changes between birth and age 10.

- Height is read along the vertical (up and down) axis.

- The age at which the height occurs is read along the horizontal axis.

- The dotted lines indicate that an average-size 4-year-old girl has a height of about 40 inches.

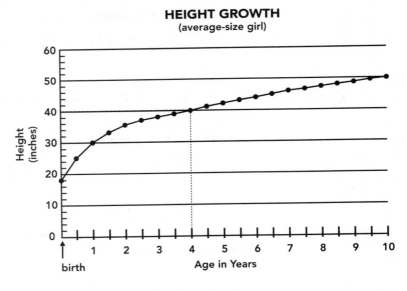

HEIGHT GROWTH
(average-size girl)

<u>**Example 1**</u>   During which year is a girl's height increasing most rapidly?

To answer this question, look at which line is rising most rapidly (is the steepest).

Answer: From birth to age 1

Example 2   What is the approximate ratio of a girl's height at age 10 to her height at age 4?

To compute this ratio, put the approximate height at age 10 over the approximate height at age 4.

Answer: $\dfrac{50 \text{ inches}}{40 \text{ inches}} = \dfrac{5}{4}$

EXERCISE 5

Part A   **Directions:** Questions 1–4 refer to the line graph on the previous page.

1. What is the approximate height of an average-size girl at birth?

2. What is the approximate height of an average-size girl at age 10?

3. At what approximate age does an average-size girl first reach twice her birth height?

4. What is the approximate ratio of a girl's height at age 10 to her height at age 1?

Part B   **Directions:** Questions 5–8 refer to the line graph below.

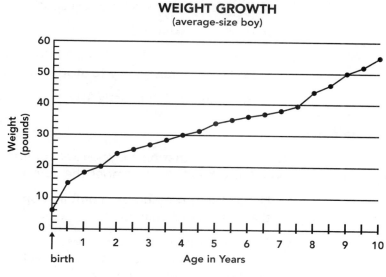

WEIGHT GROWTH
(average-size boy)

5. To the nearest pound, what is the birth weight of an average-size boy?

6. Approximately how much weight does a boy gain between his first and sixth birthdays?

7. What is the approximate ratio of a boy's weight at age 10 to his weight at age 4?

8. What age is an average-size boy when he first reaches 30 pounds of weight?

Answers are on page 832.

Probability

Probability is the study of chance—the likelihood of something happening. Have you heard statements such as these?

"There's a fifty percent chance of snow today."

"There is one chance in five that the Huskies will win."

"Chances are three to one that Marie will show up late!"

The word *chance* indicates our lack of control over what actually happens. Learning about probability helps you answer many questions involving chance.

EXERCISE 6

Part A **Directions:** The pointer on the spinner at the right can stop on either a shaded or an unshaded section.

1. Circle the number that tells the amount of equal-size sections the spinner is divided into.

   2   3   5   8   10

2. Circle the type of section the spinner is most likely to stop on each time it is spun.

   shaded   unshaded

3. Suppose you spin the pointer 20 times. Circle the number of times the pointer is most likely to stop on a shaded section.

   fewer than 10   exactly 10   more than 10

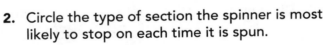

Part B

Brad remembers that his bicycle lock combination has the numbers 3, 7, and 2. But he can't remember the combination!

4. List all the three-number combinations that Brad's lock may have.

5. Circle the phrase that best describes Brad's chance of guessing the correct combination on his first try.

   very likely   equally likely as not likely   not likely

6. Suppose it takes Brad 30 seconds to try each combination. What is the greatest length of time it could take Brad to open the lock by guessing combinations?

Part C

Shelley's son tore the labels off three cans of food. Shelley now knows only that one of the cans contains carrots and that two contain beans.

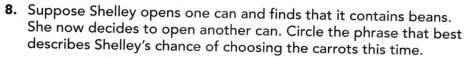

7. Suppose Shelley opens a can without knowing what is in it. Circle the phrase that best describes Shelley's chance of choosing the carrots.

   not very likely   very likely   a sure thing

8. Suppose Shelley opens one can and finds that it contains beans. She now decides to open another can. Circle the phrase that best describes Shelley's chance of choosing the carrots this time.

   1 chance in 1   1 chance in 2   1 chance in 3

9. Suppose Shelley again finds beans in the can. She has now opened two cans that contain beans. She decides to open the remaining can. Circle the phrase that best describes Shelley's chance of choosing the carrots this time.

   not very likely   very likely   a sure thing

Part D

Shauna puts 50 cards in a bag. Each card contains a single number, from 1 to 50. No two cards contain the same number. Suppose you draw a single card without first looking to see what number is on the card.

10. Circle the phrase that best describes your chance of drawing a card that has an even number.

    1 chance in 1   1 chance in 2   1 chance in 3

11. Circle the phrase that best describes your chance of drawing a card that has a number that is divisible by 10.

    not very likely   very likely   a sure thing

12. Circle the type of card you are most likely to draw. A card with a number that is . . .

    divisible by 3   divisible by 4   divisible by 5

Answers are on page 832.

Expressing Probability as a Number

Probability can be given as a fraction, such as 1 in 4, or as a percent.

- a fraction between 0 and 1, such as $\frac{1}{4}$

- a percent between 0% and 100%, such as 25%

Probability tells only the *likelihood of an event happening*; it does not tell for sure what will happen.

The spinner is divided into eight equal sections. On each spin, the pointer is equally likely to stop on any of the eight sections. Assume the pointer will not stop on a line.

Suppose you ask, "What is the probability that the pointer will stop on Green?" How do you answer this question?

In the study of probability, each possible result is called an **outcome**. A particular outcome, such as the pointer landing on Green, is called a **favorable outcome**. The probability of a favorable outcome can be written as a fraction:

$$\text{probability of favorable outcome} = \frac{\text{number of favorable outcomes}}{\text{total number of possible outcomes}}$$

To write probability as percent, change the fraction to a percent.

Example 1   What is the probability that the pointer will stop on Green?

STEP 1   There are 8 sections: 8 possible outcomes. Of the 8, only 1 is the favorable outcome: Green. So, the probability is 1 out of 8 that the pointer will stop on Green.

STEP 2   Write the probability as a fraction.

$$\frac{\text{favorable outcomes}}{\text{possible outcomes}} = \frac{1}{8}$$

Answer: The probability that the pointer will stop on Green is $\frac{1}{8}$, or 12.5%. On the average, only 1 spin in 8 will stop on Green.

Example 2   What is the probability that the pointer will stop on Red?

STEP 1   Of the 8 possible outcomes, 3 are favorable outcomes: Red. So, the probability is 3 out of 8 of the pointer stopping on Red.

STEP 2   Write the probability as a fraction.

$$\frac{\text{favorable outcomes}}{\text{possible outcomes}} = \frac{3}{8}$$

Answer: The probability that the pointer will stop on Red is $\frac{3}{8}$, or 37.5%. On the average, 3 spins in 8 will stop on Red.

EXERCISE 7

Part A   Directions: Write each probability as a fraction and as a percent. Reduce the fraction if possible.

1. a. 3 favorable outcomes out of 4 possible outcomes

_____   _____

b. 4 favorable outcomes out of 8 possible outcomes

_____   _____

c. 4 favorable outcomes out of 6 possible outcomes

_____   _____

Part B   Directions: Refer to the spinner on the previous page. Write each probability as a fraction.

2. What is the probability that the pointer will stop on

a. Green?   **b.** Blue?   **c.** either Green or Blue?

Part C   Directions: Refer to the number cube below. Write each probability as a fraction.

3. On one roll of the number cube, what is the probability that you will roll . . .

a. the number 4?

b. an even number?

c. a number greater than 4?

Part D   Directions: Answer the following questions.

4. When you flip a penny, what is the probability of flipping heads?

5. A deck of playing cards has 52 cards. Of these, 4 are Jacks, 4 are Queens, 4 are Kings, and 4 are Aces.

a. If you draw 1 card, what is the probability that you will draw an Ace?

b. If you draw 1 card, what is the probability that you will draw a face card?
Hint: A face card is any Jack, Queen, or King.

c. If you draw 1 card, what is the probability that you will **not** draw a face card?

Answers are on page 832.

Using Probability for Prediction

Understanding probability can be useful for making predictions. For example, you cannot say with certainty how many 6s will be rolled when you roll a number cube 100 times. However, you can say how many 6s are *most likely*.

- To predict the number of 6s, multiply the number of rolls (100) by the probability of rolling a 6 on each roll.

Example 1   If you roll a number cube 100 times, how many 6s will you most likely roll?

STEP 1   Write the probability of rolling a 6 on one roll.

$$\frac{\text{favorable outcomes}}{\text{total outcomes}} = \frac{1}{6}$$

STEP 2   Multiply 100 by $\frac{1}{6}$.

$$100 \times \frac{1}{6} = \frac{100}{6} = 16\frac{2}{3}$$

Answer: 17 (Round $16\frac{2}{3}$ to 17.)

Example 2   If you flip two pennies 25 times, how many times will you most likely flip heads?

STEP 1   There are four possible results: H-H, H-T, T-H, and T-T. The probability of getting H-H (two heads) is 1 in 4.

$$\frac{\text{favorable outcomes}}{\text{total outcomes}} = \frac{1}{4}$$

STEP 2   Multiply 25 by $\frac{1}{4}$.

$$25 \times \frac{1}{4} = \frac{25}{4} = 6\frac{1}{4}$$

Answer: 6 (Round $6\frac{1}{4}$ to 6.)

EXERCISE 8

Directions: Solve each problem.

1. Suppose you roll a number cube 25 times.

   a. How many 6s will you most likely roll?

   b. How many odd numbers will you most likely roll?

   c. How many numbers greater than 2 will you most likely roll?

2. Suppose you flip two pennies 50 times.

   a. How many times are you most likely to flip two heads?

   b. How many times are you most likely to flip two tails?

   c. How many times are you most likely to flip one head and one tail?

Answers are on page 833.

Data and Probability Review

EXERCISE 9

Part A **Directions:** Solve each problem.

1. Find the mean, median, mode, and range in the list of children's ages at the right.

   mean (average) = _____

   median = _____

   mode = _____

   range = _____

Name	Age
Tonio	12
Armande	8
Carla	13
Brent	12
Ty	11

Questions 2–3 refer to the table at right.

2. What is the median weight of women who are 5 feet 4 inches tall?

3. For which height is the median weight of men equal to 159 pounds?

Median Weight of Adults (pounds)

Height	Women	Men
5'2"	115	124
5'4"	122	133
5'6"	129	142
5'8"	136	151
5'10"	144	159
6'	148	167

Questions 4–6 refer to the graph at right.

4. How many 8th grade students attend Cardin School?

5. In Cardin School, what is the ratio of 8th grade students to 6th grade students?

6. In Cardin School, how many more 6th grade students are there than 7th grade students?

Cardin School Enrollment
Grades 6-8 (500 students)

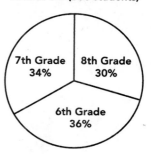

7th Grade 34%
8th Grade 30%
6th Grade 36%

7. Shauna remembers that the last three digits of Zander's phone number are 2, 7, and 8. Unfortunately, she can't remember the correct order of the digits.

555-6 ___ ___ ___

   a. List all possible orders of the three digits.

   b. Circle the phrase that best describes what probability Shauna has at guessing the correct order on her first guess.

    1 chance in 3   1 chance in 4   1 chance in 6

Questions 8–10 refer to the spinner at right.

8. Which number is the spinner most likely to land on each time the pointer is spun?

9. On one spin, what is the probability that the pointer will land on the number 10?

10. If the pointer is spun 25 times, how many times is the pointer most likely to land on 10? Round your answer to the nearest whole number.

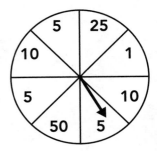

Answers are on page 833.

CHAPTER 9

Basic Algebra

Algebraic Expressions

REMEMBER

Any letter can be used as a variable.

Examples: *x, y, n, s, r, t*

Algebra is a tool that is used to solve many types of math problems. In algebra, a letter called a **variable,** or **unknown,** is used to stand for a number. An **algebraic expression** contains both numbers and variables.

Algebraic expression: $x + 4$

              ⬆——variable

The letter x stands for a number whose value is not given. Without knowing x, you do not know the value of the expression $x + 4$.

An algebraic expression may contain one or more numbers and variables combined by one or more $+$, $-$, $\times$, or $\div$ signs.

Algebraic Expression	Equivalent Word Expression
$x + 4$	x plus 4 *or* 4 added to x
$y - 7$	y minus 7 *or* 7 less than y
$9n$	9 times n *or* n times 9
$\frac{r}{3}$	r divided by 3 *or* one-third r

EXERCISE 1

<u>**Part A**</u>　**Directions:** Write an algebraic expression for each word expression.

1. x plus 9 _____　　r divided by 2 _____

2. n minus 5 _____　　one-fourth z _____

3. 8 times y _____　　5 less than x _____

<u>**Part B**</u>　**Directions:** Write a word expression for each algebraic expression.

4. $x + 5$ _____

5. $n - 8$ _____

6. $\frac{y}{4}$ _____

7. $15r$ _____

Answers are on page 833.

Algebraic Expressions with Word Problems

An important skill in algebra is to be able to represent an unknown amount as an algebraic expression.

Example 1   Julian has 840 stamps in his collection. Next week, he plans to add n more stamps to his total. Write an algebraic expression for the total number of stamps Julian will have after next week.

Answer: 840 + n

Example 2   Three friends decided to equally split the cost of a pizza. Let p stand for the price of the pizza. Write an algebraic expression that tells each friend's share of this price.

Answer: $\frac{p}{3}$ or $p \div 3$

EXERCISE 2

Part A   **Directions:** Choose the algebraic expression that represents the word problem.

1. Delman is now x years old. Which expression tells how old Delman was 5 years ago?

   (a) $x + 5$ **(b)** $x - 5$ **(c)** $5 - x$ **(d)** $5x$ **(e)** $\frac{x}{5}$

2. Barbara, Chris, and Wendy agree to share equally the money they earn on Saturday. If m stands for the amount they earn, which expression tells each person's share?

   (a) $m + 3$ **(b)** $m - 3$ **(c)** $3 - m$ **(d)** $3m$ **(e)** $\frac{m}{3}$

3. The sales tax in Amy's state is 6%. Which expression tells how much sales tax Amy will pay for a sweater that sells for n dollars?

   (a) $n + 0.06$ **(b)** $n - 0.06$ **(c)** $0.06 - n$ **(d)** $0.06n$ **(e)** $\frac{0.06}{n}$

Part B   **Directions:** Write an algebraic expression as indicated.

4. A jacket, normally selling for n dollars, is on sale for 25% off. Write an expression that tells the amount of savings (s) being offered.

5. The ratio of men to women in Jan's art class is 1 to 3. There are 18 women in the class. Write a proportion that can be used to find the number (n) of men in the class.

Answers are on page 833.

Powers and Roots

Bases and Exponents

A **power** is the product of a number multiplied by itself one or more times. For example, *5 to the third power* means $5 \times 5 \times 5$. A power usually is written as a **base** and an **exponent**.

$5 \times 5 \times 5$ is written 5^3 ← exponent

base

The exponent (3) tells how many times to write the base (5) in the product.

- To find the value of a power, multiply and find the total.
- The value of 5^3 is $5 \times 5 \times 5 = 125$.

Product	As a Base and an Exponent	Word Expression	Value
4×4	4^2	4 to the second power *or* 4 squared	16
$3 \times 3 \times 3$	3^3	3 to the third power *or* 3 cubed	27
$10 \times 10 \times 10 \times 10$	10^4	10 to the fourth power	10,000
$\frac{1}{4} \times \frac{1}{4} \times \frac{1}{4}$	$\left(\frac{1}{4}\right)^3$	$\frac{1}{4}$ cubed	$\frac{1}{64}$

Note: A number raised to the second power is *squared*. A number raised to the third power is *cubed*. These are the only two powers that have special names.

EXERCISE 3

Part A **Directions:** Write each product as a base and an exponent.

1. $2 \times 2 =$ $4 \times 4 \times 4 =$ $\frac{1}{2} \times \frac{1}{2} =$

2. $7 \times 7 \times 7 =$ $10 \times 10 =$ $\frac{1}{3} \times \frac{1}{3} \times \frac{1}{3} =$

3. $9 \times 9 \times 9 =$ $3.4 \times 3.4 \times 3.4 =$ $\frac{7}{8} \times \frac{7}{8} \times \frac{7}{8} \times \frac{7}{8} \times \frac{7}{8} =$

Part B **Directions:** Find each value.

4. $6^2 =$ $2^3 =$ $\left(\frac{1}{2}\right)^3 =$

5. $2^4 =$ $1^6 =$ $\left(\frac{3}{4}\right)^3 =$

6. $8^2 =$ $10^3 =$ $\left(\frac{5}{8}\right)^2 =$

Answers are on page 833.

Square Roots

The opposite of squaring a number is finding a **square root**. To find the square root of 36 you ask, "What number times itself equals 36?" The answer is 6 because $6 \times 6 = 36$.

The symbol for square root is $\sqrt{}$. Using symbols, $\sqrt{36} = 6$.

The table below contains the squares of numbers from 1 to 15. The numbers 1, 4, 9, and so on are called **perfect squares** because their square roots are whole numbers.

Table of Perfect Squares				
$1^2 = 1$	$4^2 = 16$	$7^2 = 49$	$10^2 = 100$	$13^2 = 169$
$2^2 = 4$	$5^2 = 25$	$8^2 = 64$	$11^2 = 121$	$14^2 = 196$
$3^2 = 9$	$6^2 = 36$	$9^2 = 81$	$12^2 = 144$	$15^2 = 225$

You can also use the table to find the square roots of the first 15 perfect squares. For example, the square root of 81 is 9 because $9^2 = 81$. Thus, $\sqrt{81} = 9$.

You can also use this table to **estimate** a square root.

Examples $\sqrt{50} \approx 7$ because $50 \approx 49$ and $\sqrt{49} = 7$.

$\sqrt{20} \approx 4.5$ because 20 is about halfway between $\sqrt{16}$ and $\sqrt{25}$.

EXERCISE 4

Part A **Directions:** Use the Table of Perfect Squares to find each square root.

1. $\sqrt{64} =$ $\sqrt{121} =$ $\sqrt{81} =$ $\sqrt{225} =$

2. $\sqrt{25} =$ $\sqrt{100} =$ $\sqrt{9} =$ $\sqrt{1} =$

Part B **Directions:** Use the Table of Perfect Squares to estimate each square root.

3. $\sqrt{10} \approx$ $\sqrt{35} \approx$ $\sqrt{83} \approx$ $\sqrt{218} \approx$

4. $\sqrt{42} \approx$ $\sqrt{110} \approx$ $\sqrt{213} \approx$ $\sqrt{72} \approx$

Answers are on page 833.

Evaluating Algebraic Expressions

MATH FACT

Ways to show multiplication:
$5 \times n$
$5(n)$
$5n$

Ways to show division:
$5 \div n$
$n\overline{)5}$
$\frac{5}{n}$

To **evaluate** (find the value of) an algebraic expression, replace each variable with a number. Then do the indicated operations.

Example 1   Find the value of $x - 2$ when $x = 5$.

   STEP 1   Substitute 5 for x. $x - 2 = 5 - 2$

   STEP 2   Subtract: $5 - 2 = 3$

   Answer: 3

Example 2   Find the value of ab when $a = 60$ and $b = 3$.

   STEP 1   Substitute 60 for a and 3 for b. $ab = 60 \times 3$
             (ab means $a \times b$)

   STEP 2   Multiply: $60 \times 3 = 180$

   Answer: 180

When more than one operation is involved, multiply or divide before adding or subtracting.

Example 3   Find the value of $4x + 5$ when $x = 3$.

   STEP 1   Substitute 3 for x. $4x + 5 = 4(3) + 5$

   STEP 2   Multiply 4 by 3. $= 12 + 5$

   STEP 3   Add 12 and 5. $= 17$

   Answer: 17

EXERCISE 5

Part A   **Directions:** Evaluate each algebraic expression.

   1. $x + 6$ when $x = 4$ $c + \$3.25$ when $c = \$1.25$

   2. ab when $a = 55$ and $b = 6$ $\frac{b}{c}$ when $b = 300$ and $c = 60$

Part B   **Directions:** Find the perimeter (P) of each figure. Perimeter = sum of sides.

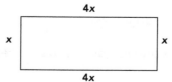

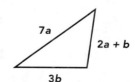

   3. $P =$ _____   **4.** $P =$ _____
       $x = 5$ inches $a = 2$ feet $b = 3$ feet

Becoming Familiar with Equations

An **equation** is a statement that says two quantities are equal. You can write an equation in words or in symbols.

- in words: fifteen minus eight equals seven
- in symbols: $15 - 8 = 7$

Each time you add, subtract, multiply, or divide, you write an equation.

Familiar Equation	In Symbols	In Words
Addition equation	$12 + 5 = 17$	twelve plus five equals seventeen
Subtraction equation	$20 - 14 = 6$	twenty minus fourteen equals six
Multiplication equation	$9 \times 5 = 45$	nine times five equals forty-five
Division equation	$30 \div 6 = 5$	thirty divided by six equals five

In an **algebraic equation**, a **variable** (letter) stands for an unknown number. The variable is often called an **unknown**. Here are examples of the four basic algebraic equations.

Familiar Equation	In Symbols	In Words
Addition equation	$x + 5 = 17$	x plus five equals seventeen
Subtraction equation	$y - 14 = 6$	y minus fourteen equals six
Multiplication equation	$9n = 45$	nine times n equals forty-five
Division equation	$s \div 6 = 5$	s divided by six equals five

EXERCISE 6

Directions: Write each equation in symbols.

1. x minus nineteen equals thirty-one _____

2. r divided by six equals seven _____

3. four times y equals forty-four _____

4. n plus twelve equals twenty _____

5. twenty-seven divided by n equals three _____

Answers are on page 834.

INVERSE OPERATIONS
Subtraction ⟶ Addition
Addition ⟶ Subtraction
Division ⟶ Multiplication
Multiplication ⟶ Division

Solving an Equation

To solve an algebraic equation means to find the value of the unknown that makes the equation a true statement. Each equation you will study in this chapter has only one solution.

Example For what value of x is the equation $x + 5 = 14$ true?

One way to solve a basic algebraic equation is to try different values until you find the solution. A second way is to use an **inverse operation**. An inverse operation undoes an operation and leaves the unknown standing alone.

STEP 1 The equation $x + 5 = 14$ is an addition equation. To undo the addition, subtract 5 from each side of the equation. Subtraction is the inverse of addition.

$x + 5 - 5 = 14 - 5$

STEP 2 Simplify the equation by completing the subtraction.

$x = 14 - 5$ (5 − 5 = 0, leaving x alone on the left side of the equation)

$x = 9$ (14 − 5 = 9)

Answer: x = 9   Notice: **9** + 5 = 14

EXERCISE 7

Directions: Find the solution of each equation with the inverse operation.

1. $x + 6 = 11$

    $x =$ _____

2. $3n = 9$

    $n =$ _____

3. $m + 9 = 10$

    $m =$ _____

4. $2z = 12$

    $z =$ _____

5. $y - 3 = 5$

    $y =$ _____

6. $\frac{r}{5} = 2$

    $r =$ _____

7. $n - 10 = 2$

    $n =$ _____

8. $\frac{t}{3} = 2$

    $t =$ _____

Answers are on page 834.

Checking a Solution

Solving an equation means finding the value that makes the equation a true statement. The **solution** is the value of the unknown that solves the equation.

To check if a value of the unknown is the correct solution, follow these steps:

- First, substitute the value for the unknown into the equation.
- Then do each operation and compare each side of the equation.

Example 1	Is $x = 5$ the solution of	$3x = 12$?
STEP 1	Substitute 5 for x.	$3(5) = 12$?
STEP 2	Multiply. Compare.	$15 = 12$?

Because 15 is **not** equal to 12, $x = 5$ is not the solution of the equation. ($x = 4$)

Example 2	Is $n = 3$ the solution of	$2n + 8 = 14$?
STEP 1	Substitute 3 for n.	$2(3) + 8 = 14$?
STEP 2	Add. Compare.	$6 + 8 = 14$?
		$14 = 14$?

Because 14 is equal to 14, **$n = 3$** is the solution of the equation.

EXERCISE 8

Directions: Check if the suggested value is the solution of the equation. Circle *Yes* if the value is correct, *No* if it is not.

1. $x + 5 = 9$ Try $x = 3$ Yes   No
2. $y - 1 = 8$ Try $y = 10$ Yes   No
3. $3n = 24$ Try $n = 8$ Yes   No
4. $\frac{x}{6} = 3$ Try $x = 24$ Yes   No
5. $y - 5 = 14$ Try $y = 19$ Yes   No
6. $7x = 29$ Try $x = 3$ Yes   No
7. $\frac{n}{4} = 4$ Try $n = 16$ Yes   No
8. $m + 3.5 = 7$ Try $m = 3.5$ Yes   No

Answers are on page 834.

Solving Addition and Subtraction Equations

Addition Equations

To solve an addition equation, subtract the added number from each side of the equation. The unknown will be left alone, and the equation is solved.

<u>Example</u>   Solve for x: $x + 7 = 12$

Subtract 7 from each side of the equal sign. On the left, $7 - 7 = 0$, leaving x alone. On the right, $12 - 7 = 5$

Answer: $x = 5$

Check the answer by substituting 5 for x.

Solve: $x + 7 = 12$
$$x + 7 - 7 = 12 - 7$$
$$x = 5$$

Check: $5 + 7 = 12$
$$\checkmark 12 = 12$$

EXERCISE 9

Directions: Solve each addition equation and check each answer. The first problem in each row is partially completed. Show all work.

1. $x + 6 = 14$ $x + 3 = 9$ $y + 8 = 20$

$$x + 6 - 6 = 14 - 6$$

2. $n + \$2 = \$10$ $y + \$5 = \$15$ $s + \$7 = \$23$

$$n + \$2 - \$2 = \$10 - \$2$$

3. $x + \frac{1}{2} = 4$ $n + \frac{3}{4} = 5$ $y + \frac{1}{3} = \frac{5}{3}$

$$x + \frac{1}{2} - \frac{1}{2} = 4 - \frac{1}{2}$$

4. $x + 3.5 = 8.5$ $n + 3.2 = 4.7$ $y + 5.1 = 14.6$

$$x + 3.5 - 3.5 = 8.5 - 3.5$$

Answers are on page 834.

Subtraction Equations

To solve a subtraction equation, add the number being subtracted to each side of the equals sign. The unknown will be left alone, and the equation is solved.

Example   Solve for x: $x - 8 = 6$

Add 8 to each side of the equal sign.
On the left, $8 - 8 = 0$, leaving x alone.
On the right, $6 + 8 = 14$.

Answer: $x = 14$

Check the answer by substituting 14 for **x**.

Solve: $x - 8 = 6$

$$x + 8 - 8 = 6 + 8$$
$$x = 14$$

Check: $14 - 8 = 6$
$$\checkmark 6 = 6$$

EXERCISE 10

Directions: Solve each subtraction equation and check each answer. The first problem in each row is partially completed. Show all work.

1. $x - 7 = 9$ $y - 3 = 4$ $n - 12 = 5$

    $x + 7 - 7 = 9 + 7$

2. $x - \$5 = \$11$ $x - \$10 = \$30$ $n - \$8 = \$13$

    $y + \$5 - \$5 = \$11 + \$5$

3. $x - \dfrac{2}{3} = 3$ $n - \dfrac{3}{4} = 1$ $y - \dfrac{5}{8} = \dfrac{7}{8}$

    $x + \dfrac{2}{3} - \dfrac{2}{3} = 3 + \dfrac{2}{3}$

4. $y - 2.5 = 4.2$ $n - 1.3 = 5$ $x - 7.4 = 10$

    $n + 2.5 - 2.5 = 4.2 + 2.5$

Answers are on page 834.

Solving Word Problems with Equations

On this page, you'll see how simple algebraic equations can be written for problems you can easily solve without algebra. Practicing algebra skills here, though, is an excellent way to become more confident with the use of equations.

To solve a word problem using algebra, follow these steps:

- First, assign a letter to represent the unknown amount.
- Then write an equation that represents the given information.
- Finally, solve the equation to find the unknown value.

Example   Len sold his bike for $300. He received $240 less than he paid for the bike four years ago. How much did Len pay for the bike?

STEP 1   Let x represent the amount Len paid.

STEP 2   Write an equation: $x - \$240 = \$300$

STEP 3   Solve the equation. $x + \$240 - \$240 = \$300 + \$240$

Add $240 to each side. $x = \$540$

Answer: $540

EXERCISE 11

Directions: Choose the correct equation. Then find the value of the unknown.

1. Barbara paid $35 for a sweater that usually costs $49. Which equation can be used to find s, the amount Barbara saved?

    a) $s - \$35 = \$49$ $s =$ _____

    b) $s - \$49 = \$35$

    c) $s + \$35 = \$49$

2. The temperature in Tucson has risen 31°F to 115°F since noon. Which equation can be used to find t, the temperature at noon?

    a) $t + 115°F = 31°F$ $t =$ _____

    b) $t - 115°F = 31°F$

    c) $t + 31°F = 115°F$

3. Holly spent $5.50 for lunch. She now has $1.25. Which equation can be used to find m, the amount Holly had before lunch?

    a) $m - \$5.50 = \$1.25$ $m =$ _____

    b) $m + \$1.25 = \$5.50$

    c) $m = \$5.50 - \$1.25$

Answers are on page 834.

Solving Multiplication and Division Equations

Multiplication Equations

To solve a multiplication equation, divide the values on each side of the equal sign by the number that multiplies the unknown. The unknown will be left and the equation is solved.

Example   Solve for x: $7x = 35$

Divide the value on each side of the equals sign by 7.

On the left, $\frac{7}{7} = 1$. On the right, $\frac{35}{7} = 5$.

Answer: $x = 5$

Check the answer by substituting 5 for x.

Solve: $7x = 35$

$$\frac{^17x}{7_1} = \frac{35}{7}$$

$$x = 5$$

Check: $7(5) = 35$

$\checkmark 35 = 35$

EXERCISE 12

Directions: Solve each multiplication equation and check each answer. The first problem in each row is partially completed. Show all work.

1. $6x = 36$ $4n = 24$ $3y = 27$ $7s = 28$

   $$\frac{6x}{6} = \frac{36}{6}$$

2. $5n = 45$ $9x = 81$ $7y = 49$ $8y = 128$

   $$\frac{5n}{5} = \frac{45}{5}$$

3. $2x = \$16$ $4x = \$64$ $6n = \$120$ $12y = 96¢$

   $$\frac{2x}{2} = \frac{\$16}{2}$$

4. $4n = 16.8$ $3y = 25.5$ $6x = 50.4$ $14z = 154$

   $$\frac{4n}{4} = \frac{16.8}{4}$$

Answers are on page 834.

Division Equations

To solve a division equation, multiply the values on each side of the equal sign by the number that divides the unknown. The unknown will be left alone, and the equation is solved.

Example Solve for x: $\dfrac{x}{4} = 20$

Multiply the value on each side of the equal sign by 4. On the left, $\frac{1}{4} \times 4 = 1$. On the right, $20 \times 4 = 80$

Answer: $x = 80$

Check the answer by substituting 80 for x.

Solve: $\dfrac{x}{4} = 20$

$\dfrac{x}{4}(4) = 20(4)$

$\boldsymbol{x = 80}$

Check: $\dfrac{80}{4} = 20$

$\checkmark 20 = 20$

EXERCISE 13

Directions: Solve each division equation and check each answer. The first problem in each row is partially completed. Show all work.

1. $\dfrac{y}{4} = 6$ $\dfrac{x}{7} = 10$ $\dfrac{z}{6} = 15$ $\dfrac{s}{9} = 5$

 $\dfrac{y}{4}(4) = 6(4)$

2. $\dfrac{x}{2} = \$12$ $\dfrac{n}{4} = \$8$ $\dfrac{y}{3} = \$11$ $\dfrac{r}{12} = \$1.50$

 $\dfrac{x}{2}(2) = \$12(2)$

3. $\dfrac{y}{3} = 1\frac{1}{2}$ $\dfrac{x}{8} = \frac{3}{4}$ $\dfrac{n}{4} = 6.5$ $\dfrac{m}{2} = 2.75$

 $\dfrac{y}{3}(3) = 1\frac{1}{2}(3)$

Answers are on page 834.

More Word Problems with Equations

On this page, you'll practice using algebraic equations to solve multiplication and division problems.

Example   Lauren lives in a state that has a 6% sales tax. On Sunday she bought a sweater on sale. If she paid a sales tax of $2.64, what was the sale price of the sweater?

STEP 1   Let *s* equal the sale price of the sweater.

STEP 2   Write an equation for *s*: $0.06s = \$2.64$

STEP 3   Solve the equation. $\dfrac{^1\cancel{0.06}}{\cancel{0.06}_1}s = \dfrac{\$2.64}{0.06}$ $s = \$44.00$

Divide each side by 0.06.

Answer: $44.00

EXERCISE 14

Directions: Choose the correct equation. Then find the value of the unknown.

1. If you multiply a number *n* by 8, the product is 176. Which equation below can be used to find *n*?

   a) $176n = 8$ b) $8n = 176$ c) $\dfrac{n}{8} = 176$

   n = _____

2. Three out of every 8 students in Leng's math class also take English. If 24 students in the math class take English, which equation can be used to find the number of students (*n*) in the class?

   a) $\dfrac{3}{8}n = 24$ b) $\dfrac{8}{3}n = 24$ c) $\dfrac{n}{24} = 8$

   n = _____

3. Chris saves $\dfrac{1}{5}$ of his monthly income. If he saves $350 per month, which equation can be used to find his monthly income (*i*)?

   a) $5i = \$350$ b) $i = \$350 \div 5$ c) $\dfrac{1}{5}i = \$350$

   i = _____

4. Yoshi paid a sales tax of $2.94 when she bought a new jacket. If Yoshi paid a 7% sales tax, which equation can be used to find the cost (*c*) of the jacket?

   a) $\dfrac{c}{0.07} = \$2.94$ b) $0.07c = \$2.94$ c) $\$2.94c = 0.07$

   c = _____

Answers are on page 834.

Basic Algebra Review

EXERCISE 15

Part A **Directions:** Write an algebraic expression for each word expression.

1. 9 times x _____   12 divided by n _____

Write a word expression for each algebraic expression.

2. $x + 10$ _____

3. $15y$ _____

Part B **Directions:** Circle the correct answers.

4. Wally, Jon, and Benji split the cost of a pizza. If the total cost of the pizza is c, which expression tells each person's share?

   a) $c + 3$ **b)** $3c$ **c)** $\dfrac{c}{3}$ **d)** $\dfrac{3}{c}$

5. The ratio of girls to boys in Judi's dance class is 4 to 3. If there are n boys in the class, which expression can be used to find the number of girls?

   a) $\dfrac{4}{3}n$ **b)** $\dfrac{3}{4}n$ **c)** $\dfrac{4}{3} + n$ **d)** $n - \dfrac{4}{3}$

Part C **Directions:** Write each product as a base and exponent.

6. $5 \times 5 \times 5 =$ $10 \times 10 =$ $3 \times 3 \times 3 \times 3 \times 3 =$ $\dfrac{1}{3} \times \dfrac{1}{3} \times \dfrac{1}{3} =$

Find each value.

7. $2^4 =$ $10^3 =$ $\left(\dfrac{1}{2}\right)^5 =$ $\sqrt{64}$

Part D **Directions:** Evaluate each expression below.

8. $x + 9$ when $x = 14$ $3n$ when $n = 12$ $c - \$2.50$ when $c = \$5.75$

Part E **Directions:** Circle *Yes* if the suggested value is a solution of the equation. Circle *No* if it is not.

9. $x - 8 = 7$ Try $x = 1$ Yes   No

10. $4x = 24$ Try $x = 6$ Yes   No

Part F **Directions:** Solve each equation. Show each step of your solution.

11. $x + 9 = 21$ $n + \$3 = \$8$ $x + \dfrac{1}{2} = 6$ $y + 2.4 = 6.5$

12. $x - \$7 = \$13$ $x - \$8 = \$21$ $n - \dfrac{3}{4} = 2$ $y - 1.2 = 7.85$

13. $6x = 36$ $4y = \$24.80$ $2n = 5$ $1.2x = 36$

14. $\dfrac{x}{4} = 8$ $\dfrac{x}{3} = \$3.50$ $\dfrac{n}{2} = \dfrac{3}{4}$ $\dfrac{x}{5} = 4.6$

Part G **Directions:** For each problem:
- Write an equation to represent the given information.
- Solve the equation, showing each step of your solution.

15. Lennie saves 5% of his earnings. If he saved \$65 last month, how much money (*m*) did Lennie earn?

    Equation: _____

    Solution: _____

16. One-third of the students in Jane's swimming class are girls. If 9 girls are in the class, how many students (*n*) are in the class?

    Equation: _____

    Solution: _____

Answers are on page 834.

CHAPTER 10

Measurement and Geometry

Units of Measurement

In the United States, two different measuring systems are used: the more familiar **customary system** and the **metric system**. Both systems use the same units of time, but each system has its own units to measure length, capacity, and weight.

Customary Units	Metric Units
Length	
1 foot (ft) = 12 inches (in.)	1 centimeter (cm) = 10 millimeters (mm)
1 yard (yd) = 3 feet = 36 inches	1 meter (m) = 100 centimeters
1 mile (mi) = 1,760 yards = 5,280 feet	1 kilometer (km) = 1,000 meters
Capacity	
1 cup (c) = 8 fluid ounces (fl oz)	1 liter (L) = 1,000 milliliters (mL)
1 pint (pt) = 2 cups	1 kiloliter (kL) = 1,000 liters
1 quart (qt) = 2 pints	
1 gallon (gal) = 4 quarts	
Weight	
1 pound (lb) = 16 ounces (oz)	1 gram (g) = 1,000 milligrams (mg)
1 ton (T) = 2,000 pounds	1 kilogram (kg) = 1,000 grams
	1 metric ton (t) = 1,000 kilograms

Time Both Systems
1 minute (min) = 60 seconds (sec)
1 hour (hr) = 60 minutes
1 day = 24 hours
1 week (wk) = 7 days
1 year (yr) = 365 days

801

Examples   Change 80 inches to feet   Change 3.5 kilograms
                 and inches.   to grams.

STEP 1   Divide 80 by 12. [12 in. = 1 ft] Multiply by 1,000.

                 80 ÷ 12 = 6 with a remainder of 8 [1 kg = 1,000 g]

                                                    3.5 × 1,000 = 3,500

STEP 2   Write the remainder as feet   **Answer: 3,500 grams**
                 and inches.
                 6 r 8 = 6 feet 8 inches

                 Answer: 6 feet 8 inches

TO CHANGE UNITS OF MEASURE

1. Use the table to find the relationship between the two units.

2. To change from a smaller unit to a larger unit, divide.

3. To change from a larger unit to a smaller unit, multiply.

EXERCISE 1

<u>Part A</u> **Directions:** Change from each smaller unit to the larger unit indicated. Three
            are done as examples.

1. 24 in. = ___2___ ft   10 c = _____ pt   24 qt = _____ gal
       $24 ÷ 12 = 2$

2. 180 min = _____ hr   40 mm = _____ cm   2,000 g = _____ kg

3. 50 in. = ___4___ ft ___2___ in.   27 fl oz = _____ c _____ fl oz
       $50 ÷ 12 = 4\ R\ 2$

4. 350 cm = ___3___ m ___50___ cm   6.5 L = _____ L _____ mL
       $350 ÷ 100 = 3\ R\ 50$

Part B **Directions:** Change from each larger unit to the smaller unit indicated. Two are done as examples.

5. 5 ft = <u>_60_</u> in.   3 gal = _____ qt   5 hr = _____ min

$5 \times 12 = 60$

6. 6 lb = _____ oz   3 kg = _____ g   2 yd = _____ ft

7. 2 ft 6 in. = <u>_30_</u> in.   4 lb 7 oz = _____ oz

$2 \times 12 = 24$

$24 + 6 = 30$

8. 2 m 50 cm = _____ cm   2 hr 40 min = _____ min

Answers are on page 835.

Reading an Inch Ruler

The 6-inch ruler is used to measure short distances. However, understanding how to read this ruler is also key to understanding how to measure longer distances when using a yardstick or a tape measure.

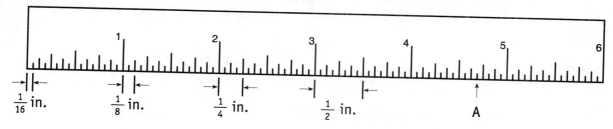

On the ruler, each fraction of an inch is represented by a line of different height. The shortest distance represented is $\frac{1}{16}$ of an inch.

Example   How far is point A from the left end of the ruler?

First notice that point A is between 4 and 5 inches.

Because point A is at a line that represents sixteenths of an inch, count the number of sixteenths from the 4-inch line to point A.

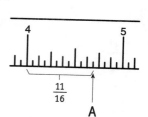

Answer: 4 $\frac{11}{16}$ inches

EXERCISE 2

__Part A__ **Directions:** Write each length as indicated.

1. $\frac{1}{8}$ in. = $\frac{}{16}$ in. $\frac{1}{4}$ in. = $\frac{}{16}$ in. $\frac{1}{2}$ in. = $\frac{}{16}$ in.   1 in. = $\frac{}{16}$ in.

__Part B__ **Directions:** Write each length as a fraction of an inch. Reduce fractions to lowest terms.

a)

_____ inch

b)

_____ inch

c)

_____ inch

d)

_____ inch

__Part C__ **Directions:** Find the length of the pencil to each fraction of an inch as indicated.

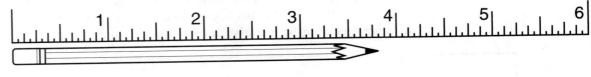

3. nearest $\frac{1}{4}$ inch _____

nearest $\frac{1}{8}$ inch _____

nearest $\frac{1}{16}$ inch _____

Answers are on page 835.

Reading a Centimeter Ruler

In the metric system, short distances are measured on a centimeter ruler. Each centimeter (cm) is divided into 10 millimeters (mm).

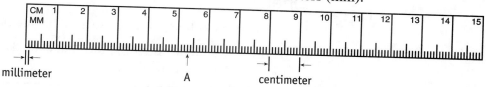

You can read a distance on a centimeter ruler in more than one way.

- as centimeters and millimeters: Point A is read *5 cm 3 mm.*
- as centimeters only: Point A is read *5.3 cm.*

Point A is 5 centimeters and 3 millimeters (5 cm 3 mm) from the left end of the ruler. You also can write 5 cm 3 mm as 5.3 cm *or* as 53 mm.

Example 1   Write 4 cm 9 mm as cm only.

Answer: 4.9 cm

Example 2   Write 6.4 cm as cm and mm.

Answer: 6 cm 4 mm

Example 3   Write 86 mm in two other ways.

Answer: 8.6 cm
8 cm 6 mm

EXERCISE 3

Part A **Directions:** Write each length as indicated.

1. Write 3 cm 9 mm as centimeters only. _____

2. Write 5.6 cm as centimeters and millimeters. _____

3. Write 147 mm as centimeters only. _____

Part B **Directions:** What is the length of each object pictured below?

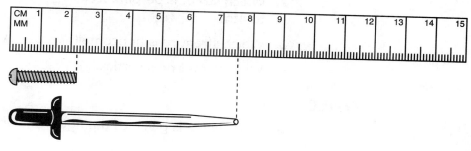

4. bolt: _____ mm or _____ . _____ cm

5. medicine dropper: _____ cm _____ mm or _____ . _____ cm

Geometric Definitions

Lines

Lines and parts of lines form the shapes that are part of our daily lives.

A **line** is a straight path of points that extends in two directions. Arrows indicate that the line extends forever.

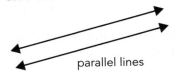

Parallel lines run side by side and never cross.

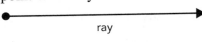

parallel lines

A **ray** is a straight path of points that has only one endpoint. A solid circle identifies the starting point of the ray.

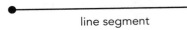

ray

A **line segment** is a straight path of points that has two endpoints. Solid circles indicate that the line stops at endpoints.

line segment

A **vertical line** runs up and down.

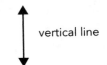

vertical line

A **horizontal line** runs left to right.

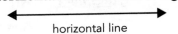

horizontal line

Perpendicular lines cross at a right angle (a corner angle).

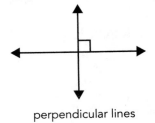

perpendicular lines

EXERCISE 4

<u>**Part A**</u> **Directions:** Questions 1–4 refer to the drawing at right.

1. Which street is parallel to Oak?

2. Which street is perpendicular to 4th?

3. Which street runs horizontally?

4. Which street runs vertically?

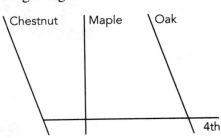

<u>**Part B**</u>

5. What name is given to the figure shown at right?

6. What name is given to figure *MN*?

Answers are on page 835.

Angles

An **angle** is formed by two rays joined at their endpoints. The symbol ∠ is used to indicate an angle.

angle

Joined line segments form the that are sides of figures such as **triangles.** An angle is formed at each point where two sides meet.

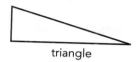

triangle

The measure (size) of an angle is given in **degrees**. The symbol for degrees is °. Degrees can be thought of as parts of a divided circle.

A whole circle contains 360°

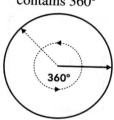

$1°$ is $\frac{1}{360}$ of a circle.

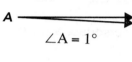

$\angle A = 1°$

$45°$ is $\frac{1}{8}$ of a circle.

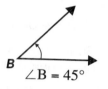

$\angle B = 45°$

$90°$ is $\frac{1}{4}$ of a circle.

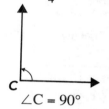

$\angle C = 90°$

An angle is classified by its size. The most common angles are shown below.

Acute Angle

36°

greater than 0° but less than 90°

Right Angle

90°

exactly 90° (The small square indicates a 90° angle.)

Obtuse Angle

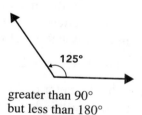

125°

greater than 90° but less than 180°

Straight Angle

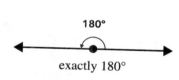

180°

exactly 180°

EXERCISE 5

<u>Part A</u> **Directions:** Name each angle below: acute, right, obtuse, or straight.

1. _____ 2. _____ 3. _____ 4. _____

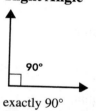

<u>Part B</u>

5. A waiter is cutting a circular pizza into 6 equal slices. At what angle should he cut the sides of each piece?

6. Suppose you want to divide a circle into 10 equal pie-shaped sections. At what angle should you cut the sides of each piece?

Answers are on page 835.

Perimeter and Circumference

GEOMETRIC FIGURES

Square

4 equal sides
4 right angles

Rectangle

2 pairs of equal sides
4 right angles

Triangle

3-sided figure

Circle

The distance around a figure such as a square, a rectangle, or a triangle is called its **perimeter** (P).

• To find the perimeter of a figure, add the lengths of its sides.

Example 1 Find the perimeter of the rectangle shown below.

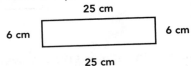

25 cm

6 cm   6 cm

25 cm

Perimeter = 6 + 25 + 6 + 25

Answer: Perimeter = 62 cm

Example 2 Find the perimeter of the square shown at right.

Perimeter = 9 + 9 + 9 + 9
(In a square all four sides are equal.)

Answer: Perimeter = 36 in.

9 in.

The distance around a circle is called its **circumference** (C).

• To find the circumference of a circle, multiply the diameter by π (pi), which is approximately equal to 3.14 or $\frac{22}{7}$.

$$C = \pi \times d \quad \text{or} \quad C = \pi \times 2r$$

Note: The diameter of a circle is equal to twice the radius.

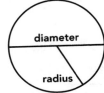

diameter

radius

diameter = distance across

radius = distance from center to edge

Example 3 Find the diameter of the circle shown at right.

Diameter = 2 × radius
       = 2 × 8 = 16

Answer: 16 in.

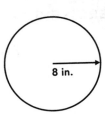

8 in.

Example 4 Find the circumference of the circle in Example 3.

Circumference = π × d
          = 3.14 × 16 = 50.24

Answer: 50.24 in.

EXERCISE 6

Part A **Directions:** Find the perimeter of each figure below.

1. _____

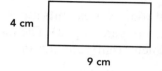

4 cm

9 cm

2. _____

3 ft   7.6 ft

7 ft

3. _____

7 in.   7 in.

7 in.   7 in.

4. _____

1.1 cm

1.1 cm

5. _____

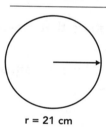

2.3 m   2.3 m

2.3 m   2.3 m

2.3 m

6. _____

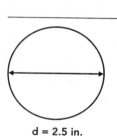

$\frac{3}{4}$ in. $\frac{3}{4}$ in.

$\frac{3}{4}$ in.

Part B **Directions:** Using the formula $C = \pi \times d$ or the formula $C = \pi \times 2r$, find the circumference of each circle below.

7. _____

r = 21 cm

8. _____

d = 2.5 in.

9. _____

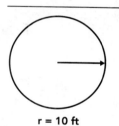

r = 10 ft

Part C

10. Kevin drove a remote-control car around a square track. Each side of the track is 65 feet long. About how many times does the car need to go around the track to go a total distance of 1 mile (5,280 ft)?

11. Allowing 3 feet for a door, how much baseboard will Carlos need to go completely around a rectangular room that is 15 feet long and 9 feet wide?

12. The radius of Earth is about 4,000 miles. What is the approximate distance around Earth at the equator?

Answers are on page 835.

Area

AREA UNIT

1 square foot

1 foot

1 foot

Area (*A*) is a measure of surface. For example, to measure the size of a rug, measure its area—the amount of floor space it covers.

The most common customary area units are the square inch (sq in.), square foot (sq ft), and square yard (sq yd). The most common metric area units are the square centimeter (cm^2) and the square meter (m^2).

The most common shape to find the area of is a **rectangle**. The area of a rectangle is given by the formula $A = l \times w$ where *l* stands for length and *w* stands for width.

- To find the area of a rectangle, multiply length times width.

Example 1 What is the area of a rectangle that is 6 inches long and 4 inches wide?

Answer: Area = *l* × *w* = 6 × 4 = **24 square inches**

The area of a **square** is given by the formula $A = s \times s$ where *s* stands for side.

- To find the area of a square, multiply the side by itself.

Example 2 What is the area of a square that measures 3 feet on each side?

Answer: Area = *s* × *s* = 3 × 3 = **9 square feet**

The area of a **circle** is given by the formula $A = \pi \times r \times r$ where $\pi \times 3.14$ (or $\pi \approx \frac{22}{7}$) and *r* = radius.

- To find the area of a circle, multiply π times the radius times the radius.

Example 3 What is the area of a circular garden that has a radius of 14 feet?

Write $\frac{22}{7}$ for π, and 14 for *r* in the area formula.

$A = \pi \times r \times r \approx \frac{22}{7} \times 14 \times 14 = $ **616**

Answer: 616 square feet

14 ft

MATH FACT

The symbol ≈ means *is about equal to.*

EXERCISE 7

Part A **Directions:** Using the area formula $A = l \times w$, find the area of each rectangle below.

1. _____

2 ft | 4 ft (rectangle)

2. _____

4 in. | 1.5 in. (rectangle)

3. _____

2 cm | 9.5 cm (rectangle)

Part B **Directions:** Using the area formula $A = s \times s$, find the area of each square below.

4. _____

5 m (square)

5. _____

$\frac{1}{2}$ in. (square)

6. _____

3.5 yd (square)

Part C

7. A tablecloth in the shape of a rectangle is 6 feet long and 4 feet wide. What is the area of this tablecloth?

8. A piece of plywood is cut in the shape of a square measuring 4.5 feet on each side. What is the area of this piece of plywood?

9. A circular wading pool has a radius of 7 feet. What is the area of the surface of this pool?

10. A sprinkler sprays water in a circular pattern. The spray reaches a distance of 12 feet from the sprinkler head. **Estimate** the total area of lawn watered by the sprinkler. (**Hint:** Use $\pi \approx 3$ for estimation.)

Answers are on page 835.

Volume

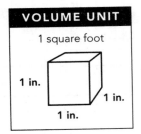

VOLUME UNIT

1 square foot

1 in.
1 in.
1 in.

Volume (*V*) is a measure of the space taken up by a solid object, such as a brick, or a measure of the space enclosed in a freezer, box, or other object.

The most common customary volume units are the cubic inch (cu in.), cubic foot (cu ft), and cubic yard (cu yd). The most common metric volume units are the cubic centimeter (cm^3) and the cubic meter (m^3).

The most common shape to find the volume of is the **rectangular solid**— the math name for familiar shapes such as boxes, suitcases, freezers, and rooms.

The volume of a rectangular solid is given by the formula $V = l \times w \times h$ where *l* stands for length, *w* stands for width, and *h* stands for height.

- To find the volume of a rectangular solid, multiply length times width times height.

Rectangular Solid

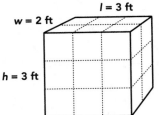

l = 3 ft
w = 2 ft
h = 3 ft

Example 1 What is the volume of a rectangular solid that is 3 feet long, 2 feet wide, and 3 feet high?

Answer: $V = l \times w \times h$
$= 3 \times 2 \times 3$
= **18 cubic feet**

A **cube** is a rectangular solid in which $l = w = h$. All sides of a cube are the same length, and this length is usually represented by *s*.

Example 2 What is the volume of a cube that is 2 meters long on each side?

Answer: $V = l \times w \times h$
$= s \times s \times s$ where *s* is the length of each side
$= 2 \times 2 \times 2$
= **8 cubic meters**

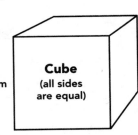

s = 2m

Cube
(all sides are equal)

EXERCISE 8

Part A **Directions:** Using the volume formula $V = l \times w \times h$, find the volume of each rectangular solid below.

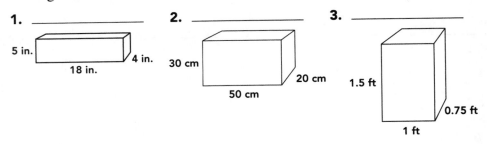

1. _____
5 in.
18 in.
4 in.

2. _____
30 cm
50 cm
20 cm

3. _____
1.5 ft
1 ft
0.75 ft

Part B **Directions:** Using the volume formula $V = s \times s \times s$, find the volume of each cube below.

4. _____

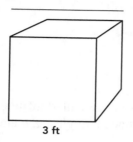

3 ft

5. _____

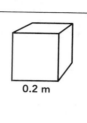

0.2 m

6. _____

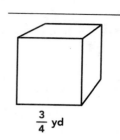

$\frac{3}{4}$ yd

Part C **Directions:** Solve each problem.

7. A contractor is putting dirt in a hole that is in the shape of a cube. If the hole measures 20 yards on an edge, how many cubic yards of dirt does the contractor need?

8. Treasure Toy Company makes plastic blocks for children. The blocks are in the shape of cubes 3 inches on each side. If Tony has 3 blocks, how many cubic inches of space will they take up?

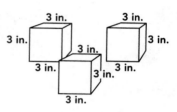

9. A freezer has the following inside dimensions: height = 4 feet; length = 2 feet; depth = 2.5 feet. About how many cubic feet of storage does the freezer have?

Answers are on page 836.

Properties of Angles

Angles can be added to form a larger angle.

- Angles that add up to 90° are called complementary angles.
- Angles that add up to 180° are called supplementary angles.

Complementary Angles

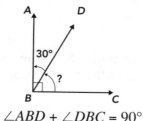

$\angle ABD + \angle DBC = 90°$

$\angle ABD$ and $\angle DBC$ are complementary.

$\angle ABD$ is the complement of $\angle DBC$.

Supplementary Angles

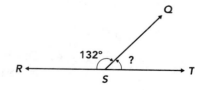

$\angle RSQ + \angle QST = 180°$

$\angle RSQ$ and $\angle QST$ are supplementary.

$\angle RSQ$ is the supplement of $\angle QST$.

Example   Angle *ABC* is a right angle. What is the measure of ∠*DBC* if ∠*ABD* = 30°?

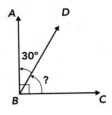

∠*DBC* = 90° − 30° = 60°

Answer: ∠*DBC* = 60°

∠*ABD* + ∠*DBC* = 90°

Angles that share a side are called **adjacent angles**. In the drawing below, there are four pairs of adjacent angles: ∠*a* and ∠*b*; ∠*b* and ∠*c*; ∠*c* and ∠*d*; and ∠*d* and ∠*a*.

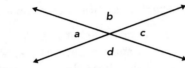

$$\angle a + \angle b = 180° \qquad \angle b + \angle c = 180°$$
$$\angle d + \angle a = 180° \qquad \angle c + \angle d = 180°$$

- Adjacent angles formed by intersecting lines are supplementary.

Angles that are opposite each other are called **vertical angles**. Vertical angles are equal.

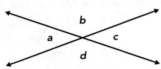

$$\angle a = \angle c \quad \text{and} \quad \angle b = \angle d$$

EXERCISE 9

Part A **Directions:** Find the measure of each angle.

1. ∠*ABD* = _____   **2.** ∠*QST* = _____   **3.** ∠*CBD* = _____

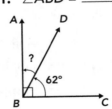 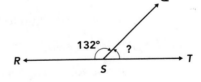 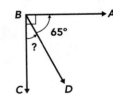

Part B

4. Draw an angle (∠*LMO*) that is complementary to ∠*LMN*.

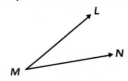

5. Draw an angle (∠*ABD*) that is supplementary to ∠*ABC*.

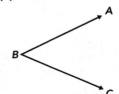

Part C **Directions:** Questions 6–10 refer to the drawing at right.

6. Which angle is vertical to ∠c?

7. Which angle is vertical to ∠d?

8. Name an angle that is supplementary to ∠a.

9. Which angle is not supplementary to ∠a?

10. If ∠b = 130°, what is the measure of each other angle?

∠a = _____   ∠c = _____   ∠d = _____

Answers are on page 836.

Properties of Triangles

Triangles can be drawn in a variety of shapes.

Types of Triangles

Equilateral	Isosceles	Right	Scalene

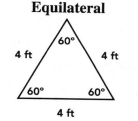

3 equal sides
3 equal angles   2 equal sides
2 equal angles   1 right angle
(90° angle)   No equal sides
No equal angles

IMPORTANT PROPERTIES OF TRIANGLES

- The sum of the three angles of a triangle is 180°.

- In an isosceles or equilateral triangle, equal sides are opposite equal angles.

- In an isosceles or equilateral triangle, equal angles are opposite equal sides.

- The longest side of any triangle is opposite the largest angle.

Example 1   In △ABC, what is the measure of ∠C?

STEP 1   Add ∠A + ∠B: 34° + 62° = 96°

STEP 2   Subtract 96° from 180°:

180° – 96° = 84°

Answer: ∠C = 84°

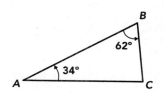

Example 2 Triangle *XYZ* is an isosceles triangle. If ∠*Y* measures 80°, what is the measure of ∠*X*?

STEP 1 Subtract:
180° − 80° = 100°
[∠*X* + ∠*Z* = 100°]

STEP 2 Since ∠*X* = ∠*Z*,
∠*X* = 100° ÷ 2 = 50°

Answer: ∠*X* = 50°

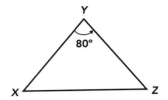

EXERCISE 10

Part A **Directions:** Classify each triangle: equilateral, isosceles, or right.

1. _____ 2. _____ 3. _____ 4. _____

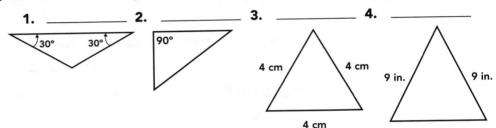

Part B **Directions:** Find the measure of each angle.

5. ∠*B* = _____   6. ∠*D* = _____   7. ∠*Y* = _____   8. ∠*T* = _____

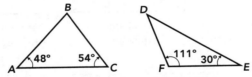 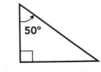 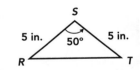

Part C **Directions:** Answer each question.

9. Can a right triangle have two right angles? If so, draw an example.

   yes or no

10. Can a triangle have three acute angles? If so, draw an example.

   yes or no

11. Can a triangle have a straight angle? If so, draw an example.

   yes or no

12. Can a triangle have two obtuse angles? If so, draw an example.

   yes or no

13. Can a triangle have three 60° angles? If so, draw an example.

   yes or no

14. Can a triangle have two 45° angles? If so, draw an example.

   yes or no

Answers are on page 836.

Measurement and Geometry Review

EXERCISE 11

Part A **Directions:** Change each unit as indicated.

1. 48 in. = _____ ft   72 in. = _____ yd

   200 cm = _____ m   32 oz = _____ lb

2. 4 ft = _____ in.   3 lb = _____ oz

   4 qt = _____ c   2.5 hr = _____ min

Part B **Directions:** Write the length represented by each point below each ruler.

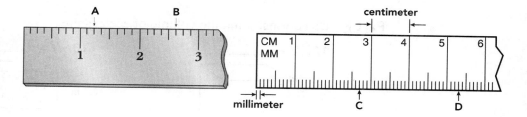

3. Point A: _____   Point B: _____   Point C: _____   Point D: _____

Part C **Directions:** Draw the lines and name the angles below.

4. **a.** Draw a line that is parallel to the line below.

b. Draw a line that is perpendicular to the line below.

5. Name each angle below: acute, right, obtuse, or straight.

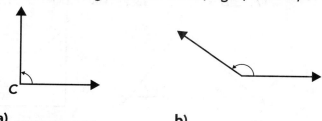

a) _____   b) _____

Part D **Directions:** Find the distance around each figure below.

6. $P =$ _____

11 yd

14 yd

7 yd

7. $P =$ _____

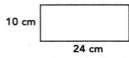

10 cm

24 cm

8. $C =$ _____

$r = 100$ ft

Part E **Directions:** Find the area of each figure.

9. $A =$ _____

8 ft

10. $A =$ _____

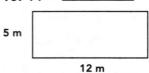

5 m

12 m

11. $A =$ _____

$r = 14$ in.

Part F **Directions:** Find the volume of each figure.

12. $V =$ _____

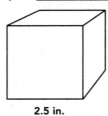

2.5 in.

13. $V =$ _____

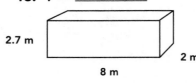

2.7 m

8 m

2 m

Part G **Directions:** Find the measure of each angle.

14. $\angle ABD =$ _____

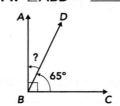

A   D

?

65°

B   C

15. $\angle OMN =$ _____

O

50°   ?

L   M   N

16. $\angle ABD =$ _____

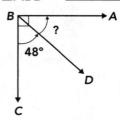

B   A

?

48°

C   D

Part H **Directions:** Find the measure of each angle.

17. $\angle B =$ _____

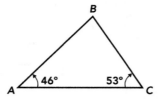

B

46°   53°

A   C

18. $\angle D =$ _____

E

40°

F   D

19. $\angle Y =$ _____

X

8 in.   58°   8 in.

Z   Y

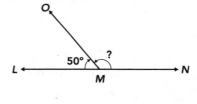

Answers are on page 836.

CHAPTER 1
WHOLE NUMBERS

Exercise 1: Understanding Place Value
(pages 653–654)

Part 1

1. **a.** <u>1</u> ten, <u>7</u> ones   **b.** <u>2</u> tens, <u>8</u> ones
2. **a.** <u>3</u> tens, <u>0</u> ones   **b.** <u>9</u> tens, <u>0</u> ones
3. <u>2</u> hundreds, <u>8</u> tens, <u>3</u> ones
4. <u>5</u> hundreds, <u>0</u> tens, <u>9</u> ones
5. <u>7</u> thousands, <u>0</u> hundreds, <u>5</u> tens, <u>6</u> ones
6. <u>9</u> thousands, <u>8</u> hundreds, <u>4</u> tens, <u>0</u> ones

Part B

7. **a.** 4 tens or 40   **b.** 2 hundreds or 200
8. **a.** 9 tens or 90   **b.** 3 ones or 3
9. **a.** 1 hundred or 100   **b.** 8 tens or 80
10. **a.** 0 tens   **b.** 6 hundreds or 600
11. **a.** 5 ones or 5   **b.** 1 thousand or 1,000
12. **a.** 4 thousand or 4,000 **b.** 0 hundreds

Part C

13. **a.** 4 thousands or 4,000   **b.** 5 thousands or 5,000
14. **a.** 1 ten thousand or 10,000   **b.** 4 tens or 40
15. **a.** 5 thousands or 5,000   **b.** 3 hundreds or 300
16. **a.** 8 ten thousands or 80,000   **b.** 9 thousands or 9,000
17. 1 hundred thousand or 100,000
18. 7 hundred thousands or 700,000
19. 3 hundred thousands or 300,000
20. 5 hundred thousands or 500,000
21. 4 millions or 4,000,000
22. 2 ten millions or 20,000,000
23. 2 hundred millions or 200,000,000
24. 3 hundred millions or 300,000,000

Exercise 2: Reading and Writing Whole Numbers
(pages 655–656)

Part A

1. 86
2. 496
3. 5,472
4. 27,634
5. 329,480
6. 6,418,624
7. 75,200,175
8. 250,500,400

Part B

9. e
10. c
11. b
12. a
13. f
14. d

Part C

15. 4,620
16. 12,275
17. 130,859
18. 2,390,160
19. 25,050,165
20. 425,600,500

Part D

21. one thousand, eighty-eight
22. one hundred eighty-six thousand
23. two hundred thirty-seven thousand, three hundred
24. ninety-two million, nine hundred thousand
25. seven thousand, nine hundred twenty-six
26. twenty-four thousand, eight hundred fifty
27. one hundred three thousand, six hundred eighty

Exercise 3: Adding Whole Numbers (page 658)
Part A
 1. 38, 88, 84, 96, 55, 29
 2. 768, 719, 932, 439, 938, 589

Part B
 3. 55, 72, 60, 104, 125, 64
 4. 336, 978, 528, 509, 1518, 1127
 5. 761, 504, 202, 662, 312, 526
 6. 1333, 1502, 1273, 1200, 1507, 1110

Part C
 7. 39
 8. 8:45 (45 minutes past 8:00)
 9. 4,134
10. $609

Exercise 4: Subtracting Whole Numbers
　　　　　(page 660)
Part A
 1. 8, 31, 34, 50, 63, 31
 2. 120, 314, 212, 201, 611, 111

Part B
 3. 38, 14, 57, 17, 139, 365

Part C
 4. 56, 274, 342, 250, 871, 771

Part D
 5. 4811, 3863, 2850, 6541, 723, 1912

Part E
 6. 558, 766, 599, 53, 587, 188

Exercise 5: Subtracting from Zero (page 661)
 1. 356, 462, 39, 254, 127, 214
 2. 459, 37, 132, 156, 383, 224
 3. 77, 567, 611, 458, 636, 433

Exercise 6: Adding and Subtracting Money
　　　　　(page 662)
 1. $7.58, $2.64, $7.75, $0.25, $9.79, $0.26
 2. $10.52, $2.17, $13.66, $3.90, $27.11, $2.87
 3. $1.15, $2.82, $2.40, $3.51, $7.17, $22.02

Exercise 7: Multiplying Single Digits (page 664)
Part A
 1. 18, 56, 9, 0, 8, 18, 56, 5
 2. 0, 6, 45, 16, 30, 0, 63, 54
 3. 12, 42, 36, 0, 14, 54, 64, 5
 4. 4, 20, 32, 21, 63, 72, 24, 15
 5. 12, 40, 16, 18, 42, 16, 45, 18
 6. 30, 27, 9, 10, 14, 48, 12, 16
 7. 27, 6, 49, 42, 45, 64, 15, 35
 8. 40, 9, 20, 56, 14, 36, 48, 9

Part B
 9. $5 \times 6 = 30$, $7 \times 3 = 21$, $9 \times 8 = 72$, $0 \times 4 = 0$
10. $5 \times 9 = 45$, $8 \times 7 = 56$, $6 \times 7 = 42$

Exercise 8: Multiplying by One-Digit Numbers
　　　　　(page 665)
Part A
 1. 63, 64, 88, 68, 39, 80, 36
 2. 328, 188, 128, 426, 720, 249, 567

Part B
 3. 936, 282, 696, 806, 639, 648, 480
 4. 1293, 2169, 1608, 2884, 1296, 7288, 1890

Exercise 9: Multiplying by Two-Digit Numbers
　　　　　(page 666)
Part A
 1. 682; 690; 480; 1196; 14,280; 12,504; 18,146

Part B
 2. 384; 528; 341; 840; 1517; 18,103; 16,384

Exercise 10: Multiplying and Regrouping (page 668)
Part A
 1. 34, 75, 96, 108, 94, 87
 2. 378, 222, 378, 450, 342, 185

Part B
 3. 535, 824, 921, 4942, 7227, 3654
 4. 1848, 6318, 2015, 7272, 2432, 1521

Part C
 5. 813, 608, 1110, 768, 753, 568
 6. 1928, 1142, 5580, 3227, 3480, 1405

Part D
 7. 252 miles
 8. 1970 calories

Exercise 11: Multiplying Larger Numbers (page 669)

Part A

1. 1892; 2444; 7790; 28,614; 24,534; 40,291

Part B

2. 2368; 4482; 1372; 3792; 1537; 4800

Exercise 12: Multiplying by 10, 100, 1,000 (page 670)

Part A

1. 830; 2400; 9000; 70; 1800; 36,000
2. 2800; 260; 7100; 4,216,000; 3300; 8500

Part B

3. 2072; 3300; 5628; 270; 42,000; 1620
4. 590; 6800; 1152; 25,000; 6675; 470

Exercise 13: Dividing Whole Numbers (pages 671–672)

Part A

1. 9, 7, 7, 6, 8, 8
2. 7, 8, 5, 5, 7, 6
3. 9, 6, 7, 4, 6, 8

Part B

4. 121, 213, 60, 50, 102, 102
5. 306, 309, 102, 106, 107, 102

Part C

6. 1 r 3, 1 r 4, 2 r 1, 2 r 1, 2 r 1, 1 r 5
7. 4 r 3, 4 r 2, 5 r 6, 6 r 7, 7 r 1, 4 r 3
8. 2 r 6, 6 r 7, 4 r 4, 2 r 4, 5 r 2, 4 r 12

Part D

9. **a.** 8 marbles   **b.** 2 marbles
10. **a.** 9 inches   **b.** 3 inches

Exercise 14: Using Long Division (page 673)

Part A

1. 14, 17, 24, 17, 23, 87
2. 18, 15, 13, 17, 12, 15
3. 34, 93, 79, 59, 62, 88

Part B

4. 18 r 3, 13 r 2, 11 r 5, 26 r 1, 52 r 1, 89 r 1
5. 12 r 2, 12 r 5, 18 r 3, 11 r 7, 28 r 1, 27 r 2
6. 94 r 4, 87 r 1, 45 r 2, 98 r 6, 84 r 3, 87 r 1

Exercise 15: Multiplying and Dividing Money (page 674)

Part A

1. $8.84, $18.00, $52.65, $80.00, $87.50, $123.75
2. $16.25, $25.30, $67.50, $750.00, $151.98, $246.25

Part B

3. $2.69, $1.55, $0.60, $2.21, $3.20, $4.34
4. $0.27, $1.05, $2.03, $3.06, $2.02, $4.50

Exercise 16: Multiplication and Division Word Problems (page 675)

1. 48 pounds [4 × 12]
2. $0.79 [$2.37 ÷ 3]
3. 325 sq ft
4. 168 gallons [672 ÷ 4]
5. $523.95 [$24.95 × 21]
6. 7 statues with 2 pounds left over [44 ÷ 6]
7. $475.00 [$12.50 × 38]
8. $39.93 [$239.58 ÷ 6]
9. $756 [$42 × 18]
10. 24 pieces of furniture [$576 ÷ 24]
11. 468 miles [52 × 9]
12. 46 minutes [2,990 ÷ 65]

Exercise 17: Rounding Whole Numbers (page 677)

Part A

1. 60; 200; 2,000
2. 90; 500; 6,000

Part B

3. 70, 80, 20, 40, 100
4. 100, 300, 200, 300, 1000
5. 1,000; 3,000; 5,000; 8,000; 1,000

Part C

6. $2, $25, $12, $7
7. $30, $90, $170, $120

Exercise 18: Estimating with Whole Numbers (page 679)

Part A

Answers will vary. Example answers are given.

1. 150, 290, $14
2. $8, 600, 500
3. 400, 4000, $60
4. 10, 30, 20

Part B

5. **d.** $595.35; estimate: $600
6. **b.** $145.45; estimate: $140
7. **c.** 212; estimate: 200 miles
8. **d.** 11; estimate: 10 counters

Exercise 19: Whole Number Review
(pages 680–682)

Part A

1. 4 thousands, 5 hundreds, 0 tens, 9 ones
2. 7 thousands, 6 hundreds, 4 tens, 0 ones
3. 9 tens or 90
4. 2 hundreds or 200
5. 3 thousands or 3,000
6. 1 ten thousand or 10,000

Part B

7. 3,830
8. 32,575
9. three thousand, four hundred eighty
10. fifty-three thousand, nine hundred eighty-nine

Part C

11. 38, 67, 26, 35, $0.74, $11.40
12. 188, 295, 410, 381, $5.37, $81.30

Part D

13. 11, 14, 8, 18, $0.47, $0.53
14. 85, 79, 199, 67, 318, $2.58

Part E

15. 45, 48, 148, 258, $52.38, $48.40
16. 1,476; 1,166; 1,835; 1,406; 1,776; 43,344

Part F

17. 7, 7, 312, 202, $0.55, $0.72
18. 3 r 7; 65; 18 r 3; 43 r 3; $0.90; $6.62

Part G

19. 70, 50, 10, 90, 40
20. 200, 200, 500, 400, 900
21. 1,000; 3,000; 4,000; 9,000; 1,000

Part H

22. Example estimates: 250; 400; 1,600; 70

CHAPTER 2
USING A CALCULATOR

Exercise 1: Adding Whole Numbers (page 684)
Part A

1. 14, 16, 20, $22
2. 62, 134, 59, $65
3. 948; 6,784; 5,420
4. $1,191; $2,411; $5,150

Part B

5. 765 miles
6. 9,293 tickets

Exercise 2: Subtracting Whole Numbers (page 685)
Part A

1. 7, 8, 5, $5
2. 26, 57, 18, $7
3. 382; 1,307; 514
4. $529; $575; $411

Part B

5. 283 miles
6. 67 inches

Exercise 3: Multiplying Whole Numbers (page 686)
Part A

1. 0, 12, 40, 63
2. 720; 468; 5,073; 1,728
3. 10,400; 21,750; 3,500; 44,100
4. $22.50; $730.40; $1,120.50; $12,535.80

Part B

5. 1,008 hamburgers
6. $28.31
7. $15.19

Exercise 4: Dividing Whole Numbers (page 687)
Part A

1. 4, 3, 11, 0
2. 17, 125, 0, 58
3. 420, 42, 146, 1,354
4. $1.22, $6.46, $4.53, $39.03

Part B

5. 46 miles each hour
6. 13 cards
7. $7.10
8. $890

Exercise 5: Calculator Review (page 688)

Part A
1. 116; 203; 3,760
2. $17.90; $82.11; $6,150

Part B
3. 15, 174, 207
4. $16.53, $5.21, $2.83

Part C
5. 133; 560; 840; 8,748
6. $12.35; $134.40; $284.80; $2,647.50

Part D
7. 356, 77, 579, 84
8. $4.45, $6.58, $8.95, $82.57

Part E
9. 75,980 people
10. $960
11. 16,094 CDs
12. 308 words

CHAPTER 3
SOLVING WORD PROBLEMS

Exercise 1: Understand the Question (page 690)
1. yearly rent
2. weight of 3 gallons of milk
3. total of federal and state tax
4. total number of items
5. mileage from Salem to Oak Ridge
6. number of pets
7. number of girls and boys
8. cost of shoe rental plus cost of bowling four games

Exercise 2: Choose Necessary Information (page 692)
1. 154 pounds, 14 pounds
2. $1.09, 5 pounds
3. 2 inches, 3 inches, 3 inches
4. 8 hours, $4 per hour
5. 147, 172, 165
6. 26,394 and 31,425
7. $0.59, 7 pounds

Exercise 3: Plan the Math (page 694)
1. Student should circle "−".
2. Student should circle "÷".
3. Student should circle "−".
4. Student should circle "−".
5. Student should circle "÷".
6. Student should circle "×".
7. Student should circle "+".
8. Student should circle "×".
9. Student should circle "+".
10. Student should circle "÷".

Exercise 4: Do the Math (pages 695–696)
Any reasonable estimates are acceptable.

1. Estimate: 30 weeks
   Exact Answer: 31 weeks
2. Estimate: $50
   Exact Answer: $49.82
3. Estimate: 40 minutes
   Exact Answer: 41 minutes
4. Estimate: 900 calories
   Exact Answer: 888 calories
5. Estimate: 600 miles
   Exact Answer: 608 miles
6. Estimate: $30
   Exact Answer: $30.21
7. Estimate: $800,000
   Exact Answer: $849,220
8. Estimate: $1,700
   Exact Answer: $1,692
9. Estimate: 850 miles
   Exact Answer: 846 miles
10. Estimate: $6.00
    Exact Answer: $6.11

Exercise 5: Think About Your Answer (page 698)
1. The student is finding the amount of change, not the total cost before tax.
   Estimate: $55   Correct answer: **(4)** $57.40
2. The student is finding the total number of papers delivered on all seven days, not the number delivered Monday through Saturday.
   Estimate: 480   Correct answer: **(4)** 468
3. Student multiplied $0.68 by 15 instead of multiplying $0.68 by 24, which gives the correct answer.
   Estimate: $15   Correct answer: **(4)** $16.32

Exercise 6: Multistep Problems (pages 702–704)
Part A
1. $11.34
2. 862 papers
3. 3 cookies
4. $6.45
5. $71.76
6. 72 tune-ups

Part B
7. labor cost = total charged – cost of parts
$43.75
8. total number of boxes = boxes carried each trip
× number of trips
192 boxes
9. each club's share = total cost ÷ 3
$207
10. total number of balloons = number given away
during April + 245
1,895 balloons
11. total change = $100 – total cost
$17.60
12. total cost of supplies = cost of 17 manuals + $27.50
$171.83

Part C
13. people served = number served Monday–
Thursday + 165
545 people
14. each share = daily rental × 6 ÷ 3
$89.20
15. total miles = 32,540 + miles driven in 1 year
48,740 miles
16. check amount = total cost of purchases + $5
$14.16
17. total number of people who voted
= total number of voters – number of
Republicans – number of Democrats
671 people

Exercise 7: Word Problem Review (pages 704–706)
Part A
1. number of cats and dogs
2. total overtime pay for the week

Part B
3. 147, 172, 165
4. 7, $2.39

Part C
5. key word: total; operation: +
6. key word: change; operation: –
7. key word: Divide; operation: ÷

Part D
Example estimates are given.
8. Estimate: 14,000
Exact Answer: 13,921
9. Estimate: 60 pounds
Exact Answer: 59 pounds
10. Estimate: 65 words per minute
Exact Answer: 72 words per minute
11. Estimate: $7,000
Exact Answer: $8,100

Part E
12. $81.25
13. 1,792 pens

Part F
14. (1) addition: 11:00 A.M.
15. (2) division: $0.05
16. (1) addition: 39°F

CHAPTER 4
DECIMALS

Exercise 1: Writing Dollars and Cents as Decimals
(page 708)
1. $0.35
2. $0.65
3. $0.33
4. $0.32

Exercise 2: Reading and Writing Familiar Decimals
(page 709)
Part A
1. 0.7
2. 0.3
3. 0.9
4. 0.5
5. 0.20
6. 0.64
7. 0.10
8. 0.36
9. 0.300
10. 0.700
11. 0.070

Part B
12. 5 tenths, 8 tenths
13. 9 hundredths, 4 hundredths
14. 25 hundredths, 41 hundredths
15. 5 thousandths, 86 thousandths
16. 2 and 235 thousandths, 3 and 126 thousandths
17. 8 cents, 4 cents

Exercise 3: Reading and Writing Decimals (page 710)
Part A
1. 0.9, 0.5
2. 0.02, 0.07
3. 0.31, 0.29
4. 0.003, 0.005
5. 0.024, 0.065
6. 0.227, 0.375

Part B
7. 2.3, 1.4
8. 5.07, 3.08
9. 6.25, 12.15
10. 1.006, 3.007
11. 3.065, 7.089
12. 9.625, 20.750

Exercise 4: Necessary and Unnecessary 0s (page 711)
1. 0.0̲8, 0.150, 0.0̲09, 5.600, 7.750
2. 0.2̲04, 0.0̲25, 6.0̲20, 0.4̲05, 6.0̲08
3. 5.000, 0.625, 0.0̲70, 1.9̲04, 3.0̲06

Exercise 5: Comparing Decimals (page 712)
Part A
1. <, <, <
2. >, =, >
3. >, <, >
4. <, <, =

Part B
5. 1st Brianne
6. 2nd Sheena
7. 3rd Nadine
8. 4th Cathy
9. 5th Maria

Exercise 6: Rounding Decimals (page 714)
Part A
1. 4 meters, $7.00, 10 centimeters
2. $31.00, 13 kilograms, 24 miles per gallon
3. 18.4 meters, $5.80, 35.8 kilometers
4. $16.50, 20.4 kilograms, $9.80
5. 6.54 meters, $1.48, 8.63 meters
6. 84¢, 10.50 meters, 0.45 inch

Part B
7. 7, 7.4, 7.36
8. 2, 2.1, 2.10
9. 6, 5.6, 5.63

Part C
10. $7.59, $13.59, $4.54, $5.75

Exercise 7: Estimating with Decimals (pages 715–716)
Part A
Any reasonable estimate is acceptable.
1. $10.00
2. 3
3. $110

Part B
4. **b.** $8.96, Estimate: $9.00
5. **d.** 2.94 m, Estimate: 3 m
6. **c.** $31.99, Estimate: $32.00

Exercise 8: Adding Decimals (page 717)
1. 1.3, 1.02, 6.1, $0.98, $6.07
2. 6.725, 4.77, 9.927, 6.542, 6.224
3. 15.525, 12.125

Exercise 9: Subtracting Decimals (page 717)
1. 0.6, 0.29, 0.215, 3.484, 6.52
2. 0.95, 1.92, 0.994

Exercise 10: Multiplying Decimals (page 718)
1. 14, 16.2, 25.4, $2.70, $22.08
2. 19.5, 13.12, 3.123, $14.00, $2.85
3. 18.55, 9.656, 1.92

Exercise 11: Dividing Decimals (page 719)
1. 2.1, 0.71, 0.421, 0.61, 0.102
2. 80, 4, 702, 77.7, 0.23
3. 200, 20, 2000, 20, 600

Exercise 12: Decimal Word Problems (page 720)

1. 4.6°F
2. 4.38 million square miles
3. 210.95 centimeters
4. 0.085 seconds
5. $13.14
6. **a.** 170.4 grams
   b. 454 grams
7. 3.9 centimeters
8. $84.00

Exercise 13: Decimals Review (pages 721–722)
Part A

1. $0.45   3. $0.07
2. $0.55   4. $0.27

Part B

5. 8 tenths, 8 thousandths
6. 12 hundredths, 12 thousandths
7. 0.7, 0.07
8. 0.15, 0.015
9. 0.004, 0.040

Part C

10. >, =, <   **11.** >, >, >

Part D

12. 5, 4.6, 4.64
13. 12, 12.5, 12.49

Part E
14. Example estimates: 22, 2, 300, 15

Part F

15. 10.725, 7.73, 11.495, 10.705, 3.047
16. 0.4, 1.9, 2.55, 0.85, 50.075
17. 41, 24.16, 202.5, 2.5, 3.9
18. 9, 36, 22, 30.1, 20.4

Part G

19. Estimate: $24 Exact: $24.11
    Estimate: $6.00 Exact: $6.22
    Estimate: $160.00 Exact: $174.00
    Estimate: $20.00 Exact: $19.71

CHAPTER 5
FRACTIONS

Exercise 1: Understanding Fractions
    (pages 723–724)
Part A

1. $\frac{4}{5}$ 2. $\frac{1}{6}$ 3. $\frac{1}{4}$ 4. $\frac{3}{5}$

Part B

5. Student should shade any 4 squares.
6. Student should shade first 7 parts.
7. Student should shade 1 of the 3 sections.

Exercise 2: Equivalent Fractions (page 725)
Part A

1. $\frac{1}{3} = \frac{2}{6}$ 2. $\frac{3}{4} = \frac{6}{8}$

Part B

3. $\frac{2}{3} = \frac{6}{9}; \frac{5}{7} = \frac{10}{14}; \frac{3}{4} = \frac{9}{12}; \frac{1}{2} = \frac{4}{8}$
4. $\frac{1}{3} = \frac{3}{9}; \frac{2}{3} = \frac{4}{6}; \frac{3}{4} = \frac{12}{16}; \frac{1}{2} = \frac{6}{12}$

Exercise 3: Reducing Fractions to Lowest Terms
    (page 726)
Part A

1. $\frac{4}{6} = \frac{2}{3}$ 2. $\frac{3}{6} = \frac{1}{2}$

Part B

3. $\frac{6}{8} = \frac{3}{4}; \frac{8}{12} = \frac{2}{3}; \frac{2}{4} = \frac{1}{2}; \frac{14}{16} = \frac{7}{8}$
4. $\frac{4}{6} = \frac{2}{3}; \frac{8}{10} = \frac{4}{5}; \frac{9}{12} = \frac{3}{4}; \frac{4}{8} = \frac{1}{2}$

Exercise 4: Improper Fractions and Mixed
    Numbers (page 727)
Part A

1. $\frac{3}{2}$ 2. $\frac{7}{4}$ 3. $\frac{13}{5}$

Part B

4. $1\frac{1}{2}$ 5. $1\frac{3}{4}$ 6. $2\frac{3}{5}$

Exercise 5: Comparing Fractions (pages 728–729)
Part A

1. <, >, <, =

Part B

2. $\frac{6}{16}, \frac{9}{12}, \frac{4}{10}, \frac{15}{24}$

Part C

3. 2, 4, 6, 8, 10;   3, 6, 9, 12, 15;   4, 8, 12, 16, 20

4. 6, 12, 18, 24, 30;   8, 16, 24, 32, 40;
10, 20, 30, 40, 50

Part D

5. 10, 20, 30
5, 10, 15

8, 16, 24
3, 6, 9, 12, 15, 18, 21, 24

8, 16, 24
6, 12, 18, 24

Part E

6. $\frac{3}{12} < \frac{4}{12}$; $\frac{7}{10} < \frac{8}{10}$; $\frac{15}{24} < \frac{16}{24}$; $\frac{18}{24} < \frac{20}{24}$

Exercise 6: Adding and Subtracting Like Fractions (page 731)

Part A

1. $\frac{2}{4} + \frac{1}{4} = \frac{3}{4}$

2. $\frac{4}{5} + \frac{1}{5} = \frac{5}{5}$

3. $\frac{7}{8} - \frac{2}{8} = \frac{5}{8}$

4. $\frac{7}{8} - \frac{5}{8} = \frac{2}{8}$ (or $\frac{1}{4}$)

Part B

5. $\frac{3}{4}, \frac{3}{10}, \frac{7}{8}, \frac{1}{8}$

Part C

6. $\frac{4}{4} = 1$; $\frac{8}{8} = 1$; $\frac{3}{3} = 1$; $\frac{5}{5} = 1$

Part D

7. $1\frac{1}{4}, 1\frac{1}{5}, 1\frac{3}{8}, 1\frac{2}{4}$ (or $1\frac{1}{2}$)

Part E

8. $\frac{1}{2}, \frac{6}{8}$ (or $\frac{3}{4}$), $\frac{4}{5}, \frac{2}{3}$

Exercise 7: Adding and Subtracting Unlike Fractions (pages 732–733)

Part A

1. $\frac{1}{2} + \frac{1}{6} = \frac{2}{3}$

2. $\frac{3}{4} - \frac{1}{3} = \frac{5}{12}$

3. $\frac{3}{4} + \frac{1}{6} = \frac{11}{12}$

4. $\frac{3}{4} - \frac{2}{8} = \frac{1}{2}$

Part B

5. $\frac{2}{4}, \frac{3}{4}$: $\frac{2}{6}, \frac{3}{6} = \frac{1}{2}$: $\frac{2}{8}, \frac{5}{8}$: $\frac{3}{6}, \frac{2}{6} = \frac{1}{3}$: $\frac{4}{16}, \frac{15}{16}$

6. $\frac{4}{12}, \frac{3}{12}, \frac{7}{12}$: $\frac{12}{15}, \frac{10}{15}, \frac{2}{15}$: $\frac{3}{6}, \frac{2}{6}, \frac{1}{6}$:
$\frac{15}{20}, \frac{8}{20}, \frac{7}{20}$: $\frac{7}{14}, \frac{2}{14}, \frac{9}{14}$

Part C

7. $\frac{1}{4}, \frac{5}{6}, \frac{5}{12}, 1\frac{5}{10} = 1\frac{1}{2}, \frac{7}{8}$

8. $\frac{1}{10}, \frac{19}{20}, \frac{1}{4}, \frac{11}{30}, \frac{3}{8}$

Exercise 8: Adding and Subtracting Mixed Numbers (pages 734–735)

Part A

1. $4, 7\frac{1}{3}, 5\frac{1}{4}, 7\frac{5}{8}, 8\frac{5}{12}$

2. $1\frac{2}{3}, 3\frac{2}{4} = 3\frac{1}{2}, 3\frac{3}{4}, 2\frac{11}{12}, 2\frac{5}{8}$

Part B

3. $1\frac{5}{16}$ inches

4. $\frac{1}{12}$ inch

5. $6\frac{3}{8}$ pounds

6. $\frac{7}{8}$ cup

7. $6\frac{3}{8}$ miles

8. $13\frac{5}{12}$ miles

9. $\frac{15}{16}$ inch

Exercise 9: Multiplying a Fraction by a Fraction (page 737)

Part A

1. $\frac{3}{8}, \frac{1}{6}, \frac{3}{16}, \frac{2}{15}$

2. $\frac{1}{15}, \frac{5}{14}, \frac{4}{15}, \frac{3}{8}$

Part B

3. $\frac{1}{3}, \frac{3}{12} = \frac{1}{4}, \frac{10}{40} = \frac{1}{4}, \frac{2}{20} = \frac{1}{10}$

4. $\frac{1}{4}, \frac{6}{15} = \frac{2}{5}, \frac{4}{14} = \frac{2}{7}, \frac{6}{12} = \frac{1}{2}$

Part C

5. $\frac{5}{32}$ pound

6. $\frac{7}{24}$ mile

7. $\frac{6}{12} = \frac{1}{2}$ pound

Exercise 10: Multiplying Fractions, Whole Numbers, and Mixed Numbers (page 739)

Part A

1. $1\frac{1}{3}, 2\frac{1}{2}, 4\frac{2}{4} = 4\frac{1}{2}, 1\frac{8}{10} = 1\frac{4}{5}$

2. $1\frac{1}{6}, 1\frac{1}{4}, \frac{12}{12} = 1, 3\frac{3}{4}$

Part B

3. $\frac{3}{5}, \frac{2}{3}, 4\frac{3}{8}, 3\frac{3}{4}$

4. $2\frac{1}{4}, 3\frac{1}{3}, \frac{6}{8} = \frac{3}{4}, \frac{24}{4} = 6$

Part C

5. $\frac{2}{3}, \frac{3}{6} = \frac{1}{2}, \frac{21}{12} = 1\frac{9}{12} = 1\frac{3}{4}, \frac{10}{6} = 1\frac{4}{6} = 1\frac{2}{3}$

6. $1\frac{11}{16}, \frac{9}{8} = 1\frac{1}{8}, \frac{27}{32}, \frac{7}{8}$

Part D

7. $14\frac{2}{5}$ ounces

8. 15 pints

Exercise 11: Dividing Fractions (page 741)

1. $1\frac{1}{2}, \frac{8}{9}$

2. $\frac{15}{8} = 1\frac{7}{8}, \frac{30}{5} = 6$

Exercise 12: Dividing Fractions, Whole Numbers, and Mixed Numbers (pages 742–743)

Part A

1. $\frac{2}{1}, \frac{4}{3}, \frac{8}{5}, \frac{3}{2}, \frac{4}{1}$

2. $\frac{4}{5}, \frac{3}{7}, \frac{2}{3}, \frac{3}{5}, \frac{5}{8}$

3. $\frac{1}{3}, \frac{1}{8}, \frac{1}{5}, \frac{1}{2}, \frac{1}{4}$

4. $\frac{4}{7}, \frac{2}{5}, \frac{3}{4}, \frac{4}{13}, \frac{3}{7}$

Part B

5. $1\frac{1}{8}, \frac{4}{3} = 1\frac{1}{3}, \frac{40}{15} = 2\frac{10}{15} = 2\frac{2}{3}, \frac{28}{8} = 3\frac{4}{8} = 3\frac{1}{2}$

6. $\frac{1}{10}, \frac{3}{8}, \frac{10}{24} = \frac{5}{12}, \frac{2}{25}$

7. $\frac{3}{16}, \frac{3}{15} = \frac{1}{5}, \frac{1}{8}, \frac{3}{25}$

8. $2, \frac{15}{8} = 1\frac{7}{8}, \frac{15}{56}, \frac{1}{6}$

Part C

9. 18 patties   12. 30 days

10. 15 forms   13. 6 washers

11. 10 people   14. 7 times

Exercise 13: Fractions Review (pages 743–744)

Part A

1. $\frac{6}{8}$ (or $\frac{3}{4}$)   6. $\frac{1}{4} = \frac{2}{8}$

2. $\frac{4}{6}$ (or $\frac{2}{3}$)   7. $\frac{1}{2}, \frac{2}{3}, \frac{3}{5}, \frac{1}{3}$

3. $\frac{2}{3}$ 8. $\frac{6}{4}$

4. $\frac{2}{5}$ 9. $\frac{13}{8}$

5. $\frac{2}{3} = \frac{4}{6}$ 10. $\frac{11}{5}$

Part B

11. $<, >, >, >$

Part C

12.. $1, \frac{3}{4}, \frac{4}{3} = 1\frac{1}{3}, \frac{17}{12} = 1\frac{5}{12}, 5\frac{9}{8} = 6\frac{1}{8}$

13. $\frac{4}{8} = \frac{1}{2}, \frac{2}{4} = \frac{1}{2}, 1\frac{4}{8} = 1\frac{1}{2}, 3\frac{5}{6}, 2\frac{7}{8}$

14. $\frac{2}{6} = \frac{1}{3}, \frac{3}{8}, \frac{3}{24} = 1\frac{1}{8}, \frac{12}{20} = \frac{3}{5}$

15. $\frac{15}{16}, \frac{15}{16}, \frac{33}{22} = 1\frac{1}{32}, \frac{5}{4} = 1\frac{1}{4}$

16. $\frac{4}{6} = \frac{2}{3}, \frac{2}{3}, \frac{24}{12} = 2, \frac{6}{5} = 1\frac{1}{5}$

17. $\frac{10}{4} = 2\frac{1}{2}, \frac{40}{6} = 6\frac{4}{6} = 6\frac{2}{3}, \frac{6}{12} = \frac{1}{2}, \frac{14}{40} = \frac{7}{20}$

Part D

18. $2\frac{5}{6}$ hours (or 2 hr 50 min)

19. 21 bracelets ($21\frac{1}{3}$ but 21 entire bracelets)

CHAPTER 6

RATIO AND PROPORTION

Exercise 1: Understanding Ratios (page 746)
Part A

1. 1 to 4, 1 to 3, 3 to 4

2. 2 to 1, 4 to 1, 4 to 3

Part B

3. **a.** 4 to 5 (8 to 10)
   b. 5 to 4 (10 to 8)

4. **a.** 7 to 5 (14 to 10)
   b. 5 to 7 (10 to 14)

Part C

5. **a.** 3 to 4
   b. 3 to 7

6. **a.** 1 to 3 (600 to 1800)
   b. 1 to 4 (600 to 2400)

7. **a.** 1 to 2 (8 to 16)
   b. 1 to 3 (8 to 24)

8. **a.** 8 to 7 (16 to 14)
   b. 7 to 15 (14 to 30)

9. 9 to 7

Exercise 2: Working with Rates (pages 747–748)
Part A
1. $1.39 per pound
2. $0.14 per pencil
3. $0.48 per bottle
4. 28.4¢ per ounce

Part B
5. **a.** $7.50 per hour
   b. $187.50
6. **a.** $3\frac{1}{2}$ miles per hour
   b. $52\frac{1}{2}$ miles
7. **a.** 66 beats per minute
   b. 3,960 beats per hour
8. **a.** 20 calories per ounce
   b. 800 calories
9. **a.** 20,000 words
   b. about 167 words per minute
   c. about 1,437 minutes (about 24 hours)

Exercise 3: Understanding Proportions (page 750)
Part A
1. No, Yes, No
2. Yes, No, Yes

Part B
3. $8n = 24$, $16n = 96$, $8x = 24$, $9n = 63$
4. $4x = 8$, $18x = 36$, $3n = 18$, $28x = 84$

Part C
5. $4n = 48$, $n = 12$; $10x = 30$, $x = 3$; $15n = 75$, $n = 5$; $16n = 96$, $n = 6$
6. $16x = 80$, $x = 5$; $3n = 36$, $n = 12$; $18x = 36$, $x = 2$; $30n = 120$, $n = 4$

Exercise 4: Proportions with Word Problems (page 751)
Part A
1. c   2. b   3. a

Part B
4. $306.90
5. **a.** 150 voters
   b. 100 voters

Exercise 5: Ratio and Proportion Review (page 752)
Part A
1. 1 to 2

2. 18 to 31
3. 1 to 3
4. $400 to $1400 (2 to 7)

Part B
5. $1.29 per pound
6. $2.89 per bottle

Part C
7. **a.** $8.75 per hour
   b. $481.25

Part D
8. $4n = 48$, $n = 12$; $18x = 36$, $x = 2$; $14n = 14$, $n = 1$; $24n = 120$, $n = 5$

Part E
9. $5.04
10. 91 miles
11. about 21 drops (≈ 21.4)

CHAPTER 7
PERCENT

Exercise 1: Understanding Percent (pages 754–755)
Part A
1. 41%
2. 80%
3. 34%

Part B
4. 40% shaded, 60% unshaded, total is 100%
5. 36% shaded, 64% unshaded, total is 100%
6. 60% shaded, 40% unshaded, total is 100%
7. 25% shaded, 75% unshaded, total is 100%

Part C
8. **a.** 89%
   b. 11%
9. **a.** 47%
   b. 72%

Exercise 2: Relating Decimals, Fractions, and Percents (pages 756–757)
Part A
1. 0.25, 0.62, 0.84, 0.37, $0.33\frac{1}{3}$

Part B
2. 3, 5, 1, 8, 6

Part C

3. $\frac{1}{2}, \frac{1}{4}, \frac{2}{5}, \frac{3}{4}, \frac{2}{3}$

Part D

4. 5%, 0.05, $\frac{5}{100}$

5. 25%, 0.25, $\frac{25}{100} = \frac{1}{4}$

Part E

6. a. $33\frac{1}{3}$%

   b. $0.33\frac{1}{3}$

   c. $66\frac{2}{3}$%

7. a. $\frac{45}{100} = \frac{9}{20}$

   b. $\frac{55}{100} = \frac{11}{20}$

   c. 0.55

8. a. $\frac{300}{1000} = \frac{3}{10}$

   b. 0.3

   c. 30%

Part F

9. $\frac{1}{8}$, 12.5%, 0.125

10. $\frac{1}{4}$, 25%, 0.25

11. $\frac{1}{3}$, $33\frac{1}{3}$%, $0.33\frac{1}{3}$

12. $\frac{1}{2}$, 50%, 0.5

13. $\frac{2}{3}$, $66\frac{2}{3}$%, $0.66\frac{2}{3}$

14. $\frac{3}{4}$, 75%, 0.75

15. $\frac{3}{4}$, 75%, 0.75

16. $\frac{1}{2}$, 50%, 0.5

17. $\frac{2}{3}$, $66\frac{2}{3}$%, $0.66\frac{2}{3}$

18. $\frac{1}{4}$, 25%, 0.25

19. $\frac{1}{3}$, $33\frac{1}{3}$%, $0.33\frac{1}{3}$

20. $\frac{1}{8}$, 12.5%, 0.125

21. $\frac{1}{4}$, 25%, 0.25

22. $\frac{1}{8}$, 12.5%, 0.125

23. $\frac{1}{3}$, $33\frac{1}{3}$%, $0.33\frac{1}{3}$

24. $\frac{3}{4}$, 75%, 0.75

25. $\frac{2}{3}$, $66\frac{2}{3}$%, $0.66\frac{2}{3}$

26. $\frac{1}{2}$, 50%, 0.5

Exercise 3: Identifying Numbers in a Percent Problem (page 758)

Part A

1. a. 30%
   b. 50
   c. 15

2. a. 75%
   b. $12.00
   c. $9.00

Part B

3. whole

4. percent

Exercise 4: Finding the Part (pages 759–760)

Part A

1. 27, 45, 138, 9

2. $2.00, $0.72, $4.14, $17.50

3. $0.99, $0.52, $1.50, 25

Part B

4. a. $76.00
   b. $114.00

5. a. $2.70
   b. $47.70

6. a. $70.00
   b. $1470

7. a. $8.00
   b. $24.00
   c. $25.68

8. a. 84 people
   b. 65%
   c. 156 people

Exercise 5: Finding the Percent (pages 761–762)

Part A

1. 20%

2. 25%

3. 20%

4. 75%

Part B

5. a. 4 students
   b. 25%

6. a. 32 quarts
   b. 50%

7. a. 80%
   b. 20%

8. 16%

9. 40%

10. a. 31.25%
    b. 68.75%

Exercise 6: Finding the Whole (page 763)
Part A
1. 132
2. $70
3. 24 pounds
4. 240

Part B
5. $584
6. $2,400
7. 30,000 people
8. 13,600 students
9. $600
10. $5,000
11. 44,000 voters
12. a. 30%
    b. $54

Exercise 7: Solving Percent Problems by Using Proportions (page 765)
1. $208
2. 63 babies
3. 8%
4. 250 people
5. a. $14.00
   b. 40%
6. a. $10.80
   b. $349.20

Exercise 8: Percent Review (pages 765–766)

Part A
1. 65% shaded, 35% unshaded, total is 100%
2. 77%

Part B
3. 0.5, 0.82, $0.66\frac{2}{3}$
4. $\frac{40}{100} = \frac{2}{5}, \frac{75}{100} = \frac{3}{4}, \frac{1}{3}$

Part C
5. 24, 170, 24
6. $4.48
7. 9,280 voters

Part D
8. 25%, 37.5%
9. 40%
10. 25%

Part E
11. $50.00, 44 ounces
12. 500 students
13. $750

CHAPTER 8
DATA AND PROBABILITY

Exercise 1: Finding Mean, Median, and Mode (pages 768–769)
Part A
1. Mean: 12 fl oz
   Median: 12 fl oz
   Mode: No mode
   Range: 8 fl oz
2. Mean: 6.8 years
   Median: 7 years
   Mode: 8 years
   Range: 3 years
3. Mean: $2.70
   Median: $2.50
   Mode: No mode
   Range: $4.00

Part B
4. 4.5
5. $9,750

Part C
6. 20 students
7. 19.5 students

Exercise 2: Reading a Table (page 771)
Part A
1. 120 carbohydrates
2. 350 carbohydrates
3. Barley
4. 660 calories
5. 21 grams

Part B
6. 5.9 mg
7. 5 g
8. 405 calories
9. $\frac{32}{15} \left(\frac{640}{300} \right)$
10. 47g

Exercise 3: Bar Graph (pages 773)

The answers in this exercise are estimated. Close estimation should be considered correct.

Part A

1. about 40 million people
2. about $\frac{26}{8}$ or $\frac{13}{4}$ (about 3 to 1)
3. about 20 to 25 million each decade
4. about 290 million people

Part B

5. about 1.8 billion people
6. about 2 to 1
7. about 4 billion people
8. about 7 billion people

Exercise 4: Circle Graph (pages 775–776)

Part A

1. 8%
2. $456
3. 7%
4. $420,000

Part B

5. $3,400
6. 28¢
7. 28%
8. $952
9. $\frac{7}{10}$
10. $51

Exercise 5: Line Graph (page 777)

Part A

1. 18 inches
2. 50 inches
3. about $2\frac{1}{2}$ years
4. a little less than 2 to 1 (5 to 3)

Part B

5. about 6 pounds
6. about 20 pounds
7. a little less than 2 to 1 (55 to 30)
8. about 4 years

Exercise 6: Probability (pages 778–779)

Part A

1. 8
2. unshaded
3. fewer than 10

Part B

4. 237, 273, 327, 372, 723, 732
5. not likely
6. 180 seconds (3 minutes)

Part C

7. not very likely
8. 1 chance in 2
9. a sure thing

Part D

10. 1 chance in 2
11. not very likely
12. divisible by 3

Exercise 7: Expressing Probability as a Number (page 781)

Part A

1. a. $\frac{3}{4}$, 75%

   b. $\frac{4}{8} = \frac{1}{2}$, 50%

   c. $\frac{4}{6} = \frac{2}{3}$, $66\frac{2}{3}$%

Part B

2. a. $\frac{1}{8}$

   b. $\frac{4}{8} = \frac{1}{2}$

   c. $\frac{5}{8}$

Part C

3. a. $\frac{1}{6}$

   b. $\frac{1}{2}\left(\frac{3}{6}\right)$

   c. $\frac{1}{3}\left(\frac{2}{6}\right)$

Part D

4. $\frac{1}{2}$

5. a. $\frac{1}{13}\left(\frac{4}{52}\right)$

   b. $\frac{3}{13}\left(\frac{12}{52}\right)$

   c. $\frac{10}{13}\left(\frac{40}{52}\right)$

Exercise 8: Using Probability for Prediction (page 782)

1. **a.** about 4
   b. about 12 or 13
   c. about 16 or 17
2. **a.** about 12 or 13
   b. about 12 or 13
   c. about 25

Exercise 9: Data and Probability Review (pages 783–784)

1. mean: 11.2 years
   median: 12 years
   mode: 12 years
   range: 5 years
2. 122 pounds
3. 5'10"
4. 150 students
5. 5 to 6 (30 to 36)
6. 10 students (2% of 500)
7. **a.** 278, 287, 728, 782, 827, 872
   b. 1 chance in 6
8. 5
9. $\frac{1}{4}$ (2 out of 8)
10. 6 times

CHAPTER 9

BASIC ALGEBRA

Exercise 1: Algebraic Expressions (page 785)
Part A
There is more than one way to write a correct answer. Example answers are given.

1. $x + 9$, $\frac{r}{2}$
2. $n - 5$, $\frac{z}{4}$ or $\frac{1}{4}z$
3. $8y$, $x - 5$

Part B

4. x plus 5
5. n minus 8
6. y divided by 4 or $\frac{1}{4}y$
7. 15 times r

Exercise 2: Algebraic Expressions with Word Problems (page 786)
Part A

1. **(b)** $x - 5$
2. **(e)** $\frac{m}{3}$
3. **(d)** $0.06n$

Part B

4. $s = 0.25n$
5. $\frac{1}{3} = \frac{n}{18}$

Exercise 3: Bases and Exponents (page 787)
Part A

1. 2^2, 4^3, $\left(\frac{1}{2}\right)^2$
2. 7^3, 10^2, $\left(\frac{1}{3}\right)^3$
3. 9^3, $(3.4)^3$, $\left(\frac{7}{8}\right)^5$

Part B

4. 36, 8, $\frac{1}{8}$
5. 16, 1, $\frac{27}{64}$
6. 64, 1000, $\frac{25}{64}$

Exercise 4: Square Roots (page 788)
Part A

1. 8, 11, 9, 15
2. 5, 10, 3, 1

Part B

3. 3, 6, 9, 15
4. 6.5, 10.5, 14.5, 8.5

Exercise 5: Evaluating Algebraic Expressions (page 789)
Part A

1. 10, $4.50
2. 330, 5

Part B

3. 50 inches (5 + 20 + 5 + 20)
4. 40 feet (14 + 9 + 17)

Exercise 6: Becoming Familiar with Equations (page 790)

1. $x - 19 = 31$
2. $\frac{r}{6} = 7$
3. $4y = 44$
4. $n + 12 = 20$
5. $\frac{27}{n} = 3$

Exercise 7: Solving an Equation (page 791)

1. $x = 5$
2. $n = 3$
3. $m = 1$
4. $z = 6$
5. $y = 8$
6. $r = 10$
7. $n = 12$
8. $t = 6$

Exercise 8: Checking a Solution (page 792)

1. No
2. No
3. Yes
4. No
5. Yes
6. No
7. Yes
8. Yes

Exercise 9: Addition Equations (page 793)

1. $x = 8$, $x = 6$, $y = 12$
2. $n = \$8$, $y = \$10$, $s = \$16$
3. $x = 3\frac{1}{2}$, $n = 4\frac{1}{4}$, $y = \frac{4}{3}$
4. $x = 5$, $n = 1.5$, $y = 9.5$

Exercise 10: Subtraction Equations (page 794)

1. $x = 16$, $y = 7$, $n = 17$
2. $x = \$16$, $x = \$40$, $n = \$21$
3. $x = 3\frac{2}{3}$, $n = 1\frac{3}{4}$, $y = 1\frac{4}{8} = 1\frac{1}{2}$
4. $y = 6.7$, $n = 6.3$, $x = 17.4$

Exercise 11: Solving Word Problems with Equations (page 795)

1. c) $s = \$14$
2. c) $t = 84°F$
3. a) $m = \$6.75$

Exercise 12: Multiplication Equations (page 796)

1. $x = 6$, $n = 6$, $y = 9$, $s = 4$
2. $n = 9$, $x = 9$, $y = 7$, $y = 16$
3. $x = \$8$, $x = \$16$, $n = \$20$, $y = 8¢$
4. $n = 4.2$, $y = 8.5$, $x = 8.4$, $z = 11$

Exercise 13: Division Equations (page 797)

1. $y = 24$, $x = 70$, $z = 90$, $x = 45$
2. $x = \$24$, $n = \$32$, $y = \$33$, $r = \$18.00$
3. $y = 4\frac{1}{2}$, $x = 6$, $n = 26$, $m = 5.5$

Exercise 14: More Word Problem with Equations (× and ÷) (page 798)

1. b) $n = 22$ **3. c)** $i = \$1750$
2. a) $n = 64$ **4. c)** $c = \$42$

Exercise 15: Basic Algebra Review (pages 799-800)

Part A
1. $9 \times x$, $12 \div n$
2. x plus 10
3. 15 times y

Part B
4. c) $\frac{c}{3}$ **5. b)** $\frac{3}{4}n$

Part C
6. 5^3, 10^2, 3^5, $\left(\frac{1}{3}\right)^3$
7. 16, 1000, $\frac{1}{32}$, 8

Part D
8. 23, 36, \$3.25

Part E
9. No   **10.** Yes

Part F
11. $x = 12$, $n = \$5$, $x = 5\frac{1}{2}$, $y = 4.1$
12. $x = \$20$, $x = \$29$, $n = 2\frac{3}{4}$, $y = 9.05$
13. $x = 6$, $y = \$6.20$, $n = 2.5$, $x = 30$
14. $x = 32$, $x = \$10.50$, $n = 1\frac{1}{2}$, $x = 23$

Part G
15. Equation: $0.05m = \$65$
　　　Solution: $m = \frac{\$65}{0.05}$
　　　　　　　$m = \$1300$
16. Equation: $\frac{1}{3}n = 9$
　　　Solution: $n = 9 \times 3$
　　　　　　　$n = 27$

CHAPTER 10
MEASUREMENT AND GEOMETRY

Exercise 1: Units of Measurement (pages 802–803)
Part A
1. 2 ft, 5 pt, 6 gal
2. 3 hr, 4 cm, 2 kg
3. 4 ft 2 in., 3 c 3 fl oz
4. 3 m 50 cm, 6 L 500 mL

Part B
5. 60 in., 12 qt, 300 min
6. 96 oz, 3000 g, 6 ft
7. 30 in., 71 oz
8. 250 cm, 160 min

Exercise 2: Reading an Inch Ruler (page 804)
Part A
1. $\frac{2}{16}$ in., $\frac{4}{16}$ in., $\frac{8}{16}$ in., $\frac{16}{16}$ in.

Part B
2. a) $\frac{7}{8}$ in.   c) $\frac{1}{4}$ in.

   b) $\frac{1}{2}$ in.   d) $\frac{5}{16}$ in.

Part C
3. $3\frac{3}{4}$ in., $3\frac{7}{8}$ in., $3\frac{13}{16}$ in.

Exercise 3: Reading a Centimeter Ruler (page 805)
Part A
1. 3.9 cm
2. 5 cm 6 mm
3. 14.7 cm

Part B
4. 22 mm or 2.2 cm
5. 7 cm 6 mm or 7.6 cm

Exercise 4: Lines (page 806)
Part A
1. Chestnut
2. Maple
3. 4th
4. Maple

Part B
5. ray
6. line segment

Exercise 5: Angles (page 807)
Part A
1. obtuse
2. right
3. straight
4. acute

Part B
5. 60°
6. 36°

Exercise 6: Perimeter and Circumference (page 809)
Part A
1. 26 cm   4. 4.4 cm
2. 17.6 ft   5. 11.5 cm
3. 28 in.   6. $2\frac{1}{4}$ in.

Part B
7. about 132 ft (131.88 ft)
8. about 7.85 in.
9. about 62.8 ft

Part C
10. about 20 or 21 times
11. 45 feet
12. about 25,000 miles

Exercise 7: Area (page 811)
Part A
1. 8 sq ft
2. 6 sq in.
3. 19 cm²

Part B
4. 25 m²
5. $\frac{1}{4}$ sq in.
6. 12.25 sq yd

Part C
7. 24 sq ft
8. 20.25 sq ft
9. about 154 sq ft
10. about 432 sq ft

Exercise 8: Volume (pages 812–813)
Part A
1. 360 cu in.
2. 30,000 cm^3
3. 1.125 cu ft

Part B
4. 27 cu ft
5. 0.008 m^3
6. $\frac{27}{64}$ cu yd

Part C
7. 8,000 cu yd
8. 81 cu in.
9. 20 cu ft

Exercise 9: Properties of Angles (pages 814–815)
Part A
1. 28°
2. 48°
3. 25°

Part B
4. any angle that, together with ∠LMN, is equal to 90°
5. any angle that, together with ∠ABC, is equal to 180°

Part C
6. ∠a
7. ∠b
8. either ∠b or ∠d
9. ∠c
10. ∠a = 50°, ∠c = 50°, ∠d = 130°

Exercise 10: Properties of Triangles (page 816)
Part A
1. isosceles
2. right
3. equilateral
4. isosceles

Part B
5. ∠B = 78°
6. ∠D = 39°
7. ∠Y = 40°
8. ∠T = 65°

Part C
9. No
10. Yes
    Example: a triangle with three 60° angles

11. No
12. No
13. Yes
    Example: an equilateral triangle, each angle having a measure of 60°
14. Yes
    Example: an isosceles triangle in which the third angle is 90°

Exercise 11: Geometry and Measurement Review (pages 817–818)
Part A
1. 4 ft, 2 yd, 2 m, 2 lb
2. 48 in., 48 oz, 16 c, 150 min

Part B
3. Point A: $1\frac{1}{4}$ in.; Point B: $2\frac{5}{8}$ in.; Point C: 2.7 cm; Point D: 5.3 cm

Part C
4. a. Example:

   b. Example:

5. a. right
   b. obtuse

Part D
6. 32 yd
7. 68 cm
8. about 628 ft

Part E
9. 64 sq ft
10. 60 m^2
11. about 616 sq ft

Part F
12. 15.625 cu in.0
13. 43.2 m^3

Part G
14. ∠ABD = 25°
15. ∠OMN = 130°
16. ∠ABD = 42°

Part H
17. ∠B = 81°
18. ∠D = 50°
19. ∠Y = 61°

POSTTESTS

17. What is the setting of the story?

(1) a boy's bedroom
(2) a school
(3) a hospital
(4) a doctor's office
(5) a car

18. What does the title of the story refer to?

(1) Schatz's application to go to school in France
(2) the nine-year-old boy's wait for his father
(3) the boy's wait for a doctor to make a home visit
(4) the boy's wait for his fever to go down
(5) the boy's waiting to die from a fever

19. What is the main conflict, or confusion, in the story?

(1) the father's feeling over possibly losing his son
(2) the doctor's handling of the boy's illness
(3) the boy's thinking a fever over 44 degrees is fatal
(4) the difference between driving miles and kilometers
(5) the boy's lack of interest in the Pirate book

20. What is the connotation (suggested meaning) of the word poor when the father says, "You poor Schatz"?

(1) disbelieving
(2) disgusting
(3) young
(4) pitiful
(5) cowardly

21. What happens at the climax of the story?

(1) The father makes fun of Schatz's mistake.
(2) The boy realizes he's not going to die.
(3) The doctor shakes his head in disbelief.
(4) The pharmacist calls to check on medication.
(5) The boy's school friends call him from France.

22. What happens at the conclusion, or end, of the story?
The boy

(1) drove at seventy miles an hour
(2) broke all thermometers in the house
(3) realized how much he loved his dad
(4) relaxed and cried easily at little things
(5) promised to learn the Celcius temperature system

23. Why did Schatz cry easily the next day?
He was

(1) still very upset
(2) relaxed and relieved
(3) disappointed in his father
(4) still very ill
(5) reacting to medication

24. What is the tone up until the end of the story?

(1) sad
(2) happy
(3) scary
(4) peaceful
(5) light

25. The theme of the story could involve all except

(1) experience

Language Arts, Writing

The Language Arts, Writing Posttest will show you how much you remember about the information you studied in this section. Take the test without looking back for help or answers.

The posttest has been divided into two sections. The first part is a test of your overall knowledge of language skills. The second part is a test of your writing ability. Once you complete the test, check your answers with the Answer Key on page 844. Then fill out the evaluation chart, which tells you which sections of the book you may want to review.

Part I: Language Skills

Directions: Each of the following sentences has an underlined part. Below each sentence are three options for writing the underlined part. Choose the option that makes the sentence correct. The first option is always the same as the underlined part of the original sentence.

1. <u>Both Tom and Jeff wanted to be elected Captain</u> of the community softball team.

    (1) Both Tom and Jeff wanted to be elected Captain
    (2) Both Tom and Jeff wanted to be elected captain
    (3) both Tom and Jeff wanted to be elected captain

2. <u>They</u> have played on the team for five years.

    (1) They
    (2) Them
    (3) Their

3. <u>Their</u> both excellent softball players.

    (1) Their
    (2) Theirs
    (3) They're

4. On Saturday, the <u>players</u> votes were counted.

    (1) players
    (2) players'
    (3) player's

5. The <u>men</u> with the most votes was Jeff.

    (1) men
    (2) mans
    (3) man

6. Jeff will assign <u>they</u> to their positions.

    (1) they
    (2) them
    (3) him

7. The games will be played at <u>Hope Valley park.</u>

    (1) Hope Valley park.
    (2) Hope valley park.
    (3) Hope Valley Park.

POSTTEST

Directions: Only one of the sentences in each of the following groups is punctuated correctly. Circle the number of the correct sentence.

8. **(1)** Terry screamed, "Shut the door."
   (2) Terry screamed, "Shut the door!"
   (3) Terry screamed, Shut the door!

9. **(1)** Sandy, will you please give me a call?
   (2) Sandy will you please give me a call?
   (3) Sandy, will you please give me a call.

10. **(1)** Ms. Popovich a true friend, cooked dinner for me.
    (2) Ms. Popovich a true friend cooked dinner for me.
    (3) Ms. Popovich, a true friend, cooked dinner for me.

11. **(1)** The movers can't get the piano up the stairs.
    (2) The movers cant' get the piano up the stairs.
    (3) The movers cant get the piano up the stairs.

12. **(1)** Science, English math, and literature are important subjects to study.
    (2) Science English math and literature are important subjects to study.
    (3) Science, English, math, and literature are important subjects to study.

Directions: Read the paragraphs below. Choose the <u>one best answer</u> to each of the questions that follow.

Dear Job Seeker:

(A)

(1) As you know, the mission of Job Finders Inc. is to match people with jobs. **(2)** We're a nonprofit organization that helps job seekers identify good employers and prepare for interviews. **(3)** Your receiving this letter because you've used our services in the past six months. **(4)** Time really flies, doesn't it? **(5)** If you've found a job, congratulations! **(6)** If not, we have some great news for you.

(B)

(7) Two new companies are opening branches in our region. **(8)** Both offer many opportunities for local workers. **(9)** Nanotech, the microchip manufacturer, is opening a new plant here. **(10)** It expected to hire 2,500 workers the first year. **(11)** Nanotech needs line workers as well as clerical and maintenance staff. **(12)** If you'd like help putting together a resumé, make an appointment with one of our professional resumé writers. **(13)** Elder Care is an assisted-living chain that is expanding into our area with five new homes for 30 residents each. **(14)** Each Elder Care home will be hiring nurses' aides, orderlies, and needs cafeteria staffers. **(15)** Job Finders is here to support you as you apply for work. **(16)** If you'd like to practice interviewing, we'll videotape a mock interview and go over it with you careful. **(17)** Remember, our services are free. **(18)** Call Job Finders at (123) 555-4321, if there's anything we can do for you.

Sincerely,

Adele Esquival, Director

13. Which revision should be made to sentence 3?

(1) Your receiving this letter because you've used our services in the past six months.
(2) You're receiving this letter because you've used our services in the past six months.
(3) Your receiving this letter because you will use our services in the past six months.

14. Which revision would make sentence 4 more effective?

(1) move sentence 4 to follow sentence 6
(2) start a new paragraph with sentence 4
(3) remove sentence 4

15. Which revision should be made to sentence 10?

(1) It expected to hire 2,500 workers the first year.
(2) It expects to hire 2,500 workers the first year.
(3) It will expect to hire 2,500 workers the first year.

16. Which revision would make sentence 12 more effective?

(1) move sentence 12 to follow sentence 15
(2) remove sentence 12
(3) start a new paragraph with sentence 12

17. Which revision should be made to sentence 14?

(1) Each Elder Care home will be hiring nurses' aides, orderlies, and needs cafeteria staffers.
(2) Each Elder Care home will be hiring nurses' aides orderlies, and needs cafeteria staffers.
(3) Each Elder Care home will be hiring nurses' aides, orderlies, and cafeteria staffers.

18. Which revision would make paragraph B more effective?

(1) Start a new paragraph with sentence 12
(2) Start a new paragraph with sentence 15
(3) Start a new paragraph with sentence 17

19. Which revision should be made to sentence 16?

(1) If you'd like to practice interviewing, we'll videotape a mock interview and go over it with you careful.
(2) If you'd like to practice interviewing, we'll videotape a mock interview and go over it with you carefully.
(3) If you'd like to practice interviewing we'll videotape a mock interview and go over it with you careful.

20. Which revision should be made to sentence 18?

(1) Call Job Finders at (123) 555-4321, if there's anything we can do for you.
(2) Call Job Finders at (123) 555-4321, if there's anything we can do for you?
(3) Call Job Finders at (123) 555-4321 if there's anything we can do for you.

Directions: Each of the following sentences has an underlined part. Below each sentence are three options for writing the underlined part. Choose the option that makes the sentence correct. The first option is always the same as the underlined part of the original sentence.

21. The rain lasted for three <u>days, but</u> the rivers were flooded.

    (1) days, but
    (2) days; so
    (3) days, so

22. The fish <u>are frying in the pan that we caught at the lake.</u>

    (1) are frying in the pan that we caught at the lake.
    (2) that we caught at the lake are frying in the pan.
    (3) are frying in the lake that we caught in the pan.

23. The nurse smelled <u>smoke, however, she</u> called for help.

    (1) smoke, however, she
    (2) smoke; however, she
    (3) smoke; consequently, she

24. The president talked, laughed, and <u>he was joking.</u>

    (1) he was joking.
    (2) he joked.
    (3) joked.

25. <u>Sally bumped into the table walking across the room.</u>

    (1) Sally bumped into the table walking across the room.
    (2) Walking across the room, Sally bumped into the table.
    (3) Walking across the room, the table bumped into Sally.

26. When the curtain <u>fell the</u> audience cheered.

    (1) fell the
    (2) fell; the
    (3) fell, the

27. Farhad wants his family to come to the United <u>States; therefore, he</u> is saving money for their tickets.

    (1) States; therefore, he
    (2) States; instead, he
    (3) States; nevertheless, he

28. Jennifer can take the <u>job if, she</u> buys a car.

    (1) job if, she
    (2) job, if she
    (3) job if she

29. Norma is <u>tired, but</u> she is still working.

    (1) tired, but
    (2) tired, so
    (3) tired, before

Directions: Underline the correct form of the verb to complete each sentence.

30. The students in the class (are, is) happy with their grades.

31. Your advice (were, was) what saved our garden.

32. Next week, Jim (will race, raced) in the track meet.

33. The manager (plan, plans) to quit her job after payday.

34. The strength of these workers (make, makes) any job easy.

35. Last night, Sheila (announces, announced) her engagement.

POSTTEST

36. Bill or I (drive, drives) the car pool every Wednesday.

37. Right now Uncle Ray (is standing, was standing) on his head.

38. You (have, has) to tell Bruce the truth.

39. My uncles (tell, tells) terrible jokes.

40. (Is, Are) everybody here?

Part II: Writing a Paragraph

Directions: This part of the Posttest will give you a chance to demonstrate how well you write. Pick one of the three suggested topics and write a well-developed paragraph. *Prewrite* by gathering and organizing your ideas through brainstorming or idea mapping. Write a topic sentence that states your main idea. Then *write*, concentrating on the content of what you're saying. When you finish writing, *revise*. Go back and reread what you have written. Check that you have used the information you learned about writing paragraphs. Also check spelling, capitalization, punctuation, and sentence structure. Then make any needed changes.

Topic 1
Think of a person you admire—a close friend, a coworker, a parent, or any person you respect. In a paragraph, explain why you admire that person. What things about him or her do you respect most?

Topic 2
Imagine what your perfect job would be like. Where would you work? What would you do? Describe your perfect job in a paragraph with lots of details.

Topic 3
Almost all of us have a good story to tell, whether it is about ourselves or someone else. It could be sweet or sad, silly or serious, or some of each. Write a paragraph telling your story.

Answers are on page 844.

Language Arts, Writing Answer Key

PART I: LANGUAGE SKILLS

1. (2) The noun *captain* should not be capitalized because it is not used as a person's title. *Both* should be capitalized as the first word in the sentence.

2. (1) No correction is necessary.

3. (3) If you substitute the contraction *They are* in the sentence, it makes sense.

4. (2) The plural noun must be made possessive.

5. (3) Only one man could have received the most votes.

6. (2) The object pronoun must be used because it is not the subject of the sentence. The pronoun must be plural to agree with *their*.

7. (3) All three words should be capitalized to show that this is the specific name of the park.

8. (2) This sentence contains a direct quote that shows strong emotion, so it takes an exclamation point inside the quotation marks.

9. (1) This sentence is a question. The name *Sandy* is used in direct address and must be set off with a comma.

10. (3) The renaming phrase *a true friend* must be set off by commas.

11. (1) The apostrophe takes the place of the missing letters when the word *cannot* is made into a contraction.

12. (3) Commas must be placed after every item in a series except the last one.

13. (2) *Your* is a possessive pronoun. The sentence needs the contraction for *you are*.

14. (3) Sentence 4 has nothing to do with the paragraph.

15. (2) *This year* is the time clue that tells you the verb should be in the present tense.

16. (1) Sentences 7–14 are about the two companies; sentences 15–18 are about the services Job Finders offers. Sentence 12 belongs with the services. See the answer to question 38 for more on how to fix paragraph B.

17. (3) The items in the sentence need to have parallel structure.

18. (2) Sentences 7–14 are about the two companies; sentences 15–18 are about the services Job Finders offers. These are two separate topics that need two separate paragraphs.

19. (2) Because it modifies the verb *go*, the modifier must be an adverb: *carefully*.

20. (3) When the clause with the subordinating conjunction *if* comes at the end of a sentence, it is not separated by a comma.

21. (3) The conjunction *so* shows that the first part of the sentence caused the second part. Note also the correct punctuation before this conjunction: a comma.

22. (2) The original sentence says that we caught the pan at the lake. The describing phrase *that we caught at the lake* should be placed next to *fish*.

23. (3) The connector *consequently* shows that the first part of the sentence caused the second part. Note also the correct punctuation for this connector.

24. (3) For parallel structure, the items *talked*, *laughed*, and *joked* must be in the same form.

25. (2) The original sentence says that the table was walking across room. The describing phrase *walking across the room* must be placed next to *Sally*.

26. (3) When a subordinating conjunction comes first in a sentence, the two ideas in the sentence are separated by a comma.

POSTTEST

27. (1) No correction is necessary.

28. (3) No comma is needed when the subordinating conjunction comes in the middle of the sentence.

29. (1) No correction is necessary.

30. are The verb must agree with the plural subject *students*.

31. was The subject, *advice*, is singular.

32. will race The time clue *Next week* tells you to use the future tense.

33. plans The subject, *manager*, is singular.

34. makes The subject is *strength*, a singular noun, not *workers*.

35. announced The time clue *Last night* tells you to use the past tense.

36. drive The two parts of the subject are joined by *or*. The verb must agree with the closer part of the subject, *I*.

37. is standing The time clue *Right now* tells you to use the present continuous tense.

38. have Use *have* to agree with *You*.

39. tell The subject, *uncles*, is plural.

40. Is This verb form agrees with the singular indefinite pronoun *everybody*.

PART II: WRITING A PARAGRAPH

In this part of the Posttest, you were asked to write a paragraph on your own. If possible, have an instructor work with you to evaluate your paragraph. If you are evaluating your paragraph on your own, be sure to put it aside for a day or two first. Then use the following questions to help you:

1. Does your paragraph have a clear topic sentence? Topic sentences are explained in Chapter 3.

2. Do the other sentences in the paragraph support the topic sentence? Supporting sentences are discussed in Chapter 3.

3. Did you have trouble coming up with enough ideas to put in your paragraph? If so, review idea mapping in Chapter 1 and brainstorming in Chapter 2.

4. Did you have trouble with punctuation, verbs, pronouns, or other areas of grammar? If so, you can find the pages to review in the Table of Contents or in the Index.

Evaluation Chart

Use the answer key to check your answers. Find the number of each question you missed and circle it on the chart below. To review the problems you missed, use the chapter in this book or the other resources listed in the chart.

Chapter/Skill	Question Number	Resources from McGraw-Hill/Contemporary	
Chapter 2 • Types of sentences	9	• Language Builder • Complete GED • GED Language Arts, Writing • Pre-GED Language Arts, Writing • MHC Interactive: GED • MHC Interactive: Pre-GED	Unit 2 105–108, 110–112, 153–156 19–24, 83–104, 115–119 13–18, 101–110, 159–161 1.6, 1.16 1.3, 4.1
Chapter 3 • Nouns • Pronouns • Contractions	1, 4, 5, 7 2, 3, 6, 13 11	• Language Builder • Complete GED • GED Language Arts, Writing • Pre-GED Language Arts, Writing • MHC Interactive: GED • MHC Interactive: Pre-GED	Unit 1 91–94 32–44 20–48 1.16 1.4
Chapter 4 • Verb tenses	15, 32, 35, 37	• Language Builder • Complete GED • GED Language Arts, Writing • Pre-GED Language Arts, Writing • MHC Interactive: GED • MHC Interactive: Pre-GED	Unit 1 73–84 51–61, 101–102 53–66, 115–117 1.13 2.1, 2.2
Chapter 5 • Subject-verb agreement	30, 31, 33, 34, 36, 38, 39, 40	• Language Builder • Complete GED • GED Language Arts, Writing • Pre-GED Language Arts, Writing • MHC Interactive: GED • MHC Interactive: Pre-GED	Unit 1 87–91 62–73 67–77 1.11 2.3
Chapter 6 • Adjectives and adverbs • Quotation marks	19 8	• Language Builder • Complete GED • GED Language Arts, Writing • Pre-GED Language Arts, Writing • MHC Interactive: GED • MHC Interactive: Pre-GED	Units 1 & 6 139 145–147 81–95 5.15 3.1, 3.2
Chapter 7 • Coordinating conjunctions • Connectors • Subordinating conjunctions • Moving sentences • Removing sentences • Beginning new paragraphs	21, 29 23, 27 20, 26, 28 16 14 18	• Language Builder • Complete GED • GED Language Arts, Writing • Pre-GED Language Arts, Writing • MHC Interactive: GED • MHC Interactive: Pre-GED	Unit 3 116–118 83, 84, 89–98 102–110 1.1, 1.2, 1.4, 1.7, 1.10 4.1 – 4.3
Chapter 8 • Describing phrases • Parallel structure • Commas	22, 25 17, 24 10, 12	• Language Builder • Complete GED • GED Language Arts, Writing • Pre-GED Language Arts, Writing • MHC Interactive: GED • MHC Interactive: Pre-GED	Unit 5 129–131, 139–142 31, 87, 93, 96, 154–156, 183–185 20, 113–114, 139–148 1.8, 1.15 5.2, 6.3

Language Arts, Reading

The purpose of this posttest is to see how much you have improved your reading skills. Take the test to see which skills you have mastered and which skills you still need to work on. Check all of your answers and use the evaluation chart on page 856.

Directions: Choose the best answer to each question.

1. Look at the following words: remark, boulder, prospector, cement. What is the correct way to divide these words into syllables?

   (1) rem-ark, boul-der, pros-pec-tor, ce-ment
   (2) re-mark, bould-er, pros-pec-tor, ce-ment
   (3) re-mark, boul-der, prosp-ect-or, ce-ment
   (4) re-mark, boul-der, pros-pec-tor, cem-ent
   (5) re-mark, boul-der, pros-pec-tor, ce-ment

2. Use your knowledge of roots, prefixes, and suffixes to match each word with its definition at the right.

   (1) archaeology   **a.** written story of
   (2) biography   someone's life
   (3) contradict   **b.** imply the opposite
   (4) intrastate   or deny
   (5) infidelity   **c.** not being faithful
                         d. study of past human
                         life and activities
                         e. within a state

3. Look at each word in **boldface type** on the left. Find its <u>synonym</u> from the four choices at the right.

   (1) **context**   **a.** contest   **c.** neighbor
                    b. setting   **d.** detour

   (2) **euphemism**   **a.** harsh   **c.** grammar
                    b. feast   **d.** substitution

   (3) **nonfiction**   **a.** fiction   **c.** true
                    b. literature   **d.** drama

   (4) **inference**   **a.** cause   **c.** fact
                    b. opinion   **d.** conclusion

   (5) **sequence**   **a.** order   **c.** set
                    b. hunch   **d.** sequel

4. Look at each word in **boldface type** on the left. Find its <u>antonym</u> from the four choices at the right.

   (1) **miniature**   **a.** huge   **c.** small
                   b. tiny   **d.** minute

   (2) **analogy**   **a.** agreement   **c.** contrast
                   b. comparison   **d.** inference

   (3) **forbid**   **a.** lie   **c.** forget
                   b. future   **d.** allow

   (4) **theme**   **a.** composition **c.** topic
                   b. detail   **d.** subject

   (5) **element**   **a.** piece   **c.** whole
                   b. part   **d.** ingredient

5. Read the following sentence. Then identify the key words that answer the questions *Who or What?* and *Did what?*

   The grocery store worker awoke to find himself in an ambulance on the way to the hospital.

   The key words are _____

   and _____.

6. Pam baked her quota of three dozen cookies for the holiday party.

   Quota means

   (1) special recipe
   (2) party members
   (3) share or amount required
   (4) contest or bake-off
   (5) club membership

Questions 7–11 are based on the following passage.

ARE ORGANIC FOODS AND PRODUCTS BETTER?

What is the definition of organic food? Is it food that is better, cleaner, or safer for you? New rules set down by the United States Department of Agriculture (USDA) say that organic foods must be produced without hormones, antibiotics, herbicides, insecticides, chemical fertilizers, genetic modification, or germ-killing radiation.

What can you buy that is labeled organic? You can buy fruits (especially grapes, apples, citrus, and tree nuts) or vegetables (especially lettuce and tomatoes). You can buy dairy (eggs and milk). You can buy meat or grains (wheat, rice, corn, barley, and oats). You can buy convenience foods (such as nutrition bars or chips and salsa). You can even buy wine and beer, diapers, baby clothes, or dog biscuits.

People buy organic food or goods even though they may cost fifteen percent more than regular items. The chief reason for the interest in organic food is superior flavor. However, people also buy organic because of concern for the environment. A person buying cereal might be concerned about the number of birds killed by pesticides. Beyond that, some people buy organic because of political or spiritual reasons. For example, a person buying pork might want it to come from animals that have lived in a natural environment.

How much of our food and goods are produced by organic methods? In 2002, it was less than two percent. But the available products have increased from fifteen to twenty percent over the past decade. Look to the future for more organic items.

—Adapted from "Certified Organic," in *Newsweek*

7. The word *organic* has many positive connotations. Circle all that apply.

(1) better tasting
(2) less likely to cause illness
(3) more expensive
(4) more natural
(5) safer for the environment

8. What is the main idea of this passage?

(1) growing interest in organic products
(2) diseases caused by pesticides
(3) fattening meat and poultry with hormones
(4) reasons to wash all your foods
(5) concern for the environment

9. Fill in the blanks with details from the selection.

a. When deciding to buying organic, you can choose from _____, _____, or _____.

b. You can consider for yourself reasons to buy organic. The main reasons could be _____ or _____.

c. Other reasons could be _____ or _____.

d. In 2002, less than _____ percent of our products were organic.

e. _____ to _____ percent more organic products have become available every year.

10. To summarize the main purpose of this article in one word, you should focus on

(1) freedom
(2) cost
(3) marketing
(4) happiness
(5) health

11. Many people eat organic foods for the superior flavor. What can you infer about chefs who serve only fresh food that is in season?

Chefs know they must

(1) protect the environment
(2) please the tastes of their customers
(3) spend more money on organic food
(4) help disease prevention organizations
(5) trust the U.S. Department of Agriculture

Questions 12–15 are based on the following passage.

Louis Pasteur was a French chemist who lived in the nineteenth century. Pasteur believed that scientists should tackle practical problems in their research. Therefore, he looked at the problem of food spoilage. Most scientists in Pasteur's time believed food spoiled because of natural chemical changes that took place within the food. However, Pasteur believed that tiny organisms in the air fell on the food, therefore causing it to spoil. He proved his theory was correct when he first heated broth to kill any organisms in it, and then sealed the broth. The broth did not spoil as long as it was sealed. But when the broth was later opened and exposed to air, it spoiled.

Pasteur applied the same principles to preventing wine and vinegar from spoiling. Then he turned his attention to preserving beer. His methods were so effective that England was able to ship beer to its colonies in Africa and India. Later, the same technique was also used to preserve milk. Even today, most of the milk we buy is labeled "pasteurized" after the man who devised ways to prevent food from spoiling.

12. Contrast what Pasteur believed with what most scientists of his day believed. Most nineteenth-century scientists believed that

food spoiled because of _____

_____ while Pasteur

believed _____ caused food to spoil.

13. In Pasteur's experiment, what caused the broth **not** to spoil? Pasteur

(1) added natural preserving chemicals to the broth
(2) heated the broth to kill organisms, then sealed the broth
(3) added organisms to the broth that prevent spoilage
(4) changed the basic chemistry of the broth
(5) used underground storage cellars for the broth

14. Pasteur used his preserving technique on several foods. Number the techniques in the sequence, or order, in which Pasteur successfully preserved them.

_____ milk

_____ beer

_____ wine and vinegar

15. What was the effect of Pasteur's preserving methods for beer? What was England able to do for its colonies?

_____

POSTTEST

Questions 16–21 are based on the following passage.

All morning that flutter of half-fear, half-doubt. At any moment Juan Pedro might appear in the doorway. On the street. At the Cash N Carry. Like in the dreams she dreamed.

There was that to think about, yes, until the woman in the pickup truck drove up. Then there wasn't time to think about anything but the pickup pointed toward San Antonio. Put your bags in the back and get in.

But when they drove across the *arroyo*[1] the driver opened her mouth and let out a yell as loud as any mariachi. Which startled not only Cleófilas, but Juan Pedrito as well.

Pues, look how cute. I scared you two, right? Sorry. Should've warned you. Every time I cross that bridge I do that. Because of the name, you know. Woman Hollering. *Pues,* I holler. She said this in a Spanish pocked[2] with English and laughed. Did you ever notice, Felice continued, how nothing around here is named after a woman? Really. Unless she's a Virgin. I guess you're only famous if you're a virgin. She was laughing again.

That's why I like the name of that *arroyo.* Makes you want to holler like Tarzan, right?

Everything about this woman, this Felice, amazed Cleófilas. The fact that she drove a pickup. A pickup, mind you, but when Cleófilas asked if it was her husband's, she said she didn't have a husband. The pickup was hers. She herself had chosen it. She herself was paying for it.

—Excerpted from "Woman Hollering Creek"
by Sandra Cisneros

[1]*arroyo:* a Spanish word for gully or dry gulch
[2]*pocked:* spotted

16. Which of the following is the best clue to the setting of the story?

   (1) "On the street."
   (2) ". . . the pickup pointed toward San Antonio"
   (3) "At the Cash N Carry."
   (4) "Like in the dreams she dreamed."
   (5) ". . . across the *arroyo.* . . ."

17. What two main characters are named in the story?

   _____ and _____

18. In whose point of view is the story told?

   (1) Cleófilas, the woman leaving quickly
   (2) Felice, the single woman driver
   (3) Juan Pedro, the husband
   (4) the spirit of Woman Hollering
   (5) the third-person, all-knowing author

19. What is the conflict or problem to be solved? Cleófilas needs to

   (1) settle on the price of the ride with Felice
   (2) find a doctor to look at her baby
   (3) get safely away from husband Juan Pedro
   (4) explain why she's laughing
   (5) get a job to support herself and her baby

20. What do you predict will happen at the conclusion, or end, of the story?

   (1) Cleófilas gains her independence.
   (2) Cleófilas learns to holler like Tarzan.
   (3) Felice is named the new Woman Hollering Queen.
   (4) Juan Pedro catches up with the two women.
   (5) Cleófilas hollers at the water.

21. Think of the actions of the two women. One lives on her own. The other is trying to make a break for a better life. Think of the meaning of crossing Hollering Woman Creek. What is the theme of the story?

(1) misunderstanding between men and women
(2) lack of satisfaction with life
(3) forgiveness and acceptance
(4) personal freedom and courage
(5) revenge of pain and rage

Questions 22–25 are based on the poem.

FRIENDSHIP

(1) OH, THE COMFORT—the inexpressive
       comfort of feeling safe with a person,
Having neither to weigh thoughts,
Nor measure words—but pouring them
(5)   All right out—just as they are—
Chaff[1] and grain together—
Certain that a faithful hand will
Take and sift them—
Keep what is worth keeping—
(10)   And with the breath of kindness
Blow the rest away.
                              —by Dinah Maria Mulock Craik

[1]*chaff:* unnecessary seed coverings that are thrown away. Therefore, the word *chaff* means something worthless or unnecessary.

22. What do the "chaff and grain" in line 6 represent?

(1) acts of friends and enemies
(2) outer covering of wheat seeds
(3) talks between brothers and sisters
(4) useless and useful words or ideas
(5) ups and downs of friendship

23. How does the poet feel about her friend?

(1) uneasy because her friend won't understand her
(2) suspicious that her friend will gossip about her
(3) sad because their friendship is over
(4) fearful that her friend will criticize her
(5) comfortable talking about anything with her

24. When the poet says, "Certain that a faithful hand will / Take and sift them—" (lines 7–8), she means that her friend

(1) throws away any unused grain
(2) helps her get her work done
(3) cannot listen when she is too busy
(4) ignores any unwise or silly comments
(5) enjoys working with her hands

25. What is the main idea of this poem?

(1) A good friendship can last a very long time.
(2) To keep a good friend, you must think before you speak.
(3) Chaff and grain are necessary to have a good friendship.
(4) A good friend focuses mainly on your positive qualities and words.
(5) A good friend mainly improves your bad qualities and words.

POSTTEST

26. Pick the word that best completes the analogy.

end : begin :: stop : _____

(1) enter
(2) move
(3) finish
(4) start
(5) halt

27. Think about the expression: "Democrats are always for change." Which of the following describes the expression?

(1) a fact
(2) an opinion
(3) a generalization
(4) a slogan
(5) a rumor

Questions 28–33 are based on the following passages.

My Fair Lady is a two-act musical play set in the early 1900s. A main character, Eliza Doolittle, sells flowers on the street. She knows her street accent will keep her from being a "lady" in London. In most of the musical, Professor Higgins tutors Eliza on her speech. Professor Higgins also falls in love with her. In Passage 1, we realize that Eliza *has* been passed off as a lady at a ball.

ACT ONE
Scene 10

The Promenade[1] outside the ballroom of the Embassy.

Time: late that evening

[Colonel Pickering is a "student of Indian dialects." Mrs. Higgins is Professor Higgins's mother and a member of London society.]

(1) PICKERING: Well, she got by the first hurdle. *(With muffled excitement)* The Ambassador's wife was completely captivated.[2]

(5) MRS. HIGGINS: I know. I've heard several people asking who she is. Do tell what happened.

PICKERING: Higgins said: "Madame Ambassador, may I introduce Miss (10) Eliza Doolittle?" and Madame Ambassador said: "How do you do?" And Eliza came right back with: "How do you do?"

MRS. HIGGINS: *(disappointed):* Is that all?

(15) PICKERING: Oh, no! When it was my turn, both the Ambassador and his wife said to me: "Colonel Pickering, who is that captivating creature with Professor Higgins?"

—Excerpted from *My Fair Lady*
by Alan Jay Lerner and Frederick Loewe

[1]*promenade:* an open area for taking a walk
[2]*captivated:* charmed or influenced

28. Use the information in the introduction and the dialogue to identify the different parts of the setting.

a. City: _____

b. Place: _____

c. Time Period: _____

d. Time of Day: _____

29. In line 1 Pickering says, "Well she got by the first hurdle." So far, this is the point of highest interest in the play. What does this expression represent?

(1) plot
(2) beginning
(3) conflict
(4) climax
(5) conclusion

ACT TWO
Scene 1

HIGGINS' *study.*

Time: 3:00 the following morning.

(1)   *(The slippers are by the desk. Eliza tries to control herself, but no longer can. She hurls them at him with all her force.)*

(5)   ELIZA: There are your slippers! And there! Take your slippers, and may you never have a day's luck with them!

HIGGINS (*astounded*):[1] What on earth? (*He comes to her.*) What's the
(10)   matter? Is anything wrong?

ELIZA: (*seething*):[2] Nothing wrong— with you. I've won your bet for you, haven't I? That's enough for you. I don't matter, I suppose?

(15)   HIGGINS: You won my bet! You! Presumptuous[3] insect. *I* won it! What did you throw those slippers at me for?

ELIZA: Because I wanted to smash your
(20)   face. I'd like to kill you, you selfish brute. Why didn't you leave me where you picked me out of—in the gutter? You thank God it's all over, and that now you can throw me back
(25)   again there, do you?

HIGGINS: (*looking at her in cool wonder*): So the creature is nervous, after all?

—Excerpted from *My Fair Lady* by Alan Jay Lerner and Frederick Loewe

[1]*astounded:* amazed or bewildered
[2]*seething:* boiling mad
[3]*presumptuous:* being too bold; acting without the right to behave that way

30. How would you describe Professor Higgins's character in relation to Eliza's feelings?

(1) professional
(2) caring
(3) wonderful
(4) clueless
(5) nervous

31. What is the overall tone of Act Two, Scene 1?

(1) amused
(2) sad
(3) angry
(4) cool
(5) calm

32. In lines 21–23, Eliza says, "Why didn't you leave me where you picked me out of—in the gutter?" She doesn't know what will become of her. This could point to a theme of

(1) creating problems with change
(2) leaving people where you find them
(3) causing bad effects with placing bets
(4) misunderstanding a teacher's role
(5) taking credit where credit is due

33. What do you predict will happen to Eliza now that Higgins has won his bet?

Answers are on pages 854–855.

Language Arts, Reading Answer Key

1. **(5)**

2. **(1) d** **(2) a** **(3) b** **(4) e** **(5) c**

3. **(1) b** **(2) d** **(3) c** **(4) d** **(5) a**

4. **(1) a** **(2) c** **(3) d** **(4) b** **(5) c**

5. *Who or what?*   *Did what?*
   the grocery store   **awoke**
   worker

6. **(3)** The clue is the phrase "of three dozen cookies." This tells how many she needed to bring.

7. **(1), (2), (4),** and **(5)** Choice (3) does not have positive connotations.

8. **(1)** Choices (2) and (5) are mentioned as details. Choices (3) and (4) are not discussed.

9. **a.** 3 of the following: fruits, vegetables, dairy, meat, grains, convenience foods

   b. flavor, environment

   c. political, spiritual

   d. two

   e. fifteen, twenty

10. **(5)** The article discusses health of people and health of the environment with the use of organic foods.

11. **(2)** Chefs depend on customer satisfaction.

12. chemical changes; organisms

13. **(2)** The broth did not spoil if it was heated and sealed. It did spoil when it was not heated, and it spoiled when it was unsealed.

14. **3, 2, 1**

15. England was able to ship beer to its colonies in Africa and India.

16. **(2)** Choice (1) could be any street, and Choice (3) could be any grocery store. Choice (4) is not a clear setting. Choice (5) is the second best clue, but it also could be any gully or dry riverbed.

17. Felice and Cleófilas   The husband, Juan Pedro, and the baby, Juan Pedrito, are referred to but are not "characters" in this passage.

18. **(5)** The all-knowing author is telling the story. Don't be confused by the fact that she does not use quotation marks for the dialogue.

19. **(3)** The *main* conflict is for Cleófilas to get away safely.

20. **(1)** Notice the last three lines of the passage: *The pickup was hers. She herself had chosen it. She herself was paying for it.* We can predict that Cleófilas will become more independent, like Felice.

21. **(4)** It took courage for Cleófilas to leave with her baby. She doesn't know whether her husband will come after her. However, Felice has her own pickup and celebrates crossing Hollering Woman Creek—showing her freedom and courage.

22. **(4)** In lines 3–5, the poet talks about words and thoughts. When she refers to *chaff* (something worthless) and *grain* (something valuable), she is referring to useless and useful ideas or thoughts.

23. **(5)** The words *comfort, safe, faithful,* and *kindness* imply that the poet trusts and feels comfortable with her friend.

24. **(4)** The poet is sure that her friend will pay attention to the ideas that are valuable and ignore the other ideas.

25. **(4)** The entire poem focuses on friends who support your positive qualities and ignore the negative ones.

26. **(4)** *End* and *begin* are antonyms; therefore, you need an antonym of *stop.*

27. **(3)** Many Democrats may favor change, but not necessarily all of them. A generalization often uses the word *always.*

28. a. City: London

   b. Place: outside the ballroom of the Embassy, the official residence of an ambassador to a foreign country

   c. Time Period: 1912

   d. Time of Day: late that evening

29. (4) The point of highest interest is the climax. Many scenes have built up to this climax in Scene 10.

30. (4) Professor Higgins takes all the credit for Eliza's hard work. He doesn't know why she's so angry. Most of all, he doesn't realize yet that they have fallen in love.

31. (3) Eliza throws slippers at Higgins, and she is "seething" with anger.

32. (1) Eliza has changed, now speaking (and dressing) well. But now that the "experiment" is over, Eliza is worried about her future. A new problem has resulted.

33. Answers may vary. However, we have been given the clue in the introduction that Higgins is in love with Eliza.

Evaluation Chart

Use the answer key to check your answers. Find the number of each question you missed and circle it on the chart below. To review the problems you missed, use the chapter in this book or the other resources listed in the chart.

Chapter/Skill	Question Number	Resources from McGraw-Hill/Contemporary	
Chapter 1 • Syllables • Word parts • Synonyms and antonyms	1 2 3, 4	• *Reading Basics*	Unit 1
Chapter 2 • Key words in sentences • Words in context • Word connotation • Main idea, supporting details • Summarizing	5 6 7 8, 9 10	• *Reading Basics* • *Complete GED* • *GED Language Arts, Reading* • *Pre-GED Language Arts, Reading* • *MHC Interactive: GED* • *MHC Interactive: Pre-GED*	37–44, Unit 4 Throughout 15–38 13–26 Throughout 1.1 – 1.4
Chapter 3 • Inference • Predicting outcomes	11, 23 20, 33	• *Reading Basics* • *Complete GED* • *GED Language Arts, Reading* • *Pre-GED Language Arts, Reading* • *MHC Interactive: GED* • *MHC Interactive: Pre-GED*	Units 4 & 5 Throughout 47–56 35–37 Throughout 2.2, 3.1
Chapter 4 • Fact opinion, and generalization • Sequence • Cause and effect • Analogy	27 14 12, 13, 15 26	• *Reading Basics* • *Complete GED* • *GED Language Arts, Reading* • *Pre-GED Language Arts, Reading* • *MHC Interactive: GED* • *MHC Interactive: Pre-GED*	Unit 5 Throughout 95–102 43 Throughout 3.3, 3.4, 5.3
Chapter 5 • Setting • Characterization • Plot: beginning, conflict, climax, or conclusion • Point of view • Theme	16 17 19, 29 18 21	• *Reading Basics* • *Complete GED* • *GED Language Arts, Reading* • *Pre-GED Language Arts, Reading* • *MHC Interactive: GED* • *MHC Interactive: Pre-GED*	Unit 5 Throughout 165–216 57–62, 131–160 4.1 – 4.5 6.1 – 6.6
Chapter 6 • Paraphrasing poetry • Theme • Reading drama • Characterization	22, 24 25, 32 28, 31 30	• *Reading Basics* • *Complete GED* • *GED Language Arts, Reading* • *Pre-GED Language Arts, Reading* • *MHC Interactive: GED* • *MHC Interactive: Pre-GED*	Unit 5 Throughout 217–277 153–156 4.6, 4.12 – 4.15 6.3, 6.6

Social Studies

The Social Studies Posttest should give you a good idea of how well you have learned the skills you have studied in this section. When you complete the test, check your answers with page 866.

Directions: Study each passage or illustration, then answer the questions that follow.

Questions 1 and 2 are based on the following speech by Sojourner Truth.

That man over there says that a woman needs to be helped into carriages and lifted over ditches. Nobody ever helps me into carriages, or over mud-puddles, or gives me any best place. And a'nt I a woman?

Look at my arm! I have ploughed, and planted, and gathered into barns, and no man could head me! And a'nt I a woman?

I would work as much and eat as much as a man, when I could get it, and bear the lash as well. And a'nt I a woman?

I have borne thirteen children and seen 'em most all sold off to slavery, and when I cried out with my mother's grief, none but Jesus heard me! And a'nt I a woman?

1. Who is Sojourner Truth?

   (1) a modern politician running for office
   (2) a black woman who was a slave
   (3) a wealthy, nineteenth-century Southern woman
   (4) an early settler in New England
   (5) a twentieth-century feminist

2. When the speaker in this passage says, "Look at my arm! I have ploughed, and planted, and gathered into barns, and no man could head me!" she means that

   (1) she could work as hard as any man
   (2) she was forced to do work that women shouldn't have to do
   (3) she loved planting and harvest time
   (4) she appreciates the help that men have given her
   (5) a real woman must do hard physical labor

Questions 3 and 4 are based on the following passage.

How many languages do you speak? Actually, whenever you speak you use a particular form of language called a dialect, and your dialect probably changes to suit your listeners. A dialect consists of a special vocabulary, unique pronunciations, and certain habitual ways of organizing words in sentences.

No two people speak in exactly the same way, but any group of individuals that spends time together or shares interests will develop unique speech patterns that eventually become a dialect. For instance, residents of the same geographic area will share an accent and vocabulary. Similarly, people with the same occupation, like astronauts and doctors, usually develop their own special jargon.

3. What do people who speak the same dialect have in common?

   (1) Their voices are almost identical.
   (2) They were born in the same generation.
   (3) They put sentences together in similar patterns.
   (4) They share the same opinions and beliefs.
   (5) It is difficult for outsiders to understand them.

4. Which of the following groups of people would most likely speak the same dialect?

   (1) people with red hair
   (2) people who grew up and surf at Huntington Beach
   (3) people who write a lot of letters
   (4) people who hate their jobs
   (5) people who eat Primo brand spaghetti sauce

857

Questions 5 and 6 are based on the following graphs.

BEVERAGE MARKET SHARE 1976–1992*

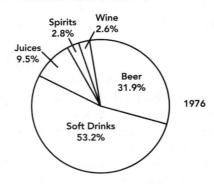

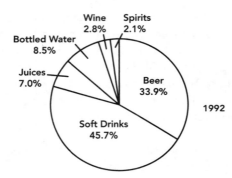

*Includes only bottled beverages.
Coffee, tea, and milk are excluded.

5. Which of the following was a **new** factor in the drink market in 1992?

(1) juices
(2) soft drinks
(3) beer
(4) bottled water
(5) wine

6. From 1976 to 1992, which type of beverage suffered the greatest loss of market share?

(1) beer
(2) bottled water
(3) wine
(4) juices
(5) soft drinks

Question 7 is based on the following passage.

"I can't make a . . . thing out of this tax problem," complained President Warren G. Harding to a friend. "I listen to one side and they seem right and then—God!—I talk to the other side and they seem to be right. . . . I know that somewhere there is a book that will give me the truth, but I couldn't read the book. I know somewhere there is an economist who knows the truth, but I don't know where to find him and haven't the sense to know him and trust him when I find him. God! What a job."

7. The main idea of this paragraph is that President Harding

(1) provided leadership on the tax issue
(2) did not know what to do about the tax problem
(3) needed to hire a new economist
(4) wanted to read more books about taxes
(5) thought that taxes were not a serious problem

Question 8 is based on the following passage.

The culture of Renaissance Italy was important because there were many large cities and not one main capital. Unlike England and France, Italy had no main capital city or central government, but rather many cities that served as regional capitals. For example, Rome was the major city for the Papal States, and Venice for northeastern Italy. During the later years of the Renaissance, foreign governments took control of the various Italian regions. For instance, in 1494 France invaded Italy. The age of Leonardo da Vinci, Raphael, Titian, and Michelangelo followed the French invasion, and culture and art became an important part of daily life. But as Italy began to be ruled by other countries, interest in the arts gradually shifted to other parts of Europe.

POSTTEST

8. According to the passage, Italian leadership during the Renaissance ended because

(1) Italy did not have one dominating capital city

(2) Italy never developed democratic institutions

(3) Italy had difficulty maintaining its independence

(4) there was no one to replace its greatest artists

(5) the period of peace hurt creativity

Questions 9 and 10 are based on the following passage.

Africa is a continent that is struggling to overcome the impact of colonial rule. Just as the United States used to be governed by the British, many African countries used to be ruled by governments in Europe.

One goal of the colonial governments was to make as much money as possible from the individual colonies. To do this, they forced the people to work long hours without the benefit of modern machines or technology. These laborers were not paid and, in time, stripped the land of its ability to grow crops. Natural resources, such as forests, were also used up. The agricultural revolution that had helped farmers in many parts of the world was never introduced to colonial Africa.

Unlike most colonies that fought for independence, African colonies did not have a middle class to lead the governments once they gained independence. In the United States, businessmen such as Thomas Jefferson, George Washington, and James Madison were able to lead their newly independent country. In many African countries, however, the colonial governments kept people from becoming leaders. When these countries finally gained independence, civil wars often occurred between the people who were trying to take control. Many of the problems facing African nations today can be directly linked to the days of European colonialism from 1880–1960.

9. The main idea of this passage is that in Africa

(1) colonial governments prevented modern machines from being shipped to Africa

(2) today's problems should be blamed on the middle class

(3) the global economy will be the key to African progress in the future

(4) colonial governments caused many of the problems facing African nations today

(5) progress has been helped by the middle class

10. Given the information in this passage, you might predict that in ten years

(1) African economies will modernize and grow rapidly

(2) Africa will continue to struggle with the effects of colonialism

(3) colonial powers will be asked to take over again

(4) democratic forms of government will be set up through much of Africa

(5) Africa will follow the strategies of East Asia

POSTTEST

Questions 11 and 12 are based on the following chart.

GROSS DOMESTIC PRODUCT (2000) AND LAND AREA FOR SELECT NATIONS		
Nation	**GDP (trillion $US)**	**Land Area (sq km)**
Brazil	1.34	8,511,965
China	5.56	9,596,960
Germany	2.184	357,021
Japan	3.45	377,835
The Netherlands	0.413	41,526
Russia	1.2	17,075,200
South Africa	0.412	1,219,912
United States	10.082	9,629,091

Source: CIA - The World Factbook 2002

11. Which nation has a land area most similar in size to the United States?

(1) Russia
(2) The Netherlands
(3) Japan
(4) Brazil
(5) China

12. If the nations on the chart were first listed in order of the size of their Gross Domestic Products, and then were listed in order of their land areas, which would have the greatest difference between the two rankings?

(1) Russia
(2) The Netherlands
(3) Japan
(4) Germany
(5) South Africa

Question 13 is based on the following cartoon.

Background Clues: In 1995, Congress considered several welfare reform bills. Members of Congress wanted the states, instead of the federal government, to control major welfare programs. This would mean that each state would decide which welfare programs to fund and in what amounts.

Mike Keefe, *The Denver Post*

13. The cartoonist thinks that welfare programs are

(1) full of problems
(2) best run by state governments
(3) very helpful
(4) a good way to retrain workers
(5) encouraging people to have children

Questions 14–16 are based on the following passage.

Sociologist David Riesman, in his book *The Lonely Crowd,* describes two types of Americans. First is the inner-directed person whose life is controlled by his or her own strongly held inner values. An example of an inner-directed man is the rugged frontiersman, who has to rely on himself while he works on his homestead.

The second type of American is other-directed. Other-directed people are more interested in the approval of other people than in personal values. A member of a teenage gang and a successful mid-level manager in a large company are examples of other-directed people.

14. Which ad might appeal to an inner-directed man?

(1) A lone, good-looking cowboy on a horse is lighting a cigarette. The ad reads, "This is Marlboro country."
(2) "Subaru is the Largest-Selling Car in New England."
(3) "Come join millions! Celebrate the 100th Anniversary of the Statue of Liberty in New York."
(4) "Come to Disney World, the Dream Vacation for Every Child!"
(5) "Buy Crest, America's Best-Selling Toothpaste."

15. An other-directed person generally

(1) is a gang member
(2) needs the approval of others
(3) likes to be in the wilderness
(4) is an independent thinker
(5) works as a manager

16. An example of an other-directed person is

(1) an independent, millionaire oilman
(2) a bad-tempered, foul-mouthed tennis star
(3) a former politician
(4) a practicing member of a religious sect
(5) a hermit who lives in a cave

Question 17 is based on the following ad.

WOMEN!

Fight the Equal Rights Amendment!
It will not help you—It will hurt you.

The Equal Rights Amendment is a threat to all women.
If it passes, it will rob you of

• your right to be a homemaker

• your protection from being drafted and serving in combat

• your right to alimony

17. The writers of the above ad wanted women to believe that passage of the Equal Rights Amendment would have

(1) taken privileges away from women
(2) promoted male control of society
(3) required that men and women use the same bathrooms
(4) ensured that women dominated society
(5) been fair to both men and women

Questions 18 and 19 are based on the following passage.

Over one hundred years ago, Henry David Thoreau went to jail to protest the Mexican War. In recent times, many people have followed Thoreau's example and openly broken a law in order to bring public attention to injustice.

The great Indian leader Gandhi took Thoreau's ideas further. When convicted of breaking a law, Gandhi would serve a prison sentence rather than pay the smallest fine. In prison, he went on hunger strikes to draw even more attention to himself and his cause, the independence of India from Great Britain.

When good and caring people are thrown in jail for their beliefs, it often makes others think about the laws and conditions that they are trying to change. Peaceful but determined protesters in the United States, such as Martin Luther King, Jr., were inspired by Gandhi and adapted his ideas to the struggle for racial equality. When King and others were jailed for their beliefs, they helped many Americans realize that segregation was wrong. Their example helped strike down the laws that kept segregation alive.

18. After Martin Luther King, Jr., went to jail,

  (1) Thoreau was jailed for his beliefs

  (2) segregation laws in the United States started changing

  (3) India won its independence from Great Britain

  (4) Gandhi went on a hunger strike

  (5) the United States fought the Mexican War

19. It is the author's opinion that

  (1) Thoreau opposed the Mexican War

  (2) Gandhi went to jail rather than pay fines

  (3) Martin Luther King, Jr., used the nonviolent tactics of Gandhi

  (4) Gandhi was a great leader

  (5) segregation laws are no longer legal in the United States

Questions 20 and 21 are based on the following passage.

Of all the original thirteen colonies, Pennsylvania attracted the most non-English settlers. It was also the colony that had the greatest tolerance of religious and cultural differences. It was founded by Quakers, led by William Penn, who wanted to create a colony based on religious freedom and fairness to all people.

20. An important value of the founders of Pennsylvania was

  (1) economic freedom

  (2) separation of nationalities

  (3) conversion of the Indians to Christianity

  (4) religious freedom

  (5) return to nature

21. A likely reason that Pennsylvania attracted more non-English settlers than any other colony is that

  (1) the climate was better than in any other colony

  (2) it was the most tolerant of different people's beliefs

  (3) English settlers preferred to go elsewhere

  (4) it had the best natural resources

  (5) the Quakers were good managers

POSTTEST

Questions 22 and 23 are based on the following map.

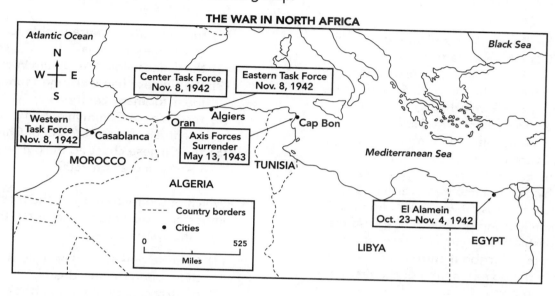

THE WAR IN NORTH AFRICA

22. In what country did the Axis forces in North Africa surrender?

(1) Egypt
(2) Libya
(3) Tunisia
(4) Algeria
(5) Morocco

23. How much time elapsed from the first Allied victory in North Africa at El Alamein on November 4, 1942, to the landing of the Western, Center, and Eastern Task Forces at Casablanca, Oran, and Algiers?

(1) 6 months
(2) 3 months
(3) 23 days
(4) 1 week
(5) 4 days

Questions 24 and 25 are based on the following passage.

After the Opium Wars and various rebellions of the 1800s, Chinese leaders began to change the way the government was run and stopped following many of the old traditions. For the first time, books from other countries were translated into Chinese. The Bible was also translated, along with other important religious writings. Eventually, books about history, science, military arts, technology, novels, philosophy, and politics were translated.

During the 1870s, newspapers and magazines grew in number and popularity. Because these were published frequently, Chinese citizens were able to learn about current events and changes in the government. For the first time, people living across China could read about the same topics at the same time. The newly formed interest in current events stimulated debate and the expression of public opinion.

The publication of newspapers and magazines, combined with translations of foreign works, gave Chinese readers new information about politics and the economy. Concepts such as evolution and progress became known to the general public. Gradually, Chinese scholars gave up the idea that history operates in a cycle. In its place emerged the idea that history moves forward through stages. This change in thinking signaled the end of the Chinese dynastic system.

—Adapted from *Microsoft® Encarta® Encyclopedia 2000*

24. The passage contains enough information to explain why

    (1) ruling dynasties were unable to adapt to changes in China
    (2) the Chinese lost the Opium Wars
    (3) the Chinese had welcomed foreign ideas for many centuries
    (4) the Chinese Communist Party eventually gained control of China
    (5) the Chinese changed their view of history in the late 1800s

25. Which of the following was the most important cause of the end of the Chinese dynastic system?

    (1) Chinese defeats and rebellions made them open to new ideas.
    (2) the translation of foreign books into Chinese
    (3) the rising and falling of the dynastic cycle
    (4) the development of democracy at a local level throughout China
    (5) the enormous changes taking place as a result of industrialization

POSTTEST

Question 26 is based on the following passage.

Canada is the second largest nation in the world, but it is defended by a tiny military less than half the size of the United States Marine Corps.

The Canadian army has fewer than 300 troops protecting 3.5 million square miles of northern territory. An amusement park in Edmonton has more submarines than the Canadian navy. In fact, Canada's territories are so sparsely monitored that a Nazi weather station, built secretly on the Canadian coast in 1943, went undiscovered until 1981.

Nevertheless, Canada's military has earned an international reputation for protecting the peace in other nations. Canadian troops are regularly deployed on more than a dozen different United Nations peacekeeping operations.

26. According to the passage, the Canadian armed forces are unable to

(1) defend themselves
(2) purchase submarines
(3) monitor Canadian territory
(4) recruit enough soldiers
(5) stay out of United Nations operations

Answers are on pages 866–867.

Social Studies Answer Key

1. (2) The speaker says she could "bear the lash," and the last paragraph states that she had borne thirteen children and seen most of them sold as slaves.

2. (1) She describes heavy farm work that she did. When she says that no man could "head" her, she means that no man could do any more work than she.

3. (3) The first paragraph tells you that a dialect includes certain ways of organizing sentences.

4. (2) The second paragraph tells you that people develop a dialect when they spend time together or share an interest. The surfers at Huntington Beach do both.

5. (4) All of the choices except bottled water appear on the graph for 1976 as well as on the graph for 1992.

6. (5) Among the choices, both juices and soft drinks lost market share. However, soft drinks lost a larger percentage of market share than juices did.

7. (2) The first sentence states the main idea: "I can't make a . . . thing out of this tax problem." In the rest of the paragraph, Harding describes his confusion and need for guidance.

8. (3) The passage states that as Italy fell under foreign domination, leadership of the Renaissance moved to other parts of Europe.

9. (4) The main idea of the passage is that colonialism caused many of the problems facing African countries today.

10. (2) The passage makes it clear that the negative impact of colonialism will not be easy to overcome. Even as progress is made, Africa will still struggle to overcome colonialism.

11. (5) The land area of the United States is 3,717,796 square miles. China's land area of 3,695,500 square miles is closest in size to the United States.

12. (1) In land area, Russia ranks first of the eight nations listed, while its Gross Domestic Product ranks sixth. None of the other nations listed have as great a difference in the two rankings.

13. (1) The symbol labeled *welfare* is a can of worms. When we call something "a can of worms," we mean that it is full of problems.

14. (1) The lone cowboy looks like a tough, independent individual, an inner-directed person.

15. (2) *Other-directed* is defined in the second paragraph as a person who is more interested in the approval of other people than in values.

16. (4) A devout member of a religious sect would look for approval from others in the sect.

17. (1) The writers of the ad listed some privileges that women might want. The ad says that if the Equal Rights Amendment passes, women will not be able to have these privileges.

18. (2) The last sentence states that after King and others were jailed, the laws began changing.

19. (4) Gandhi did many important things, and many people consider him a great leader. This is a personal belief. The other choices are facts that can be proven.

20. (4) The passage states that the colony had the greatest tolerance of religious differences and that the Quakers wanted to create a colony based on religious freedom.

21. (2) Since the colony was the most tolerant of other people's beliefs, it makes sense that it would attract people who were different from the English.

22. (3) According to the map, the Axis forces surrendered on May 13, 1943, at Cap Bon in Tunisia.

23. (5) According to the map, the Western Task Force at Casablanca, the Center Task Force at Oran, and the Eastern Task Force at Algiers, all landed on November 8, 1942, just four days after the end of the battle of El Alamein.

24. (5) The passage fully explains why the Chinese changed their view of history in the late 19th century. The view had been of an unending cycle of rising and falling dynasties. The new view was the Western view of history as a constantly evolving process.

25. (2) The passage states that the introduction of newspapers and translations of foreign works gave Chinese readers much new information about political systems and economic strategies which in turn led to the end of the dynastic cycle.

26. (3) The passage tells you that Canadian territory is sparsely monitored. It also tells you that the tiny Canadian military must protect a lot of territory. There is no evidence for the other choices.

Evaluation Chart

Use the answer key to check your answers. Find the number of each question you missed and circle it on the chart below. To review the problems you missed, use the chapter in this book or the other resources listed in the chart.

Chapter/Skill	Question Number	Resources from McGraw-Hill/Contemporary	
Chapter 1			
• Finding details	15	• *Complete GED*	297–443
• Restating information	2	• *GED Social Studies*	Ch. 1
• Summarizing information	8, 26	• *Pre-GED Social Studies*	Ch. 1, 62–63, 73–78
• Main idea	7, 9	• *MHC Interactive: GED*	Throughout
• Inference	1	• *MHC Interactive: Pre-GED*	Throughout
• Political cartoons	13		
Chapter 2			
• Using charts	11, 12	• *Complete GED*	297–443
• Using graphs	5, 6	• *GED Social Studies*	Throughout
• Using maps	22, 23	• *Pre-GED Social Studies*	19–21, 36–48, 51–53, 57–61, 240– 242
		• *MHC Interactive: GED*	Throughout
		• *MHC Interactive: Pre-GED*	Throughout
Chapter 3			
• Application of ideas	14, 16	• *Complete GED*	297–443
		• *GED Social Studies*	Ch. 2
		• *Pre-GED Social Studies*	Ch. 2
		• *MHC Interactive: GED*	All
		• *MHC Interactive: Pre-GED*	All
Chapter 4			
• Sequence	18	• *Complete GED*	297–443
• Cause and effect	25	• *GED Social Studies*	Ch. 3
• Compare and contrast	3	• *Pre-GED Social Studies*	Ch. 3
• Fact, opinion, and hypothesis	19, 21	• *MHC Interactive: GED*	Throughout
		• *MHC Interactive: Pre-GED*	Throughout
• Predicting outcomes	4, 10		
Chapter 5			
• Adequacy of information	24	• *Complete GED*	297–443
• Errors in reasoning and propaganda	17	• *GED Social Studies*	Ch. 4
		• *Pre-GED Social Studies*	Ch. 4
• Values	20	• *MHC Interactive: GED*	Throughout
		• *MHC Interactive: Pre-GED*	Throughout

This Science Posttest can be used to evaluate your science reading skills after you have worked through the science section. The questions will test your ability to understand science passages and answer questions with multiple-choice format. When you have finished the posttest, check your answers with the Answer Key on page 878.

Directions: Read each passage and study the illustrations carefully. Then circle the <u>one best answer</u> for each question. Feel free to look back in the passage to help yourself answer the questions.

Questions 1 and 2 are based on the following passage and graph.

John Washington is a wildlife manager in a national forest. His job is to make sure that all the animals in the forest are doing well and that there are not too many or too few of any one species of animal.

In the forest live a few wood ducks. For the past five years, John has been trying to increase the number of wood ducks by setting out artificial nesting boxes near streams and ponds. To see if his experiment is working, John has kept records of the number of wood ducks seen in the forest each year. Here is a graph of his results.

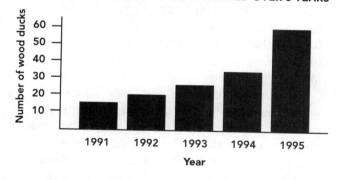

NUMBER OF WOOD DUCKS SIGHTED OVER 5 YEARS

1. About how many wood ducks were sighted in the year John started his experiment?

   (1) 5
   (2) 15
   (3) 25
   (4) 40
   (5) 60

2. What is the hypothesis John is testing with his experiment?

   (1) Wildlife managers should take care of animals.
   (2) There aren't enough wood ducks in the forest.
   (3) More nesting places will help to produce more wood ducks.
   (4) People can count wood ducks accurately.
   (5) Wood ducks breed every five years.

Questions 3 and 4 are based on the following passage and chart.

Physicists use the idea of density to describe different materials. Very dense materials are very heavy. Iron and lead are dense materials. In contrast, Styrofoam is not dense at all and is quite light.

The density of something is expressed in the number of grams that a cubic centimeter of that substance weighs—in the metric system of measurement. For example, 1 cubic centimeter of pure iron weighs 7.86 grams; we say that iron has a density of 7.86 grams per cubic centimeter. The density of a pure substance is always the same. If you had 2 cubic centimeters of iron, they would weigh exactly twice as much, or 15.72 grams. The chart below shows the densities of some common substances.

Material	Density (in g per cm³)
Gold	19.3
Mercury	13.6
Lead	11.3
Silver	10.5
Iron	7.86
Diamonds	3.5
Aluminum	2.7
Water	1.00
Alcohol	0.79
Gasoline	0.68
Air	0.0013

3. How much would a 6-cubic centimeter diamond weigh?

(1) 3.5 grams
(2) 6 grams
(3) 9.5 grams
(4) 21 grams
(5) 35 grams

4. An archeologist dug up an old crown. There were 30 cubic centimeters of metal in the crown, and it weighed 315 grams. What material was used to make the crown?

(1) gold
(2) lead
(3) silver
(4) iron
(5) aluminum

Questions 5 and 6 are based on the following passage.

Space travel of the future is likely to be very different from what it is today. Scientists predict that space travel will be as common as air travel. The launch site on Earth will be a spaceport that operates like a commercial airport, readying each reusable launch vehicle (RLV) for another flight within hours of landing. The RLV will take off like an airplane from a rail system instead of lifting off vertically.

In outer space, RLVs and other spacecraft will operate from giant orbiting platforms or permanently manned bases on the Moon. These stations will be the springboards to other planets and the stars. Travel to these distant places will take much less time than it does today. What is now a nine-month journey to Mars, for example, will take only three months using new propulsion systems such as hot-gas plasma rockets, ion engines, and solar sails. If any of this seems familiar, perhaps you've read similar ideas in science fiction books. It seems that science fiction authors are often light-years ahead of real science!

POSTTEST

5. Which of the following can you best infer from the prediction that spaceports will operate like commercial airports?

(1) Spaceports will have the same restaurants and stores found in airports.
(2) RLVs will look like airplanes.
(3) Space travel will be as common and popular as commercial air travel today.
(4) Funds for building spaceports will come from federal and private sources.
(5) Citizens will oppose the construction of spaceports near their homes and businesses.

6. A light-year is the distance that light travels in one year, about 6 trillion miles. What do you think the writer means by the last sentence in the passage?

(1) Most people are familiar with science fiction books, films, and other works.
(2) Science fiction authors often predict the science of the future.
(3) Real science happens too slowly to hold most people's attention.
(4) The giant orbiting platforms in space will be bigger than the international space station.
(5) After humans travel to Mars, our next venture will be to the stars.

Questions 7–9 are based on the following passage and diagram.

We humans rely on our sense of sight to see the world around us. What we see is called light. The organ with which we sense light is the human eye. Even though the eye is such a small organ—only about one inch across—the way it works is really quite amazing.

When light enters the eye, it passes through the cornea, the clear outer layer in the front of the eye. Then the light moves through a clear, watery material called the aqueous humor and into the pupil, an opening in the iris. The iris is the colored part of the eye. Next the light

passes through a lens, which bends the light as it passes through a clear, gel-like substance called the vitreous humor. Finally, the light becomes focused on the retina, which lines the back of the eye.

The retina contains two kinds of cells called rods and cones. Rods are sensitive to dim light, and cones are sensitive to bright light and color. When the light hits these cells, a chemical is formed that creates nerve impulses in the optic nerve. The optic nerve transmits the impulses to the brain, where they are interpreted as light.

PARTS OF THE EYE

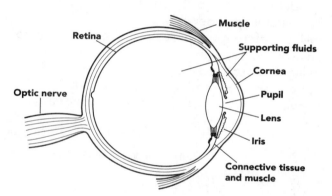

7. What is the first paragraph mainly about?

(1) how humans rely on the world around them
(2) how to use the sense of sight
(3) how the human eye differs from the eyes of other animals
(4) how people see light
(5) how to keep an eye healthy for perfect vision

8. Which of the following can you infer from the passage?

(1) The human eye is a very complex organ.
(2) The cornea is more important than the lens.
(3) The aqueous humor is a clear, watery material.
(4) Light travels in straight lines.
(5) The optic nerve sends impulses to the brain.

9. According to the diagram and passage, which of the following best describes the *cornea*?

   (1) the opening in the front of the eye
   (2) the fluid covering the iris and pupil
   (3) the clear outer layer in front of the eye
   (4) the colored part of the eye
   (5) the nerve that extends from the back of the eye

Questions 10 and 11 are based on the following passage and graph.

Below is a solubility graph showing how a new vitamin powder called Vitamix dissolves in milk at different temperatures. Use this graph to answer the next questions. **Note**: Liters and milligrams are measurements from the metric system. You can read the graph without knowing exactly how much a milligram or a liter is.

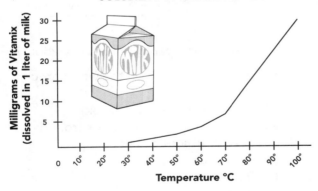

SOLUBILITY OF VITAMIX IN MILK

Milligrams of Vitamix (dissolved in 1 liter of milk)

Temperature °C

10. What does the general trend of the line graph show?

    (1) Hot liquids dissolve powders better than cool liquids.
    (2) The higher the temperature, the less Vitamix will dissolve.
    (3) The more liquid used, the more Vitamix will dissolve.
    (4) The more Vitamix is dissolved, the lower the temperature will get.
    (5) The higher the temperature, the more Vitamix will dissolve.

11. How was the information for this graph probably obtained?

    (1) Many people noticed Vitamix would dissolve at different temperatures.
    (2) Someone did an experiment on dissolving Vitamix in water.
    (3) A survey was taken.
    (4) Several people did experiments on dissolving Vitamix in milk.
    (5) A famous scientist predicted how Vitamix would dissolve in milk.

Questions 12 and 13 are based on the following passage.

Artificial selection has been used for centuries by people who wanted to develop new, more useful types of animals. In artificial selection, a breeder chooses animals having the traits that he or she wants and then breeds the animals together. Later, the most desirable of the offspring are bred together again.

This process of breeding can continue for many generations. For example, to develop a type of dog to go down holes after badgers, some German dog owners bred together dogs with short legs and long bodies. From the offspring, they chose the puppies with the shortest legs and longest bodies and bred them together. After many years, they developed a dog with a low, long body and very short legs called the dachshund, or "sausage dog."

12. According to the passage, who uses artificial selection?

   (1) people who want an improved breed of animal

   (2) only Germans

   (3) mostly dog breeders

   (4) only people long ago

   (5) mainly people who like to hunt and fish

13. Which of the following can you infer about why dachshunds are nicknamed "sausage dogs"?

   (1) Dachshunds eat a lot of sausage.

   (2) Dachshunds used to cost the same as a sausage.

   (3) Dachshunds are the same color as sausage.

   (4) Dachshunds are shaped somewhat like a sausage.

   (5) Dachshunds were originally bred by a person named Sausage.

Questions 14 and 15 are based on the following passage and diagram.

The first record player was a very strange-looking machine. It was patented by Thomas A. Edison in 1877. It didn't play records as we know them but instead played cylinders covered with tinfoil. A recording could be made on the cylinder by speaking or singing into a mouthpiece that led to a large diaphragm, a flexible disk similar to the top of a drum. This diaphragm was connected to a needle. Sound waves from the voice caused the diaphragm to vibrate, which made the needle move up and down, pressing grooves into the foil.

To play the recording, the process was simply reversed. The cylinder was turned, making the needle move up and down in the grooves. The needle made a small diaphragm vibrate, causing it to reproduce the original sounds. These sounds came out through the mouthpiece, which amplified them—or made them louder. As you may imagine, the sounds were not very clear. Also, the foil records wore out very quickly. The music industry has come a long way since 1877; in fact, most people today use CD players.

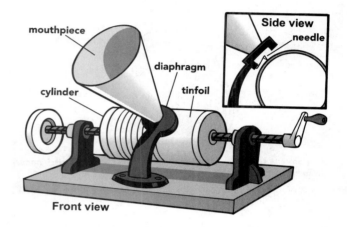

Front view

14. According to the passage, which of the following is **not** true?

   (1) There were recording machines before 1900.

   (2) Thomas Edison invented an early type of record player.

   (3) Early record players had a needle.

   (4) Early amplifiers were not electronic.

   (5) Foil records could be played over a period of many years.

15. Which of the following can you best infer from the passage?

   (1) Sound waves cause things to wear out.

   (2) Sound waves cause solid objects to vibrate.

   (3) Sound waves cause cylinders to turn.

   (4) Sound waves are amplified by tinfoil.

   (5) Sound waves are not used in modern record players.

Questions 16 and 17 are based on the following diagram.

THE HUMAN HEART

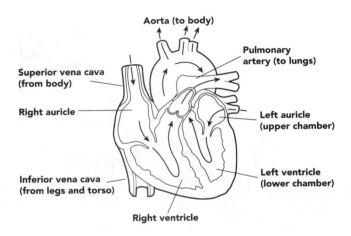

16. According to the diagram, which of these statements is true?

    (1) There are three main chambers, or sections, in the heart.
    (2) Some veins lead directly into the ventricles.
    (3) Blood flows from the auricles into the ventricles.
    (4) No arteries or veins lead directly to the body.
    (5) Blood flows from one ventricle directly into the other.

17. The diagram suggests that the word *pulmonary* probably has something to do with which of the following?

    (1) the heart
    (2) the brain
    (3) the lungs
    (4) the body
    (5) the blood

Questions 18 and 19 are based on the following passage and diagram.

Many ecologists today are concerned about the problem of acid rain. Acid rain is rain that picks up sulfuric acid pollution in the air and then falls into lakes and streams. After a while the water acidifies, endangering many of the fish and plants that live in it.

No one has proved what causes acid rain. Some scientists believe that burning coal in power plants puts too much sulfur in the air that then forms sulfuric acid when it rains. Other scientists think that most of the sulfur in the air comes from car exhaust fumes. Still others say that the lakes are getting acid from the soil around them or the plants in them and not from the rain at all. Right now, different groups of scientists are testing their own hypotheses. They need to find out what causes acid rain and how it affects lakes and streams.

Acid Rain Formation

18. Which of the following best describes what happens when something *acidifies*?

    (1) It dies.
    (2) It falls like rain.
    (3) It becomes less acidic.
    (4) It helps plants and animals.
    (5) It becomes more acidic.

19. The author of this passage would probably agree with which of the following?

(1) The problem of acid rain will be easy to solve.

(2) Acid rain is not very important.

(3) There should be more research on the acid rain problem.

(4) Most people know the cause of acid rain.

(5) Acid rain is a problem only for fishermen and boaters.

Questions 20–22 are based on the following passage and diagram.

The periodic table is a chart that organizes the 112 known elements by their properties. Each box in the chart contains information about one atom of a specific element. The diagram shows the box for flourine. The first things to look for are the element name and symbol.

The numbers in the box give information about the structure of one atom of the element. The atomic number, for instance, shows the number of protons in the nucleus of the atom. This also represents the number of electrons circling outside the nucleus. The atomic mass shows the sum of the protons and neutrons in the nucleus.

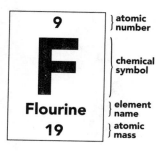

20. According to the diagram, which of the following is the chemical symbol for fluorine?

(1) F

(2) Fr

(3) Fe

(4) Fm

(5) Fl

21. How many protons does an atom of fluorine have in its nucleus?

(1) 9

(2) 10

(3) 19

(4) 27

(5) 28

22. How many neutrons does an atom of fluorine have in its nucleus?

(1) 9

(2) 10

(3) 19

(4) 27

(5) 28

Questions 23–25 are based on the following passage and diagram.

Photosynthesis is the process by which a green plant makes its own food for growth and repair of the plant's cells. Most photosynthesis occurs in a plant's leaves. Inside the leaves are cells called chloroplasts that contain chlorophyll—the green pigment that gives leaves their green color. Several other substances in a plant's leaves are necessary for photosynthesis to occur. Light energy from the Sun strikes a plant's leaves and is absorbed by chlorophyll in the chloroplasts. Carbon dioxide from the air enters a plant's leaves through tiny openings. Water enters a plant's leaves after it is absorbed through the roots and moved upward through the stem. The diagram shows the chemical reaction that occurs during photosynthesis.

```
                    PHOTOSYNTHESIS

                         sunlight
  carbon                            glucose
         + water  ───────────────▶          + oxygen
  dioxide               chlorophyll  sugar
```

23. Which of the following substances is **not** needed for photosynthesis to take place?

  (1) carbon dioxide
  (2) sunlight
  (3) oxygen
  (4) chlorophyll
  (5) water

24. Which of the following best describes glucose sugar?

  (1) a substance needed for photosynthesis
  (2) a sweet-tasting substance
  (3) a gooey substance, like maple syrup
  (4) a food made during photosynthesis
  (5) a special type of chlorophyll

25. Which of the following best describes the chemical reaction for photosynthesis?

  (1) Carbon dioxide uses water and sunlight to make light energy.
  (2) Water uses carbon dioxide and glucose sugar to make water and oxygen.
  (3) Glucose sugar uses oxygen to make carbon dioxide and water.
  (4) Sunlight uses glucose sugar and oxygen to make carbon dioxide and water.
  (5) Chlorophyll uses sunlight to change carbon dioxide and water into glucose sugar and oxygen.

Questions 26–28 are based on the following passage and illustrations.

Have you ever wondered why a roller coaster doesn't fly off the track as it speeds around a curve? The roller coaster moves in a circular path because the track applies a force that causes the roller coaster to continually change direction. This force, called centripetal force, keeps an object moving in a circular path.

To prove to her students that centripetal force causes circular motion, a teacher conducted the experiment shown in the illustrations below.

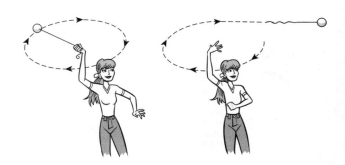

POSTTEST

26. Which of the following best defines centripetal force?

(1) the force that acts toward the center of the circle in which an object is moving
(2) the force that pulls a moving object away from the center of the circle
(3) the force that pushes back in reaction to an action force
(4) the force that keeps an object moving in a straight line
(5) the force that accelerates a moving object

27. Which of the following is **not** a step in the teacher's experiment, as shown in the illustrations?

(1) Let go of the string.
(2) Grab hold of the loose end of the string.
(3) Measure the mass of the small rubber ball.
(4) Whirl the ball overhead.
(5) Tie the ball to one end of a string.

28. What happens when the centripetal force, created by the student's hand on the string, is removed?

(1) The string snaps apart from the force.
(2) The ball moves in a straight line.
(3) The ball keeps moving in a circle.
(4) The hand holds tightly onto the string.
(5) The string exerts more force on the ball.

Questions 29 and 30 are based on the following passage and equation.

When the atoms of two or more elements combine, a chemical reaction occurs and a completely different substance is formed. That substance is called a compound. During the chemical reaction, the forces holding the atoms together break down and the atoms rearrange themselves to form the compound. Scientists use a chemical equation to show what happens during a reaction.

The equation below shows the chemical reaction that occurs when iron rusts. The starting substances in a chemical reaction are called reactants. In the equation below, the reactants are shown on the left side of the arrow. The new substance that is formed is called the product. The product is shown on the right side of the arrow. The chemical equation for rust can be read "iron plus oxygen produces iron oxide—sometimes called rust."

$$4Fe + 3O_2 \longrightarrow 2Fe_2O_3$$

29. What are the reactants in the chemical reaction for rust?

A. iron   **B.** oxygen   **C.** iron oxide

(1) A and B
(2) A and C
(3) B and C
(4) C only
(5) A, B, and C

30. A catalyst is a substance that speeds up a chemical reaction. Water and salt are catalysts that speed up the chemical reaction that produces rust. Based on this information, which type of iron product would tend to show the **least** amount of rust?

(1) a cruise ship that sails often in the Caribbean Sea
(2) a ski lift at a mountain resort in the Swiss Alps
(3) a water-collection barrel in a South American rain forest
(4) a flagpole at a resort on the coast of Florida
(5) a military tank in the Sahara Desert

Answers are on pages 878–879.

Science Answer Key

1. (2) The bar for 1991 is halfway between 10 and 20. This can be estimated at 15.

2. (3) John is hoping that providing more nesting places will increase the number of ducks.

3. (4) According to the chart, 1 cm³ (cubic centimeter) of diamonds weighs 3.5 grams, so 6 cm³ would weigh 6 times 3.5, which equals 21 grams.

4. (3) If you divide 315 grams by 30, you get 10.5 grams per cubic centimeter, which is the density given in the chart for silver.

5. (3) This answer is implied by the sentence in the first paragraph about "readying each RLV for another flight within hours of landing" and by your knowledge of airports and air travel today.

6. (2) Using the definition of light-year and your knowledge of the types of spacecraft described in science fiction works, you know that science fiction writers often predict future science.

7. (4) The first paragraph describes how humans see light. Choice (1) does not cover all that is in the first paragraph. Choices (2), (3), and (5) are not covered in the first paragraph at all.

8. (1) You can tell that the eye is a very complex organ from the description in paragraphs 2 and 3 of how the eye works.

9. (3) The diagram shows the cornea as the outer layer surrounding the eye. The passage describes it as a "clear outer layer in front of the eye."

10. (5) Choice (1) is not correct because this graph gives information only about Vitamix dissolving in milk, not about all powders in all liquids. The graph line shows that more Vitamix dissolved as the temperature of the mixture got higher, so choices (2) and (4) cannot be correct. Choice (3) is not right because the graph did not show using different amounts of liquid.

11. (4) The graph shows data from experiments. Choice (1) is wrong because it is unlikely that people would just "happen" to notice exact temperatures and amounts of Vitamix dissolved. Choice (2) is wrong because the experiment is about Vitamix and milk, not water. Choices (3) and (5) are incorrect because this graph is based on observed facts, not just opinions.

12. (1) See the first sentence.

13. (4) The passage describes dachshunds as being long and low, with very short legs—thus, somewhat sausage-shaped. Choices (1), (2), (3), and (5) are not mentioned in the passage at all.

14. (5) The passage says that the "foil records wore out very quickly."

15. (2) The passage says that "sound waves from the voice caused the diaphragm to vibrate," and the diaphragm is a solid object.

16. (3) On each side, the arrow comes down from the auricle into the ventricle.

17. (3) The pulmonary artery leads to the lungs, and the pulmonary veins come back from the lungs.

18. (5) The passage says that water acidifies when acid rain falls into it. As more acid rain falls into the water, the water becomes more acidic.

19. (3) In the last sentence, the author says that scientists need to find out what causes acid rain. Choices (2) and (5) are not correct because the author says that this is a problem that many people are worried about.

20. (1) The diagram shows that the symbol for fluorine is *F*.

21. (1) Paragraph 2 states that the atomic number shows the number of protons. The atomic number of fluorine is 9.

22. (2) Paragraph 2 states that the atomic mass shows the sum of the protons and neutrons in the nucleus. We already know from the atomic number that the atom has 9 protons. To find the number of neutrons, subtract the 9 protons from the atomic mass: $19 - 9 = 10$.

23. (3) The passage does not mention oxygen as a substance needed for photosynthesis. Oxygen is a product of photosynthesis.

24. (4) The first sentence of the passage explains that a plant makes its own food during photosynthesis. Other sentences describe the substances needed for photosynthesis to occur. The diagram shows those substances on the left side of the arrow and glucose sugar and oxygen on the right side of the arrow. From your experience, you know that oxygen is a gas. Therefore glucose sugar must be the food made during photosynthesis.

25. (5) The diagram shows that carbon dioxide and water combine in the presence of sunlight and chlorophyll to produce glucose sugar and oxygen. The passage also gives this information.

26. (1) This definition is explained in paragraph 1.

27. (3) The illustrations do not show the mass of the ball being measured. Every other choice is shown in the illustrations.

28. (2) The second illustration shows that the centripetal force, created by the hand on the string, has been removed. The ball and string stop moving in a circle and instead move off in a straight line.

29. (1) Paragraph 2 explains that the reactants are the starting substances on the left side of the arrow in the equation. The substances on the left side of the arrow are the elements iron and oxygen.

30. (5) Rain and snow are forms of water, and salt is both found in the ocean and used to melt snow on sidewalks and streets. Choice (5) is the only product in an area with no rain, snow, or salt.

Evaluation Chart

Use the answer key to check your answers. Find the number of each question you missed and circle it on the chart below. To review the problems you missed, use the chapter in this book or the other resources listed in the chart.

Chapter/Skill	Question Number	Resources from McGraw-Hill/Contemporary	
Chapter 1 - Science Knowledge and Skills • Scientific method • Building vocabulary	 2 26	• *Complete GED* • *GED Science* • *Pre-GED Science* • *MHC Interactive: GED* • *MHC Interactive: Pre-GED*	Throughout Throughout Chapters 1–3 Throughout Unit 1
Chapter 2 - Life Science • Understanding what you read • Understanding illustrations • Analyzing ideas • Building vocabulary	 12, 23 1, 25 13 24	• *Complete GED* • *GED Science* • *Pre-GED Science* • *MHC Interactive: GED* • *MHC Interactive: Pre-GED*	459–496 155–254 71–172 3.4, 3.8, 3.12, 3.16, 3.20, 3.24 Unit 2
Chapter 3 - Human Biology • Understanding what you read • Understanding illustrations • Analyzing ideas • Building vocabulary	 7 9, 16 8 17	• *Complete GED* • *GED Science* • *Pre-GED Science* • *MHC Interactive: GED* • *MHC Interactive: Pre-GED*	459–496 155–254 71–172 3.4, 3.8, 3.12, 3.16, 3.20, 3.24 Unit 2
Chapter 4 - Physics • Scientific method • Understanding what you read • Understanding illustrations • Analyzing ideas	 27 14 3, 28 4, 15	• *Complete GED* • *GED Science* • *Pre-GED Science* • *MHC Interactive: GED* • *MHC Interactive: Pre-GED*	556–577 289–336 205–236 3.3, 3.7, 3.11, 3.15, 3.19, 3.23 Unit 3
Chapter 5 - Chemistry • Scientific method • Understanding what you read • Understanding illustrations • Analyzing ideas	 11 21, 22, 29 10, 20 30	• *Complete GED* • *GED Science* • *Pre-GED Science* • *MHC Interactive: GED* • *MHC Interactive: Pre-GED*	533–554 257–288 175–204 3.2, 3.6, 3.10, 3.14, 3.18, 3.22 Unit 4
Chapter 6 - Earth and Space Science • Analyzing ideas • Building vocabulary • Evaluating ideas	 5, 6 18 19	• *Complete GED* • *GED Science* • *Pre-GED Science* • *MHC Interactive: GED* • *MHC Interactive: Pre-GED*	497–532 337–385 237–283 3.1, 3.5, 3.9, 3.13, 3.17, 3.21 Unit 5

Mathematics

The purpose of this posttest is to see how much your mathematics skills have improved. When you have completed the test, check your answers with the Answer Key on page 889.

1. Which of the following numbers is greater than 2,100 but less than 2,400?

   (1) 1,950
   (2) 2,015
   (3) 2,150
   (4) 2,450
   (5) 2,624

2. Which of the following numbers can be described as

   5 ones, 8 tens, 9 hundreds, and 4 thousands?

   (1) 5,984
   (2) 5,894
   (3) 5,498
   (4) 4,985
   (5) 4,489

3. Jocelyn drove 247 miles on Tuesday and 193 miles on Wednesday. How many total miles did she drive these two days?

   (1) 330 miles
   (2) 370 miles
   (3) 390 miles
   (4) 440 miles
   (5) 480 miles

4. By plane, Dallas is 795 miles from Atlanta. Also by plane, Dallas is 936 miles from Minneapolis. How many miles farther is Dallas from Minneapolis than from Atlanta?

   (1) 141 miles
   (2) 143 miles
   (3) 259 miles
   (4) 459 miles
   (5) 1,731 miles

5. Julian has 12 identical packages to mail. Each package weighs 29 pounds. What is the total weight of these packages?

   (1) 228 pounds
   (2) 248 pounds
   (3) 288 pounds
   (4) 328 pounds
   (5) 348 pounds

6. Allison applied for an administrative job that required a typing speed of 65 words per minute. On a 6-minute typing test she typed 348 words. How many words per minute (wpm) did Allison average on this test?

   (1) 58 wpm
   (2) 59 wpm
   (3) 65 wpm
   (4) 390 wpm
   (5) 2,088 wpm

7. At a hardware sale, Royce bought a drill on sale for $38.49 and a wrench set on sale for $21.99. What is the best **estimate** of the total amount Royce paid for these items?

   (1) $40
   (2) $50
   (3) $60
   (4) $70
   (5) $80

8. For her home, Barb plans to buy 28 rolls of insulation. If she pays $31.95 for each roll, what is the best **estimate** of the total that Barb will be charged?

(1) $500
(2) $600
(3) $700
(4) $800
(5) $900

9. On Monday's shopping trip, Marilyn bought a lamp for $23.49, a table for $49.50, 2 vases for $19.95 each, and a serving plate for $12.79. Which expression below can be used to find the amount Marilyn paid for the lamp and the vases?

(1) $23.49 + $12.79
(2) $23.49 + $19.95
(3) $23.49 − $19.95
(4) $23.49 + $19.95 + $19.95
(5) $23.49 − $19.95 − $19.95

10. For the following problem, what is the necessary information (the numbers needed to answer the question)?

Tommy is buying a used pickup that has a sticker price of $12,500. The dealer agrees to lower the price an extra $500 and give Tommy $4,500 for his car as a trade-in. Tommy buys the pickup and makes an additional down payment of $2,000. Tommy will pay off the balance of what he owes in 24 equal monthly payments. For what price is the dealer selling the pickup to Tommy?

The necessary information for this question is

(1) $12,500 and $500
(2) $12,500 and $4,500
(3) $12,500 and $2,000
(4) $12,500 and $4,000 and $500
(5) $12,500 and $4,000 and $2,000

11. Jenni drove 483 miles in 9 hours. **Estimate** Jenni's average speed (miles per hour) for this trip.

(1) 60 mph
(2) 50 mph
(3) 40 mph
(4) 35 mph
(5) 30 mph

12. Each Monday through Friday, Leanne delivers a newspaper to each of her 67 customers. Last weekend she delivered a total of 149 additional papers. How many total papers did Leanne deliver last week?

(1) 216 papers
(2) 382 papers
(3) 434 papers
(4) 484 papers
(5) 618 papers

13. How is the number 0.018 read in words?

(1) eighteen thousandths
(2) eighteen hundredths
(3) eighteen tenths
(4) one point eight thousandths
(5) one point eight hundredths

14. How is the following number written using digits?

two hundred forty-three thousandths

(1) 243,000
(2) 2.043
(3) 0.243
(4) 0.0243
(5) 0.00243

15. Put the following decimals in order from least to greatest:

A. 0.428 **B.** 0.071   **C.** 0.607   **D.** 0.009

(1) D, B, C, A
(2) D, B, A, C
(3) A, C, B, D
(4) C, B, A, D
(5) C, A, B, D

16. Round 0.183 to the nearest tenth.

(1) 0.1
(2) 0.11
(3) 0.18
(4) 0.2
(5) 0.21

17. Sid measured the distances along the four sides of his garden space. The lengths (in meters) are shown on his drawing. What is the total distance around the outside edge of Sid's garden?

(1) 31.825 m
(2) 33.25 m
(3) 34.5 m
(4) 36.175 m
(5) 38.025 m

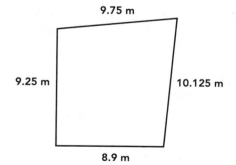

9.75 m

9.25 m

10.125 m

8.9 m

18. Jill's normal body temperature is 98.6 degrees. When Jill had the flu, her temperature went up to 103.2 degrees. By how much did Jill's temperature rise when she was ill?

(1) 4.6 degrees
(2) 4.8 degrees
(3) 5.0 degrees
(4) 5.4 degrees
(5) 5.6 degrees

19. The distance between Lon's house and his workplace is 7.8 miles. He drives this distance twice each day, 4 days each week. How many total miles does Lon drive to and from work each week?

(1) 31.2 miles
(2) 42.6 miles
(3) 53.4 miles
(4) 62.4 miles
(5) 187.2 miles

20. Kendall Construction Company is fixing potholes along Airport Drive. The crew can fix about 0.25 miles of road each day. How many days will it take this crew to fix 2.75 miles of highway?

(1) 6 days
(2) 9 days
(3) 11 days
(4) 14 days
(5) 17 days

POSTTEST

21. Which fraction tells what part of the following group of figures is shaded?

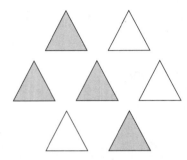

(1) $\frac{4}{3}$

(2) $\frac{3}{4}$

(3) $\frac{4}{7}$

(4) $\frac{3}{7}$

(5) $\frac{1}{4}$

22. Express the fraction $\frac{16}{24}$ in lowest terms.

(1) $\frac{16}{24}$

(2) $\frac{8}{12}$

(3) $\frac{3}{4}$

(4) $\frac{2}{3}$

(5) $\frac{1}{2}$

23. Which improper fraction is represented in the shaded part of the drawing below?

(1) $3\frac{2}{7}$

(2) $2\frac{3}{4}$

(3) $2\frac{2}{3}$

(4) $2\frac{3}{11}$

(5) $1\frac{2}{7}$

24. Kim mixed $3\frac{1}{2}$ cups of flour, $1\frac{3}{4}$ cups of flour, and $\frac{3}{4}$ cup of sugar in a mixing bowl. How many cups of ingredients did she place in the bowl?

(1) 6 cups

(2) $5\frac{1}{2}$ cups

(3) $5\frac{1}{4}$ cups

(4) 4 cups

(5) $3\frac{3}{4}$ cups

25. Last month, Paul lost $7\frac{1}{2}$ pounds. This month, Paul lost $3\frac{3}{4}$ pounds. How many more pounds did he lose last month than he lost this month?

(1) $\frac{4}{14}$ pound

(2) $3\frac{1}{4}$ pounds

(3) $3\frac{1}{2}$ pounds

(4) $3\frac{3}{4}$ pounds

(5) $4\frac{3}{4}$ pounds

26. Valley Meats sells diet hamburger that has only a $\frac{1}{8}$ fat content. How many ounces of fat are in a 12-ounce hamburger made of this meat?

(1) $1\frac{3}{4}$ ounces

(2) $1\frac{1}{2}$ ounces

(3) $1\frac{1}{4}$ ounces

(4) $\frac{3}{4}$ ounce

(5) $\frac{2}{3}$ ounce

27. Willie has $\frac{7}{8}$ of a pizza that he wants to divide into 3 equal parts. What fraction of a whole pizza will be in each part?

(1) $2\frac{1}{8}$

(2) $\frac{7}{11}$

(3) $\frac{3}{8}$

(4) $\frac{7}{24}$

(5) $\frac{7}{38}$

28. Malina's compact car gets 48 miles to the gallon during highway driving and 32 miles to the gallon during city driving. What is the ratio of this car's highway mileage to city mileage?

(1) $\frac{3}{16}$

(2) $\frac{2}{3}$

(3) $\frac{7}{8}$

(4) $\frac{5}{4}$

(5) $\frac{3}{2}$

29. Melissa earns $366.00 each week for 30 hours of work. What is Melissa's pay rate in dollars per hour?

(1) $12.20

(2) $11.40

(3) $10.80

(4) $ 9.20

(5) $ 8.60

30. What is the value of *n* in the following proportion?

$$\frac{n}{24} = \frac{5}{8}$$

(1) 3

(2) 12

(3) 15

(4) 16

(5) 20

31. A recipe for 9 servings of dessert calls for 2 cups of sugar. How much sugar is needed to make 25 servings?

(1) $4\frac{2}{3}$ cups

(2) $4\frac{5}{6}$ cups

(3) $5\frac{1}{4}$ cups

(4) $5\frac{5}{9}$ cups

(5) $6\frac{1}{3}$ cups

32. What percent of $1.00 is represented by the group of coins shown below?

(1) 176%

(2) 126%

(3) 76%

(4) 38%

(5) 24%

33. How is 74.5% written as a decimal?

- **(1)** 74.5
- **(2)** 7.45
- **(3)** 0.745
- **(4)** 0.0745
- **(5)** 0.00745

34. How is 36% written as a fraction that is reduced to lowest terms?

- **(1)** $\frac{9}{25}$
- **(2)** $\frac{16}{25}$
- **(3)** $\frac{13}{50}$
- **(4)** $\frac{18}{50}$
- **(5)** $\frac{36}{100}$

35. Gene's Men Store is offering a 30% discount on all shirts. How much can be saved by buying a shirt on sale that normally sells for $26.00?

- **(1)** $3.60
- **(2)** $4.00
- **(3)** $6.30
- **(4)** $6.50
- **(5)** $7.80

36. On her math test, Latisha got 42 questions correct out of 50. What percent of the questions did Latisha get correct?

- **(1)** 8%
- **(2)** 16%
- **(3)** 21%
- **(4)** 58%
- **(5)** 84%

Questions 37–38 refer to the table below.

Little Tykes Day Care	
Name	**Age**
Brittany	3
Kyle	5
Henrietta	4
Sam	2

37. What is the mean (average) age of the four students listed in the table?

- **(1)** $2\frac{1}{2}$
- **(2)** 3
- **(3)** $3\frac{1}{2}$
- **(4)** 4
- **(5)** $4\frac{1}{2}$

38. What is the median age of the four students listed in the table?

- **(1)** 3
- **(2)** $3\frac{1}{2}$
- **(3)** 4
- **(4)** $4\frac{1}{2}$
- **(5)** 5

39. When he bought a new TV, Dwight made a 25% down payment of $92.00. What was the total price of the TV?

- **(1)** $ 67.00
- **(2)** $117.00
- **(3)** $184.00
- **(4)** $314.00
- **(5)** $368.00

POSTTEST

Questions 40 and 41 refer to the circle graph.

Sandmeyer Mountain Bicycles
Percent of Sales per State

40. What percent of sales of Sandmeyer mountain bikes are made in states other than California, Washington, and Oregon?

(1) 7%
(2) 11%
(3) 15%
(4) 47%
(5) 93%

41. Sandmeyer bicycle sales for June were 2,400. How many of these sales were in Oregon?

(1) 1,500
(2) 1,200
(3) 870
(4) 360
(5) 280

42. A sock drawer contains 5 pairs of blue socks, 7 pairs of black socks, and 4 pairs of white socks. If Denny randomly chooses a pair of socks from the drawer, what is the probability that he will pick white socks?

(1) $\frac{5}{16}$
(2) $\frac{1}{4}$
(3) $\frac{4}{11}$
(4) $\frac{1}{3}$
(5) $\frac{1}{2}$

43. What is the value of 2^3?

(1) 1
(2) 6
(3) 8
(4) 16
(5) 23

44. What is the value of $x - 18$ when $x = 27$?

(1) 4
(2) 9
(3) 23
(4) 36
(5) 45

45. If you add 32 to a number, the sum is 41. If n stands for the unknown number, which equation can be used to find n?

(1) $n = 32 + 41$
(2) $n - 41 = 32$
(3) $n + 41 = 32$
(4) $n - 32 = 41$
(5) $n + 32 = 41$

46. What is the value of *x* in the following equation?

4x = $25.60

(1) $ 4.60
(2) $ 5.20
(3) $ 6.40
(4) $ 9.60
(5) $12.80

47. How is 35 ounces written as pounds and ounces?

(1) 1 pound 3 ounces
(2) 1 pound 13 ounces
(3) 2 pounds 1 ounce
(4) 2 pounds 3 ounces
(5) 4 pounds 3 ounces

48. What is the approximate circumference of the circle below? Use the formula $C = \pi d$. (**Hint:** $\pi \approx \frac{22}{7}$)

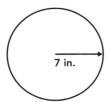

(1) 44 inches
(2) 86 inches
(3) 122 inches
(4) 154 inches
(5) 178 inches

49. What is the volume of the rectangular solid below? Use the formula $V = l \times w \times h$.

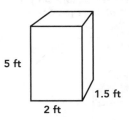

(1) 3.5 cubic feet
(2) 8.5 square feet
(3) 8.5 cubic feet
(4) 15 square feet
(5) 15 cubic feet

50. What is the measure of $\angle ABC$?

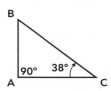

(1) 52°
(2) 64°
(3) 90°
(4) 142°
(5) 232°

Answers are on page 889.

Mathematics Answer Key

1. **(3)** 2,150
2. **(4)** 4,985
3. **(4)** 440 miles (247 + 193 = 440)
4. **(1)** 141 miles (936 − 795 = 141)
5. **(5)** 348 pounds (29 × 12 = 348)
6. **(1)** 58 wpm (348 ÷ 6 = 58)
7. **(3)** $60 (40 + 20 = 60)
8. **(5)** $900 (30 × 30 = 900)
9. **(4)** $23.49 + $19.95 + $19.95
10. **(1)** $12,500 and $500
11. **(2)** 50 mph (500 ÷ 10 = 50)
12. **(4)** 484 papers [(67 × 5) + 149 = 484]
13. **(1)** eighteen thousandths
14. **(3)** 0.243
15. **(2)** D, B, A, C
16. **(4)** 0.2
17. **(5)** 38.025 m (9.75 + 9.25 + 8.9 + 10.125 = 38.025)
18. **(1)** 4.6 degrees (103.2 − 98.6 = 4.6)
19. **(4)** 62.4 miles [(7.8 × 2) × 4 = 62.4]
20. **(3)** 11 days (2.75 ÷ .25 = 11)
21. **(3)** $\frac{4}{7}$
22. **(4)** $\frac{2}{3} \left(\frac{16 \div 8}{24 \div 8} = \frac{2}{3} \right)$
23. **(3)** $2\frac{2}{3}$
24. **(1)** 6 cups $\left(3\frac{1}{2} + 1\frac{3}{4} + \frac{3}{4} = 6 \right)$
25. **(4)** $3\frac{3}{4}$ pounds $\left(7\frac{1}{2} - 3\frac{3}{4} = 3\frac{3}{4} \right)$
26. **(2)** $1\frac{1}{2}$ ounces $\left(12 \times \frac{1}{8} = 1\frac{1}{2} \right)$
27. **(4)** $\frac{7}{24} \left(\frac{7}{8} \div 3 = \frac{7}{24} \right)$

28. **(5)** $\frac{3}{2} \left(\frac{48 \div 16}{32 \div 16} = \frac{3}{2} \right)$
29. **(1)** $12.20 $\left(\frac{366}{30} = \frac{n}{1} \right)$
30. **(3)** 15
31. **(4)** $5\frac{5}{9}$ cups $\left(\frac{9}{2} = \frac{25}{n} \right)$
32. **(3)** 76% (.25 + .25 + .10 + .10 + .05 + .01 = .76 = 76%)
33. **(3)** 0.745
34. **(1)** $\frac{9}{25} \left(\frac{36 \div 4}{100 \div 4} = \frac{9}{25} \right)$
35. **(5)** $7.80 (26 × .30 = 7.80)
36. **(5)** 84% $\left(\frac{42}{50} = \frac{n}{100} \right)$
37. **(3)** $3\frac{1}{2}$ (3 + 5 + 4 + 2 = 14; 14 ÷ 4 = $3\frac{1}{2}$)
38. **(2)** $3\frac{1}{2}$ (5, 4, 3, 2; halfway between 4 and 3 is $3\frac{1}{2}$)
39. **(5)** $368.00 $\left(\frac{92}{25} = \frac{n}{100} \right)$
40. **(1)** 7% (100 − 15 − 28 − 50 = 7)
41. **(4)** 360 (2,400 × .15 = 360)
42. **(2)** $\frac{1}{4} \left(5 + 7 + 4 = 16; \frac{4}{16} = \frac{1}{4} \right)$
43. **(3)** 8 (2 × 2 × 2 = 8)
44. **(2)** 9 (27 − 18 = 9)
45. **(5)** $n + 32 = 41$
46. **(3)** $6.40 (25.60 ÷ 4 = 6.40)
47. **(4)** 2 pounds 3 ounces (35 ÷ 16 = 2 r3)
48. **(1)** 44 inches (7 + 7 = 14; $\frac{22}{7} \times 14 = 44$)
49. **(5)** 15 cubic feet (2 × 5 × 1.5 = 15 cubic ft)
50. **(1)** 52° (180 − 90 − 38 = 52)

Evaluation Chart

Use the answer key to check your answers. Find the number of each question you missed and circle it on the chart below. To review the problems you missed, use the chapter in this book or the other resources listed in the chart.

Chapter/Skill	Question Number	Resources from McGraw-Hill/Contemporary	
Chapter 1 • Place value • Basic operations • Estimation	1, 2 3, 4, 5, 6 7, 8,	• *Complete GED* • *GED Mathematics* • *Pre-GED Mathematics* • *MHC Interactive: GED* • *MHC Interactive: Pre-GED*	742, 743 25–28 23–25, 44, 45 5.1 1.1 – 1.6
Chapter 3 • Necessary information • Estimation • Multistep problems	9, 10 11 12	• *Complete GED* • *GED Mathematics* • *Pre-GED Mathematics* • *MHC Interactive: GED* • *MHC Interactive: Pre-GED*	702–710 51–74 34–56 5.7 6.1, 6.2
Chapter 4 • Understanding decimals • Ordering decimals • Rounding decimals • Basic operations	13, 14 15 16 17, 18, 19, 20	• *Complete GED* • *GED Mathematics* • *Pre-GED Mathematics* • *MHC Interactive: GED* • *MHC Interactive: Pre-GED*	725–746 75–92 57–77 5.4 2.1 – 2.5
Chapter 5 • Understanding fractions • Basic operations	21, 22, 23 24, 25, 26, 27	• *Complete GED* • *GED Mathematics* • *Pre-GED Mathematics* • *MHC Interactive: GED* • *MHC Interactive: Pre-GED*	747–774 103–136 78–111 5.3 3.1 – 3.6
Chapter 6 • Understanding ratio • Using rates • Word problems	28 29 30, 31	• *Complete GED* • *GED Mathematics* • *Pre-GED Mathematics* • *MHC Interactive: GED* • *MHC Interactive: Pre-GED*	785–792 137–148 112–124 5.5, 5.7 4.1 – 4.3
Chapter 7 • Understanding percent • Relating decimals, fractions, and percents • Solving percent problems	32 33, 34 35, 36, 39	• *Complete GED* • *GED Mathematics* • *Pre-GED Mathematics* • *MHC Interactive: GED* • *MHC Interactive: Pre-GED*	793–808 149–182 125–143 5.6 5.1 – 5.4
Chapter 8 • Mean and median • Reading a graph • Probability	37, 38 40, 41 42	• *Complete GED* • *GED Mathematics* • *Pre-GED Mathematics* • *MHC Interactive: GED* • *MHC Interactive: Pre-GED*	814–819 212–219 114–148, 173–186 5.15, 5.16 8.1, 8.2
Chapter 9 • Powers and roots • Evaluating expressions • Solving equations	43 44 45, 46	• *Complete GED* • *GED Mathematics* • *Pre-GED Mathematics* • *MHC Interactive: GED* • *MHC Interactive: Pre-GED*	711–714, 730–733 32–36, 93, 94, 127–129 187–192 5.2, 5.17 9.1 – 9.4
Chapter 10 • Units of measurement • Circumference and volume • Measuring angles	47 48, 49 50	• *Complete GED* • *GED Mathematics* • *Pre-GED Mathematics* • *MHC Interactive: GED* • *MHC Interactive: Pre-GED*	873–892, 897–904, 907–914 183–193, 235–275 212–220, 225–245 5.8, 5.10, 5.11 7.1 – 7.6